Praise for Age Well and Feel Great

"Al has written a book of inspiration and hope, reflecting his impressive and passion-filled journey to transform - radically - not just his own existence but countless others, into one of vibrant longevity. As a physician in functional medicine and a researcher in longevity, I cannot tell you how thrilling, how satisfying, it is to see someone outside of medicine and science "get" that he can make lifestyle choices that will absolutely impact his well-being, and then decide to share all he's lived and learned with others."

—Dr. Kara Fitzgerald, author of *Younger You: Reduce Your Bio Age and Live Longer, Better*

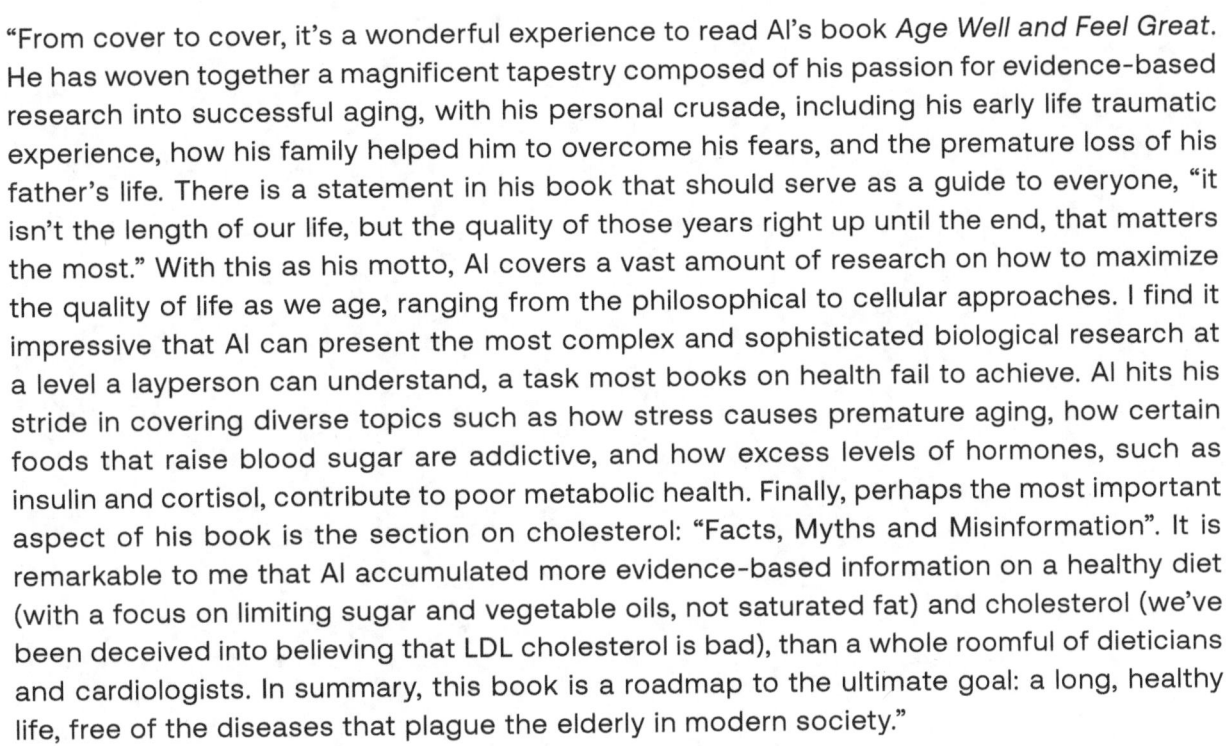

"From cover to cover, it's a wonderful experience to read Al's book *Age Well and Feel Great*. He has woven together a magnificent tapestry composed of his passion for evidence-based research into successful aging, with his personal crusade, including his early life traumatic experience, how his family helped him to overcome his fears, and the premature loss of his father's life. There is a statement in his book that should serve as a guide to everyone, "it isn't the length of our life, but the quality of those years right up until the end, that matters the most." With this as his motto, Al covers a vast amount of research on how to maximize the quality of life as we age, ranging from the philosophical to cellular approaches. I find it impressive that Al can present the most complex and sophisticated biological research at a level a layperson can understand, a task most books on health fail to achieve. Al hits his stride in covering diverse topics such as how stress causes premature aging, how certain foods that raise blood sugar are addictive, and how excess levels of hormones, such as insulin and cortisol, contribute to poor metabolic health. Finally, perhaps the most important aspect of his book is the section on cholesterol: "Facts, Myths and Misinformation". It is remarkable to me that Al accumulated more evidence-based information on a healthy diet (with a focus on limiting sugar and vegetable oils, not saturated fat) and cholesterol (we've been deceived into believing that LDL cholesterol is bad), than a whole roomful of dieticians and cardiologists. In summary, this book is a roadmap to the ultimate goal: a long, healthy life, free of the diseases that plague the elderly in modern society."

—David Diamond, Ph.D., *Professor, University of South Florida*

AGE WELL *And* FEEL GREAT

The Proven Path to Solving the Aging
Puzzle and Going the Distance!

Al Lyman

For more information, email coachal@coachal.com

ISBN 979-8-88759-022-6 - paperback
ISBN 979-8-88759-023-3 - ebook

Get Your Free Gift and Start Using the Concepts In This Book. *Go the Distance!*

FREE GIFT

Would you like a FREE downloadable guide with INSIDER TIPS and STRATEGIES to help you start making progress quickly?

I've found the readers who are most successful and make the quickest progress download this FREE 32-page E-BOOK!

You can get a copy by visiting:
www.theallyman.com/free-guide

Or scan this QR code on your device:

DEDICATION

For Pops.
I miss you.

The Modern Evolution of Boy to Man.

The Choice Is Yours. Choose Wisely.

CONTENTS

PART 3: MOVEMENT

PART 4: STRENGTH

PART 5: CARDIO

PART 6: FINAL THOUGHTS AND RECOMMENDATIONS

EPILOGUE

PREFACE

I have often dreamt, of a far off place
Where a hero's welcome, would be waiting for me
Where the crowds will cheer, when they see my face
And a voice keeps saying, this is where I'm meant to be

I'll be there someday, I can go the distance
I will find my way, if I can be strong
I know ev'ry mile, will be worth my while
When I go the distance, I'll be right where I belong

Down an unknown road, to embrace my fate
Though that road may wander, it will lead me to you
And a thousand years, would be worth the wait
It might take a lifetime, but somehow I'll see it through

And I won't look back, cuz I can go the distance
And I'll stay on track, no, I won't accept defeat
It's an uphill slope, but I won't lose hope
Till I go the distance, and my journey is complete

But to look beyond the glory is the hardest part
For a hero's strength is measured by his heart

Like a shooting star, I can go the distance
I will search the world, I will face its' harms
I don't care how far, cuz I can go the distance
Till I find my hero's welcome, waiting in your arms

I will search this world, I will face its harms
Until I find my hero's welcome, waiting in your arms

Lyrics from the song, *Go The Distance*, from Disney's 1997 animated
feature film, *Hercules*. Music by Alan Menken, lyrics by David Zippel.

When I was 25, I made a conscious decision that would change my life forever. That decision was **to *die healthy***.

How I got there is a bit of a long story, but I want to share it with you - it's ultimately why I decided to write this book. But first, let me set the stage and ask you some direct questions:

- Do you believe it's possible to feel healthier and better as you get older, living your 60s and 70s and beyond with little to no pain?
- Do you believe you can avoid the all-too-common chronic diseases we associate with getting older, that often end up killing us?

Whether you believe it now or not, by the time you finish reading this book and putting my words into action in your life, I'm confident you'll say YES, I believe! So, what's the key? *You must envision a healthier you* and throw away the negative stereotypes so many of us have about aging. *You must see your life play out in your mind's eye* the way you want it to. *You must know in your heart you can impact how that happens* by being more intentional. *To do that, you must take consistent action that aligns with that vision.* That's what this book is all about.

So back to my story of how I got here and the decision that would change my life: I started running in my early 20s to try and get in shape. While I was motivated to give running a try, I found it to be hard, and it wasn't all that much fun. Shocker, right? ☺ Thinking back on my childhood, I was always the slowest in gym class and among the last to get picked for any team, so it's not surprising I found running hard.

In high school, I wasn't athletic, I didn't do sports. And I remember in my senior year, my gym teacher said he'd fail me if I didn't get out there and complete the mile run.

In 1983 – I was 24 at the time - things got more serious with running because I decided to join some friends and do the Boston Marathon. Not as an official runner mind you, but as a "back of the packer," or "scab," a term used to describe unofficial runners back in those days. I finished that first *unofficial* Boston in 4 hours. That's a picture of me right before the start in my favorite yellow Mustang t-shirt next to my running buddies and musician colleagues, Ken and Kirk. What a day it was!

As time went on, running got a little bit easier because I was slowly improving. I was also getting into the running lifestyle, which included taking better care of myself. I was eating better, trying to sleep better, and thinking more about how to manage stress. I guess you could say I was starting to see the bigger picture. Running put me on a path to become a healthier, better person. It wasn't *just* about getting faster or leaner. Yes, I still wanted to get faster! But beyond that, I started to see running as only one part of improving my overall health.

One thing led to another and soon, I became more curious about aging - not why we age, but why some people seemed to be more prone to getting sick and often ended up with a chronic disease, and others didn't. I also wondered what, if anything, could be done to avoid what seemed like an inevitable downturn in health. I remember buying my first book on the topic of "anti-aging" in the late-1980s. It was a book written a few years earlier by Durk Pearson and Sandy Shaw called *Life Extension*.

During those years when I was turning my life around a little bit and getting into a healthier lifestyle, learning about fitness, and aging, my immediate family – the people I lived with and loved the most – seemed to be on a very different path.

Look at this picture, taken on Christmas Eve in 1993. The man all the way to the right is my dad. He's sitting with some close friends and my mom who is second from the left with glasses.

In this picture, my dad is 59 years old.

Fifty-nine.

Three years YOUNGER than I am right now.

Here's a picture of me taken just a few weeks ago.

When he died six years later from brain cancer – a cancer that was diagnosed only 10 months earlier, he was suffering and in pain; he weighed about 80 pounds, and he was *really* angry.

His two close friends to his right both died in their mid-70s, one from complications associated with amyotrophic lateral sclerosis and the other, from heart disease.

Take a *close look* at my dad. It is shocking how *old* he looks in this picture.

My dad was a great person – genuine, hard-working, loyal, a salt-of-the-earth kind of guy who was universally loved by friends and family alike. All his friends knew if they needed it, he'd have given them the shirt off his back. What I remember most about him was how much he cared for my mom. He would do anything for her and for us kids.

What I also remember was how fast he seemed to age. How, even at a relatively young age, he struggled to get up out of his chair – pushing himself up with his arms. Or how tired he seemed to be so much of the time, and the bloated puffiness in his face and legs. Maybe you know someone right now who's in pain or is struggling with an illness. It's not easy to watch. You want to do something to help them; your heart aches for them. But most of the time, you just sigh and realize there's not much you can do.

Sure, my dad could have been more proactive with how he took care of his health. But I know he did the best he could with what he knew at the time. Like many of his generation, he just accepted whatever was going to happen would happen. *He relied too much* on his doctors and on the health care system. *He didn't understand* the addictive nature of the pre-packaged convenience foods that had become so popular for so many of his generation. *He didn't realize* how muscle and strength disappear as we get older if we don't do something to reverse the trend. *He didn't understand* the damaging effects of the environment he worked in every day. **He never acknowledged how he lived – his habits and his lifestyle – could play such a pivotal role in how and when he died.**

I hated watching my dad struggle and die from cancer. It made me so sad. Angry. And if I am being honest - scared. As I look back on my life, especially when he was here, I realize the reason I decided to write this book was to help others learn what he didn't learn. Or simply couldn't.

I made that conscious choice at 25 to die healthy because somehow, I knew the only way to be, do, and have all I wanted out of my own life was to learn from his struggle, his pain, his innocence, and my, and our family's, heartache. I wanted to look at life through a different lens than he did. Since then, in many ways my life has been defined by learning whatever I could about how to live healthier and longer and putting what I learned into action. So, that's what I did and continue to do to this very day.

Fast forward to the past few years that will forever be identified with the COVID-19 pandemic. I made another life-altering decision to embark on a speaking career. I've done some public speaking in the past, but the topic of those talks was always related to running, triathlon or injury prevention, reflecting my experience as an endurance athlete, therapist, and coach. This speaking journey is different because what I see around me – how our collective health as a society is worsening - is shocking.

I've spent my entire life learning how to be healthier, yet right now in the U.S., it's entirely possible we're less healthy than we've ever been. Increasing numbers of Americans are either overweight or obese. *One-third of the children in the U.S. today struggle with obesity. What's worse, that number has more than tripled over the last four decades. It was 5% in 1978 – it's more than 20% today.* Greater than one in three Americans are prediabetic and insulin resistant. And of those, over eight out of ten don't even know it. *And that's not the half of it.*

In 2020, nearly 1.9 million new cases of cancer were diagnosed in the U.S. and more than 600,000 died from the disease. [1] That's more than 1700 people a day. Cancer is a leading cause of death worldwide, accounting for nearly 10 million deaths in 2020. That's nearly one in six.[2] In the U.S., it's the second leading cause of death, right behind heart disease.

Right now - and this should shock everyone to their core, roughly 88% of Americans are metabolically unhealthy, which means these five biomarkers are higher than they should be: 1. hypertension, 2. insulin resistance, 3. triglycerides, 4. low HDL cholesterol, and 5. overweight. It's predicted that by 2035, upwards of 80% of Americans will be prediabetic. That's outrageous. And scary.

By a wide margin, the U.S. spends more on healthcare than any other developed country. In 1970, we spent 70 billion annually; today it's about four trillion, and it's expected to rise to over six trillion in the next five to seven years, accounting for about 20% of our GDP.[3] But this spending spree doesn't seem to be helping us live healthier lives. And these problems are not just about our metabolic health, it's also about our *mental* health.

Even before the COVID-19 pandemic, the numbers of people seeking help for anxiety and depression skyrocketed. 20% of adults are experiencing some type of mental illness. Between 2005 and 2017, rates of depression increased by more than 50% among kids aged 12 to 17 years old.[4] Between 2007 and 2018, the suicide rate among 10 to 24 year-olds increased 60%, making it the second leading cause of death for that age group. From January through September 2021, children's hospital cases related to self-injury, suicidal ideation and attempts in kids ages 5 to 17 rose 53% from the same period in 2020.[5]

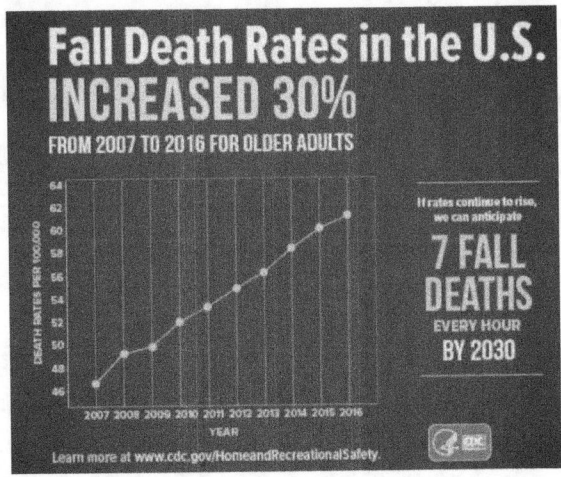

And here's the kicker - now more than ever, we're turning to our healthcare system – doctors, nurses, hospitals - to solve these problems for us. It's a medical establishment that is very good at certain things, but unfortunately bad at others. To understand what that means, imagine being in a car accident or falling down a set of stairs. You go to a hospital, and while that care will inevitably be expensive, it will be great care – better than ever. The same is true if you need treatment for symptoms from an acute illness. But the same system that is skilled at treating acute illness and trauma is not very good at helping us **prevent** the chronic diseases and lifestyle related illnesses that are literally, and often silently, killing us.

And then there's our body, including the joints, bones, and soft tissues like muscles. Many are suffering from debilitating back pain and arthritis leading to rising numbers of joint replacements. Death from falling has increased 30% from 2007 to 2016. At this rate, by 2030, there will be seven deaths from accidental falls every hour! *We're weaker and more frail than we've ever been.*

Not only has the cost of prescription drugs skyrocketed, so has the cost of the side effects that go with those drugs. Mounting medical bills are the single biggest reason for people filing for bankruptcy in this country.[6] Think about that.

Every one of these statistics is *screaming at us* there is a big problem, and if something doesn't change soon, we're going to be in even bigger trouble down the road.

And then, there's something we rarely ever talk about but is so important: underlying health issues often go unnoticed because they haven't manifested as actual symptoms, yet, and thus aren't being addressed.

For example, imagine you've had a water leak in your ceiling. Water is dripping down and there's a brown spot dirtying that nice white paint. So, you put a bucket underneath the drip and get some paint to cover up the ugly brown. But the next time it rains, the same thing will happen. Because there's still the underlying problem that is causing the leak. You can't see it, but it's there, causing the symptoms – the drip and the stain. The same is true with things like arthritis and back, hip, or knee pain. In addition, diabetes, hypertension, and fatty liver, to name just a few, are chronic health issues that are becoming more common with each passing day.

We're treating symptoms, and doing it in a reductionist way, without looking at the big picture. Thus, we're missing the very real possibility that something much more insidious is going on – something that at the very least is preventing us from enjoying life to its fullest.

I Wrote This Book Because I Know We Can Do Better.

I'd like to share a story with you. Because, even as I got more into the running lifestyle and improved, I also felt like something was *missing*. I noticed many of the runners I saw at races didn't *look* healthy to me, they looked weak and emaciated. Truth be told, I was starting to feel this way too, and I didn't like it. So, I looked around at other sports and one group I saw that seemed much healthier than I was feeling were triathletes. You know the sport, right? It's a combination of swimming, biking, and running. The most famous triathlon in the world is the Hawaii Ironman. Every year I looked forward to seeing it on TV and would often fantasize about being able to do it. For me, this was a pipedream; it was never going to happen. Or so it seemed.

You see, when I was 10, I was goofing around with some friends in a river and suffered a near fatal drowning. But that wasn't the worst of it. You've heard the old adage about getting back on the horse, right? Well, a couple of months after that experience, my parents signed me up for a town sponsored summer swim program taught by some teenagers who were lifeguards. It's crazy, but I was 10-years-old at the time, and as I sit here and write as a 62-year-old, I don't have any memory of the near-drowning, but still have vivid memories of those swimming lessons. If I'm being honest, there are times when I still feel like I'm the same frightened, humiliated, 10-year-old kid.

So, what happened? On the first day of the program, my mom dropped me off at school so I could board a bus to the local lake. As soon as we arrived, despite the instructors cajoling me, I refused to join the group. I never wanted to go and wanted no part of it when the bus arrived at the lake. I sat by myself, pouting, already feeling isolated and alone.

The whole morning went by, and I sat there watching the other kids playing and swimming. It was almost lunchtime, and as lessons were wrapping up, and the other kids who were in the water were drying off and changing, a couple of the instructors came over to me. It was the first time they'd spoken to me since I arrived a few hours before.

One of them looked at me and told me to come with them. I didn't say anything and just followed behind them as we headed toward the water's edge. As we got closer, one of the teenage instructors grabbed my arm and started to pull me into the water. I was resisting, kicking and yelling. But to no avail. It didn't matter. They were bound and determined to get me into the water and "teach me" the elementary backstroke.

I don't know how much time went by. However, one of the most vivid memories I have of that whole experience is watching as the bus, loaded with all the other kids, drove off. I can still see in my mind's eye, a few of the kids staring out through the glass windows, looking at me, pointing, laughing. All I remember from that point on is one of the instructors telling me to call my mom so she could come and pick me up. I don't remember how the whole fiasco ended in the water, only that I was crying, and felt embarrassed and humiliated. I wanted to die.

I would not get into water more than waist deep for the next 26 years, from that summer day in 1970 until January 1996.

Now if you're following along, you're wondering what happened that would get me into the water in January of 1996. A month earlier, in December 1995, I was watching the Ironman on TV like I did every year, this time with my then 9-year-old daughter, Erin. We were sitting, watching anxiously, literally at the edge of our seats. I was in awe. The race was so exciting that year – Mark Allen and Thomas Hellriegel duking it out on the run, with Allen coming from 13 minutes down at the start of the run portion to claim the men's crown. And then there was the women's battle between Paula Newby Fraser and Karen Smyers. Unfortunately, Paula collapsed just a few hundred yards from the finish to open the door for Karen, who claimed the women's crown in glorious fashion.

Of course, every time I'd watch the Ironman, I never believed it could happen for me. Even worse, while I wouldn't have admitted it at the time, with each passing year, I was feeling even more sorry for myself - ashamed because I was *still afraid* to go into the water. I mean, through all the years I was growing into adulthood, I carried that with me. I still feel a little embarrassed thinking back on it.

I don't know if you know that feeling? Is there something you secretly carry with you from your past that you're ashamed of? Maybe it's a "dark little secret" that most if not all your friends don't know about? That was me.

So, Erin and I were watching intently and the energy was building to a fever pitch, just like the temperature in Hawaii. This picture shows Mark Allen steadily closing in on Thomas Hellriegel just ahead, during the late stages of the run.

Then, in what has turned out to be one of the most pivotal and unanticipated moments of my life, I turned to Erin and shouted:

I'm gonna do the Ironman!

She turned and looked at me, paused for a moment, and chuckled, in the innocent, unassuming way that a 9-year-old daughter would do when her dad said something kind of ridiculous, at least to her. Like, what in the hell was I thinking. ☺ Right?

I never could have dreamed or imagined how much my life would change because of that one moment – that one bold statement. That one *wish*.

Fast forward, four long years later, I finally made it. At Ironman Lake Placid in 2000, in what was my second Ironman distance race that year and my third total, I achieved my dream by finishing near the top of my age-group to claim a coveted qualifying slot for the Ironman World Championships in Hawaii. Every time I think about it, I'm still amazed that it actually happened.

Here's the photo of me crossing that Ironman Lake Placid finish line, with Erin and her little brother, A.J., on my arms. That would become a family ritual – every Ironman finish line I would cross from that point forward would *always be* with them on my arms. I wouldn't do it without them.

And in case you're wondering, yes, that long four-year journey to overcome PTSD and my deathly fear of the water, and also learn how to swim, was just about THE hardest thing I've ever done in my life. The only thing that I can say was more difficult was watching my dad die a little bit each day after his cancer diagnosis.

Prior to that first Kona Ironman, in what became another ritual, Erin and A.J. secretly wrote me a letter of encouragement to read before the race. It was their idea. And they continued to do it for every one of my Ironman races, beginning with that first Hawaii Ironman on October 13, 2000. Erin would write it, then stick it under my pillow so I would find it on race morning when I woke up. Looking back after all the years that have passed, the letters they wrote to me before each of my ironman races are my most prized possessions. The love and compassion just pours out of each one.

Here's that first letter. I know it might be hard to read so I've transcribed it on the next page.

10/15/00

Daddy-

I just want to let you know that no matter what happens tomorrow (or today- depending on when you read this) we all LOVE YOU! We are so proud of you, just because you've gotten this far. I remember when you told us you were going to do THE Ironman. We all just laughed.

But you made it here in just a few years, despite our laughs. YOU HAVE EARNED YOUR WAY TO THE IRONMAN WORLD CHAMPIONSHIP. You've worked so hard. You are prepared, I promise.

I am proud to call you my dad. Whenever you cross any finish line, no matter what the clock says, I'm like "Hey, that's my father. He raised me (w/ mum) Isn't he awesome?" I know that none of this makes you feel better, but it makes me feel better to know that you know how I feel. (Did you get all that?) Just do your best + have fun. Enjoy the finishing. The cake is all your hours staring at a black line, sweating, + working hard.

As for the swim? Well, I can't really help you because I just don't understand what you're going through. But I do know that you CAN DO THIS. You know that you'll get through it, and just think about what you're going to feel like after. Powerful. Proud. Awesome!

After the swim, you're set. Show em your stuff. Show yourself your stuff. Be careful. Have fun.

Just keep telling yourself, you can do it. Think of "I believe I can Fly." Think of "Go the Distance." Face your fear. Finish what you have the courage to start. Think of how much worse it could be. Think of why you started this. Think of what family + friends have said. And if you miss us, do what you told me to do in a postcard a long time ago: sing the song "Somewhere Out There" by Kenny in your head.

So this is it. The Big Dance. You did it, you earned your way here, just enjoy it. (you're thinking "yea, right!")

I don't know what else to say but I ♡ U so much. I'm SO PROUD OF YOU. This is the Hawaii Ironman that you're going to finish. Awesome.

Love always + forever.
Erin

Daddy,

I just want to let you know that no matter what happens tomorrow (or today – depending on when you read this), we all LOVE YOU! We are so proud of you, just because you've gotten this far. I remember when you told us you were going to do THE Ironman. We all just laughed.

But you made it here in just a few years despite our laughs. YOU HAVE EARNED YOUR WAY TO THE IRONMAN WORLD CHAMPIONSHIP! You've worked so hard. You are prepared, I promise.

I am proud to call you my dad. When you cross that finish line, no matter what the clock says, I'm like, "Hey, that's my father. He raised me. (w/ mom). Isn't he awesome?"

I know that none of that makes you feel better, but it makes me feel better to know that you know how I feel. (Did you get all that?) Just do your best – have fun. Enjoy the frosting. The cake is all your hours staring at a black line, sweating + working hard.

As for the swim? Well, I can't really help you because I just don't understand what you're going through. But I do know that YOU CAN DO THIS. You know that you'll get through it and just think about what you're going to feel like after. Powerful. Proud. Awesome.

After the swim, you're set. Show em your stuff. Show yourself your stuff. Be careful. Have fun.

Just keep telling yourself you can do it. Think of "I believe I can fly." Think of "Go the Distance." Face your fear. Finish what you have the courage to start. Think of how much worse it could be. Think of why you started this. Think of what family + friends have said. And if you miss us, do what you told me to do in a postcard a long time ago: sing the song, "Somewhere out there" by Kenny in your head.

So this is it. The Big Dance. You did it. You earned your way here. Just enjoy it. (You're thinking "Yea, right!")

I don't know what else to say but I LOVE u so much + I'm SO PROUD OF YOU. This is the Hawaii Ironman that you're going to finish. Awesome.

Love always + forever.

Erin (w A.J.)

Here's my finish line photo from the 2000 Ironman World Championships, again with Erin and A.J. on my arms. Pure joy.

As I neared the end of the race, turning the corner from Hualalai onto Alii Drive, and then down Alii to the finish line – the emotion – well, it's something I'll never be able to describe, and will never, ever forget.

And, amazingly, I've finished five more Ironman races (nine total) since then and qualified two more times for the Hawaii Ironman World Championships. And I haven't drowned yet! ☺

I share that story with you for one reason: **I'm living proof that it's never too late to start something new or to go after and achieve your dreams.** That's what the song, *Go the Distance,* is all about, and why I shared the lyrics with you at the beginning of this Preface.

We CAN DO better my friends. This book is your guide for finding that "better" and living the life you have dreamed of and going the distance.

What do you say we make it happen? Let's get to work and GO THE DISTANCE. I'll see you in Chapter 1!

By the way, if you're thinking that is one amazing letter from a 14-year-old young lady and her little brother to their dad, I think you'd be right about that. I still cry every single time I read it. ☺

INTRODUCTION

Start over, start again. It's time for a new beginning. The triumphs will be sweet and the regrets will sting. Take it all in, whatever it may be, and move on steadily ahead.

Whatever experience life may bring your way, find in it something to value. Take that value and make the most of it as you apply it in a positive, purposeful direction.

Concern yourself not with what is wrong, but with how you can make it better. Concern yourself not with what might have been, but what could be. Take pleasure not in what you have, but in what it can enable you to do.

Let go of any envy, anger, or despair. Hold on to the love, the joy, and the hope. In each ending, find the new beginning that is surely there. With every finish line, there is another starting line not far ahead. In each setback, find the will to go forward, and use each success to create value that goes far beyond yourself.

Appreciate every moment, whatever that moment may bring. And from those moments will come a remarkable life. Let's get started!

~AI

Everything can be taken from a man but one thing; the last
of the human freedoms – to choose one's attitude in any
given set of circumstances, to choose one's own way.
— Victor Frankl

Do not regret growing older. It's a privilege denied to many.
— Anonymous

Imagine you can see your future in your mind's eye. Whether you're now in your 30s, 40s, 50s or beyond, as you pause and look into the future - what does your life, especially your health, look like? What about the next decade and the decade after that? How do you feel? What do you see? Do you see yourself feeling good for many years to come? Are you healthy and physically capable of doing whatever you would like? Are you enthusiastically looking toward the future with hope and promise? Or... are you feeling betrayed by your body? Are the youthful hopes and dreams you once believed were possible, dissolving into aches, pains, and debilitating disease?

If you answered honestly, you probably saw yourself struggling with increasing health issues as you aged. And in fact, isn't that something we all, as a society, have come to *expect*? If you're not sure what I mean, take a moment to look around you. You know those indignities of aging we're all too familiar with, such as arthritis, back pain, diabetes, dementia, heart disease, and cancer, to name a few? It seems we've reached a point where most believe these afflictions are *normal* and an inevitable part of getting older. That's just the way it is, and there's nothing we can do about it.

I think it was early 20th century American movie star and actress, Mae West, who said, "getting old isn't for the faint of heart." Boy, was she ever right!

Or was she?

Life Can Become a Series of Compromises.

The truth is, now, more than ever, many are sadly *dying slow gradual "deaths"* before their actual demise. All around we see increasing rates of chronic disease such as cancer, dementia, and diabetes. We're also witnessing increasing rates of functional decline and the associated emotional pain from isolation because of that decline. Every one of these ailments can leave us with lasting pain and rob us of our ability to enjoy life to its fullest.

Medical science might be keeping us alive longer with new drugs and treatments that are helping to increase our *lifespan*, but our *healthspan*, which is the *quality* of those years, is worsening. Day by day, week by week, year by year. Left with no choice, life becomes nothing more than a *series of compromises*. That might sound depressing, but I'm here to tell you, **it doesn't have to be that way.** While many accept the picture I've painted as common and "normal," it *isn't inevitable*. All of us are capable of aging while feeling and looking younger than our chronological age.

This book is the resource you've been looking for to help you live a healthier, happier life that isn't defined by pain and suffering as you get older. The idea is to be able to **go the distance,** feeling good right up until the very end. It's written specifically for people like you and aims to be inspiring, even empowering, giving you just enough practical and actionable knowledge without confusing buzzwords or information overload.

Healthy in Your 50s, 60s, 70s, and Beyond? YES!

Yes, my friend, there IS hope. And it doesn't matter what age you are. Anyone CAN make positive changes that will have a lasting impact and improve their life. A future full of possibility is what we dreamed about when we were young. I know there is more you want to do and so much joy left to experience that will take you into your future. *All you need is belief, and the right kind of practical, actionable guidance to show the way.* And of course, a willingness to commit and take action. The fact that you've picked up this book and are reading this right now tells me you are that kind of person!

Can You Envision a Healthier, Happier Path For Yourself?

Let's pause again and this time, in your mind's eye, envision a future that isn't as bleak or filled with endless compromise. Imagine your 60s and beyond, being able to live life entirely on your terms, feeling strong, not fragile! Imagine being able to do the things in life that matter the most to you – being able to create lasting memories with family and friends with very few if any physical limitations.

Then, finally… one day very far off into the future, perhaps at the "young" age of 110 or 120, after spending a fun-filled day doing something important and enjoyable - you lie down at night, go to sleep, and don't wake up the next day.

You Die Healthy.

In this scenario, you don't miss out on the opportunity to enjoy life's most important occasions. You get to watch grandchildren grow up and perhaps even get married. You have the opportunity to travel with family and friends and create lasting memories – for you AND for them.

At the same time, you're able to avoid years of physical, emotional, or financial pain and hardship that come from long term hospital or convalescent care, participating fully in whatever activities you'd like to! *Isn't that the way you'd like to live out the time you have left here on earth?* Of course, the only possible answer to that question is YES!

We Can Do Better.

If dying young at an old age sounds unrealistic, I'm here to tell you and show you, it isn't. It is possible with the right kind of intentional approach to getting older, and a touch of good fortune. It's possible for anyone who begins to make small but important positive changes, regardless of their age. Science and our understanding of the human body advance every day. We're living in a new age with greater understanding of what matters the most. Even if you're in your 70s or 80s, you can do things NOW that can add quality years to your life. I know it's true – I've seen it happen! Of course, you must believe it too. It won't happen just by wishing.

In this book, you'll find everything you need to know to begin to make those positive changes, giving yourself the best possible chance to live out your final years feeling good, and then die a natural, "healthy" death.

We're at a Crossroads – a Moment of Truth.

Just in case you're thinking this is only about living longer or some fantasy like immortality, it's not. Yes, modern medical science is becoming more sophisticated every day and is keeping us alive longer than ever.

But think about this: by the year 2050, for the first time in human history, the number of people OVER the age of 65 will exceed the number of people under the age of 15.

That's astounding, especially when you consider according to the very latest statistics, **right now in 2022, more than 93% of those 65 or older suffer from one or more chronic diseases.**[1]

Who wants to live longer if it means more years of pain and suffering? The answer is **no one.** It's the quality of our years that matters the most. And that's what this book is all about.

Let's face it, life is hard. If you're in your 20s, 30s or 40s, and have a family and a profession or job, I know much of the time you're just trying to get through your day. You've got too many responsibilities. You're busy balancing multiple roles including supporting other people. You probably don't sleep very well or enough. You don't have enough time OR energy to take care of YOU - to do the things that you, deep down inside, know you need to do to thrive, physically and emotionally, not just for today but for your future.

When it comes to things like exercise and nutrition, you're confused. How could you not be? There's so much conflicting information out there about what you should eat, what you shouldn't eat, what kind of exercise you should do, blah blah blah. I get it. The solutions you seek are available if you're willing to open your mind and take action. I'll show you the way.

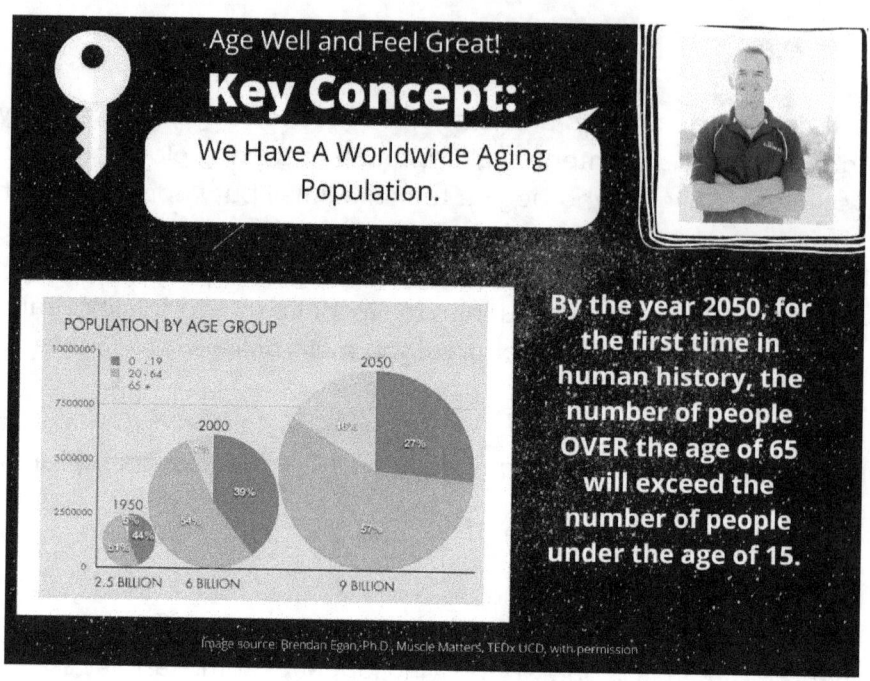

Age Well and Feel Great!

Key Concept:

We Have A Worldwide Aging Population.

By the year 2050, for the first time in human history, the number of people OVER the age of 65 will exceed the number of people under the age of 15.

POPULATION BY AGE GROUP

Image source: Brendan Egan, Ph.D., Muscle Matters, TEDx UCD, with permission

Your Future Is Now. It's NEVER Too Late.

Your confusion ends now! In this book, I am going to share with you what I've learned through an entire lifetime of thinking about exercise, nutrition, stress, chronic disease, and how to achieve and keep good health. *And it's what I've been putting into practice for more than 40 years.* It's what I've taught hundreds of people – just like you – over the last 20+ years as a sports therapist, coach, and personal trainer.

I will also decipher some of the very latest in scientific research and thinking on important topics related to *why* we age. I'll bring together wisdom from other experts so you get to hear it from the horse's mouth. I wrote this book as a 62-year-old who, other than antibiotics after dental work, has never taken a prescription drug. It has truly been my life's work to learn how to age better and **go the distance**. You get the benefit of that experience and my never-ending thirst for knowledge by reading this book and taking action with the information and guidance I provide.

Being Healthy ISN'T About Trying to Live "Perfectly."

Being healthy isn't about exercising for hours or trying to find the perfect diet or having to give up many of the things you enjoy. What it is about is discovering for yourself, with guidance from a trusted source, what the positive and sustainable changes are you can make to your daily routine, that if done consistently, can add up to a powerful transformation. And a whole new you. You just might find you get many more of what could ironically be the very best years of your life! In fact, I challenge you right now to make sure they ARE the best years. I believe you can do it.

This Book Isn't Like Any Other Book.

Sure, there are other books on aging, some written by scientists with Ph.D.'s after their name, that are a bit dry and filled with endless pages of technical jargon. While those books can be great resources, they often lack practical, easy-to-follow actionable advice on what to do and how to proceed. In this book, you'll find easy-to-understand guidance and wisdom gleaned from real experience and science, along with the extra inspiration you need to take action.

There are also books with "anti-aging" titles that slyly glorify youth and beauty. They promise quick, often unrealistic results. Phrases like "turn back the clock," "halt aging," and "dramatically reverse sagging skin, age spots, thinning hair, and wrinkles," are telltale signs to be very skeptical. These books often use scare tactics to grab your attention. And the radical "promises" they present are sure to be accompanied by a sales pitch for supplements, as the sole purpose of that type of book is to sell something and earn profits for the author and the supplement company. Not surprisingly, you'll often notice the author has obviously had plastic surgery or that pictures have been photoshopped.

However, in THIS BOOK, you won't find radical promises, just sound advice based on real science combined with 40+ years of practical experience and thinking every day about how to become truly healthy and age well. And you can rest assured *I'm not selling anything.*

Still other books are filled with graphics that are poorly designed, or the opposite – pictures of professional exercise models – both of which often miss out on the most important details. This isn't that kind of book. Here you'll find real people striving to age well just like you, demonstrating time-tested important details that matter the most for *your* success.

Inside this book, you'll find realistic, actionable guidance to help you feel better, stay younger and healthier, so you can truly **go the distance**. Your job will be to stay the course and never give up in your pursuit of a better you. I know you can do it!

I also designed this book to be modular, so you can read it any way you want. You can dip in and out of chapters, skim for the most relevant nuggets, or revisit chapters whenever you want a reminder or fresh shot of inspiration.

My Friend, If You Don't Have *YOUR Health*, Nothing Else Matters...

No amount of money or status matters very much, if you're in pain or sick with a chronic illness that robs you of the things that make life worth living. It's easy to forget this as we go through life. We're focusing on our career path or caring for others – those often take priority. Until, that is, we're hit square in the mouth with a health problem that forces us to deal with a new reality.

Here's another truth that might be hard to hear – but it IS the truth. Take a few seconds to ponder this: **If we don't make time *now* for our wellness, at some point in the future, we'll be *forced to* make time for our illness.**

If we become sick or end up struggling with a chronic condition, in what's an ironic twist, we might not be able to be there for others or fulfill our responsibilities. In a worst-case scenario, we become a burden *to those loved ones we least want to burden.* The thing is, you and I know prioritizing self-care when you're busy and stressed and have so many responsibilities, **is hard.**

But so is needless pain and suffering, chronic illness, medical bills, becoming a burden to others, and even early death. *The quality of your health and therefore your life is defined most by the values you are willing to struggle for.* So, let me ask you point blank: What kind of pain do you want in your life?

Because there is no such thing as a life without some kind of hard.

You must *choose your hard.* It's that simple.

The Great News Is...

Are you less healthy than you want to be or looking toward the future anxiously and want to be proactive now? Are you frustrated with endless doctors' visits that never seem to help? Are you saddled with low-back pain so much that you can't stand it anymore? If any of those sound familiar, *you're in the right place.* That's the great news. And it really doesn't matter how old you are right now. That's the other great news. Anyone can make positive changes in their health when they know what to do and what matters the most. No looking back. No regrets. Just positive, proactive steps moving forward. You can do it, I know you can.

I Am Going to Make You a Promise – But I Can't Do It Alone – You Have to Act.

If you read this book and consistently act on the guidance I provide, one tiny step at a time, I promise you will feel, look and act younger AND most importantly, you will have the best possible chance to live longer AND go the distance and ultimately die healthy. I *guarantee it.*

If you're wondering where my willingness to make this promise comes from, it's simply this: I have *lived virtually everything* I will share with you. I know my recommendations about eating and exercise work because I've tried and tested them throughout my lifetime, then waited patiently while the research validated them. And I've seen it work in others.

I wrote this book for YOU – the person who simply wants to live their best life and feel good all the way to the end – to **go the distance!**

What Will You Find Inside This Book?

o   How you can feel better and be healthier now and into the future with a few simple yet profound changes to your daily routine.

o   The optimal approach to eating better, without dieting, so you will be healthier, have more energy, and better body composition.

o   The simplest and most effective evidence and experience-based strategies to incorporate exercise in as little as 10 minutes a day.

o   Why you find it difficult to find the motivation to exercise consistently, and what you can do to make it part of your daily routine with less struggle.

o   How to build a more stable, stronger, healthier "chassis" so you can do all the things you love to do with little physical limitations.

o   How to think about and handle your relationship with your doctor and the healthcare system, so you're less frustrated and healthier overall.

o   The truth about the debate between lifestyle habits and family history, so that you're empowered to make positive changes that WILL help you live better, longer, and die healthy.

o   What those people who live to 100 or more in "blue zones" around the world know, that you don't.

o   The most important things to know about stress, sleep, dental health, early diagnosis, and more.

o   The latest scientific advice from some of the world's leaders in aging research, simplified and broken down into easy-to-understand ideas and tips without the jargon.

o   My practical experience and time-tested tips from my more than 40 years as an endurance athlete, coach, and sports therapist. I've lived everything I will share with you!

Nothing Happens Without Action—DON'T Wait To Get Started.

Learn what it actually means to die healthy, and how you and anyone willing to believe and then act can achieve that goal. Learn how to improve your life by living intentionally, so that you can live free of disease and dysfunction and then die healthy. *I know you can do it.*

It won't always be easy, but nothing worth achieving ever is. And I'd argue THIS achievement is more valuable, more meaningful than any other.

When I was 25, I made a decision. I was going to die healthy. I am asking you to make the same decision. Today. Right now. *I believe in you and I know you are worth it.*

Get started reading Chapter 1 now. Don't wait!

During the run portion of my 2001 Hawaii Ironman, my kids Erin and A.J., wrote "GO THE DISTANCE" on the road in chalk to inspire me to the finish line. My race number was #241.

PART 1

THE BEGINNING

CHAPTER 1

WHAT DOES IT MEAN TO DIE HEALTHY?

Strangely, life gets harder when
you try to make it easy.

Exercising might be hard, but never
moving makes life harder.

Uncomfortable conversations are hard,
but avoiding every conflict is harder.

Mastering your craft is hard, but
having no skills is harder.

Easy has a cost.

> *Until you make the unconscious conscious, it will*
> *direct your life and you will call it fate.*
> — Carl Jung

'm going to tell you a story but before I do, if you skipped over the Preface and Introduction to get to Chapter 1, I implore you to go back and read those two chapters first. You won't be sorry you did.

So, it was 23 years ago. I don't think I'll ever forget it. Dad mentioned he was having trouble seeing. He brushed it off for a while, trying to tune out that voice in his head saying something is wrong. Finally, after almost driving off the road, he couldn't ignore it any longer. My mom arranged an appointment with the doctor and after a series of tests came the news we all least wanted to hear.

He had a brain tumor.

Receiving that diagnosis was like being sucker punched in the gut. We were all so scared. I vividly remember the frightened and angry look on his face, listening to the oncologist talk about treatment. The moment I heard his diagnosis I looked over at him. For the first time ever, dad looked so vulnerable. And scared. It was a look I had never seen before.

Dad was born on a farm in Vermont and grew up around the railroad and farming. He was a blue collar, "salt of the earth" kind of guy. Strong, tough, and rough around the edges. To anyone who didn't know him well, his gruff exterior was intimidating. And that's exactly how he arrived for a follow up visit with the doctor. He scoffed. He wasn't having any of what the doctor had to say and wasn't going to go through with any treatments. We all begged him. *Fight it*, we said. He scowled.

I felt helpless searching for answers, for some way to help him. In a desperate attempt for some ray of hope, I made some calls to Sloan Kettering Cancer Center in New York City to speak with a doctor who was an expert in this type of cancer, a glioblastoma.[1]

After about a dozen attempts, I finally got a doctor on the phone. He heard my desperation and told me to send the scans to him for review and he'd call me back in a few days. I was encouraged by his willingness to help and felt hopeful. But when I spoke with him a week or so later, he squashed any sense of hope. "I'm not sure what you've been told," he said. "I'm sorry to be the one to have to tell you this, but there is no way – the type of cancer your dad has is nearly always terminal. He probably has only a few months."

When someone you love becomes sick with a disease like terminal cancer, you're never ready for it. Hearing a diagnosis like that is sickening; you want to go somewhere and throw up. At that moment, the fear, anger, and sadness I felt was overwhelming.

In the U.S. in 2020, 602,350 people died from cancer, nearly 1700 a day.[2] Today it's the second leading cause of death in the U.S. right behind heart disease. Regrettably, cancer may soon take over that unenviable "lead."

One of my most gut-wrenching memories from that day occurred when we arrived home. We walked slowly and silently inside. Dad went off on his own to a spare bedroom in the back of the house. This tiny bedroom was mine growing up and had since become his own quiet space. He had a small TV with an old VCR attached to it. One of his favorite things was watching videos of old trains. My grandfather worked for the Central Vermont Railroad, so my dad grew up around the rails and loved anything having to do with trains.

After going inside, I sat down in the corner and just stared at a blank wall, still numb from what had just happened. After a while, I followed him back there to see how he was. I was still in shock. I'm sure he was too. He was sitting in his chair in the middle of the room, motionless, watching one of the train videos. I went back there to talk with him, to tell him I loved him – to say I was so grateful for all he had taught me. For all he did to provide for all of us. I didn't want any of that to go unsaid. But standing behind him where he couldn't see me, I froze and just *couldn't say a word*.

As I watched him from behind – I started to cry – tears were running down my face. It felt so hopeless, so sad. My dad was only 65 at the time. He'd just retired from his job. There was so much he still wanted to do, so much still to share with my mom and his kids and grandkids, so many memories that hadn't yet been created. All I could think was, *why did this have to happen?*

What Do You See for Yourself?

Life is short. Every single day is a gift. At any moment, our life can be turned upside down and the person we hold most dear can be taken away. If there's one harsh potentiality my dad's brain cancer taught me, it was that.

Most of us want to live a long life, but don't we also want to live an active, *energetic, vibrant* life, right up until the end? When you think about being older, do you see yourself feeling good right up until the end or do you expect to lose the ability to do some of the things you love to do? Do you believe you'll be physically, mentally, and emotionally capable of enjoying whatever years you have left?

When I was in my teens, it sometimes felt like I'd live forever. Sure, I knew that Father Time would someday prevail, but when you're young, that someday seems far off in the distance.

(image source: cartoonists, Glen and Gary McCoy)

When I was in my early-20s, the whole idea of *getting old* and dying was still so foreign. As time when on, I learned that no one really wants to talk about it or even think about it. It can be depressing. But in my mid-20s, I started thinking more about what it would be like to *grow old*. I wondered if there was a way to avoid the physical decline I saw in so many others.

When you're in your 40s, you look in the mirror and notice subtle changes. You might even worry you're starting to look like your parents. ☺ By the time you hit 60, if you aren't struggling with a chronic condition or haven't had a hip or shoulder replacement yet, you can count yourself among the rare and fortunate few.

David Sinclair, Ph.D. is a well-known author, Harvard professor, and one of many aging researchers learning more about what makes us *grow old*. In his book, *Lifespan: Why We Age and Why We Don't Have To,* he references a research study that found 85-year-old men "are diagnosed with an average of four different diseases, with women of that age suffering from five. Heart disease and cancer. Arthritis and Alzheimer's. Kidney disease and diabetes." He then points out they're all "different ailments with different pathologies, studied in different buildings at the National Institute of Health and in different departments within universities."[3] All these different diseases and what is the single risk factor for every one of them? If you guessed aging, you'd be right.

Regardless of your age, have you wondered what it would be like to *feel even* older? When Dr. Sinclair speaks to large groups about his research on aging, he says he often brings an *age suit* with him and asks a young volunteer to wear it. Here's how he describes this age suit: "A neck brace reduces mobility in the neck, lead-lined jackets and wraps all over the body simulate weak muscles, earplugs reduce hearing, and ski goggles simulate cataracts." He goes on to say "as you might imagine, after only a few minutes of walking around in the suit, the young test subject is very relieved to take it off – and fortunately they can. Imagine wearing it for a decade."[4]

In his book *Constructive Living*, author David Reynolds talks about those with chronic illness and how their quality of life suffers, describing a routine full of compromises and practical adjustments. "Their daily lives require rescheduling and new pacing of activities, rerouting of market trips in order to utilize wheelchair curbs or to avoid hills, arranging for backup support in case of accident, education so that families can help intelligently, dietary control, skill in recognizing changes in their own bodies, rearranging furniture for accessibility to equipment and medications, adjusting bathroom and bed facilities at home, changes in exercise habits, contact with others who share the same difficulty, and much more."[5] He goes on to say "chronic illness and pain, like neurosis, are forms of suffering. People who moan endlessly about what is happening to them, lost in their misery and self-centered despair, focus almost exclusively on their own suffering and thus feel it more acutely. They actually hurt more, subjectively, than their counterpart who has precisely the same disease but lives constructively."[6]

So, let me ask you, what if we could slow down the rate at which we age? Could we reduce the risk of becoming slaves to these conditions of disease and dysfunction? I believe we can. That's what this book is all about.

We Can Do Better.

There is a much happier and more hopeful flip side to the unnerving images of decline I just painted for you. For example, imagine being able to attend your great grandchild's college graduation, or their wedding. Not just being there, but actually enjoying it physically, mentally, and emotionally. Imagine the moments with your family you could be a part of, meaningful not only for you, but also for them. Aren't these moments what truly makes life worth living? I'd argue that *nothing matters* more – nothing *means* more – than those moments.

For years, I've looked around and watched as the health of so many friends and family gradually declined. I've watched as many were forced to spend the last third or even half of their life in physical or mental anguish and pain. I've watched as they've battled physical decline and chronic disease, often one after another – their lives defined by endless doctors' visits or the amount of prescription drugs they had no other choice but to take. All to ease the pain and manage whatever symptoms they were dealing with.

Without Good Health, Does Anything Else Matter as Much?

I have a very good friend battling stage 4 cancer. Over the last few months, I've noticed, as have many others I'm sure, how his frightening diagnosis has resulted in a subtle shift in his priorities and seems to have brought even deeper meaning to his relationships. Sometimes it takes something awful to happen for us to finally see and understand what matters most in life.

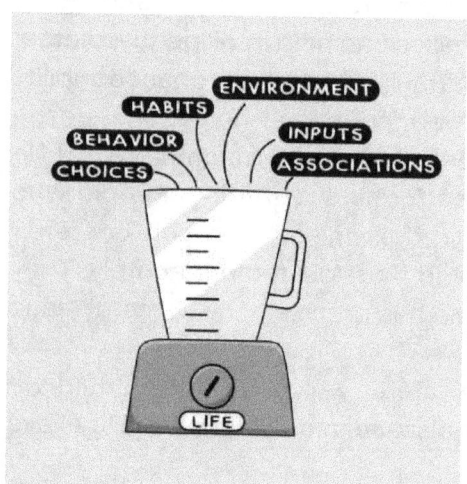

Living through my dad's 10-month long battle with brain cancer, combined with all I've learned, has helped me realize the single, most profound TRUTH you will read in this or any book: **without good health during the course of our lives, nothing else matters quite as much.**

If you're sick and in pain or suffering, you can't enjoy valued relationships with loved ones or be involved in meaningful personal or work-related activities, or even enjoy the inherent beauty of mother nature. You desperately want to, of course. You just can't. Pain and suffering changes everything.

Countless scientific studies have shown as we age, material possessions matter less. Strong emotional bonds with family, friends, and community take on more importance. We spend so much of our lives acquiring possessions and chasing career success or other accomplishments, only to at some point realize *you can't take it with you.*

It doesn't matter how much money you have made, how much you've saved, or how many possessions you own, if you can't take advantage of those special moments that create memories - memories that will last forever in the hearts and minds of you and your loved ones.

The idea is to die young as late in life as possible.
— Dr. Ashley Montagu

What Is Your Perfect "Dream" Life?

After high school, many of us go to college looking toward the future and a promising career. Others start working right away or decide to do something vastly different like take off on a wild adventure. We build friendships and join communities of like-minded people. If we're fortunate, we might even meet a person we want to spend our life with and start a family. Hopefully we find the "perfect" job or career, watch our children grow and prosper, and settle down to live our perfect "dream" life. And of course, we look forward to the day we're paid well for our hard work, adding value and richness to our lives, a beautiful place to call home, a nice car, even regular vacations, or a vacation home. I'm guessing some of this might sound like a "dream" life to you.

I'm here to remind you that NONE OF THOSE things can possibly mean as much or be as enjoyable as they might be if you're sick or in pain and suffering. *Being truly healthy and feeling good* creates the platform that gives us the opportunity to enjoy the most meaningful things in life. To experience life to its utmost.

When my dad was diagnosed with brain cancer, chronologically speaking, he was *only* 65. But his *biological age*, which is the age our body *seems* based on how we feel or look or act, was so much older than that. Even when he was in his 40s and 50s, I remember watching him struggle to get out of a soft chair. I saw the pained look on his face when he *tried to* bend over to pick something up off the floor. I knew he was out of breath walking up a flight of stairs. That didn't make sense to me, he wasn't *that* old. In the end, sadly, his perfect "dream" life was cut short.

The Ah-Ha Moment That Changed My Life.

When I was in my early 20s, I started running to get in shape. I was feeling very much OUT of shape at the time – the "freshman 15" had turned into 20. Like, not being able to button my pants! You know that feeling? ☺

Strangely though, something else happened at the same time. I noticed that some older people around me, like my dad, were a*ging faster than I thought they should be.* And that was alarming. I wondered why people age differently – why some people get sick with a disease like cancer and others don't. We all know aging happens to everyone. Our hair grays, our skin wrinkles and sags, our joints begin to ache, which leads to some moaning and groaning when we get out of bed in the morning. And then people die. We're all going to die someday. But none of this is about dying – it's about *how we are able to live.* To this day, I'm not sure what made me so keenly aware of how people around me aged, and along with it, what they did or didn't do that might have contributed to how they were aging.

Looking back, I vividly remember how my grandfather looked during the last weeks of his life. He spent his final years in a nursing home. The gnarly texture of his unshaven face, and the hollow look in his eyes - he was nothing more than shriveled-up skin and bones. Nursing homes are sort of a modern-day invention. Centuries ago, people didn't live long enough to make nursing homes necessary. If someone *did* survive to "old age," they would typically be cared for by their family. That's now changed, particularly in the U.S. We've got more people than ever living longer but not necessarily better. I remember how depressing the whole nursing home scene was. It seemed everyone who was there hated being there, including the staff. And I dare say many of the families had moved on.

I saw how my grandfather's final years played out – in pain and barely able to speak. And I saw what was happening with my dad. All around me, there was an increasing number of "older" people who weren't healthy and more reliant than ever on prescription medications and endless doctor's visits.

I wanted something different for myself. That's one of the reasons I started running. Which wasn't easy. I mean, as a kid, I sucked at sports. Really, I did. Is there any chance you were also the slowest in gym class like I was? ☺ In elementary school, during recess out on the playground, I was *always* the last kid to get picked for a game of kickball. By the time I got to high school, I knew I wasn't talented, so I didn't try to do sports, other than play freshman baseball where I warmed the bench for the entire season.

As time went on, my fitness was improving. Still, some days, I had a hard time getting out the door. Motivation is hard at times, right? ☺ Slowly but surely, I saw myself transforming. I embraced this new active lifestyle and felt good about myself. And I became even more curious. I wanted to learn more about what was happening physiologically, inside my body, how this fitness journey I was on was impacting me in ways I couldn't see in the mirror.

The Epiphany.

One day during lunch break, as I was walking over to the gym with a friend, he asked me why I ran. He was like a lot of people, maybe even you. He'd tried running once and hated it. I do think sometimes folks give up too soon, before it starts to get a little easier, but there's no denying distance running isn't for everyone.

For whatever reason his question caught me off guard. No one had ever asked me that before. Instantly our walking pace slowed. Sometimes the harder you think, the slower you move, you know? I was thinking about his question - *why am I doing it?*

Sure, I had signed up for some races and was excited and also a little nervous about them. But at that moment, I didn't think about the races. I believe deep down, I knew there was something *more* to it, but I don't think I ever actually acknowledged what that "something" was.

Then, like a bright light in a dark room, I had one of those *ah-ha* moments. I stopped, turned to him, and said...**"I run to square the curve."**

I have no idea where I'd heard that phrase or where it came from. But the meaning behind it was so clear to me. It seemed, in that exact moment, these ideas that had been swirling around in my mind about growing older and staying younger and feeling better, all coalesced into this defining three-word phrase – **square the curve**. Not surprisingly I guess, he was totally confused. He looked back at me with this puzzled look and laughingly said, "What the hell are you talking about? Square the curve?"

We continued walking slowly toward the gym without saying anything for the next few minutes. I could tell he was wondering if I'd heard his question. I was fumbling for the right words as I wrestled with all the thoughts going through my mind at once. As we neared the entrance to the gym, I stopped, turned to him, and tried to explain it this way:

"Imagine living for a very long time not in pain or with a disease, but feeling great, able to do the things you want to whenever you want to, nothing holding you back. And then one day far off in the future, maybe you're 105 or even 110, you go to sleep and don't wake up the next day. You *die healthy*."

"Squaring the Curve": Lifespan vs. Healthspan.

On the next page, you'll see an image comparing two square boxes. Take a good look at these boxes and the lines drawn in and around them. Our focus is what is inside these boxes, not the boxes themselves. I drew a very rough version of this graphic on a blank piece of paper a few days after that walk with my friend. Many years later, I created what you see here to paint a visual image of how I had envisioned the way I wanted my life to go – the way everyone's life *should* go.

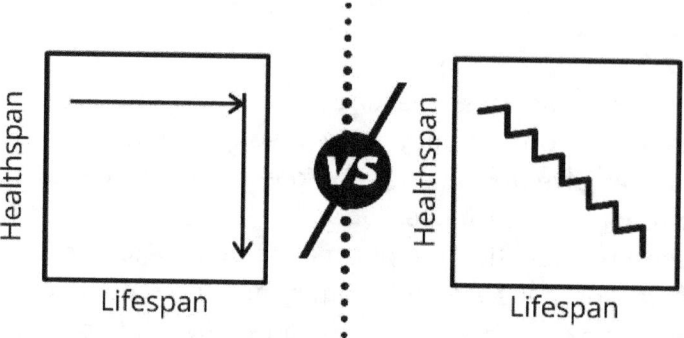

Across the bottom of both boxes is the word **Lifespan,** which I think of as the horizontal axis. On the side is the word **Healthspan,** which is the vertical axis. As you might have guessed, these axis represent a time continuum for a person. For our purposes here, that person will be me.

Lifespan is defined as the total amount of time I am alive here on earth. **Healthspan,** on the other hand, is defined as the amount of time I am able to spend in *good health, free from serious pain and debilitating chronic disease. Do you see the difference between healthspan and lifespan?*

Now look below, this time at a slightly modified version of the previous image. This version has some additions in red. The bold red arrow in the box on the left is pointing at the intersection of the horizontal arrow and the vertical arrow. The horizontal arrow **represents my lifespan** - the total amount of years I am alive, and the vertical arrow represents **the *day I die.*** If you look at those two lines with arrows, horizontal and vertical, and the intersection point, that is the "squared curve" I was referring to.

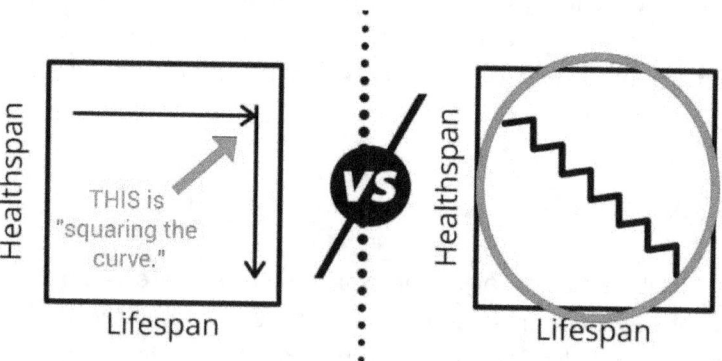

To put it another way, this "squared curve" image of two arrows meeting at a right angle is a theoretical ideal life continuum where I was able to maintain good health throughout my life right up until the end, when I went to sleep and didn't wake up the next day.

In the box on the right, you see a jagged line trending downward. As you might now be able to imagine, that jagged line is meant to graphically represent the gradual decline and erosion of good health typical of so many in this day and age.

As a well-spent day brings happy sleep, so life,
well used, brings happy death.
— Leonardo da Vinci

The Trajectory of Our Lives Has Changed.

In *Being Mortal: Medicine and What Matters in the End*, author, doctor and Harvard professor, Atul Gawande, M.D., takes a deep dive into how the trajectory of our lives has been transformed by modern medicine and public health. He says for "all but our most recent history, death was a common, ever-present possibility. It didn't matter whether you were five or fifty. Every day was a roll of the dice."[7]

A hundred or more years ago, anyone could be fine one day and gone the next. Whether it was a virus or bacteria born of poor sanitation, or an accident or a heart attack, there was neither the trauma care nor the medicine available then to save a life the way we can now. In his view, that was the natural "curve" of our lives.

As the years went on though, in Gawande's words, "medicine found ways to cut the mortality of heart attacks, respiratory illnesses, stroke, and numerous other conditions that threaten adult life. Medicine has pushed the *fatal* moment of many diseases further outward."[8] The key word here is *fatal*. Because when it comes to our health, for the overwhelming majority of us, the last few decades have been defined by the inability to save ourselves from the health issues that ruin our quality of life in the first place. It's only death that saves us.

"We have drugs, fluids, surgery, intensive care units to get people through. They enter the hospital looking terrible, and some of what we do can make them look worse. But just when it looks like they've breathed their last breath, they rally. We make it possible for them to make it home – weaker and more impaired though."[9] Think about it. He's actually describing the jagged line inside the red circle on the right of my graphic. **That jagged line represents the up and down of illness followed by a temporary recovery, only for illness to rear its ugly head and strike again.**

Death occurs eventually, of course. But the path there isn't like it might have been at one time, or what it should ideally be. What I mean is, in this modern world, it's often a slow gradual yet steady downward trend with occasional "recovered ground" leaving us worse off than before, but still alive. Until that is, the day finally comes.

Looking back to the day I said, "*I run to square the curve*," I hadn't had the opportunity to read Gawande's book. It hadn't been written yet. I purchased my first copy while researching for this book. But the way he described how the trajectory of our lives has changed represents how I originally thought of the "curve." Both as it should be – a squared right angle where we go to sleep one day and don't wake up the next – and as it plays out all too often today - a step-like gradual deterioration of our health – or even, I would suggest, *a gradual death over a long period of time.*

I was listening one day to a podcast episode of *The Drive* with Dr. Peter Attia, M.D. I don't recall which episode it was, but he was speaking about this idea of how so many are now dying a slow, gradual death. What he said stuck with me. You see, when we "die," our life is over and nothing matters at that point, right? But I want you to think of the word "death" a little differently. It's not the death you typically think of. Because obviously, when you hear the word *death*, your first thought goes immediately to someone's *demise*.

For example, "so and so" died of a heart attack or "so and so" died in a car accident. Those are the kinds of *actual* deaths where someone's life ends. With that kind of actual death, it's easy to see your heart and lungs stop working. That's the end of life as we know it. However, here's the difference and it's what I meant with "square the curve." And it's what Gawande was speaking about in his book, also. *It's what that downward trending jagged line inside that box on the right is all about.*

I recall Dr. Attia alluding to this idea that most people, as much as 80%, die a different sort of "death" first, before their actual "demise." Perhaps it'll be a *cognitive* death. That is, because of some form of dementia, their minds will become so dull or diseased, they won't be able to be the people they want to be. Sadly, they may not even know the people they love, or who love them.

Maybe their body will begin to *physically* break down so much, the things that at one time gave them so much joy – whatever it is, playing golf, skiing, running, hiking, or playing with their grandkids, will no longer be feasible. They'll be deprived of those things. *Perhaps even getting out of a chair or bed will become impossible.*

Or they'll die *emotionally*, becoming despondent, depressed, secluded even. Robbed of life's greatest joys, in what would be the saddest thing of all - the *desire to keep on living*, might also die. For some, those changes might begin in mid-life as something very subtle. For others, it will begin later, but the trajectory will be the same.

Now if you think that's a depressing way to look at how life usually goes, I agree! It's not pretty. Here's the thing: whether you think that's realistic or not, the truth is, from the dramatically rising rates of obesity in children and adults, to the 26,000 people a day worldwide who die from cancer, to the three out of four Americans who are now metabolically unhealthy and pre-diabetic, to the four trillion dollars a year spent in the U.S. on healthcare, to the worsening mental health crisis – depression, anxiety, suicidal ideation increasing at an alarming rate, *things look pretty grim.*

Every one of those statistics is screaming there's a big problem, and if something doesn't change – if *we don't change* - we're going to be in even bigger trouble down the road.

When you want to help people, you tell them the truth. When you want to help yourself, you tell them what they want to hear.

– Thomas Sowell

A Scientific Paper That Changed Everything.

James F. Fries was a professor at Stanford until he retired in 2017. When he was an undergraduate student, he majored in philosophy, so it's "no surprise as a medical researcher he was obsessed with how to lead a good life, even though his interest was more about physical than moral well-being."[10]

In 1980, he wrote a seminal paper that was published in the New England Journal of Medicine where he presented his hypothesis that has since become known as his "compression of morbidity."[11] Earlier in his career, he noted along with some of his colleagues, that life expectancy had dramatically improved thanks to improvements in vaccinations and sanitation that reduced deaths from acute, transmissible disease, but that increase in lifespan "did not mean an accompanying increase in 'healthspan,' or the duration of one's life free from chronic conditions like hypertension, diabetes, and heart disease."[12]

In his landmark paper, Fries wrote: "*Think about two points on a typical human lifespan, with the first point representing the time at which a person becomes chronically ill or disabled and the second point representing the time at which that person dies. Today, the time between those two points is about 20 years or so. During the early portion of those years, chronic disease or disability is minor, but increases nearer to the end of life. The idea behind compression of morbidity is to squeeze or compress the time horizon between the onset of chronic illness or disability and the time in which a person dies.*"[13]

Looking back, it's possible I learned about Fries' hypothesis, I just don't remember. What I do know is for the very first time, someone with notable cache in the field of medical and scientific research proposed the idea that lifespan and healthspan are distinctly different and focusing on extending healthspan was worthy of our individual and collective effort.

In 2008, a professor at the University of Illinois at Chicago, James A. Swartz Ph.D., wrote an article for The American Journal of Public Health, titled *James Fries: Healthy Aging Pioneer*. In it, Dr. Swartz summed up the enormous impact of Fries' work by writing, "Since Fries' seminal article on his hypothesis was published in *The New England Journal of Medicine*, compression of morbidity has been intensely discussed and argued for nearly three decades. Today, with data strongly confirming the hypothesis, compression of morbidity has become widely recognized as the dominant paradigm for healthy aging, at both individual and policy levels, and is thought to have laid the foundation for successful health promotion and programs."[14]

Lifespan vs. Healthspan.

For me, as it was for Fries', *how I live* isn't about extending how *long I live*, although it would be foolish to say I wouldn't want to be alive for as long as possible. In other words, **it isn't the length of our life, but the quality of those years right up until the end, that matters the most.**

No one ever knows when it's our time. The upper limit of a human being's lifespan remains a mystery in scientific circles. But we do know how to enhance whatever time we have while we're alive. We do know we can impact, to some degree, when our dying day may come, improving the chance that we can continue to do what we love to do, be the people we want to be, and be there for the people we care most about, without suffering needlessly during those years. THAT is what it's about. *Healthspan. Not lifespan.*

Decide to be intentional about how you age and focus on what you can control. If you do that, you can reduce and perhaps even avoid altogether the needless pain and suffering so recognizable for most people as they get older.

Take Control.

For as long as I can remember, I've wanted to learn how to live a life where I could do what I wanted for as long as I wanted, hopefully right up to the age of 110 or so, and then one day go to sleep and not wake up. That is, to die of "natural causes."

To *die healthy means you accept that you won't live forever, but you want to live in the best way that you can for as long as you are here. And then when the day comes for you to move on to whatever is next, you do so with very little, if any, pain and suffering*. It's as simple as that.

I will acknowledge that sometimes the reason someone dies an early death is a mystery. Many events and experiences and environmental exposures occur throughout the course of our lives that can sometimes lead to diseases or accidents that often seem to come out of the blue. Why certain things happen is often a mystery. *Life* is a mystery.

But the latest discoveries in aging science about how and why we age proves we have much more control over *how* we will die than we might have believed at one time. Scientists like Dr. Sinclair and others believe that lifestyle – how we live our lives, which is under our control – determines as much as 70-80% of the outcome and genetics are responsible for only about 20%.[15]

Simply put, how we choose to live, the decisions we make about what we eat, the exercise we get, how we manage stress - all of these things play a huge role in how healthy we will be over the course of our lifetime and will determine to some degree, whether or not we die healthy. In order to achieve this, we need to take control of what we can. Take control of your health, and by doing so, your life!

What Prevents It?

After reading this far, I am hoping you're excited to learn more about how to look and feel better, stay younger and healthier, and have more energy and time for the most important people and things in your life. And then ultimately, die *of natural causes* at a ripe old age, very far into the future with a smile on your face.

With so much hope and promise about what we can do to control our destiny, you might be thinking, what could possibly go wrong? Odds are some reading this right now will say they absolutely *want what I've described here,* but unfortunately, they'll struggle with consistently doing the things that need to be done to actually *make it happen*. And that's frustrating. Because I want more than anything for you to see the possibilities for a long life without disease or disability, but I also know it won't happen unless you **take action**. The secret IS in the doing, not in the reading or talking.

So, the next question is, what might prevent us from being able to live to a ripe-old age and then die of natural causes? I have some ideas, which I'm sure doesn't surprise you. ☺ And I'd like to share some of them with you. After all, if we know in advance what might derail us or even keep us from starting in the first place, we'll have a better chance for success.

Confusion.

We live in an information age, a time in history when we can easily pick up our phone or jump on a computer and in a nanosecond have endless pages of information about absolutely any topic. That is amazing and often, it's super helpful. Other times, however, all that information can just create massive confusion.

For example, the more options and opinions and points of view you hear about diet and exercise, the greater the chance you may ask yourself questions like *what should I do first? Is fat bad for me or not? What kind of exercise is the best for me? What experts should I listen to for advice?* And the biggest question of all, which is, *what I do or don't do, and how I live – does it actually matter?*

The confusion is multiplied ten-fold or even a hundred-fold by the relentless marketing all around us from profit hungry companies. And then there's social media, where it seems everyone has an opinion, often driven by greed. In other words, they're telling you what they want you to believe so you'll buy their product. The whole of this adds up to a lot of confusion! This is one of THE reasons I wrote this book. You can trust the information I'll share, but if you're ever in doubt about anything you read, I beg you to do your own research and dig deeper. Ask questions. Be inquisitive and curious. Challenge the status quo.

Awareness.

Imagine you're driving a racecar, zooming around a speedway at top speed. Obviously, if you're a good driver, you'll closely monitor the gauges in your dashboard while you grip the wheel carefully to stay on the right line around the track. Those gauges show oil pressure, water temperature, and other important information that help you monitor the health of the car while you're racing. I think of it as real-time feedback that will give you a clue about a potential problem with the car *before* it might happen. That feedback just might save your life, depending on what it is.

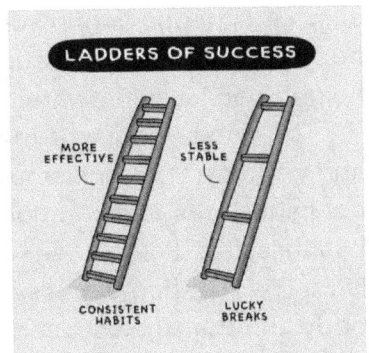

Unfortunately, very few of us are monitoring our own body's "gauges" to see what is going on "under the hood." We're not as aware as we should be about what's happening inside our body. Sadly, many of us know more about our cars than we do about our own body! Also, as important, some of us are unaware or ignorant of what it actually means to *BE HEALTHY*. To put that another way, what most people think of as good health, isn't actually "good" health at all.

For example, chronic disease often begins as an insignificant or benign "minor" issue that people shrug off as a "normal" aspect of getting older. How many times have you heard someone say, "it's just old age." And if you think about it, if you do believe you're basically in "good" health and there's nothing "wrong," what impetus do you have for making real changes in your lifestyle? The answer is you don't. Human nature dictates that we don't act until it's "panic time" – until we get scared to death.

Think about this: I could walk up to anyone in the grocery store today and ask them if they believe they're "healthy." Most would say yes. After all, if they aren't fighting a cold virus or dealing with any overt symptoms of an illness impacting them right in that moment, they are likely to believe they're in good health. Along the same line of thinking, they will likely believe the extra belly fat or the swelling or joint pain they're experiencing is a normal part of getting older. Or normal, period! For the majority, they're wrong. Those symptoms aren't "normal." They're not healthy.

The things that accelerate how fast we age or contribute to the slow death I spoke of earlier, are usually insidious and not always obvious to us unless we're looking closely and paying attention. *Unless we're more aware.*

Many are not faced with the truth until their annual doctor visit. That's when they find out their blood pressure might be elevated, or their liver enzymes are abnormal, or their white blood cell counts aren't as they should be. They may not have felt a single symptom that was obvious to them unless they were aware and could know the difference. They're sailing along in life thinking things are fine. That they're healthy. Until they're not.

I've always believed one of the greatest benefits of achieving a high level of fitness and health is knowing what that feels like, even if it's only for a short time. For example: having a high level of energy throughout the day, sleeping soundly, and even having a daily bowel movement at the same time every morning. I've had those moments in time when I felt very fit and healthy, almost invincible and, honestly, it's an amazing feeling.

Ironically, being at the top of their game physically gives a person a unique awareness of just the opposite - when things *aren't* as they should be. It's like having an insider's look at what is happening in your body – and being sensitive to any changes, long before they become major health issues. It would be awesome if more people could experience that heightened level of awareness.

The most important markers of ill-health like insulin resistance, chronic inflammation, and visceral fat are insidious. They aren't initially obvious to us. As a result, we're blind to the consequences of our actions and habits until troubling symptoms finally manifest as serious health issues. For this reason, what most people think of and believe is "good health," often isn't. The take home message for you is BE. MORE. AWARE. Be mindful. Pay attention to your body and the signals it sends your way.

Giving In to Impulse and Instant Gratification.

It's human nature, I guess. It's hard to keep our eyes on the long-term prize. I get it. Still though, why do we all have such a difficult time delaying gratification? Why do we often trade what *we want most*, for what we want - *in the moment?*

I can't think of anyone who has expressed this better than one of my all-time favorite writers, Mark Manson, who said "nearly every culture around the world encourages sacrifice today for a better tomorrow. So why is delayed gratification so hard?"[16]

Perhaps it's because, as he points out in his article, we are also wired to be instinctively lazy. He writes we tend to "get lazy about really important stuff" (like exercising and taking good care of ourselves) "because at some level, they're stressful. As such, we go to extreme lengths to avoid them, procrastinating for days and weeks, even months or years, even though we know they're best for us. Until we feel permanently stuck."[15]

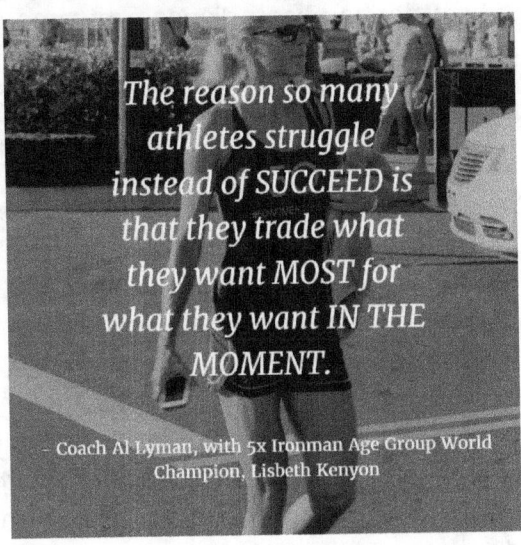

The reason so many athletes struggle instead of SUCCEED is that they trade what they want MOST for what they want IN THE MOMENT.

— Coach Al Lyman, with 5x Ironman Age Group World Champion, Lisbeth Kenyon

I don't know if Manson has hit on the reason or not, but I do know when we seek to understand our nature a bit better and come to realize when we make choices every day about important things like our health, we've got to know we're fighting human nature. And we won't always win. And that's OK. As long as we "win," most of the time. ☺

Apathy.

When I was in middle and high school, I always assumed I would age much like my dad. As the years passed and he grew overweight and suffered from a variety of ailments I assumed were just associated with getting older, things like losing muscle mass and achy joints, I figured I was in for the same fate.

After all, I shared the same DNA, I reasoned, so I was certain to look and feel like he did. Thankfully, I was wrong. I know that because I'm sitting here as living proof. What I didn't know at that time was how we live and age and ultimately die, is much more about our lifestyle – the choices we make day in and day out - than it is about our DNA.

Sure, we all have a lot of things in common with our siblings and parents, and often experience the same kinds of health issues. It's natural to place the blame for those health issues on family history – on genetics. But what I hope you'll learn is we share many of those health issues, not because of DNA, but because we often have the same habits and share the same environment.

For example, it's common to see the children of parents who are obese become overweight or even obese themselves. Is the reason they all share the same genes, or is it because they're all eating the same things and living in the same way? Of course, we know family history does play a role in some diseases. As do our ethnic backgrounds.

The truth is many overstate these as the primary reasons for the prevalence of illness and disease. If I've heard it once, I've heard it a thousand times. It goes something like this: "My father had heart disease, my grandfather had heart disease, my grandmother had heart disease. It's in our genes. So, it's no surprise I also have it." My response to that is: Nope, it's in your pantry and fridge. It's in the choices you make. **Think of it this way: genes load the gun. Lifestyle and your diet pull the trigger.**

In some instances, people who are not genetically related but share the same household have strikingly similar health outcomes. The bottom line is the research and data show unequivocally that heart disease, and in fact many of the other most common diseases, are primarily lifestyle diseases. Which finally, leads me to **apathy.**

It's a fact people's behavior reflects what they believe. **Most people don't believe what they do matters enough to change, it's that simple.** To put it another way, most people don't believe the actions they take every day to care for their health – their daily habits, their choices - impact their longevity or their ability to die healthy. They lack belief in the power of the choices they make. They're apathetic.

In some instances, the apathetic among us will build arguments (in their own mind and in discussions with others) against taking time in their day to do things like exercising or eating better. They don't have the faith it will make a difference long term. In a worst-case scenario, *cognitive consonance* rears its ugly head, expressed this way: *we believe what we're doing is right because we're already doing it.*

Or they express *confirmation bias.* They point out and focus only on the evidence which supports family history and genetics matter the most. (The data which supports this is old – outdated – and no longer valid. Don't believe it!). If you don't believe IT WILL matter, you won't act like it will. My hope is everything you read in this book convinces you that it matters, more than you could possibly imagine. I'm living proof of it, as are many others. By the time you finish this book, I know you will believe it! Keep reading!

Another obvious reason for our apathy is it's difficult to accept or face up to the idea that our health IS our responsibility, and no one else's. Why is it difficult? Because accepting it often means we must change. Looking in the mirror and changing habits *is hard*.

It's been said that changing and improving your life requires you to destroy a part of yourself and replace it with a newer, better version. Growth is therefore, by definition, painful to some degree. It also means taking care of ourselves, first. And we know prioritizing self-care is also hard.

But so is needless pain and suffering, chronic illness, having expensive medical bills, becoming a burden to others, and early death. The quality of your health and thus your life is defined most by the values you are willing to struggle for. What kind of pain do you want in your life? As I said in the introduction to this book, **you must choose your hard.**

Small Daily Actions That Lead to Lifestyle Transformation.

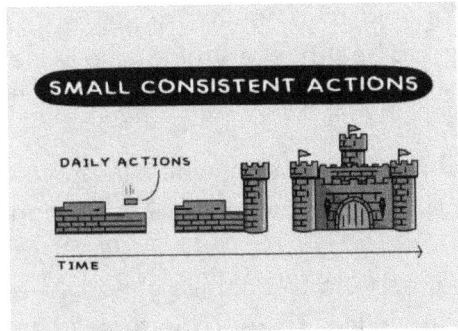

To achieve our ultimate goal, we need to accept where we are, acknowledge our feelings, and choose to take ownership of our health by doing something which demonstrates self-worth and self-actualization, *every day*. In other words, in the words of Andy Dufrene in the movie, *The Shawshank Redemption*, we need to **get busy living or get busy dying.**

Here's a short list of five things you can do right now, a quick primer on some of the things you'll learn more about in this book.

1. **Set time aside each day for 5 minutes of exercise of your choice.** Don't get crazy and overdo it - start small if you haven't exercised before or if it's been a while. Afterward, check how you feel. I'm willing to bet you'll feel great. Remember that feeling.

2. **Substitute one positive food choice for what would have been a less optimal choice**. Afterward, check how that choice made you feel. Remember, a single small improvement applied consistently is a LOT more powerful for positive change than is a gigantic series of changes you can't or won't sustain.

3. **Become more aware of sugar and processed foods in your diet and seek to reduce them.** Sugar is everywhere in processed foods. If it has a label, chances are it has added sugar.

4. **Eliminate snacking most days of the week and seek to have eating "windows" of time that result in increasing hours without eating, thereby lowering insulin levels**. You'll learn more about this in the next section of the book.

5. **Get to bed earlier and create the most optimal environment for quality sleep**. That means a dark space, going to bed at the same time every night if you can, and making sure to get off your smart phone or other technology, at least 30 minutes before bedtime.

Not only will these five things help you achieve your goal, you'll get the added benefit of slowly and steadily building new habits that ultimately lead to a lifestyle transformation, which is the best path to long-term change and success.

As is usually the case, the secret in starting and keeping momentum is to start small. Walk five minutes. Meditate for one minute. Skip one dessert. Get to sleep five minutes earlier. Then challenge yourself to do more. You'll find doing something small often motivates you to do more and keep going.

The changes you make will enrich and improve every other aspect of your life – empowering you to become a better parent, spouse, co-worker, and citizen. And you will inspire others as you advocate for a healthier approach to living by caring for your own health first.

A great life starts and ends with good health. Without good health, everything else in life suffers. And because doing those important things which are good for our health is difficult and often a struggle, the positive effects last much longer.

Self-love and self-actualization begin with caring for our physical health, which improves mood, energy levels, self-esteem, and adds meaning to our lives. If we love ourselves enough to do the work, we can create the life we deserve!

The human body is remarkable in its ability to adapt and respond to positive stress. As a result, there is always hope for positive change, even very late in life. To keep learning, keep reading! I'll see you there!

CHAPTER 2

WHY WE AGE:
EXPLORING AGING AT THE CELLULAR LEVEL

Maintaining order rather than correcting disorder is the ultimate principle of wisdom.

To cure disease after it has appeared is like digging a well when one feels thirsty, or forging weapons after the war has already begun.

— Nei Jing, 2nd century BC

> *As long as you live, keep learning how to live.*
> — Seneca

I was standing at the start line of a 5k race a few weeks ago. It was before the gun went off and I was bouncing up and down to stay loose and chatting with this guy next to me, who happened to be my age. We were talking about this book. Our conversation started when we ended up together during our warmup. He said he'd always wondered *why* we age. He asked me, "Al, what's going on inside that's causing the changes I see in the mirror?" I looked back at him and said the first thing that came into my head. "Well, it's complicated." We both chuckled, and then turned our attention back to the race.

Later on, as I was cooling down, I thought about his question. I pondered not just his question about *why we age,* but whether I should even broach the topic in the book. Because I'll tell you, when I was putting that first rough draft of the outline together, this chapter wasn't in there. It's a topic that can get pretty sticky, you know? Lots of chemistry and biology techno-jargon can creep in if you let it. And I did promise I was going to keep this book simple and easy to read, right?

The fact that he wondered though, made me believe that YOU, too, might be wondering. If you can understand this aging process a bit better, I'm hoping you'll be even more empowered to take control of your health. That's my goal: to get you pumped up and ready to make some changes. So, I made the decision to forge ahead with this chapter.

There is lots of important activity happening inside our cells from the moment we're born until our last breath. If you're interested in learning more about how that activity impacts how we age, keep reading. At the end of this chapter, I'll merge this cellular activity with a broader perspective of aging so you're empowered to act on what you learn. But, if you're not so excited to hear about some of the gory details and want to move on to the next part of the book, that's OK too. You can always come back to this chapter.

There is a recurring theme in this chapter that is also consistent throughout the book. It's this: <u>when it comes to how and when we age, nothing happens in isolation</u>. All of the various elements that ultimately determine how we age, such as our attitude and outlook, activity, what and when we eat, and our reason for getting up in the morning, to name a few, are all related. As you will see, the mind-body connection is real!

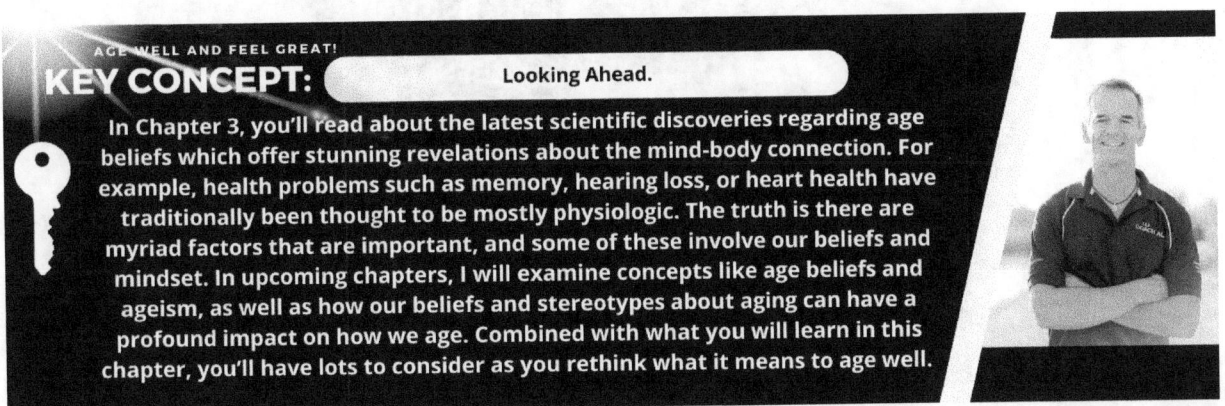

AGE WELL AND FEEL GREAT!

KEY CONCEPT: Looking Ahead.

In Chapter 3, you'll read about the latest scientific discoveries regarding age beliefs which offer stunning revelations about the mind-body connection. For example, health problems such as memory, hearing loss, or heart health have traditionally been thought to be mostly physiologic. The truth is there are myriad factors that are important, and some of these involve our beliefs and mindset. In upcoming chapters, I will examine concepts like age beliefs and ageism, as well as how our beliefs and stereotypes about aging can have a profound impact on how we age. Combined with what you will learn in this chapter, you'll have lots to consider as you rethink what it means to age well.

This Is A NEW and Exciting Time For Aging Research.

Discoveries are happening almost daily. That's what I am learning as I follow the latest news on longevity and aging research. Like most areas of study, *the more you know, the more you realize you DON'T know, you know?* ☺ That's both exciting and a little frustrating too. I'm convinced we're on the cusp of some amazing discoveries in the next few years. Just imagine being able to know with almost 100% certainty what is actually happening inside our bodies as we age – to our genes, to our DNA, to our cells. Does that sound futuristic or even crazy? Imagine if the scientists doing the research at the grass-roots level could know with certainty what is happening inside our cells, wouldn't they be that much closer to knowing how to slow down aging or even stop the aging process all together?

As we age, the communication and interaction that happens inside a cell is wildly complex. On the plus side, most if not all of these interactions have been identified and listed. Most scientists agree as to what is on the list. What they don't agree on, is which of these is the *most important.* In a way, that makes sense. Each of them has their own specialty, and it's natural they'd get some tunnel vision. Even so, let's talk about that list, and then we can discuss a few of the most recent discoveries and why they matter, OK?

(image source: cartoonists, Glen and Gary McCoy)

What Is Happening at a Cellular Level That Might Be Most Responsible for What We See and Feel as We Age?

Well, we could start with *cellular senescence*, which means cell death, or when a cell stops dividing, and then dies.[1] The accumulation of *senescent cells* is considered one of the hallmarks of aging. Then there's *apoptosis*, which is programmed cell death. *Apoptosis* can lead to diseases like cancer if it doesn't happen correctly. *Cellular senescence (cell death)* is often accompanied by the *shortening of telomeres*. What are those you ask?

Telomeres form the ends of human *chromosomes*. *Chromosomes* are what contain the actual genetic information making us unique. *Telomeres* are made of repetitive sequences of DNA that protect the *chromosome* from damage. In essence, they form caps at the ends of the *chromosomes* and keep the genetic material from unraveling. Shortening with each cell division, they help determine how fast a cell ages. When *telomeres* become too short, the cell stops dividing altogether. Although *telomeres* do shorten each time a cell divides, progressive and increased shortening is what is associated with aging and disease.[2] I'll share more information on *telomeres* shortly.

Then there's *oxidative stress* [3] and *DNA damage*. I'll discuss DNA and the damage that can occur a bit later in the chapter. And finally, there are the changes "programmed" by way of our own genes and DNA. If you're thinking the list is getting longer, you're right. If you were to do a Google search, you'd come up with an increasingly long list of theories about what happens to cells as we age. Everyone has an opinion, and there are lots of different kinds of studies being done all the time.

For example, one article written by professor, Leonard Hayflick, of the University of California at San Francisco titled, *Entropy Explains Aging, Genetic Determinism Explains Longevity, and Undefined Terminology Explains Misunderstanding Both,* points out "age changes can occur in only two fundamental ways: by a purposeful genetic program driven by genes or by random, accidental events." This means it's either our DNA or something that happens to us that is driving aging. [4]

As for longevity itself, Hayflick believes *entropy* is central to the discussion and "clearly, the genome governs the processes that determine longevity." Before I go on, you may be asking what is the *genome*? And what is *entropy*? The genome is the entire set of genes present inside a cell or an organism. Entropy is a basic law of the universe that says everything will gradually decay into some kind of disorder. For example: think of how metal will rust if it's left exposed to the elements, or how a campfire gradually burns away, or how ice melts. These are all *entropy* in action.

Another article published in 1981 titled *The Aging Process* written by Denham Harman, offers a very different perspective. Harman, now deceased, was a former American medical academic most well known as the "father of the free radical theory of aging." In his article, he states "accumulating evidence now indicates that the sum of the deleterious *free radical* reactions going on continuously throughout the cells and tissues constitutes the aging process or is a major contributor to it."[5] That's a whole lot of words there, right? ☺ What was Harman trying to say? This theory of aging says the damage is caused by "free radicals," those pesky little unstable molecules that are supposed to be repaired by "antioxidants." I'm sure you've heard this theory. Who among us hasn't at one time or another taken a pill or eaten something because we believed it contained "antioxidants," or that it was an antioxidant rich food? I know I have.

Not surprisingly, a multi-billion-dollar global industry of "antioxidant" drinks and pills and potions is booming! Think about this: a 2017 article by the journal *Nutraceuticals World* said in 2015, global sales of antioxidants totaled $2.9 billion and would reach $4.5 billion by the year 2022![6] This despite the fact that in the time frame since Harman wrote his article, scientists have pretty much invalidated the whole idea. The current belief seems to be an antioxidant rich diet stimulates our natural defenses rather than acting alone. So, is an antioxidant rich diet healthy? It can't hurt. And it *might* even help. Will it have the powerful impact and slow the rate of aging as claimed in advertising? Current research says, probably not.

Which brings me to two areas of research that are among the most exciting. It has to do with DNA itself and the changes that happen as we age. Remember me mentioning earlier that I'd talk soon about DNA damage? In my mind, this is the cutting-edge in aging science.

So, you may recall from high school biology class DNA is the chemical name for the molecule that carries genetic instructions in all living things.[7]

DNA consists of two strands that wind around one another to form a shape known as a double helix. It's wrapped in a coil shape. Simple enough, right?

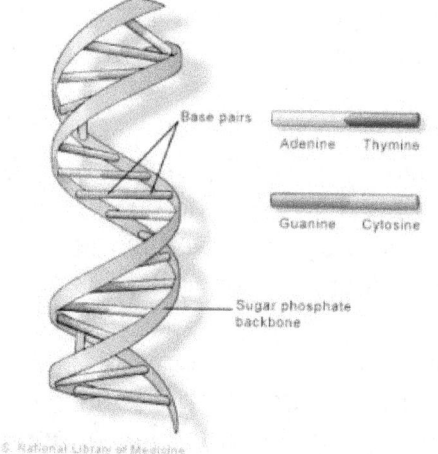

U.S. National Library of Medicine

Well, one very interesting theory about the key to what is happening inside our bodies when we age has to do with how DNA can become damaged and *unwrap*. This theory comes from well-known author and Harvard research professor Dr. David Sinclair, who says there is "unspooling" or "unpackaging" of the DNA. In the process of that unspooling, cells become more of a generalized cell type vs. a specific cell type, essentially losing their identity and thus begin to act abnormally. What "abnormally" actually means differs depending upon cell type. He believes this is cell "confusion" – what he refers to as the "information theory of aging."[8]

He refers to this unspooling or unwrapping as *ex-differentiation*, believing it is actually the root cause, *not just of aging, but of most diseases*, and the key to slowing aging and extending lifespan is to "slow down *ex-differentiation*."[9] As one example, in diseases like Alzheimer's, genes lose their "identity" through this unpacking or unspooling. This process begins many years before the symptoms appear as some form of dementia.

What's another, simpler way to think of it? Well, are you old enough to remember compact discs? ☻ Sinclair says the equivalent of this *ex-differentiation* are "the scratches on CDs which cause songs to play incorrectly. In other words, the messaging becomes distorted."[10]

So, what causes this *ex-differentiation* or unwrapping of the DNA and subsequent cellular confusion? In his eyes and that of many other researchers, it is the *epigenome.*

The *epigenome* is a multitude of compounds that tell the genes what to do. Sinclair calls them the "readers of the DNA." The preface "epi" means above. In this context, it's "above" the genome. In her book, *Younger You,* author and naturopathic physician, Dr. Kara Fitzgerald, ND, IFMCP, when talking about this *epigenome,* uses an analogy of a computer to simplify. Imagine for a moment your DNA is the *hardware* part of the computer. As you know, the computer hardware is the case and the components inside the case. It's all plastic and metal and pretty much useless without the *software* that runs on the computer, telling the hardware what to do, right? The software is what makes the hardware go; it tells the hardware how to act, so to speak. *That's what the epigenome is.*[11] This new science of aging focusing on our epigenome is referred to as **epigenetics.** If you've read any articles or books about aging recently or listened to any podcasts, you've heard this word, *epigenetics,* the study of how behaviors and environment can cause changes that affect the way genes work.[12]

This leads me to the other theory I wanted to discuss. That theory is an *epigenetic process* called **DNA methylation.**[13] To keep it simple, let's go back to Dr. Fitzgerald's analogy of a computer I shared earlier. *DNA methylation* is the operating system of the computer. It's the part of the software telling the hardware – in this case, your DNA – what to do.[14] Imagine certain molecules that can be measured (known as methyl groups) which sit *on top* of certain sites on genes. These molecules "stick" to the genes by way of chemical bonds and cause changes to the DNA. These methyl groups determine which genes are turned on and which are turned off.[15] The take home message that's most important is this: because these modifications occur on the DNA molecule and occur by means of *environmental influence,* we have some control over this process through our own behavior and lifestyle.

Another interesting aspect to this methylation process is chromatin remodeling, which is particularly noteworthy because it produces a complex of proteins on top of the DNA that will determine the shape of the DNA inside of the cell nucleus. If you aren't sure what chromatin is, it's simply the complex of DNA and protein whose function is to package long DNA molecules into tighter, compact structures. Certain types of chromatin may cause the DNA to become more tightly packed; when that happens, genes in these areas tend to not be expressed. As a result, epigenetic changes on this chromatin and how tightly packed the DNA is, can determine whether that particular gene will be expressed or ignored.

DNA methylation isn't anything uniquely new; it's happened to all organisms from the beginning of time. What is unique is our ability to measure the methylation patterns and see how certain things, such as diet, exercise, stress, and lifestyle, impact them. Think of it simply as giving the "orders" and "regulating" how the DNA should express itself. Generally speaking, *more* DNA methylation turns genes *off*, and *less* DNA methylation turns genes *on.*

What's also interesting is the methylation process has *patterns* that can and do change over time. By measuring the DNA methylation *patterns,* scientists can then measure how old you are. Not your chronological age, but rather something much more important - your *biological* age. Remember chronological age is the number of years a person has been alive, while biological age refers to how old a person *seems*.

As you're reading through this very brief summary of what DNA methylation is, you might come to the conclusion that more of it is better. However, that is definitely not the case, more is not necessarily better. DNA methylation activity needs to be balanced. For example, you wouldn't want to under activate tumor-suppressor genes or genes that are responsible for DNA repair. Doing so could increase cancer risk. Similarly, you wouldn't want to limit the expression of a gene that helps proper bone formation.

To make sure methylation patterns are balanced, Dr. Fitzgerald and other experts recommend a regular intake of what are called "methylation adaptogens." Adaptogens are used in herbal medicine and are said to help stabilize and balance physiological processes in the body, promoting better overall health and balance.[16] A good analogy is the thermostat in your home, which regulates the temperature either up or down based on how the weather changes outside. It isn't important to know all of the names of the huge variety of methylation adaptogens. What is important to know is most of them are plant compounds you can get in your diet by eating lots of colorful plant foods. All varieties of cruciferous vegetables like broccoli, cauliflower, kale and brussels sprouts, are particularly good sources to name a few. Berries (my personal favorites are blackberries, raspberries, and blueberries), shitake mushrooms, rosemary and turmeric are also good sources. Eat up!

If you were to do some additional research on epigenetics, you'd soon discover there are now companies offering what is called an **epigenetic aging clock** testing, to test for your biological age. It is known as "Horvath's Clock," because it was pioneered by well-known aging researcher, Dr. Steve Horvath, around 2013. He used human samples to determine 353 biomarkers correlated with aging to develop this test.[17]

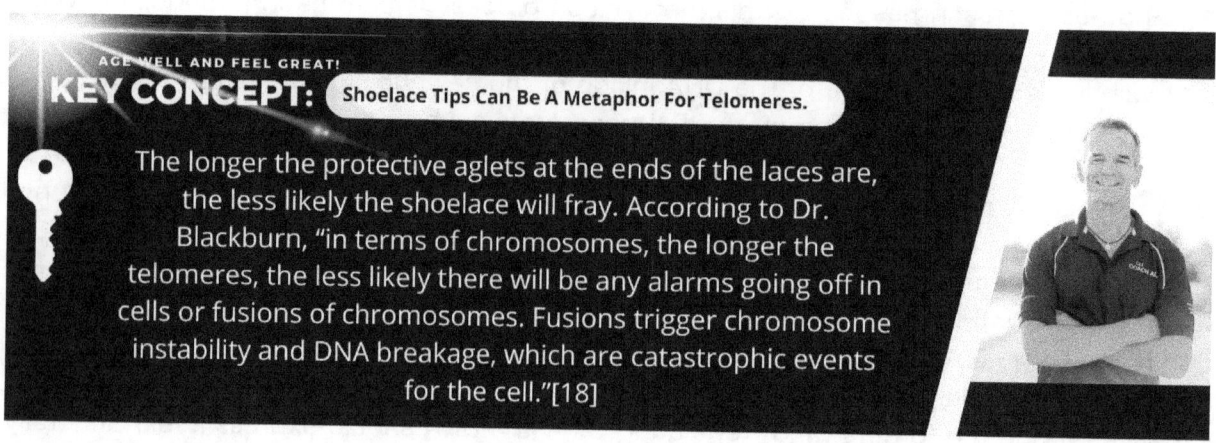

AGE WELL AND FEEL GREAT!

KEY CONCEPT: Shoelace Tips Can Be A Metaphor For Telomeres.

The longer the protective aglets at the ends of the laces are, the less likely the shoelace will fray. According to Dr. Blackburn, "in terms of chromosomes, the longer the telomeres, the less likely there will be any alarms going off in cells or fusions of chromosomes. Fusions trigger chromosome instability and DNA breakage, which are catastrophic events for the cell."[18]

Can You *Think* Your Way to Faster Cellular Aging?

Earlier I told you about *telomeres* and how their shortening with each cell division helps determine how fast a cell ages. Remember telomeres are essentially repeating segments of DNA that live at the ends of the *chromosomes*. These "caps" at the ends of the chromosomes keep the genetic material from unraveling. Author, Elizabeth Blackburn, who won a Nobel Prize in 2009 (along with Carol Greider and Jack Szostak) for discovering the enzyme known as *telomerase* (an enzyme in cells that helps keep telomeres in good shape) can extend *telomeres*, believes there are thought patterns that can be either healthy or unhealthy for our *telomeres*. In a way, according to Blackburn, your *telomeres* are listening to you and responding to the foods you eat, your response to challenges, the amount of exercise you get, and especially, *the thoughts you have, both positive and negative.*

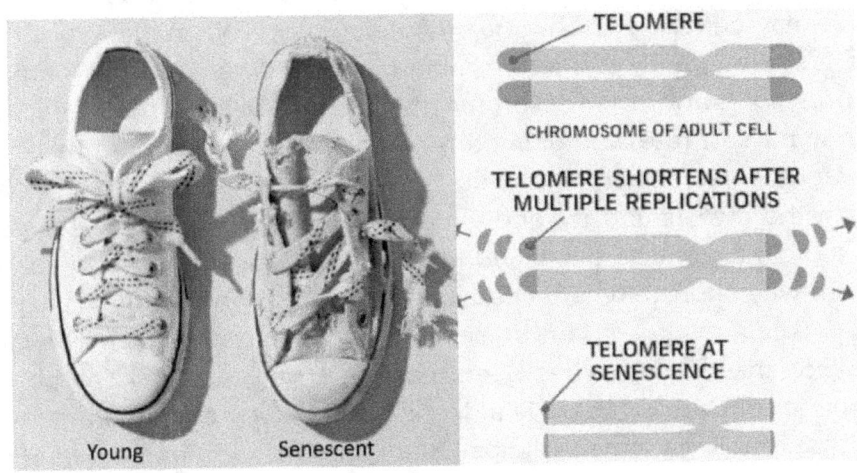

(image source: https://www.oumere.com/blogs/news/the-biology-of-aging)

So, do you think of yourself as sometimes cynical? Do you ever become angry or even hostile? Most of us at one time or another, especially in this day and age, can relate. Blackburn and a number of other colleagues, in a study of British civil servants, discovered men who scored high on measures of cynical hostility had shorter telomeres than men whose hostility scores were low. The most hostile men were 30 percent more likely to have a combination of short telomeres and high telomerase, a profile that seems to reflect the unsuccessful attempts of telomerase to protect telomeres when they are too short.[19] The research showed people who score high on measures of cynical hostility tend to get more cardiovascular and metabolic disease and often die at younger ages.

Are there other factors related to your thoughts that might influence your telomeres and increase premature aging at the cellular level? The answer apparently is yes, and as a result, you might want to rethink that pessimistic view of yours and how you routinely ruminate on problems. ☺ In her book, *The Telomere Effect: A Revolutionary Approach to Living Younger,*

Healthier, Longer, Blackburn says, "pessimism is the second thought pattern that has been shown to have negative effects on telomeres. When our research team conducted a study on pessimism and telomere length, we found that people who scored high on a pessimism inventory had shorter telomeres. This was a small study of about 35 women, but similar results have been found in other studies, including a study of over 1,000 men. It also fits with a large body of evidence that pessimism is a risk factor for poor health. When pessimists develop an aging-related illness, like cancer or heart disease, the illness tends to progress faster. Like cynically hostile people — and people with short telomeres, in general — they tend to die earlier." [20, 21]

Blackburn additionally points to *rumination* — the act of rehashing problems over and over — as another destructive thought pattern. If you're wondering how to tell the difference between ruminating and simply reflecting on something, which would seemingly be harmless, Blackburn says, "reflection is the natural, introspective analysis about why things happen a certain way. It may cause you some healthy discomfort, but rumination feels awful and never leads to a solution, only to more ruminating."[22] When you ruminate, stress sticks around in the body long after the reason for the stress is over, perhaps leading to a rise in blood pressure and heart rate, and ultimately raising levels of the harmful stress hormone, cortisol. Your vagus nerve, which helps you feel calm and keeps your heart and digestive system steady, withdraws its activity, and remains withdrawn long after the stressor is over.

Since Blackburn's book was published in 2017, there have been additional discoveries that may point to why short telomeres cause *senescence*, which as you may remember, is cell death. David Sinclair writes about these discoveries in detail in his book, *Lifespan*, and believes the reason this happens "has been mostly worked out."[23] The bottom line is, as you'll read throughout this book, there is a definite mind-body connection that impacts how fast we age. It's a prevailing theme in almost every chapter. I remember years ago reading a book titled, *Don't Sweat the Small Stuff*, and that's the message here, my friend: when you allow stuff that happens to all of us on a routine basis to fester and build up inside of you, and then make it worse by ruminating on it, the end result is you're aging faster at the cellular level.

There's also research showing when you allow your mind to wander and can't let things from the past go, you will end up with shorter telomeres. You'll also not be nearly as happy as you could be. For example, Blackburn and co-author, Elissa Epel, along with their colleague Eli Puterman, studied close to 250 healthy, low-stress women ranging from 55 to 65 years old and assessed their tendency to mind-wander.[24] They asked them two questions: "How often in the past week have you had moments when you felt totally focused or engaged in doing what you were doing at the moment? How often in the past week have you had any moments when you felt you didn't want to be where you were, or be doing what you were doing at the moment?" Then they measured the women's telomeres. The women with the highest levels of self-reported mind-wandering had telomeres that were shorter by around 200 base pairs. The study demonstrated the connection between perceived stress and mind-wandering and the length of telomeres.

Finally, in his Ted Talk titled, *Want to Be Happier? Stay in the Moment*, aging researcher Matt Killingsworth reinforces this same idea that in order to maintain healthy telomeres AND also feel better, you need to be present where you are. It comes back to mindfulness - staying in the moment.[25]

So, what to do? As you'll read throughout this book, the solution is to **be more aware**. You're welcome to have a thought in response to something happening and get angry for a moment, but then you NEED to let it go. Don't allow negative thoughts to rule your life. After all, they're just thoughts. In an article titled *Two Minds*, author Mark Manson, says "as soon as you try to eliminate a thought or emotion, you make it stronger."[26] Or as Tony Robbins says, "you feel what you focus. The more you focus on an emotion, the more powerful it becomes. Thus, negative emotions are like quicksand, the more you struggle to get out of them, the further into them you sink."[27]

I don't have to tell you there are a lot of troubles and problems in the world right now; it's a challenging time in history. As such, our lives are often defined by stressful moments that can make us angry and more cynical. Sometimes it is hard to avoid. A smart person once told me something that has stuck with me: "If you can't affect it, don't let it affect you." Good advice. The bottom line, be more aware of when these emotions build up inside you. Then focus on letting them go. Be mindful. Stay in the moment. Be present where you are – be where your feet are. Practicing these life skills will go a long way toward keeping your telomeres longer and allow you to also feel much happier most of the time.

Self-Induced Physical Stress = Hormesis.

Before we wrap up this chapter, I'd like to turn the dial away from negative stressors and introduce a positive stressor, *hormesis* (which you'll read more about in the upcoming chapter on **Time Restricted Eating**). While I'm at it, I'll also discuss "survival circuits" at the heart of a lot of current scientific research. The simplest way to think of **hormesis** is self-induced *physical stress* that causes a *positive* physiological response. As opposed to the more *negative* emotional stress that's a lot less desirable. As you'll learn, we NEED physical stress and its effects to thrive.

To help you better understand hormesis, I'd like to share a story about **Biosphere 2.** In case you're not familiar, this is a science research dome made of glass and steel tubing in Arizona, built between 1987 and 1991, to study and demonstrate the viability of living in a completely enclosed ecological system designed to support and maintain human life.[28] It was intended to replace the earth's biosphere.

Here's what happened, providing a huge insight into hormesis. Naturally, they grew trees inside of Biosphere 2. They found *trees grew much faster than they did in the wild but would not fully mature. In fact, they collapsed on themselves before they could reach their full height,* snapping under their own weight.[29] The reason for this turned out to be one of the most fascinating and unexpected findings of Biosphere 2. It was *that wind plays a role in the lives of trees.* Researchers learned the trees snapped due to a lack of *stress wood,* a wood that forms in place of normal wood as a response to external forces.

The underlying principle here is, you guessed it, *hormesis.* Stress from wind blowing in all directions on the tree, creating a wide variety of forces for the tree to counterbalance against, makes the tree more resilient. In the same way, self-induced physical stress can make *us more resilient,* too. Kind of interesting, right? ☺

Stress Induced "Survival Circuits."

Hormetic stress is also how vaccines work – a low dose virus is introduced into your body, which causes your immune system to produce antibodies to fight it. It's how muscles adapt and grow; those little microtears that occur because you did something at the edge of your strength level help you recover and become stronger. The point being it isn't the formation of things like *stress wood* that build up in response to external forces that's most important. There's something much more significant happening in response to this stress.

In humans and in other species too, *hormesis* causes certain "survival circuits" to switch on, involving these compounds: *AMPK and mTOR.*[29] Don't worry, you don't need to know what these acronyms mean or remember exactly what they are, except that these are other "regulators" controlling what happens to the DNA, similar to the DNA *methylation* mentioned earlier.

These compounds respond to **how we live** – our lifestyle. That is, how and what we eat, the exercise and sleep we get, etc. And in particular, how we stress ourselves in ways that make us stronger inside and out. That's the real take home message. How we live our lives, day in and day out, matters.

For example, mTOR responds to the energy you expend and how often you eat. So, *low* mTOR activity is a good thing. It's a "signal" to your body that times are tough, so it needs to hunker down, so to speak, to build back stronger and become more resilient. Think of it this way: you exercise or do some time restricted eating or fasting and the message to your body is it *must become stronger*. That's part of that "survival circuit."

AMPK it is a sensor of energy, particularly low energy. It ramps up the energy producing centers of the body, which are the mitochondria, those little powerhouses inside the cell where energy is produced. We want more activity of AMPK. Not surprisingly, the way we get more AMPK activity is by eating less.

Reducing mTOR and increasing AMPK activation elevates metabolism and kickstarts *autophagy.* And although it literally means "self-eating," autophagy is actually the positive process of the body cleaning out damaged cells to regenerate newer, healthier cells. One additional note about AMPK, it increases sensitivity to insulin, helping to get sugar out of the bloodstream. That's a very good thing as you will learn in Chapter 9, when we go into detail about *insulin resistance* and *hyperinsulinemia.* In that chapter, you'll learn about the dangers of insulin resistance and why the opposite, which is insulin sensitivity, is so important to age well. The bottom line is these "survival circuits" that are hormetically activated are all very good for our long-term health and vitality.

These recent and groundbreaking scientific discoveries teach us if we can kickstart our "survival circuits" and experience hormesis as the result of exercising more or eating less often, all which promote healthy DNA methylation, and do less of the actions that damage DNA and cause the unspooling to occur (which you remember is the *ex-differentiation*), we can achieve our goal of increasing our healthspan.

And remember, most experts agree that genetics – our family history - only accounts for about 20% of the reasons we age. Only 20%. **The remaining 80% is, you guessed it, lifestyle.** *How we live our lives.*

It is up to us. The choices we make about how to live our life, matter! Fortunately for you, as it turns out, that's what the rest of this book is all about! Let's get to it.

Age Well and Feel Great!
Key Concept:
Our Future Is Largely Up To Us:
It's Simple But It Isn't Always Easy.

Healthy Food Choices

Lean and Healthy

Exercise

Sunlight

Junk Food

Dark and Drab

Television

Overweight

Inflammation

Image source: Brendan Egan, Ph.D., Muscle Matters, TEDx UCD, with permission

CHAPTER 3

AGE BELIEFS AND THE AGING PUZZLE:
WHAT'S MISSING?

It is too late! Ah, nothing is too late
Till the tired heart shall cease to palpitate...
Chaucer, at Woodstock with the nightingales,
At sixty wrote the Canterbury Tales;
Goethe at Weimar, toiling to the last,
Completed Faust when eighty years were past...
What then? Shall we sit idly down and say
The night hath come; it is no longer day?...
Something remains for us to do or dare;
Even the oldest tree some fruit may bear;...
For age is opportunity no less
Than youth itself, though in another dress,
And as the evening twilight fades away
The sky is filled with stars, invisible by day.

— In 1875, Henry Wadsworth Longfellow, then 68, penned this poem and read it at his fiftieth class reunion at Bowdoin College.

*Anyone who dreams of an uncommon life, eventually discovers
there is no choice but to seek an uncommon approach to it.*
– Gary Keller

When I finally decided to write this book, I thought to myself *it's about time*. Part of me believed I should have written it ten years ago. After all, for years I've thought about how to age better and live longer and have been putting what I learned into practice. Ironically, now that I'm finally writing, I know there is no possible way I could have written this book ten years or even one year ago.

I don't know about you, but when I was in my 20s and 30s, the vision I had of someone in their 60s, 70s, and 80s, was mostly of frailty, rocking chairs, and mental decline. I'm sure part of the reason was what I was seeing with my grandparents and my dad. If I were to ask you what comes to mind when you think of that older age group, depending on who you may think of, perhaps words like "stubborn, grumpy, slow, or sick" would come to mind. Or perhaps similar to what someone in Okinawa (where there are many centenarians) may say if asked the same question, you might respond with vastly different words like "wise, active, vibrant, or carefree." These words all represent age stereotypes of older people. Stereotypes are widely held and fixed but oversimplified images or ideas of a person or a thing. In this instance, the age stereotypes I just described, which represent vastly different visions of aging both positively and negatively, determine how older people are treated and thought of as they go through life, as well as how they think about themselves. Research also shows these age stereotypes evolve into *age beliefs* that play a role in how well and long people live.

Age Beliefs Are Stereotypes.

Author, professor, and expert on the psychology of aging, Becca Levy Ph.D., says her research shows negative age beliefs "are internalized from society starting in childhood and continue throughout the lifespan," and they "operate unconsciously and increase in power as they become more self-relevant."[1] Her studies have shown children as young as three have already internalized these stereotypes enough to express them. In Dr. Levy's book, *Breaking the Age Code: How Your Beliefs About Aging Determine How Well and Long You Live*, she references a study of American and Canadian children that "found that many of them already viewed older people as slow and confused."[2] She says age beliefs are "mental maps of how we expect older people to behave."[3] These expectations, she goes on to say, are like many stereotypes, "they are the product of natural, internal processes that begin when we are babies as a way of sorting and simplifying the overwhelming amount of stimuli in the world. But they're also the products of external societal sources, such as schooling, movies, or social media and the ageism that operates in these realms."[4]

When I was much younger, I assumed most *negative* age stereotypes I'd heard about older people were true. As I mentioned, I'm sure my age beliefs stemmed from what I saw in the older members of my family. Add to it the fact that in the U.S., old age has been stigmatized and youthfulness glorified. Examples of negative age stereotyping are easy to find. All one need do is look through a magazine rack or watch television commercials. You'll inevitably see pictures and ads glorifying youthfulness and selling products like "anti-aging" creams and pills developed to help the 60+ set look and perform better. What is frustrating is the "anti-aging" ads aren't the half of it. We're all shown and told from an early age what

is "beautiful" and what isn't. Any woman who's given birth and then struggled with stretch marks or losing the extra pounds afterward can relate. And then there's menopause! Oy! What often begins as a subtle form of body shaming can easily evolve into negative age stereotyping. And it's all around us, in places we aren't even aware of.

We've all been programmed throughout our lives to judge ourselves. It's hard to not let negative thoughts fester and inevitably lead to negative self-perceptions and self-doubt, especially when living in a society that glorifies a "perfect" body and complexion. Every person reading this has, at one time or another, looked in the mirror and wished what they saw was, somehow, *different*.

I'm here to tell you if you aren't already aware, it doesn't get easier as you get older. When you hit your 50th birthday, you begin to notice the changes. When you hit your 60th birthday, the changes are there in the mirror staring back at you. If you're fortunate, they're subtle. I mean, when I was in my 20s, I thought 60 was really old! Now that I'm here, I've got a different opinion! ☺ Gray hair, male pattern baldness, arthritic pain and stiffness are just a sampling. I fully admit at times, these signs of aging have made me feel, well, uneasy. I realize I'm not 30 anymore and time is marching on.

If all this sounds like I've had my doubts, I wouldn't disagree. I'm human, which means I'm subject to the same ebb and flow of emotion as any other human. Still, we can't let a number determine how we live our lives. I've learned, as you will too, there is much we can do to alter our future path for the better. It starts with awareness and a better understanding of our own perceptions about aging.

The last idea I want anyone to come away with after reading this book is "perfect" or "skinny" or "unblemished" is what I'm after and what you should be after. Don't get caught up chasing something that is not only unrealistic, it's not necessary to age well and be happy. Taken to extremes, it can ruin your life and make you miserable. Your happiness should never hinge on something so changeable, so variable. None of this means it's OK to let yourself go and gain unwanted excess bodyfat or skip out on exercise. What it does mean is that aging well isn't about how "perfect" we look in the mirror as much as how healthy and whole we are from the inside-out, in mind, body *and* spirit.

You *Are* Perfect As You Are...

If that sentence seems counterintuitive in a book loaded with information and tips about how to become heathier and age better, I get it. But in truth, it shouldn't. Throughout life and certainly as we get older, there will always be this inherent tension between **self-acceptance** and **self-improvement.** It exists inside each of us, me included. On one hand, we all want to be at peace with ourselves and feel good about where we are and what we've accomplished, that we're good people deserving of love and respect. Conversely, there are all of the concepts you'll read about in this book, such as eating better, getting outdoors more, putting in some effort to include exercise in your day. It's all hard much of the time. And for many, there's a long seemingly uphill climb to get to where they ultimately want to be. A big part of aging well is finding the right middle ground between these two spaces – self-acceptance and self-improvement. I don't think this internal tension ever goes away, no matter what kind of positive action you take today. There's still tomorrow and the next day and what you'll believe you "failed" at doing. Or not doing.

The truth is, no matter how many times you trip up or how much room you still have to grow and improve, you are worthy and lovable *as you are*. In the end, we need both self-acceptance and self-improvement; having one without the other inevitably leads to dysfunction. As author and modern day philosopher Mark Manson once said in his newsletter, "if you're all self-acceptance without self-improvement, then you become a lazy, indulgent, selfish twat. If you are all self-improvement with no self-acceptance, then you become a neurotic, hyper-critical, over-anxious mess." The point is, if we're growing and learning and doing the best we can, chances are we'll always be trying to strike that balance. It's just part of being human.

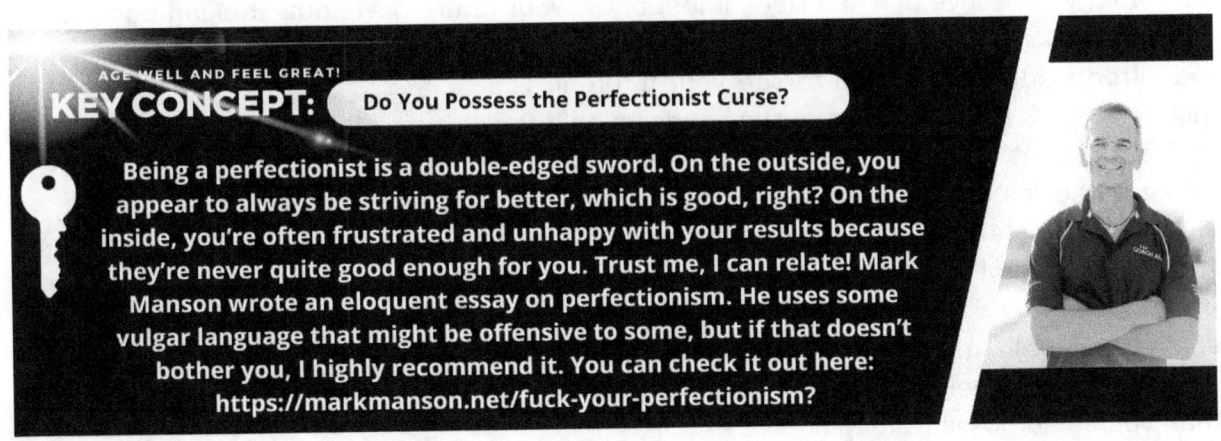

AGE WELL AND FEEL GREAT!

KEY CONCEPT: **Do You Possess the Perfectionist Curse?**

Being a perfectionist is a double-edged sword. On the outside, you appear to always be striving for better, which is good, right? On the inside, you're often frustrated and unhappy with your results because they're never quite good enough for you. Trust me, I can relate! Mark Manson wrote an eloquent essay on perfectionism. He uses some vulgar language that might be offensive to some, but if that doesn't bother you, I highly recommend it. You can check it out here: https://markmanson.net/fuck-your-perfectionism?

We know our entire world is filled with different stereotypes, discrimination, and biases, most of them extremely harmful. We're all guilty to some degree, though it often isn't our fault. Kids unfortunately learn a lot of these early in life. And yet **ageism**, defined as the discrimination against an individual strictly on the basis of their age,[5] seems to be more prevalent than ever. None other than the World Health Organization calls ageism "the most widespread and socially accepted prejudice today."[6]

Whether we want to admit it or not, we all have our opinions about the aged and aging. How we think is largely a social construct that emanates out of the unconscious programming we all receive as we grow and mature. Dr. Levy calls the unconscious process "implicit bias," which she says, "automatically influences us to like or dislike certain groups of people." Perhaps most important, she also says it's "hard to mitigate or even just to accept, because it so often goes against the grain of what we consciously believe."[7]

If you're wondering why I'm sharing all this, it's because our own often long-held *age beliefs*, both positive AND negative, have a huge impact on *how we age and how we think about others as they age*. As I said earlier, how we think about aging is largely a social construct. **The expectations each of us has about what it means to age will, in part, play a role in what actions we take and, ultimately, how we experience our later years.**

More to the point, if you think life will suck the older you get, if you expect to experience increasing pain, have fewer freedoms, and to disengage from life as the years pile on, then to a very large degree, you will experience a self-fulling prophecy.

With a negative outlook on aging, you're much less likely to act on the advice and recommendations in this book, or from any other resource meant to help you navigate the aging process more successfully.

Throughout this book, you'll read over and over again how what you believe can and does impact how your future plays out. Looking back to the Preface, I asked if you believe it's possible to feel healthier and better as you get older. In the Introduction, I asked you to see your future in your mind's eye, to envision what getting older would look and feel like. I asked whether you'd be looking toward the future enthusiastically with hope and promise, or if you saw yourself fighting chronic pain and disease. Because I revisit this idea of our own beliefs about aging so much, part of me wonders whether you'll simply get tired of seeing it! ☺ Well, I'm here to tell you, again, whether your age beliefs are largely positive or negative matters more than you could possibly imagine.

In this book, I present statistical evidence that demonstrates our collective health is getting worse, not better. On the flip side, there are also lots of examples of people who are truly rocking their later years, and I don't mean in a rocking chair. In her book, Dr. Levy tells the story of filmmaker and actor, Carl Reiner, who at ninety-five, "starred in an HBO documentary called *If You're Not in the Obit, Eat Breakfast*, about life as a nonagenarian." She adds, the "people he interviews (which include Mel Brooks), are funny, self-deprecating, and happy. They describe their lives as productive and full of meaning and complain about the condescension they face from society for being old. Norman Lear, who created many of the most memorable sitcoms of the 1970s (including *All in the Family*, *Maude*, and *The Jeffersons*) tells Reiner in the documentary: "Because I'm ninety-three, I'm supposed to behave a certain way. The fact that I can touch my toes shouldn't be so amazing to people." He is now 100 and just created a new sitcom with an all-Latino cast.[8][9]

Perhaps the person who best exemplifies what it means to age well and is truly rocking his later years is the incomparable composer extraordinaire, John Williams, who at age 90, displays the work ethic one might expect from a young, up-and-coming composer trying to get that first big break, rather than the greatest living composer of our time. After all, among other things, he recently released an album of his music with cellist Yo-Yo Ma and the New York Philharmonic and scored the music for a semi-autobiographical film of Steven Spielberg's called *The Fablemans*, and is at present, simultaneously writing a piano concerto for renown pianist Emanuel Ax, and composing music for *Indiana Jones 5*, starring Harrison Ford.[10]

It isn't just the fact Williams continues to be knee deep in his work as a composer, spending hours at his Steinway piano with a pencil in his hand – a process he describes as "cutting a stone at your desk,"[11] it's that he doesn't spend much time reflecting on what he's accomplished. He's always looking forward to what's next. For example, in a recent interview, when asked about his relationship with Spielberg and the fact that they've now worked on 30 films together, he says "It's been 50 years now. Maybe we're starting on the next 50." In the interview, he mentions this film score for *Indiana 5* may be his last but goes on to say, "I don't want to be seen as categorically eliminating any activity. I can't play tennis, but I like to be able to believe that maybe one day I will."[12] He's humble, and while clearly proud of his accomplishments, remains completely engrossed in the now, as well as what lies ahead. He has two birthday concerts planned this summer at The Kennedy Center and at Tanglewood, the summer home of the Boston Symphony. He also "has a number of concerts planned for the rest of the year, including performances in Los Angeles, Singapore and Lisbon."[13] As the author of the interview describes him, Williams remains "enchanted by cinema, and the ability of sound and image, when combined, to achieve liftoff."[14] William's outlook on aging and living in the moment, while also looking toward the future with hope and promise, is one we all should strive to emulate.

In an upcoming chapter, *The Mainstays of a Healthy Life*, you'll learn about *Blue Zoners* – those people who live in certain regions of the world where there is a higher percentage over age 100 than anywhere else. You'll learn some of their secrets – the things that seem to empower them to not only live longer, but live better. They all believe the benefits of life outweigh the hardships – and debilitation in later life isn't inevitable. These beliefs are a cornerstone of their way of life.

Think about this: Dr. Levy points out for the last 100 years, the average age of the Nobel Prize winner is 65. She says "Frank Gehry designed Seattle's hip new rock museum at the age of 70. Add to the list Hitchcock, Dickens, Bernstein, Fosse, Wright, Matisse, Picasso, and Einstein."[15] All these people produced some of their best work at a time when others may have thought they were over the hill.

Aging does not have to be a slow gradual degradation of our cognitive, emotional, and functional health like the depressing descriptions I wrote about in Chapter 1. The truth is the second half of our lives can be some of the most productive and happiest years. But we have to believe it and then take the action necessary to manifest those positive age beliefs.

The bottom line is, if you don't believe you have the power to impact how you age and how you will feel as the years add up, you won't be inspired to eat better or find new and fun ways to incorporate movement and exercise into your life. You won't care how much sleep you get or how you manage stress, or work to foster a sense of community and purpose in your life.

The science is clear. *Lifestyle factors, including age beliefs, determine as much as 80% of our longevity.* And thinking back to what you learned in Chapter 2 and *epigenetics*, the 20% of our longevity thought to be determined strictly by our genes may be even lower still. According to one 2020 study titled *When Culture Influences Genes: Positive Age Beliefs Amplify the Cognitive-Aging Benefit of APOE ε2*, it's clear age beliefs also impact whether, and if so how, certain genes are expressed.[16]

Whether you think you can, or you think you can't—you're right.

— Henry Ford

Alzheimer's and Age Beliefs.

Among the diseases that can have the greatest impact on our lives as we age, perhaps the one that is most feared is Alzheimer's disease, a neurodegenerative disorder known to kill off brain cells. It's the most common form of dementia.[17] Most people know there is some genetic basis, in that people who are born with a certain gene called APOE4 are more prone to developing the disease.[18] Naturally, if you found out you have this type of APOE4 gene (which is the case for about 15 percent of the population) instead of the more common APOE3 variant or less common APOE2 variant, you'd immediately believe you'd have a much greater chance of getting Alzheimer's. Interestingly, according to Dr. Levy and her research, only about half of the people who have the APOE4 variant, go on to develop Alzheimer's.[19] Why?

To understand the answer to that question, Dr. Levy and her team of researchers "tracked a national sample of more than five thousand older people over a period of four years," and discovered "among participants who carried the risky APOE4 gene, *those with positive age beliefs were 47 percent less likely to develop dementia than those with negative beliefs.*"[20] In fact, those people with positive age beliefs had about "the same likelihood of developing dementia as those *without* the risky gene who had positive age beliefs."[21] One thing I've learned writing this book, is this kind of revolutionary research finding has been repeated over and over again, across continents and in many different labs. The incredible impact the mind-body connection can have on our health and well-being is undeniable!

That which does not kill us, makes us stronger.

— Friedrich Nietzsche (and Kelly Clarkson) ☺

A Positive Mindset.

Looking back to very early on in my own experiences of running long races like the Boston Marathon, and later in my Ironman triathlon racing, I learned the importance *of visualization* before race day. Visualization, as you might imagine, is similar in execution to meditation. I've shared this same advice with the athletes I've coached for more than 20 years.

The goal is to sit down well in advance of the race itself and go through each phase of race day, one step at a time; every detail, from the moment you wake until you cross the finish line. As you go through every part of the race in your mind's eye, you visualize yourself successfully executing your race plan and accomplishing your goals.

Of course, anyone who has attempted a race as long and difficult as an Ironman triathlon knows to expect unforeseen obstacles and challenges that might make it more difficult to accomplish your goal. Therefore, your mission during visualization is to rehearse, in advance, how you will respond to those obstacles in a positive way. In order to be successful, you want to be able to take every challenge you're faced with and turn it into a possible advantage that will help you get to the finish line faster.

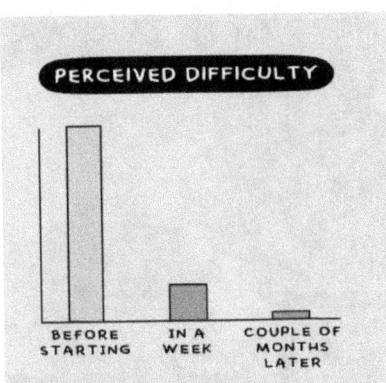

Let's be clear. None of this means you can *wish* your way to a great race. Seeing something happen in your mind's eye doesn't automatically make it happen in real life. But on the flip side, I do believe *if you don't first see yourself having success and meeting every challenge head on in a positive way, when the time comes, the chance of it actually happening is reduced.*

The take home message is the entire journey, regardless of what it might be, begins by *fostering an increasingly deeply held belief that you can be successful.* As you reinforce positives and see yourself taking positive action, you begin to see yourself, in your mind's eye, having success. You only need to then go out and make it happen just as you've visualized it. So where does this belief come from? Where does the confidence to toe the line of a race or in fact, face any obstacle you might face, come from? Surely it can't be created out of thin air?

It comes from prior experience, from having done the work and preparation ahead of time. It comes from the commitment displayed in the weeks and months leading up to the event. The same could be said for a student taking an exam, an attorney taking the Bar, or any athlete approaching a competition. The great Ethiopian champion marathoner, Juma

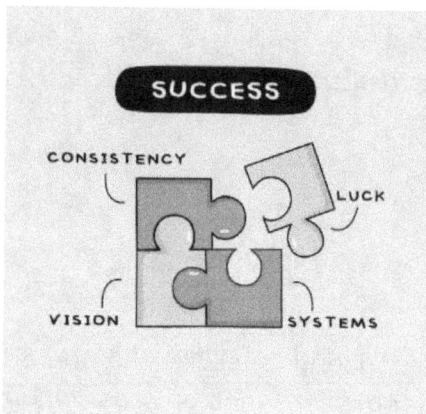

Ikangaa, once said "the will to win is nothing without the will to prepare." I've repeated a similar version of Ikangaa's quote to myself a thousand times, especially during weak moments when my own will to do what I needed to do to prepare, was waning.

When it comes to age beliefs, we know anyone who has positive age beliefs is likely to also be intentional about how they eat or stay active. Odds are, they're a generally optimistic, happy person most of the time. The point being *it all goes hand in hand*. A positive mindset leads to more positive actions, which in turn reinforces the positive mindset, which in turn filters back to more discipline and a commitment to positive action, which feeds our positive age beliefs, and so forth and so on. Our own age beliefs and that of the society in which we live strongly influence what we'll do, how proactive we'll be, and in the end, how the late stages of our life play out.

Of course, we also know having positive age beliefs is only one important part of aging well. In other words, it's only one *piece to the aging puzzle*. Aging well, like so many things in life, won't happen to the degree it can when we only have one piece of the puzzle – you need them all to finish the deal and increase your odds for success.

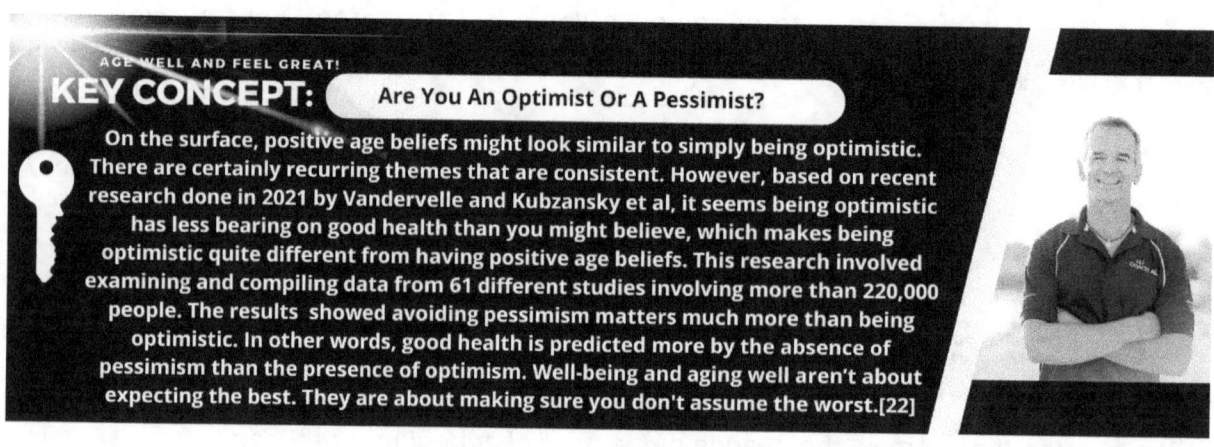

AGE WELL AND FEEL GREAT!
KEY CONCEPT: Are You An Optimist Or A Pessimist?

On the surface, positive age beliefs might look similar to simply being optimistic. There are certainly recurring themes that are consistent. However, based on recent research done in 2021 by Vandervelle and Kubzansky et al, it seems being optimistic has less bearing on good health than you might believe, which makes being optimistic quite different from having positive age beliefs. This research involved examining and compiling data from 61 different studies involving more than 220,000 people. The results showed avoiding pessimism matters much more than being optimistic. In other words, good health is predicted more by the absence of pessimism than the presence of optimism. Well-being and aging well aren't about expecting the best. They are about making sure you don't assume the worst.[22]

So, What Are the Pieces to the Aging Puzzle?

Paying attention to one or only a few of these pieces of the puzzle *isn't enough*. For me, I think of putting all the pieces of the aging puzzle together as essentially "checking" all the boxes of lifestyle habits and actions that, together, add up to what it means to age well. To achieve what we hope – to become truly healthy so we can live our best life right up until our last day, we need to "check" most of the boxes of good habits and positive lifestyle changes and reaffirm *positive age beliefs*. Along the way, we should also discard negative age stereotypes of what it means to be "beautiful" or to age well.

What does it look like to check only one or two of the "boxes?" Here are some examples:

- Someone who eats organically grown food but isn't physically active and doesn't get much exercise.
- Someone who does some strength training to maintain muscle tissue, but eats a lot of junk food, or doesn't get any cardiovascular exercise or do any mobility work to protect joint health.
- Someone who has positive age beliefs but doesn't eat well or exercise in a way that reflects those beliefs.
- Someone who, in order to feel more worthy, chases an unrealistic image of "perfect," and ends up imbalanced, unhappy, and even further from truer, more meaningful and authentic good health.
- Someone who gets plenty of "cardio" exercise but doesn't do anything to maintain muscle tissue or enhance joint health.
- Someone who exercises and doesn't eat much junk food but has periodontal disease and won't see their dentist to have it addressed.
- Someone who might have a great family history/genetics, and just assumes (hopes) that will be enough, so they allow themselves to become overweight and don't exercise.
- Someone who exercises regularly and generally eats well but has negative age beliefs and is generally pessimistic about their future, expecting the worst will happen.
- Someone who religiously takes their supplement pills but never ventures outdoors to get some natural sunlight.
- Someone who does yoga routinely to maintain joint mobility and balance but doesn't do anything to improve or maintain muscle strength or get any cardio exercise.
- Someone who does eat well and gets some kind of exercise occasionally but is under tremendous stress and doesn't sleep well.

We're Human.

There are myriad reasons why this hit or miss approach, where we act on some things but miss on others, is common. One reason is simply that it reflects our humanity. It's often easier to passively accept aging is just going to happen the way it happens and there isn't much we can do about it. You know, this idea that "it is what it is" so we might as well get used to it!

Another reason is striving to fit every piece of the puzzle together isn't easy. In fact, it's often just the opposite. And after all, life is already hard enough without worrying about eating better or fitting in exercise, right? These reasons often manifest as self-talk that usually leads to passivity and inaction. Nothing changes. As a result, we aren't able to build enough positive age belief. We don't think what we do matters enough to then commit to the actions that reinforce the positive belief. Add to this the idea that we all – including me – tend to want to spend our free time doing what we most *like* to do, what feels good, what we're good at, instead of the hard stuff we don't enjoy as much. No one wants to do something they don't enjoy or think they aren't good at.

But what if our own perceptions are wrong. That is, maybe we are actually good enough. Maybe there's a way to make something more enjoyable. The time when we most feel like giving up and letting things just be the way they are, is the time when we most need to be more creative, open-minded, and sometimes, just try a little harder.

Simply put, one of the most important keys to living your best life right up until the end is doing some of the other things you may not like as much, but you do them because you know it's worth it. You are worth it. Your loved ones are worth it.

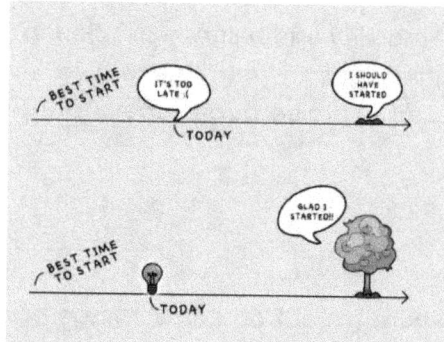

When it comes to doing the hard stuff – the things I have to really motivate myself to do - I usually say to myself, *this is the* **price you pay to play**. I've literally said that five-word phrase to myself thousands of times. To me, living without chronic disease and keeping all my joints functional right up until the end is worth it! In so many ways, this message you're reading right now is the most important one I hope to convey to you in this book. I can't say it enough or put more emphasis on it. Feeling good and being able to experience all the joys of life with the people you care for the most, until the very end, is worth it.

Seek To Check Every Box.

If you consider yourself to be physically strong and muscular, yet you're fighting some chronic disease that's diet-related, or perhaps you go out every day and run/walk a few miles, yet you're also battling low-back or hip pain that sometimes ruins your day, decide now to change and begin to look at things in a new way. Consider the missing pieces to your puzzle and your personal areas of opportunity to make the puzzle whole and complete. If you do, you'll be much happier and feel much better about yourself. At the same time, *avoid the tendency to* focus on where you might have come up short in the past, or you'll continue to suffer and feel increasingly frustrated. As the old adage says, don't look back, you're not going that way. Rather, focus on the lessons you are learning here and look at them as opportunities to grow and improve, instead of more tasks you *have to* fit in. Without a balanced and positive approach to diet, stress, exercise, movement quality, and sleep, *you will have less chance to live your best life right up until the end.* And that is what this book is all about.

It Isn't About Being Extreme in Any One Area.

You don't need to get crazy or be maniacally committed. In fact, going to the extreme in any one area usually leads to a whole different set of problems. For example, an overzealous approach to exercising can cause a musculoskeletal injury that leads to more pain and frustration. Likewise, arbitrarily deciding to eliminate a certain food or an entire food group in an effort to eat "better" might lead to an imbalance that, over the long term, makes you feel worse. And after all, life is meant to be enjoyed! Trust me, my healthy eating mindset and lifestyle doesn't mean I don't enjoy dessert, or theater popcorn (and a box of Junior Mints to go with it), or pizza and beer on occasion.

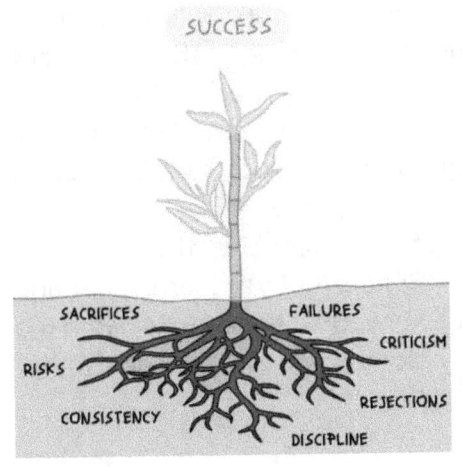

What you want to foster in your own life are balanced, consistent, positive lifestyle habits that you can maintain for the rest of your life. It's not about being "perfect" one week and letting things blow up the next. It's a true lifestyle transformation you're after.

Think about it: when you consider a dietary approach as something you only need to do for a certain amount of time, say to lose weight, you're going to try and be more strict. While that approach might produce some short-term results, over time it's also a recipe for frustration. On the flipside, if you look at exercising and how you eat as a *lifestyle* – the way you live most of the time – you are able to give yourself a little leeway because you know what you're doing is something you will continue to do throughout your life.

Regardless of whether it is exercise or how you eat or sleep or manage stress, you don't have to be "perfect" every day. Look at all the pieces of the aging puzzle as a long-term, lifestyle transformation. Ironically, that kind of mindset will give you more leeway for the occasional missed opportunity, provided you jump right back at it as soon as feasible. Consistency, not extremism, is the path you want to choose.

What Are *Your* Areas of Opportunity?

A few years ago I attended an extensive certification program to become a certified *Functional Range Conditioning Mobility Specialist*. The course was challenging. It wasn't the type of certification program where the attendees sit and take notes while listening to lectures. The training was predominately hands on. Admittedly, I struggled with a lot of what we were tasked to do. Of course, there's almost no better way to learn and really understand new concepts and ideas than to try to apply them in real time.

One of the recommendations the instructors shared as they watched some students struggle was to think of our limitations not as something that was "wrong" or "bad" but, rather, as *areas of opportunity*. At the time I thought that subtle shift in mindset was brilliant. I latched onto it and have used it repeatedly ever since.

I recommend you approach everything you read about and learn in this book the same way, including each of the puzzle pieces or boxes that need to be checked. Don't think of them as something wrong you have to "fix," but rather as *areas of opportunity*. This mindset reinforces a positive age belief. It presents challenges as something akin to the glass being *half full* rather than *half empty*.

I have to admit I love this kind of thinking – it's a positive mindset and proactive approach to living and learning that will more easily lead to positive changes. I have always found it's

the best approach when working with athletes as a coach and therapist.

It is not now and never will be about looking in the mirror and seeing something "wrong." What it IS about is embracing the idea we are always and will forever be growing and learning. This is our human experience. Every new discovery about our body and our health is another opportunity to improve.

When you think of each piece of the puzzle to aging well as an area of opportunity to learn, grow, and prosper, you will empower yourself and look toward the future with hope and optimism. You will free your mind to seek new ways to improve, rather than feel badly about the past.

> *The harder I work, the more I live.*
> - George Bernard Shaw

Learn From Rocky.

One of my favorite movies is *Rocky III*. The movie starts with the "Italian Stallion" having become so famous his likeness is everywhere. Of course, fame and complacency catch up with him and he proceeds to lose his title to the young thug, Clubber Lang, who had caused the death of Rocky's beloved trainer, Mickey, before their first bout. Somewhat expectedly, Rocky sinks into depression and can't find the hunger he once had to train. Needing to regain the love and support of his family, as well as the elusive "eye of the tiger," he goes to a former opponent, Apollo Creed, who at this point is the only one who seems to believe in Rocky.

There's an incredible training sequence where Rocky can't seem to find a reason to work or even to care. Apollo is pleading with Rocky to get with it, to try harder. Rocky murmurs, "tomorrow." Apollo fires back "There IS NO tomorrow! There IS NO TOMORROW!" Do you remember that part of the movie? It's intense!

Fear of the unknown, or even fear of what we're capable of, can consume us. Sometimes that fear can keep us from committing. We can all learn from Rocky not to waste another day. Life is too short. As you embark on this journey of learning and exploring and experimenting and creating your best life in the process, do it with commitment and in as balanced a way as you can. Find that little sense of urgency.

The word balance can have different meanings depending upon the context. In this chapter, balance means recognizing there are many different pieces to the aging "puzzle" that ALL need at least a little bit of your attention *if* you're going to become truly healthy and stay that way right up until the end.

It's all up to you – and how you view life and getting older. Failure and frustration and mistakes teach us lessons. The end result will be the success we're looking for, as long as we act every day and don't give up or give in. Onward and upward!

CHAPTER 4

CONSCIOUS AGING:
HOW TO REWRITE THE NARRATIVE

The word anti-aging has to be struck.

I am pro-aging. I want to age
with intelligence and grace and
dignity, and verve, and energy.

— Jamie Lee Curtis, *actress*

We all have those pictures of ourselves we latch onto because they portray us the way we want to appear to others. Perhaps the lighting was just right or it was a good hair day. Those are the pictures that show our best side and of course, are the ones we'll also use for our profile picture on Facebook, right? Speaking of which, have you ever noticed that sometimes when one of your Facebook friends finds that "perfect" photo, they never change it, even years after the picture was taken? Celebrities are often the same way with their websites and photo ops. I believe part of the reason might be they want to portray themselves as "perfectly" as possible - as they see themselves in their mind's eye on their very best day, which is to say, attractive and dare I say, youthful.

My girlfriend Terry often giggles while watching me go through my after-shower routine in front of the mirror. I'm particularly fussy about my hair, making sure it lays just right. I'll brush it then adjust it with my hands. She enjoys teasing me by messing it up right after I've gotten it just the way I want it, which ticks me off. ☺ So, of course I'll grab her hand and push it away.

I sometimes wonder what I'm going to do when it becomes even more obvious I'm going bald. I promise you, I'm never going to do that awful "comb over" I see on others. I'll be the one that decides when I go bald, not mother nature, thank you very much! ☺ A few months ago, I told Ter one day she'll look over at me and realize it's all shaved off! Immediately, we both laughed out loud. I mean, how ridiculous, right? Who cares about my hair? The answer is no one.

If you backed me into a corner and asked me to be honest, I'd admit there are some days when the whole idea of getting older scares me. It's the idea that I'm much closer to the end of my life than the beginning, you know? On those occasional days when I'm feeling as "old" or older than my age, it's easy to slip into a little self-pity, which of course makes me feel even worse.

Some days, I experience the same kind of emotional roller-coaster when I'm out running. I mean, the days of "personal bests" and running really fast are long gone. I know that. But at times, it's hard to accept how much slower I am now than I used to be, or how much harder it can feel. Ironically, had I begun running only a few years ago instead of 40+ years ago, and running as fast as I am now, I'd be going faster than most others my age and likely feeling ecstatic about it. It just depends on your perspective which is based on your past experience. It's the difference between achieving something when you're younger and then trying to sustain it into the later years, vs. starting something later and feeling really good about yourself in the present. I have to admit I'm chuckling to myself as I type this. Oh, the stories we tell ourselves as the years pile on, you know? I mean, who cares? It shouldn't matter that much, but somehow, it does.

Naomi Woodspring, author of the book, *Baby Boomers, Age, and Beauty*, has written on the topic of how we all lament the aging process, and says in her research, "most people readily admitted that there was a certain amount of grief connected with aging."[1] Asked in an interview why she would spend so much time researching about the relationship between aging and beauty, she says "it is an essential aspect of our humanity. As we move through the trajectory of our lifespan, from babyhood to old, that embodied reflection of who we are and how we appear to ourselves and others is part of the rich story of our species. There is evidence from prehistory that we painted ourselves for our gods and others. Highly polished metal reflecting devices were all the rage in ancient Egypt and were used in antiquity throughout the Mediterranean civilizations. Had Narcissus lived he might have been an old man staring at his own reflection in the pool. Self-presentation looms large in our human history and beautification of the self is an important and abiding aspect of that."[2]

Aging is no accident. It is necessary to the human condition, intended by the soul. We become more characteristic of who we are simply by lasting into later years; the older we become, the more our true natures emerge. Thus, the final years have a very important purpose: the fulfillment and confirmation of one's character.

— James Hillman, author, and psychologist

Rewrite the Script – Reshape the Narrative.

As I type this, I'm about three months into this book writing process. I've been learning a lot and am gradually reinventing in my own mind, what it means to age "well." I've even changed my opinion about the words we use to describe this process of getting older. My working title for this book continued to change too, in part because of how my own perceptions and ideas have evolved. The term "anti-aging," as actress Jamie Lee Curtis said, should be struck. Aging isn't a "problem" that needs to be fixed. Sure, we can improve HOW we're aging. But "anti-aging" promotes the idea youth should be glorified and aging should be viewed as undesirable, which is wrong. And it isn't only how we use the term anti-aging; it's also how we treat ourselves and others as we age.

On the "Blue Zone" island of Sardinia, about 125 miles off the coast of Italy, one of the most salient elements of their society is how they treat older people. In his Ted Talk, *How to Live to Be 100+,* author Dan Buettner says "You ever notice here in America, social equity seems to peak at about age 24? Just look at the advertisements. Here in Sardinia, the older you get the more equity you have, the more wisdom you're celebrated for. You go into bars in Sardinia, instead of seeing the Sports Illustrated swimsuit calendar, you see the centenarian of the month calendar." [3] Our collective goal should be to honor the aging around us, while we ourselves embrace aging by doing it intentionally, with *confidence*.

I know I will never run as fast as I did when I was 25 or 30, nor can I dramatically undo the deepening wrinkles on my face, despite what marketing and advertisers would have me believe. The really important question is, how can I, or anyone else, *reshape the narrative inside our heads* that equates running speed or our complexion, or anything else for that matter, with attractiveness and youthfulness and even our own innate value as human beings. What's ironic is as a man, I have it a lot easier than most women. There's something about wrinkles and gray hair that make men look "distinguished." To prove that point, a survey conducted by the online dating site Match.com, found 72% of women find gray haired men very desirable. [4] Most women would agree it isn't quite as easy for them.

I'm sure there are some men reading this thinking, *are you kidding, Al? I never look in the mirror when I'm brushing my hair. Get over yourself.* ☺ My point being, for every one of us, feeling self-conscious and even struggling with the reality of aging, is normal. We're all a little different in how we think about it, and because we all age at different rates and are at a different point on the timeline of life, it's understandable we don't see it the exact same way. I've learned the most important thing is to not judge myself. And accept whatever I might feel from one day to the next.

About a year and a half ago, while I was working on my Conscious Aging "talk" with a group of Speaker Lab colleagues [5], I was studying and learning about storytelling and came across an author named Kindra Hall. I bought her first book, *Stories that Stick,* read it in about two days, enrolled in one of her online courses, and in the process, learned much about the power of storytelling. Not just storytelling for marketing or business purposes mind

Good Heavens! This towel weighs 14 pounds.

you, but also the stories we tell ourselves that drive how we live and feel about our lives. As I was thinking about the narrative that goes on inside our heads about what it means to be "beautiful" and "youthful," I realized most of what we believe about aging and how we're going to manage the inevitable changes, comes back to *the stories we tell ourselves that inevitably shape our lives and especially, our self-perception.*

It seems we always want to place a label on something – calling it good, bad, ugly, or pretty. We use a lot of those same labels on ourselves when looking in the mirror. That kind of judgement doesn't serve us well. Those labels manifest into scripts that swirl around in our heads and become the way in which we see the world, and ourselves. If we're going to make the years we have here on earth as good as they can be, **we need to not only accept**

ourselves and the aging process as normal, we need to also accept the power of our minds and our capacity to heal ourselves and adapt as we age.

I often think back to a phrase you may have heard too. It goes something like, "life sucks and then you die." It's usually said in jest, but there's sometimes a hint of seriousness too. I mean, how awful is that, right? Don't allow that kind of negativity to infiltrate your subconscious. Focus on taking *control of those stories, shift your perspective, reshape the narrative inside your head, commit to being more mindful, and take control over how you live by gradually changing your habits.*

We need to be intentional about how we look at and handle getting older, or it will happen without us having any say in the matter. Our goal is to see getting older – the whole aging journey – in a new and better light, rather than something that will be awful, but we've got to simply endure.

Choose to focus on what age gives you, not what it has taken away.
— Arthur C. Brooks, author of *How to Build a Life*

So, if you're even a little bit like me and sometimes find you're thinking and repeating the same old stories about your untimely demise and decline into someone less youthful, or attractive, who is closer to the end than the beginning, it's time to discuss how we can change that narrative. ☺ After all, while it might not have an exact correlation, there are more than a few scientific studies that have shown the "placebo effect" is very real and our self-perception matters. And as you learned in the previous chapter on age beliefs, if we believe our thoughts have power, that also matters.

When we embrace the power of our mind by working to change a physical or mental habit, we engage the brain's plasticity. The new behavior, when done consistently, rewires our neuropathways. We do have the ability to be intentional about our thoughts and actions, we simply need a system or path to make it easier to be consistent.

In an article titled, *Aging Gracefully Can Be Scary, But Psychologists Reveal How to Shift Your Narrative*, freelance journalist Vanessa Nirode,[6] shares some thoughts on **cognitive behavioral therapy**. For her article, she interviewed a leading psychologist, Goali Saedi Bocci[7], and through that interview, Nirode learned "cognitive behavioral therapy is a lot about changing our thoughts, which isn't an easy thing to do." In the interview, Nirode freely admits "I have a very loud and insistent voice in my head that, at times, spews all sorts of negative things. I suspect many of us do. It's difficult to change that perspective. That, though, is exactly what I needed to do."[8]

"Cognitive restructuring, cognitive reframing, and thought distortions are challenging," Saedi Bocci said. "One kind of thought distortion is catastrophizing. An example would be taking notice of a line or a wrinkle and catastrophizing by thinking something like, *my aging is premature*. By the time I'm a specific age, I'm going to look a specific way."[9] Nirode goes on to say, "the subtext, of course, being that that specific way will be old and no longer attractive." "One thing doesn't have to lead to this rabbit hole of thoughts," continued Saedi Bocci. "I can make an observation, take a step back and say (to myself), *OK, I'm assessing, yes, this is a true physical change. I'm not going to say this wrinkle isn't here, but I can change the meaning of it.*"[10]

In Kindra Hall's newest book, *Choose Your Story, Change Your Life*, she says, "where the mind goes, the body follows."[11] In her words, "most of the self-stories you tell yourself – the kind of person you say you are and the things you are capable of – are invisible to you because they have become such a part of your everyday mental routine that you don't even recognize they exist. Yet, these self-stories influence everything you do, everything you say, and everything you are."[12]

The more I've learned about this part of our universal human nature, the more I tend to agree with Kindra. If we're going to change and rewrite the script about our self-perceptions as we age, we need to unravel our thoughts and learn more about the stories we're telling ourselves, so we can begin to do more of the things we need to, to take better care of ourselves both mentally and physically. In a nutshell, what you tell yourself about yourself, matters. A lot.

There are resources that can help us. In her book, Kindra provides a specific set of strategies to help us learn how to rewrite the narrative inside our head. She presents the strategy in three steps. Step one is to "catch your stories at work." That means to be more aware of your own self-talk and thoughts. Step two is to analyze and ask yourself whether what you're telling yourself is true, or not. Step three is to choose a story that serves you. The word "choose" is central to step three. We *always have* the power to choose. [13] I recommend grabbing a copy of the book to learn more.

It's about awareness first and being more intentional with your words. Words have great power to either reinforce a negative or to change the narrative. You can decide. You *must* decide. It isn't up to me, or the media, or society, or your friends or coworkers, to write YOUR story of what it means to get older, or how you see yourself in your journey. **It's up to you to write YOUR story, and then reinforce it with action.**

Focus on Your Strengths and Where You're Taking *Action.*

When I'm working with an athlete who happens to be on the other side of 60 like I am, I encourage them to find new ways to get "personal bests" by learning new skills and starting to engage in new (for them) activities. Beyond "aging up," (which is what happens when you enter a new age-group to compete with and against others who are also your age), doing something new and different is among the best ways for them to keep growing and finding new ways to excel. After all, when you're learning a new skill, each time you go back at it you're liable to be better than you were the time before.

I also like to encourage them to think about what they ARE doing well, and focus on that, vs. the things they don't do as well simply because they're older. This also means recognizing what we are doing each day to help ourselves age better and more intentionally. For example, if you're eating better or starting to include more movement into your daily routine, or you're focused on getting stronger and taking action in that regard, be sure you change that inner monologue to include positive phrases such as, *I'm honoring my health. I'm eating better. I'm controlling stress better. I'm more in control of my life and can impact how my years will play out.* The more you're able to pat yourself on the back and reinforce what you ARE doing to better care for yourself, the more empowered you'll be to continue consistently doing those things you need to. And as a result, you'll be able to take control and shape how the rest of your life will play out.

Even though I know I won't ever run as fast as I used to, the way I try to think of it is as long as I'm working hard and smart each day and having fun learning and exploring new ways to age better, by moving, getting stronger, learning new skills, and racing every once in a while, I'm doing what I *need to do*. I may not be as young as I once was, but I still find I can think of myself as the same 30-year old athlete setting personal goals and striving every day to be better, to learn more and then put what I learn into practice. When I'm out there running, I might not be going as fast as I used to, but the effort I'm putting into it feels the same. *That's what counts the most.*

The biggest goal I set for myself when I decided to write this book was to provide a complete blueprint of strategies to help you, the reader, age better through *intentional actions* and *conscious choices.* As we all know, aging and the human body and disease is somewhat a mystery, but if there's one thing I hope you learn reading this book, it's there are so many ways you can script how the rest of your life plays out.

In the article by journalist Vanessa Narode that I referenced earlier, she mentions a metaphor told to her by author and expert, Ann Kearney-Cooke.[14] Kearney-Cooke uses this rowboat metaphor when she's counseling people about beauty, aging and acceptance. She says, "imagine you're in a rowboat and the rudder that steers the boat is stuck. There's also water in the bottom of the boat. You have a bucket with holes in it, but still, you keep trying to bail out the water. You spend all your time and energy on the water problem that you can never solve, while completely ignoring the fact that the rudder on the boat is stuck and is what you should be paying attention to."[15] What I take from Kearney-Cooke's metaphor is we should stop trying to bail water and accept we can't stop the process of getting older chronologically, but at the same time, there are things we CAN do to better unstick our own rudder and redirect the course of our lives. In doing so, we'll reshape our inner narrative and take control of our aging journey.

Focus your time and energy on reinventing the personal narrative about *your life*. Celebrate the small victories and the obstacles you've overcome while also being intentional about not only your daily habits, but also the stories you tell yourself, about yourself.

Learn to turn the page. Beauty IS more than skin deep. The next chapters of your life have yet to be written, but you can and must be the author. Rather than something terrible to be endured, aging can be more like a series of new chapters with different objectives and new, yet to be discovered joys and experiences. It's up to you.

Practicing Mindfulness.

You know, I've always been, shall I say, intense. In high school, I remember friends telling me I was sometimes too "serious." It's taken a long time for me to learn and realize sometimes that seriousness can be intimidating to others. ☺ Of course, I'd rather think of myself as an "achiever," not intimidating. Yes, I've always pushed myself and others around me to do more. Over the course of my life, I've learned the hard way - that kind of focus and determination is both a blessing *and* a curse. The curse was me being a perfectionist. Too much of the time, it seemed like nothing I did was ever good enough. Have you heard the saying, credited to Shakespeare I believe, that goes something like "our greatest strength is also our greatest weakness?"

In my early running days, I focused on getting faster and making sure I did the work to be ready for the next race. When I began my triathlon journey with the singular goal of qualifying for the Ironman World Championship in Kona, Hawaii, I took that serious approach to a new, higher level. And then when I decided to go into business for myself and opened a gait analysis lab with a sports physician partner, I was 100% sure we were going to change the world of running and triathlon. I thought I had learned what it took to be successful, that I had it figured out. Boy, was I ever wrong.

I know now that writing this book has, in many ways, helped me learn more about myself than anything else. Why? Well, as I've researched and learned more every day about aging, I've been looking more inward than outward, reflecting on my life, and letting go of some of that intensity and perfectionism that in so many ways defined the first half of my life.

As I sit here right now, all I can say to those I've met that I may have intimidated, and to my kids, Erin and A.J., for sometimes making them feel it was never good enough, please *forgive me.* In many ways I didn't even know what I didn't know, especially about business.

Rewrite the Script. Start New. Keep Learning. Keep Growing.

Over these last few years, as I've looked back and reflected on the times when I made myself look naïve, and ignorant, I had no other choice but to reconsider what it means to grow old *while also* reflecting on what it means to live a meaningful life – a life well-lived. I've made so many mistakes in my life, yet at the same time I hope I've made a positive difference in other people's lives. Over time, I knew if I kept working at it, I would eventually learn how to rewrite the script in my own mind and learn how to forgive myself for those mistakes. Just like you, I'm human. We're all just doing the best we can. I'm learning to accept the past can't be changed and I can't allow myself to fall victim to the typical stereotypes about getting older. I need to be intentional and strive to find the right balance between my thoughts, feelings, and daily actions. I can now look to the future with a heightened understanding of the facts about aging and feel confident. The future is bright! As you are learning, the mind-body connection is real and more powerful than we have realized. **We are the only creatures on earth that hold the power to change our biology with how we think and what we feel.**

Scholar, philosopher, and researcher, Jean Houston, Ph.D., summed it up best when she said, "we are gradually coming to see that the years beyond sixty five or seventy, the years of our second maturity, may be evolution's greatest gift to humanity."[16] Hmmm...second maturity...I like thinking of it that way. However, I can vouch for that process having started, at least for me, a little earlier than 65. 😊

Nothing ever goes away until it has taught us what we need to know.

— Pema Chodron

All this is to say I've become even more aware of how being mindful can help us to age better and more gracefully. It's about being present – in the moment. It was Eleanor Roosevelt who said "tomorrow is a mystery. And today? Today is a gift. That's why we call it the present."

Whenever I attend a coaching conference or educational seminar of any kind, I always commit to going into it with a "beginner's mind." That means emptying my mind, as much as I can, of what I've learned before that experience so there's room for new wisdom to enter. When I can do that, I'm more curious. I'm more intrigued with what I can learn that I hadn't before. The possibilities become endless when our mind and our thoughts are in the present and open to listening and learning. I'd even go so far as to say curiosity can drive how we approach aging, and all the things that go along with it. When I'm curious and embracing whatever it is I'm experiencing, I'm more at ease, more relaxed, more at peace with myself and the journey I'm on.

Now What Needs To Be Done?

There are some days when we just don't want to get out of bed. Sometimes we feel overwhelmed and may not even want to keep fighting. Whenever that kind of emotion manifests, I know the best way out of it is to **take action. I need to go and do something.**

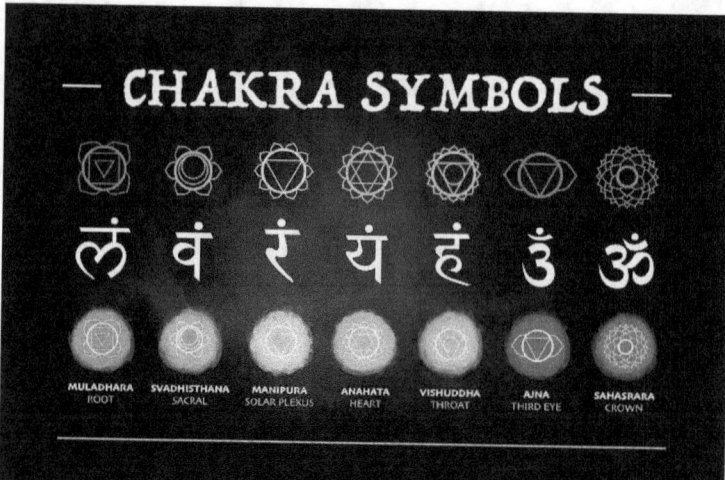

In his book, *Constructive Living*, author David Reynolds shares a phrase which to me, represents the power of self-mastery. What is it? You guessed it: *Now what needs to be done?*

Are you feeling unmotivated to get in a quick workout "snack?" Repeat these words: *Now what needs to be done?* Reaching for some junk food in a weak moment when the cravings hit? Repeat these words: *Now what needs to be done?* Wondering if it will all really be worth it in the end? Repeat these words: *Now what needs to be done?*

It's a mantra to try harder, live better, live with more integrity. Take control of yourself. Thinking about this reminds me that one of these days, I'm going to get a tattoo of the Sanskrit symbol for the third chakra, *Manipura*, associated with fire and the power of transformation.

Let Go.

While you're reading this book, I encourage you to let go of any previously held beliefs or stereotypes about aging, even if only for a few moments. If you can, try to internalize any new ideas and carry them with you as you embark on a new day. You may find a new way of thinking and a new lifestyle and mindset that together, will light a path that assists you in honoring your health and improving your odds of feeling good for the rest of your life.

While I've never done very much of it myself, this is also the effect many people report from experimenting with and practicing meditation. There seems to be a better ability to disengage from our own inner-critic and become more aware of our thoughts and feelings without judgment. In his book, *The Seven Graces of Ageless Aging*, author Jason Elias brings his own experiences in Chinese medicine and speaks to the power of meditation. He says "meditation directly addresses the root of the stress response. It releases memories of stress and lowers levels of cortisol and adrenaline in the body." He goes on to point out practicing meditation isn't a "one size fits all" choice. It's "best to truly resonate with the chosen type of meditation. For one individual, silent sitting may resonate, for another, walking quietly in nature works."[17]

Mindfulness seems to have a direct connection with stress, too. In the next chapter, *The Mainstays of a Long, Healthy Life*, you'll read and learn how negative stress can add up and impact our health, causing us to age faster. The challenge as we get older is how that stress can accumulate and suck the joy out of life, leaving us feeling helpless and hopeless.

One of the things I've noticed in elderly people who are reaching the last years of their life is how they lament the past. Their minds are focused on how life *used to be* – the "good ole days." Thinking back on those memories pulls them OUT of the present, and while many of those memories are happy ones, the end result is they feel sad that it isn't "good" anymore. Deepak Chopra calls this the "curse of memory." He says it "ages us from the inside; our inner world is getting older, shutting us out from reality, which is never old."[18]

It's not a coincidence the elderly in convalescent homes or those forced to stay in their own home where they have only their television to keep them company, end up more sad and depressed due to the never-ending negative news cycle. For sure, we can't control that news cycle, but we can control our exposure and response to it. Be mindful of the impact of that news cycle on your emotions and choose not to watch or worry about what's happening out there. Instead, go for a walk, journal or write, listen to music, get some exercise, garden. The options are endless if we open our minds to it.

Also, in the upcoming chapter on the *Mainstays of a Long, Healthy Life*, I discuss the importance of early detection, which I briefly alluded to in Chapter 2. This is one more place where mindfulness is important. We all need to be in better tune with our body and our thoughts. If we listen inward, we will know what our body is trying to tell us and what we should do next. Will we listen and act accordingly?

In his book, author Jason Elias references a quote from close personal friend, psychiatrist, and spiritual teacher, Andrew Ferber, who says we all need to stay "tuned in, present, mindful, to what feels right for them, at every level, and to honor that. Trusting that belief has been my guide since an early age. From there we can take full responsibility for ourselves and our lives. We must practice self-inquiry. I say be evermore aware of yourself and trust what you find!"[19]

We would all age better if we could be more aware of our breath and every sensation we feel, be less of a perfectionist, decide to join a class or meditation group and be more present each hour of every day. I will give you more tools to help with all of these in other parts of the book. Be on the lookout.

We Don't Know What We Don't Know.

I'm sure you've heard of the **Dunning-Kruger effect**. But in case this is the first time, let me explain. It's a "cognitive bias whereby people with low ability at a task overestimate their ability.[20]

Take a close look at the graphic below. It tells the story.

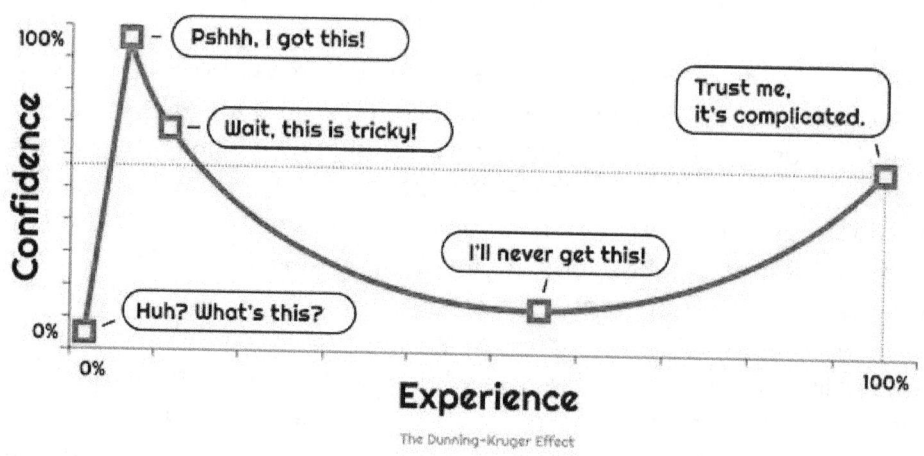

The Dunning-Kruger Effect

I am positive I've spent a *lot of time* at the top of **"Pshhh, I got this!"**, that's for sure. I'm fairly certain that particular point in time has also been referred to by some of the smartest people I know as the top of "Mount Stupid." ☺ In other words, sometimes you don't know what you don't know, right? Well, little *did I know*. It was Darwin who said, "ignorance more frequently begets confidence than does knowledge: it is those who know little, and not those who know much, who so positively assert that this or that problem will never be solved by science."[21]

Even as I sit here and type away, I will admit I feel a little bit of "imposter syndrome." In case you've never heard the phrase before, it's generally defined as the inability to believe one's success is deserved or has been legitimately achieved as a result of one's own efforts or skills. In other words, I sometimes wonder if I've learned enough and put what I've learned into practice enough, to be in a position to write this book. One thing I am sure of is, I couldn't have written it any sooner than now. There's so much to learn and you've got to live it to know it. Trust me, it's complicated. The funny thing is (yes, I am chuckling to myself right now as I type this), I've found most of the folks I work with and admire are the same way. That is, they are serious and hard on themselves. I call some of them members of the "self-berating" club. As goal-oriented people, we go through transitions that in many ways, mimic those larger changes that happen to us over the course of our lives. Like chapters in a book, all with a new story to tell and a different focus. There's always more to learn.

Regardless of where you are on this continuum of life, whether you're just trying to keep what you have now and hopefully slow the aging clock a little bit, or you are younger and focused on planning ahead so you won't have any regrets down the road, one thing is certain...

...if you don't take the time to truly enjoy every step of this journey you're on and savor each moment for what it is, a gift, you will miss out on the most important things...

...how far you've come, how much you've grown, how much better and smarter you are now than you were at one time, and how rich your life is now because of who you are, your goals, your commitment and your support group of loved ones who help you make it all happen.

If you had all of the time and the money in the world, what would you do?
— Deepak Chopra, from *The Seven Spiritual Laws of Success*

It's About Balance: Are You Striking It?

Has anyone ever said to you (or have you said to them), "have fun," when you were about to embark on a new chapter or a task that you or they expect is going to be very difficult or challenging? Maybe the first day at a new job, or starting school, or if you happen to be an athlete, at the starting line of a hard or long race? "Have fun!" Ha-ha! Sometimes when I think about it, it makes no sense! How can pushing yourself to extreme levels of fatigue and suffering, or going into an unfamiliar environment with so many unknowns, be "fun?"

Yes, you have to work "hard." There aren't any shortcuts or hacks to creating our best selves, and then creating our best chance at dying healthy of natural causes. You need to sacrifice and continue to keep learning and growing. You need to get up and out of bed ready to do the things you need to do, even on those days when every fiber of your being is telling you to ignore the alarm. *But you also need to sleep in once in a while* - savor and appreciate how fortunate you are to be alive for one more day. Because every single day is a gift. Don't take your goals or yourself so seriously. Take nothing for granted and don't act (or talk to yourself) like this amazing adventure of life is *guaranteed,* because as you know, it *isn't.*

Every day is a new beginning - a new starting line. Treat it that way. *Calm yourself. Take a deep breath. Smile. Be patient and compassionate with yourself. You are amazing.* As each day comes, just do the best you can. And, as you get ready to literally turn the page and move on to the next chapter of this book, I'd like to share a few more things I've learned the hard way that I hope will help you get the most from your learning and aging journey.

Margin of Error.

If you're like me, your *margin of error* is shrinking. Margin of error is defined as an amount (usually small) that is allowed for in case of miscalculation or change of circumstances. For me, it means, well, I'm not 20 anymore. Or 30. Or even 40 for that matter! ☺ The things I might have taken for granted in the past, I can't take for granted any longer. Whether it's doing daily mobility or movement practice or taking the time to shop for the healthiest foods, or getting regular blood work, *there's no faking it or masking what I need to pay attention to and take action on, any longer.* Some might say, "Coach, you're among the most diligent people I know when it comes to exercising and doing the little things." Well, maybe that's true, but as you've heard me acknowledge a few times already, the reality is, I'm human. And like all humans, I'm subject to the same struggles, frustration, and even complacency. I have to wake up every day and earn it again, just like you and everyone else. It's a daily challenge that really sucks sometimes, but I know it's worth it, and when pressed, *you do… too.*

Turn the Page.

You would think that anyone who writes a book about intentional aging and staying healthy, or who has contemplated what it takes and studied it as much as I have, might be afraid to get old. We all struggle with it at times. After all, it's complicated, right? ☺

Despite all the emotions that go with watching the years pass by, I can say I'm not trying to relive my youth or the past. As I said earlier, no, I won't ever run as fast as I did when I was 30, that's a fact. And that's OK. Because I'm not looking back - I'm committed to turning the page, every day.

As amazing as some of my experiences have been, such as the many Boston Marathons or my three Hawaii Ironman races, I'm never going to try and recreate those experiences, even though they were truly life-changing moments in my life. If that sounds strange, it's probably because our inherent human nature is to do just that – keep trying to recreate our best experiences from the past, reliving those moments in our mind. The thing is, even though it might be our nature, I know trying to do that won't serve me well, and it won't serve you well either.

The thing is, while I don't have the youthful joints or the elasticity in my muscles or the maximal aerobic capacity I once had, I do have more knowledge, wisdom, and experience. There are many more experiences left out there to try and to learn from. New mountains to climb. I'm not looking back. Today is what I have. Tomorrow is unknown. The past is in the past.

Enjoy the Journey.

I mean it. Enjoy the journey. Relish every experience. Good and bad. Learn from the stoics who believed in *Amor Fati* – which means *love of fate*. It was Epictetus – both a crippled slave and one of history's most beloved philosophers, who said, "do not seek for things to happen the way you want them to. Rather, wish that what happens happen the way it happens: then you will be happy."[22]

If I've learned anything, it's this: when things are easiest and when we're going along feeling almost ageless, like we can do anything, that's when we can take those moments for granted. It does seem easy when we're clicking on all cylinders.

The fact that you're reading – that you want to live and age better and you're willing to do whatever it takes – is awe-inspiring. But still, take time to step back and appreciate where you are right now and all the amazing things you have accomplished, the people you've met and the experiences you've had. Good and not so great. All of it. Relish it. Enjoy the moment. Smell the roses as they say. Time does fly. And there's no going back.

Though human affairs are not worthy of great seriousness it is yet necessary to be serious; happiness is another thing. I say that a man must be serious with the serious, and not the other way about. God alone is worthy of supreme seriousness, but man is made God's plaything and that is the best part of him. Therefore, every man and every woman should live life accordingly, and play the noblest game, and be of another mind from what they are at present. What, then, is the right way of living? Life must be lived as play, playing certain games, making sacrifices, singing, dancing, and then a man may be able to propitiate the gods, and defend himself against his enemies, and win the contest.

— Plato, Greek philosopher (428-328 BC)

from his Laws.[23]

Be More Like a Kid!

That Plato was a smart guy, you know? Even as early as 300 BC, he was speaking and writing about living life *as play*. Singing, dancing, playing games, just like kids, who are amazing in part because they haven't yet become afraid of failure. They get up, fall down, get up again, fall down again, laughing and playing every step of the way. They don't care about winning and losing until they're taught to care. They move constantly, trying and learning. Every which way. Unstoppable.

Play prepares you for the future.
— Isabel Behncke

Isabel Behncke, a recent guest on the Tim Ferris Show, is a field primatologist and applied evolutionary ethologist who studies social behavior in animals (including humans) to understand our urgent challenges with each other and the planet. On the show, Isabel talks about how she "grew up at the foothills of the Andes mountains in Chile, where she developed a life-long love for nature and wildness as well as culture and the arts. An explorer-scientist, she is the first South American to follow great apes in the wild in Africa. She walked more than 1864 miles in the jungles of Congo for her field research observing the social lives of wild bonobo apes, who, together with chimpanzees, are our closest living relatives."[24] The thing she most wanted to share in her conversation with Ferris is how "play is at the root of creativity, social bonding, and healthy development, (which are) findings that have relevance in education, innovation, complex risk assessments, and freedom."[25]

Chimpanzees, just like kids, don't need much to be happy. Provided their basic needs are met, their lives are simple, joyful, and filled with pleasure. They love to play! Well, my friend, *that energy is still in me, and it's in you too*. No matter what happens, if you smile and remember to be grateful for the opportunity to just be here and be learning, you'll feel so much better about yourself and all the more ready for the next adventure, the next challenge. Remember, to succeed, we must grow. To grow, we must change. To change, we must learn. To learn, we must be curious. *Stay curious. Stay learning. Stay succeeding. And keep it fun!*

Nothing is enough for the man to whom enough is too little.
— Epicurus, Greek philosopher (341-270 BC),
the author of an ethical philosophy of simple pleasure, friendship, and retirement.

I saw the movie, "Father Stu," recently. For me, the best quote from the movie was this: "Life is going to give you a gut full of reasons to be angry, you only need one to be grateful."

It has been said that **gratitude** is like a portal - a doorway to another dimension where all the best things in life reside - acceptance, hope, appreciation, and happiness.

Since you are a person who values your health and *also* values the time spent with friends and family, let me offer a suggestion. When you find yourself craving something decadent to eat or drink, don't deny yourself in the name of "being good." Instead, try running it through a **gratitude filter,** first. Not sure what I mean? Think of it this way: Imagine seeing a food or drink and there's absolutely no doubt in your mind that you want it. Before you grab it, take a moment, and say this to yourself: *I'm grateful for this food.* Or *I'm grateful for the opportunity to eat this.* By pausing a moment and using a gratitude *filter,* you give yourself an opportunity to consider if you *really* want it, in a much different way than saying "I deserve it," or the reverse, guilting yourself into turning away because it's the "best" choice. Even if you're focused on making good choices, sometimes the best choice is to remember how fortunate you are.

I know some of you might be shaking your head and thinking this has little to do with aging well, but honestly, there's something about gratitude - about feeling grateful, that seems to *increase our desire to care for ourselves.* We need to be smart and work hard and persevere, but I believe we need to be grateful and kind to ourselves, too. And yeah, sometimes the right choice is to eat the damn pie. ☺

Try it. I for one, am grateful you're choosing to read this book. Thank you! Let's move on to the next chapter on the *Mainstays of a Long, Healthy Life.*

CHAPTER 5

THE MAINSTAYS OF A LONG, HEALTHY LIFE:

EARLY DIAGNOSIS, STRESS, SLEEP, FINDING HAPPINESS AND A LONG, HEALTHY LIFE THE BLUE ZONE WAY

We can't change the cards we are dealt, just how we play the hand.

— **Professor, Randy Pausch,** *from his Last Lecture*

> *Ikigai translated means the happiness of always being busy.*
> — *Japanese concept from the island of Okinawa*

> *An ounce of prevention is worth a pound of cure.*
> — Benjamin Franklin

In a way, modern life and all that comes with it has advanced some myths about our destiny. One of those myths is as we age, our health and our enjoyment of life *will* steadily decline. I imagine there are a few reading this who, after complaining about one of the many indignities of getting older, have had their doctor say to them "it's all pretty much downhill from here," or something like that.

The truth is it doesn't have to be that way. We can do better. After all, it's the reason I wrote this book. In upcoming chapters, you will read much more about nutrition and diet, movement, exercise, and stress, among many other things. To preempt what is to come, in this chapter I'm going to introduce what are the three or four most important mainstays for a long, healthy life. These concepts provide the foundation for how to build a healthier mind, body, and spirit, and naturally involve moving, sleeping more and better, eating better, and reducing "bad" stress in our lives. In many ways, they represent a *lifestyle transformation*. Without these, the other additional positive changes I hope you'll be empowered to make after reading this book will have far less impact. As you work your way through the book and reflect back on the "puzzle" concept I introduced in Chapter 3, you will gradually learn more about which of those pieces you might be missing, as well as where your own greatest areas of opportunity are. You'll be able to construct your own "mainstays" list that is yours and yours alone. I hope you do!

Giving each of these elements their proper due and improving our own awareness is how we can each build the kind of healthy, vibrant life we deserve – one filled with joyful experiences and good health right up until our very last day.

Early Diagnosis.

I begin this discussion on the mainstays of a long, healthy life by talking about *early diagnosis*. It's such an important topic, you'll read more about this in the next chapter, *Self-Assessment: What Are Your Risk Factors and Family History?* If this seems like a strange place to begin, it shouldn't. You see, as I type this right now, I'm thinking about a very close friend battling stage 4 colon cancer. Stage 4 means it has advanced - it has spread from his colon to other parts of his body. He's been through at least a dozen chemo transfusions, each lasting more than 40 hours. He recently said in the last six months, he's gone through 540 hours of chemotherapy. Five-Hundred-and-Forty HOURS. Think about that. And he's only in his mid-50s.

Looking from a distance, it appears he's lived a generally healthy life and made some of the right lifestyle choices. That he's contracted this awful disease doesn't make sense; he's never seemed like a person at risk of getting cancer, let alone at such a young age. So, what gives? Why is he in this predicament, where he practically needs a miracle to survive? Such is the mystery of an insidious disease like cancer. And other diseases too. Despite what we *have* learned that can help lower our risk, unfortunately there is still so much beyond our understanding. And so, we're left to wonder why.

Thinking about my friend reminds me of the story of Carnegie-Mellon professor Randy Pausch. His "Last Lecture" recorded in 2007 has been viewed almost 21 million times on YouTube and was also the title of a book he coauthored and published in 2008.[1] In case you haven't heard this story, about one month before his last lecture, he was diagnosed with terminal pancreatic cancer and given six months to live. For Randy's friends and family, losing him was beyond tragic. It can't be overstated. Unfortunately, what is almost as tragic is his death might have been avoided had he been diagnosed earlier. And while I don't know what will happen with my friend and his own battle with cancer, had he been diagnosed earlier, his situation might not be quite as grim.

We have a healthcare system that is very reactive, but not at all proactive. Other than routine annual exams, we typically don't see our doctor until we have some troubling symptom that we can't easily explain away. At the time of his "last lecture," Randy Pausch was in "good" health and said as much at the outset of his talk. He even got down on the stage and performed a few one-arm pushups to prove it. He showed his audience something I often say myself: *fitness and health are mutually exclusive*. At any one moment in time, *you can be "fit" and yet not be truly healthy*.

But think about this: When caught in stage 1, pancreatic cancer that has remained localized has a five-year survival rate of 42%.[2] Had he been diagnosed earlier, given how active and healthy (other than the cancer obviously) professor Pausch seemed to be, you would think his chances of at least meeting or even exceeding those odds would have been good.

It is true pancreatic cancer gives very few early warning signs and is difficult to diagnose with routine tests. As time goes on, I know the technology that's required to improve early detection is advancing.

The obvious take home here is that *early and accurate detection of diseases is a huge part of the puzzle of how to prevent early death and premature suffering*. Unfortunately, our healthcare system, which I often joke should be called our "sick care" system, is in crisis mode and ill equipped to help us as much as we would like. And in case you hadn't noticed, your doctor is already overworked and under a lot of stress him or herself.

I'm here to tell you that one of the solutions and what is our best chance at getting an early diagnosis when we most need it, is this: *be more in tune with your body and be more proactive.* I've often said what an incredible feeling it is to be in great physical condition and *truly* healthy, and what a shame it is more people don't know what it feels like to feel *really* good - to be in great physical shape. When you're fit and in very good physical condition, you're more in tune with nuanced feelings and sensations that could make a big difference down the road. Being in better physical shape makes it easier and simpler to be **in tune** with your body and know intuitively when things are "off," or when something isn't quite right with how you're feeling. Think about it: If you can tune in well enough to subtle signals your body may send you, you can start asking questions long before whatever it is manifests on a clinical test down the road. It could mean the difference between a stage 1 diagnosis and a stage 4 diagnosis. Of course, the second part of this equation is taking action when you do sense something isn't right. Too many sit idly by and wait for something to go away on its own. Sometimes it does, and sometimes it doesn't. I'd say it's better to be safe than sorry, you know?

So, how do you reach the point where you are able to really tune in? You must do the work to dial in your lifestyle habits and follow the guidance I'll give you in this book. You also need to work with your healthcare provider to get the detailed bloodwork you need more often and seek out routine diagnostic testing before an issue arises. If you do these things, you'll be more *in tune* and able to get early detection when you need it most.

It's very likely you won't get the help you need from the healthcare system. It's overwhelmed at the moment. In fact, in a study done of almost 30 million doctor consultations in 67 countries, the average time a doctor spends with his/her patient is five minutes or less. And in the U.S., the average time is less than 20 minutes.[3] That's not a lot of time to learn much about you and your health and habits. When you combine that with the fact that it's impossible for doctors who are busy with their work and their lives, to keep up with all the latest research and developments that might be particularly important for you, what you learn is YOU are your own best advocate. My advice? Accept and embrace the fact that your health is your responsibility and no one else's. No one will ever care as much about your health as you!

In his book, *The Science and Technology of Growing Young*, author Sergey Young, points out "232 million people live with undiagnosed diabetes; 15 percent of all people with HIV and 30 percent of all people with tuberculosis are similarly unaware of their diseases. Up to 30 percent of Parkinson's sufferers and up to 80 percent of those with Alzheimer's disease are not diagnosed. And of the more than one billion people worldwide living with hypertension, as many as half do not know about it."[4]

Living here in Florida where the sun shines almost daily, I make it a point to visit the dermatologist at least once, and often twice a year. Even if I still lived in the northeast U.S., I'd schedule that appointment. Why? I've spent a lot of time in the sun over my lifetime. That 10-minute appointment doesn't take much time for either him or I, but it could make all the difference in early detection.

The same is true for dental appointments. I've been seeing a hygienist for a cleaning every three months for at least the last 25-30 years. Yes, it's more expensive than once or twice per year. And yes, I know a lot of these appointments aren't covered by insurance, so it means paying out of pocket for some percentage of it. But the way I look at it, a dental cleaning may be 80 dollars, but a more serious and invasive procedure that wasn't addressed earlier could be thousands of dollars.

As I stated in the introduction to this book, it comes down to **choosing your hard**. It's a pay me now or pay me later kind of thing. And that later payment could be a serious one that isn't just financially painful, it could also be physically painful. Think about the pain of a biopsy, where a large needle is used to extract tissue from an area of the body, or a cardiac catheterization, where a tube is inserted into an artery in your groin to flush a dye that allows the technicians to get a better look. Ouch.

The bottom line is, when it comes to cancer and most of the other diseases killing us, early diagnosis can literally mean the difference between life and death. It is up to us to make it happen. It's our responsibility and no one else's. No one is going to do it for us.

So, what to do? Here are a few things you can start with to get the jump on an illness or disease before it's too late:

- **Listen to your body.** To have a better sense of what's going on inside, work to improve your fitness and health so you are more "in tune" with the often subtle, nuanced signals your body may be sending you.

- **Speak with your healthcare provider and be proactive about getting every diagnostic test you think might be warranted**. Have the discussion before it's too late, and then continue the discussion into the future for as long as needed.

- **Be willing to spend whatever it takes earlier, before you have to spend a lot more, later**. For example, a diagnostic test to detect cancer early might be a few hundred dollars, but compare that to months of chemotherapy, which will cost hundreds of thousands of dollars and be difficult to endure as well. Some will say they simply can't afford it. Trust me, I know how expensive things can be. But here's the thing: if you are paying for daily lattes at the drive-through and always have the latest iPhone, consider what is really most important for your long-term health and vitality.

- **Do some research on epigenetic testing and learn more about this new technology**. This is one way to get to know more about your genome to help predict and prevent disease. Companies like *23andMe* offer genotyping to shed light on your genetic predisposition for certain diseases. I predict this epigenetic diagnostic technology is going to explode in the coming years. Author Sergey Young references a 2019 study that says the market may approach 22 billion by the year 2026.[5]

- **Be proactive about bloodwork to look at the most important biomarkers**. I've used a company like *Inside Tracker* to get bloodwork done that goes beyond the normal tests.

- **See your dentist and dermatologist early and often.** And if you're a woman, your gynecologist. Be inquisitive and keep learning more about the early warning signs for these and other areas of your body. It may make a big difference down the road.

- **Get screened.** Most experts agree an optimal frequency for colon cancer screening can vary based on your individual risk factors. Because colonoscopy testing is accurate and colorectal cancer tends to grow, most experts recommend people at average risk should have a baseline colonoscopy at age 50, then repeat the exam every 10 years.[6] Risk factors warrant more frequent screening. For example, a physician may recommend more frequent colon cancer screening for you if:

- You have been diagnosed with inflammatory bowel disease.
- You have been diagnosed with ulcerative colitis or Crohn's disease.
- You have a history of multiple, large, or high-risk adenomas.
- You have a parent, sibling or child diagnosed with colorectal cancer or adenoma.

It ain't what you don't know
that gets you into trouble.

It's what you know for sure
that just ain't so.

— Mark Twain

Stress.

You're a human being living in our modern world. Experiencing some form of *stress is inevitable*. The stress we each experience is often unique, but also in many ways, universal. And, as you've learned in earlier chapters of this book, not all stress is "bad" stress. One such example is the *hormetic* stress you learned about in Chapter 2. It's the type of "positive" stress that comes from physical exertion and strain, such as when we exercise or experience hunger. Scientific research has shown us this kind of stress elicits positive effects by turning up the knob on our "longevity circuits."

Interestingly, hormetic stress is how vaccines work, by introducing an invader to our body that elicits an adaptive response from our immune system. Hypoxia (insufficient oxygen in the body's tissues) and exposure to extreme temperatures such as cold-water immersion, are other forms of hormetic stress. On the flip side, as you read about in Chapter 2, a lack of this kind of stress is one reason the trees planted inside of Biosphere 2 died an early death. It's also how muscles adapt and grow so we can do more work with them. The bottom line is these "survival circuits" that are initiated from this kind of positive stress involve a cascade of chemicals in the body that appear to be positive for improving our healthspan. That's good stress!

Hormetic stress isn't the only positive type of stress. Given some time to think about it, I bet you could come up with other positive stressors, and even some that you actually love to experience. In his book *Behave, The Biology of Humans at Our Best and Worst*, author Dr. Robert Sapolsky points out the "stressful menace of a roller-coaster ride is that it will make us queasy, not that it will decapitate us; it lasts for three minutes, not three days. We love that kind of stress, clamor for it, pay to experience it."[7] These are the kinds of stressors that are fun, in part because they're both a tiny bit unpredictable and even a little scary. For example, imagine you're on that roller coaster and you know a BIG drop is coming but you don't know when. That kind of anticipatory stress makes you feel alive and is usually fun! The same thing might be said for the interactive "haunted houses" many love to go through on Halloween. One common aspect to these kinds of fun stressors is we trust that they're also safe. That is, even though we don't have control on that roller coaster, we are willing to get on and are excited about it because we believe we'll be fine when the ride is over.

There's also the positive stress that helps us be at our very best in important high-leverage moments. Think of that important job interview you had, or a game you were in where the results of the game mattered. Most of us are stimulated by a little dose of pressure – it can help us focus and get better results. I've often repeated the phrase *fear is a great motivator*. For example, I can think back on many times when I felt the stress of an upcoming musical performance or a race I had signed up for. Having to be ready to perform when the time came put a little fear in me, which in turn, gave me the impetus to get into the practice room and prepare, or to get up early ready to train.

I don't think stress kills you outright very often, but it sure makes other things that kill you more effective at doing it.
— Robert Sapolsky, Ph.D.

What About the Negative Stress That Accelerates Aging?

To this point, I've talked about positive stressors. No doubt if you stopped reading this chapter right now, you might think everything is coming up roses and all the stress we experience is going to be in some way, good for us. The truth is far from it, unfortunately. To understand, let's review something I shared with you earlier and then discuss what it means in the context of stress.

You'll remember in the chapter titled *Why Do We Age*, I introduced the concept of *DNA Methylation*. Do you recall the computer analogy from Dr. Fitzgerald that I shared in that chapter? To quickly review, remember that *DNA methylation* is like the operating system of a computer. It's the part of the software that tells the hardware what to do. In the case of your body, it's your DNA. As you know, when you don't have the software on your computer to tell it what to do, the hardware can get wonky, right?

Remember that I also told you there are certain molecules known as methyl groups that sit on top of certain sites on genes, and these can be measured. These molecules "stick" to the genes and cause changes to the DNA. These methyl groups determine which genes are turned on and which are turned off.[8]

Thanks to some new scientific research, what we've learned is *negative stress* plays an important role in *DNA Methylation*. **Stress can alter how DNA functions and determine which genes are turned on and turned off.** Think about this: Almost 25% of the methylation sites in the epigenetic clock I referred to in the earlier chapter on *Why Do We Age* are related to stress.[9]

What's more, it's now clear there is a genetic component we weren't aware of until relatively recently. According to Dr. Fitzgerald, an expert on *DNA Methylation* and herself a researcher in this area, "cumulative life stress, earlier trauma that's resulted in PTSD, and even how much stress your mother was exposed to when she was pregnant with you can negatively impact your epigenome."[10] And thus in turn, influence the stress *you* might experience.

It can be a little frightening to consider the implications of this, you know? Except any fear you or I might feel could add to our stress! ☺ In all seriousness, when I became acutely aware of this, I realized *how vital it is for us to do all we can to be in control of our stress response*. After all, we know these kinds of stressors are inevitable. The thing is, we DO HAVE control over *how we react* to what happens to us.

It's empowering and exciting to realize there are so many ways we CAN positively impact this process. It isn't predestined or out of our control by any means. In fact, there's research showing we can reverse negative changes in *DNA Methylation* with things like short periods of meditation and yoga and other forms of relaxing exercise and even just being out in nature. These all can help us handle stress more effectively and as a result, positively change how genes are expressed.[11]

Don't lose hope, and always remember with every negative stressor, *there's something positive you can do at that moment which will help turn things around*. **That's your mission moving forward – to learn what those are for you and put them into action when it matters the most.**

What Happens When We Feel Stressed?

Stress causes the release of two hormones in the body. The first is *adrenaline*. The other is *Glucocorticoids*, released from the adrenal glands and better known as *cortisol*. This is the "stress hormone" you may be familiar with. The stress response isn't under our conscious control. When you're stressed, you're experiencing a "fight or flight" response, which is our Sympathetic nervous system kicking in depending on what it is that's causing the response and how significant it is. On the flip side, our Parasympathetic nervous system relaxes and calms us. That's turned off as soon as "fight or flight" kicks in.

So, how do these two hormones behave when we're feeling stressed? To better understand it, I'm going to share this metaphor I pulled from Dr. Peter Attia's *The Drive* podcast interview with Dr. Sapolsky. It conveys in simple terms how these two different hormones act in the body: "*Adrenaline* in two seconds is handing guns out of the gun locker to whoever's going to defend you. (On the other hand) *glucocorticoids* are building the aircraft carriers that a year from now are going to be essential. It does some of the slower components in the stress response, stretching out over minutes to hours."[12] Remember though, while adrenaline feels immediate in its actions and might therefore take a higher priority in your mind as a result, it is the *cortisol* or *glucocorticoids* that seem to be linked most closely with the epigenetic changes to the DNA I mentioned earlier.

Hormones don't determine or cause behaviors. Instead, according to Dr. Sapolsky, they "make us more sensitive to the social triggers and exaggerate preexisting tendencies."[13] The key thing to remember is each of us will have a different response to stressors, which in turn results in different levels of hormones being secreted. There are also variations from one person to another in the number of receptors for these hormones. This points out that in many ways, when it comes to how much we feel stress and how we are able to handle it, we're all an *experiment of one.* No shocker there, right? We are all unique.

The bottom line is negative stress in one sense, seems to be about a *loss of control and predictability.* And there's not a lot about our modern lives that IS predictable, that's for sure! We are forced to give up control almost on an hour-by-hour basis. So, again, **our mission is to exert control in our lives wherever the opportunity exists.** That starts with improving our routine habits regarding nutrition, exercise, and sleep, for starters. You'll learn more about how to make positive changes regarding these in upcoming chapters. It is also critical to begin to change the narrative in our mind, which you learned about extensively in previous chapters.

What Are Some of the Other Ways Negative Stress Can Shorten Our Healthspan?

The science is clear, negative stress not only shortens our life, it can hurt the quality of life. Looking at it physiologically, it seems to come back to increased, even chronic, levels of cortisol, the hormone mentioned earlier, that's most often associated with stress.

There seems to be a very strong relationship between cardiovascular disease and negative stress. Stress may lead to high blood pressure, which can pose a risk for heart attack and stroke. Stress may also contribute to cardiovascular disease risks such as smoking, overeating and lack of physical activity.[14] Stress altered epigenetics, which you learned about in Chapter 2, increases inflammation, dysregulates blood sugar, and imbalances our immunity.[15] All these alterations aren't good if you want to be healthy and feel good right up until the end!

Higher levels of cortisol reduce melatonin secretion and hurt sleep quality. It also hampers brain function, resulting in memory loss, impaired judgement, long-term planning and strategizing, and impulsiveness.[16] Not surprisingly, negative stress seems to be associated with dementia and is definitely associated with addiction and depression. When we are stressed, we react more emotionally to events happening around us and we tend to process information more quickly, but ironically, less accurately. We're also less social and more likely to disconnect from the world around us.

It's obvious to anyone paying attention that higher *chronic* levels of cortisol and adrenaline are going to have a big and exponentially increasing negative affect on our health, short and long term. The key word here is "chronic." After all, similar to inflammation in the body, with stress, the difference between an *acute response,* which is normal, and a *chronic level* that never dissipates, is often the difference between good health and disease.

What Are the Main Causes of Negative Stress for Most?

For the great majority of us, life is, shall I say, complicated. In many ways, more complicated than ever before. Between school and career, long hours at work, crying newborn babies, relationship issues, family problems, and the rising cost of living, not to mention big picture issues like global warming, mass shootings, and warring nations, it's easy to see how life can feel almost overwhelming at times. So, if you're wondering why you're not sleeping very well, or you're cranky and can't seem to focus, think of the impact of these things. That might give you a clue.

There are also the negative impacts of lockdowns during the recent pandemic, especially for those in lower social classes. In research that Dr. Sapolsky and some of his colleagues did with baboons, they discovered **the lower the social rank, the greater the stress.** "They're not being stressed by lions chasing them all the time. They are being stressed by each other," Sapolsky said. "They're a perfect model for westernized stress related disease."[17]

There is research that confirms "your socioeconomic status, your wealth, your objective measure of wealth, is indeed a predictor of your health."[18] When your social status is lower, that generally means you're not being listened to very much, you're likely being left out of much of the decision-making that goes on around you, and you're also likely being paid less and working longer hours. All of which can lead to increased stress, frustration, and feeling powerless. Interestingly, the stress each of us feels seems to be more about our subjective view of how we compare ourselves to others, vs something more objective.

Do Age Beliefs Influence Stress?

In Chapter 3, you learned of the importance of *age beliefs* and heard from an expert, Dr. Becca Levy, who tells of her and other's research looking at how *positive age beliefs* can serve as a barrier against negative stress. Time and again, when individuals were presented with positive age stereotypes, stress levels dropped, and cortisol and heart rate levels were lower, consistently helping the participants achieve a sense of calm sooner in stressful situations.[19] Additionally, studies also showed age beliefs significantly influenced psychiatric conditions, especially later in life, in part because stress is often a major factor in mental health issues for older people. I'm willing to bet this information doesn't come as much of a surprise to you, reflecting on what you learned earlier in the chapter on ageism and age beliefs. The take home is there's a strong mind-body connection that results in real chemical changes in the body that absolutely impact how we age.

What About Genetics and Family History?

We learned earlier there's little doubt we're all born with epigenetic programming from previous generations. If you ask me, that's profound information right there. Think about it. I mean, if you're like me, you might be thinking right now about those traits you've seen in yourself and in your parents or your children, and how they could have been passed on via epigenetic programming from an even earlier generation. There's evidence this programming can be passed on for as many as four generations, something that I find shocking.[20] In truth, this topic deserves an entire chapter all to its own, it's that important. But there are other things to write about. At least now you know. ☺

What About the Media, Especially Social Media?

Not surprisingly, Facebook, Instagram and all the other forms of social media that have become institutionalized in modern life seem to amplify the effects of stress. Any time you look around, you can find someone who seems to be having more fun, is better looking, wealthier, who has a better job, or even seems to be aging less than you are. None of it might actually be true, but something simple like seeing someone drive a nicer car can leave us feeling less successful.

What About the Silent, Insidious Stressors?

As we mature, it's logical we'd each develop more effective strategies to deal with stress. The thing is, as the years pass and the world around us evolves, there tends to be new kinds of stress instigators, sometimes not so obvious. I'd even say the worst kinds of stress many of us are dealing with in our modern world are just that – not very obvious at all. In my mind, they're more insidious – *almost invisible* even.

You're probably very familiar with the more obvious kinds of visible stress, such as a screaming baby at 2 AM or sitting in rush hour traffic and being late for an important appointment, or the stress you might feel after being on social media. However, it's the silent variety that may be more damaging to our health, short and long term. These tend to become chronic and worst of all, sometimes we aren't even aware of them. If enough of them build up, you begin to feel awful, as though the weight of an entire building is collapsing down on you. If you allow these kinds of stressors to manifest, it's likely you'll also become more complacent and less willing to put energy and time into your health, fitness, and life goals, which is what you need to do for a healthier, better you.

So, what are some of these silent stressors I'm referring to? The first that comes to mind for me is **burnout.** You know, that feeling that is sometimes hard to put a finger on but makes you feel overwhelmed, and emotionally exhausted? In today's modern world, women are at a much higher risk of this feeling, in part because many are trying to balance the expectations they themselves and others have placed upon them. In their book *Burnout: The Secret to Unlocking the Stress Cycle*, coauthors (and twin sisters) Emily and Amelia Nagoski point out it's difficult to "love your body" when every magazine cover has ten diet tips for becoming "your best self." Or, how it can seem impossible to "lean in" at work when you're already operating at 110 percent and don't feel you're being recognized for it. These kinds of feelings definitely lead to the chronic "fight or flight" stress mentioned earlier. From this example, it's easy to see how negative age stereotypes also play a critical role in our stress.

One of the most effective ways to get out of this "fight or flight" stressed out, emotionally exhausted feeling is to do some kind of exercise or physical activity. Getting outdoors and exposing yourself to sunlight, and moving - whatever the activity, is a great way to counteract this feeling so you can get back to a point where your body doesn't feel threatened. The authors also point out deep and slow breathing, laughter, and connecting with others on an emotional level with a cry or a hug, can be just what you need.[21]

The next silent stressor that comes to mind is **technology and information overload.** Modern life and all the gadgets, smart phones, and access to today's internet come as a double-edged sword, like a lot of other things in life. The sharpest and more dangerous side of this "sword" is the endless gobs of techno-related information coming at us, non-stop! It's worse for the increasing numbers of people who have jobs where constant email, messaging, and zoom calls are engrained in the workplace. Then, ironically, when we get home, we do the thing we should least do – we start swiping through our smart phone or watch YouTube videos or turn on the television. All of it adds up to even more media and technological information coming at us. How do you know if you're suffering from **technology and information overload?**

- Do you find yourself getting angry at what you're hearing or reading?
- Do you feel like it's all just "too much?" Does the term "rat race" really resonate with you?
- Do you feel like you just don't know where to put your attention, or that you can't focus on any one thing for very long?

If you answered yes to any of these, it's time to start consciously filtering information and consider whether being in your own "rat race" is the best thing for you. When it comes to "filtering," think of it as triage in an emergency department at a hospital.[22] The staff needs to determine whose emergency is most important so they can get to those that need help the soonest. You need to triage information the same way. And no, it's not always easy to filter information. In the end, you need to decide what matters most to you and then act in your best interest. If need be, go cold turkey on social media for a while. Remember if you're giving attention to things that in reality, are just noise, you'll have less of yourself to give to yourself and others around you that matter the most.

Next is a stress inducer of the highest order I call **sensory information overload!** Think of this as **noise.** Or better still, not enough **peace and quiet.** Here's an example: a few times a week I take my leaf blower and go outside around our home to clean up the debris that's fallen from the trees. We have lots of trees near the house that deliver a never-ending supply of "tree junk." Each time I go out, I think my neighbors must be so tired of hearing that annoying whine from the leaf blower. And this kind of *sensory overload* doesn't only come from leaf blowers. It could be a neighbor's barking dog or music blaring from one of the bedrooms, or the sound of traffic or a never-ending car alarm going off in a parking lot. The possible sources are endless.

As humans, we're wired to respond to certain sound signals and often do it without any thought. Whether it's a car horn – that makes us jump and take notice – or the quiet hum of a dishwasher – that we ignore, our response just happens. But what if it all adds up and combines with other kinds of stressors and becomes too much? The end result can be anger or aggression, elevated blood pressure and a greater desire to reach for a bag of chips or a candy bar for comfort, none of which will serve our health goals very well.

Once again, it's smart to remember we're all unique. Some of us thrive on the noisy shopping mall environment and don't like the peace and quiet of a walk in the woods. Others are the opposite. The solution is to know yourself better, learn your triggers, and make sure you do what YOU need to in order to find the right balance. If you're sensitive to **sensory information overload**, schedule "quiet breaks" into your day. If time allows, stop on the way home from work to relax in a quiet spot for a few minutes. For me, I often like to go to bed a little earlier than normal, so I can lie there and enjoy the peace and quiet of silence, just staring at a blank ceiling.

The last of the hidden, silent stressors harmful to our health is best described with the phrase, **emotional labor,** coined by sociologist Arlie Hochschild in 1983 in her book, *The Managed Heart*.[23] One simple way to think of **emotional labor** is the combined "internal work of actively managing the feelings of others, as well as control our(selves) and our response."[24]

To help you imagine what this means, let me tell you about my girlfriend Terry, who spends a few days a week as a server in a breakfast and lunch restaurant. If you've ever done this kind of work, you know how hard it can be. One of the hardest aspects is you *have to be* nice, cheerful, and engaging to every person you interact with, as you take care of their needs. You have to be that kind of person even if they're rude or leave a bad tip, and even if you're physically tired or just having a bad day. That kind of forced behavior because it's your job, can be exhausting.

My work as a coach is another good example. Any coach or teacher knows your primary responsibility is to be encouraging and positive. Your coaching clients rely on you to boost their feelings of hopefulness and competence and give them confidence. The problem sometimes comes when you aren't feeling any of those things for yourself yet are forced to conceal those feelings to do your job. If you're a parent or a caregiver for the elderly, you're also intimately familiar with this feeling.

And what about bus drivers, store checkout clerks, hospital workers and other first responders? Anyone and everyone in some kind of service industry. If you add the internal work that's involved in being nice and courteous all the time and the effort required to keep your feelings to yourself, to the loud noises that are often part of these environments, it's easy to see how this can add up and make you want to scream. The stress can lead to frustration, angst, and our own health taking the brunt. When this kind of stress builds, it's difficult if not impossible to be content and look toward the future with hope or find the mental and emotional space to care for our own health and well-being at a time when it's most important to do so.

Age Well and Feel Great!

Key Concept:

Negative Ions

One of the things I love most about living on the gulf coast of Florida is the amazing beaches that are a few minutes from home. Whenever I feel a strong need to de-stress, the beach calls. Walking along the water's edge, listening to the waves crashing – it's always had a powerful calming effect on me.

One day quite a few years ago, I became curious if it was just me, or if there was something unique about the beach that made it such as special place of healing and peacefulness. That curiosity led me to learn more about negative ions, which are often described as an invisible calming force in nature. These ions are created in nature as air molecules break apart due to sunlight, radiation, and moving air and water. As our body absorbs them, it releases serotonin – a "feel good" chemical messenger in the body.

Think of a waterfall or just walking in the woods or the mountains. It's about being outside. So, can you imagine what advice I might offer you to reap the positive benefits? Get outside!!

What About Nutritional Stress?

In 2010, I gave a presentation on optimal daily and training nutrition to a group of student-athletes at the University of Hartford, in Connecticut. In anticipation of my talk, I'm sure the student-athletes were expecting me to give them the regular dose of "make sure to get adequate protein for recovery," and to eat their fruits and veggies. However, there was one topic I brought up that caught them a little off guard. What was it? Below are two slides from that presentation. As you can see, I refer to stress as the "fire" in our lives. That is, whether it's the rat-race mentality or poor sleep or even feeling a little depressed, it's all either creating stress or manifesting itself as the result of it.

The "FIRE" in our lives is: <u>STRESS</u>
The root cause of many issues...

❑ What causes or creates stress?
- Not eating nutrient dense foods
- Eating refined processed foods
- Change!
- Training
- **Lack of sleep**
- RAT RACE mentality: *emotional / intellectual stress*

❑ What are the results?
- Weakened immune system: *sickness*
- Poor recovery from training
- Poor sleep: ***reduced GH release***.
- **Cravings:** *sugar burning, NOT fat burning!*
- **Chronic hunger**
- Poor motivation or inner drive
- Depression: *Lowered Serotonin release (comfort foods!)*
- Chronic disease!

The "FIRE" in our lives: <u>STRESS</u>
What should we do?

❑ "Good" and "Bad" (uncomplimentary) Stressors
   ❑ Cultivate the good – Eliminate the bad

❑ Nutritional Stress:
   ❑The *stress* to your entire body created by:

   - eating *refined, processed* foods
   -*not eating* nutrient dense foods

❑ *Nutritional Stress accounts for 70% of uncomplimentary stress for most of us..*

❑ *What is the largest contributor to Nutritional Stress?*
* *Eating refined, processed foods...*

The thing I'd most like to draw your attention to is how the kinds of **food we eat** can become a huge inducer of stress – *nutritional stress* - that not surprisingly, comes from routinely eating junk and processed, refined foods, which then leads to chronic inflammation, increased bodyfat, a very unhappy gut microbiome, and poor energy levels, and that's for starters. As you can imagine, the more nutritional stress you have in your life, the worse you feel and the worse you feel about yourself! It's like a cascade that leaves you feeling badly physically and emotionally. **Nutritional stress is yet ONE MORE reason to do all you can to minimize the junk, processed, refined foods in your diet and eat more REAL foods.**

How Can We Recover to Feel Better and Become Healthier and More Resilient?

There are no quick fixes or "hacks" that will make it easier to manage stress. Awareness, as in many things, goes a long way toward helping us manage it more successfully. It goes without saying, but I will say it anyway, eating better most of the time will help. A lot! You'll feel better physically, and feel better about yourself. Exercising regularly, which if done in a smart way that doesn't result in you putting more pressure on yourself, is a fantastic way to counterbalance the negative stress in our lives.

Schedule more "me" time. Make plans for relaxation. And as you can imagine, it's important to be careful not to consume too much alcohol. Shortly, you'll read more about what I've learned from the "Blue Zone" regions of the world. These are geographical pockets around the world where the greatest percentage of centenarians live. One universal trait in all these Blue Zones is taking time to relax and downshift. Paradoxically, they don't "retire", nor do they do a lot of *intense* exercise. Their lives are structured so they're constantly nudged into physical activity, yet they always set aside time to relax. That's something we could all learn from. Balance. I'll talk more about these Blue Zones later in this chapter, and what we can learn from them.

Here are some extra TIPS from the resources and authors I've enjoyed reading and exploring over the last few years. These folks have learned a lot about how to better handle stress in their own lives and have been willing to share with others what has worked for them.

Secret service agent and author, Evy Poumpouras, in her book, *Becoming Bulletproof: Protect Yourself, Read People, Influence Situations, Live Fearlessly,* reminds us hormetic stress isn't just the stress that comes from adapting physically. In her words, "it's also about adapting mentally as well." Her secret service training was designed around this concept. She shares "over the course of months, the instructors incrementally exposed her and her colleagues to greater and greater amounts of stress to the point where they could function highly, both mentally and physically, while under extreme conditions." She calls this "micro stress" that if we're incrementally and repeatedly exposed to, can help strengthen our minds.

In her opinion, "ironically, today we seem to be constantly pushed toward seeking a life that is stress free. But what these *purveyors of placidity* don't realize – or choose not to tell us – is that we need a certain amount of stress to make us stronger. Think of your mind like a muscle of adaptability. If you train it, it will get stronger. If you let it lie on the couch in sweatpants while stuffing your face with nacho chips and binge-watching Netflix, not so much."[25] I have to agree with her. Part of the challenge is taking control and incremental and repeated exposure to the right kinds of mental stressors. It can be tricky to manage and balance.

In his book, ***High Level Wellness: An Alternative to Doctors, Drugs, and Disease,*** author Don Ardell has three recommendations for dealing successfully with stress: He says to "take stock of your own power. Distress, when you think about it, is not really outside of you – it is in your subjective response to a situation. This being the case, you can learn to recognize and almost completely manage your feeling-level by working on the notion that you have the power to control your own stress response."[26]

When I read that some time ago, it brought me immediately back to the great stoic philosopher, Marcus Aurelius who said: "If you are distressed by anything external, the pain is not due to the thing itself but to your estimate of it. This you have the power to revoke at any time." And this, which may be his most well-known quote: "The happiness of your life depends upon the quality of your thoughts: therefore, guard accordingly, and take care that you entertain no notions unsuitable to virtue and reasonable nature."[27]

I've enjoyed reading every book I can find by author Kindra Hall, who I told you about earlier. As I mentioned, her first and most well-known book is *Stories That Stick*. The stories she and I are referring to are the kind of stories *we tell ourselves*. Think about it: the thoughts you have and the things you tell yourself about you and the world around you has much to do with how you're able to control and manage stress.

For example, in her newest book, *Choose Your Story, Change Your Life*, she speaks about something called *negativity bias*. To imagine what this is, think of an instance in your own life where someone said something negative that shocked you or even better, a situation you were in that you felt was dangerous. Kindra says "research shows we tend to remember traumatic incidents better and learn more from negative experiences and tend to make decisions based more on negative information than positive," which tends to influence the "stories we tell ourselves, giving them a negative slant."[28]

Thinking of this from the standpoint of our ancestors and how we've naturally evolved over tens of thousands of years, it makes sense. As Kindra points out, the "more in tune to danger and risk we are, the more likely we are to live longer."[29]. While she was referring to our ancestors and the idea they'd always assume a noise in the bush was a bear and not a cool breeze, for me it's about driving defensively and taking smart precautions around the home, all with the idea of improving our safety, which leads to a sense of calm.

I'll leave this section and you with a little something from one of my all-time favorite books that has been on my shelf since I bought it in 1995, *The Aladdin Factor*, by authors Jack Canfield and Mark Victor Hansen. It's this: "Anything is possible if you dare to ask."[30] This is a great book for pinpointing the major stumbling blocks to asking, and then learning simple techniques to overcome them. Just in case you're wondering, the message isn't about blindly wishing upon a star or hoping for change. It's one that puts the onus on us, encouraging and inspiring us to not try to go it alone, but be willing to ASK FOR HELP when we need it. They teach you how.

So much of the stress we experience could be more easily resolved if we reached out more when we needed it. We all get here on the backs of those that came before us. We need each other to thrive. Friends, colleagues, co-workers, and family, all play an important role in OUR success and happiness. No one does this thing called life, alone. And to age consciously, you need the help and support of those closest to you.

What a pity that so many people would rather believe their doubts and doubt their beliefs. Why don't we just decide to have no doubts and believe our beliefs! Fear and worry are just the misuse of the creative powers we originally got to dream.

-- Jannie Putter

You Can't Pour From An Empty Cup.

Out on a run yesterday, I was thinking how much social media has changed our lives. From a goal-oriented athlete's perspective, if Facebook and Twitter are great for one thing that's *positive* (as opposed to the *negative* political banter), it's the **inspiration** we can enjoy from seeing lots of posts and messages from the folks we are connected with.

On that topic, is it me or does it seem like every day, everywhere we look on social media, we're barraged with motivational messages, memes, positive quotes, and folks sharing their workouts to inspire and motivate not only themselves, but their friends too?

Yet at the same time, as I look around and talk with others, many are not making the progress they'd hoped to. Could it be we're so distracted and drained and often running on empty, we're finding it difficult to do the things we need to?

Don't get me wrong. I believe there is some power in motivational messages and I know having a community of people supporting us is often a large part of our individual success. Very often we need that little extra boost. But still, look around. A lot of us are struggling. We're stressed and it seems like we're always distracted. Despite those positive messages, we're often no further down the "success" path than we were before.

So, what gives? I'm no expert on the changes we see happening in the world around us, that's for sure. However, I do know this: it's very **hard to pour from an empty cup**, you know? Simply put, in what is definitely a recurring theme in this book, we all must find better, more effective ways to care for ourselves, first. That starts by taking a hard look at where we are putting our energy and making some often difficult choices.

Sometimes the biggest challenge is not falling victim to the "quick fix" mentality that is so pervasive, in part because of social media. I mean, because you watch (or *think* you watch - be careful what you believe) someone "be awesome" on Facebook or YouTube doesn't mean those skills and abilities and results are magically transferred to you. It's not about "trying" harder or giving more. It might be about knowing where to give, and where to let go. We can't allow ourselves to look for the quick fix, "instant" cure, or some kind of special secret sauce whenever we get anxious or impatient. And we sure as hell would be better off if we stopped comparing ourselves to others, something that social media has, at times, made nearly impossible.

One of my all-time favorite "personal growth" speakers and leaders, Jim Rohn, once said: "Success is the predictable result of doing the right things, in the right way, at the right time." The well-known writer and professor, John Gardner, once said: "Excellence is doing ordinary things, extraordinarily well." Those who are able to make the positive lifestyle changes I'm encouraging you to do in this book aren't born that way. Rather, they've learned and embraced the idea that we *can* have it all, just not all at the same time! Success is a *growth process* that requires *focus, determination, hard work, a little humility*, and most of all, a *willingness to do the things you often least want to do, when you least want to do them!* ☺ It also requires enough energy to do the little things well, which won't ever happen if we're trying to do it all.

Humility is a tough one. To me, it means you're willing to listen, hear the truth, and commit to life-long learning. It also means seeing supposed "failures" not as failures at all, but rather, as *one more steppingstone moving you closer to where you want to be*. When it comes to so much of what I do on the exercise and movement front, I'll admit I'm a bit of a fanatic about "doing things in the right way," as Jim Rohn, said. My former partner Dr. Kurt Strecker has often said that you can do any exercise 95% correctly and get very little benefit from it.

So, are you doing the *right things*, in *the right way*, *at the right time*? Are you doing the *ordinary things, extraordinarily* well? Also, are you trying to *pour from an empty cup* or *wasting energy comparing yourself* to others? Our future success and happiness aren't dictated or limited by our DNA, our parents, where we grew up, or who we know. Far greater achievement, satisfaction, and fulfillment are available to each one of us, regardless of our background, talent level, or gender. Of course, for many of us, the process of learning what the right steps to take are, begins by *simplifying our lives, and* learning what we need to do.

A constant see-saw

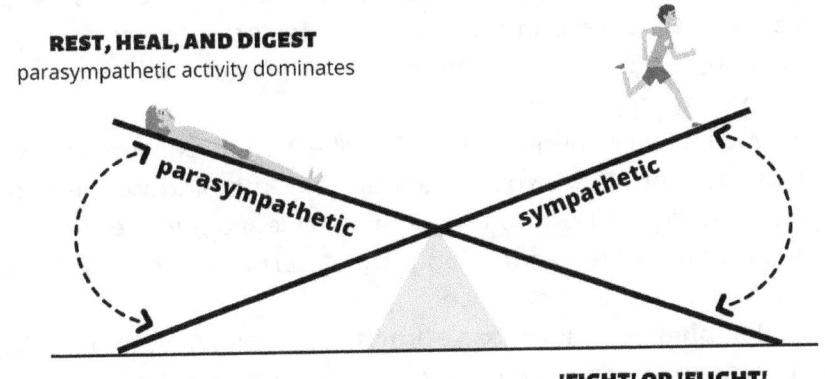

REST, HEAL, AND DIGEST
parasympathetic activity dominates

parasympathetic

sympathetic

'FIGHT' OR 'FLIGHT'
sympathetic activity dominates

Motivation and Stress: An Inverse Relationship?

So often we go through periods in our lives where for one reason or another, stress and anxiety levels are higher than we want them to be. Maybe it's the time of year, dissatisfaction at work, health issues with someone close to us, economic challenges, or flux and change which in and of itself, can cause a ton of stress. During times like these, it's helpful to remember when those stress levels are UP, it is often natural and normal for our energy and motivation to do the things we need to for our own self-care, to go in the opposite direction – DOWN.

In other words, *stress and anxiety exist in inverse of boundless energy, internal drive, and motivation.*

I bet that makes sense as you're reading it, yet we all struggle with this dilemma at times. It comes when we don't see this inverse relationship, and we begin to ADD to our stress levels by berating ourselves for not "wanting it" more, or working harder, or having the same level of motivation we may have had in the past.

The issue ISN'T that you don't care, it's more likely your body is in a "fight or flight" mode and stress hormones like cortisol are soaring throughout your bloodstream. When that's the state of mind you're in, the best thing for you to do at any moment *might* be to exercise, but sometimes that's the last thing you can motivate yourself to do! So why am I mentioning this? The reasons are important and multifaceted. Let's review a few tips to better understand how we can navigate this inverse relationship.

- **Stop beating yourself up for any lack of drive or motivation**. See this for what it is, an *inverse* relationship.
- **Seek productive ways to ease the stress, but remember at the same time,** facing those issues which are the primary cause, and taking action to change the situation as best you can, is a smart strategy too! Don't bite off too much at any one time. Easy to say, hard to do, I know!
- **Get out and move!** Even when you don't feel like it, if you can just start with something small, almost nothing at all, you'll have done something positive for YOU, which will leave you feeling better about yourself and leave a few endorphins as well, to enhance your mood. I'll talk more about this "start small" mindset in the upcoming chapters on movement and exercise.
- **If all else fails, please be kind to yourself.** Seek balance, and if at first you don't succeed, try, try again. Keep smiling, keep it fun, and remember – don't be so hard on yourself! ☺ None of this gives you permission to slack, but rather, to be honest with yourself and kind to the most important person in the world, YOU!

Age Well and Feel Great!

Key Concept:

Mental Health Is the New Fitness Goal

The physical fitness and health benefits of exercise are well known to most people. In this day and age however, with stress from work and burnout at an all-time high in some circles, perhaps the biggest benefit to an exercise routine is for your mental health. The newest data seems to support this. For example, according to a just released report from online fitness-class scheduling platform Mindbody, the top two reasons Americans work out now are to reduce stress and feel better mentally. That's a striking change from 2019, when according to Mindbody's report from that year, controlling weight and looking better were top motivators for many exercisers. [31][32] Perhaps this shouldn't be surprising – the link between exercise and stress reduction, improved sleep, and enhanced mood is well established. And after all, runners have been talking about a "runner's high" for as long as I can remember. 😊

The key is knowing yourself and making sure you have some options. Some days you might feel like a gut-busting intense workout to blow off some steam; other days something more recovery-oriented, such as a tai-chi or yoga class, or simply a walk in the woods, might be just what the doctor ordered.

Don't fall victim to turning your workouts into another form of stress that makes you feel unworthy or like a failure. It's one thing to try to be mindful and to focus on improving yourself, but if the hustle and bustle of a stressful work day leaves you feeling fried, the last thing you may want to do is put more pressure on yourself to perform in the gym. Sometimes the best "workout" is rest and being kind to yourself.

Take Action: Breathwork and Three Dimensional (3-D) Breathing Practice.

Here's one thing you can do on a routine basis to help reduce stress and improve your health – relaxed breathwork. It's so simple and easy to do, yet it is something we rarely do enough. It works! It'll help you manage stress, sleep better, and release tension all over your body. Breathwork doesn't have to be complicated. It can be as simple as taking a few very deep breaths over a slow count of 4 or 5, in and out. Repeat a few times over a minute or two and you'll feel better. You can come back to it at any time.

If you want to take it a step further for even more benefits, that's also easy and simple to do. I call it 3-dimensional (or 3-D) breathing.

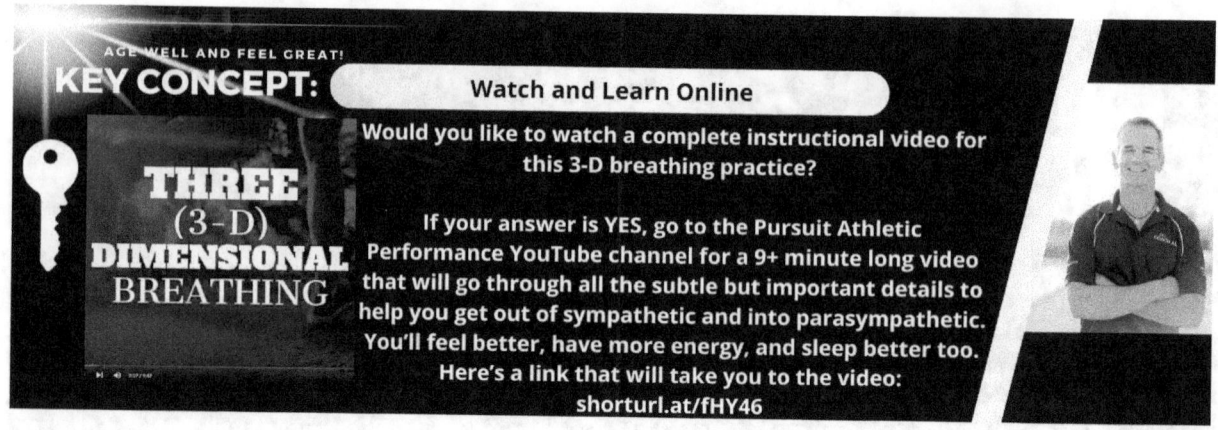

Breathing happens automatically, right? You don't need to think about it. Well sure, that's true if we're talking about surviving. The thing is, living your best life, feeling good and avoiding chronic disease is about more than just surviving.

The way we breathe reflects the physical, mental, and emotional state we're in. Even more, the kind of breaths we take can greatly impact those states.

We can change our health and how we feel by becoming more mindful about our breathing. It can be as simple as taking a few very slow, deep breaths to relax our mind and body. We can also go a bit deeper and take our *optimal breathing* to the next level for even more benefits. Take a look at this image of the diaphragm which comes from my online program, *Restore: The Foundation Program*. Imagine how it moves up and down, expanding and contracting with each deep breath you take.

Keep in mind stress, exercising, and our hectic lifestyles can all lead to *less optimal breathing habits*. That's another way of saying that stressed out feeling you're carrying around with you may result in lots of *chest breathing*, which isn't an optimal way to breath. Shallow chest breathing can lead to headaches, neck and back pain, and a host of other issues. Even more, it can lead to conditions ranging from those that are hardly noticeable, such as malaise or fatigue, chronic tightness, and anxiety, to those that are a lot more problematic, such as

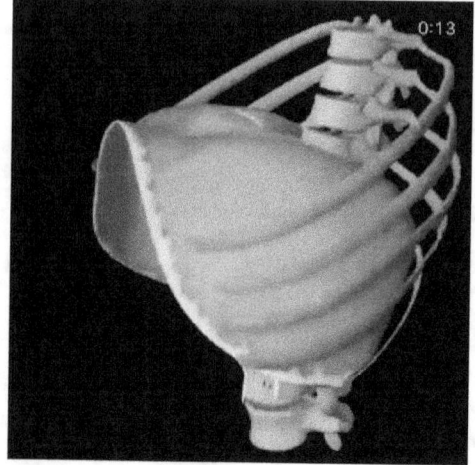

back pain, and even hypertension/high blood pressure.

Deeper, focused 3-D breathing can help undo the tension and stress and provide your body with more of the oxygen it needs to thrive. So, what is 3-D or three-dimensional breathing? It's our ability to expand and relax ALL the cavities of our upper body from the lower abdomen and pelvis to our rib cage and trunk, both front to back and side to side, rather than using only our chest and upper cavity. Learning and practicing the next-level dynamic integration of all the parts of your trunk, rib cage, and lungs is what makes this practice different than just taking a few deep breaths.

What Are Your Goals With 3-D Breathing Practice?

1. To move away from always being in or close to a sympathetic – shallow breathing in the chest, "fight or flight" state of being, and into a more restorative, relaxed, parasympathetic state.

When *parasympathetic* nervous system activity is higher, you're more relaxed and better able to recover, sleep, and generally feel less tired – and more rejuvenated. Conversely, what are some of the typical signs of being chronically in *sympathetic?* Having a higher resting heart rate, sweating, or feeling anxious, muscle fatigue and achiness, and inflammation, to name a few.

2. To improve your general, overall health and in particular, your core stability, especially when used in conjunction with the other fundamental skills such as the basic abdominal brace that you will read about in Chapter 20, *How to Improve Your Stability*.

In terms of your health, 3-D breathing can improve your spine's ability to move, improve digestion and organ health, and improve the functioning of your gastrointestinal system, among many other things.

3. And as mentioned, to improve the capacity to use ALL these breathing regions – thoracic, abdominal, pelvic – during a typical respiratory cycle. For various reasons, one area may dominate over another at certain times, but you need the ability to access all three to be truly healthy, feel good and have more energy.

Here Are Some TIPS to Enhance Your Practice:

- I love practicing first thing in the morning when I wake, or on the flip side, right before bedtime. In fact, while lying in bed before falling asleep can be the ideal time. You'll notice a slower respiratory rate and be able to feel more relaxed and at peace. This is one way to set up a great night's sleep.
- Breathing practice can happen in many different positions. None are perfect for every single person. Lying down in a face up position is the best position for most people, but feel free to bring this practice into a host of different positions and at different times of day.
- Feel free to place a pillow under the head to create optimal alignment/comfort.
- None of these breathing skills should ever be forced. Relying too much on muscle strength or force can lead to compensation which will reduce the potential benefits you may receive.
- Always focus primarily on the exhale, which should happen through your nose and pursed lips! And always exhale for twice the amount of time you inhale.

- A 2 – 1 – 4 – 1 count strategy can work very effectively, however, feel free to choose a rhythm that works best for you. As mentioned, the key is to remember to exhale for twice as long as you inhale.
- In case you're wondering, a 2 – 1 – 4 – 1 count looks like this: 2 seconds inhale through the nose, 1-second pause, 4 seconds exhale through your nose and pursed lips, 1-second pause, then repeat. Doing this will give you 8 seconds per breath and around 7-8 breaths a minute.

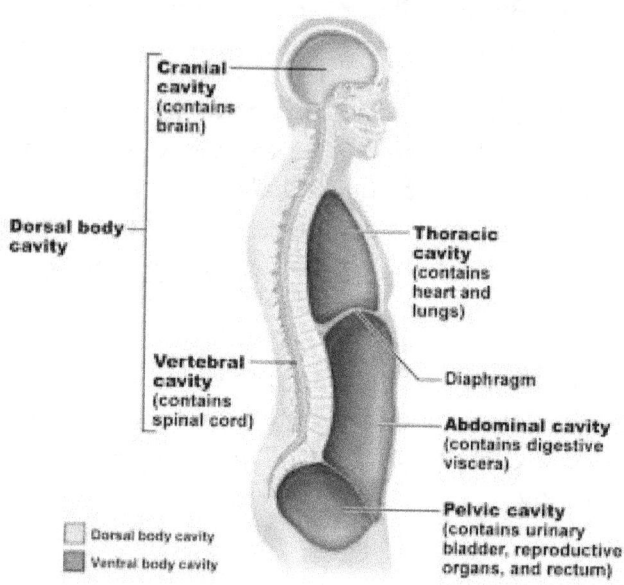

Spending as little as 1 minute up to 5 minutes practicing these skills can help restore optimal health, improve recovery and rejuvenation, and lead to enhanced sleep and a feeling of well-being.

So, let me ask, do you have any chronic shoulder, neck, mid-back, chest, or rib pain? Have you struggled with gastroesophageal reflux? Have you been told or found to have low blood oxygen levels? Do you have any breathing "issues"? All these daily challenges could be the result of your breathing habits, which among other things, could lead to some diaphragm dysfunction. The diaphragm is the most important muscle of inhalation. It separates the *thoracic* cavity, containing the heart and lungs, from the *abdominal* cavity.

As the diaphragm contracts, the volume of the thoracic cavity increases, and air is drawn down into the lungs. It has very important fascial connections to the sternum, the ribs, the thoracic and lumbar spine, and abdominal organs. It also plays an important role in non-respiratory functions (think of your bathroom habits as one example) by increasing abdominal pressure when needed. It can prevent acid reflux by exerting pressure on the esophagus as it passes through the esophageal hiatus. What's more, diaphragm muscle trigger points can lead to referred pain in the rib cage or shoulder.

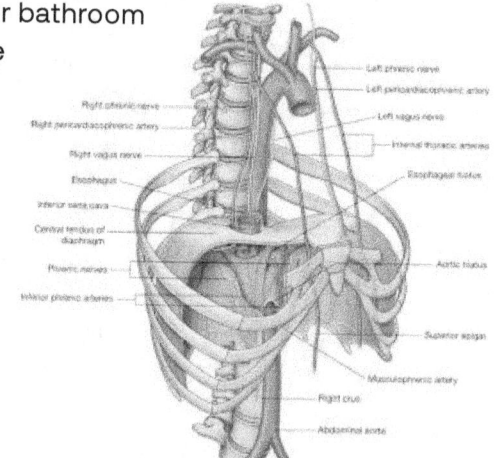

Why am I sharing all this technical information? It's to make the point that proper breathing is critical for your health and daily rejuvenation. It's often overlooked and taken for granted. Don't!

Feelings come and go like clouds in a windy sky.
Conscious breathing is my anchor.
— Thich Nhat Hahn

What About Meditation?

I'll admit for a long time when I heard the word "meditation," I tended to fluff it off and disregard it, thinking it was a bit poo-poo for this "serious" endurance athlete. ☺ As time went on and I learned more, I came to the realization I was already meditating, I just didn't think of it that way. You see, each of us can meditate in whatever way works best, for us. We can make it whatever we want it to be. The end goal is always the same: *to develop a deeper calmness, reduce stress, and gain some clarity.*

A quiet walk or jog in the woods can be meditation. I find sitting at the beach to be a great way to meditate. For you, it may be sitting alone in whatever place you find comforting. Closing your eyes and removing any thought or judgement from your mind while listening to the quiet, may be your preferred form of mediation. The trick is letting your thoughts go and clearing your mind.

One of my mentors in this book writing journey is author, Scott Allan, who works with a company called the Self-Publishing School. Recently, Scott wrote an email to his list titled *The Meditation Habit.* In that email, he shared his own discovery of the power of meditation, including his early skepticism and how, once he discovered it, he realized it was the thing he'd always been searching for. His advice is great and worth sharing.

He says "meditation can be difficult at first if you're not used to it. But you can do it anywhere regardless of how much noise pollution surrounds you. Meditation is nothing more than training your mind to move into a silent place that already exists. You have to find it and then, once there, focus on staying in that place for as long as you can. It's easy to start meditating. Here is a simple process I use that works:

- Situate yourself in a secluded location. This can be a room at home or if you are in the middle of a workday, you might have an empty room or space not being used at the office.
- Turn off devices and anything else that could distract you.
- Sit comfortably, close your eyes, and begin deep breathing.
- Observe your thoughts. You don't have to do anything about them. Just let them go.
- Stay focused on breathing. Absorb the sounds and sensations around you.
- Focus on your awareness of the environment.
- Commit to this practice of meditation twice a day. It has many positive health benefits for both your mind and body."[33]

Earlier I shared some guidance on how to approach 3-Dimensional Breathing. That practice alone, but especially when combined with some quiet time as Scott describes above, could be your saving grace for reducing stress in your life. It might be worth a try. ☺

When you fight biology, and sleep is one of the most conserved behaviors across all living organisms that we've observed, when you fight that kind of innate hard grained biology, you normally lose.

And the way that you know that you've lost, is disease and sickness, either acute or chronic. At some point a lack of sleep will get you.

— Matthew Walker, Ph.D.

Sleep.

I've always been fascinated with ultra-running and have tried my hand at a few long ultra-endurance races in my lifetime. One of the most famous of those events I've been enamored with is the **Badwater 135**. As the name implies, it's a *one-hundred- and thirty-five-mile running race* through Death Valley California. The race website describes it this way:

> "Covering 135 miles (217km) non-stop from Death Valley to Mt. Whitney, CA, the Badwater 135 is the most demanding and extreme running race offered anywhere on the planet. The start line is at Badwater Basin, Death Valley, which marks the lowest elevation in North America at 280' (85m) below sea level. The race finishes at Whitney Portal at 8,300' (2530m). The Badwater 135 course covers three mountain ranges for a total of 14,600' (4450m) of cumulative vertical ascent and 6,100' (1859m) of cumulative descent. Whitney Portal is the trailhead to the Mt. Whitney summit, the highest point in the contiguous United States. Competitors travel through places or landmarks with names like Mushroom Rock, Furnace Creek, Salt Creek, Devil's Cornfield, Devil's Golf Course, Stovepipe Wells, Panamint Springs, Darwin, Keeler, Alabama Hills, and Lone Pine.[34]

If you're thinking this sounds like a ridiculously hard, insanely dumb race, well, you might be right. ☺ Temperatures at the hottest time of the year rarely go below 100 degrees and can easily reach 120 to 130 degrees during the hottest times of the day. After all, Death Valley is a barren desert comprised of chalky white salt flats and gnarly scrub (with painful pointy things sticking out of them) and is one of the hottest regions anywhere on Earth. In fact, when I was at this event in 2011 and arriving to the village of Stovepipe Wells at the 42 mile-mark of the race, I remember seeing the thermometer say 129 degrees!

At one time, I thought I wanted to try my hand at this race. The best way to prepare for doing a race like this is to first, go there and see it up close yourself, firsthand. You learn about it by being there. At Badwater, that means being part of a support crew for a runner who is in the race. Each runner competes with the support of his or her own crew of anywhere from three to five people who usually follow the runner in two vehicles, one of them a van. The race itself doesn't provide during-race support, so having a crew is considered essential to complete it.

The crew's responsibilities range from getting and providing ice, water, energy foods, and of course the assortment of medical supplies needed, such as tape and band aids for the runner's feet. As you can imagine, almost anything can happen in 135 miles of running in the desert, to both the runner and the crew!

A couple of months before the July race dates, I contacted the race director to tell him I was interested in joining a support crew if he happened to hear of anyone who needed some extra support. About two weeks before the race, I got an email from an Italian runner, Roberto, who said he needed support crew help. He asked if I'd be willing to meet him and the rest of his crew for the race. I jumped at the opportunity. And what an experience it was. A lot of highs, and a lot of lows, too. I'd argue it was as hard for the crew as it was for Roberto, who achieved his dream of becoming a Badwater finisher in around 42 hours!

Another member of the crew for that race told me that he too, wanted to do the race. If he was ever able to qualify and put it all together, when the time came he said he would only do it if I would agree to be on his crew. I guess that was his vote of confidence for me that I'd been a positive, contributing member of the team. I told him of course, I'd be honored, should the time come. One year later, he sent me an email saying he had qualified and was going to race! Just like that, it was Badwater 135, here we go again!

This time, I knew what to expect. Long days, even longer nights, and not very much sleep along the way.

The support crew "routine" is to drive on the same roads as the race but stay a little ahead of the runner. It would be typical to drive a mile ahead, park alongside the road, then wait until your runner arrives, at which point you'd go out onto the road and see what they might need. It's your job to be ready with almost anything. Here is a picture of our support van alongside the road during the race. The name of our runner is on the side of the van.

As you can imagine, sometimes the runner needs moral support, or to rest momentarily by getting out of the sun, or the typical water bottle refill or ice packs on the neck. Once they're set, you get back into the van and drive ahead for another mile or so. As you can imagine, there's a lot of "hurry up and wait" for the crew in a race like this. It can ebb and flow between being excruciatingly boring, and then instantly nerve wracking.

In this picture, I'm behind the wheel of the van and another crew member, Jon, is sitting alongside.

In this 2012 race, some things transpired that made it particularly difficult for our entire team. First, about halfway into the race, one of the crew members got sick and needed to be driven to a motel miles back, using one of our two vehicles. We were already shorthanded to begin with, as one of the crew members who was scheduled to be there hadn't yet arrived. To make a long story short, by the time we reached the halfway point of the race at the top of Townes Pass at around midnight of the first day, I was the only support crew member there. At the time, I was hoping the driver who had taken the sick crew member back to the motel wouldn't be gone long, but as I said earlier, I knew a lot of unforeseen things can happen in a race of this magnitude, in the middle of the hottest place on earth. Keep in mind the race had begun at 5 AM and we'd been out in the desert sun all day long. This next picture shows my back as I wait for our runner to make his way closer to us on day two, about 70 miles into the race.

Anyone who has ever worked a double shift or been forced to stay awake knows the feeling. As you get more tired, it feels like something has a grip on you and is crushing down on you. I remember sitting on the side of the road behind the steering wheel of the car – it's 3 AM and I'm waiting for my runner to come up alongside. It's as dark as the blackest black,

and I am finding it so hard to keep my eyes open. But I have to, because my runner is liable to show up at any moment and will need my support.

Those dark and lonely hours before the sun rose were absolutely excruciating. And while I'm used to feeling refreshed when the sun does come up on a typical day, that's not how I felt that morning. Fast forward, by the time we reached the 72-mile mark, our runner bedded down for a couple of hours, but I couldn't. I had too much work to do to be able to support him through the race. Eventually, the two additional crew members, one who arrived late and the driver for our sick member, arrived and were able to assist.

We finally arrived at the finish line in 42 hours, the same as Roberto had done in 2011. This picture is our runner leading the way with the crew behind, as we're approaching the finish line at the Mount Whitney portal. In the end, I never slept at all during the race, going roughly 45 hours without shutting my eyes for more than a few minutes. No deep or sustained sleep. After the celebratory finish, we drove back down to our hotel in Lone Pine. During the hour or so drive, the urge to sleep was absolutely overwhelming.

So, why tell the story of these two Badwater experiences? During both races, to say I didn't sleep much would be a huge understatement, but in the 2012 race it was worse. During

those last hours before I was finally able to get to bed, I couldn't function, nor could I think about anything else. I felt like I was going insane. I felt like I had been drugged, like I was in this awful trance. I've never taken a hallucinogenic drug, but I imagine that is what it might be like. I was at times hostile, disoriented, my head was spinning, and as I said, definitely hallucinating. Those 45 hours had wreaked complete havoc on me.

Until then, I don't think I ever thought much about the importance of sleep. When I finally woke up after hitting the motel bed about 12 hours later, I went outside to see the others. I said something to the effect that I was thinking the lack of sleep might kill me, long before going without food or water would. It hit me *that hard*.

Years later, as I learned more, I realized as shocking as it seemed, what I said that day wasn't far from the truth. I was listening to *The Drive podcast* with Dr. Peter Attia, M.D.. and his guest at the time, one of the world's leading experts on sleep, Matthew Walker, Ph.D.. I remember Dr. Walker emphatically repeating this notion that sleep is SO crucial for our health and well-being, a lack of it could kill you long before you'd die from starvation. In fact, there was a study done in 1983 with mice where they deprived the mice of sleep until they died. (Sounds awful, I know!) The results were the animals died 20% sooner than they would from starvation.[35]

When It Comes to Optimal Aging and Good Health, Sleep is One of the Most Common Missing Pieces.

It's always interesting to me when I'm talking to someone about aging or their health, how they'll tell me some of the things they believe they're doing well to be healthier and age better. Their pride shines, whatever it might be. What I've found though, is while there are always things we can "hang our hats on" as things we are doing well, there is usually something missing.

And that something is often very important. I alluded to these "missing pieces of the puzzle" in Chapter 3. Getting the necessary hours of regular sleep, as well as adequate sleep *quality* is one of the most common "missing" pieces. I believe one of the reasons is because *quality* sleep seems elusive to so many. I'm always having the conversation with someone who tells me they either have a hard time falling asleep, staying asleep, or getting enough sleep.

One of the goals of this book is to help you improve your life *before* aches and pains arrive. Make no mistake about it my friend, **high quality sleep is one of the MOST important pieces of the puzzle as you age.** You can do so many other things right – get proper exercise, eat well, and get stronger, and even become part of a loving community where you've found your true purpose in life, **but if you don't sleep well or enough, those other things might be wasted.** It may sound extreme, but I assure you that is what I've learned digging into this topic myself.

Dr. Walker gave a Ted Talk in 2019 titled *Sleep Is Your Superpower.* In it, he said "men who sleep five hours a night have significantly smaller testicles than those who sleep seven hours or more, and a lack of sleep will age a man by a decade. We see equivalent impairments in female reproductive health, caused by a lack of sleep. And that is the best news I have for you today."[36]

My advice to you is to follow his lead and focus on making sleep *your* superpower. If you learn nothing else from this book, it should be this: **Without proper and consistent sleep, you will have a very hard time aging well and living a long healthy life.** Or being as productive as you would like to be. In Dr. Walker's words, "nutrition and exercise are important, but sleep is the foundation on which those two other things sit. It's not the third pillar of good health, (I think) it is the foundation."[37]

Anyone over the age of 40 knows it is common to begin to experience a decline in sleep quality and quantity. And according to Dr. Walker, it's a myth that older people don't need as much as those younger. He also believes a lack of sleep is why we see a cognitive decline as we age. In fact, I'd argue that much of what we think of as typical signs of aging are signs that the body needs more, and higher quality, sleep. We shouldn't think of sleep interruptions as something we're forced to deal with as we age, although it is obvious to any woman who has been through menopause that night sweats and having to get up to pee more often can present some challenges.

In case you're wondering, you won't find a lot of details about the various stages of deep or REM sleep in this chapter. Why? Entire books have been written on it and after all, I'm not an expert. I'll leave it to you to explore some of the resources I've provided if you're interested. I heartily recommend Dr. Peter Attia's podcast, *the Drive*, with guest Dr. Matthew Walker.

At last count, Dr. Walker, has been a guest on the podcast eight times. He's a neuroscientist, professor at the University of California at Berkeley, and founder of the Center for Human Sleep Science, as well as being the author of the best-selling book, *Why We Sleep: Unlocking the Power of Sleep and Dreams.* All the episodes can all be accessed via this link: https://peterattiamd.com/matthewwalker1/

According to Dr. Walker, "sleep is your life-support system and Mother Nature's best effort yet at immortality."

Chronic Disease and Sleep.

One thing a lot of us aren't aware of is the degree to which poor sleep quality is associated with chronic disease. In his book, *The Science and Technology of Growing Young*, author Sergey Young says "getting even one hour less sleep on a single day can increase your chances of a heart attack by 24 percent! Getting one hour more sleep can reduce that risk by 21 percent. More than 15,000 studies link sleeping less than seven hours per night with coronary heart disease, stroke, asthma, atherosclerosis, chronic obstructive pulmonary disease, arthritis, depression, high blood sugar, diabetes, kidney disease, even after adjusting for other factors like smoking and obesity."[38] Other studies have linked sleep deprivation with hormones that regulate hunger and impulse control, and the link between cancer and poor sleep is said to be so strong, according to Young and Walker and other experts, "the International Agency for Research on Cancer (IARC) has classified night-shift work as a probable carcinogen, alongside sinister-sounding suspects like vinyl fluoride and diethyl sulfate."[39]

When it comes to the connection of sleep deprivation and cancer, think about this: On his podcast, Dr. Peter Attia, M.D., points out "I don't think people necessarily appreciate that we pretty much always have cancer, and our immune system is pretty much always protecting us. It's actually the exception when the cancer develops into something clinically."[40]

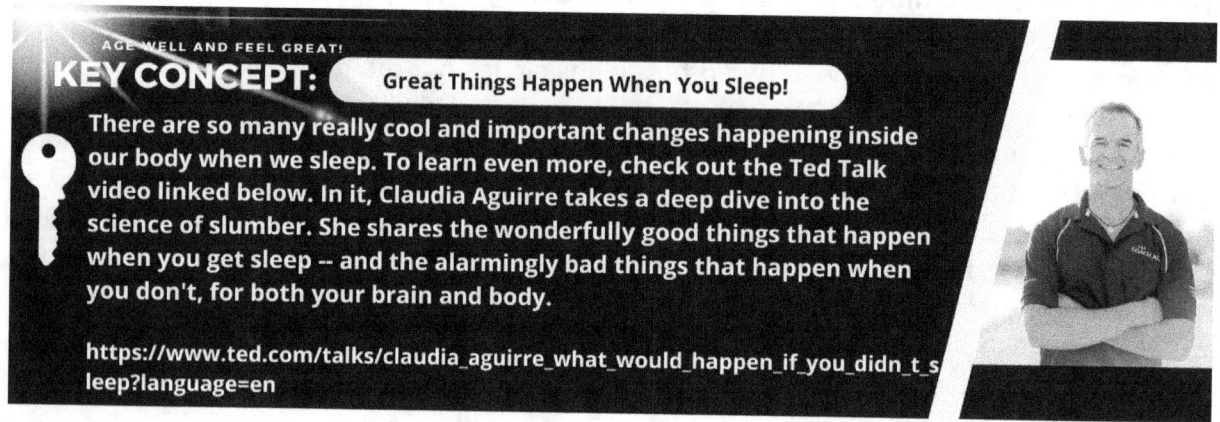

AGE WELL AND FEEL GREAT!

KEY CONCEPT: Great Things Happen When You Sleep!

There are so many really cool and important changes happening inside our body when we sleep. To learn even more, check out the Ted Talk video linked below. In it, Claudia Aguirre takes a deep dive into the science of slumber. She shares the wonderfully good things that happen when you get sleep -- and the alarmingly bad things that happen when you don't, for both your brain and body.

https://www.ted.com/talks/claudia_aguirre_what_would_happen_if_you_didn_t_sleep?language=en

Your Immune System and Sleep.

Anyone reading this understands as your immune system function goes, so goes your health. You can't have good health IF your immune system is compromised or isn't functioning as effectively as it needs to. So, how does poor sleep quality or a lack of enough sleep impact our immune system?

There was a study done at UCLA, discussed on the podcast interview by Dr. Attia with Dr. Walker, that shows "partial sleep deprivation reduces natural killer T-cell activity."[41] According to Dr. Walker, the study demonstrated that after one night of poor sleep, when "they measured natural killer cells (which identify foreign elements like cancer cells and destroy them), (that) one night of poor sleep caused 70% drop in natural killer cell activity."

He went on to point out: "imagine what it could be after months of insufficient sleep." Simply put, sleep is one of the most powerful and potent regulators of your immune system. As you get older, if sleep quality gets worse, your immune system will also get worse. Clearly, if your goal is to die earlier, it should be easy to do – just don't sleep!

Our Healthcare System and Sleep.

I don't know about you, but in my experience, rarely do doctors or other healthcare professionals emphasize how important sleep actually is. The fact that doctors themselves rarely get enough sleep compounds the issue. As a society, we put a lot of emphasis on working hard. Many are forced to work overtime to make ends meet but fail to realize how that negatively impacts sleep quality.

Most experts believe the same could be said for children and school start times. The way most of our systems are set up right now, sleep quality and quantity are way down the list in order of priority. And our kid's learning and adaptation is suffering as a result. Dr. Walker says, "when sleep is abundant, minds will flourish, and if our goal as educators is to educate, and not risk lives in the process, then I feel that we are failing our children in a quite spectacular manner, with this incessant model of early school start times."[42]

Age Well and Feel Great!

Key Concept:

Is the Quality Of Your Sleep Related To Your Circadian Rhythms?

One of the many daily habits I have is going outside right after I wake up in the morning. I'll get a tall glass of water after rinsing my face with cold water then mosey out to greet the burgeoning sunlight. It's a great way to start the day. One of the reasons I do it is to set my circadian rhythms in motion. For the same reason, I try to avoid exposing my eyes to a lot of light late at night before bedtime.

If you're wondering why I follow this morning routine, it is because most people are overexposed to bright light late in the day and underexposed to light early in the morning. As a result, our bodies often don't know what time of day it is. And yet we expect to get right to sleep as soon as we put our heads on the pillow.

Think about this: Thirty thousand years ago, our ancestors didn't have that problem. There was only one true source of light: the sun. Their body knew well when it was time to wake and when it was time to sleep. The take home is, get off your computer and away from the I-pad and smart phone at least an hour before you plan on laying down. Turn down the bright lights. And follow my lead by getting outdoors to get your day started. You won't regret it!

Sleep and Chronotype.

One of the most interesting facts I've learned in my own research is each of us has our own unique sleep *chronotype*. Chronotype is the natural inclination of your body to sleep at a certain time, or what most people understand as being an early bird versus a night owl. I used to believe that "night owls" should get to bed earlier and were being lazy sloths when they slept in, and people like me (early risers) were more "motivated," but those generalizations are not true. Studies have shown that besides regulating sleep and wake time, your individual chronotype has an influence on appetite, exercise, and core body temperature. It is why you feel more alert at certain periods of the day and sleepier at others.[43]

Are We Good Judges of Our Own Sleep Quality?

I'll often ask the athletes I coach how they're sleeping. Sometimes they'll let me know they've had a poor night's sleep. And sometimes they're using some other kind of technology or metric that gives them some feedback on their sleep quality. In my experience, we are terrible judges of our own sleep quality and quantity. Very often when we "think" we get a great night's sleep, the reverse is true.

There are a number of reasons why this is the case. Being in good general health can mask temporary sleep issues. Very often, changes in sleep quality are subtle and difficult to ascertain ourselves. And if you snore or suffer from some other kind of sleep disordered breathing, that can make things even harder to self-assess. The truth is most people with disrupted sleep don't know what they're missing because they've often never experienced anything different.

How We Sleep Is How We Live.

Author and dentist, Dr. Mark Burhenne, DDS, in his book *The 8-Hour Sleep Paradox*, says sleep disordered breathing is an epidemic and public health crisis affecting millions of us – as many as 42 million in the US alone with most being undiagnosed. It isn't just about not sleeping well. He says, "it affects our judgement, emotional capacity, creativity, and just about every cognitive process." He goes on to say "science has found that there's a strong link between anxiety and depression and sleep disorders. Yet, when someone is diagnosed with anxiety or depression, they're rarely offered a sleep study."[44]

After speaking with my own dentist about this, I've become a believer that just about everything inside of our mouths affects how we breathe, and therefore how well we sleep. It goes without saying when you aren't sleeping well, nothing else works very well. Sleep, or lack of it, plays a huge role in how much stress we experience and how well we manage that stress.

So, what is "disordered breathing" when you sleep? Essentially, it's mouth-breathing. If you snore or wake up with dry mouth, or you grind your teeth at night, those are all telltale signs you're mouth-breathing when you should be nose-breathing. You might also have some type of obstruction in your airways creating breathing or sleeping issues. Chronic heartburn or GERD can also be an indication there's an obstruction that needs to be rectified.

According to Dr. Burhenne:

- About 42 million American adults have sleep disordered breathing, up to 90% of which are undiagnosed.
- One in five adults has mild obstructive sleep apnea.
- One in fifteen adults has moderate to severe obstructive sleep apnea.
- 80-90% of people with diabetes have obstructive sleep apnea.
- Up to 95% of people who have had a stroke also have sleep apnea.
- Up to 35% of people with heart failure have obstructive sleep apnea.
- People with moderate to severe sleep apnea have an up to 15-fold increased risk of being involved in a traffic accident.[45]

In his words, "the sleep-disordered breathing crisis is making us exhausted, sick, unhappy, and stupid. Sleep disordered breathing now rivals obesity and smoking as our greatest public health crisis."[46]

In later chapters on exercise, especially type 1 cardiovascular exercise, I discuss the **importance of nose-breathing to assess your effort level and to achieve even more health benefits**. Most people never stop to think about the fact our mouths aren't designed for breathing the way our nose is. Among other things, when you're breathing through your mouth, your blood isn't getting oxygenated the way it needs to.

I know when I'm feeling more anxious, I find myself doing more mouth-breathing. It makes sense, right? More "fight or flight" nervous system actions mean our body is calling for MORE air! Unfortunately, the habit of mouth-breathing can become chronic and that's where the

problems often start. The answer is to be more aware. Check yourself often when you're driving, sitting around reading or watching TV, or at any other time, to see if you're nose-breathing (good) or mouth-breathing (bad).

Some experts have recommended using a tape across your lips at night to make sure your mouth remains closed. There are many resources online to learn more about this technique. Here's one of them: https://thesleepdoctor.com/snoring/mouth-taping-for-sleep/

So, what can you do to both sleep more and sleep better? That's the million-dollar question, but let's take a stab at it. As I mentioned earlier, in *the Drive* podcast episodes with Dr. Walker, he and Dr. Attia discuss anything and everything you could possibly think of related to sleep, so go there to learn more. I will share what I feel are the most important take-aways for you!

- **Most people need seven to nine hours of sleep.** If you're in the habit of watching television or flipping through Facebook on your smartphone and can honestly say that is cutting into your sleep time, you need to change it. The same is true with late night work responsibilities. Get off the email! You have to take control of your life when it comes to sleep – IF you want to be around long enough to enjoy a full life.
- **A television in your bedroom is a big NO.** Among other things, the artificial blue light from the screen seems to inhibit melatonin production (which is your body's natural sleep hormone). The same is true for an iPad or laptop.[47] Do NOT take those to bed.

Remember, you need adequate amounts of natural melatonin release in order to sleep well. So, should you supplement with melatonin? According to Dr. Walker, that depends. And, if a little is good, is more better? He says some people are dosing too high, and there is evidence that if you use too high a dose, you may actually shut down your body's own production of natural melatonin. His recommendation is to start with the minimum dose of 0.5 milligrams and cut it off at 3 milligrams. In my opinion, in nearly every instance, more usually *isn't* better. Dr. Walker says some older people can benefit from moderate supplementation. He also says it can be helpful for offsetting the effects of jetlag if you're traveling. Listen in to *the Drive* podcast interviews he does with Dr. Attia to learn more.[48]

- **Keep out the bright light – create what I think of as a dark cave.** There are numerous studies that show light also interferes with melatonin release. If you think about it, this is one thing that is very different now vs a couple million years ago, or even just a few hundred. There's a natural cycle of light and darkness that when respected, will enhance our normal awake and sleep rhythms. The thing is, we often mess up this natural rhythm by keeping bright lights on at night, when mother nature would have the environment less bright. What to do? Turn down the bright lights well in advance of bedtime. And make sure your bedroom is totally dark. Use blackout curtains and tape over some light infiltration if you need to.
- **Keep it cool.** Just like too much light, a too warm environment will increase core body temperature and inhibit the production of beneficial sleep hormones. Keep the thermostat low, open the windows if you need to, or get yourself a ceiling fan or room air conditioner. A temperature of between 65 to 68 degrees seems to be ideal.
- **I love my morning coffee. But I've learned as I've gotten older I need to shut it down no later than noontime to 2 PM.** And that includes that afternoon latte you've grown to love. You probably knew that, but I said it anyway. ☺ Caffeine can have a half-life of seven hours, meaning that seven hours after you drink a cup of coffee, half of the caffeine is still in your body.
- **Does alcohol help or hinder sleep? This is where there is a misunderstanding about the effects of a drink before bed. The truth is alcohol disrupts the sleep cycle** and while it might help you wind down before bed, it will almost assuredly

disturb your sleep quality. And of course, beer and wine are high in carbs and sugar, which is also a big NO prior to bedtime. (At the 42 minute mark of this podcast interview, Matt Walker discusses how alcohol disrupts sleep and also raises the risk for Alzheimer's disease: https://peterattiamd.com/matthewwalkerama/)

- **Create some bedtime rituals and stick with them.** This could mean making your space a bit darker, shutting down the electronic devices and instead spending a few minutes reading or meditating, so you can prepare for your best night's sleep.

- **Experiment with some sound devices or apps that can help you track your sleep better or create the ideal environment for optimal sleep.** Sleep Cycle and Sleep Score are apps that might help. Low-level white noise like ocean waves crashing can also be very helpful.

- **Have a consistent wake up time.** While it might not seem to matter what time you get up from one day to the next, many studies have identified a consistent wake up time as being crucial to help your body align with your natural circadian rhythms. Getting outside first thing in the morning and exposing your eyes to sunlight will also help. It's always the very first thing I do after peeing and then drinking 12 to 16 ounces of water. Try it!

- **Anxiety, being overweight, and not getting enough exercise or activity in your routine, are all contributing factors to a poor night's sleep.** Rather than try to "fix" the sleep problem, address the root cause of the problem, first. I realize that's often easier said than done, but if there's one thing I've learned, it's there are very few if any "quick fixes" to address something as important as sleep quality and quantity.

- **If you ARE trying to lose bodyfat, many studies have shown that sleep deprivation will make it much harder.**[49] The same is true if you're an athlete trying to maximize recovery and adaptation to training. Sleep rocks!

- **Taking naps during the day can often be a great way to catch up on missed sleep and feel better, provided they're short** (10 minutes up to 1 hour maximum), but if you're having trouble sleeping at night, taking a nap might not be a smart thing to do.

- **What are some other good resources to learn more?** Try these: https://thesleepdoctor.com/, https://project-sleep.com/, https://academic.oup.com/sleep

There are so many more things I could include here. As I've said before, entire books have been written on this topic, and I've read many of them! ☺ The fact of the matter is if we want to live our healthiest life right up until our last day, we can't downplay the health benefits and healing powers of uninterrupted, high quality sleep. Taking control of our sleep habits and doing all we can to make it as good as it can be isn't easy. There are no quick fixes that work overnight (pun intended!) ☺ But it can be done. And I'd say it is well worth the attempts. I hope you agree!

Follow your passion. Stay true to yourself.

Never follow anyone else's path
unless you're in the woods and you're
lost and you see a path. Then by all
means you should follow that.

— **Ellen DeGeneres,** *comedian, and actress*

> *How far you go in life depends on you being tender with the young, compassionate with the aged, sympathetic with the striving, and tolerant of the weak and strong. Because someday in life you will have been all of these.*
> — George Washington Carver, *scientist*

Finding Happiness and a Long, Healthy Life, the *Blue Zone* Way.

In 2008, author Dan Buettner, in partnership with National Geographic and the National Institute for Aging, published a book called *The Blue Zones: Lessons for Living Longer From the People Who've Lived the Longest.* The book was inspired by a decade plus long investigation by Buettner to explore the mysteries of human longevity. His journey began earlier when he was "leading a series of interactive, educational projects called Quests, in which a team of Internet-linked scientists investigated some of Earth's great puzzles."[50] These quests led him to learn more about the island of Okinawa, in Japan – how it was among the places on earth where people seemed to live the longest.

Years later, after being hired by National Geographic to write a cover story about the "Secrets of a Long Life," he would return to Okinawa with a new team of experts to learn what their secrets were. He says, "this story profiled three areas of the world with concentrations of some of the world's longest-lived people – areas that we dubbed "Blue Zones.""[51] In his words, "somehow Okinawans managed to reach the age of 100 at a rate up to three times higher than Americans did, suffered a fifth the rate of heart disease, and lived about seven good years longer."[52] Buettner learned it isn't just the Blue Zoner's extra years of life expectancy, it's that by and large, they're able to spend these extra years healthier, remaining active and enjoying life to its fullest.

As you can imagine, the first time I heard about these Blue Zones, I got curious and couldn't order Dan's book fast enough. I found his Ted Talk on the topic and listened in as soon as I could. The entire time, all I could think was, is there something I can learn from these regions of the world and the people who live there, that could change my life and those I care about, for the better?

I imagine that most of us, if only for a brief moment, have wondered about the habits and surroundings of these people, sometimes called "Super-Agers," who live to 100 and beyond. For instance, is there some kind of magical superfood they eat native to their location that gives them great health? Is there something about their lifestyle that gives them all those extra years of vitality? Or is it genetics? I needed to learn more!

Beuttner wrote about four Blue Zone regions including the island of Sardinia, specifically an area up in the highlands called the *Nuoro province*, off the coast of Italy. Then there is a small patch of land on the main Island of Okinawa (which is actually 161 small islands) – a rural town called *Ogimi*, with a population of about three thousand. "This town boasts the highest life expectancy in the world – a fact that has earned it the nickname of the Village of

Longevity."[53] Next is the *Nacoya Peninsula* on the coast of Costa Rica, and finally the city of *Loma Linda*, a longevity oasis of sorts in Southern California. While Buettner didn't write about it, a fifth Blue Zone is included in this list, *Ikaria, Greece*. One of every three people on this island near the coast of Turkey is over ninety years old, compared to less than 1 percent of the population of the U.S. It's been called the "Island of Long Life."

As you know, this book isn't about longevity or primarily about living longer. For me, I only want a long life if I can *also* be healthy and feel good for the great majority of it. No one wants more years of suffering, right? The thing is, Blue Zoners don't just live longer, they *also* live healthier, and better. So, what is it about these regions of the world and the people who live there? Are there secrets that can also help us live longer and better? Is it possible that any of us might reach the age of 100 or beyond and be healthy too?

Most if not all the scientific research I'm aware of seems to agree, exceptional longevity is VERY rare. Depending on which study you read or what expert you listen to, you might find slightly different odds, but they are all very small odds. Scientist and researcher, Dr. Nir Barzilai, M.D., says only 5 in 10,000 people worldwide will live to see age 100.[54] Dan Buettner, in his Ted Talk, said "about one out of 5000 people in the U.S. will live to be 100."[55]

Beyond the fact at least at this point in time, very few of us will reach 100, is the idea that exceptional longevity usually runs in families. In his book, *Age Later: Healthspan, Lifespan, and the New Science of Longevity*, Dr. Barzilai, one of the world's leading researchers on centenarians, says "one of the questions I asked (several centenarians) was whether longevity ran in their families. It turned out that it usually did, with many of them saying they had family members who had lived to be one hundred or older. This supported our theory that exceptional longevity is based on genetics, and so did the centenarians themselves. When asked why they think they live longer, their number one response was genetics. None of this surprised us though, because Tom Perls, director of the New England Centenarian Study at Boston University, Paola Sebastiani, genetics professor, and other investigators had already shown that exceptional longevity is often inherited."[56] If you remember in the earlier chapter, *Why Do We Age?*, I closed by telling you "virtually all the experts agree that genetics – our family history - only accounts for about 20% of the processes I've introduced here, and thus how fast we age." All the research I've read on this statistic bears this out as a completely true statement.

In his book, Dr. Barzilai says in studies done on "identical twins who were separated early in life and had different levels of health and different diseases in midlife suggest that genetics account for about 25 percent of the variations in life span."[57] Only 25 percent. He goes on to say this "means that even if you have genes that increase your risk for type 2 diabetes, if you're physically active, eat healthy foods, and manage your stress, you may never develop the disease."[58] In his Ted Talk, Dan Buettner, also discusses the "Danish Twin Study that established that only about 10 percent of how long the average person lives, within certain biological limits, is dictated by our genes."[59] What I took from all of this is the research seems to be very clear that genetics plays only a small role, yet exceptional longevity runs in families.

If you're like most people reading this, you're probably wondering at this point, what gives. I mean, if most centenarians live to be 100 or more because of genetics, and yet genetics only accounts for about 20 percent of what happens, and yet at the same time, living a very long life seems to run in families, then what is going on? The truth is researchers aren't sure. Dr. Barzilai believes "something must be protecting the centenarians, some undiscovered genetic alteration that helps, not hurts."[60] He also believes they've discovered some of what those alterations might be. He presents some of those findings in his book published in 2020, which can be seen as a contemporary review on the latest science.

There's something else going on that I haven't yet discussed, and that is **families who live together and grow together, often eat the same foods and have many of the same habits.** We see this over and over again in these Blue Zone regions. Think of it this way: it's a myth that all *diseases* run in the family. What does run in the family is diet. If more people focused on changing their diet, more would be able to escape the family history of disease. To put it another way, *genes predispose but do not predetermine.* ☺

Let's take a closer look at what some of the world's experts on Blue Zones have learned and shed some extra light on what we can learn about longevity and happiness. Keep in mind entire books have been written on these topics. My goal is to see where we can draw some parallels that could enlighten and empower us to make some positive changes where we have areas of opportunity to do just that.

Begin by answering this question in a single, memorable sentence: Why do you get up in the morning?

— Dan Buettner, *author and journalist*

Diet.

It may not surprise you that all the Blue Zone regions share some very similar ways of eating born from many generations. There's no doubt whatsoever their approach is vital to their longevity success. First, they all eat a primarily plant-based diet full of vegetables with lots of color. And all the Blue Zoners eat a wide variety of foods. A study "found that Okinawans ate 206 different foods, including spices, on a regular basis. And they ate an average of eighteen different foods each day,"[61] which in my mind, is in striking contrast to the nutritional "poverty" of our fast-food culture here in the U.S. Eighteen different foods a day!

Blue zoners rarely eat sugar, especially processed sugar. Most don't even know what it is. They also rarely overeat, which again is in contrast to our "super-size it" mentality in the U.S. Okinawans have this "3000-year-old adage known as *Hara Hachi bu.* It's a saying they repeat before their meal to remind them to stop eating when their stomach is about 80% full".[62] They use smaller plates and keep portions small. Food isn't served the way it is in the U.S., as appetizers, then main courses, and then dessert. It's more common to see it presented all together on one smaller plate. This practice is also common in Buddhist temples in the east.

Across all the Blue Zones, *moderation* rules. And while the diet is primarily plant-based, it doesn't mean they don't eat meat. They just don't eat it very frequently. Nuts and legumes are also a mainstay. And then there's the regular consumption of green or white tea and red wine. Again, all in moderation.

Eat your vegetables, have a positive outlook, be kind to people, and smile.
— Dan Buettner, *author and journalist*

Physical Activity.

All the Blue Zoners get lots of regular low-intensity activity during their days, but they don't "exercise" in any structured way that is typical of the way we think of exercise. Instead, their lives revolve around being active most of the time. Everything they do seems to nudge them into physical activity. They don't stay at home and watch the world go by.

In Okinawa, women typically get up and down off the ground 30 or 40 times a day. And all Okinawans pride themselves on never retiring, at least in the way we think of retirement. In fact, there isn't even a word in their language for retirement. In his Ted Talk, Dan Buettner says "Sardinians live in vertical houses, and are always going up and down the stairs. Every trip to the store or to church or to a friend's house occasions a walk. They don't have conveniences. There is not a button to push to do yard work or house work. When they do intentional physical activity, it's the things they enjoy. And they all have a garden."[63] In Loma Linda, California, another Blue Zone, the Seventh Day Adventists who live there follow a weekly ritual where they stop what they're doing and take "nature walks." Buettner says the power in these "isn't that they're done occasionally, it's that they're done every week."[64]

For Blue Zoners, it isn't just about staying physically active. They all believe in (and live by) the classic saying, *"mens sana in corpore sano,"* which means "a healthy mind in a healthy body."[65] Their mental "workouts" might surprise you. It's almost always informal. They play games and interact with others, remaining curious and always learning. Because they don't generally have televisions, they aren't drawn to sitting and watching, something which isn't interactive.

What I've learned as I've studied and read about the Blue Zoners is how important it is to expose ourselves to and *embrace change*. Even if it means stepping outside of our comfort zone and feeling a bit anxious. Change, provided we prepare for it, challenges our mind and body to be adaptable, and thus, to thrive. I'll talk more about this shortly, when I tell you a story about how I accepted a new role as an orchestra librarian – something that got me way out of my comfort zone!

So far, we've learned these Blue Zoners are always active, they rarely do strenuous structured exercise but they don't rely upon comforts or conveniences to make their lives easier. We've also learned their diets are varied, don't contain much processed or refined sugars or fast food, and they usually grow their food in their own gardens. They don't drink alcohol or use tobacco excessively, either. We also know each of these cultures takes time to relax and unwind. Whatever it may be, taking time to pray, a walk in nature, or time spent hanging out and relaxing with friends or family, it isn't forced. It's a part of their lifestyle, and there's no sense of guilt, ever. On the contrary, it's central to their entire existence. And history. In truth, if we took what I've just shared with you in this paragraph and learned from it, we'd be way ahead of the game. Which brings me to one more thing I've learned that makes these regions somewhat unique and very special. I alluded to it in the previous chapter on aging *intentionally*.

Ikigai: A Reason For Living (and So Much More).

I don't remember exactly when it was that I first read Victor Frankl's book, *In Search of Meaning*, but I'm certain I was in my 20s. I remember at the time, I was interested in learning more about the Holocaust and was also, like some other 20 somethings, curious about existentialism and the meaning of life. I'd often ask myself, *why am I here? Why are WE here? What's my purpose?* I'm sure most reading this, at some point, go through some variation of wonderment and what might be termed an existential crisis and begin to seek some answers to these questions. At that age, many are unsure of where life will take them and what might lie ahead, and often get caught in the crosshairs between doing what is expected of us or what we're told to do, rather than what we might want to do.

What I took from Frankl's heartfelt book and experiences at the Auschwitz concentration camp was that he was able to survive because he made it his singular mission – his ultimate purpose – *to* survive. He wanted others to learn from his experience and then begin to consciously discover their life's purpose. He felt this would also be the best way to confront neuroses, be it depression, anxiety, feeling lost or empty, or even simple complacency. He believed if you could fulfill your life's destiny, you'd be more motivated to relentlessly forge ahead in your life journey, not looking back on past failures, while also being better equipped to deal positively with whatever obstacles lie ahead.

Okinawans believe that finding **this purpose for being** is the key to a happier and longer life. The word they have to describe this is *Ikigai*. According to authors Hector Morales and Francesc Miralles, who wrote the book of the same name, *ikigai* means *a reason for living*. This ikigai is so central to the Okinawan way of life, it can't be separated from who they are and how they live. In my opinion, **it might be THE most important thing we can learn from the Blue Zoners**. Having a strong sense of *ikigai* – the place where passion, mission, vocation, and profession intersect – means that each day is infused with meaning. [66]

For my entire life, I've always said that I won't ever "retire." Now, I'll admit I've never had a "real" job in my entire life either. ☺ (Don't hate me). I've been so fortunate in that regard.

This doesn't mean I won't relax, or take a vacation or three, or even disappear every once in a while to recharge. What it does mean is, *if the day comes when there isn't a compelling reason for me to get up in the morning and to keep learning, sharing, and working, then that, in my mind, is when it might be the beginning of the end for me.* This might be one of a few things I have in common with composer, John Williams, who you read about in Chapter 3 and who is continuing to write and work, even at age 90! After all, Mark Twain said find a job you enjoy doing and you'll never work a day in your life.

It isn't about seeking enjoyment or pleasure, it's more about something you're passionate about. As a father, I tried to teach my kids, if they can find that thing that when they're doing it, time both stands still *and* seems to fly, they should find ways to do more of *that thing.* The same could be said when it comes to who we spend our time with. I think John Williams has figured this out and then some. As have many others.

I'm sometimes asked how I could still be so enthusiastic about exercise and training and talk for hours about it, even after all these years. My answer is always the same. I believe it's my destiny – my purpose. I'm writing this book for exactly the same reason. Most days, I get up excited to try and be better in some way, and open mentally and emotionally for what I might learn. And I am learning every single day. There's always something new to discover, about myself and about the topic at hand, be it aging well, or something movement or sport related. And it isn't enough for me to learn it, I also want to *share it.*

I recognize that for many, knowing your purpose isn't that easy. It can elude us, depending on where we put our energy or how we might be distracted. I'd only suggest you remain open to it. Trust your heart, while remembering nothing comes without some kind of effort. Through consistent effort and work, we can find our way. To think of it another way is to remember the Japanese idea of *ikigai* as "the happiness of always being busy."[67] Of course, it isn't just about being busy. There's something much more going on there.

I remember as a kid visiting my grandparents when they were in a convalescent home. Those places seemed so sad to me. While there was always a collection of people around including staff and residents, there seemed to be an aura of loneliness. And desperation. Do you know anyone right now who is older and spends more time alone than they would like? In his Ted Talk, Buettner reiterates something we all know to be true: *isolation kills.* "Fifteen years ago, the average American had three good friends. We're down to one and a half right now. If you were lucky enough to be born in Okinawa, you were born into a system where you have a half a dozen friends with whom you travel through life. They call it *Moai.* And if you're in a *Moai* you're expected to share the bounty if you encounter luck, and if things go bad, a child gets sick, parent dies, you always have somebody who has your back."[68]

Authors Garcia and Miralles talk about the friendliness of the residents when they arrived in the village of *Ogimi.* They laughed, joked around. They reported this "uncommon joy (that) flows from its inhabitants and guides them through the long and pleasurable journey of their lives."[69] All the Blue Zones are places with a strong sense of community. They work together, supporting each other, nurturing friendships. And when combined with eating right and the moderate but consistent exercise they get each day, it adds up to a winning formula for a long healthy life.

These elements all align with one other aspect that's been found to be universal in these Blue Zone regions: people who live the longest seem to have a *positive attitude* and a high degree of *emotional awareness*. One study done by Yeshiva University and Albert Einstein Institute for Aging Research, co-authored by Dr. Nir Barzilai, the researcher I referenced earlier, found "personality traits like being outgoing, optimistic, easygoing, and enjoying laughter as well as staying engaged in activities may also be part of the longevity genes mix."[70]

"When I started working with centenarians, I thought we'd find that they survived so long in part because they were mean and ornery," said Dr. Barzilai. "But when we assessed the personalities of these 243 centenarians, we found qualities that reflect a positive attitude towards life. Most were outgoing, optimistic, and easygoing. They considered laughter an important part of life and had a large social network. They expressed emotions openly rather than bottling them up. Also, the centenarians had lower scores for displaying neurotic personality and higher scores for being conscientious compared with a representative sample of the U.S. population."[71]

In 2017, shortly after moving to the gulf coast of Florida, I was offered the opportunity to play percussion in the Venice Symphony, a professional, 75-member part-time regional orchestra near my new home. Needless to say, I jumped at the chance and haven't regretted it for a moment. Two years later, in what was a surprise development, the position of librarian for the orchestra opened up. I got a call from the personnel manager who asked if I might consider taking on this new role in addition to playing percussion. To say I was taken aback with his phone call is an understatement. My first gut reaction was, of course not. No, thank you! After all, I'd never done anything like that in my life. I'm already busy with my coaching business and other commitments, I don't need to take on a job as big as that one. I mean, becoming a normal librarian requires learning a host of unique skills. There's so much that goes on behind the scenes. When it comes to being an orchestra librarian, the argument could be made it's even more challenging. And the thing is, I didn't even know the half of it. Talk about being out of my comfort zone!

Well, as you might have already figured out, after thinking about it and talking with my girlfriend, Terry, I decided to accept the position. Now, I won't kid you, I was very apprehensive about what kind of job I would do and what unforeseen problems would arise. I questioned whether I had what it would take to do, not just an acceptable job, but a great job. I didn't even know where to start.

Weeks later, at one of the first rehearsals for the upcoming season of concerts, I stood in front of the orchestra and asked for their patience and support, and then shared why I decided to jump at the opportunity to become their librarian. I said, "there are two main reasons I'm standing in front of you right now. The first is that I am excited to be part of a great organization comprised of a lot of great people and in the midst of incredible growth. To be able to play a small role in future successes and be a part of this symphony family and community is exciting. The second reason is, I can't think of a better way to build more friendships and get to know all of you on an individual basis."

It's now 2022. The librarian role has grown on me little by little. I still have those days when I question why I decided to do it, but most of the time, I'm grateful for the chance to contribute. I'm challenged mentally and physically to do the job as well as it needs to be done, something I know Okinawans would applaud.

One of my favorite contemporary philosophers and authors, Mark Manson, often says a great life isn't a life devoid of problems. Rather, he says a great life is a life with the *right kinds* of problems. I can certainly relate. This job, while frustrating at times – I call them growing pains – is filled with the right kinds of problems. What I mean is, this IS a great organization bringing so much good music to so many and it's growing. It is a terrific community of people that often feels like family. I'm fortunate to be building friendships with each member, which has been among the most enjoyable aspects of this job. Little did I know at the time but taking that opportunity and running with it was akin to finding my own version of *ikigai*. It's been one of the best decisions I've made.

A few weeks ago, my daughter, her husband, and my four-year-old grandson came to visit. I was so excited in the weeks leading up to it, I could hardly control myself. If you're a parent or a grandparent or an aunt or uncle and spend time with a toddler who's four, think about what life is like for them. It's often a huge roller coaster of emotions. They don't have many filters to control how they feel from one moment to the next, that's for sure. They can go from laughing out loud to a screaming tantrum in a heartbeat. One thing is undeniable, and it's something we can all learn from them. *They live in the moment.* They never look back to the past, and they have no concept of the future. For a four-year old, it is only about what is happening at that very moment. To watch them when they're having fun in their best moments is pure joy.

That same quality of being present in the moment is rampant in Blue Zone regions. It's about the *here and now*. The Okinawans have a word - "*wabi-sabi*" – that to them, represents the inherent beauty of the temporary or fleeting, changeable, and imperfect nature of the world. They believe instead of searching for *beauty* in perfection, we should all look for it in things that are flawed and incomplete.[72] That's a remarkable point of view, don't you think?

A complimentary Japanese concept is that of *ichi-go ichi-e*, which could be translated as "this moment exists only now and won't come again."[73] They focus on being present, mindful, and intentional, valuing each day as it might be their last, yet embracing all that comes their way. The good and the bad. Accepting there are certain things for which they have very little control, yet there is much they can do to help make the world a better place to grow and thrive in. Especially as the years march on.

In the U.S., as a society it seems we've become increasingly obsessed with comfort and convenience and seeking pleasure. In some ways, modern life is leading us further from what is in our hearts – our true nature. Happiness isn't something that comes to us if our lives are easier. It comes when we've found meaning in our lives. Our *ikigai*.

The Okinawans believe we shouldn't obsess about finding our *ikigai*. They also believe it doesn't have to be some big thing – it could be as simple as helping our neighbors or being a good parent or grandparent. To connect with your *ikigai*, trust your intuition. Listen to the internal compass inside your head that guides you closer to the things you were meant to do and further away from those that don't suit you. In the end, in the words of authors Morales and Miralles, you'll be very "busy doing what you love while being surrounded by the people who love you."[74]

- **Find a reason to get up in the morning**. Live a life of purpose. Set goals. Be a lifelong learner. Engage. Avoid "retirement."
- **Avoid the "bad-news" news cycles on TV and in newspapers**. You'll feel better and realize whether you watch or not, life goes on - the future will be here soon!
- **Reach out more. Laugh more. Connect with others more**. Even as we're technically apart, we can and need to be more together.
- **Keep moving**. Make physical activity a part of your daily life.
- **Our society's preoccupation and obsession with comfort and making things easier on ourselves is killing us**. Think about it.

Let's move on to the final chapter in Part 1, where we discuss more about risk factors, family history, and then review an important self-assessment questionnaire. I'll see you there! Keep going!

CHAPTER 6

SELF-ASSESSMENT:
WHAT ARE YOUR RISK FACTORS AND FAMILY HISTORY?

Between stimulus and response,
there is a space.

In that space is our power to
choose our response.

— Victor Frankl

If there's one thing I've learned from a lifetime of studying and experiencing what it means to be truly healthy, it's that our lifestyle choices day in and day out make the biggest difference when it comes to our individual risk for chronic disease and early death. Scientific studies confirm this, and as you know, it's what this book is all about. What you eat, how much exercise and sleep you get, and how you handle stress, among other things, all matter when it comes to becoming truly healthy, living your best life, and aging well.

Early Detection.

We also know genetics and family history play a vital role in determining our risk. The more we can learn about our family history, the better equipped we'll be to detect any potential health problems as early as possible. Now, more than ever, *early detection* is often the difference between life and death, or at the very least, being able to manage a condition more easily so that it won't severely impact our lives as much.

Most people aren't aware of how early some diseases and conditions actually begin manifesting in the body. Think about this: Dr. Peter Attia, M.D., a Stanford/Johns Hopkins/National Institute of Health-trained physician focusing on the applied science of longevity, says when it comes to heart disease, very often "fatty streaks start forming in artery walls in the first decade of life."[1]

And if that isn't scary enough, a study from 2001 done with a large group of over 200 heart transplant recipients, all with hearts that had been donated by teenagers, seemed to confirm this. The results of the study showed one out of six of the recipient's hearts had significant evidence of hardening of the arteries.[2] Amazingly, none of them had any symptoms that would have given them a clue that early heart disease was lurking beneath the skin.

Even as early as age 40, it's a good idea to begin to have regular cancer screenings for breast, colon, lung, cervical, and prostate, for starters. If you're a man, having a regular colonoscopy could be the most important health decision you make in your lifetime. My recommendation is to make sure you have frequent discussions with your doctor to be sure you're getting the proper screenings at the most important times. To do otherwise is to ignore one of the most important things you have control over to remain healthy and avoid early death.

Your Individual Risk Factors.

I don't know about you, but I've asked myself the question, *what are my risk factors?* many times over the years, especially when considering my family health history. I bet you've asked this question too.

We're at a point now where we can create a medical risk profile to look at our relative risk for certain diseases. We can do this a variety of ways. My advice is to start with the three areas I lay out for you in this chapter.

1. **First is to make sure you complete my "essential six" tests/screens I've outlined below with the aid of your doctor.** As mentioned, these are a minimum for both men and women. Women should add, at the very least, an annual mammogram and pap smear.
2. **Next is to research your family history,** which I'll discuss in more depth soon.
3. **Third is to go through the self-assessment** which you'll read about soon, to give yourself a more accurate, objective view of where you are, and what areas you might have to improve in to lower your risk.

With all the above information laid out in front of you, you'll have an accurate view of your present status and what your risk factors are. Your goal will always be to improve in the areas you have the greatest control over, which is inevitably going to be the factors directly related to lifestyle. Remember, *you can't change your genes, but you CAN change how they're expressed.*

My Essential Six: Blood Testing and Screening.

So, what are the most important screens and tests I would recommend?

For both men and women, I would start with these six, in no particular order. For women, I would add a pap smear and a mammogram, as well as routine self-exams. These by no means make up a complete list. They're just a starting point. Speak with your doctor or health care provider for more information and guidance, not just on the tests I'm recommending here, but on any others as well. Don't wait! Do it now.

1. **Fasting blood glucose:** This is the most common diagnostic tool on this list – it's usually a part of every blood test associated with an annual checkup. It's a starting point to check for prediabetes and diabetes, as it measures the amount of sugar (glucose) in your blood after you have not eaten for at least eight hours. A level

between 70 and 100 milligrams per deciliter (mg/dL) is considered normal. Above this, your body is showing signs of insulin resistance and even diabetes.[3]

2. **Hemoglobin A1C:** Unlike a test of blood sugar, this test reveals an "average" blood sugar over a ninety-day period and provides a far better indication of overall blood sugar control. You don't have to be fasted for this test.[4]

3. **Fasting insulin:** Long before blood sugar begins to climb as a person becomes diabetic, the fasting insulin level will rise, indicating the pancreas is working overtime to deal with the excess of dietary carbohydrate. It is a very effective early warning system for getting ahead of the diabetes curve, and as you will read in this book, it has tremendous relevance for every single aspect of your health.

4. **C reactive protein (CRP):** This is a marker of inflammation throughout the body. As you'll learn in an upcoming chapter on chronic inflammation, we want as little of it as possible. Learning where you are in the moment will give you a good starting point.

5. **Skin screening:** Especially as we age, we can't ignore what has likely been a lifetime of exposure to UV-A and UV-B rays from the sun. Seeing a dermatologist at least annually, if not more frequently, is smart. This is a no brainer if you've spent a lot of your years outside being active like I have.

6. **Bone density:** The gold standard to assess bone health is a DEXA scan. The benefit to a DEXA, is you'll learn much more than just bone density.

There's also *genetic testing* that identifies changes in genes, chromosomes, the genome, or proteins. One example? The screen for the APOE4 gene to assess the risk of developing dementia. This test evaluates a person's DNA to determine what combination of APOE forms (genotype) is present.[5]

According to the National Institute for Health, "certain genes can increase the risk of developing dementia, including Alzheimer's disease. One of the most significant genetic risk factors is a form of the *apolipoprotein E* gene called *APOE4*. About 25% of people carry one copy of *APOE4*, and 2 to 3% carry two copies. *APOE4* is the strongest risk factor gene for Alzheimer's disease, although inheriting *APOE4* does not mean a person will definitely develop the disease."[6] There are others of course. As you can see, there's a lot to consider when determining exactly which tests and screens are important for you, depending on your age AND your family history.

Your Family History:

It's very important you learn as much as you can about your own family history. Whatever you can learn will help you assess your risk. It won't be what determines your future, but it can help empower you to make changes where needed. The more you know, the more empowered you should feel.

Learn What You Can:

Your primary goal should be to learn as much as you can about your parents, grandparents, aunts and uncles, and even great grandparents. Ask questions like, is there anyone who had a stroke, a heart attack or who had cancer? What about any history of Alzheimer's or other dementia? You'll also want to learn about any evidence of metabolic disease or diabetes.

Context Matters:

Don't settle for simple answers, however. You need context to flush out how much of what you learn matters. For example, you might find out your grandfather died of lung cancer. Once you dig deeper to learn more, you might also find out he smoked 3-packs of cigarettes a day for most of his adult life. That's the kind of context that will bring additional clarity.

Look for Patterns:

Are there any patterns of disease or even habits that stand out to you? The goal is to identify these so you can put the pieces together to accurately assess your risks. In summary, once you've learned as much as you can about both the health history itself as well as any personal habits that could have impacted that history, and then looked to see if there are any patterns that could give you a clue about something which might well be a true risk factor in your family, you'll be armed to make better decisions moving forward about your OWN habits and choices.

Genetic Fatalism:

I don't know about you, but when the topic turns to discussing family history, I find it's easy to get hung up trying to learn more, and even reach a point where you throw up your hands and decide it just doesn't matter. It makes me think of a term I've often referenced in conversations with others, *genetic fatalism,* which is people having genetic risk information that might induce a sense of fatalism, or a belief that little can be done to reduce the risk. There's been quite a bit of scientific research into the implications of this sense of fatalism, including one study that examines this outlook and its impact on government policy and genetics research.[7]

I think of genetic fatalism as the "blessing OR curse of choice." It's that sometimes distorted yet dominant cultural narrative out there that says we're mere subjects of our destiny and fate - we have no control over what happens to us. If you've ever heard other people, or yourself utter phrases like, "I must have bad genes," or "my parents were fat, so that's why I'm going to be fat," or "my grandparents both had high blood pressure, so I'll have it too," then you know what genetic fatalism is. I consider all these statements a complete cop-out. Why? Because while family history is one important element in assessing our risk for disease, in the majority of instances it only accounts for a small percentage of the total risk. In a way, this is the same kind of negative mindset that traps so many into thinking it doesn't matter what you do or how you live – you're going to die when you're going to die, so why bother. In the end, it comes down to your outlook and mindset.

As you think, so you are.
Proverbs 23:7

What we all need to acknowledge is we *can't change our genes, but we CAN change how they're expressed.* You've already read a bit about the science surrounding this in Chapter 2, which you may remember as *epigenetics.* Most aging experts agree that up to 80% of your *chronic disease risk comes back to lifestyle. Family history only accounts for 20-30%.* The take home message is don't get caught up thinking your choices won't change your destiny. They will and they do!

It's human nature to be a little bit anxious about the fact we have so much control over our present and future health. It places the responsibility for our health solely in our laps. There are no pointing fingers at our ancestors or our parents. It certainly is a lot easier to just passively let things happen. Many religions are built on the idea we should surrender our control to a higher power, that we should "let go" and let things be what they'll be. When it comes to your health, I don't have to tell you I believe you should embrace your individual power and dismiss any idea of passively letting go. Of course, while I believe *you have much more control over your health and your future than you realize,* I also accept that in some respects control is a myth. One thing there is zero debate over, is the fact that we have full control over our attitude and our reaction to what happens. You must believe that too, and then act accordingly. ☺

Self-Assessment Questionnaire:

To this point we've discussed some of the most important tests and screens you should have while also consulting with your doctor or other healthcare provider. We have also discussed the importance of learning more about your family health history. The last piece of the puzzle for now, is to go through this simple 17-question **questionnaire** that may reveal habits that could be silently harming you.

The goal of this TRUE/FALSE questionnaire is to gauge your risk factors for many of the most common chronic diseases. Respond to these statements as honestly as possible. Don't think about the connections to disease that might be implied and don't take them personally. Just respond truthfully. No one will have the answers to these questions but you.

In upcoming chapters you'll begin to understand why I used these particular statements and where you stand with regard to your risk factors. If you feel like you're in between true and false, and would answer "sometimes," then you should choose true.

1. I don't get any kind of cardiovascular or aerobic exercise.
2. I typically eat some kind of packaged or processed food daily.
3. I drink fruit juice.
4. I don't do any type of strength training.
5. I always have some type of bread with my meals.
6. I don't buy organic produce.
7. I drink soda.
8. I try to eat low-fat foods whenever possible.
9. I am overweight.
10. I occasionally eat cereal or pastries as breakfast foods.
11. I drink energy drinks.
12. I typically eat more than five servings of fruit daily.
13. I drink some kind of alcoholic drink every day, be it beer, wine, or liquor.
14. I typically eat dessert after dinner more than one time per week.
15. I get less than seven hours of quality sleep per night.
16. Negative stress sometimes keeps me from being happy and contented.
17. I take at least one prescription drug daily (such as a statin) that has been prescribed by my doctor, to manage high blood pressure, high cholesterol, or a similar health-related issue.

So, what was your score? How many "trues" did you have?

Guess what, you shouldn't have had any. In other words, a perfect score on this test would be zero "true" answers. Yes, if you answered true to one or more questions, you are at greater risk for chronic disease than if you scored a zero. The more "trues" you have, the higher your risk. Now, THAT's true. ☺

But, as you'll learn in the next chapter and throughout the book, this journey of discovery we're on together isn't about being perfect. It IS about an opportunity. My advice is to combine this questionnaire with what you learn from screening and testing and research into your family's history, and then look at it as nothing more than a beginning. And an opportunity.

Go right to the next chapter to learn more of what I mean. I'll see you there.

PART 2

FOOD

CHAPTER 7

INTRODUCTION:
CONFUSION AND CHAOS

Right now, lying in bed, sick and remembering a lifetime, I realize that all my recognition and wealth that I possess is insignificant in the face of my impending death.

You can hire someone to drive for you, make money for you - but you can't hire someone to get sick for you.

Steve Jobs
...who died with a $7 billion fortune, at 56, from pancreatic cancer.
These are some of his last words...

When in doubt, tell the truth.

– Mark Twain

Once upon a time, there was a man whose goal was to be as good as he possibly could be – to pursue a path of personal excellence in whatever he did, as an athlete, a parent, partner, musician, or citizen. Beyond pursuing excellence, he also grew to become more passionate about living a rewarding life filled with adventure and challenges!

And of course, he wanted to live for a long time to experience the joys of family, friends, and the many adventures he'd inevitably throw himself into. He knew it wasn't the number of years that mattered the most, but the quality of those years. To him, the goal wasn't just to live longer, but to live better. To go the distance.

Above all, he grew to understand that without good health along the way, none of the other things would matter quite as much. It's so much harder – perhaps even impossible - to experience life's true joys when we are sick or battling a disease. He knew – especially as he listened and learned more and studied harder - that *how he ate, what he ate, and when he ate,* would play a huge role in how much he'd wrestle out of his natural ability, regardless of the endeavor. After all, it only makes sense. In many ways, we are - and become - *what we eat.*

As the years went on and he grew older, he discovered his biggest challenge was finding the right balance between (1) enjoying the fruits of his labor, which in one respect meant enjoying the food he ate and who he ate it with, and (2) achieving his goals of a long, healthy life. After all, humans are social beings and eating is social, right? If we're fortunate and have access to good-tasting food, savoring it while we eat in the company of friends and family, is absolutely one of the true pleasures of life.

As you have probably guessed, this man is me.

So, what have I learned in my more than 62 years? I've learned it isn't always easy or even possible to get what we want. I've learned when it comes to our health and fitness, it'll always evolve as a series of ebbs and flows, not a straight line. I've learned how to be patient with myself and start anew each day. That's important. And most of all, I've learned if we find our own reasons for doing the hard things that aging intentionally requires - our "why" if you will - we CAN dramatically increase the odds of achieving what we want most. Which is good health for as long as possible. Of course, we need to BELIEVE, and then learn how.

This might come as a surprise to some, but **there's nothing more important for your long-term health than when and what you eat – it's the cornerstone of good health throughout the lifespan.** Which is, in a way, ironic. After all, when it comes to the topic of food, there's more confusion than ever. That confusion is one reason we're in the mess we are as a global community. Chronic diseases and deaths across the globe that can be attributed to our diet are escalating at increasing rates. It's frightening. Never before has there been so much misinformation and even flat-out lies from so called "experts" including our own government, as well as relentless advertising and marketing from all facets of the food industry. For the latter, know their goal is to manipulate how we think about food and what we believe, get us hooked, and ultimately influence our choices as we walk the grocery store aisles and check out at the cash register.

Regardless of the reasons you have for reading this book, my goal is to help clear up some of this confusion and the resulting chaos inside your mind. Mark Twain would approve, because **I'm going to tell you the truth about what matters the most.**

As you'll learn, the key to success in any of the areas I'll discuss is making *small, incremental* changes. And then being mindful as you adopt those changes. If you can be patient and stay the course, you will have the best possible chance of feeling and looking better as time goes on. So, let's get to it.

Looking ahead, each chapter of Part 2 will have a different focus. In Chapter 8, I'll review some common myths and introduce some concepts that will form the foundation for learning more, and then discuss the "enemy" – or "enemies," we're all battling on a daily basis. In Chapter 9, in what may be the most comprehensive and information laden section of this book, I do a deep dive into the topic of insulin resistance and hyperinsulinemia. As you may recall in the Introduction to the book, I promised I'd keep things simple and avoid information overload. Well, I think I broke my promise with this section. ☺ But hang in there anyway – if it wasn't important, I wouldn't be discussing it. Remember you can always break it into chunks and return at any time.

When thinking about disease and what, how, and when we eat, the one thing that ties them all together is insulin and our metabolic health. That's what makes Chapter 9 so comprehensive and important. Whether it's meal timing and frequency, sugar-laden processed foods and the food industry, or the diseases we're suffering from because of the food we eat or don't eat, *insulin, hyperinsulinemia,* and *insulin resistance* are deeply related to all of it. In fact, as time goes on and more good scientific data emerges, we may learn that ALL our modern-day health problems circle back to our metabolic health, or lack thereof. And that means they will be tied directly to the foods we eat or don't eat, and when. I know the more you understand the underlying science with this master hormone, insulin, the more you'll feel compelled to make changes that will lead to better health.

In Chapter 10, I'll review **Time Restricted Eating** – what it is and isn't (spoiler alert: it's not calorie restriction or starvation), how to do it, and whether it's for everyone. I'll then offer a variety of options for how you can begin to integrate this approach to meal timing in a way that leaves you more confident it could work for you, as well as feeling satisfied and with more energy than ever.

In the remaining chapters, I'll cover nutrition-related topics like sugar, cholesterol, chronic inflammation, our gut microbiome, and what really matters when discussing both red meat eaters and vegetarians. Finally, we'll finish with actionable tips, common questions, and advice to answer any doubts or questions you might still have.

Who and What Should We Trust?

Let's talk about the reason there is so much confusion about diet and our health. As you can imagine, over most of my adult life, I've purchased or borrowed hundreds of books on nutrition, diet, health, and fitness. A couple of years ago I bought a book titled *The Longevity Paradox: How to Die Young at a Ripe Old Age,* by Dr. Steven Gundry, MD. It's a huge book, more than 500 pages. On the cover, it says Dr. Gundry is a "New York Times" best-selling writer. It was published in 2019, which means the information inside should be somewhat current.

Given Dr. Gundry is a doctor, and because it appears at first glance he has a history of writing good books, you'd think this would be a very good resource full of trustworthy and important information about how to age well, wouldn't you? That's what I thought, too. When I first got the book, I was anxious to learn more about Dr. Gundry and what he had to say, so I went to YouTube to watch some of his videos. I also did some online research.

The first thing I noticed on YouTube was that Dr. Oz (who many fans of daytime TV think of as an "expert" on health-related topics) endorses Dr. Gundry. *Oops, that's the first red flag.* Why? In the eyes of most true experts in the scientific community, Dr. Oz is a charlatan who shares, shall I say, pseudoscientific nonsense. Not much of what he says or endorses should be trusted. Nevertheless, I went to one of the videos I found on YouTube and listened to Dr. Gundry. He begins by saying he's a "best-selling author of the Plant Paradox." He then picks up a tomato and says, "think this is good for you? Think again."

I'm like, *what?* So that's *another red flag.*

He's saying tomatoes are unhealthy. While we could disagree as to their true benefit, there's no question this statement doesn't tell the whole story. Like many things, to understand it fully is to accept there is some nuance. Tomatoes contain a nice array of healthy compounds called polyphenols and a compound called lycopene that, in the eyes of many peer reviewed studies, makes them a good choice. Lycopene is one of the compounds that gives this fruit (or vegetable, depending upon how you slice it), its red color.

On the flipside, tomatoes belong to a family of fruits and vegetables referred to as nightshades, that contain a compound called alkaloids.[1] And yes, alkaloids in very high amounts can be dangerous, and there are some people who are sensitive to this compound. Naturally, those people should avoid tomatoes and other nightshades. The other ailment that is sometimes linked with nightshades is chronic inflammation. The bottom line is, to date there hasn't been a scientific study (that I'm aware of) to show the moderate amount of this compound found in these foods is dangerous for everyone.

When I have helped others with food sensitivities, and found that nightshades appeared to act as a "trigger" for inflammation or other problems, it's usually been a "signal" for another underlying problem perpetuating chronic low levels of inflammation, and the nightshades are fuel for the fire, so to speak. As is often the case, the solution is to be mindful; pay attention to how you react when eating these or any other kind of food for that matter. If in doubt, leave them out. And of course, consult your doctor for more specific advice.

So, back to the video with Dr. Gundry: I listened in a bit more and then skipped ahead to the end, only to find he's actually *selling supplements* for a company he's affiliated with. Strike three. My bullsh*t alarm was going crazy inside my head! ☺

When I began to read his book, it only took me about two pages to figure out what the entire 500 pages was all about, which is our gut microbiome. He contends our gut bacteria gone awry is the single cause of all our ill health, and also the only part of us that, when working right, keeps us healthy and allows us to live to a ripe old age. I laughed and thought to myself, *are you kidding me right now?* I am absolutely sure that gut bacteria play an important role in our health, but I'm even more sure it isn't the only thing that matters.

What's my point in sharing this story? THIS is one big reason we're confused. In my humble opinion, when it comes to nutrition, he appears to be a greedy charlatan. He's not someone I would recommend anyone take advice from. The problem is, he has all the credentials and the credibility that goes along with it – he's even apparently performed many surgeries. If you didn't know any better, you'd have no reason not to trust what he says. For example, if you were cruising down the aisle at the local bookstore and found this book and bought it, you might take it home and read it thinking it contains trustworthy advice and guidance. And if that happened, I'm afraid you'd be off on a "wild goose chase" of sorts, with very little hope of making real progress toward living a happier, healthier life.

It's no wonder, especially when you look at how the COVID-19 pandemic was handled by the government and medical establishment, many of us have lost complete trust in "experts" and even in science. Do any of them really know what they're talking about? We've got reason to wonder, that's for sure.

Let's be honest, every five or ten years, a new set of "guidelines" comes out telling us what we *should* do, and how we *should* eat. First it was low-fat and then no-fat, then low-carb and then no-carb, and on and on. One expert says grains are evil, at the same time the government comes out with a food pyramid telling you grains should be the foundation of your diet! How many times have you watched the evening news and heard the broadcaster say, "a new study was released by the (insert well-known organization of experts) saying that x or y food has been found to be bad for you." Right? Over and over again, talking heads telling the viewer what "science" has found, that we absolutely *must know*. (My advice? Never believe what you hear on the news about nutrition!)

The difficulty of knowing who to trust or believe doesn't stop there. I'd add that it even bleeds into the actual data and scientific studies we all assume are done well, but very often aren't. For example, let's start with the fact who funds a research study has a lot to do with what the results of the study are. I mean, you don't think a research study on milk and other dairy foods, funded by the dairy industry itself, might determine it's *good for you*, or even essential for your health? The truth is much if not most of the research done, is funded by the very companies who stand the most to gain financially – if the results turn out "right," of course. If it doesn't, the results are liable to end up buried. That happens all the time.

The other big issue is most of what we know or think we know about food and health come from "observational" studies, not from actual double-blind, controlled experiments.

In observational studies about diet, the researchers do exactly as the name implies – they "watch" and observe people over a period of time who have different diets and see how they fare. The problem with this kind of scientific "research" is obvious. For starters, people who eat different foods very likely also have other differences that aren't being tracked, things like exercise, sleep, work-life balance, stress, etc. All of it impacts how they eat. As a result, the researchers aren't able to control the variables that need to be controlled and accounted for, to draw conclusions that can be trusted.

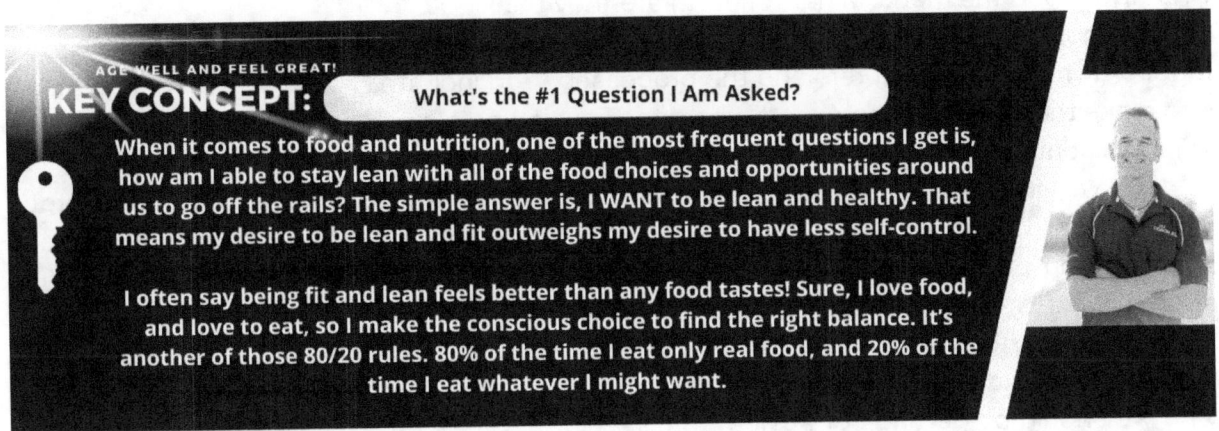

AGE WELL AND FEEL GREAT!

KEY CONCEPT:

What's the #1 Question I Am Asked?

When it comes to food and nutrition, one of the most frequent questions I get is, how am I able to stay lean with all of the food choices and opportunities around us to go off the rails? The simple answer is, I WANT to be lean and healthy. That means my desire to be lean and fit outweighs my desire to have less self-control.

I often say being fit and lean feels better than any food tastes! Sure, I love food, and love to eat, so I make the conscious choice to find the right balance. It's another of those 80/20 rules. 80% of the time I eat only real food, and 20% of the time I eat whatever I might want.

Interestingly, this is the same kind of problem that hampered the research on tobacco and smoking. After all, you can't require people to smoke in a controlled experiment because it's obvious to anyone paying attention, smoking increases your risk of dying! The bottom line is all the research that's been done on nutrition has, to some degree, been hampered by the fact we don't have enough objective, controlled experiments to tell us what it is we most need to know.

What About Dieticians and the Academy of Nutrition and Dietetics (AND), Formerly Known as the American Dietetic Association (ADA)?

When the topic is food and the question is who we can trust, we naturally assume any dietician would be a reliable and trustworthy source of information. Well, I'm not sure about that. Far be it for me to throw an entire group of professionals under the bus, so I won't do that. What I will do, is share my experience and then leave it up to you to draw your own conclusions.

Most dietitians I've known over my adult life, and I've known many, have been some of the smartest people I've had the pleasure of knowing and working with. But unfortunately, most have stuck to the established dogma that has defined the profession. For example, they tend to think of a *calorie as a calorie*. It's not, as you'll learn more about in upcoming chapters. Also, many have traditionally focused on what is IN food, when everything I've learned tells me what matters as much if not more, is what has BEEN DONE to the food, such as through manufacturing, processing, and distribution. But the **biggest** evidence I have that we should all seriously question this profession, is what is served in schools around the nation. It is BAD. And it's a huge reason our kids are less healthy than they've ever been, and all of it is prescribed, orchestrated, and managed by a registered dietician. (I'd add the food isn't much healthier in most hospitals, ironically).

Let's be honest: When the standard fare in the lunch line at a secondary school is some kind of fake juice box and rectangle shaped fried fish, or pizza, candy, and french fries, among other less-than-ideal foods for growing children – you have to seriously question the person who developed the menu. What on earth are they thinking?

The most cynical among us would go one step further and argue the industry is largely funded by food manufacturers and the processed food industry. I don't know enough about it to make the case, but one expert who does have an opinion is author, Robert Lustwig, MD, who has something to say when it comes to this contention.

He says, and I quote: "104,000 dieticians are registered with the Commission on Dietetic Registration (CDR). Their mission statement is to administer valid, reliable, and rigorous credentialing processes to protect the public."[2] What are some of the companies who sponsored this organization in 2019? Among others, his research concluded some of the biggest supporters were these processed food companies: Nestle USA, Campbell Soup Company, Splenda sweetener, and Pepsi Co.[3] This list has to make you think and question who we should be getting our advice from.

Where to go from here? Well, thankfully we've got some options. We can start by looking at tens of thousands if not millions of years of our evolution as a species for clues. And there are many. We can also learn to trust our instinct to some degree and always remain skeptical as we read and peruse the available information. We must become and then remain lifelong learners. After all, while a lot of diet programs are marketed as being "new" and contemporary, the truth is almost nothing is actually "new." Even veganism and raw food diets have been around for hundreds of years. Keto goes back to the 1920s. Nothing's new. ☺ (Except of course, the explosion of industrialized food - that is definitely new, and it's not good!)

And then there's at least one more option, which is what I've done over most of my adult life. It's a common-sense application of the previous ideas - combined with my own *mindful* experimentation. And yes, the addition of that word mindful was very intentional. **You won't learn as much about your own body and your own metabolism if you aren't paying close attention, before, during, and after you eat.**

Because there is one thing I am 100% sure of, and that is while we are all the same species - human beings - we are also somewhat unique. There are absolute differences in the way food is metabolized in our bodies, from one person to another. If you stop and think about this, you realize how true it is. That is, we've all got slightly different genetic predispositions, intestinal microbiota, and livers, for starters. The other thing I'm very sure of is that over time, our bodies change. What might have been a good food choice at one time, might not always be in the future.

Here's something I've seen in others and experienced myself and is worth considering: Even if we do nothing more than decide to remove a certain food or type of food from our diet, over time our digestive system's ability to handle that food and digest it successfully, can be diminished or disappear entirely. At some point in the future when we try that food again, it may not "agree" with us, causing stomach upset, cramps, or nausea. I'm willing to bet most of you have experienced this firsthand. And naturally, we would come to the conclusion that this uncomfortable or nauseating experience confirms removing that food was a smart thing to do! *But was it?* Did we lose the ability to digest the food because the makeup of our gut changed, or because it really isn't good for us? That's the million-dollar question.

This is one of the reasons why as a general rule, *I don't believe it's smart to arbitrarily remove an entire food type or group from our diet.* That doesn't mean you can't be successful by doing so (see my earlier note about how we're all unique and an experiment of one), but the odds are reduced. If you consider what this advice means, you'll quickly realize you should never consider any diet program that has you arbitrarily remove a food group or type. I'll talk more about diets and diet programs in the next chapter.

Once again, it is worth looking at our ancestors who very likely ate a wide variety of wild plants, fruits, roots, nuts, and seeds, and hunted wild animals and fish. The word variety is key! In the end, any approach to eating that causes you to become more mindful – to pay closer attention to what, how much, and when you're eating, is very likely going to be productive and may lead to a true lifestyle change for the better. And that really is the take home message.

1. **Eat mindfully.** In fact, do everything mindfully! Listen to your body. Be willing to consider all the factors when determining whether something is good or not-so-good for you. Think about what you're eating, and why. Is it because it's convenient? Or tastes good? Or is better for you? Be aware. At least, if you're aware, you can make a choice in good conscience and with no regret one way or another.

2. **Experiment yourself to find what works best for you.** Enjoy the journey of nutritional exploration! Keep learning. Don't rely *exclusively* on what anyone else says or assume it's the gospel truth.

3. **Focus on REAL food,** first. I'm willing to bet if you begin to remove some processed foods in favor of real food, you'll be shocked at how MUCH processed food you actually eat. Every single person who makes this change and starts to become more aware is usually shocked. Which often motivates them to continue to be mindful and aware.

All in all, there's nothing more valuable than what we learn from *doing* - from actually trying different things and experimenting and learning and listening to what our mind and body and intuition is trying to *teach* us. And then making our own best-informed decisions about how to move forward.

With that, let's move on to some Myths, Magic-Bullets, and the Enemy We're all Doing Battle With. I'll see you in the next chapter!

CHAPTER 8

MYTHS, MAGIC BULLETS, AND THE ENEMY

If your doctor prescribes you medication without first asking about your diet, your sleep, your exercise routine, your water consumption, whether you have any structural issues and the stress in your life, then you don't have a doctor, you have a drug dealer.

— Unknown

'd just sat down with some musician colleagues to enjoy dinner after an afternoon concert. Playing music has long been something I've loved, and it was a vocation for much of my life. I've also always enjoyed the chance to sit down over some food and drink with my musician friends whenever the opportunity arises.

We were all sitting around a large table, hungrily looking over the menu, when one of the ladies – her name is Sue - reached into her purse and pulled out a book called the "18-Day Diet." Without talking to anyone in particular, she mentioned she started reading this book - and that she thinks it'll help her lose some weight – weight she's been struggling to lose. Without seeming too anxious, I asked Sue if I could take a look.

Glancing through it, I quickly found out this "diet" book's concepts were a bit, shall I say, shaky. Like a lot of these kinds of books, there seemed to be a random mix of good information and myths. The menu of allowed foods? Nothing more than varying combinations of grapefruit, oranges, toast, eggs, and vegetables. That's IT. Now I'll admit those aren't the worst assortment of diet foods ever, but the idea that those are the only foods you can eat while on this diet, tells you all you need to know about how sustainable this eating plan might be. I chuckled to myself but didn't want to make her feel uncomfortable or appear like I was judging. I couldn't keep from smirking though. She was looking back at me – waiting for me to say something.

As I continued to flip pages, I thought to myself: *don't get drawn into a conversation you know won't end well. You're smarter than that. Keep your mouth shut and keep your opinion to yourself.* ☺ Then the person next to me asked to take a look, grabbed the book out of my hand, and started flipping through. Without hesitation, she looked straight at Sue and said, "wow, that looks crazy. Like, really restrictive. Are you going to try and follow this? Looks like another fad diet to me." The whole table got quieter. Everyone was trying to be discreet while waiting to see what Sue would say. Would she defend the book, laugh along, and agree, or would she feel a little embarrassed and change the subject?

Short of politics, there isn't a topic that will churn up the anxiety level and create divisiveness in a group conversation more than food and diet. I mean, eating *is personal*. It's a topic we can all become very emotional about. Taken to extremes, we can end up defending our own beliefs to the point where it morphs into something that feels like religion.

In his book, *Diet Cults: The Surprising Fallacy at the Core of Nutrition Fads*, author Matt Fitzgerald says "the rituals of promoting and adopting special diets is not really all about better health. Since as far back as the Kosher dietary laws of the ancient Hebrews and even before, human beings have formed group identities and derived a sense of moral superiority from eating by strict rules. The modern obsession with identifying (and identifying with) the 'healthiest' diet is merely a new twist on the same old phenomenon." He goes on to say, "people who become convinced that a certain way of eating is best for everyone believe they are making a rational choice in pursuit of improved health, whereas they are primarily making an emotional and moralistic choice to join a special group that makes them feel good about themselves." [1]

Whether you agree with Fitzgerald's point of view or not, it's safe to say it is one of those topics everyone has an opinion about. And we're not usually shy about sharing what we think. So, why does it seem like eating well should be simple for us all, yet it isn't that way? It's because there are so many dimensions to consider when thinking about how food influences our health, AND our waistline. And how we enjoy life.

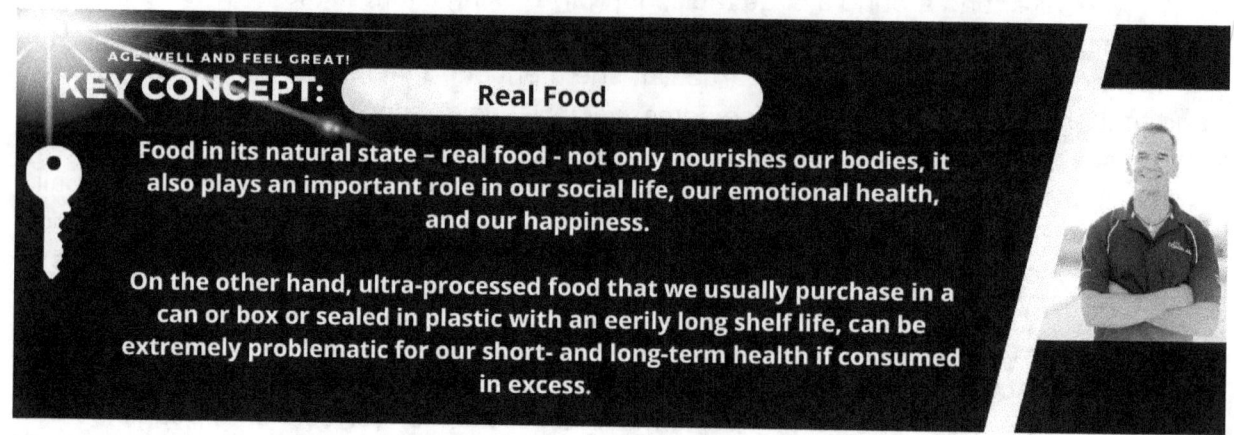

AGE WELL AND FEEL GREAT!

KEY CONCEPT: Real Food

Food in its natural state – real food - not only nourishes our bodies, it also plays an important role in our social life, our emotional health, and our happiness.

On the other hand, ultra-processed food that we usually purchase in a can or box or sealed in plastic with an eerily long shelf life, can be extremely problematic for our short- and long-term health if consumed in excess.

Part of the problem is the word "diet." All of us, at one time or another, has had a love/hate relationship with this word. On the surface, it's associated with some kind of restriction that is usually sold to the reader or consumer as "the solution" to a whole host of problems. One thing we'd all agree on: There are a lot of reasons we eat what we do the way we do, and those reasons go far beyond what we *need* for sustenance.

We've Got a Big Problem and We're Looking in All the Wrong Places for the Answers.

In my early running years in the early 1980s, I bought every nutrition book I could find, thinking there *must be* some kind of advice – some "magic bullet" that would help me get leaner and faster. My thought process was always the same: *what did the authors of these books know that I didn't?* I wanted to find out! And the sooner the better. Everyone has stories about looking for some "secret" that would make eating the right kinds of foods easier or lead to quick fat loss. And I'm sure you've seen those TV commercials featuring a celebrity promoting a diet and guaranteeing it works. (I don't know about you, but I've always wondered if those celebrities actually follow those diets or if they're just getting paid to say so. I guess we'll never know).

Did you know that US News and World Report has a search function on their website where you can "search" different diet plans? I found a total of 47 DIFFERENT diets![2] According to Nielsen Bookscan, roughly 6 million diet books are sold each year in the U.S.[3] The "South

Beach Diet" book alone sold 23 million copies. Dr. Atkins sold another 15 million. And our collective search for the "perfect" diet to give us the results we want isn't something new – the origins go back hundreds of years.

Every one of those books promises results, if you do exactly what they tell you to do. They're all marketed as having the final answer to our problems. It goes something like this: we (said author, also known as a self-pronounced expert) states that he/she has found the solution, and it just so happens it's this thing they're selling.

Dieting and Diet Books.

Books like the "18-Day Diet," the one my colleague Sue purchased, wouldn't exist if it wasn't for us. We're part of the problem, whether we want to admit it or not. Because what many people *really* want is a pill. And if we can't have a pill, we want the functional equivalent of a pill – simple, neat, tidy, easy. You know, eat these particular five or six foods for a few days or weeks, and bingo - your problems are over. The other thing we want is *certainty*. We need a guarantee. (Spoiler alert: there aren't any).

Despite how appealing they seem to be at times, diet plans and diet books telling you to cut certain kinds of foods or macro-nutrients like carbs, fat, or protein, or those that are based on restricting calories by eating less, **never work long term.** Similarly, diets that lead you to make a change resulting in temporary weight loss, also don't work, because as soon as you return to your regular way of eating, you usually regain any lost weight. It's easy to fall victim to the kind of thinking, for example, that claims one food or food group is "bad." Part of the reason people latch onto this approach is it boils down the often-difficult decisions about what to eat, to something black and white – cut and dried.

Author and researcher, Dr. Roy Baumeister, whose research spans multiple topics including self and identity, self-regulation, interpersonal rejection, and the need to belong, wrote a book titled *The Paradox of Choice*. This paradox of choice is an important variable to consider with diet cults and fitness routines. We have so many food choices available to us, but most people don't handle unlimited choice well. It's an emotional drain to face limitless choices day in and day out. It can be very taxing on willpower and decision-making. For example, it's a lot easier to just pick a one-sided approach and go with it, such as when someone decides to become a vegetarian. That eliminates meat from the long list of possible choices. Similarly, for someone who decides to go ketogenic. They can cross carbohydrates off the list of choices. It's easier to be leaner when you constrain your choices. Nobody wants OTHER people limiting choices for them, but if you can do it for yourself, you can make your life a lot easier and make success a matter of habit, not a battle of will.

That being said, for most people, the solution will come back to reducing the intake of processed, addictive sugar-laden foods that alter our body chemistry and, in the process, drastically increase our risk of chronic disease. We want to adopt a way of eating that's sustainable, that doesn't leave us hungry all the time. One key to losing weight and more specifically, body fat, is understanding hunger. More to come on this important topic! Keep reading.

*The definition of insanity is doing the same thing over
and over again and expecting different results.*

– unknown

The Great News Is, There Is an Approach That Does Work.

You can become leaner and healthier and improve the chance you will **go the distance** and eventually die healthy of natural causes. It's an approach you can stick with over the course of your life and become the "norm." Because as mentioned, if it isn't sustainable and can't be adopted as a normal way of eating and living, it won't help.

In this chapter, I'm going to share with you the nuts and bolts of what I've learned. It's based on my own practical experience but is also backed by solid, evidence-based science. I learned through trial and error and my own research and observations and then waited for the science to catch up and confirm my findings. At the same time, there's so much we *still don't know* and we're learning every day. Science is always evolving, but when you've decided to write a book, you can't wait decades for the final answer.

So, what have I learned? *No one has the nutritional "magic bullet" for weight loss or optimal health. There is no pill or quick fix.*

There Is No Such Thing as the "Perfect" Diet for Every Person.

In other words, there isn't *one singular way* for all human beings to eat. We're all an experiment of one to some degree. Yes, there are some basic principles that should guide us; I will discuss them as we go. But beyond those, we need to find what works best for us – not for today or this week, but for a lifetime.

What's more, I'll add *there is no such thing as a "bad" food.* I mean, all food is inherently good. The problem is what is done to that food if it's processed – what's been taken out (like the germ) or what's been added, which might be a whole host of chemicals that could potentially be dangerous. Let's not forget while I believe there aren't any "bad" foods per se, there are certainly *bad habits.* And that is usually where folks go wrong. I'll talk more about this important distinction later in this chapter.

My experience tells me when we try and achieve "perfect" by eliminating a food that someone else has deemed "bad" 100% of the time, it can often lead to even more frustration. The key is focusing on the bigger picture – on our **daily habits.** The way we eat day in and day out, for weeks and months and then years. We'll talk more about this later in this chapter, too. So, what's the one thing I *can* say with absolute certainty?

What We Eat (and Don't Eat) Matters MORE for Our Well-Being Than Anything Else.

It's what more than 40 years of practical experience and study has taught me. It matters even more than exercise, more than reducing stress, or sleeping better. *Food is the #1 tool we have at our disposal to create our best health and increase the odds of us going the distance and dying healthy.* Nothing else impacts our health more than what we eat.

As you will learn – by the same token, what we *don't* eat will have just as profound an impact. Specifically, eating *less*, and *less often*. Not coincidently, *these are also the #1 things most people really struggle with.* So, if what and when and how we eat is so important for our health and for avoiding chronic disease, why do so many of us struggle with food? Why do so many of us struggle to maintain healthy eating habits? I've thought about these questions for most of my adult life, as I observed others and, in many instances, tried to help them when they reached out to me.

I'm here to tell you most of the reasons people struggle aren't their fault. It's about bad mainstream health misinformation and myths surrounding the best ways to feel good, stay lean, and age well. To learn what I mean, keep reading.

Body Composition and Aging.

When someone buys a diet book, most of the time they're doing so hoping to lose weight. Sometimes it's vanity, driven by a promised upturn in status and to improve self-esteem. Other times it's simply a desire to be healthier and feel and look better. Common thinking would tell us leaner is *always* better, right? Yet, my experience tells me it's not always that cut and dried.

Yes, the research to date says there is an obesity crisis worldwide. In the U.S. alone, according to the Centers for Disease Control and Prevention, "in 2017–2018, the age-adjusted prevalence of obesity in adults was 42.4%."[4] That's more than 4 out of 10. Looking closer, approximately 2/3 are overweight. That should scare every one of us. But beyond that shocking statistic, the larger question is this: is what we are seeing in rising obesity rates a symptom of a larger problem, or is it *the* problem itself? Particularly as it relates to our health and ability to eventually die healthy. That's a huge question.

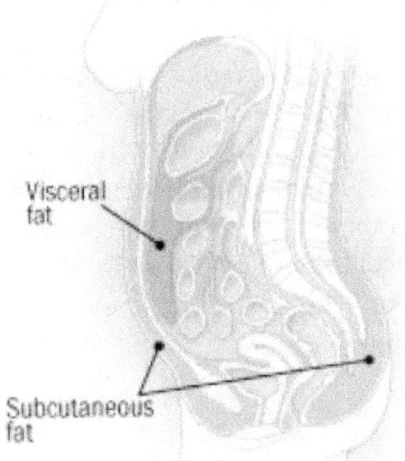

Visceral fat

Subcutaneous fat

In many ways, the research on obesity is still in its infancy. There's a lot we don't know. It's easy to say being over-fat is the problem that needs to be solved to improve our disease risk and our hoped-for opportunity of dying healthy. But, like many things in life, it might not be that simple. And here's why:

You can be a *little* above your "ideal" body composition and still be in good health, with low disease risk. On the opposite end of the spectrum, you can be "skinny" and not necessarily be in very good health. In other words, "skinny-fat." What's that mean, you ask? "Skinny-fat" is an unhealthy phenotype. The word phenotype is defined as "the observable characteristics of an organism, resulting from the interaction of the organism's genes with its environment." "Skinny-fat" refers to a person with a normal Body Mass Index (BMI), who has a low amount of muscle mass and a high amount of body fat.[5] It's a commonly used measure by health professionals to determine where someone fits into a category, with their attendant health risks. The way I define this term is, having a high percentage of body fat and a low amount of muscle mass.

In actuality, BMI doesn't capture the true health risks associated with body composition. It isn't very useful for many people as it is a poor substitute measure of the two most important body components, which are:

1.   the amount of muscle you have.
2.   the amount of visceral (hidden) body fat you have.

To think of it a different way, a "skinny-fat" person is someone who is a "normal" weight, but whose relative proportions of fat and muscle are skewed in the wrong direction. Think of it as skinny on the outside and fat on the inside. Being "skinny-fat" is about the difference between having most of your fat deep inside your body around your organs – something called *visceral* fat or having it more near the surface – underneath the skin – something called *subcutaneous* fat. The latest science seems to support the theory that people with higher levels of *visceral* fat – the fat that is deep and not something we see in a mirror – are at heightened risk of developing chronic disease.

As author Sam Apple states in his book, *Ravenous: Otto Warburg, the Nazis, and the Search for the Cancer-Diet Connection*, this "displaced fat may be invisible from the outside, but it is far from benign. It drives inflammation and interferes with how our cells respond to insulin. To overcome that interference, or resistance, the pancreas has no choice but to secrete more insulin, and a dangerous cycle takes off."[6]

Also, somewhat ironically, Robert Lustwig, MD, *a Professor of Clinical Pediatrics at University of California, and the author of a host of different books on diet-disease connections, adds that* "being thin is not a safeguard against metabolic disease or early death. Up to 40 percent of normal-weight individuals harbor insulin resistance – a sign of chronic metabolic disease. Of those, 20 percent demonstrate liver fat on an MRI of the abdomen. Liver fat, irrespective of body fat, has been shown to be a major risk factor in the development of diabetes."[7] He adds these words: "you think you're safe? You are so screwed. And you don't even know it."[8]

How Do You Know If You Might Be "Skinny-Fat?"

The gold standard for assessing where you have most of your stored fat is to have a DEXA scan to determine the amount of visceral fat you have. A DEXA scan is an imaging test that also measures bone density, body composition, and overall muscle mass.[10] DEXA is short for "dual-energy X-ray absorptiometry." I've gone through this test and would highly recommend it, although you should know going in you might be surprised (shocked?) because it does tell you the truth. On the plus side, it's quick and painless, and as a bonus, most experts consider DEXA scans to be the most useful, easy, and inexpensive test for helping to diagnose osteoporosis.

A much less accurate, but fast and easy method is to measure your waist. If your waist size is more than half your height, odds are you might be skinny fat. Here's another: *Is it hard? Does it jiggle?* One way to quickly assess the type of storage fat you have is to grab some around your waist and shake it. If you can actually grab it and shake it, that's *subcutaneous* fat which resides under the skin. That's better. If your stomach is round, big, and hard and you can't grab it and shake it, it's likely you have more *visceral* fat. That's worse.

You see, sometimes being able to jiggle your fat is a good thing! ☺

Age Well and Feel Great!
Key Concept:

The Fat Acceptance Movement: What Is It Based On?

Earlier I told you it's possible to be a tiny bit over your "ideal" body composition and still be generally healthy. But I'd be remiss if I didn't also mention there are lots of scientific studies that show the more excess fat you carry, the higher your risk for chronic disease. [11]

I have to question what basis a "Fat Acceptance" movement has for saying otherwise.[12] Some might say that being critical of anyone who is severely overweight or obese is a form of body shaming. I discussed this in Chapter 3 on age beliefs and ageism. It's often a fine line between self-acceptance and self-improvement.

I believe it's never OK to body shame anyone, but I also know being overweight carries potentially serious negative health consequences.
On the other end of the spectrum, being underweight is also a problem. These are the frail and weak who lack protein and don't get enough of the essential nutrients they need to thrive.

Good Health Is Too Complex to Be Boiled Down to a Number on a Scale.

The notion you can be healthy *only* if your weight is at some "ideal" number or if your body mass index ranges between some numbers such as 22 and 25, is flawed. And misleading. We know the jury is still out on the definitive connection between body composition and risk of chronic disease. There's a lot more we need to learn. As you go through this book and then consider changing your daily eating habits, *focus on the overriding lifestyle principles and concepts I present, while working toward making very small but consistent improvements to your daily habits.*

If you attempt to make large changes all at once, you'll frustrate yourself. Small consistent positive changes will allow you to reach an optimal body composition *without forcing it.* Being overweight won't be an issue for you. Yes, you'll need to be patient and persistent. Sorry, but few things worth achieving happen quickly. Focus on adopting lifelong sustainable eating and exercise habits – that's the path you want to follow. I tell you more about what that means in this chapter and in future chapters. Keep reading!

Self-discipline is one of the greatest acts of self-love.
— Coach Al

Willpower vs. *Skill* Power.

Back in the late 1980s, I was working as a part time Wellness Program Coordinator at the Coast Guard Academy while a member of the U.S. Coast Guard Band. Part of my responsibilities included helping regular people like you who were asking this important question: *How can I eat healthier to look and feel better, but also not give up the foods I really enjoy?*

Because on top of handling our daily stressors and trying to eat healthy, I know many of you are sitting there thinking, life is short – why would I want to deprive myself of the things I most enjoy, especially when there aren't any guarantees. That's a great question!

I asked myself that same question many times, especially during the 1980s. Researching and reading to see how nutrition experts would respond, and asking others their opinions, and also experimenting myself, it seemed like most of the answers came back to – you guessed it - *deprivation and willpower*. You know, "controlling yourself." We just need more "willpower." Along the same lines, haven't we always been told if we exercise more and eat less, we're guaranteed to lose weight? And if you can't lose weight, it's *your* fault. You just need more willpower. I'm here to tell you this isn't true. It's not your fault. Not entirely, anyway.

Yes, of course we are responsible for our actions – we do have control over what we put in our mouth. Any thinking person would agree some self-discipline is important – you don't get very far in this world without a little self-discipline, that's for sure. But is it really about having more willpower? The truth is, it isn't that simple. There's something making it even harder for the average person to do the right thing when it comes to food choice. That something is more powerful than discipline. It starts with *awareness*. Being mindful. It's about understanding the enemy we're all lining up against. It's also about understanding our own personality and knowing whether we're better at *moderating or abstaining*. I'll talk more about that soon.

Rather than thinking "willpower," why not think SKILL power! This is the way Dr. David Katz, the founding director of Yale University's Prevention Research Center, thinks of it. He states the good news is "the skills required aren't the classic triad of suffering, sacrifice and struggle. Rather, the skills required are organization, planning, and thoughtfulness."[13] I agree. With those skills, it is possible to not only experience healthy, more permanent fat-loss, but also more importantly, a healthy, and friendly relationship with food.

As I'll discuss more in this chapter, "skill power," does take time to master and gets easier with time, because the more practice a person has with a particular skill, the better that person will be at it, and the more natural it will become. The bottom line for now: We shouldn't try to achieve "perfect," just better. Little by little, small positive changes can add up without having to go to extremes.

Avoid the temptation to think of a food as "good" or "bad." Our goal is to be mindful and understand the difference between an occasional indulgence and something very different – which is what we do day in and day out - our daily habits. I've found understanding this to be key to my own and other's success.

Super EASY to Make the *Wrong* Choice – Super HARD to Make the *Right* Choice.

So, who is this enemy I mentioned earlier? Simply put, it is the food industry. Or what is sometimes referred to as industrialized food. I like to call them "BIG FOOD." Not sure what I mean? Think about this reality:

- We live in a world driven by the media, corporate marketing, and increasing corporate profits, where as a consumer, it's super easy to make the wrong choice, and super hard to make the right choice.
- We live in a world where 80% of the food sold in grocery stores is processed and contains sugar.
- We live in a world where if you cover the front of the package and simply read the ingredients, you can't tell what's in the box – whether it's a breakfast fruit tart, a pizza, or a hot dog.

When you consider all those things, it's clear if we want real change to healthier eating habits that are sustainable long-term, we need to be more aware of the battle we're fighting and understand the inherent challenges in it.

Listen, I'm not here to tell you that "BIG FOOD" is all evil. It's fair to recognize there have been some positives, including that acquiring food has become more convenient and accessible for many. But part of the message I need you to understand is this: a large majority of what is being produced and sold in grocery stores as pre-packaged "convenience" food, is in reality hurting us a lot more than helping us. I'll discuss more about this and the addictive nature of these foods later in this chapter. Keep this in the back of your mind as you keep reading: Be aware. Be mindful. Understand the enemy.

The Big Myth.

In 1989, I traveled to the *Cooper Institute for Aerobics Research* in Dallas to become certified as a physical fitness specialist. You may have heard of Dr. Kenneth Cooper. He was the doctor and scientist who pioneered the term "aerobics," espousing the benefits of doing aerobic exercise to improve cardiovascular health. When I was at the clinic, I met one of the doctors on staff, Dr. Roy Vartabedian, who had just published his own book on nutrition called *Nutripoints: Healthy Eating Made Simple*. I grabbed a copy of his book and read it cover to cover.

It's based on a very smart concept – this idea we should rank foods based on their nutrient value, NOT on how many calories they contain. For years, there's been this prevailing myth, arguably one of the biggest myths that's ever been told by doctors, nutritionists, the government, and the food industry, which is the number of calories is what matters the most. Or when it comes to losing weight or eating healthier for our long-term wellbeing, all calories are *the same*. We've all heard this a million times: when the number of calories you take "in" exceeds the calories that you burn or go "out", you gain fat. And when the opposite occurs, you lose it.

While this is technically true, there's a *lot more* to it. For example: If you try to lose weight by cutting calories, you may be hungry all the time. Then you would be miserable and couldn't sustain what you were doing. Nor would you want to! Also, certain kinds of foods, irrespective of their calorie count, make you hungrier. A 2019 study gives us some insight into a reason people consume more calories than they spend, and it's alarming for those who eat ultra-processed food.[14] Here's a summary of the study: A group of people were admitted to a metabolic ward, which is the gold standard for research of this kind, since researchers can control everything the participants eat. The subjects ate either ultra-processed food or whole foods for the first two weeks, then switched to the other type of food for two more weeks. Meals were designed to be matched for calories, energy density, macronutrients, sugar, sodium, and fiber. The subjects were allowed to eat *as much or as little as they wished*. What were the results?

When they ate ultra-processed food, the *subjects gained nearly 2 pounds*. When they ate whole foods, *they lost 2.4 pounds*. Simply put, the processed food made them hungrier, so they ate more. Cravings increased. The whole, unprocessed food satisfied their appetites, so they ate less. Ultra-processed food is designed to be appealing and is less able to satisfy hunger, so you often eat more of it. When you think about it, it makes sense, right?

Obesity as we know it was rare until a century ago and uncommon – less than 10% of the population – just a few decades ago. That's because humans didn't always eat such huge amounts of ultra-processed food. Compare that to today where, unfortunately, more Americans than ever are consuming a large majority of their calories as ultra-processed food.

Our goal must be to create an eating lifestyle that by design, *limits processed foods*. That's one extremely important key to successful, permanent fat loss and enhanced health.

What About Self-Control?

When you eat processed foods, cravings soar. You're rarely satisfied for long. Soon, you realize you need to have more control. You're always asking yourself, *where's my willpower? Don't I "want it" badly enough to stop eating this?*

Does this kind of self-talk sound familiar? The misinformation you usually get from mainstream health sends this message: it all comes back to "controlling yourself." Reading Dr. Vartabedian's book helped me understand for the first time these ideas aren't true. That basing what and how we eat to be healthier, solely on calorie count, without considering the KIND of food we're eating, is a huge mistake.

All Calories AREN'T the Same. In Fact, a Calorie is NOT a Calorie.

Living healthier and free of disease and improving our odds of going the distance ISN'T about how many calories we take in or how many we can drop from our diet. For too many years, the mainstream medical establishment, the American Dietetic Association (ADA) and dieticians, food corporation marketing, the fitness industry, and poorly written diet books, have ALL largely and mistakenly put the emphasis on calories *alone*. And misled us in the process.

This campaign started in the early 1900s when a scientist named Atwater standardized how much heat energy (how many calories) three specific macronutrients would liberate when burned in a device that measures such things. Since then, dieticians and the ADA have clung to this mistaken idea that a person's plate of food can be exactly calculated using this math. The problem is the math *doesn't* account for the role of fiber (which isn't absorbed and doesn't add any calories to the total but *does* have an impact on the total you absorb). The other element I'll discuss in more detail later in this chapter? The importance of our intestinal microbiome and the fact it metabolizes up to 25-30% of everything you eat.[15]

So, if it's not about math and counting calories, what *is it about?* It's about the impact different kinds of food (especially the ultra-processed foods which make up the average American diet) have on your body, brain, and your metabolism. Food is a drug. Food is medicine.

Different foods have different effects on your entire body that can't be reduced to a simple math equation. I'll talk more about this soon.

It's also about emotion. And instinct. And even how the average consumer is being manipulated by the large corporations that manufacture processed foods. It's "BIG FOOD." The industrialized food industry. The government is culpable as well, as is the American Dietetic Association. The bottom line: Calories tell you NOTHING about *vitamins, minerals, protein, type of fat, oxidation status, bioavailability, absorbability, level of processing, antinutrients, how an animal was raised, soil health, pesticides or estrogen content, allergens, toxins, heavy metals, microplastics,* or any *other additives.*

One of my goals with this book is to get you OUT of calorie mode, and into insulin mode. Keep reading to learn more – I'll do a deep dive into this hormone in the next chapter. It's important!

Are You a Moderator or an Abstainer?

Have you ever been told, or said yourself, the "secret" is *everything in moderation*? Sounds simple enough, right? You can have whatever you want, just eat it (or do it) in "moderation." If only it was that simple! ☺ But it's not. And one reason is we're all unique. For one thing, some of us are "moderators" and others are "abstainers."

For the most part, I've never been an all or nothing kind of person. I'm what I would call a "moderator." For example, I can open a bag of chips and have just a few and then close the bag and throw it back into the pantry. "Abstainers," on the other hand, will have a very hard time closing the bag once they open it, even when they try really hard. An abstainer is terrible at moderating and finds it much easier to abstain from something rather than trying to use it moderately. If an abstainer opened a bag of chips and had just a few, they'd have a hard time thinking about anything else UNTIL those chips were gone! Can you relate?

I used to think of abstainers as "weak" or lacking willpower. I considered it a fault until I learned that all people are either moderators or abstainers and there is no moral superiority to either predisposition. If you're thinking that moderators also happen to be the kind of people who lose weight more easily, you'd be right. It's the reason you need to know if you're a moderator or an abstainer. It points out once again, we're not all wired the same.

The take home message is, if you're an abstainer, focus on setting yourself up to succeed by manipulating your environment to best suit your temperament. In other words, don't routinely buy or store the foods you know you can't trust yourself to eat in moderation. You'll find you have more success when you rearrange your daily life to maximize good habits and limit exposure to temptation.

Choices: A $2.78 Frozen Pizza or A $5.00 Pint of Organic Blueberries.

In his book *Hooked: How Processed Food Became Addictive*, author Michael Moss explains how a 1.5 trillion dollar processed food industry rose to power - primarily through its relentless pursuit and manipulation of our own instinctual desires. As one example, it makes sense one of the basic instincts that drives our food choices relates to price.

As Moore puts it, "evolutionary biologists frame our development as humans in terms of energy – in terms of how we spend the energy we derive from food and how much energy we have to expend to obtain that food. For the latter, it only made sense that our forebears learned to take the easiest path in eating. Walking upright meant less effort in foraging: using fire to cook increased the efficiency of our digestion; in eating fresh meat, we chased down the sloth, not the springbok. Today, there seems to be some of this ancient behavior at play in the choices we make in food. Cheaper food means having to work less in order to pay for that food, and thus we are drawn by instinct to grocery and restaurant bills that are smaller."[16]

This isn't meant to minimize the very real challenge many among us have, who are financially strapped, where cheap food might be the only option. However, again as Moore puts it, "how else but through the nature of evolution can you explain the large number of Mercedes and BMWs that flood the parking lots of Aldi's everywhere."[17] ☺

Beyond the short-term cost, we know when you eat *real food* as opposed to processed, manufactured food, you are much more satisfied. Instinctively, your body has a much keener sense of when you've eaten enough. You need to listen to it. Part of the reason you're more satisfied is you're getting the nutrients you need by way of that food. On the other hand, when you eat processed or junk foods, you aren't getting the nutrients your body needs. You will usually eat more than you should, and still feel hungry.

Perhaps the real epidemic that's going on right now is this: being over<u>fed</u> but malnourished. If that seems counter intuitive, look around you. It's real – and the typical American diet is the reason. One key to being more satisfied, healthier, and leaner, is eating *real food* most of the time. No calorie counting required! No dieting required!

Age Well and Feel Great!

Key Concept:

Can A Person Be Overfed and Malnourished At the Same Time?

The answer is an absolute YES. People with metabolic syndrome or who are insulin resistant frequently fall into this category.

They eat lots of calories, yet those calories are "empty." In other words, they are often lacking in important nutrients such as the amino acid tryptophan, which is essential to make serotonin, and methionine, which is needed to make glutathione, an important liver antioxidant.

Remember, when grains are processed, they're stripped of their germ which is where most of the vitamins, minerals, and polyphenols live.[9] When the majority of someone's diet is made up of empty calories, the risk of being under-nourished increases. It only makes sense. Food for thought.

What Are the Processed Foods We're Talking About?

Simply put, it's pretty much everything in the middle aisles of the grocery store, and almost everything you'll find on convenience store shelves. And no, it's not a coincidence those stores place those shelves right near the cash register. It's anything in a box or plastic wrapper. Think of the things in those middle aisles that can sit on those shelves (or on yours at home) for months at a time, sometimes years, without going bad.

It's worth noting federal regulators don't require the manufacturers to list the chemical compounds used in their products. Rather, when it comes to the stuff that literally gives these foods their smell and taste, they're clumped together under the vague category of "natural and artificial flavors." Loaded with white flour, white sugar, high-fructose corn syrup, trans fats and a host of other chemicals produced in a laboratory, these convenience foods are at the heart of the real problem we're facing on the food front. Most people are concerned about what is inside a food they eat, but for me, it's always been more about what happened in the manufacturing process that made the food in the first place. Again, I'll ask you to pause for a moment, and think. If you're thinking you'd "like" to not eat those foods but you simply can't resist them, keep reading.

Food Is a Drug.

If we have any chance of changing our eating habits for the better, it's critical we understand **processed foods are addictive** – every bit as much as tobacco, alcohol, and other drugs. They're designed by the manufacturers to be biologically addictive. The food industry uses scientific research and massive, data-supported marketing ploys aimed at getting us addicted to highly processed junk food brimming with sugar, salt, and chemicals, none of it having any real lasting nutritive value.

They know how to create that perfect mouthfeel, that perfect brain hook. These foods change our brain chemistry and hormones in a way that affects our ability to control our behavior. And, by the way, the same wonderful folks who are pushing that addicting junk food ALSO own companies that will "help" you diet to lose the weight their other companies caused you to gain. It's win-win for them! And a big lose-lose for us.

And here's the thing: when life gets hard, when you're stressed, when you're tired, it's more difficult to make good choices. Who hasn't experienced driving down the road after a stressful day, smelling the McDonalds french fries or Kentucky Fried Chicken as you get closer? You have to focus so hard on NOT succumbing to that, right? It draws us in. And plenty of research has been done where brain scans show the brain is affected exactly the same way as it is with cocaine or heroin use.

It's not an emotional addiction, it's a *biological* addiction. Read that again and again, until it sinks in. Even I am drawn in, and I get it. Listen, we're all human. It's the same battle for all of us, to become more mindful and make the best choices we can on any given day, in the face of our brain chemistry. The only way to break the addiction is to get away from the temptation long enough for the craving to subside. That isn't easy, but it's worth it. As I said earlier, food is medicine. And so is sleep, stress reduction, exercise, and connections with others. We need to make sure we're choosing the best medicine more often, for our long-term health.

A Summary: 10 Lessons.

Here are 10 take aways to summarize what I've discussed so far that provide the foundation for what is to come. Keep smiling. ☺ With knowledge comes power.

1. **Food is the #1 tool we have** at our disposal to create our best health and increase our odds of being able to die healthy.
2. **There is no such thing as a nutritional magic bullet or pill**, nor are there any guarantees.
3. **When it comes to eating well, all calories aren't the same**. The type of food that makes up those calories, and its impact on your body chemistry, matters. A LOT. Get out of calorie mode and into insulin mode. You'll learn more in the next chapter about what that means and why it's so important.

4. **There is no such thing as the "perfect" approach to eating for every single person**. Despite all being human, there are some unique aspects to our biochemistry. We are all an experiment of one to some degree. Through a little experimentation and an open mind, we can each find what works best for us.

5. **Restrictive diets (and the diet books that go along with them) don't work long-term and won't help you become healthier or feel better**. Your ultimate goal is to adopt better, more easily sustainable lifestyle and eating habits that will let you enjoy life!

6. **Avoid the temptation to categorize foods as either "bad" or "good."** Focus on habits instead. Understand it isn't the occasional indulgence that matters as much as do our daily habits – how and what we eat, day in and day out, over the course of months and years.

7. **It's not about being "perfectly" skinny**. You can be a little bit above your "ideal" weight and still be quite healthy. What matters more than what you see on the outside when looking in the mirror, is the visceral fat you don't see that surrounds your organs.

8. **We need to know the enemy if we're going to win the battle**, and make no mistake, we do have a battle on our hands. Who's the enemy? It is industrialized food. One key to winning the battle is awareness and the mindful eating that follows. A little bit of self-discipline helps too.

9. **Food is a drug**. It often has drug-like effects on our body chemistry, which impacts our mood and behavior. Have you or someone you know ever been "hangry?" If so, you know what I mean. Habitually considering the drug-like effects the foods we eat can have will help us adopt the smartest sustainable eating habits.

10. **Our relationship with food and how we approach daily eating should become a lifestyle that is sustainable over the long term**. If it isn't something we can stick with, it won't last and it won't help us become healthier or increase our chances of dying healthy.

Now let's move on to the next chapter where I will get down and dirty about insulin, insulin resistance, and hyperinsulinemia! Buckle up, it will be quite a ride!

CHAPTER 9

INSULIN RESISTANCE AND HYPERINSULINEMIA

The truth will set you free.

But first it will piss you off.

— Gloria Steinem

*If doctors ran insulin reduction clinics, we'd get rid
of 75% of chronic disease in the world.*
—Robert Lustig, MD

Whether you realize it or not, in many respects, as a species we are sicker now than we've ever been. In the U.S., the children being born today may well end up with a lower life expectancy than those from earlier generations. The latest statistics show life expectancy in the U.S. has actually gone down over the last couple of years.[1] If that sounds hard to believe, just look around you. We're witnessing alarming increases in chronic disease nationwide and worldwide that, as a whole, have never before been experienced by our species at this level.

Our collective and individual health is declining, while chronic conditions that cause disability, pain and suffering, and even early death, are on the rise. Remarkably, this is happening despite many advances in modern medical science. I often wonder how that is even possible, but it is happening.

I'm here to tell you **hyperinsulinemia and insulin resistance** *are at the root of nearly every chronic illness we struggle with today, especially in the U.S and other developed countries.* How common are they?

According to the latest statistics, as many as 85% of people in the U.S. are insulin resistant![2] That's more than eight out of ten of us! At least half of all adults in other developed countries are insulin resistant. Ironically, many people who have *hyperinsulinemia* don't have any obvious (to them) symptoms at first, and thus don't even *know* they have it. What's even more frightening is more than 10% of American children are *insulin resistant*. There are now documented reports of insulin-resistant four-year-olds![3] And of a three-year-old who was diagnosed with type-2 diabetes![4]

Most experts agree. *Hyperinsulinemia* and *insulin resistance are the most widespread health disorders worldwide. There's also consensus they directly or indirectly are related to virtually every other chronic disease.* I would argue if we were able to "fix" this problem of hyperinsulinemia and insulin resistance across the population, reducing the epidemic of chronically high insulin, we'd see the occurrence of other more familiar (and more feared) diseases like cancer, heart disease, and Alzheimer's, go way, way down. We might even all but eliminate them.

I believe *hyperinsulinemia* and *insulin resistance* are the central lynchpins that tie all of these diseases together. They "connect the dots" of the diseases we all fear the most, the ones that are ruining our quality of life and in many instances, eventually killing us. Yes, that's a bold statement to make. But it's what I believe and what the latest science shows.

Before I delve deeper into the topic of *hyperinsulinemia* and *insulin resistance*, what causes them, how they're different, and most importantly, what we can do about it, I want to say: I'm not an endocrinologist or any other kind of doctor. Nor am I a laboratory scientist. What I am is a sports therapist and coach who, because of some personal goals I was chasing in the sport of running, became curious and went on to spend part of almost every day of my life studying and learning more about this topic. The more I learned, the more I wanted to learn.

Because I'm not a laboratory scientist or a doctor...

- I won't make claims that only someone who is an in-lab scientist or doctor could make.
- I'll refer to published and peer-reviewed scientific studies where appropriate, and there are many which exist that provide the scientific consensus to support my own experiential findings.
- I'll share what I have learned from other experts that my own experience tells me is the most important information to share, giving credit where it's due.

So, if you're thinking you haven't heard much about *hyperinsulinemia* and *insulin resistance* before, despite how common they are, you're not alone. I wasn't familiar with either of them until my goals and interest in running and endurance performance pulled me in that direction.

Back in my early days as a runner in the early 1980s, my initial goal was to see if I could extend endurance by *"burning" more bodyfat as a fuel source for my running, instead of sugar, and in the process, become more sensitive to insulin and its effects.* This is actually a key component of what I hope to teach you, so hold onto this thought. I'll talk about it in more detail, later in this chapter. As time went on though, it became obvious that becoming more sensitive to insulin had profound implications that went beyond my running performance – effects that were even more profound for improving and maintaining optimal health, which includes avoiding chronic diseases and aging well.

What I learned was these two seemingly different goals of...

1. Improving athletic performance and
2. Improving health

...were actually linked together in an important way. That might not be surprising to you, but for me, I've been aware that fitness and health are not mutually exclusive. That is, you CAN be fit and still be unhealthy or at risk for disease. And everything I've learned since those early running days in the 1980s has reinforced this important distinction.

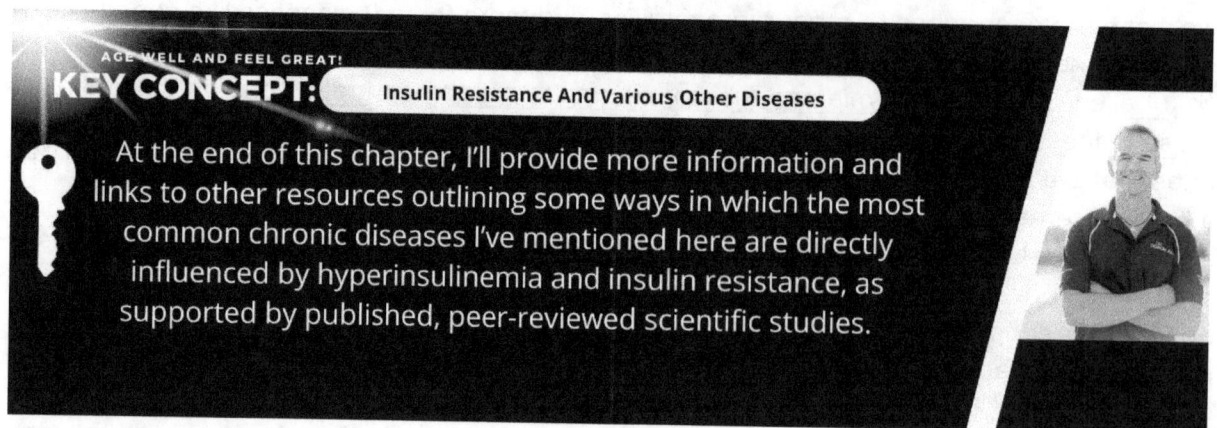

AGE WELL AND FEEL GREAT!
KEY CONCEPT: Insulin Resistance And Various Other Diseases

At the end of this chapter, I'll provide more information and links to other resources outlining some ways in which the most common chronic diseases I've mentioned here are directly influenced by hyperinsulinemia and insulin resistance, as supported by published, peer-reviewed scientific studies.

Consider This a Primer: Science Is Complex and Traditional Ways of Thinking Are Always Going to Be Challenged.

There's no possible way I could cover all the things you might want to know about insulin in this section. There's too much to learn and know. Entire books have been written on this topic alone. And our traditional ways of thinking about this are always evolving. They have to because there are always new discoveries. I would venture a guess what is taught in medical school today will have to change as time goes on. Traditional paradigms about health AND about how and why we age are always being challenged, for good reason!

Similarly, when describing complex actions in the body, especially at the cellular level, it is easy to make things sound simpler than they actually are. I will occasionally do this for simplicity's sake. ☺ Also, as you continue reading, know there will be some things I'll be forced to glance over due to space limitations and the desire to keep things as simple as possible. So, look for my recommendations on where to go for other reliable sources of scientific information to learn more about this topic should you want to. I will provide that information when appropriate.

Experiments never fail. They just yield new and useful experience and learning.

— unknown

I've Spent My Life Learning and Making Mistakes, and Then Learning Some More...

...by way of study, application, and experimentation. After all, that's what this book is all about – my personal experiences as a coach, athlete, curious layperson, and therapist. Sharing what I've learned in the trenches. By doing, then reviewing and adjusting, then doing again.

In most instances, after years of trial and error applying what I learned, I've come to draw my own conclusions, while always being open-minded and looking for more answers from the latest scientific findings. Along the way, what usually followed was me waiting patiently for evidence-based peer-reviewed science to confirm what I had, in many cases, already learned myself.

Think of it this way: In some fields of study, progress seems to move ahead at very fast speeds, because that particular field doesn't demand the same *evidence base* as does medicine. Think of the technology responsible for our smart phones as one example. It's been said that evidence-based medicine is not a search for truth, it's a search for consensus.[5] I tend to agree. In contrast, companies like Apple and Google aren't waiting for consensus to move forward and create change.

That's one very big reason progress in *preventive* medicine and holistic health practices is so slow. And why I've been motivated to continue marching ahead, often experimenting on myself and others I have coached and worked with, without the *consensus* that many others in the medical community sit back and wait for.

The bottom line is, <u>it's beyond time for all of us to better understand *hyperinsulinemia* and *insulin resistance* as THE primary underlying factor in every chronic disease, as well as accelerated aging, and early death.</u> It is finally time to make *hyperinsulinemia* and *insulin resistance* part of the public lexicon.

How I Became So Familiar with a Disorder Most Haven't Heard of.

Back in those early days as a runner, I usually drank plain water to stay hydrated on the hottest days in the summer and also during my long training runs and races to replace the fluids I was losing via sweating. The idea of using anything other than water never occurred to me. Because for the kinds of events and training I was doing, there wasn't any need for anything else.

Until, that is, in the mid-1990s, when I ventured into the sport of triathlon and started preparing for longer triathlon races – the Ironman triathlon in particular. You see, in very long endurance races, it was assumed you'd need something *in addition* to plain water to finish without completely running out of energy. That "in addition" would be calories taken in via sports drinks, gels, and other "energy foods," as well as some electrolytes.

To understand why this is the case, and why it's important, we need to take a step back and talk about what insulin is, what hyperinsulinemia is, and what insulin resistance is. Finally, *looking at how our body stores energy and uses it* - will be important to understand what we need to do and why, to improve our health and age well.

What is Insulin?

When most people hear the word insulin, they think of a medication that people with type-1 diabetes need. But it is much more than that. Insulin is a hormone produced in the body. Hormones are substances that act like chemical messengers. To imagine what a chemical messenger like insulin does, think of something that is manufactured in one part of the body, then travels through the bloodstream to affect other parts of the body.

Insulin is produced and secreted by the pancreas, which is a small organ located near the stomach. I think of insulin as truly the "master" hormone, meaning it has many, many functions in the body – it's difficult to know every single thing that insulin handles. It's a lot!

You see, unlike most other hormones, insulin affects *every single cell in the body* in many ways. How cells replicate, whether they live or die, how they change in size, and how they influence growth in many parts of the body, are just a few examples. The specific effect it has depends on the type of cell. For example, when insulin binds to a muscle cell, the muscle cell then makes new proteins. When it binds to a liver cell, the liver cell then makes fat.

But Its Most Well-Known Job Is...

...to regulate our blood sugar levels, to keep them at a "normal" level. It does this by taking sugar, or more correctly, glucose, out of the bloodstream. You see, our body needs to have blood glucose maintained within a very narrow range, as sustained high levels of glucose in the blood are dangerous, even potentially lethal. Insulin, along with glucagon[6], are the hormones that make this happen.

Now, if you're like me, it is easy to get confused when you hear sugar referred to in this context, with different terms such as glucose, sucrose, dextrose and so on. Keep in mind that there are many types of sugars including one familiar example: *table* sugar (which is technically sucrose and is made from a combination of fructose and glucose). It is easy to get confused! ☺

So, to simplify things for you the reader, when I'm discussing the sugar *in our bloodstream*, I'll stick with using the correct term which is *glucose*. The reason is simple: Glucose is the end product of the digestion of all the different forms of sugar and carbohydrate we eat. In other words, regardless of the type of sugar or carbohydrate we consume, it all ends up as glucose.

So, in a healthy body, how does insulin work to regulate blood glucose?

- You eat or drink something, some of which is absorbed into your bloodstream, resulting in an increase in your blood glucose (or sugar) level.
- The higher the food is on the glycemic index, the faster the rise in blood glucose.

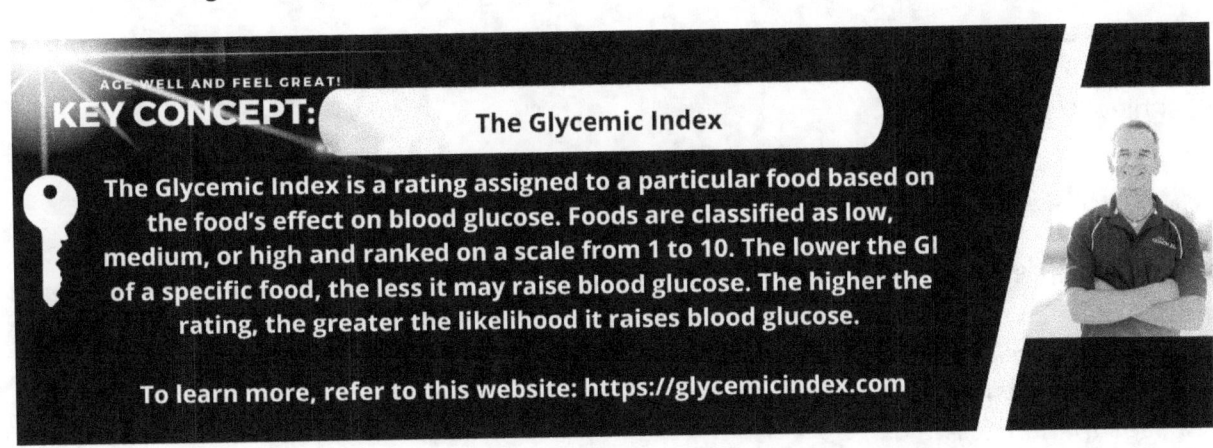

AGE WELL AND FEEL GREAT!

KEY CONCEPT: The Glycemic Index

The Glycemic Index is a rating assigned to a particular food based on the food's effect on blood glucose. Foods are classified as low, medium, or high and ranked on a scale from 1 to 10. The lower the GI of a specific food, the less it may raise blood glucose. The higher the rating, the greater the likelihood it raises blood glucose.

To learn more, refer to this website: https://glycemicindex.com

In response to the rise in blood glucose, the pancreas then secretes insulin to bring the level of glucose back down to a normal level.

Where does the glucose go once it is shuttled *out* of the bloodstream? In very simple terms, it goes into storage. We'll talk more in a minute about what kind of storage, but suffice to say, that's another way to think of insulin - as a *storage* hormone. It's also a *pro-building* hormone. So, as you can see, insulin is a powerful substance and does amazing things in the body that are essential for life, when it's working as it should. And when there isn't too much of it floating around. And when we are *sensitive* to it. *Which is the problem.*

What are Insulin Resistance and Hyperinsulinemia?

Very often insulin doesn't work as it should. When that happens, it's called insulin *resistance*. When insulin builds up to very high levels in the bloodstream, that's called *hyperinsulinemia*. (In this instance, hyper as a prefix in front of insulin, meaning more, or greater, or increased beyond normal).

One theory of current mainstream thinking in the medical community is that insulin *resistance* causes *hyperinsulinemia*. It's often difficult to know for sure, but my belief is they usually happen concurrently, although very often some initial amount of *resistance* leads the way. That's why I am presenting them in this way. These conditions are often the beginning of a cascade of many other potentially serious health issues, the most common being type-2 diabetes.

At various times throughout this chapter, you will read references to diabetes. In every instance, I'm referring to type-2 diabetes, NOT type-1 diabetes. Type-1 and type-2 are very different conditions with very different treatment strategies and outcomes. Type-1 is considered to be genetic and is referred to as an auto immune condition.[7]

Are Insulin Resistance and Hyperinsulinemia Different?

Yes, they're different. But very much related, as you will see a bit later in this chapter when I delve deeper into the specific differences and get to the heart of how we can all can become healthier. Keep reading.

How Serious Are These Conditions?

Remember in the first paragraph of this chapter, I boldly stated that *hyperinsulinemia and insulin resistance are at the root of nearly every chronic illness we struggle with today, especially in the U.S and in other developed countries. My thesis is that these two issues together – hyperinsulinemia and insulin resistance, are the hidden epidemic behind most illnesses that are killing us.*

They are the driving force behind the increases we're seeing in various kinds of cancer, as well as many if not most of the illness' modern day humans struggle with, such as heart and kidney disease, fatty liver disease, neurologic diseases and reproductive issues. And of course, obesity and what is known as metabolic syndrome, both of which lead directly to an overall decline of our health. And early death.

Also, if you're an athlete or someone who wants to be active and wants to continue to feel good, know that *insulin resistance* leads to decreased mitochondrial function.[8]

Mitochondria are present in every single cell in the body. They are the powerhouses of the cell – providing much needed energy for the cell to do its job. Since mitochondrial function is already deteriorating as a "normal" byproduct of aging, when insulin resistance and hyperinsulinemia are present, the situation is even worse. Without optimal functioning of these little powerhouses of the cell, you won't be at your best, especially as you age.

Keep in mind this isn't only my opinion or personal observation. It's supported by dozens of research articles and ongoing scientific studies. And we're learning more every day. Additionally, it's obvious to anyone paying attention that as a medical community, we're not doing as good a job as we need to of understanding OR managing these problems. We're at a critical stage in healthcare where "our medical systems are best suited to diseases of the past, not those of the present or future." [9] So, with that being said, let's first define insulin resistance:

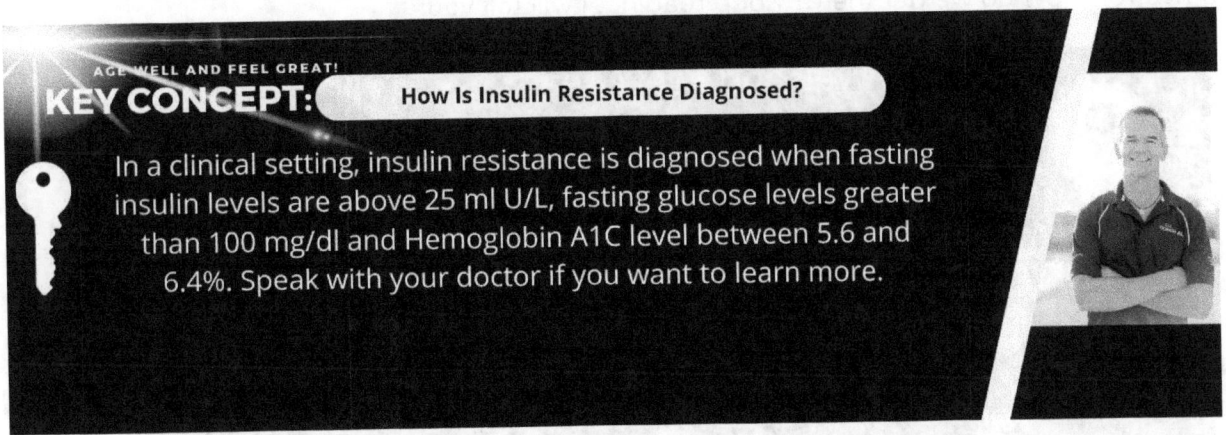

AGE WELL AND FEEL GREAT!

KEY CONCEPT: How Is Insulin Resistance Diagnosed?

In a clinical setting, insulin resistance is diagnosed when fasting insulin levels are above 25 ml U/L, fasting glucose levels greater than 100 mg/dl and Hemoglobin A1C level between 5.6 and 6.4%. Speak with your doctor if you want to learn more.

Simply put, **insulin resistance is a reduced, or diminished, response to insulin**. To put it another way, it's an impaired ability for insulin to do all the things it is supposed to do. In its advanced state, insulin resistance often leads directly to *hyperinsulinemia* and then eventually, to type-2 diabetes.

What Happens Inside Our Body When We Become Insulin Resistant?

Looking back to the earlier example of how insulin works to regulate blood glucose in an otherwise healthy body, you'll recall:

- You eat or drink something, some of which is absorbed into your bloodstream, resulting in an increase in your blood glucose (or sugar) level.
- The higher the food is on the glycemic index, the faster the rise in blood glucose.
- In response to the rise in blood glucose, the pancreas then secretes insulin to bring the level of glucose back down to a normal level.

So, what happens when someone becomes insulin resistant? The process is exactly the same. But it would stand to reason once you become insulin resistant, *more insulin is required to get the same response as before*. What's also happening is the amount of insulin is building up in the bloodstream, which is, you guessed it - *hyperinsulinemia*. Soon you have a very dangerous cycle beginning. One that negatively impacts every facet of your health. The more you eat, the more insulin you produce and the less sensitive you become to it. And the more it then builds up. And the more you need of it to get the same job done, and the more insulin you produce. And the more it builds up. And so on. You get the point.

On the opposite end of the spectrum is being more insulin *sensitive*. This means exactly what it says – less insulin is required to achieve the same effect of reducing glucose to normal levels. <u>Consistently normal levels of blood glucose, with very few swings up or down, is exactly what we all want and need</u>. Small variations in insulin fluctuation are what we should strive for! How do we get there? Keep reading, I will tell you!

Age Well and Feel Great!

Key Concept:

Is There An Evolutionary Explanation For Insulin Resistance?

Gerald Schulman, M.D., Ph D., Professor of Medicine, Cellular & Molecular Physiology, and the Director of the Diabetes Research Center at Yale, has a fascinating theory that insulin resistance was an important component of our evolution as a species, preventing starvation during very lean periods of time. He is quoted on Dr. Peter Attia's The Drive podcast as saying:

"In my view, insulin resistance was a protective mechanism throughout evolution that allowed us to survive starvation which was probably the predominant environmental exposure we've had for the last many, many millennia. It's only in recent years, recent decades and now we're in this toxic environment of over-nutrition and it's when these same pathways now are going the opposite direction—promoting disease by doing what they were at one time was protective. And now they're actually being called metabolic disease."[10]

In my opinion, this very interesting theory provides a window into how, what was once important for our survival a very long time ago, can become something which is hurting us. Much of this can simply be traced back to the present availability of food.

Is the Problem Excess Glucose, or Excess Insulin?

In a healthy person, when blood glucose is at a normal level, insulin is also (usually) normal. However, with insulin resistance, insulin levels are higher than expected relative to glucose. This is what *hyperinsulinemia* is. In his book, *Why We Get Sick*, author Benjamin Bikman Ph.D., states "in the story of insulin resistance and diabetes, we've been treating glucose as the main character, but it's really the sidekick. That is, glucose is the typical blood marker that is used to diagnose and monitor diabetes, but we really should be paying attention to insulin levels first."[11] So, is the problem excess glucose or excess insulin? The answer, at least according to Dr. Bikman, is too high, or excess insulin. In other words, *hyperinsulinemia*. I happen to agree with him, and here's why:

Remember I mentioned earlier that insulin has many functions in the body, only one of which is shuttling glucose out of the bloodstream and letting it enter into cells. This fact is super important when understanding the real paradox and problem we're facing. Because the truth is, if we look at the body holistically and consider not just glucose circulating in the bloodstream, but ALL the glucose in other parts of the body as well, we know those other parts of the body can be *quite sensitive* to insulin, even when a person has been described clinically as being insulin *resistant.*[12] There are many examples of this, such as something called *de novo lipogenesis*,[13] which occurs in the liver. Describing that in detail now simply goes beyond the scope of this chapter. And truthfully, it isn't necessary to know all the details of *de novo lipogenesis* (or any other similar process) to understand what we need to do to "fix" this problem of *hyperinsulinemia*.

If this idea of being at once resistant but also sensitive to insulin, depending on the body part, sounds counterintuitive to you, you're not alone. I would argue many medical professionals don't understand this fundamental concept yet. Most are trained to look primarily at blood glucose vs. more holistically at insulin. As an aside, resting glucose levels are easier to test for than is insulin, which contributes to this challenge.

The bottom line: Stay with me. These concepts are so important for understanding not only what we need to do to make sure we're on the right path, but also WHY we are on this path in the first place. After all, I've always believed if a person can understand better why they should do something a certain way, they'll be much more empowered to do it. The "why" is empowering. When we know the "why," we're encouraged to keep practicing and learning and experimenting. There are reasons behind the "do" that are important for growth and progress.

So, considering this fact that a person can be BOTH insulin resistant and insulin sensitive at the same time, depending on which part of the body or which cells we're talking about, I will now turn my focus specifically to *hyperinsulinemia* – as the primary problem we are facing. In other words, as you will soon learn, the real problem isn't just that we need to be more sensitive to insulin. The bigger problem is there's no place for the excess glucose to go! To put it another way, in a person who is insulin resistant, having insulin available to push more and more glucose into the cells can't happen. Why?

Because the cell is already too full! What we're left with are two major challenges we need to fix. And as you probably guessed already, they are directly related to each other. I call these two challenges...

The "Cycle of Doom."

1. Cells are too full of overflowing glucose, so more insulin has little to no effect.
2. We're not accessing and using the glucose that is already there, hence why challenge #1 is a problem.

If you're not clear on what this means and how it works, keep reading. It will all make more sense soon. ☺ First, to learn more and discover what we can do to turn this problem around, I need to discuss *how our body stores energy and then uses it.*

A Two-Tiered Strategy: A Healthier Metabolism = A Healthier You

Earlier in this chapter, I told you when glucose is shuttled out of the bloodstream, it is sent into storage. In this section, I'll teach you where those storage sites are and why they matter for your health, body composition, and vitality, so you can age well and live a life free of chronic disease. After all, that's our goal, right? To accomplish these goals, we'll look at a two-tiered strategy to a healthy metabolism.[14]

1. **Tier #1** is enhancing our body's ability to burn more fat – not sugar - for energy.
2. **Tier #2** is using the stored sugar in muscles and liver so there is space for glucose to go, besides into fat cells.

Before I go on, just to review, let's remember our metabolism is simply all the chemical reactions that go on in our body that turn food into energy. Remember also the body has to store energy for use when you're not actually digesting or consuming food. This is normal since your body needs a constant supply of energy and needs to be able to access energy stores whenever necessary.

We have two forms of energy storage:

1. Body fat stored as deposits inside of fat cells, and
2. *Glycogen,* which is the storage form of sugar or carbohydrate. The storage sites for glycogen are in muscles and in the liver.

Also, you'll remember me telling you earlier that I was, at one time, ignorant to the importance of insulin and the many jobs it has in the body - UNTIL my running goals pulled me in the direction of needing to learn more. As I mentioned, my goal at that time was to see if I could extend endurance by burning more body fat as a fuel source for running.

And if you think about it, that makes sense, right? Because, in theory, if I (or any other person) could use stored body fat as a source of fuel for running or any activity, where there are almost limitless amounts available (more on this coming up), I could go further before becoming depleted and then feeling exhausted. **This is the tier #1 approach or strategy to a healthier metabolism.**

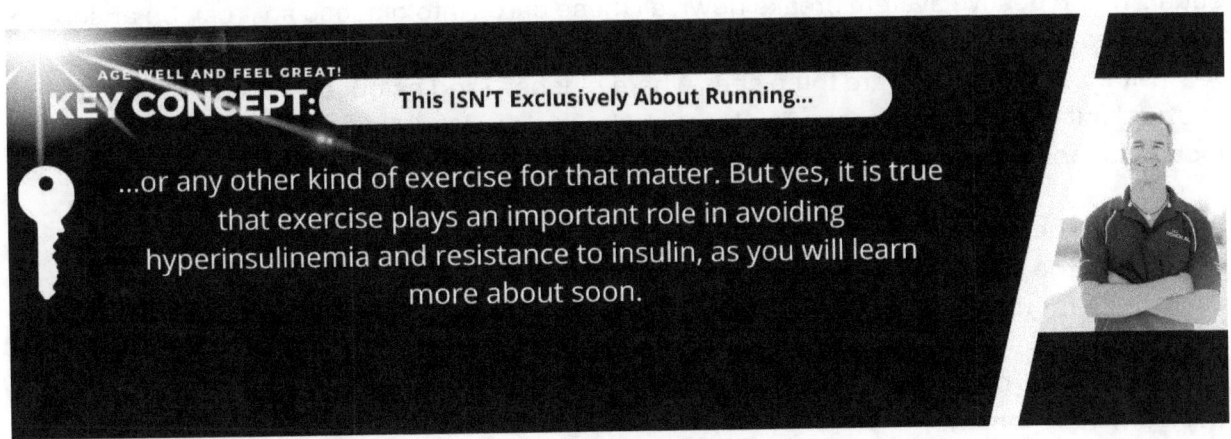

AGE WELL AND FEEL GREAT!

KEY CONCEPT: This ISN'T Exclusively About Running...

...or any other kind of exercise for that matter. But yes, it is true that exercise plays an important role in avoiding hyperinsulinemia and resistance to insulin, as you will learn more about soon.

As it turns out, this is true and exactly what happened for me as I experimented and learned through my own practice. And scientific studies have since validated everything I learned.

What I most need you to know, is this information is important for *any person*. I recommend you keep reading even if you've never run for fitness and never intend to, because what you are learning is important for every single human being.

In case you're wondering – I will discuss **tier #2** soon – it's as important for us to achieve our goals of a healthier metabolism and for optimal aging as is **tier #1**. Before we do that, though, let's back up for a moment to be sure we understand the basics. To do that, we'll go through a quick primer on carbohydrates, henceforth referred to as "carbs." We'll also look at where they're stored in the body, because understanding this is central to also understanding the Cycle of Doom I referred to earlier.

You could say our food supply has changed more in the last 100 years than it has in the last 10,000.

— Paul Grewal, M.D.

A Quick Primer on Carbohydrates: Storing Them and Using Them.

Carbohydrates (carbs), as you may know, are a type of macronutrient (along with fat and protein) found in foods. They're generally classified as simple or complex, depending on their chemical structure. Complex carbs are also called starches. These take a little longer to digest and result in less of a spike in blood sugar. Examples of "complex" carbs are beans and other legumes, most vegetables, fruits like berries and apples, and some grains.

"Simple" or refined carbs or sugars are those found in some fruits, juices, sodas, and many other processed foods. They usually result in a much quicker and higher spike of blood sugar. Your digestive system breaks down all these carbs into glucose so it can be absorbed through your bloodstream.

Inside our body, there are three sites where glucose (and calories) are stored, after being shuttled out of the bloodstream. The location determines *what* form of glucose is stored. The locations (once glucose is absorbed and digested) are:

- In the muscle, stored as muscle glycogen.
- In the liver, stored as liver glycogen.
- In fat cells, throughout the body, stored as, you guessed it, fat.

Perhaps not coincidently, this is also the actual order in which glucose is stored, as we will learn in a moment.

What Is Our Capacity for Storing Glycogen?

Remember glycogen is the storage form of glucose, or sugar, within the muscle and liver. And as you can imagine, we have the ability to store vastly more fat in our body - than we can store glycogen in muscles and the liver. While the exact amount varies, we might only be able to store 1500 to 2000 total calories of glycogen in both our muscles and liver.

What Is Our Capacity for Storing Fat?

In contrast, we have limitless capacity to store body fat! In fact, even a very lean man with a low percent of body fat might have 80,000 or more calories stored as fat. In other words, even the leanest among us have more than enough stored fat for any purpose.

What Fuel Source Gets Used First?

When your body needs energy – especially when it needs energy quickly – it goes first to circulating glucose in the bloodstream and stored glycogen in the muscles and liver. For example, when you're under stress and rushing to get to work, or when you're exercising intensely - running, jumping, and even when you're panicked.

Similarly, muscle glycogen and liver glycogen are where your body *deposits* glucose first. That's what happens when insulin shuttles it out of the cell. However, if those glycogen stores are FULL, the only thing that can happen is the liver turns the glucose into fat – more specifically *triglycerides* (a word used to describe fat in your bloodstream) – so it can then be deposited into fat cells. And we know, in contrast, there *is unlimited capacity* for your body to store glucose as fat, right? ☺ Obviously, we don't want this to happen, because that means we'll be getting fatter. And NO ONE wants that.

Age Well and Feel Great!
Key Concept:

This is NOT About Restricting Calories.

As you read through this chapter, you will notice I don't mention calories very much, nor is there much reference to a certain number of calories as being important to age well. Focusing only on calories won't produce the results you desire – it's outdated thinking! The message here isn't what you've likely heard and read in other places, to simply "eat less."

When you read something in this book about eating less frequently (be it time-restricted-eating, or intermittent fasting), I am NOT referring to caloric restriction. In actual practice, you will sometimes discover you are in fact, eating fewer calories. That's usually a byproduct of timing, not a specific intent to restrict calories.

What matters the most? It isn't how many calories you consume that matters the most, it's about the relationship between what you eat AND when, and the hormonal response to that.

Tier #2: What Does It Mean to Deplete Glycogen?

You may be asking at this point, why is this important for me to learn? What's the point? The point is this very important concept: *glycogen depletion*. This concept is powerful – this is **tier #2** of the strategy I introduced earlier. Depleting glycogen means you're getting rid of stored carbs. And in the process, you're creating more healthy storage capacity for the glucose being shuttled out of your bloodstream. This is exactly what you want to happen!

The problem is, for most people – especially those who are insulin resistant, it never happens to the degree that it needs to! In other words, *most people never actually tap deeply into those stored carbs in the muscle and liver.* To put it succinctly, most people never actually experience a meaningful level of glycogen depletion!

For that matter, the same holds true for accessing those nearly unlimited fat stores. Many people simply never tap into stored body fat to any measurable degree. Why not? Most people eat too often, resulting in ample supplies of glucose floating around in the bloodstream. After all, there's no reason for your body to go after those in storage, when it's readily available in the bloodstream, right?

The other very important reason is most aren't exercising or moving enough. When you exercise, particularly strength train, you create an energy deficit. That deficit means you're clearing out glucose and stored glycogen – again, exactly what you want. Also, any time you eat a food that results in a rise in blood glucose, making circulating blood glucose the preferred source of immediately available energy for your body, you negate any chance you have to access those fat stores. And, for the person who is even marginally insulin resistant, their body is also primarily relying on and using circulating blood glucose for energy, NOT the stored glycogen or stored body fat.

In most cases, it does come back to a person eating too often – usually snacking - or eating too many refined carbs. As a result, there's chronic secretion of insulin – resulting in both *hyperinsulinemia* and, you guessed it - *insulin resistance.*

One answer? **Eat less often.** That means avoid snacking, too. The idea is to change our behavior so we become more fat-adapted, and less reliant on sugar in the bloodstream. I'll talk more about how to approach this and to cut cravings and feel satisfied most of the time in the next chapter. Keep reading.

The other answer? **Get moving.** That can come from daily chores, exercise, and other fun activities that use up stored sugar and enable you to access stored bodyfat for energy. One little known fact which I will talk about more in the upcoming chapter on strength and resistance training is skeletal muscle is the largest single reservoir in the body for glycogen. When you contract that muscle, you increase the use of stored glycogen and help the transference of sugar out, so that more can be taken up out of the bloodstream. The benefit? You need less insulin to bring down blood sugar!

THIS is one important reason I always recommend leaving a 2-to-3-hour window of no-eating time between food consumption and when you start to exercise. This is a basic principle of "fueling" for every athlete I have ever coached.

In other words, do NOT take in any food or consume any calories up to 3 hours before starting to exercise. I adopted this philosophy many years ago and it has served me, and the people I have coached, very well. If you're worried you won't have enough energy to exercise and feel good doing it, don't be. Unless you're heading out for many hours, you have more than enough on board to get the job done.

Eating too close to exercise can result in an insulin spike that inhibits our ability to access free-fatty-acids and stored glycogen for energy. It can also disturb digestion and normal blood flow to working muscles during exercise. The effects of this are somewhat dependent on the intensity of the exercise, but as a rule, this holds true for any person.

Ironically, many people who hope to lose bodyfat and improve their endurance fitness sabotage their attempt to do so because they're eating too close to the start of exercise.

Age Well and Feel Great!
Key Concept:

Have You Ever Heard Of A Marathon Runner "Hitting the Wall"?

The term is common in marathoning circles for this reason: runners and walkers burn about 100 calories per mile, regardless of the speed. Assuming one has ~1500-2000 total calories stored as glycogen in the muscles and liver, doing the math confirms that stored glycogen will take the runner to only about the 20-mile mark.

The marathon distance is 26.2 miles. (100 calories per mile x 20 miles = 2000 calories). There's still another 6.2 miles (10k) the runner has to cover, but if they've run out of stored glycogen, chances are their pace will slow dramatically and they may even be forced to stop. Hence the term, "hitting the wall."

I personally experienced "hitting the wall" in my very first official marathon, the Marine Corp Marathon, in 1986. I was cruising along and on goal pace until I passed that dreaded 20-mile mark.

All of a sudden, it was like I had hit a wall. I started to stumble a little bit, felt lightheaded, and as a result, my pace understandably slowed. Fortunately, I was soon able to regroup and finished strong enough for an official finish time of 3:01:20. I would have undoubtedly finished even faster had I not hit that wall! 😊

An Analogy That May Help.

On episode #39 of Dr. Peter Attia's *The Drive* podcast[15], his guest, Dr. Jason Fung, M.D., talks about what is actually happening metabolically in instances such as I am describing. He shares this great analogy of packing a suit case for a trip. I transcribed Dr. Fung's description from the podcast to help you make sense of what can be a complex topic. It goes like this:

"Imagine you're packing a suitcase. The suitcase is getting full, but despite that, your wife (or significant other) tells you to put in more shirts. So, you do. But she keeps telling you to put more shirts in the suitcase. Finally, you say no more. There are three reasons why you finally said no more.

1. The suitcase won't open any more so you can't add more shirts.
2. The suitcase is too full to add more.

3. You decided to stop listening to her.

Whether you are willing to do what she says and add shirts, or you are defiant to her request to keep adding shirts, the outcome looks exactly the same; there are *excess shirts outside the suitcase.*

- In the case that you're being stubborn and not listening to your wife, this is just like excess insulin (in this case, the shirts) in the bloodstream being rammed into the cells (or in this case, the suitcase).

What's also happening, and this is key in understanding the implication of this analogy:

- The actual problem is there's no room for more shirts. Trying to force more shirts into the suitcase is not a solution to the problem."

The real solution is to get rid of the excess shirts in the suitcase. Or in the case of the cell, to *empty the cell of glucose.* So, there you have it. Now let's get to the specifics about what you can do to reverse the trend and create the healthiest metabolism imaginable!

What You Can and Must Do NOW.

Everything I have shared with you in this chapter has led us to this point. Are you ready to take some action? I hope so! If you want to normalize insulin levels and improve your metabolism and your overall health and increase your chances of living without chronic disease, you can do so. *It's up to you.*

There are three changes you MUST start to make now, and I've alluded to them frequently throughout this chapter. You'll read more about these in other chapters as well.

1. **Increase your physical activity,**
2. **Eat less sugar and processed foods, and**
3. **Eat less often.**

The gold is in these three changes. They will help you age better and feel and look better like nothing else you could possibly do! I'm going to teach you all you need to know about these essentials for healthy living in the next chapters. For now, let's wrap this with some basics so you're empowered to keep learning and are ready to take your metabolic health to the next level.

MOVE! The Addition of Exercise to Your Daily Routine is So Much More Important Than Simply Improving Your "Fitness."

Moving your body in whatever way you can – the more vigorously the better, will result in a lot of great things happening inside your body.

- For one, glucose gets pulled OUT of the bloodstream into the muscles without the aid of insulin. When you MOVE – when you do any kind of physical activity, you get the end result of clearing glucose from the blood without insulin having to do any of the work.
- For another, you create the open space, or "reservoir," for glucose to be pulled into the muscle. Muscle is, after all, the primary "eater" of glucose.
- As such, you've also created the opportunity for your muscle to pull free-fatty-acids (fat) directly into the muscle from the bloodstream!

In that earlier analogy of the suitcase and attempting to stuff it with more shirts, you hopefully created a picture in your mind's eye of what is actually happening at the cellular level in your body. Another analogy that might help is to think of the *gas tank* in your car or truck. You'll have to use your imagination just a little bit for this analogy to make sense.

Imagine your car's *gas tank* is akin to BOTH your body fat stores and muscle and liver glycogen stores. It is the storage location for gas for your vehicle after all, right? Now imagine that gas tank in your vehicle is nearly full because you're hardly ever driving anywhere. That's akin to eating lots of processed, refined carbs and eating them often, but not moving very much or exercising. When you aren't driving, you aren't using up the gas in your tank. What would happen if you went to the gas station often and kept trying to fill the tank, despite not driving very much. Before long, that tank is "full" and the gas is overflowing onto the ground and making a big mess of things.

The more often you go to the station to "fill up," the more the tank overflows. That's exactly what's happening when you eat often and don't move very much. You aren't creating any space for that glucose (or in the case of your car, the gasoline) to go! When you keep "topping off" the tank of circulating blood glucose, there's nowhere for the glucose to go except to be converted into triglycerides and then dumped into fat cells. Your body composition worsens. And you never actually experience glycogen *depletion*.

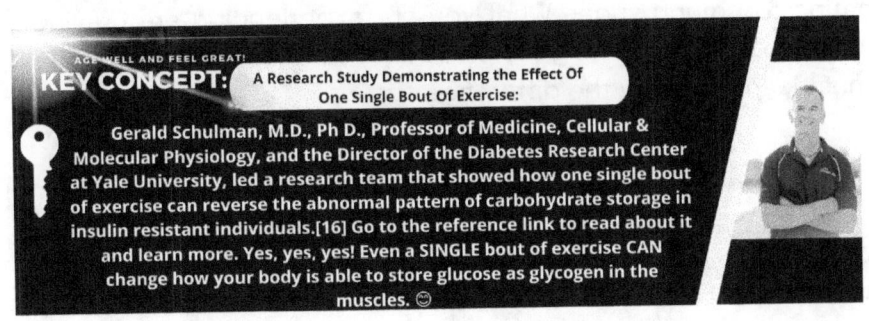

AGE WELL AND FEEL GREAT!

KEY CONCEPT: A Research Study Demonstrating the Effect Of One Single Bout Of Exercise:

Gerald Schulman, M.D., Ph D., Professor of Medicine, Cellular & Molecular Physiology, and the Director of the Diabetes Research Center at Yale University, led a research team that showed how one single bout of exercise can reverse the abnormal pattern of carbohydrate storage in insulin resistant individuals.[16] Go to the reference link to read about it and learn more. Yes, yes, yes! Even a SINGLE bout of exercise CAN change how your body is able to store glucose as glycogen in the muscles. ☺

If we could tap into those stores of glycogen in the muscles and liver more often, we'd create a positive "deficit" – glycogen depletion - that would allow more "space" for glucose to go.

- When you exercise at a slightly higher intensity, glycogen stores can be depleted faster, creating the positive deficit we desire. Many peer-reviewed well-designed scientific studies have shown this is the case not only immediately after the bout of exercise, but also over the longer term.[17] This is an "after-burn."
- When you eat less often, your body will use up more of that stored glycogen for energy, creating that positive deficit we desire.
- When you eat less refined, processed foods, and sugar, you end up with a lower insulin response and more normalized blood glucose.

As an aside, if you exercise for longer durations, you can create larger glycogen "deficits," and set up a more ideal scenario where you always have a place for glucose to be transported, rather than fat cells.

Eat. LESS. Sugar.

If there was only one change you could make right now, my advice would be to cut down on refined and processed sugar. Even better, eliminate it from your diet completely. When we come right down to it, there's nothing more harmful to our health than frequent feastings on refined sugar! Nothing.

What's the obvious stuff I'm talking about? Start with soda, fruit juices (which are just as harmful as soda), cookies, cakes, candy, and cereals. Honestly, refined processed sugars in these foods should scare you. Why? Because they're addictive. They stimulate the same areas of your brain as heroin and cocaine.

When you eat them frequently, you lose any control you might normally have. It's as though someone else is occupying your body and mind and making decisions FOR you. The more you eat, the more you want to eat! Once you've developed the "habit," it's very hard to break. This is happening to kids at an early age and as a result, we're seeing more of the negative impact society wide, earlier in life than ever before. Kids are insulin resistant at four or five years old!

If you're eating too much sugar, what you are experiencing are cravings. Cravings are nothing more than your body wanting more of the substance it's addicted to. Cravings aren't hunger! You must learn to know the difference.

Start Small: The Goal Is to Make That One Small Change - a New Daily Habit.

Like most things, the best path to success is not to bite off too much at one time or try to make too large a change all at once. So, if you want to succeed at cutting sugar down or out of your diet, the best approach is to start with something small. Make THAT one small change a habit you can repeat over and over.

Very often that small change to start with can happen in the grocery store. DON'T buy that sweet treat you're in the habit of buying. After all, if it's not on your shelves at home, you can't eat it, right? Especially late at night when you're least motivated to improve and change your habits. Consider if you're a moderator or an abstainer, remember?

A recently released article looking at the prevalence of insulin resistance in children and young adults demonstrated data collected between 1999 and 2018, showed among those aged 12 to 18, one in five are prediabetic![18] Approximately 1/3 of those diagnosed with prediabetes will progress to full-fledged diabetes within 1 year. That should scare you.

Start by cutting back on dessert to only once per week. In our society we think of dessert as a normal part of a meal, and sometimes as a reward. In reality, it's often just a punishment for your body and your health. Perhaps it is weaning yourself off the sugar you use in coffee, to sweeten the flavor. Try pure Stevia as a substitute to transition away from needing that sweetness.

And of course, if you have vending machines in the workplace, avoid them at all costs. The goal isn't to substitute one type of sweet for another one. The goal is to retrain your taste buds and palate to STOP craving sugar.

We're all familiar with the obvious names of many refined sugars, but the truth is it can and does hide behind many different names on ingredient lists, making it sometimes impossible to discover. For example, although "evaporated cane juice" might be easy enough to spot – what about "diastatic malt" or "panocha?" To learn more, check out Robert Lustig's book, *Sugar Has 56 Names – A Shoppers Guide,* and become an enlightened consumer.

Key Concept:

Here Is One Reason Our Skin Ages More Quickly...

We all know how soft and smooth a baby's skin is. Unfortunately, it doesn't stay that way, eventually looking more like beef jerky or an old baseball glove than the smooth and silky way it starts out. This is largely due to a chemical reaction known as glycation, which is simply the binding of proteins to sugar.[19]

It's what happens when you grill a burger and also what happens in your body when you habitually keep blood sugar levels above what the medical profession considers to be the normal fasting range (70 to 99 mg./dl). Once these blood sugar levels start to hover over 85 mg/dl – long enough, high enough, and often enough – glycation becomes a problem. In other words, you start to "cook" yourself; you start aging prematurely and your face takes on the appearance of an old baseball glove way earlier than it might otherwise. Not only does having perpetual high blood sugar cause you to slow-cook yourself, externally and internally, it also leads to a host of metabolic problems, including insulin resistance and obesity.

What can you do to reduce the incidence of glycation? Follow the advice in this chapter and also in the chapter on Time Restricted Eating. In other words, optimize insulin sensitivity and keep resting blood glucose as low as possible.

Think about this: thousands of years ago, our ancestors didn't have constant access to easily accessible food loaded with added sugars, all of which create more cravings. They'd have to forage – and hunt for food. It wouldn't be uncommon for a human to go many hours without eating. Contrast that with present day, where we are exposed to constant messages everywhere we go, and everywhere we look, to eat, eat, eat! Where a convenience store, loaded with pre-packaged foods laden with sugar is never more than a few minutes or miles away. No matter where we are.

Do Insulin Resistance and Hyperinsulinemia Play a Prominent Role in Other Diseases?

My personal belief is, yes, the supporting data and scientific evidence is strong in establishing clear connections between these conditions and other often fatal chronic diseases. All one need do is take the time to examine the evidence objectively. That being said, as mentioned, I'm not a doctor nor am I a laboratory scientist. So, I won't pretend to have first-hand knowledge of how all the mechanisms of disease work. That would be silly, and likely damage my credibility.

Thus, what follows is a summary of ideas and opinions along with many references to other materials, books, and studies, for your continued learning. Because the research into these diseases and their causes is happening at break-neck speed, I have no doubt as soon as this book is published, the list of references will likely become somewhat outdated. At the same time, the work that has been done to this point does help us understand these connections. My hope is you'll be inspired to learn more, and you will follow the advice I present so you can experience the positive effects for yourself, firsthand!

Much like the ancient riddle, "which came first, the chicken or the egg?", the question that's often asked is this: Are *hyperinsulinemia* and *insulin resistance* merely symptoms of obesity, heart disease, cancer, and other diseases, or are they important leading causes of those diseases? I invite you to keep reading, learning, and being curious. You'll then be able to decide for yourself. Onward we go!

Insulin Resistance, Hyperinsulinemia and Heart Disease:

The term "heart disease" refers to a variety of different but related ailments of the cardiovascular system such as high blood pressure (also known as hypertension), and also disorders such as stroke, vessel plaque, and even thickening of the heart muscle and its walls.

In his book, *Diabetes Epidemic and You*, author Dr. Robert Kraft, in discussing the origination and pathology of this disease, says "investigations and research in the 1970s identified increased insulin (hyperinsulinemia) as the primary cause affecting all arterial vessels including capillaries. They accounted for the microangiopathy of the retina, the neurotology of the central and peripheral nervous system, and the arteriosclerosis of all major and minor arteries."[20]

In his book, *Why We Get Sick*, author Benjamin Bikman, Ph.D., describes in detail in Chapter 2, the relationship between insulin resistance and hypertension/high blood pressure and many other heart ailments. To learn more, read this book!

Insulin Resistance, Hyperinsulinemia, and Inflammation:

When you hear the word inflammation, a few different things might come to mind. Had you recently twisted your ankle and watched it swell up, you'd be thinking about that *acute* inflammatory response that led to the increasing fluid buildup in your ankle. And very likely, the subsequent increasing degree of pain you experienced. The message here is that acute inflammation is how your body fights infections and helps speed up the healing process.

On the other side of the spectrum, if you've spent any time reading or learning about some of the hallmarks of aging – the things we all assume are natural byproducts of getting older – you might think of the word a little differently. When we think of aging, it's the often hidden, *chronic* inflammation throughout the body we're most concerned about.

According to Dr. Robert H. Shmerling, M.D., medical editor of *Understanding Inflammation* from Harvard Health Publishing, and an associate professor of medicine at Harvard Medical School, "when inflammation gets turned up too high and lingers for a long time and the immune system continues to pump out white blood cells and chemical messengers that prolong the process, that's known as *chronic* inflammation. From the body's perspective, it's under consistent attack, so the immune system keeps fighting indefinitely."[21]

So, acute inflammation is a necessary part of how our immune systems function. Chronic on the other hand, has been linked with a whole host of diseases and among other things, is surely very tightly connected with insulin resistance, cardiovascular health, and cholesterol levels. I'm going to share more details with you about chronic inflammation in an upcoming chapter, but I did want to briefly discuss its connection to insulin resistance and hyperinsulinemia. The science is becoming clearer each day as old myths are put out to pasture and new discoveries are heralded.

When it comes to cardiovascular disease, serum (blood) cholesterol levels, insulin resistance and chronic inflammation, let me say I am now very skeptical about the dangers of that elevated LDL-C cholesterol (typically referred to as the "bad" kind). In other words, I don't believe it is the culprit or driver of inflammation or a huge factor in cardiovascular disease that was once believed. I'll share more about this in an upcoming chapter when I do a short but deep dive into cholesterol – what we once believed and what I've learned most recently. The point I want to share is, as I alluded to a moment ago: The data does confirm that at the very least, chronic inflammation and the markers we use to measure it inside the body, more accurately predict cardiovascular disease than does cholesterol level.[22] Here's the kicker: "Whereas insulin elicits anti-inflammatory actions in an **insulin-sensitive** person (with normal levels of insulin), insulin activates inflammation in **insulin-resistant** people with high levels of insulin."[23]

If you think about it, it almost seems counterintuitive, but it speaks to the power of insulin and the importance of being more insulin *sensitive*. What this means is insulin resistance is at least a partial CAUSE of chronic inflammation, not just a factor associated with it.

Understanding this is so important when it comes to your health. Practically speaking, what I am saying is, <u>YOU need to pay much more attention to insulin sensitivity and chronic inflammation, than you do your cholesterol levels.</u>

I'll wrap this section with a great bit of information from author Benjamin Bikman, Ph.D.: "Implicating insulin resistance as a cause of inflammation places insulin resistance at ground zero for heart disease – it's waging war on the blood vessels by doing everything to promote atherosclerosis. First, insulin resistance increases blood pressure, increasing the likelihood of blood vessel damage. Next, it increases lipid deposition in the blood vessel walls. Finally, insulin resistance increases inflammation, promoting the ongoing infiltration of the blood vessel with macrophages, which become increasingly laden with oxidized lipids, changing into foam cells." The end result of this insidious cascade? The increasing buildup of atherosclerotic plaque. Just like that, you've now got heart disease.[24]

Insulin Resistance, Hyperinsulinemia and Cancer:

We would all agree cancer is an absolutely devastating disease that often causes unspeakable emotional and physical pain and suffering. Unfortunately, experts think it will soon overtake heart disease as the leading killer of people in developed countries. The origins of cancer are complex. There is too much we still don't know. The body, and disease, are often a mystery. There continues to be so many different points of view in the medical and scientific community about how normal cells become cancerous, and then how those cancerous cells grow and spread.

Despite the things we don't know, there is much we do. And so, we must move forward with the information we have access to and act in the best way we can. Which leads me to this basic question: are most cancers that afflict us as we get older, simply diseases of aging itself that almost all of us can expect to face as we reach "old age"? Also, are the origins of most cancers primarily genetic, where family history plays a more important role, or are there other equally important factors such as lifestyle or environment (both inside and outside the body), that make an individual more likely to have cancer?

As it relates to the discussion of *insulin resistance* and *hyperinsulinemia*, are there specific lifestyle factors like diet and exercise and sleep and stress, that contribute to increasing or decreasing our risk for cancer? To me, these are some of the million-dollar questions that still need definitive answers. The thing is, while we may not have the definitive answers yet, we do know much more now than we did even as little as a year ago.

To examine a potential connection between aging itself and cancer and other diseases, I'll refer to one researcher in the field of aging, well-known author and Harvard professor, Dr. David Sinclair, who says there are unequivocally "hallmarks of aging that lead to disease," such as "unspooling of genes and DNA," which he identifies as one fundamental cause of aging. As you learned a little bit about in Chapter 2, he argues that this unspooling alters the "clocks" that determine cell function.[25] Most importantly, from the standpoint of the questions I'm asking here, is his belief that this is the root cause of *not just aging*, but of *most diseases*.[26]

Along with this is his belief our healthcare system unfortunately focuses on the end stages of this process. And very often too late – essentially "putting a band aid on the problem." I happen to agree. In fact, this is one of my biggest concerns with our entire healthcare system, which I've already told you I think of as a *sick-care* system.

Think about it. It's a system that is quite good at treating *individual* diseases once they've been diagnosed, but not nearly as good at helping to prevent them from occurring in the first place. As Sinclair puts it, it's "whack-a-mole" medicine - addressing one specific disease, he says, "ignores the rest of the body."[27] For example, a person who has been diagnosed with lung cancer might successfully be able to recover from that specific disease with chemotherapy and radiation, but what about the damage that may have been done to the rest of the body by the treatment itself? What about the idea that the rest of the body has largely been ignored through this process, and continues to age at the same rate? In

Sinclair's opinion, his research and that of other similar experts in the field shows that, in fact, the "same process occurs for ALL diseases."

What's that process? Again, as you learned in Chapter 2, he calls it "ex-differentiation," which is "unspooling of the DNA," or "cellular confusion – cells becoming more of a generalized cell type vs. a specific cell type." So, we really are back to that ancient riddle again, aren't we? Is it the chicken or the egg? In other words, what are the origins of cancer, and are there important lifestyle factors at play such as diet and exercise, that impact insulin resistance?

The link between cancer and lifestyle is becoming clearer and easier to see as we learn more about the true nature of this disease. But what about the more specific question of insulin resistance, hyperinsulinemia, and cancer? A good case can be made it all comes back to our *metabolism*.

Remember earlier in this chapter, I presented a two-tiered strategy for a healthier *metabolism*, where I discussed how we can enhance <u>how glycogen is deposited in the liver and muscles and how body fat is accessed for energy</u>. Could there be a connection between our metabolism – how cells produce and use energy – and cancer? There are experts in the field of cancer research that believe this is the case – that the root cause of many cancers are metabolic in nature. If this is true, it would be related to the role that insulin plays within the cell.

To learn much more about this particular metabolic theory of cancer pathology, we need to look at the work of Boston College professor, Dr. Thomas Seyfried, M.D., who says "emerging evidence indicates *impaired cellular energy metabolism* is the defining characteristic of nearly all cancers regardless of cellular or tissue origin." He contrasts this with normal cells, which derive energy differently. His hypothesis is that a "view of cancer as primarily a metabolic disease will impact approaches to cancer management and prevention."[28]

While the jury is still out about whether cancer is metabolic in nature, there's much to see here. There's a very good chance we'll see the case made for cancer having a strong connection to how cells use and get energy become stronger as time goes on. As it turns out, a lot of other experts in the field agree. And it makes sense, doesn't it? After all, cancer cells need energy to multiply. And "cancer cells often have more insulin receptors."[29]

How do they get the energy they need to grow so quickly? In my opinion, this is where the action of insulin and the amount of insulin at any one time, plays a role. To learn more, we can look at a recently published book, *Ravenous: Otto Warburg, the Nazis, and the Search for the Cancer-Diet Connection*, where author Sam Apple closely examines the insulin-cancer connection. He says, "by the 1980s, scientists already knew that many tumors have an unusually large number of insulin receptors and that insulin, a growth factor, causes both healthy and cancerous cells to multiply."[30]

He goes on to highlight that many other researchers in the field have also looked at the insulin/cancer connection. He says "in 1995, Harvard professor Edward Giovannucci, found that people diagnosed with colon cancer also tended to have high insulin. Giovannucci was soon followed by Rudolf Kaaks, who published a ground breaking paper titled *Nutrition, Hormones, and Breast Cancer: Is Insulin the Missing Link?* He goes on to say "it wasn't just breast and colon cancer. Each year seemed to bring evidence of yet another cancer that could be connected to insulin. The list includes cancer of the pancreas, uterus, kidney, esophagus, and prostate. People who have high insulin when they are diagnosed with cancer also tend to have worse outcomes."[31]

We can also look at the work of another well-known cancer researcher, Cornell University Professor of Cancer Biology in Medicine, Dr. Lewis Cantley, M.D., who Sam Apple interviewed for his book. Dr. Cantley offers additional insights into the insulin/cancer connection, by explaining that "elevated insulin seems to be especially hazardous to the epithelial cells that form a protective layer around our organs. Under normal circumstances," Dr. Cantley explained, many such epithelial cells "rarely see insulin." But when hyperinsulinemia (the condition of continuously elevated insulin) sets in, the situation is very different. Someone with hyperinsulinemia might have "50 times more insulin" than normal circulating in the blood all day and night."[32] That last statement is, in my opinion, fascinating, and shows the clear indication there's a strong connection deserving further investigation.

Another well-known expert, researcher Gerald Schulman, M.D., Ph D., Professor of Medicine, Cellular & Molecular Physiology, and the Director of the Diabetes Research Center at Yale, said in his interview on *The Drive* podcast with Dr. Peter Attia, M.D., "if we can understand insulin resistance, then that's going to be the best way to fix diabetes, heart disease, fatty liver disease, and slow down cancers."[33] Dr. Schulman goes on to state "insulin resistance is driving the huge increase in cancers which are associated with obesity, such as breast, colon, pancreatic, and liver cancers and that there is strong preclinical evidence for this in animals. Insulin resistance is not necessarily causing the cancer but is promoting its growth."[34]

To summarize, regardless of whether you believe cancer is a metabolic disease or not, there's no debate about the direct connection between insulin and cancer. What's more, there is also no debate that even when a person is declared cancer free, they will still need to manage the disease for the remainder of their life. And that is again, in my opinion, where their ability to avoid becoming insulin resistant or being able to reduce hyperinsulinemia can be so vital to remain cancer free.

The connection is clear: maintaining normal insulin levels and optimizing metabolism through a smart approach to eating and exercise has a direct effect on remaining cancer free and living a healthier, happier life. I could go on and on. To learn more, I highly recommend Sam Apple's book, *Ravenous*. Read it!

Insulin Resistance, Hyperinsulinemia and Hearing Loss:

We know there will be some degree of hearing loss as we get older. There are many studies which have shown a direct connection between insulin resistance and hearing loss. Losing hearing OR eyesight for that matter, is something we all fear as we age. Certainly, for those where insulin resistance has progressed to type-2 diabetes, there are conditions such as diabetic retinopathy, glaucoma, and cataracts, that can cause vision loss and even blindness.

In his book *Why We Get Sick*, which I referenced earlier, author Dr. Bikman provides numerous links to published, peer-reviewed studies connecting Meniere's disease and insulin resistance. Meniere's disease is a disorder of the inner ear that causes severe dizziness (vertigo), ringing in the ears (tinnitus), hearing loss, and a feeling of fullness or congestion in the ear. Meniere's disease usually affects only one ear. Dr. Biman states "the connection between Meniere's disease and insulin resistance is strong. One study found that 76% of patients with Meniere's disease were also insulin resistant. Other data reveal that up to 92% of people with tinnitus have hyperinsulinemia."[35] Additionally, he says "the most common – and most overlooked – cause of vertigo is a disorder of glucose metabolism."[36]

Insulin Resistance, Hyperinsulinemia and Muscle Loss:

One of the most well-known and infamous signs of getting older is the gradual deterioration of our muscle mass, referred to as *sarcopenia*. We have to fight this with all the energy we can muster, because there's a direct link between the amount of lost muscle and our ability to function normally and enjoy life as we age. I will discuss this in much more detail in the chapters on movement and exercise.

Studies do show in people with insulin resistance, there is a higher degree of protein breakdown and muscle loss that goes beyond that which is considered normal. One study, published in February 2020, showed "skeletal muscle mass is an important factor in glucose and energy homeostasis and is positively correlated with insulin muscle sensitivity.[37] This means the more muscle you have, the greater the likelihood your muscle cells will be more sensitive to insulin, which is a good thing!

Other studies have shown "increased muscle mass increases skeletal muscle glucose uptake and improves insulin sensitivity. *Sarcopenia* can cause skeletal muscle mass and strength to decrease, thereby reducing skeletal muscle insulin sensitivity."[38] Bottom line: If you're insulin resistant, you'll have a harder time taking up glucose into storage sites and also maintaining muscle or trying to increase it and improve.

Insulin Resistance, Hyperinsulinemia and Fibromyalgia:

According to author Benjamin Bikman, Ph.D., there are very recent findings that suggest "insulin resistance could be a (direct) cause of Fibromyalgia."[39] In his book, he references a published report titled "Is Insulin Resistance the Cause of Fibromyalgia: A Preliminary Report." The report states that "people with this condition are much more likely to struggle with insulin and glucose control."[40] And this makes sense, doesn't it? After all, we're fundamentally talking about a condition that is about energy, being able to have more of it and having that energy we're feeling be on a more even keel.

Insulin Resistance, Hyperinsulinemia and Non-Alcoholic Fatty Liver Disease (NAFLD):

Of all the many chronic diseases that are metabolic in nature, few are increasing at a faster rate than is fatty liver, which is one form of NAFLD. I'm guessing that fact is coming as a bit of a surprise to many who are reading this. After all, many people haven't even heard of this disease which is, ironically, not directly associated with alcoholism but is in many ways, destroying our livers and dramatically increasing the odds of early death.

I think that's shocking when you consider the fact this disease was practically unheard of 30 years ago and, according to experts, has become the most common liver disorder in western countries.[41] What is it? It is simply fat that accumulates in the liver. And along with it, untold amounts of inflammation – a hallmark of virtually all chronic diseases.

The results of a study to look at the relationship between insulin resistance and liver fat was just completed in April 2022. It was funded by the National Institutes for Health and conducted by researchers at Yale University as well as other universities, led by Dr. Kit Petersen, MD, a professor of medicine at Yale who, among other things, has spent the last 20 years of her career studying young, lean people with insulin resistance.[42] The researchers stated they've been able to "redefine a key metric for diagnosing non-alcoholic fatty liver (NAFL) in young, lean, healthy people. Too much liver fat can lead to insulin resistance, type 2 diabetes, hepatic steatohepatitis (NASH), and cirrhosis, as well as an increased risk of cardiovascular disease.[43] What was their main takeaway from this study?

"The day they didn't have any more liver fat, their blood sugars were normal, they were not insulin resistant, and their diabetes was gone." Petersen said. Just one more piece of evidence that reducing the amount of fat which builds up inside the liver is critical to reduce disease risks.

What's its prevalence? According to recent statistics, 25% of the global community has it and as of 2015, more than 80 million Americans have it![44] There seems to be a disproportionate number of Hispanics with NAFLD. According to experts, NAFLD has become the most common cause of chronic liver disease worldwide and will soon become one of the leading causes of cirrhosis. Additionally, it's believed if it isn't already, it will soon be the leading reason for liver transplant in the U.S.[45]

One thing that is especially frightening about this disease is its connection to fructose, a type of sugar that is similar to alcohol in how it's metabolized by the liver. High fructose corn syrup (as well as other forms of fructose) is one of the most common ingredients in many processed foods and a major contributor to metabolic disease, in my opinion and in the opinion of many experts.

One recommendation I'll make right now: if you're drinking fruit juice of any kind, reduce your consumption of it or even stop all together. You don't need it. As a society, we're consuming more of it now than ever before and it's a major contributor to all the problems that have been discussed in this chapter. The evidence is clear: there's an undeniable link between all these conditions. And our health is suffering for it!

Insulin Resistance, Hyperinsulinemia and Obesity:

All the evidence we now have confirms being overweight and obesity are clearly linked to insulin resistance and hyperinsulinemia. In my opinion, the reasons are fairly obvious and they're twofold:

1. When you have elevated insulin levels and are becoming increasingly insensitive to that insulin, combined with...
2. Having no (or limited) places for circulating glucose to be deposited in muscles and liver (because glycogen storage is already full), there's no other choice but for the liver to turn that glucose into triglycerides and deposit it into fat cells.

This is a twofold problem I've delved into in detail in this chapter. That being said, most experts would agree the connections between obesity and insulin resistance are complex. And not always simply explained. The reason? Just as I alluded to in the introduction to this section, it comes back to the ancient riddle of the chicken or the egg – which came first? In other words, is hyperinsulinemia a symptom of obesity and being overweight, or is it an important leading cause? We know there is much more to learn. We don't have all the answers.

But I certainly feel confident saying the prevalence of being overweight and obesity in the U.S. and worldwide is skyrocketing! That is obvious! That increase parallels our increasing intake of processed, sugar-laden convenience foods that have been shown to also increase the chances of being *hyper insulinemic* and *insulin resistant*.

To learn more, read Dr. Bikman's book, *Why We Get Sick*. Also, there are many other very good books on this topic, including Gary Taube's *Good calories, Bad Calories*, Dr. Jason Fung's *The Obesity Code*, and Dr. David Ludwig's *Always Hungry*.

Insulin Resistance, Hyperinsulinemia and Dementia, Alzheimer's, and Other Neurodegenerative Diseases:

Dementia is a broad term that describes changes in memory and other cognitive functions. There are many types of dementia and many clear causes, with Alzheimer's being perhaps the most well-known. I have found through my study there are many experts in the field of geriatric research, aging, and neurodegenerative diseases, that believe *metabolic dysfunction*, which certainly describes what insulin resistance and hyperinsulinemia are, is at the root of these diseases.

In an article published in 2012 in the journal *Research Rejuvenation*, the idea that Alzheimer's might even be called Type-3 diabetes was put forth. The author's abstract reads: "Alzheimer's disease (AD) and metabolic syndrome are two highly prevalent pathological conditions of Western society due to incorrect diet, lifestyle, and vascular risk factors. Recent data have suggested metabolic syndrome as an independent risk factor for AD and pre-AD syndrome. Furthermore, biological plausibility for this relationship has been framed within the *metabolic cognitive syndrome* concept. Due to the increasing aging of populations, prevalence of AD in Western industrialized countries will rise in the near future."[46]

With regard to Parkinson's Disease, insulin is known to alter dopamine in the brain which, according to author Benjamin Bikman, Ph.D., "provides a direct causal relationship between insulin and Parkinson's."[47] He goes on to point out "regardless of the factors directly linking insulin with Parkinson's disease, a clear association exists."[48]

A 2012 study and article also referenced in Dr. Bikman's book, said "up to 30% of patients with Parkinson's disease have type 2 diabetes, with possibly up to 80% having insulin resistance (or prediabetes)."[49] The bottom line: In many ways, the research and understanding of these diseases is in its infancy. That being said, we can see a clear relationship if we are honest and looking objectively. As mentioned, there is much more to learn!

For more information about Alzheimer's, check out Dr. Peter Attia's *The Drive* podcast, episode #164, where he hosts Amanda Smith, M.D.. The title is *"Diagnosing, Preventing, and Treating Alzheimer's Disease, and What We Can All Learn from Patients with Dementia."*[50] It's a fascinating conversation!

Insulin Resistance, Hyperinsulinemia and Menopause:

Let's face it, if you're a woman that's gone through or is going through menopause, which is that plethora of changes marking the end of a woman's reproductive years, you've no doubt experienced firsthand how unpleasant many of these changes can be. Naturally, I haven't experienced these but I live with someone who has. ☺ Things like hot flashes, night sweats, and a host of other physical changes, often make life even more challenging than it already is.

Menopause is marked by the changing levels and loss of female hormones, estrogen, and progesterone. There's strong evidence in the literature that estrogens are extremely important in a woman's metabolic function and ability to maintain an even-keeled blood glucose, so it stands to reason women that have gone through menopause have a greater risk of ultimately becoming insulin resistant. One study I learned about through my own investigation, looking at an individual's inability to produce estrogen due to a deficiency in aromatase, gives a clue about what may be happening.[51]

Also, according to many experts, "women with the metabolic syndrome (which includes but isn't limited to obesity, insulin resistance, and dyslipidemia) are known to be at especially high risk for cardiovascular disease (CVD). The prevalence of the metabolic syndrome increases with menopause and may partially explain the apparent acceleration in CVD after menopause."[52] My advice, understand the challenges you may be facing as the years go on, and as always, speak with your doctor to learn more, or if you have additional questions.

Lower testosterone levels in aging men seem to have a similar effect, which doesn't surprise me because in some ways, reduced testosterone in men is similar to menopause in women. Numerous studies have linked lower testosterone and increased insulin insensitivity and hyperinsulinemia in aging men.[53] To me, this is simply one more example that as the years go on, our "margin of error" shrinks. Which, I guess, is the definition of aging.

The key is to start as early as possible with consistent and smart eating and exercise habits that reduce the risks and stay on course as the years pile on. It's not always easy, but it is worth it.

Insulin Resistance and Japanese "Blue Zone" Eating Habits:

In Chapter 5, you read about some mainstays of a healthy life and the living habits of the "Blue Zone" region of Okinawa. One of the habits that was mentioned and is a big part of life there is the concept of *Hara Hachi Bu*, which translated means to eat until you are 8 parts (out of 10) full. In Japan, stopping before you are full is a sign of self-control and seen as a highly regarded character trait. This is in stark contrast to the U.S., where NOT cleaning your plate, especially if you're a man, is a sign of suspect virility.

There's another centuries old tradition in Japan called "kaiseki," and while it has various manifestations, it essentially involves starting with some light soup or broth, followed by a vegetable dish and then a protein dish, and concluded with a rice dish. [54] This "one soup, three sides" concept isn't just arbitrary, though. The soup or broth sets the tone of the meal. You start off slowly and patiently with a gut-friendly dish. It would also stifle any ravenous hunger you may be experiencing so you won't wolf down the rest of the meal. Vegetables come next because of their fiber content; they help your body start to feel full and allow you to embrace the concept of *Hari Hachi Bu*. Protein and fat come next, and then, when you are close to being 8/10ths full, comes the invariably small portion of carbs.

This style of eating makes sense but it's also got some real science to back it up. A scientific study done in 2017 demonstrated eating the protein and vegetable components (the patty, lettuce, and tomato) of a hamburger 10 minutes before eating the carbohydrate portion (the bun) led to far lower elevations of post-meal glucose and insulin levels.[55] Given that eating a hamburger that way isn't realistic, the researchers conducted another "nutrient order" study, this time using a more realistic eating pattern.

They rounded up 16 subjects with type 2 diabetes. On three separate days, one week apart, after a 12-hour fast, all 16 subjects ate meals with the exact same calorie and carb/protein/fat content. The three meals were based on the following conditions:

1. Participants ate carbs first (ciabatta bread and orange juice) over a 10-minute period. They then rested 10-minutes before eating protein (skinless chicken breast) and vegetables (lettuce, tomato, and cucumber with Italian vinaigrette), again over a 10-minute period.

2. Participants ate protein and vegetables first over a 10-minute period, followed by a 10-minute rest period, then finished with the carbs (bread and orange juice), again eaten over a 10-minute period.

3. Participants ate only vegetables first. Again, they got 10 minutes to finish the first course. They then took a 10-minute rest, followed by protein and carbs eaten over a 10-minute period.

All study participants had blood drawn just before mealtime and at 30-minute intervals up to three hours after the start of the meal. So, what did they find? Eating the carbs last reduced the insulin response! In effect, it had the same effect as do two popular diabetes drugs, acarbose and nateglinide, we can assume are prescribed for the same purpose. The researchers figured that reduced insulin response had to do with "delayed gastric emptying." More precisely, the fiber in the vegetables acted to slow the speed of the various chemical reactions, somewhat like control rods do in a nuclear reactor.

As you've learned, a muted insulin response is not only important for diabetics to keep insulin/blood sugar levels from spiking too high after meals, it's also really healthy for everyone else. As an aside, the researchers also found eating carbs last reduced *ghrelin*, the hunger hormone, thereby suggesting that a kaiseki style, carbs-last meal might make you eat less when the next meal rolls around.

So, what's the take home message from all of this? Clearly, eating the bun last isn't going to work if you're enjoying a hamburger. ☺ However, what you can do is simply consider eating most of the carbohydrate rich foods in any meal last. For example, having a baked potato along with your steak? Eat the steak first, then the potato. Do you typically enjoy bread prior to your main meal, something that is a tradition in restaurant eating? More often, see if you can hold off on the bread until you've eaten some protein and fat. One thing we can safely assume, eating that salad as the first course is a really good idea. Soup or broth is optional. ☺

Some Personal Reflections on How We Got Here and What We Can Do About It:

How did we get ourselves into this situation, where I would sit down to write a book about aging well and feel compelled to include an entire section on *insulin resistance* and *hyperinsulinemia*? More to the point, how on earth did we reach a point where more than half of all Americans are overweight, and potentially pre-diabetic and insulin resistant? Looking back on the years I've tried to answer these questions for myself, I shake my head. If I had to simplify the reasons and was forced to choose only two, I'd say it boils down to these two factors:

1. Government mandates, and
2. Industrialized food. Or as I like to call them, "BIG FOOD."

In 1977, the U.S. Senate Select Committee on Nutrition and Human Needs, under the chairmanship of Senator George McGovern, issued the first set of dietary guidelines that fundamentally changed our attitude about what we should eat. What were the recommendations of this committee? I quote: "To avoid overweight, consume only as much energy as is expended; if overweight, decrease energy intake and increase energy expenditure. Increase the consumption of complex carbohydrates and "naturally occurring" sugars from about 28 percent of intake to about 48 percent of energy intake." The report also recommended Americans eat less fat and less cholesterol. Wow, what bad advice!

These guidelines, which are rumored to have been written by a young intern with no formal education in nutritional science, made carbohydrates a "health food" and demonized fat, producing what we call *lipophobia* – the fear of dietary fat. In a nutshell, the government mandated we get the fat out of food, and the food industry responded by pouring more sugar in. The result has been a perfect storm, disastrously altering our biochemistry and driving our eating habits out of our control.

Know this: Despite what you may have read in the past or heard from so-called "experts" or may have believed yourself, **the fat from food ISN'T the culprit in our epidemic of chronic disease.** Fat that comes from healthy foods such as the saturated fat from red meat or the monounsaturated fat from Olive Oil - DOES NOT make you fat. And there's zero evidence, in well done published, peer-reviewed scientific studies, connecting it directly to the diseases that are killing us. On the contrary, what we've learned is it's dietary sugar, especially ultra-refined sugars from processed foods, that is the culprit.

For what it's worth, looking back it is clear corporate profits are what drove the decisions that were made in Washington. In fact, a few years earlier, in 1971, the Secretary of Agriculture, Earl Butz, orchestrated a major change in agricultural policy, establishing his goal of bringing down the price of food. Butz decided the solution was to industrialize the production of corn with the use of massive subsidies to farmers. This drove down the price of corn and in the process, increased its use in processed foods, making it more available everywhere, irreversibly changing what we have eaten since then. Within 5 years of the widespread adoption of these guidelines, rates of diabetes and obesity increased exponentially. It's estimated obesity rates went from 15% in the early 1970s, to nearly 40% by the time the decade had ended. The other complicit partner in this?

Of course, it's industrialized food – the large food manufacturing companies that make up the food industry. You heard me refer to them in another chapter of this book as the "enemy." Look around you. Fast food restaurants pop up every day. On every street corner and in the most populated towns and cities, they're ready to suck you in with what is truly biologically addictive food.

Whether you realize it or not, the food industry uses scientific research and massive, data-supported marketing ploys aimed at getting all Americans - yes, you, me, everyone - addicted to highly processed, no-nutritive-value, junk food brimming with salt, fat, and chemicals. Processed foods are addictive – every bit as much as tobacco, alcohol, and drugs.

As I mentioned earlier (my apologies for the redundancy), food manufacturers know how to create that perfect mouthfeel, that perfect brain hook, referred to as a "bliss-point" of food. These foods change our brain chemistry and hormones in a way that affects our ability to control our own behavior. So how do different foods impact brain chemistry, you ask?

1. **It can change gene expression**. Yes, the food you eat can literally turn genes on and off. If you eat broccoli, you can turn on genes that detoxify by way of a compound called glutathione. If you drink green tea, you increase the level of catechins, which can detoxify heavy metals and activate various enzymes. If you eat the right foods,

you can balance your hormones. If you eat the wrong foods, you can throw hormones completely out of whack. See insulin as one example!

2. **It can hijack your mood,** making you anxious or the reverse, making you calm and peaceful. Food dramatically impacts mood!

3. **It can change your microbiome**. You have trillions of bacteria in your gut that control almost every function in your body – and when you eat the wrong foods, you grow the bad bacteria that make you sick – when you eat the right foods, you grow the good bacteria that improve your health.

Of all the recommendations I offer in this book, none of them will come at you as strongly as will this: **Avoid "fast" ultra-processed foods as much as possible.** The less you eat them, the less you'll want them. Soon, you'll begin to learn what you thought was actual hunger, was just cravings.

Does a food have an ingredients list? If it does, try to avoid it. And if you do consume something with an ingredients list, read it. *The longer the list, the greater the risk*. In the end, it's simple to know what to eat most of the time: Leave the food that man made, eat the food that God made.

In Summary:

In this chapter, I've probably gone into much greater detail than you may have wanted or expected. After all, I promised earlier to be brief and not overload you with information. I'd say I failed in that regard, but for good reason. ☺ Despite sharing many interesting aspects of both *hyperinsulinemia* and *insulin resistance*, I've really only touched on some basics. And there are certainly some important things I've very likely missed. There is so much more to cover that goes beyond the scope of this book. We've really just begun to learn.

Similarly, we've scarcely touched on some of the reasons a few of the many chronic diseases I've argued are killing us, such as heart disease, type 2 diabetes, obesity, stroke, cancer, and Alzheimer's disease and other dementias, could very possibly be thought of as *metabolic diseases*. That is, diseases of *hyperinsulinemia* and *insulin resistance*. If nothing else, you have much more to think about as you consider making positive changes to your lifestyle. We all want to do better - to age better - and live our lives out to their fullest, ultimately creating the best chance to die healthy at a ripe old age!

Wondering If You May Be Insulin Resistant?

If you are concerned you may be hyper insulinemic or becoming insulin resistant, and on your way toward metabolic syndrome or even type 2 diabetes, the first thing you should do is seek out your doctor and have a conversation about it. You'll want to have some bloodwork done to assess for certain markers in the blood, which can help you find out where you are.

Some of the best doctors will have their patients wear continuous glucose monitors, so they can get real-time feedback about this important marker. Also, if you are overweight or obese, know that your risk is higher.

Here are some important questions recommended by experts to determine whether you may be insulin resistant. Do any of these apply to you?

- Do you have more belly fat than you'd like?
- Are you overweight?
- Do you frequently feel thirsty?
- Do you have high blood pressure?
- Do you start to feel hungry a short time after eating a meal?
- Do you urinate frequently or retain water easily?
- Do you have tingling sensations in your hands and feet?
- Do you have high levels of blood triglycerides?
- If you're a man, do you struggle with erectile dysfunction?
- If you're a woman, do you have polycystic ovarian syndrome?[56]

Wondering What Is the Best Way to Test for Insulin Resistance?

Glucose is easily measured with a finger prick and the requisite test strip. Insulin is more difficult to measure. If you think you may be insulin resistant, speak with your doctor as soon as possible and follow up with his/her recommendations. According to most experts, measuring fasting insulin via fasting bloodwork is the most common method, but the most practical and accurate might be something known as the **Oral Glucose Tolerance Test.**

To learn more, search oral glucose tolerance test on the web or go here: https://www.mayoclinic.org/tests-procedures/glucose-tolerance-test/about/pac-20394296

Keep Reading - Keep Learning:

To learn more about how you can improve your eating patterns to combat these diseases and lead a healthier, happier life until you eventually, at a very old age, die healthy - head to the next chapter on **Time Restricted Eating.** In that chapter, I'll go into depth about all things "TRE" related and tell you why I prefer this term to intermittent fasting. You'll learn all the benefits, whether it's right for you or not, how to get started should you choose to give it a try and perhaps even make it a part of your daily habits.

CHAPTER 10

TIME RESTRICTED EATING

To be sick of sickness is the only cure.

-The Tae Te Ching

It's often been said by nutritionists and moms the world over, breakfast is the *most important meal of the day*. Who among us hasn't been chided at one time or another by their mom or significant other to not skip it as we ran out the door? I don't know if it's the most important meal, but I will say it is my favorite meal.

For the better part of the last 30 years, I've hardly ever eaten breakfast when most people do. Most of the time, I'm eating "breakfast," or what might be better described as my first meal of the day when everyone else is eating lunch - sometime between the hours of 11 am and 2pm.

In 1944 General Foods introduced the phrase "breakfast is the most important meal of the day" at the center of a huge advertising campaign designed to put their refined sugar and chemical-laden cereal on the tables of every single American home.[1] Whether or not it's the most important, there's no doubt it's the most marketed meal!

So, why am I routinely eating my first meal later in the day? There are many reasons, but the bottom line is, *there isn't another habit or routine you could adopt that is more powerful for improving your health, than this.* Amazingly, it's a habit that if done consistently, can simultaneously:

1. Bolster your short- and long-term health and ability to age well,
2. Help you lose unwanted or excess bodyfat to stay leaner,
3. Help you feel and look better.

I call this simple approach **Time Restricted Eating (TRE)**. In this chapter, I'm going to tell you why TRE works for most people, and how to go about it. In the past, I've referred to it, as have others, as simply having an *eating window*. Some in the health and science field call it time restricted feeding (TRF). It's also been called *intermittent fasting*, which is a common phrase used by others in science circles and in lots of programs.

As time goes on, I like the term *intermittent fasting* less and less. Why? Well, I'd much rather look at it as a positive – making the conscious *choice* to eat only during certain hours of the day, whereas the word "fasting" sounds more restrictive. My eating "window" is usually between noontime and six o'clock. Six hours out of 24. This timing translates to a six-hour period when I'll eat, and an 18-hour period when I won't.

Is this specific timing mandatory or essential to get benefits? No. But it is what I do most days of the week. You can achieve most benefits in that 18-hour non-eating window of time. With practice and experimentation, you might find there's a different window that is ideal for you! We're each an experiment of one. As well, our activity level and daily schedule play a role. I'll talk more about that, as well as different strategies, a bit later in this chapter.

So, back to the name - does it matter what we call it? Nope, it doesn't matter. Whatever the name, it's what I have done for most of my adult life, after some experimentation to find the most practical and worthwhile approach.

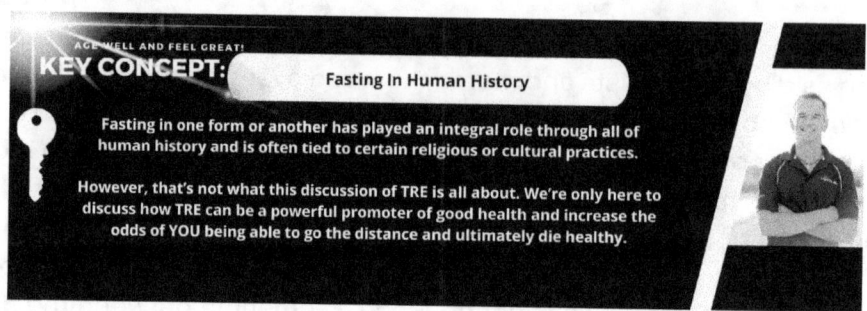

Which brings me to this: the bulk of what I will share with you in this chapter is my own personal experience with TRE – what I've learned through years of trial and error (and study) about the benefits you can expect and the best way to approach it. Of course, I'll also include specific references to pertinent research occasionally, and some tidbits and tips from the scientific community as well.

It's the Hot Topic in Fitness.

If you've been following the trends in the fitness industry at all, you know intermittent fasting has been one of the hottest topics over the last few years. Every week it seems there's a new magazine or podcast touting the benefits. Much of what I've seen has been good information. However, what you'll learn in this chapter will be skewed toward a very practical approach focused on keeping things simple. I want you to be able to get the greatest benefits by grabbing the low-hanging fruit, first.

In this chapter, I will teach you...

- What TRE IS and what it ISN'T.
- Why it can be powerful for improving health, short and long term.
- Who might not want to do it and why.
- What the different approaches are you can experiment with to find what works best for you.
- Recommendations for how to best combine it with exercise.
- What the smallest effective dose is, or the least you can do to get the most benefits.
- How to rotate your approach based on factors such as the time of year and your activity level.

- How it affects natural circadian rhythms or your body clock, and central nervous system.
- And more.

So, let's jump in. First, as you can imagine or may have experienced yourself, there are many different approaches, myths, and misconceptions about what TRE is and isn't. So, let's start by discussing some basics and then take it from there.

What is Time Restricted Eating NOT About?

You may be reading this and thinking, shouldn't he talk about what it *is* before he talks about what it *isn't*? Well, let's just say I'd like to get the biggest myths and misconceptions out of the way first. Let me be clear up front: the biggest misconception is TRE is about calorie restriction or that it requires depriving yourself of the foods you most enjoy. Or, that you'll walk around hungry most of the time! No, it isn't about any of those things. Let me say it again: time restricted eating or intermittent fasting, isn't about dieting OR deprivation or especially calorie restriction. Nor is it about teeny-tiny portions or starving yourself! No, no, and no!

If you've read or followed any of what the scientific community focused on aging and longevity has been up to for the last 50 to 100 years or so, you know calorie restriction (besides being a basic tenet of most diet programs), has been *the most relentlessly studied* topic in aging labs the world over.

There have been hundreds of scientific studies on calorie restriction using every type of organism from yeast to mice to humans. Perhaps the most infamous experiment on humans was the Biosphere 2 experiment, where in 1991, eight people lived for two years inside a three-acre, closed ecological dome in southern Arizona. While the researchers certainly learned a lot during that time, the consensus is it didn't pan out the way they'd hoped, primarily because after a few months, the soil spawned an explosion of oxygen-gulping bacteria. The result was the scientists felt like they were living at the equivalent of 14,000 altitude![2]

The bulk of calorie restriction research as it pertains to extending *lifespan*, has had mixed results. Some of it has shown the potential to extend lifespan or improve longevity, but other times we have seen the opposite effects. Regardless, remember that longevity *isn't the primary focus* of this book. Sure, we'd all enjoy living longer but only if we can do it in good health. It's our *healthspan* that is the focus. We want to improve our health and the quality of the years. When it comes *to that* goal, purposefully restricting calories over the long term is NOT going to help us.

Our focus and goals are also NOT about depriving yourself of eating what you most enjoy. As you will read in this chapter and in other parts of the book, you can to some degree, "have your cake and eat it too." I still occasionally enjoy some "cheat" meals and dessert, but I balance that against smart TRE. And exercising. The key is finding the appropriate balance and accepting too much of a "bad" thing won't help you achieve your goals. The bottom line is, as you've already read repeatedly in this book, it's not about achieving "perfection," it's about your daily habits – what you do or don't do the majority of the time.

Never discourage anyone who consistently
makes progress, no matter how slow.
-Plato

Do You Eat Less?

Yes, you may experience a daily calorie deficit and in fact, eat less when employing TRE. And that's a good thing! The key is most of the time, it shouldn't be your explicit goal to restrict calories. Rather, it's about adjusting meal timing so you can normalize insulin and along the way, experience a little bit of "want." If you're wondering what I mean by "want," let me explain.

Admit It, We Don't Like to Be Hungry.

Those of us who live in a privileged world know what it's like to have food available at every moment. And we like it that way, right? We've become accustomed to answering the call when we hear or feel that rumbling in our stomach telling us it's time to eat again. We live in an industrialized world of ultra-processed food - produced by companies that want our money. On every street corner, in every gas station or convenience store – those companies whose primary goal is $$ – are more than happy to help. Let's face it, you can't go anywhere without seeing food, hearing about food, or simply being encouraged to eat. Well, I'm here to tell you the food industry is playing us. And they're making us sicker in the process. You read about that in Chapters 7 and 8.

The thing I want to share with you here is this: most of the time *that rumbling or growling in your stomach is a big fat lie. It's not hunger. It's a temporary craving.* If you wait a little while, or drink some water, it'll likely go away. But because any kind of food we might want is easily available, and we mistakenly believe we are actually hungry and in need of food, we usually choose to eat something to quiet the rumble. This is where we go wrong.

Choose to ignore that initial rumble and learn to understand and differentiate between a temporary craving and real hunger. You can then begin to experience that mild state of "want," that is very healthy and good for you. And here's why: **hormesis.**

You'll recall from the chapter on *Why We Age: Exploring Aging at the Cellular Level*, I briefly discussed hormesis, sharing the story about the role of wind in a tree's life, something that was learned firsthand at Biosphere 2. If you've forgotten, pause here and go back and read it. The easiest way to define hormesis is to say it is "good" stress.

While I promised in the introduction to limit buzzwords and keep things simple and not technical, please bear with me. There are two main reasons you need to understand hormesis:

1. It's critical for you to come away from reading this book with the short list of the *most* important things that will have the greatest impact on your health – and hormesis IS one of those things.
2. It will come up once more when we're discussing the incredibly beneficial effects of various forms of exercise later in the book.

What's "Good" Stress?

Good stress is simply different kinds of self-induced *physical* stress. It is NOT the emotional stress we're all too familiar with that makes us anxious and weary. It's things like exercise and exposure to hot and cold temperatures, that kickstart or up regulate our "internal defense" systems to guard us against premature aging and strengthen our immune system. *Mild hunger or a feeling of "want" is just that kind of thing.* According to some experts and research studies, when we are emotionally stressed, the ability of our immune systems, specifically our T-cells and lymphocytes, to multiply in response to infectious agents is drastically reduced. That makes us more vulnerable, not stronger. Without our immune cell's ability to "redeploy" so they may seek out and protect other vulnerable areas in our body to prevent viruses and other pathogens from gaining a foothold, well, let's face it, we'd have no chance to live healthier OR longer.

What does help us stay healthier though, is what scientist and author, David Sinclair, reiterated in his recently published book *Lifespan – Why We Age and Why We Don't Have To. He says* hormesis is a powerful activator of "longevity genes" and "survival circuits" which help us age better.[3] If you recall, I introduced you to these concepts in Chapter 2. Also, according to Sinclair and many other researchers in this field, eating less often and eating less in general, both result in the kinds of cellular stress that is extremely "good for our epigenome, because (they) stimulate our longevity genes - the disaster response teams" in our body."[4] Additionally, Sinclair states, "when hormesis happens, all is well. And in fact, all is better than well, because the little bit of stress that occurs when the genes are activated prompts the rest of the system to hunker down, to conserve, to survive a little longer. That's the start of longevity."[5]

Similarly, in his recently published book "Path to Longevity," aging researcher, Dr. Luigi Fontana, states "fasting can act as a mild stressor or hormetic agent that provokes a survival response in the organism, helping it to endure adversity by activating longevity pathways. This explains why animals kept on a regime of intermittent fasting are also more resistant to a wide range of stresses."[6] There's a large body of research that supports the idea "hormesis is an evolutionary process where a cell or organism exposed to a mild stressor adapts and can later resist another more intense stressor. It does this by activating an adaptive response that triggers cellular protective and anti-aging pathways.[7]

The message I need you to hear is this: **don't be frightened or run from a feeling of mild hunger**. Know that when you're a little bit hungry – the kind of hunger than can happen when you haven't eaten for 12 to 24 hours, *good things are happening* in your body, and keep in mind the more used to eating frequently you are, the harder these changes will be.

---

*The surest way to prevent yourself from learning
a topic is to believe you already know it.*
– James Clear, author of "Atomic Habits"

Finding the Right Balance.

Before we discuss what TRE actually is and how to do it, let's talk about *balance*, and why that word is so vital. It goes back to something you'll see repeatedly in this book: if you decide to make a change, with diet, exercise or anything else, to be successful, the change *must be something you can sustain over the long-term.* That's why following super restrictive diets never work. That's true even for a ketogenic diet (aka "keto"), which has become popular recently. Sure, followed strictly, keto can result in fat loss simply because it is so carbohydrate restricted. The problem is, very few people can or want to sustain that level of restriction indefinitely. So, when they eventually return to another more natural (for them) way of eating, the fat they may have lost when following Keto, often returns.

This is true for almost any type of high-protein or high-fat, low-carb diet, including Atkins. When a normal diet returns, so does the bodyfat. This is WHY *Time Restricted Eating* is so powerful! It IS sustainable. It is something you can use over a very long period with great success.

One of the first questions you might ask is, "do I have to do it every day?" The answer is no. You have options. You can be flexible with it. Depending on what you learn as you experiment and what your goals are, you can approach it more moderately or commit to more frequency. It's up to you, and it's all dependent upon your goals.

You don't have to give up all your favorite foods. Notice I'm not saying you can eat whatever you want, because that's the last message I want you to hear. The quality of what you eat matters, a lot. What I am saying is with TRE, you can find the right balance between days when you're more strict, and other days when you loosen the reins a bit, so to speak. My personal experience and observations have shown TRE gives you that small extra element of freedom when done consistently over a long period.

When you can find that right balance, you have an approach – a philosophical approach – that you CAN sustain for the rest of your life. This is exactly what I've discovered for myself.

What is Time Restricted Eating ALL About?

TRE is simply about adjusting the **timing** of your meals, to extend the amount of time when you are *not eating*. The earlier "window" I descried with my own approach, works in part because it takes advantage of the overnight period when I'm sleeping. My experience has been it's easier to extend that overnight fast, by delaying breakfast. (It's easy to see where the term, break-fast, came from). However, one could just as easily move the "window" earlier to connect the evening hours with the overnight hours, thus extending the non-eating "window." The goal is a longer period than might be normal for you, *between* meals, where you aren't taking in any calories.

Age Well and Feel Great!
Key Concept:

When Did I Start To Experiment And Learn About the Benefits?

It goes back to my early days as a runner. In the beginning, I had many days when there were long time periods between meals, because I did a bad job of timing or planning my early morning runs and work schedule. ☺

You see, some days I'd be up early to run, and then rush off to work, not allowing myself enough time to eat. Sometimes I'd grab something on my way, but very often I wouldn't actually eat until the first mid-morning "break."

At the same time, I was always training in a "fasted" state, something I will talk about later in the book. (There are so many benefits to exercising in a fasted state, it can't be overstated). As time went on, I realized both approaches were very good at "teaching" my body to access more fat stores as fuel sources, and in the process, normalize insulin levels.

Later, I experimented with planned back-to-back "depletion" training sessions to see how I performed when glycogen was depleted from the muscles and liver. Looking back those were productive experiments that I approached very cautiously. As this well-known phrase straight out of the urban dictionary says, I recommend you "don't try this at home!"

Remember in the earlier chapter on insulin resistance and hyperinsulinemia, you learned about the importance of being insulin sensitive and maintaining normal insulin levels. **Simply put, when there are longer periods without eating, insulin can reset to normal levels. That's exactly what you want to happen.**

Learn the Difference Between Hunger and Cravings.

True hunger is something you've likely *not* experienced, even though you may think you have. It's difficult to generalize as there will be many different types of people reading this, but most people who are fortunate to live in developed countries don't know what it's like to be *truly hungry*. True hunger can only be experienced when you stop eating for a prolonged period of at least a day or more.

Cravings are a completely different story. Cravings are something *you have* likely experienced. And they do "feel" like hunger. But they're not. What they are is a byproduct of living an unhealthy lifestyle chock full of wheat and grains, sugars, refined carbohydrates, and other junk food that exhausts your pancreas and might be as much as 100% responsible for your unwanted bodyfat. When you eat a diet rich in refined sugars and other processed foods, you get the quick sugar peak and then the subsequent crash. It's a vicious cycle. The more you eat foods like bread and pasta and other sugar-laden snack foods, the more your body will continue to crave it. You experience a brief surge of energy and then a crash. This kind of roller coaster isn't any fun!

You may recall in Chapter 8, I told you how food manufacturers spend millions of dollars to create food that is addictive. I told you it's a biological addiction, not an emotional one. When you realize and accept this, you begin to see cravings mean you aren't in control – *the food is*. And the food manufacturers are, too. That's what they want – for you to act as though you have *no choice*. That's not a good place to be. And I know you agree. The time has come to differentiate between these two things, true hunger, and cravings. They are different. Understand it, accept it, and learn to deal with it.

Humans, like you and I, thrive off of true hunger. Cravings are like a curse. Trust me, when you finally defeat them with smart eating and meal timing, you'll feel absolutely amazing.

Teach Your Body to Become a "Fat-Burning Machine."

You'll remember in the chapter on insulin, I presented this idea that when glucose is floating thru the bloodstream and insulin is elevated, you're not depleting stored glycogen and not accessing stores of body fat for energy. In that situation, you're using blood glucose for energy. To encourage your body to access stored fats for energy, you need to normalize insulin and reduce the amount of sugar in your diet. You'll also benefit from the right amount of both strength training and aerobic exercise like walking, running, and cycling. I'll discuss this "fat burning" element in the chapter on "cardio" exercise. Keep reading.

You can become a "fat burning machine" through TRE. Circulating glucose gets used up, resulting in your body accessing more of its body fat stores for energy. Remember, *no food means no insulin*. As an aside, don't hesitate to return to Chapter 9 on insulin, for a refresher. There's a lot of information there. The better you understand it, the more empowering it will be.

Eat More Fat. Especially Omega-3.

One last thing on this topic: one important way to enhance your body's ability to access fat for fuel, is to eat more of it. As I stated earlier, and you'll hear repeatedly throughout the book, fat from food is NOT the enemy, sugar is. *You need lots of good fats in your diet to promote good health.*

Fat from nuts, seeds, avocado, grass fed and finished red meat, and even dairy, are all important staples to include in your meal planning to burn more fat for energy. The idea that things like nuts are high-calorie and should be avoided is false thinking! And the idea that we should be drinking and eating "low-fat" dairy foods because the fat isn't good for us, is also false.

At the end of Chapter 9 on *insulin resistance*, I shared some personal reflections. Among those was how, because of some government mandates in the early 1970s, the fat in food, especially saturated fat, became vilified, so much so that **low-fat** foods became all the craze through the 80s and 90s. **Don't be fat phobic!**

All this being said, yes, there ARE certain types of fat we'd be smart to avoid eating. Here are a few to be on the lookout for:

1. **Trans-fats**[9]: these fats that are in all kinds of processed foods, are created when hydrogen is added to vegetable oil to make it a solid. What are the typical foods where you'll find this kind of fat? Let's start with cake frostings, pie crusts, biscuits, microwave popcorn, coffee creamers, frozen pizza, refrigerated dough, vegetable shortenings and stick margarines. The fats help give a more solid texture and richness to certain foods, like baked goods and ready-to-eat frostings. You get the picture – if you avoid packaged processed foods, you can avoid trans-fats. Read the labels of any packaged foods before you buy – avoid these like the plague! Thankfully there is much less of this type of fat in foods now than a decade ago.

2. **Polyunsaturated vegetable seed oils are best avoided whenever possible. Choose Extra Virgin Olive Oil.** The names are misleading. You'd THINK they're healthy for you when the truth is far from it. The problem comes largely from the processing. As mentioned earlier, it isn't about the food itself so much, it's what is done to the food that matters.

The real challenge for many of us is what to use when we want an oil to cook with. There's reason to be concerned about the choice we make. After all, fats and oils can get damaged when exposed to heat. With some, toxic compounds are created which can lead to disease. If you want to cut your exposure to potentially harmful and carcinogenic compounds, you should only cook with fats that are stable at high heat. According to experts, there are two properties of cooking oils that matter most:

- **Smoke point:** The temperature at which the fats begin to break down and turn into smoke.
- **Oxidative stability:** How resistant the fats are to reacting with oxygen.

The winner on both counts is Olive Oil. While it does have a slightly lower smoke point, it is rich in antioxidants like polyphenols, which prevent the oil from oxidizing at high heat. It also holds up well during heating due to its low polyunsaturated fat content (the opposite of most seed oils).

In one study that used several types of olive oil for frying, extra virgin olive oil proved particularly resistant to oxidation.[10] Other studies note that olive oil does not oxidize much when used for cooking, while vegetable oils like sunflower oil do. [11] It is also a myth that heating olive oil leads to the formation of unhealthy trans-fatty acids. In one study, frying olive oil eight times in a row only increased the trans-fat content from 0.045% to 0.082% — still a negligible amount.

I'll reintroduce seed oils in Chapter 12 when I talk about chronic inflammation. These are very inflammatory, and as you'll learn inflammation has a big negative impact on our health. Keep reading.

Here's a chart to help you make the healthiest choices for you and your family.

A Guide for Choosing Your Best Cooking Oil.

#saynotoseedoils

The oil we choose to cook with has a major impact on our health. Choosing the best kind helps prevent chronic disease. Always choose the most natural source with the least amount of added ingredients or processing.

The BEST to use anytime.	Use moderately.	Always avoid these.
Virgin Olive Oil	Ground Nut Oil	Canola Oil
Cold Pressed Coconut Oil	Sesame Oil	Rice Bean Oil
Ghee	Safflower Oil	Soybean Oil
Butter		Mustard Oil
Avacado Oil		Margarine
Lard		Lite Butter
Beef Tallow		Cottonseed Oil
Virgin Coconut Oil		Corn Oil
		Grapeseed Oil
		Vegetable Oils

*Virgin Olive Oil, Avacado Oil, and Ghee are your best choices for high temperature cooking. *Virgin Coconut Oil is made from coconut milk. Cold pressed is made from dry coconut.

The old saying you are what you eat, is actually NOT accurate.

The perfect example of this is the fat that comes from nuts, grass fed meat, and avocados, as three examples. Those highly nutritious foods don't make you fat, they improve your health. Almost every one of us would be healthier if we increased our good fat intake.

-Coach Al

Can *Anyone* Do TRE?

Virtually any person can use some form of TRE or intermittent fasting for the health benefits. There's absolutely nothing dangerous about it if done in a smart way. That being said, there are two age-groups of people I believe wouldn't be as well served, as I'll discuss soon.

So, if almost anyone can do TRE successfully, what's the problem? Many are told it isn't "smart" or safe to skip breakfast, or to go very long without eating. It isn't difficult to find studies that reinforce this idea if you look for them. Some of them say "skipping breakfast is common in the U.S." and doing so could be unhealthy. One states, "limited evidence suggests that skipping breakfast is associated with atherosclerosis and cardiovascular disease."[12] I wouldn't vouch for the quality of these studies, that's for sure. It's worth noting again that I hardly ever skip breakfast, I just eat it much later than most. ☺

It's obvious to anyone paying attention, traditional medicine and the medical profession as a whole, haven't kept up. Old paradigms die hard. To say I'm not impressed with traditional approaches to the problems that are plaguing Americans would be an understatement. I won't point the finger at doctors; it's a system-wide problem that ignores the root causes of one of the most troubling problems of modern life – a health issue I've already discussed in great detail: insulin resistance and along with it, metabolic syndrome.

If you think about it, it's easy to see good health isn't profitable. Sickness is. I hate to put it that bluntly, but it's the truth. If you are proactive, take good care of yourself, achieve true good health, and then work to keep it, the system won't make much money off you. Have you ever stopped to think your local hospital wouldn't be very happy if their Intensive Care unit was empty all the time? That means a direct hit on that hospital's bottom line. Don't misunderstand. I'm not saying hospitals are "bad." What I am saying is profits drive a lot of what we're seeing in how healthcare is facilitated in this country. They are fundamentally in business to make money for shareholders. Think about it. For now, let's simply say that mainstream medicine has failed when it comes to helping us become healthier, lose unwanted fat, and extend the length of our healthy years.

You must be informed, and skeptical of everything you read. Educate yourself, and most of all, listen to your intuition and consider what actually makes sense. I for one, encourage you to challenge my thinking and my advice! I welcome it. Goodness knows I've challenged myself on everything I'm sharing with you – the fear of my own confirmation bias has forced me to.

Should *Everyone* Do TRE?

As I briefly alluded to earlier, no, I don't believe TRE or intermittent fasting is a good idea for every single person. The exceptions? Two age groups, the very old and the very young, both benefit from more frequent mealtimes. As a result, these two age groups would not be candidates for TRE in my opinion. Toddlers and young children do need to be careful about consuming too much sugar, but because they're in a growth stage of the life cycle, we should focus simply on making sure they're eating the highest quality foods. Doing anything other than letting them eat when their hunger dictates, would be foolish and could potentially impact their development.

On the other end of the spectrum are the eldest among us, who may lack the simple desire to eat, and thus under normal circumstances, might not get the nutrients they need. Most of the folks who fall into this category need calories! And often.

Lastly, I would also say anyone who is extremely lean – less than 10% body fat for men, and 12-15% body fat for women, should be very careful about how often they employ TRE or any type of intermittent fasting. This isn't to say that occasionally employing TRE wouldn't be beneficial – it might be. However, people who fall into this category should place greater emphasis on building and maintaining muscle tissue.

What Are Some Additional Benefits of TRE and Eating Less Often?

- **It can induce a process inside cells called *autophagy*,** which is the body recycling and cleaning out dead or damaged cells and removing toxins. In science circles, it's thought of as an evolutionary self-preservation mechanism so the body can rebuild and regenerate newer, healthier cells. "Auto" means self and "phagy" means eat. So, the literal meaning of autophagy is "self-eating."[13] This might be one of the most important benefits to help you age well!

- **It can help cut down on the amount of oxidative stress in cells**, which simply means through the process of eating less often, we can expect to have less accumulation of oxidative free radicals, less oxidative damage, and we can see an increase in our body's cellular response to stress. Because of that, there will be less oxidative damage to other components in cells also, such as cellular proteins, fats/lipids, and things like nucleic acids, associated with aging and disease.[14]

- **It can help you lose unwanted bodyfat.** By focusing on only eating during a window of time, you can more easily get into an energy, or calorie deficit, which can lead to fat loss. As important, you're going to have more normal insulin levels, and combined with exercise or carbohydrate restriction, you will see a much greater chance of achieving optimal body composition. All without having to starve yourself or follow a diet program you won't enjoy or simply can't sustain long-term.

- **It helps boost the hormone, glucagon, which is the opposite of insulin**. I briefly mentioned glucagon in the previous chapter on insulin resistance. Remember, glucagon is a hormone that acts as the opposite of insulin. Insulin works to store energy, while glucagon does the opposite – it wants to spend it. Which is exactly what we want! Naturally, glucagon rises during periods when you are not eating. Think of these as two-sides of the same metabolic coin.

According to Dr. Benjamin Bikman, in his book, *Why We Get Sick*, "glucagon wants the body to release its stored energy by pushing the fat cells to share their fat and the liver to share its glucose. Because insulin and glucagon work against each other to activate and inhibit metabolic processes, the balance of these two hormones dictates which processes actually occur."[15] Simply put, insulin leads to fat storage. Glucagon leads to fat release for use as energy. Win-win.

The formula is quite simple: *Less insulin = more glucagon = more lipolysis = more fat burning*. Lipolysis is the breakdown of lipids into fatty acids, which are then oxidized and used as fuel. In simpler terms, lipolysis is the process of burning fat, which is what we all want, right? Glucagon regulates lipolysis, while insulin inhibits it. How does TRE allow us to mobilize fatty acids? It promotes the release of glucagon, so yes, not eating is effective for removing body fat.

- **It helps boost growth hormone release**. Growth hormone and insulin are sort of mutually exclusive, much in the same sense that glucagon and insulin are mutually exclusive. They don't go together. So, when insulin is around, you can rest assured growth hormone will not be. Natural human growth hormone is produced by our pituitary gland, and as we get older, less is released. That's unfortunate since it is hailed by many in scientific circles as the actual fountain of youth. Why? Growth hormone helps to increase muscle mass, decrease bodyfat, increase bone density, increase our energy levels and vitality, acts to defend our cells by warding off pesky proteases (which are destructive enzymes), increases our levels of strength and stamina, and even aids in elevating our mood and sex drive.

The bottom line, my friend, is *virtually every single risk factor for disease and ill health* - inflammation, insulin resistance, cardiovascular risk factors, blood fat profiles, and body composition, to name just a few, have been shown by many well-designed scientific studies (including the one referenced at the end of this paragraph, published in 2021) to be drastically improved when you eat less often and especially, when you combine that approach with some form of exercise![16] And while I'm only one person, I'm here to tell you I've lived this and can vouch for its benefits firsthand.

Are There Any Potential Downsides to TRE?

For most people, there are very few downsides to TRE. However, it is important to remember there are many factors contributing to our health and vitality, and we are all unique and an experiment of one. Thus, an honest review of TRE should also look at any potential downsides. If in doubt, discuss it with your doctor or healthcare provider. Have the conversation and be informed.

Are You Getting Enough Protein?

One of the biggest challenges anyone beyond the age of 50 has is maintaining muscle tissue. It's increasingly harder to build it as we age. Losing muscle mass, known as *sarcopenia* – the term for muscle wasting, is the last thing we want to happen. To keep what we have and even build upon it, we need to consume enough protein in our diet. This is the challenge – it's difficult even under the best of circumstances sometimes, but if we're employing TRE or intermittent fasting, it can be even harder.

According to longevity expert, Dr. Peter Attia, M.D., most people don't consume enough protein. He points out this is particularly common among middle-aged women. **His recommendation is to get at least 1 gram of protein per day, per pound of bodyweight.** That's the minimum.[17] When you sit down and do the math, this seems like an awful lot. But I agree with his recommendations. There's been a little bit of an uptick on protein-phobia recently in the media, and as a rule, it's unfounded.

Make sure to eat quality protein in each meal, and if you do choose to use TRE, put extra focus on including enough protein in your meals during your window so you meet the minimum requirement of 1 gram per pound of bodyweight. As Dr. Attia points out, and I completely agree: "The older you are, the more important it is to emphasize anything that's going to allow you to maintain and build strength and maintain muscle mass."[18]

What About Cortisol?

Another potential downside to TRE is that long periods of time without eating may lead to an increase in the stress hormone, cortisol, which may lead to even more food cravings. Cortisol levels are worth monitoring if you're at risk for chronic diseases such as diabetes or heart disease. Speak with your doctor if you have questions.

What About Overeating or Binging?

One other obvious potential downside is you may be at risk of overeating and binge-eating. Why? It's a complicated topic to discuss but the reality is, for some who take TRE or any other kind of fasting to an extreme, perhaps leading to acute caloric deficit in the process, there's the risk in a moment of weakness, you could end up binge-eating.

The risk of this happening is higher when you're stressed. Or late in the day when your self-discipline is most easily challenged. The take home here is don't overdo it and put yourself in a situation where you lose control. Perhaps easier said than done for some people, but at the end of the day, you are in control of what you put in your mouth and what you don't.

One rule of thumb that's so important? **Eat more slowly.** Chew your food completely. The slower you eat, the better the chance your stomach will catch up with your chewing speed, and the sooner you'll feel satisfied. One habit that helps me is putting my fork down after each mouthful. Try it, it works.

What About the Risk of Dehydration?

Why? When we're eating less, we might also forget to drink. And we know that dehydration can lead to headaches, kidney stones, fever, and eventually it can kill you.

Some studies show we are more sensitive to hunger than to thirst, which might lead one to drink less than he or she should.

Here are my rules about daily water intake and maintaining the right level of hydration:

1. **Start every day with a tall glass of water**, at least 12 oz., every single morning. Before coffee, or your morning chores, before doing anything else. Doing this will get your day started the right way and may even kickstart a bowel movement, in part due to that wonderful gastrocolic reflex.
2. **Continue to drink water throughout the day**. A good starting point or goal should be at least ½ ounce (and even up to 1 ounce if you're active or during the summertime) for every pound you weigh. For example, a man that is 160 pounds would want to drink at least 80 ounces total, which is a little more than half a gallon.

The best time to plant a tree was 25 years ago. The second-best time to plant a tree is today.
— Chinese parable

Why Will Some Have Difficulty with TRE?

Like anything else you may try that is new to you, there's always the potential to trip up. And there's usually a learning curve to find what works best. Fear will keep some from even trying TRE. Fear of how uncomfortable it might be. Fear that it won't work for them. And that's a shame. If you're reading this and you aren't in those two age-groups I mentioned earlier, I hope you give this approach to eating a sincere try. If you do, you won't be disappointed in the results.

Beyond the fears I mentioned, what are some of the other things that might keep people from trying TRE? My experience tells me the obstacles to being successful with TRE come down to *these three factors*. There are more that can sabotage our success, but these are the most common in my experience. If you want to increase your chances for success, my advice is to make sure you think about these, and plan in advance so you can address each one head on!

1. **They lack a supportive environment.** We all need supportive people AND a supportive environment to give us a little extra help or encouragement when we are going through a challenging time or working on changing and self-improvement. If you look at the many cultures around the world who practice some sort of fasting, such as Muslims, they're able to be successful in part, because they support each other.

The solution is to seek out others who believe in you and in this process. Block the negative noise around you by ignoring those who tell you it isn't smart or good for you, or that you can't do it. Team up with a partner and do this together – that will make it much easier for you to plan meals, too!

Your goal is to set up your environment, which means your home and your office or workplace, for the best chance for success. And when it comes time to shop, don't buy the foods you know will increase your odds of self-sabotaging your chance for success, especially if you're an abstainer! Plan your days and meals ahead of time to increase your success. A supportive environment is so important!

2. **Their expectations are too high.** It's human nature to expect changes to happen quickly when we begin new habits. But the reality is, things often take more time and effort than we might hope.

Know and accept right up front you may feel hungry and will have to work through it. You may also experience other symptoms temporarily, such as headaches, and cramping or diarrhea. In my experience, the people who have had more of these kinds of symptoms have been the people who needed to make these changes the most. In other words, the harder it is, the more you need to do it. We're each an experiment of one – and we all come into these changes with a unique perspective and habits. Be patient, persistent, and don't expect too much too soon. If you stick with it and adjust and adapt as you need to, you will be rewarded!

- **Losing sight of the fact that whatever difficulty or discomfort you experience is temporary.** Remember, the benefits are powerful and will last!

Don't forget why you are reading this book and what your ultimate goal is – to age well, feel and look better throughout your life, and hopefully go the full distance and ultimately die healthy very far off into the future. Hold those goals near to you and remind yourself of them when the going gets a little tough.

HOW TO DO Time Restricted Eating – What Are Your Options?

Before getting into the details surrounding the many approaches or strategies for TRE, I want to bring up the important idea of *experimenting* and understanding we're all an experiment of one. And above all else, *start conservatively with whatever approach you decide.* Read that again. Start conservatively, ok? ☺

Now, the opposite of conservative would be to decide in one day, to start using TRE every single day thereafter – essentially making a dramatic overnight change to your routine. That's not conservative OR smart for that matter! What it is, is an approach that's likely to set you up for binging or feeling crappy and becoming very frustrated or unhappy. A *much smarter approach* is to begin with one of these three progressively challenging strategies:

1. Once or twice a week, every other week at first.
2. Once or twice a week.
3. Alternate days, where you do it every other day.

Do number 1 and 2 look ridiculously easy to you? If so, that's good. Still, you should start conservatively. And here's why: Every single time we try to change too many things about our daily routine or habits too quickly, regardless of how much we want the change to occur, we set ourselves up for failure and frustration.

It is much better to change a tiny bit more than not changing at all AND KEEP IT GOING over time. The "going" itself – <u>the consistent approach you can sustain over time – the day after day of doing these things</u> – that is where the power is.

What are the Best Strategies for Timing TRE?

I told you earlier what I typically do, which is an 18-hour window of not eating, with (you guessed it!) a 6-hour eating window. I like to keep the overnight "fast" going and will normally exercise in the morning, and typically have my first meal sometime between 11 and 2 PM. I'll keep that window open until 6 o'clock.

As I describe a variety of strategies below, remember these are general guidelines. It's about the big picture, my friend, OK? My goal is to teach you some principles and concepts you can mold to best fit your life and your goals. So, it isn't about following the script exactly, it's about following it "for the most part," keeping in mind the overall goals and philosophy. This is always and forever a "most of the time" kind of thing. Don't become a slave to your goals!

Can you do exactly what I do if you'd like to? Of course! Just remember, it took me decades of experiments and practice and study to reach this point. It's what works for me, most of the time. You can learn from what I've learned and will certainly make faster progress than I have in that regard. Just be patient with yourself and the journey you're on. The irony is once you do this long enough for it to become habit, it will feel surprisingly easier than you may think. Cravings will largely go away, and your energy levels will stabilize. The time will fly, and you won't even realize it!

Let's call what I told you is typical for me, **Option 1.** I consider this strategy to be an "ideal" that would be a great option for most people on a routine basis once you have a little bit of experience with it. So, let's keep going. What's the next thing to remember?

Keep It Simple.

While I'll present a variety of strategies here that may, on the surface, look complex or even difficult to do, don't be scared. It's really as simple as you make it. So, make it simple! For example, let me give you a reframing of **Option 2**, (which you can skip ahead to read through first if you like) that keeps it SO simple and practical, it's almost hard to believe:

A couple of times a week, have dinner on the early side and then the next day, have your first meal on the later side, leaving around 16 hours in between.

That's it! Not that difficult, right? Reframed in a practical way, it should seem very easy. You simply sleep for 7 to 8 hours (hopefully), and then when you wake up, you make sure you have that large glass of water and perhaps a cup or two of coffee, and then wait a few hours before that first meal, with no snacking at all in between. *Voila!* You did it! The power in this approach isn't its complexity obviously, it's in being consistent over a long period of time. Making it a habit.

With that very simple and practical perspective as a backdrop for more learning, let's now look at a few of the approaches timing wise, that you might choose. Always keep in mind the simple and profound idea that it's NOT about being exact, or even crazy! It's about setting up what will be the most productive way to extend that **non-eating window of time for you**. That's your goal.

Five Different Strategies for Time Restricted Eating:

The options are similar to one another, which should make sense to you. The simple and ultimate goal is some form of break from eating throughout the course of the day. You definitely want to be smart and choose a conservative place to start so you can build momentum and keep it going. Over time, with some experimentation and practice, you'll learn what works best for you. And what works best will change depending upon your schedule and lifestyle. As I'll discuss in the next section, it's important to be flexible with your options and vary things routinely so you and your body don't get stuck in a rut. Keep reading to learn more about that.

As you embark on what may be a new journey for you, please remember to be patient with yourself and the process. And persistent, of course. I know I've said this multiple times and sometimes redundancy can be frustrating if you're a reader, so please accept my apologies! The thing is there's a reason I'm beating this idea into the ground. Rome wasn't built in a day, right? Change never happens as quickly as we would like it to. Just stay the course and keep learning. It will be worth it! ☺

1. **Option 1 (this is what I do and my "ideal") - Time Restrictive Eating window of 6 hours: not eating from 6 PM until Noontime the next day.**
   a) This can be done every other day, or on only a few days during the week. Until you're very experienced with this approach and comfortable with it, I wouldn't suggest doing it every day. Over time, you may find doing it every day works well for you *most of the time.* Start conservatively!

2. **OPTION 1a – Essentially the same as Option 1, except the time of day: not eating from Noontime to 6 AM the next day.**
   a. As with Option 1, it can be done on some days, such as day 1, 3, and 5, or only during the weekdays or only on weekends, at first.

3. **OPTION 2 – Time Restrictive Eating window of 8 hours:** This approach is a variation on Option 1 and Option 1a, where you either start earlier or finish later.
   a. This can be an easier way to start for some people as it is a little bit more forgiving than Option 1 or 1a. Research does support that a 6-hour window which you have in Option 1 and 1a is more beneficial when done consistently.

4. **OPTION 3 – Time Restrictive Eating window of 0 hours: not eating from 6 PM on one day to 6 PM the next day. Or Noontime on one day to Noontime the next day.**
   a. This would typically only be done once per week. Generally, it is better for those who have already experienced some success with a 6 to 8 hour eating window, first.
   b) It is above the "ideal" 6-hour eating window. It isn't ideal as the potential risk exists for excess tissue/ muscle breakdown and lower overall energy and reduced recovery.
   c) It is more taxing mentally.
   d) It CAN be a good option on occasion for those who are experienced with TRE. We all need to experiment to find what works best for us!

5. **OPTION 4 – The ONE MEAL PER DAY approach.** Focusing on simply eating only 1 meal per day (without any snacking of course) still provides an 18–20-hour net fasting window.

a. You could ideally use a 4-hour eating window such as from 6 to 10 PM, or 5 to 9 PM, or 4 to 8 PM, as three examples.

Should You Vary How You Approach TRE? Yes!

Now that we've covered some different strategies and hammered home the idea that this is really simpler than it might seem at first, the next question you may have is, should you stick with the exact same strategy for weeks or months or even years at a time? The short answer is, no, you shouldn't do the exact same thing week in and month out. Varying your food choices and eating routines, whether it is TRE or not, is a very smart thing to do. In this case, variety really IS the spice of life!

The reality is, things like your activities or your sport training if you're an athlete, your individual goals, the time of year and the weather, your work schedule and social life too, all impact how you approach this. And in fact, any other changes that inevitably occur during the course of a year, ALL should play some role and dictate to some degree, how you approach TRE and ultimately, your food choices.

There are going to be times when you're less active, or when the weather keeps you indoors. During those periods, you should eat less carbohydrate and would benefit from a more progressive approach to TRE. On the other hand, there are going to be times when your activity levels are higher – if you're an athlete in a challenging training cycle, for example. During THOSE times, you'll need more energy from the food you eat. Perhaps a higher percentage of carbohydrate as well, to fuel more intense activities. That would be a bad time to get really aggressive with TRE! Do you see the difference?

On top of it all is the simple idea that changing up the strategy for the sake of it, is very often a good thing to do. Why? There are many reasons, but it really comes down to the fact it's how we have evolved as a species. Not sure what I mean?

In his book, *Sapiens – A Brief History of Humankind,* author Yuval Noah Harari, describes how for 2.5 million years of human history, Sapiens continued to live by "foraging for and gathering wild plants and hunting wild animals."[19] Think about it: our ancestors were hunter-gatherers - nomads, moving from one place to another to find food and shelter – there were times when food was abundant, and other times when it was scarce.

With the changing seasons and changing landscape, came a completely new array of wild plants. They truly ate what was in season. They pretty much ate whatever they could find, and it varied a lot from one week or month, to the next. They were forced to go periods where they didn't eat much at all, and at other times, when options were plentiful, they would happily gorge and stuff themselves! Until they began to domesticate as farmers, that is.

As Harari describes, all this changed during the "agricultural revolution that occurred about 10,000 years ago, when humans began cultivating wheat and expanding farming."[20] Ironically, Harari goes on to say "studies of ancient skeletons indicate that the transition to agriculture brought about a plethora of ailments, such as slipped discs, arthritis, and hernias."[21] ☺

Some things never change, right? We herald the dawn of new ways of doing things that theoretically should make life easier and better, and very often the reverse happens – we end up worse off than before!

In what is profound and a harbinger of things to come, Harari goes on to say "rather than heralding a new era of easy living, the Agricultural Revolution left farmers with lives generally more difficult and less satisfying than those of foragers. Hunter-gatherers spent their time in more stimulating and varied ways and were less in danger of starvation and disease."[22]

History shows us "humans are omnivorous apes who thrive on a wide variety of foods. Grains made up only a small fraction of the human diet before the Agricultural Revolution. A diet based on cereals is poor in minerals and vitamins, hard to digest, and really bad for your teeth and gums."[23] If you're wondering why our ancestors changed and became farmers, to a large extent, it was because more and more gathered into larger groups and communities. Farming seemed like the easiest way to feed larger and larger groups of people.

The take home lesson here is, *be more like your ancestors*. Vary your approach to TRE and meal timing, and make sure to get foods in their natural state. Choose fruits and vegetables that are in season, as often as you can. This will bring a natural variety to your eating, just as nature intended. One thing I've always thought and sometimes said, more often than I'd like to admit, is *the day we (as a species) left the food chain, the sh*t began to hit the fan!* Think about it. ☺

Should We Trust the "Science?"

On April 22, 2022, as I was in the midst of writing this book, the *New York Times* published an article titled *Scientists Find No Benefit to Time Restricted Eating*.[24] When I saw the article and read through it, I realized the authors truly were screaming out to the reader there's NO BENEFIT TO TRE! I was shocked. I had to take a step back and take a big deep breath. Could this actually be the kind of trustworthy, science-based information the thousands who subscribe to the *New York Times* have come to expect?

I was even more surprised when I read the article was based on and cited a *just-released* study published in the *New England Journal of Medicine* titled, *Calorie Restriction with and without Time Restricted Eating in Weight Loss*. [25] Yikes. As you can guess, from my perspective this was not looking good. Imagine you're sitting drinking your morning coffee and you come across this article in print or online. It would naturally pique your curiosity. You might read through it and then decide to go look at the actual research article, just like I did. After reading through both, my guess is you might be questioning what you've learned while reading THIS book of mine, and even wondering if I know anything at all about the topic. After all, the *New York Times* is one of the largest newspapers on the planet and surely must be a reliable source of information, right? And even if you would question the reliability of the *Times*, the fact the article was based on research published in the prestigious *New England Journal of Medicine* (NJM), surely makes it accurate and reliable information, yes? I mean, that NJM research article shows more than a dozen scientist's names, all with Ph.Ds. This has to be trustworthy, right???

Which brings me to why I'm sharing this information with you. And yes, this is frustrating for me, let me tell you. But it is what can happen when it comes to journalism, selling newspapers, and the very precarious nature of "research" and "science." Here's what I mean: You can NOT trust headlines or even "research" presented as "scientific," until you look closer and seek to understand the <u>often-nuanced</u> details about how studies were done and what the information shared has to say.

Newspapers print headlines that give false impressions, sometimes as click-bait. In other instances, the article's authors do what a lot of us do, which is make quick, often inaccurate assumptions after a quick review of the research. Sometimes it's due to deadlines, and other times it's because they may not fully understand the subject matter. And then there's our own confirmation bias. Any or all of these can lead to a set of conclusions based on false information, without necessarily understanding the details that make all the difference, including what the research actually says, OR how the research was actually done.

Let me explain why I believe this is exactly what happened with THIS article, by digging into the details of the study. Please follow along with me as I go through this study in detail. I promise it will make sense at the end and you'll understand why you can't trust headlines.

In the study, <u>139 people</u> were randomly assigned to one of two groups, called Group 1 and Group 2. Group 1 was the *control* group. Group 2 was the experimental group.

Remember a *control group* is a group that does not include any change to the variable being tested. Why is a control group important in an experiment? The control group is important because it acts as a benchmark to compare the results of the experiment to. The *experimental group* is the group that is the object of the testing.

1. Group 1 were those doing a calorie restricted diet (1200-1500 total calories for women, 1500-1800 total calories for men) alone.
2. Group 2 were those following the same calorie restricted diet as Group 1, PLUS time restricted eating (TRE).

Note being in the 2nd group meant the participants could only eat for 8 hours of the day, between 8:00 am - 4:00 pm. As you'll soon learn, this is an important factor in the results they achieved.

Keep in mind BOTH groups were on *calorie restricted* diets, which is important in the context of this study and as you'll soon see, was a big problem. Why? Over the short term, calorie restriction almost always leads to some weight loss, depending on the weight and body composition of the person. Therefore, it would be easy to then draw the conclusion that whatever weight loss was achieved happened *because* of calorie restriction, and *not* TRE. This is clearly a poor study design element and essentially killed any chance of the researchers learning what they hoped to about TRE! Why? To achieve accurate results and reliably test the effect of TRE, the study should have had both subjects eating a *moderate calorie diet* that *isn't either* restricted or excessive. As an aside, scientific studies have reliably demonstrated eating too few calories chronically, which is essentially what a "calorie restricted" diet is, *doesn't work long-term* and isn't healthy.

That being said, let's find out if the TRE folks, who could only eat between 8 and 4, actually did lose more weight? According to the study, not really. To be clear, after 12 months, the TRE group *did* indeed lose 4 pounds, but this amount was deemed "not statistically significant," hence the headline in the article, "Scientists Find No Benefit to Time Restricted Eating."

As you might imagine, there's a lot more to this story than meets the eye, or the headline for that matter. There are a lot of problems with how the study was conducted, starting with the calorie restriction I mentioned earlier. To see what I mean, see the next two missteps on the part of the researchers.

1. This study did not have enough participants to show the difference the researchers were looking for. Without enough subjects, there's a too small sample size and thus, you cannot prove the conclusions are valid. This is what is deemed a classic "underpowered" study.
2. What was the standard they set to be able to call the weight loss "statistically significant?" They stated there must be a 40% increase in weight loss from only 16% increase in fasting time! Anyone would agree that's a ridiculous expectation, especially considering the control group wasn't particularly overweight to begin with. Their average weight was only 194 pounds.

If you're not sure what I mean by saying the expectation was unrealistic and even ridiculous, let me explain: The control group (not TRE) lost approximately 13 pounds over the 12 months of the study, which is, to put it into context, a good result. Here's the kicker: according to the research design, in order for the study of 139 subjects to have shown TRE works, there needed to be an *additional 5.5 pound weight* loss in the TRE group compared to the control group. That would mean a total of 18.5 pounds, or about a 40% increase!

Was this a reasonable weight loss target for the design? To really find out, let's look closely at some more of the variables. The control group (not TRE) had an eating window of 10.2 hours per day, which means they didn't eat for 13.8 hours. The TRE group ate over 8 hours a day and didn't eat for 16 hours. The increase in "fasting" time is 2.2 hours, or *only* 16%. That's not a huge difference in time between the two groups, yet this is what the researchers expected would cause an extra 5.5 pounds in weight loss.

Think about this for a second. To expect an extra 40% weight loss because of only a 16% decrease in the eating window, is ridiculous, especially considering the amount of time the TRE group was given to eat. A full 8 hours. That's a nearly "normal" window for many people. Anyone who understands how challenging it is to lose weight understands how unrealistic and poorly designed this was. As you know from having read this chapter, my recommendations for TRE are for a smaller eating "window" than 8 hours, yet that is what they used for this study group.

If you're wondering WHY this difference in the eating window is significant, consider that most well-designed studies have *shown people eat LESS when they have less time to eat.* [26] That makes sense doesn't it? After all, if you only have 2 hours to eat, there's no way you're going to eat as much as you would if you had 4 or 5 or 6 hours to eat, right? To think of it another way, I've found many people eat too much simply *because* they are eating too often.

The other obvious issue here is this study was designed to test independent variables instead of dependent ones. After all, the time you spend eating and the total amount you eat are not independent variables and treating them as such will miss the key fact that for some people, this is the ultimate cause of why they are eating too much, and then gaining weight.

There's a huge difference between a 4 or 6 hour window, and an 8 hour window.

Here's a graphic that offers a clear visual representation of this difference, taken from a 2020 study published in the magazine, *Cell Metabolism.* [27] Here are the highlights of this study:

- 4 hour and 6 hour time-restricted feeding regimens were tested in adults with obesity.
- Both regimens produced similar weight loss over the 2 months of the study.
- Both regimens reduced energy intake by ~550 kcal per day without calorie counting.
- Both regimens produced similar reductions in insulin resistance and oxidative stress.

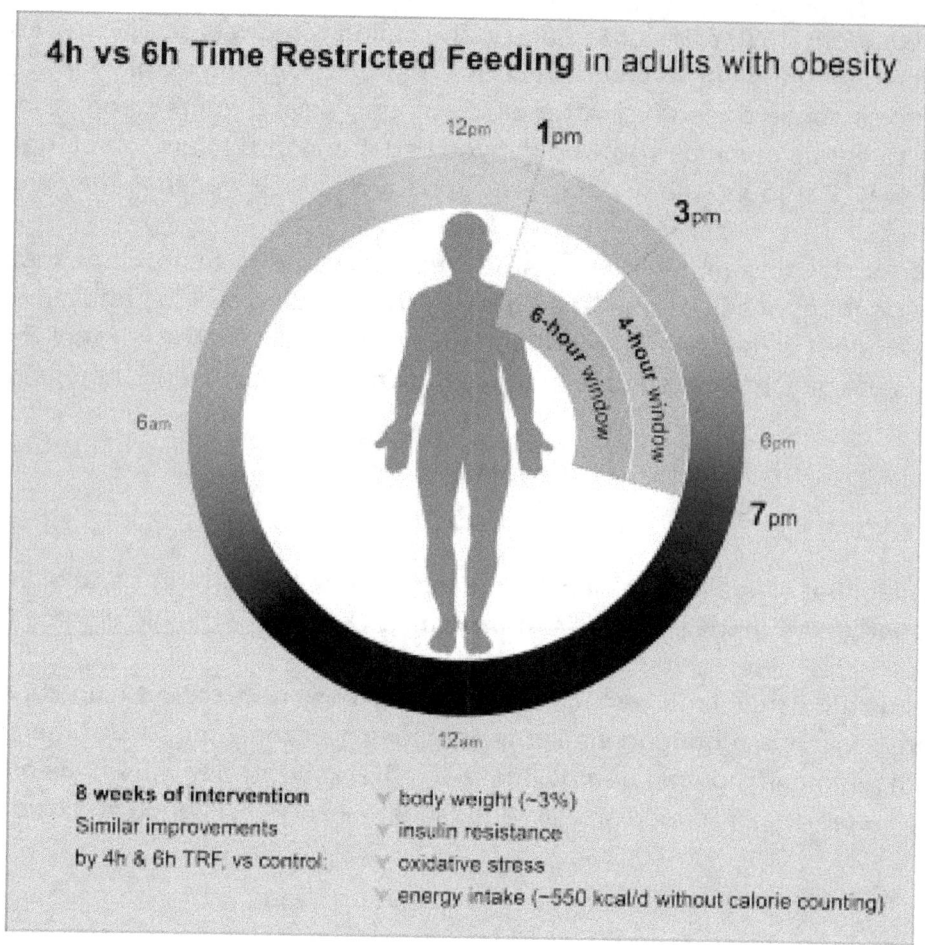

4h vs 6h Time Restricted Feeding in adults with obesity

12pm · **1**pm · 3pm · 6pm · 7pm · 6am · 12am

6-hour window · 4-hour window

8 weeks of intervention
Similar improvements
by 4h & 6h TRF, vs control:

▼ body weight (~3%)
▼ insulin resistance
▼ oxidative stress
▼ energy intake (~550 kcal/d without calorie counting)

One important take-home from those highlights is both the 4 and 6-hour TRE regimens reduced caloric intake of around 500-600 calories per day *without* calorie "counting." That's a positive benefit – no one wants to count calories!

The bottom line is this: the *New York Times* article's subject heading is terribly misleading, and the study cited that was the basis for the article was poorly designed and doesn't, in fact, show that TRE is NOT effective. But that IS what you would believe if you just read the headline and didn't dig a little deeper into the details.

What it does show is we always have to look closer for nuance that tells the whole story. You simply can't believe what you read, no matter what the source is, without first looking further and investigating all the facts. Which is something I hope you do with this book too.

Key Concept:

Other Reasons TRE Can Work Well For Most People

Dr Jason Fung has worked with thousands of obese and overweight individuals and helped many achieve their optimal weight and reverse type-2 diabetes. He says TRE is one of the tools he teaches his patients to achieve their weight loss and health goals. Here are some of the reasons he believes TRE works![28]

1. TRE creates a structure to your eating day. Instead of the rule "eat whenever you want," you have a rule "eat only between 8am and 6pm" or whatever time interval you want to follow.
2. TRE creates consistency by having the same eating window.
3. TRE makes it easy to turn this approach into a habit. Consistency builds habits. Once it becomes habit to avoid late night eating, you no longer need as much willpower to avoid late night eating because this has become your new normal.
4. TRE is free. It doesn't cost money, it saves money.
5. TRE doesn't take more time, it saves time.
6. TRE can be applied to any type of approach to diet.
7. TRE simplifies your life. It doesn't make life complicated, it makes it simpler.
8. TRE is easy for anybody to understand. The "rules" can be explained in a minute or less.
9. TRE is a traditional way of eating, allowing time for the body to digest the food eaten. It's not a new-fangled fad, it's the oldest eating rule in the book. DON'T EAT ALL THE TIME.

OK, now that you have a good understanding of what TRE is and the many benefits as well as how to approach it, let's move on to the next chapter to learn more about the dangers of processed sugar. Brace yourself. You won't ever look at it the same way again. I'll see you there!

CHAPTER 11

SUGAR

The three most harmful addictions are heroin, carbohydrates, and a monthly salary.

— **Nassim Nicholas Taleb**

Is glucose a sugar? Yes. Is fructose a sugar? Yes.
Are they the same? Not even close.
—Dr. Peter Attia, M.D.

S-u-g-a-r.

Just saying it brings rise to a slew of emotions, doesn't it? It's a blessing, because it makes everything it's in, taste so good. And as you'll see, it's also a bit of a curse. As simple as that one word is, though, the impact of it in our diet and our American way of life, is far from simple.

Besides being delicious, it's also addictive, and toxic, especially in larger amounts. I don't think it's overstating it to say it's the central *linchpin* for the widespread and dramatic decline of our overall health. Not just us as individuals, but also globally. Think that's too strong a statement to make?

What about this: Our nationwide intake of sugar is as much as 400x more than what it was two decades ago. It's estimated the average American consumes 152 pounds of sugar a year![1] 152 pounds!! That's equivalent to three pounds a week! And it's not just in the "obvious" places like candy and soda. You'll find it hiding in salad dressings, "'health" sports drinks and bars, pasta sauces, breakfast cereals, and even "good for you" foods like yogurt. It is in virtually every single processed food.

Think about this:

- We live in a world where about 25 million Americans, especially those in lower income areas, live in a "food desert" where it's nearly impossible to find a vegetable. *But there are fast food restaurants and gas stations on every corner.*
- We live in a world where more than 8 out of 10 products on the grocery store shelves are processed and contain added sugar, where the food we're eating is all essentially a commodity.
- We live in a world where 60-70% of the foods we eat are basically derived from a small number of raw materials – wheat, corn, and soy, which are flour, sugar, and refined seed oils, turned into all varieties of processed foods.

Entire books have been written about the sugar molecule and why it's responsible for our expanding waistlines and growing list of chronic diseases. You may have heard at one time that the evil lurking in our food was saturated fat. As you've already read in this book, *that was a myth.* The real evil is sugar, in all its forms.

My goal here isn't to reiterate what has already been said countless times or quote the advice of experts who have written about their own research. It's also not to go on and on about the dangers of too much sugar, although you will likely be thinking that way by the time you finish this chapter.

Rather, my goal is to give you, the reader, a little bit of <u>a wake-up call</u> about *the dangers to your health that are associated with the chronic consumption of sugar in all its forms.* And to wake you up to the goings on and propaganda that has come at us in all forms of marketing and messaging from the food industry.

I'm also here to remind you that because of this, the problems we're facing aren't entirely your or my fault. As I alluded to in an earlier chapter, we're lining up to do battle with an enemy that unfortunately doesn't have our best interest at heart. The enemy that wants our money, every day in every way, is <u>BIG FOOD</u> as I've often referred to them – the corporations whose primary focus is making cheap, plentiful, delicious food available to as many people as possible, so their profit margins go up-up-up! They're running the show. If you're wondering what "show" I'm referring to, it's what has become the typical American *way of life.* Alongside a government that's failed to hold them accountable and is in some ways, equally culpable, as is a modern medical establishment also profiting from illness, we've got a battle on our hands to get our collective health moving in the right direction.

Let me ask you a rhetorical question: *is it better to be cured of cancer or to have never gotten cancer in the first place?* Statistics say only 33 percent of people treated for cancer survive past the five-year mark. That's scary. At the same time, according to estimates, as a country we spend 97.5% of our healthcare budget on treatment and only 2.5% on prevention. Drugs after all, don't treat the *cause* of chronic disease, they only treat the *symptoms.* There's no profit in good health, but there sure is a lot of profit to be made in treating symptoms.

One might argue our healthcare system is collapsing under the extreme demand to treat disease. After all, again according to estimates, only three out of ten baby boomers report they're in good health. The fact is more people than ever, especially those 50 and older, are struggling with some kind of chronic disease. I'd say the acronym "SAD," which I've heard used in various circles including from longevity expert, Dr. Peter Attia, pretty much describes the "show": The (S)tandard (A)merican (D)iet.

Nestle, PepsiCo, Coca-Cola, Tyson Foods, not to mention McDonalds - those are a few of the <u>Big Food</u> goliaths creating the irresistible food contributing to skyrocketing rates of metabolic disease and insulin resistance, overweight and obesity, and chronic diseases that are literally killing us.

And, if you think government is on our side and is standing up to make things right, you might want to think again. Sometimes I really do believe the often-repeated phrase "government is not the solution to our problem, it IS the problem." At the very least, the government is complicit in not getting things right like the low-fat fiasco, the labeling rules, and the food pyramid. If you'd like to learn even more about government's role in many of the nutrition challenges we face as a nation, a great resource is the chapter titled *What Has the Government Wrought,* in Dr. Robert Lustwig's book, *Fat Chance.*[2]

Admit It - We're Addicted.

It's easy to forget food is a drug. But trust me, the companies I mentioned – THEY haven't forgotten it, that's for sure. The fast food and processed foods we all think of as a normal part of American life today – they are all addictive – every bit as much as tobacco, alcohol, and drugs. We don't just become addicted to the taste of these foods – we're addicted to the smell, the texture, the colors, and even the memories that we associate with them. They're designed by the food manufacturers to be *biologically* addictive.

It comes back to the pleasure centers in our brain and one very specific neurotransmitter called dopamine. Our brain likes for us to be "rewarded," and it certainly seeks pleasure. Think of it this way: it's about what some experts refer to as our "hedonic pathway, where primal emotions, reproductive drive, and survival instincts are all housed and expressed."[3] So, what's the basic connection to dopamine?

As you may know, dopamine seems to be the motivator to drive us to do the things that give us pleasure. Social media and sex are two things that immediately come to mind. As it relates to what we eat, words like "yumminess" and "euphoria" are often associated with dopamine release. It's a feeling of joy. Dopamine is sometimes called the "pleasure" juice. The key thing to remember is it isn't just the feeling you get *after* eating an Oreo cookie or McDonald's french fries, it's also *the anticipation* - as you drive down the road, pull up to the drive-thru window, and reach into the bag you can almost taste them!

I appreciate how author Michael Moss summarizes this incredible series of chemical reactions in our brain driven by dopamine and all designed to keep us fully engaged: Imagine yourself walking into McDonalds or pulling up to the drive-through window, you "wouldn't be chasing mere happiness, as the company likes to say in its advertising. (You) would be pursuing a feeling that comes from doing something far more important: staying alive. (Your) brain would be letting (you) know in no uncertain terms that nothing in the entire universe – not (your) self-respect, or finances, or the plan (you) had for losing some weight – could be more important than placing that order."[4]

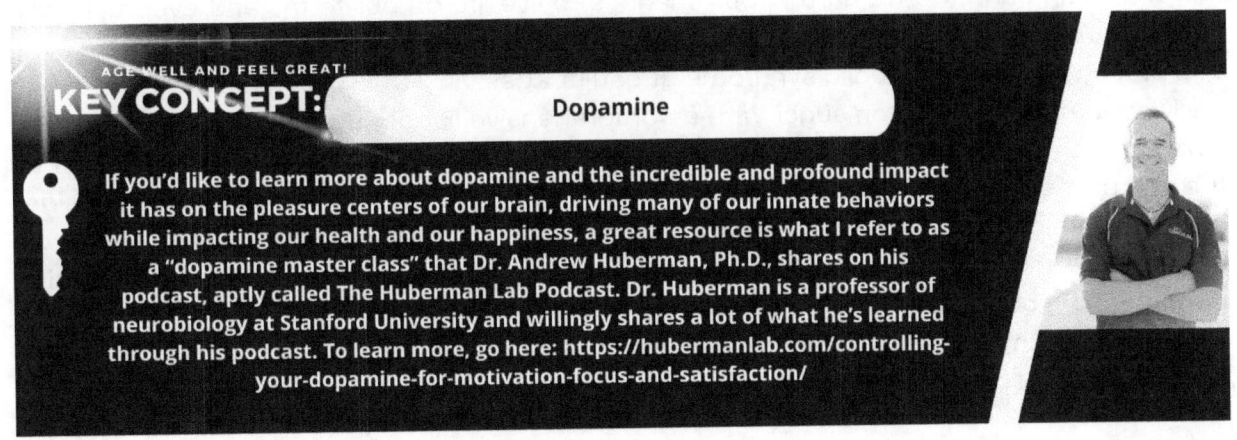

AGE WELL AND FEEL GREAT!

KEY CONCEPT: Dopamine

If you'd like to learn more about dopamine and the incredible and profound impact it has on the pleasure centers of our brain, driving many of our innate behaviors while impacting our health and our happiness, a great resource is what I refer to as a "dopamine master class" that Dr. Andrew Huberman, Ph.D., shares on his podcast, aptly called The Huberman Lab Podcast. Dr. Huberman is a professor of neurobiology at Stanford University and willingly shares a lot of what he's learned through his podcast. To learn more, go here: https://hubermanlab.com/controlling-your-dopamine-for-motivation-focus-and-satisfaction/

Sugar ISN'T Just One Thing or Type of Molecule.

We typically use the word *sugar* to describe what we put in coffee or sprinkle on our oatmeal or what is sometimes hidden inside packages of food, as though we're describing only one kind of molecule or substance. We often talk about "natural" sugars found in vegetables and fruits, and the opposite, "artificial" sugars found in processed foods. The truth is, there are a LOT of different types of sugar. The most dangerous is the type you can't see or may not even know exists in the food you're eating.

The type of sugar (whether it's fructose, glucose, allulose, dextrose, or some combination, like sucrose, which is what we know as "table sugar"), isn't what I want to focus on here. In truth, you could easily research and read more if you're interested. I recommend you take the time to do that.

What I want to focus on to help you make the most informed decisions, is the *effect* that each type has on you and me. You see, they all share nearly identical molecular make up. What's different is the effect they have on us. And our health.

Let's start with insulin resistance. In Chapter 9, I went into great detail about *hyperinsulinemia* and *insulin resistance* and all of the chronic diseases that come from them. Across the board, regardless of the type of sugar, insulin resistance is very largely a direct effect of *excess* sugar consumption. Note I used the word, *excess*.

So, the question is, what is *excess* for you? Or most people? Well, that depends on your current health and health history, and your activity level, for starters. For example, someone who is pre-diabetic or has high blood pressure or a high fasting glucose, and who might also be moderately overweight, has much less "margin of error" than a physically active and fit person who has normal and/or "ideal" metabolic health markers. The bottom line, as you've read many times in this book, the effects of *excess* sugar intake are devastating for our health and well-being and they're hurting our chances to live life on our terms and eventually die healthy. To add insult to an already growing problem, kids are being affected more than ever and presenting with metabolic syndrome at earlier ages.

I'll wrap this segment on sugar with a comprehensive list of suggestions, tips, and links where you can go to learn more about a particular subtopic. Before I do, though, remember at the end of the day, it comes back to processed food and the hidden dangers lurking inside. It's just that simple. **If you learn one single thing from this book, it should be the more you can replace the processed food in your diet with some kind of REAL food, the healthier and happier you will be. It's that simple.**

Next, for a more nuanced approach to eating, remember these THREE things. And don't forget you can come back often to re-read this if it helps!

1. **We're an experiment of one:** I've said it before here in this book and I'll say again at some point: your relationship with food as a whole and sugar in particular, is all your own. We're all an experiment of one. Some of us have a wider "margin of error" than do others, such as the serious athlete who is burning lots of carbohydrate due to many hours of sports training. Be honest with yourself, know yourself and the battle you're facing and act accordingly in your own best interest.

    Along these lines is accepting ourselves and our own faults, our own unique strengths and weaknesses, and the unique challenges we each face. And still loving ourselves! It could be long work hours, a long commute, the lack of high-quality organic foods where you live or the cost, or the people you live with who, despite their best intentions, make things more challenging – whatever it is!

    It's human nature to want to compare ourselves to others and when we do, we almost always come up on the short side of things – feeling worse about ourselves. DON'T do that! Wherever you are, be there, right where your feet are. Learn to love yourself for who you are. Strive to be better, a little bit each day.

2. **This *isn't and won't ever* be about "perfection" or giving up some of the foods you love.** Let it go, "perfection" is not what it's about! I enjoy a lot of different kinds of treat foods, like an occasional chocolate bar or one of my favorites, carrot cake! But I don't do it frequently. And when I do indulge, it's usually on a day when I've gone through an extended period of not eating, or a day when I did more than the usual amount of exercise. The minute I feel the urge that I must HAVE it, that lets me know to be even more keenly aware of what I'm putting in my mouth.

    While it isn't and won't ever be about "perfection," it IS about understanding *and* accepting that while a piece of chocolate or a cookie isn't evil or something you have to "give up" forever, eating it every day (or every other day) for weeks or months or years on end, may contribute to an evil, poor health-related outcome. There isn't any such thing as a "bad" food, (although some experts would argue this). It's about "bad" habits. I'll say it again: don't get hung up thinking this is about being "perfect." It isn't. But at the same time, you need to accept that your habits create your outcomes. You can't have it all, all the time.

3. **Strive to change only one tiny thing about your habits or routine at a time.** In other words, avoid the temptation to make massive changes all at once. If I've seen it once I've seen it a hundred times – someone gets excited about a new lifestyle change or makes a decision to try and improve or change something, and they go all gangbusters with massive changes in a short amount of time. Then, because they put so much pressure on themselves to *keep it going*, eventually their motivation starts to wane a bit and before you know it, that big transformation becomes a memory. *Don't let that happen.*

eat less sugar

{ you're sweet enough already }

The path to success is paved with tiny repeatable "tweaks" to our routine or habits – that sometimes feel like no change at all. What you want is something sustainable, *without* placing too much pressure or stress on yourself to keep it going. Start by eating dessert one less time per week. That's a small change. But your goal is to keep that change. Establish it as a new habit.

Or start by making a commitment to not eat after 6pm for at least one day/night per week, and then make it two, and then if you can keep that commitment, challenge yourself to go for a Monday – Friday routine. Sometimes you won't be able to stick with it because of a social outing or some other unforeseen factor but get right back on the horse the next day. Commit to it!

Take control. Small changes you can truly sustain are the key to your success. I'll talk more about this in the chapter on exercise, so keep reading.

What About Sugar Substitutes?

There's so much to learn about all the types of sugar substitutes such as aspartame, saccharin, and stevia, to name a few. My best recommendation is to limit how much you consume of any of these. Don't use them routinely. That means as an addition to your coffee OR as part of your diet soda kick. In this instance, it is about moderation. In other words, a very occasional sip of a diet soda isn't going to be harmful, unless it turns into a one or two a day, every day, habit. Then you've got a problem you need to address.

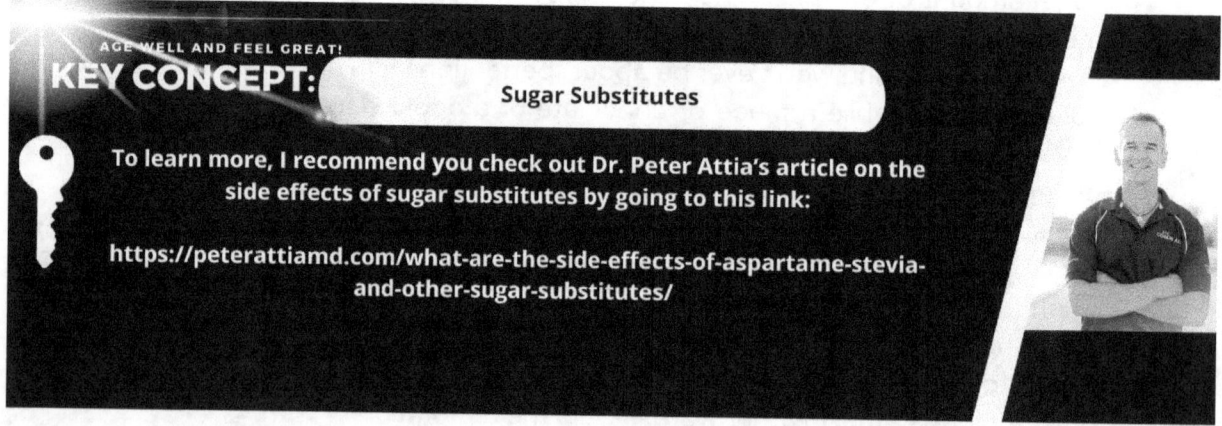

AGE WELL AND FEEL GREAT!

KEY CONCEPT: Sugar Substitutes

To learn more, I recommend you check out Dr. Peter Attia's article on the side effects of sugar substitutes by going to this link:

https://peterattiamd.com/what-are-the-side-effects-of-aspartame-stevia-and-other-sugar-substitutes/

Tips, Recommendations, and Links for More Information:

Become more aware. Advocate for your own health by knowing what it is you're putting in your mouth. Be honest with yourself. We're all fighting the same battle. It isn't easy, but the benefits are well worth it.

- **Eat REAL food.** Sometimes when I'm talking to someone about nutrition and want to drill the keys down to the simplest concepts, I go right to this: **Eat Real Food.** And yes, while that might seem to make it simpler than it might be sometimes, the truth is simple: <u>The closer you can get what you eat to be what God made *most of the time*, and not what a food manufacturer made, the better off you will be</u>. The better you will feel. <u>The less cravings you will experience. The leaner you will be</u>. For example, did God make Twinkies or Cheez Whiz? No, but he did make raspberries and avocados! Think about it.

- **Give up the fruit juices. They're not "healthy."** As a society, we drink much more sugar than we eat, which is ironic. And a lot of it is because we mistakenly believe fruit juices are healthy or as healthy as the fruit themselves. Not true. So, if you're in the habit of a daily glass of orange or apple juice, start to wean yourself off. Have the fruit instead.

- **Real fruit, especially organically grown, is fine. And recommended.** Fruit juices aren't recommended, but real fruit is! In real fruit, you'll get the benefits of increased soluble and insoluble fiber, nutrients, and water. As always, try to eat more of the low-sugar variety, such as berries. Vary what you eat and go with what is in-season at the time. Eat organic whenever you can.

- **Skip the soda and sports drinks, "most" of the time.** Together, these are the most highly advertised and marketed foods on the planet, and for good reason. They're not only addictive, they're also highly profitable for the companies that make them. The profit margin on this sugared water is through the roof! Again, start to wean yourself off them, little by little.

- **Be on the lookout for hidden sugar. Get into the habit of reading food labels.** The truth is, if it has a label, it probably has added sugar. Beet sugar, dextrose, cane sugar, and on and on it goes. Get to know where it is and avoid it whenever you can.

- **Remember, a craving isn't hunger.** Know the difference. For example, if you ate 3 hours ago and are feeling hungry, that likely isn't hunger, it's a craving. If you haven't eaten in 36 hours or so and are feeling hungry, that probably IS hunger. Know the difference.

- **Avoid High Fructose Corn Syrup (HFCS) like it is poison,** as this might be the most simultaneously ubiquitous and evil processed sugar in all of processed food manufacturing. Stay away from anything with added HFCS. Learn to recognize it. Fructose can be an especially harmful type of sugar depending upon the source. To learn more, check out this enlightening episode of *The Drive* podcast with Dr. Peter Attia, titled "How Fructose Drives Metabolic Disease," with well-known expert on fructose, Dr. Rick Johnson, MD. https://peterattiamd.com/rickjohnson2/

- **Want to know how to move forward?** *Start eating ONLY real food,* you'll begin to see disease disappear. And your waistline will shrink. It's very difficult to get "fat" on real food. *Get out into the sunshine,* you'll begin to see anxiety disappear. *Begin doing a little bit of exercise,* you'll begin to see muscles reappear. *Set up your ideal sleep environment, begin to sleep better,* and you'll see energy start to reappear. Focus on these basics to see the bad disappear and the good reappear.

- **Keep the foods OUT of your house that you know you can't resist.** If it's not in your pantry, you won't be able to indulge. Shop wisely and be disciplined. You'll be rewarded by eventually building new habits and in time, losing the cravings all together.
- **Don't buy your food where you buy your gasoline.** Despite there being some good food options if you look hard for them in your favorite quick stop shop mart, the overwhelming majority of choices are best left on the shelves.
- **Think of your food choices like stock market returns.** Would you invest in something that gives you negative returns OR positive returns? The difference is one is unpredictable to some degree (the market, obviously) whereas the other is very predictable.
- **When you switch from eating junk food to REAL whole foods, like our ancestors did, your brain is not going to like it.** It may try every trick in the book to sabotage your success. Why? The brain likes habits and doesn't like change, whether it's good or not so good for us. You must resist and persist! You can do it!
- **Remember your favorite alcoholic beverages are sometimes also a source of sugar.** In moderation, wine and other alcoholic drinks can be part of a healthy diet. The problem arises when it evolves to excess. My recommendation? No more than 3 to 5 glasses a week, even if those glasses are only red wine.
- **See your doctor at least once per year and have regular blood work done.** Know your fasting blood glucose level. Watch your uric acid levels as there are many studies that have drawn a close correlation between uric acid and development of fatty liver.[5] The bottom line, be aware of things like liver enzymes and blood pressure and glucose. Your doctor will know more, but the message here is to be an educated consumer. Advocate for YOUR health.

In his book, *Philosopher's Notes*, author Brian Johnson tells the story of how "Abraham Maslow liked to say that in any given moment we have a choice: Will we step forward into growth or back into safety?" I think that's a great question. Brian says, "Moment by moment by moment, we make a choice. And we shape our destiny. Brian says he likes to think of it like this: It's almost as if we have a little subconscious computer that's keeping score for us. +1 if we choose to step forward into growth. -1 if we choose to step back into safety.

+1 or -1. +1 or -1. +1 or -1.

Let's say the alarm goes off tomorrow morning. Do we step forward and do the thing we said we'd do – whether it's jumping out of bed and immediately meditating/going for a run/whatever? OR do we step back into safety and pull the covers over our head as we try to forget what we said we'd do and come up with some lame rationalization about how we need the rest, blah, blah, blah whiny blah?"[6]

+1 or -1.

I believe the same could be said when you're walking through the aisles of the grocery store. Based on some of what you learned in this chapter, do you stick with the promise you made to yourself to shop near the perimeter of the store, or do you fall victim to the fancy packaging and ease and convenience of processed, packaged junk food taking up space in the middle of the store?

The good news is that a few positive steps forward can have a mysteriously positive effect. You can build some momentum that can make all the difference. And we always have the choice to take that step forward! So, what's a +1 step you can take right now?

PS: Now's a good time to take it. I'll be here when you get back. ☺

CHAPTER 12

CHRONIC INFLAMMATION

It's not how old you are,
but how you are old.

– Marie Dressler

Like a lot of other people, I have a few weird quirks. One of them is I like to observe other people – "people watching" I call it – look at them and mostly observe how they "move." When I say "move," I mean whether they seem to be in pain or have a limp or if there's something that shows me their overall structural status. Do they sit or stand or walk or even run easily, or is it a struggle? That kind of thing.

If you know me at all, that won't come as a surprise. After all, throughout the years I've spent as a sports therapist and coach – owning and operating a gait analysis lab for about 10 years alongside a sports physician – I've always been a detail-oriented person and that's no different when I'm observing people. Suffice to say, I like to look and notice things! I also tend to over *think* things, but that's for another chapter. ☺

Anyway, beyond how someone might move, I also look to see if there are any telltale signs that might clue me in to their general health status. You can sometimes learn a lot about someone's health by how they look. The key is knowing *what it is* you're looking for. It isn't always obvious.

One area I'm always looking at is the feet, ankles, and legs. I'm looking to see if they're puffy, or if there is a more defined look to them. Often as people get older, they tend to have that puffy, inflamed look. Sometimes there will be a reddish color to their skin. That's one telltale sign of *chronic inflammation*, which is, coincidentally, the topic of this chapter.

Laying out the first draft of the outline for this book back in March of 2022, I knew I'd include a chapter sharing what I've learned about chronic inflammation – the impact it has on our health, markers for it, and obviously what we have learned might be the primary causes. I decided to include it in Part Two, simply because now more than ever, we're coming to understand the critical link between diet and the degree of chronic, often damaging inflammation that may be lurking inside our body.

Looking at it from a distance, inflammation is one of those subjects that can easily be misunderstood. It is easy to look at inflammation and see it as a singular "problem," when in truth, it isn't that simple. Sometimes, as in the case of acute inflammation, it's not a "problem" at all – it's a normal process that occurs as the body is healing itself, as in the period of time following a sprained ankle. As in many things, we're reminded that understanding inflammation requires a little nuance.

One thing seems clear: chronic inflammation is now negatively linked with Alzheimer's and other dementias, cancer, fatty liver disease, cardiovascular disease, and the list goes on. All the chronic diseases that are literally killing us. Author and researcher, Dr. David Sinclair, believes chronic inflammation is so central to the development of age-related diseases, he and other scientists often refer to the process as "inflammaging." As I alluded to in Chapter 9, there's also an undeniable connection between *chronic inflammation* and *insulin resistance* and *hyperinsulinemia*. The question that remains as the debate in the scientific community rages on, is what comes first, the insulin resistance or the chronic inflammation?

Chronic inflammation is *murkier* than insulin resistance. That is, it isn't always obvious to us that it exists. For example, many people know what fluctuating energy levels feel like, but most don't feel bloated all the time, and thus may not be aware they have an inflammatory problem. I also believe many mistakenly believe the symptoms of redness or swelling to be somewhat "normal," especially as we age.

One other aspect to be aware of is inflammation is often linked with something called *cellular senescence*, which I briefly alluded to in Chapter 2, *Why We Age*. To review, what is a *senescent* cell? According to one of the world's experts on the topic, Ned David, Ph.D., it's a cell that stops dividing and is no longer functional. The number of these *senescent* cells increases as we age.[1] Some experts believe *senescent* cells can't become cancerous, but they can do lots of other damage to cells around them and are known to produce toxins and other inflammatory mediators that do most of the damage we associate with aging and mortality.[2] Says author Daniel Levitin, Ph.D., they are akin to "zombies in a horror movie," that just "won't die."[3]

So, what are some of the damaging toxins produced by the senescent cells? One example is a protein called a *cytokine*. According to Dr. Sinclair, *cytokines* "cause inflammation and attract immune cells called macrophages that then attack the tissue." In Sinclair's view, being chronically inflamed is unhealthy. We need look no further than to anyone battling multiple sclerosis, inflammatory bowel disease, or psoriasis. He says, "all these diseases are associated with excess cytokine production."[4]

In December of 2019, the Journal *Nature Medicine* published a groundbreaking report with a very long list of highly respected authors, titled: *Chronic Inflammation in the Etiology of Disease Across the Lifespan*, which was funded by the National Institutes of Health and more than a dozen other academic institutions. In the report, the abstract says "recent research has revealed that certain social, environmental and lifestyle factors can promote *systemic chronic inflammation* (SCI) that can, in turn, lead to several diseases that collectively represent the leading causes of disability and mortality worldwide, such as cardiovascular disease, cancer, diabetes mellitus, chronic kidney disease, non-alcoholic fatty liver disease and autoimmune and neurodegenerative disorders. In the present Perspective we describe the multi-level mechanisms underlying SCI and several risk factors that promote this health-damaging phenotype, including infections, physical inactivity, poor diet, environmental and industrial toxicants, and psychological stress."[5]

The take home message here is simple: There's certainly enough scientific evidence to show chronic inflammation is closely associated with virtually every chronic disease. In my opinion, it's a silent killer. If you believe you may be battling some chronic inflammation, ask your doctor to test your level of *C-Reactive Protein*, which is a protein in your blood that rises as your level of chronic inflammation rises.[6] It is important to seek your doctor's input and guidance, to be sure you're looking at all your options and being tested appropriately.

Age Well and Feel Great!
Key Concept:

Is There A Connection Between
Depression And Chronic Inflammation?

Some good research does show a link between depression and systemic, chronic inflammation.[7] That might not be surprising considering how important our emotional state is to our overall health. We're reminded once again the human body doesn't recognize the medical profession's or our own sometimes artificial separation of physical and mental illnesses. Emotional stress or anxiety can absolutely manifest a serious physical disease, and vice versa, making the recovery from a disease more difficult. Mind, body, and spirit form a critical three-way street.

As you recall, I discussed this briefly in Chapter 6: The Mainstays of a Long Healthy Life. Our physical health is closely tied to our emotional state of mind. We need a strong sense of purpose, a supportive community, and to be around those we love and who love us, to be truly happy and healthy, regardless of our age.

These things do become even more crucial as we reach our later years, but for reasons that probably seem obvious to you, they sometimes get harder to hold onto as we age. Children grow and often move away, we retire from our primary vocations, and as a result, our sense of purpose can also "retire." We need to find new ways to energize ourselves and our lives! The possibilities are endless, but they won't fall down upon us like magic pixie dust. We need to seek them out. Be proactive. And never give up.

What Treatments Lower Chronic Inflammation?

Most treatments to lower chronic inflammation involve cutting back on or removing altogether the two most common foods that can cause it, which are wheat and dairy. If you're thinking there's a recurring theme here, especially with regard to wheat, you're right. With our societal propensity for fast-foods and processed foods, many health issues can be traced to eating too much junk food. Not coincidently, being overweight and obese seems to also increase inflammation directly.

Are there other factors that seem to help? Staying active and moving, including exercising, absolutely helps. Sleeping better and more soundly also seems to help. There also appears to be a relationship between our gut microbiome and our energy levels. If you recall from Chapter 10 on *Time Restricted Eating*, I pointed out the highly inflammatory nature of polyunsaturated Omega-6 rich vegetable seed oils. These seed oils found in most homes and restaurants and often touted as "healthy," in part because the word "vegetable" is in the name, aren't healthy!

Why are seed oils hazardous for your health? Primarily, it has to do with the manufacturing process, where chemicals are used as solvents, as well as what happens to them as these seed oils age or when they're heated. Seed oils are unfortunately used in almost all factory-made foods, and are used by virtually every restaurant, even high-end 4-star expensive ones.

Here's my sincerest advice: target the following seed oils and remove them from your diet as much as you can: **corn oil, cottonseed oil, canola oil, grapeseed oil, and sunflower oil**.

So, what are the MOST inflammatory foods in the average person's diet? They are, in no particular order:

- Bread, cookies, pastries, and other similar processed foods with added refined sugars.
- Fried foods – anything cooked in vegetable oils. French fries, "Americanized" Chinese food, and anything cooked in a deep fryer.
- Soda and sugar-sweetened drinks including energy drinks.
- Processed meats like hot dogs, sausage, and lunch meats.
- Butter substitutes like margarine.

Having looked through the list of foods that are inflammatory, I'm sure you've noticed all of them contain *refined sugars, are processed and manufactured in a factory, and are made with or from seed oils. I can't say it strongly enough. Avoid eating these foods on a regular basis. On an every so often occasion, OK. Regularly? No way. Don't.*

In Summary, to Reduce Chronic Inflammation...

- **Limit the use of artificial sweeteners.**
- **Make sure to read about oral / dental health later in this book and pay close attention**. There's a strong correlation between poor oral health and systemic inflammation, and thus chronic disease. Keep your teeth clean by flossing and brushing daily, along with limiting the sugary drinks you consume. It's super important to reduce whole-body inflammation.
- **Get started on *Time Restricted Eating***. Head back to that chapter and get started. Having a non-eating window of time is linked with lower levels of chronic inflammation.
- **Get started on strength training**. You'll learn more about that in an upcoming chapter – it has a dramatic impact as does aerobic exercise, in diminishing chronic inflammation.[8]
- **Get outside more often**, especially in the morning, and whenever you can get more sunlight. That's always how I start my day – with a very tall glass of water and then a walk outside, all good habits that reduce chronic inflammation.

Do most if not all of these recommendations sound somewhat familiar to you? By the time you've reached this point in the book, I would think so. There IS a recurring theme here. ☺

Key Concept:

Quick Reminder: None Of What I've Shared Has To Be An All Or Nothing Proposition.

As I've said repeatedly, there's no such thing as a "bad" food, there are only those habits that will get us into trouble.

Take the foods above that I just mentioned. Do I occasionally indulge in a hotdog or a soda? Yes, I do. Occasionally. And that's the key word. As in a couple of times per year. When they become something you consume regularly, that's a problem.

One way I think of it? When I can't instantly imagine what a food tastes like, then it has probably been enough time since I last chose to eat it. Think about it that way and it'll help you make the best choice.

Can you really have your cake and eat it too? In the end, you will need to find your limits. Some find that they need to go "cold turkey" if they're struggling with health issues. Others can strike the right balance, and that's great as long as you're being honest with yourself. In the end, you are the person most responsible for your health. That's a good thing to remember.

CHAPTER 13

CHOLESTEROL: *FACTS, MYTHS, AND MISINFORMATION*

The new guidelines are based on shoddy science and misinterpretation of the data. This is a gift to Big Pharma. The American Heart Association has become little more than a propaganda arm of Big Pharma and Big Food. It's a disgrace.

— **Dr. Barbara Roberts,**
cardiologist and director of the Women's Cardiac Center at The Miriam Hospital and associate clinical professor of Medicine at the Alpert Medical School of Brown University, speaking about the new guidelines recently published by the American Heart Association. She is the author of *The Truth about Statins: Risks and Alternatives to Cholesterol-Lowering Drugs.*

When I first thought of writing this book, the idea was to share my experiences and whatever wisdom I had gleaned so others could learn from my mistakes and experimentation. I didn't intend to do a deep dive into any specific medical or clinical topics. After all, I'm not a doctor or laboratory researcher. Of course, if you've read through the chapter on *insulin resistance* and *hyperinsulinemia*, you know that I felt it was important to go way beyond simply sharing my practical experience and look closer at the science surrounding that very important topic.

I'm approaching cholesterol in a similar way. Again, I won't pretend to be a doctor or a researcher who is working day in and day out in the cholesterol arena. In truth, I feel like a bit of an imposter for even broaching this topic. But I've had my experience, and this is my book after all, right? So, I'm forging ahead into deeper waters.

What I'll share is a very simplified version of what is actually going on inside your body. One might also say it's a subjective, scaled down version. It's hard to keep cognitive bias out of the equation. Additionally, there are entire textbooks written on blood fats – what they are, and what they mean, etc. There is no way to cover it all here and I'm not going to try. But at the same time, this is a topic that is very important if the goal is to become truly healthy. I'm compelled to share what I have learned. I'll leave the rest up to you. You decide for yourself. Sound like a plan? Good. Let's get started.

There is so much to discuss about cholesterol: the potential dangers of high blood levels, its connection to heart disease risk and inflammation, where it comes from, and the idea that in my opinion, there exists a lot of misinformation about it. This makes it a complicated AND controversial topic.

And on top of whatever scientific research exists, is the fact if you watch any television at all, you know drug companies are spending millions of dollars to get their message out. What's that message, you ask? Taking statin drugs to treat "high" cholesterol is an essential part of the "solution."

So, before I get to my own story and cholesterol numbers, I need to repeat, this topic is *controversial*. There are differing opinions among experts, and a lot is at stake for not only the medical profession and the drug companies, but most importantly, you and me! After all, if we don't know the truth, how on earth are we going to know who to trust or listen to? And how will we make informed decisions about what is best? So, at the outset, my advice is to keep all of this in mind as you read.

There's No Such Thing As "Good "and "Bad" Cholesterol.

Let's start by discussing some important terms, starting with cholesterol itself. What is it? Cholesterol is a fat-like molecule – a "lipid" - that your body uses to make cells, hormones, and acids, among other things. The idea that cholesterol is "bad" is a myth. Not only is it not bad, it's essential for life and part of every single membrane in your body. If you're wondering where cholesterol comes from, every single cell in the body synthesizes it and we also get a small amount of it in the food we eat.

What are HDL and LDL? Is HDL "Good" and LDL "Bad"?

The acronym HDL is short for "high density lipoprotein." LDL, as you probably guessed, is short for "low density lipoprotein." The first thing to know is that HDL and LDL aren't even cholesterol, they're proteins that *carry* cholesterol and other fatty substances through the bloodstream. Think of them as somewhat like natural oils, waxes, and steroids, that are *blood fat transport particles.* If you're wondering why cholesterol needs a "carrier," it's because fat doesn't mix well with water, so a carrier is necessary.

Again, the words "bad" and "good" don't mean very much when it comes to cholesterol, even though they've become part of how we think of it. I'll say it once more: _there is no such thing as "good" or "bad" cholesterol._ Read that again. I'll wait. ☺

Keeping It Simple.

When it comes to *low density lipoproteins,* for the purposes of simplifying and zeroing in on the most important facts for you to learn, I'll refer only to "LDL," even though that is actually a gross oversimplification. In reality, there are many different types of low-density lipoproteins, including LDL-P, LDL-C, and even V-LDL, which is short for *very low-density lipoprotein.* If you'd like to learn more about the differences, I encourage you to research it on your own.

My Own Personal Stake in This Topic.

I'll say up front I have a personal stake in this topic. Why? Just like you, I get blood work done for my annual physical. This is smart, as you read about in Chapters 5 and 6, where I discussed the importance of early diagnosis.

My Lipid Panel

A few years ago, the results from my blood draw showed my total and LDL cholesterol were high. See the picture below, which is a clipped image of one portion of my report. I've highlighted both the TOTAL and LDL in yellow. You'll notice the total cholesterol is 228. And the LDL is 152.

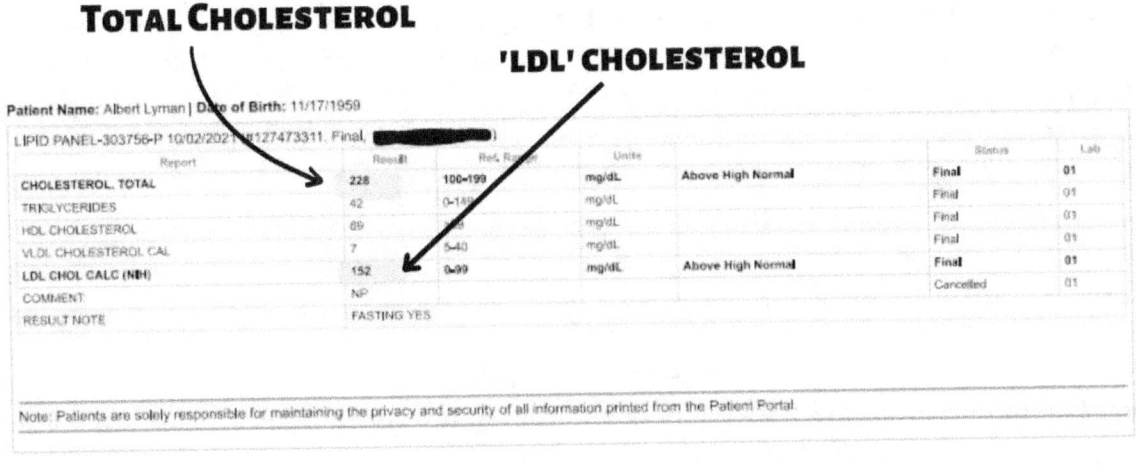

TOTAL CHOLESTEROL

'LDL' CHOLESTEROL

Patient Name: Albert Lyman | Date of Birth: 11/17/1959

LIPID PANEL-303756-P 10/02/2021 #127473311, Final,

Report	Result	Ref. Range	Units		Status	Lab
CHOLESTEROL, TOTAL	228	100-199	mg/dL	Above High Normal	Final	01
TRIGLYCERIDES	42	0-149	mg/dL		Final	01
HDL CHOLESTEROL	69		mg/dL		Final	01
VLDL CHOLESTEROL CAL	7	5-40	mg/dL		Final	01
LDL CHOL CALC (NIH)	152	0-99	mg/dL	Above High Normal	Final	01
COMMENT	NP				Cancelled	01
RESULT NOTE	FASTING YES					

Note: Patients are solely responsible for maintaining the privacy and security of all information printed from the Patient Portal.

My general physician was moderately concerned with these "too-high" numbers. If you look at my results, you'll notice according to the reference range, the total cholesterol *should be* less than 200 and the LDL cholesterol *should be* less than 100. As it turns out, every other health marker I have was at or above the recommended levels, according to the established standards anyway. But still, my doctor felt it was worth "keeping an eye on."

As you can imagine, the idea that I had a cholesterol level and an LDL level (which is typically considered to be the "bad" type, remember) above the recommended range, didn't sit very well with me. I asked myself the obvious questions: *How could this be? What was I doing wrong? What am I missing?* Perhaps you've had the same experience and have had numbers that surprised and even worried you, leading to you wanting to learn more? It can be a little disconcerting if you're like me and want every series of numbers to fall in line with where they "*should*" be, you know?

I could keep going, but before I go too far, let's review some basic definitions so I can be sure we're on the same page. Then we'll discuss more about what these numbers actually mean in both my opinion and in the opinion of some of the experts and doctors I trust. I'll also talk about some other myths and misconceptions.

What Have We Been Told About Cholesterol?

For as long as I can remember, there's been this public perception that having a cholesterol level over 200 is associated with a higher risk of heart disease and if it is too high, we need to reduce the amount of foods containing cholesterol in our diet. I question the validity of both of these assertions. I'll discuss more in a moment about why I believe we should all be questioning this.

It's also been accepted as fact and conveyed to the general public as such, that in severe cases of a high cholesterol level or where there might be a genetic component where diet interventions haven't helped, we should consider a statin drug to lower cholesterol, and by doing so, will have a lower risk of heart disease. In case you're wondering what statin drugs are, they're a family of drugs developed to *artificially* lower blood fat and cholesterol levels. The most well-known is a drug named Lipitor.

Where Did These Accepted Standards for Cholesterol Levels Come From?

Are you wondering just as I was, where these established standards for cholesterol came from? Without going into the gory historical details, what I've learned is it all started in the early 1960s with a man named Ancel Keys.[1]

His picture on the cover of Time Magazine demonstrates how influential he was at that time. Besides being perhaps the most influential nutritionist of his day, he is also known as the developer of the "K-Ration" used by the military.

I encourage you to do your own research and learn more about Keys. I present this here only for context. What is undeniable is that what he shared through his study called the *Seven-Countries Study*,[2] has become widely accepted as dogma.

So, what was Key's message? Americans eat too much fat in general and too much saturated fat in particular, and to reduce the risk for heart disease, we should replace our too-high intake of saturated fats with polyunsaturated (vegetable, or seed oil) fats. His hypothesis was those polyunsaturated fats were healthier for you and me. From Key's work, what followed in the 1970s was the creation of a set of dietary guidelines for all Americans telling us to reduce our fat intake.

To reiterate, anyone old enough to remember back to the 1980s and 1990s knows there was and continues to be a massive media-wide campaign from governmental agencies and high profile heart disease organizations, such as the American Heart Association [3], the European Atherosclerosis Society (EAS), and others, telling the public high fat foods are "bad" and should be avoided. The present-day messaging continues to largely mirror Key's original recommendations. Similarly, the amount of cholesterol contained in food continues to be linked to dietary fat intake. If you were to assume this information from these influential heart disease organizations was true, you'd most likely believe high fat foods are "bad" and correspondingly, that "high" total cholesterol and especially LDL cholesterol, leads to increased risk of cardiovascular disease and heart attack.

Was Keys correct in his belief that American's eat too much fat and polyunsaturated fats are healthier? Should the fat contained in food and saturated fat in particular, be demonized? Do we need to reduce our intake of fat to lower our risk for heart disease? Does cholesterol, especially LDL cholesterol, build up and stick to artery walls and increase our risk of heart disease and clotting? As I'm sure you're saying to yourself right now, those are "million-dollar questions" at the heart of this controversial topic.

To review, Key's hypothesis as well as what the public has been told since the 1970s is known as the **Diet-Heart Hypothesis**. In practical terms, it simply says that 1) the fat you eat in food 2) raises your blood cholesterol level which 3) leads to increased risks for heart disease, heart attack, and stroke. So, again I'll ask, is this hypothesis correct? Is there a direct relationship between dietary fat and cholesterol levels and heart disease?

In 1985, Michael Brown and Joseph Goldstein received the Nobel Prize for their research on LDL cholesterol in people with a genetic condition called familial hypercholesterolemia (FH). This condition involves impaired binding of LDL to its membrane receptor, which results in dramatically elevated blood levels of LDL. Simply put, people with this genetic condition have elevated levels of LDL, which as you've read, is typically thought of as "bad" cholesterol.

Because people with FH exhibited premature cardiovascular disease (CVD), Brown and Goldstein declared there was a "causal relation between an elevated level of circulating LDL and atherosclerosis" [4], thereby providing support for the idea that elevated LDL cholesterol causes heart disease. Since then, as mentioned, this pejorative view of LDL as the "bad cholesterol" has been promoted by many high-profile heart disease organizations. In fact, the European Atherosclerosis Society (EAS) says "LDL is unequivocally recognized as the principal driving force in the development of ASCVD" (atherosclerotic cardiovascular disease).[5]

So, were Brown and Goldstein correct? To begin to answer that question and the other related rhetorical questions I've asked, I'd like to share what I learned in a conversation I had with one of the world's leading authorities on this diet-heart hypothesis, Dr. David Diamond, Ph.D., a professor in the Departments of Psychology and Molecular Pharmacology and Physiology at the University of South Florida. A google search of his name will give you access to a host of videos and articles.[6] This reference link will take you to an article entitled: *Bad Cholesterol May Not Be So Bad for You After All.*[7] This reference will also lead to the research paper on the same topic, addressing this myth that LDL is "bad."[8]

In a paper currently published in the public opinion section of the *Journal of Endocrinology and Diabetes*, Dr. Diamond and his colleagues respond to the finding from Brown and

Goldstein – that there's a causal relationship between circulating LDL and heart disease and atherosclerosis. This paper states the work Dr. Diamond and his colleagues have done demonstrate subsequent "studies on the FH population show extensive inconsistencies with the lipid hypothesis" (proposed by Brown and Goldstein.[9] In other words, they don't believe a causal relationship exists. The paper goes on to state, "if LDL is inherently atherogenic, the burden of atherosclerosis should increase with time of exposure to LDL. Thus, cardiovascular mortality would be predicted to increase with age as a direct consequence of time of exposure to LDL. But, to the contrary, studies show heart disease mortality in FH individuals declines with age. [9, 10] Elderly individuals with FH exhibit equivalent risk of heart disease mortality to those in the non-FH population, despite a lifetime of exposure to high LDL. This finding directly conflicts with the twin beliefs that LDL is inherently atherogenic, and that heart disease risk increases with the duration of LDL exposure.[11] That elderly FH individuals exposed to decades of high LDL demonstrate no increase in heart disease mortality, as well as no increase in morbidity from stroke [12] compared to the general population, undermines the lipid hypothesis - that high LDL is inherently atherogenic." The paper goes on to state that one more challenge to this "lipid hypothesis is FH individuals have a lifetime all-cause mortality rate equivalent to that of the general population." [10, 13-15] Clearly, it's Dr. Diamond's view and that of his colleagues who co-wrote this paper, that when you look at all of the research honestly, the hypothesis linking higher levels of LDL and increased risk of heart disease isn't supported.

I consider Dr. Diamond to be a trustworthy source of information. To understand one reason why, I'd like to provide some additional context by sharing a little of his own personal experience with cholesterol, which comes from a video transcription of a talk he gave in 2019 at a CrossFit Health Conference, titled *Deception in Cholesterol Research: Separating Truth from Profitable Fiction*.[16]

Dr. Diamond originally developed an interest in cholesterol and statin drugs in 1999 after being diagnosed with a familial disease called hypertriglyceridemia, a genetic anomaly that causes triglyceride levels in the blood to rise and can often lead to other health issues like obesity. He followed dietary recommendations, reducing saturated fat and meat consumption and ate more carbohydrates such as oatmeal and beans. What happened? Well, the only thing he succeeded in doing was raising his triglycerides even more (not a good result), lowering HDL (also not a good result) and to top it all off, gaining weight. So, what happened next? His doctor recommended he take a statin drug to lower his numbers. At that point he realized, "well, I've got a Ph.D. in biology. The least I can do is read about what a triglyceride is and what I should do about it."

After taking a deep dive into the research, he realized, "Damn! It's the bread, and the potatoes, and the sugar I've been eating that is driving up my triglycerides." He continued, "I was struck by this epiphany that I was given the wrong information." He decided to begin investigating how his doctor and the dietary guidelines could have gotten the science on cholesterol so wrong. Naturally, he traced the misinformation to Ancel Keys, who he says, had "a bachelor's degree in economics" and "knew nothing about nutrition, knew nothing about heart disease, and unfortunately was in charge, to a great extent, of nutrition and heart disease research in America."

Dr. Diamond continued to review cholesterol science and statin research and while doing so, experienced a few more epiphanies that went against the established dogma. For instance, he found "people with high cholesterol have a significantly lower rate of cancer, infectious disease, and live an overall normal lifespan." An investigative paper has been published that speaks to this. This paper calls into question the relationship between LDL and risk of dying in the elderly.[17] The results of the investigation? Those with HIGHER LDL live longer. As you might be thinking right now, this investigative paper calls into question the entire cholesterol hypothesis that's been presented to the public for years.

To add insult to injury, the methods of statistical manipulation researchers and drug companies use actually inflate statins' effectiveness for lowering heart disease risk while downplaying the drug's adverse effects. For example, Dr. Diamond said he determined the authors of the trial for cholestyramine (a drug which is prescribed to lower LDL cholesterol in the blood) were able to make a statistically *insignificant* .4% improvement in heart disease risk appear to be 24% by reporting *relative* rather than *absolute* risk.

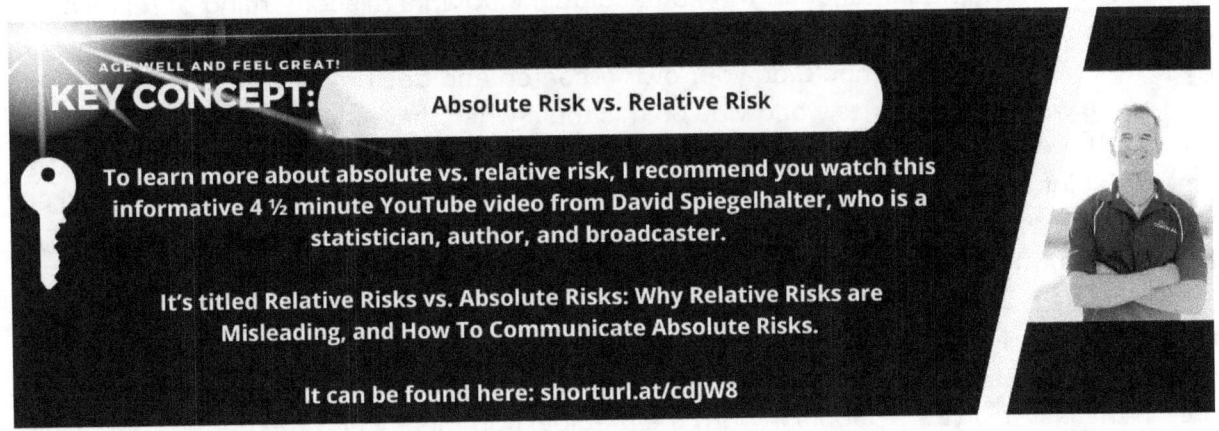

KEY CONCEPT: Absolute Risk vs. Relative Risk

To learn more about absolute vs. relative risk, I recommend you watch this informative 4 ½ minute YouTube video from David Spiegelhalter, who is a statistician, author, and broadcaster.

It's titled Relative Risks vs. Absolute Risks: Why Relative Risks are Misleading, and How To Communicate Absolute Risks.

It can be found here: shorturl.at/cdJW8

To understand how this gross misinformation could have happened, we need to first understand the difference between **absolute risk** and **relative risk**. Note the talking heads on television and headlines in newspapers use relative risks data all the time. I suspect they do it to capture your attention. It's an easy way to hype a subject and create a buzz. Here's the bottom line: *relative risk is a meaningless number without the context of absolute (or baseline) risk.* Absolute risk numbers are needed to understand the implications of relative risk and how specific factors or behaviors affect your likelihood of developing a disease.

In his investigation, Dr. Diamond also looked at the study on Lipitor (a widely prescribed statin drug), which helped generate $100 billion in revenue for the company that makes it and found the same thing: The study claimed the drug could decrease heart disease risk by 36%, which he says, "is a gross manipulation of the 1% (absolute) risk that actually matters." Dr. Diamond also argued the adverse effects of statins are multifaceted and significant. The peer reviewed literature, he explained, "has demonstrated an association between statins, type 2 diabetes, rhabdomyolysis, cognitive disorders, cataracts, renal failure, and liver dysfunction, to name a few." And if all that isn't enough, there's more. Recently an important paper was published calling into serious question the results and findings of the well-known Women's Health Initiative study done in the 1970s, that shows following a low-fat diet may in fact, be harmful.[18]

Nevertheless, statins remain the most widely prescribed class of drugs in the U.S.. To explain this, Dr. Diamond cited a quote from his colleague Paul Rosch, published in the Scandinavian Cardiovascular Journal: "That belief that coronary atherosclerosis is due to high cholesterol has been perpetuated by powerful forces using tactics to preserve the profits and reputations of those who promote the doctrine." Dr. Diamond concluded by saying, "the only person that potentially can benefit from a statin is someone that really wants to depend more on medication than a lifestyle change."

Beyond the obvious misuse of relative risks, I want to acknowledge *there have been* studies done through the years that *appeared* to back Key's findings and draw an association between cholesterol and heart disease. The problem is, as you've already learned, if you do a deep dive into those studies and examine how the data was represented to the public, you see frequent misrepresentation of the actual data including a misconstruing of relative and absolute risk. In my opinion, the studies simply weren't presented to the public ethically or honestly. In the end, you should do your own research and decide for yourself.

I agree with many experts worldwide on this topic when they say Keys was wrong. Dietary fat isn't the cause of heart disease and in fact, there isn't any *direct correlation* between dietary fat intake, cholesterol, and our risk of heart disease. I might go even further and say there is a lot of data supporting the idea those with the highest total cholesterol levels live LONGER than those with lower levels!

There are many experts who agree with these assertions that what we've been told *isn't the whole truth*. Many studies have been done questioning the validity of those original 1970s dietary guidelines.[19] This unfortunate misinformation has been out there for decades – it's only in the last few years people in both the medical community and the public at large, are beginning to catch up.

So, having read all this information, you might now be asking what *does* increase our risk of heart disease, heart attack, and stroke? **The research clearly points to the risks for these ailments being prevalent in people who are insulin resistant or who are prediabetic or have type 2 diabetes, which is currently afflicting millions of people in the U.S.**[20] Not surprisingly, chronic exposure to high levels of glucose and insulin are driving factors in the development of cardiovascular disease.[21-24] Additionally, modest improvements in the diet, including cutting back on refined sugar and other refined, processed carbohydrates has shown to be more effective in treating insulin resistance, metabolic syndrome, and cardiovascular risk, than many of the commonly used anti-diabetic drugs.[25] I'm sure those findings don't come as a surprise to you after reading the chapter on *insulin resistance* and *hyperinsulinemia*.

The fact is, there is study after study demonstrating **reducing the amount of sugar in the diet, especially refined and processed sugar, is vastly superior for reducing any risk**

of heart disease related ailments, compared to reducing dietary fat. The American public appears to have been sold a bill of goods by both the media, the government, and to some degree, the medical establishment. In case you're interested in reading more, I'm referencing 38 additional research studies that all, in one form or another, confirm these findings.[26-64]

As I've said, my advice is to do your own research and dive deeply into the topic. Learn more. Question everything, including what I've shared with you in this chapter. There are many opposing viewpoints.

Thankfully, we are witnessing some progress! The latest Dietary Guidelines for Americans do call for a drastic reduction in sugar (finally!), while indicating fats *can now be considered a part of a healthy diet*.[65] So, that's evidence that we are making progress.

There IS some work that still needs to be done though, because there are plenty of medical professionals out there that have stopped learning and are still buried in old ways of thinking. In the end, you must do your own research and make up your mind about who to believe. So up to this point:

- **Total and LDL cholesterol levels don't tell us very much about our risks, in and of themselves.** They don't tell you anything about your risk of dying or anything specific about your heart health. If anything, ironically, having higher numbers seems to support you'll live longer.

- **LDL cholesterol is NOT bad or toxic.** We've been deceived into believing it is "bad." In fact, it actually plays a very important role in our immune system. When we have an infection or invasion by a pathogen, it's LDL that works with your white blood cells to attack the pathogen.

- **Saturated fat intake does not increase your risk for heart disease.** Dietary fat isn't what we ought to cut back on. Believe it or not, it's sugar. I imagine by this point in the book, this isn't coming as a big surprise to you. Fat in the diet has been blamed for so many health problems that in truth, are actually because of sugar.

- **High LDL cholesterol does not cause heart disease.** There are other factors such as excess sugar intake, a lack of adequate physical activity and exercise, excess levels of stress, to name a few, that likely play a much larger role in heart disease risk.

- **The cholesterol you eat has very little impact on the cholesterol level in your body, despite what you've been told.** In fact, one example of misleading advertising from food manufacturers, is when a processed or vegetable-based food is labeled as "low or no cholesterol." Why? Only animal foods contain cholesterol. And because more than 50% of the cholesterol we ingest from food is *esterified*, we don't absorb very much of it at all.[66]

Keep in mind at this very moment somewhere, someone is being told they need to lower their cholesterol levels and should go on a statin drug! Not surprisingly, my older sister, Lyn, was given this exact advice a few weeks ago. While there are some who may benefit and indeed may need to be on a drug, the actual number of those people is less than drug companies would have you believe. Honestly, it's scary. We must be informed. Do your research and decide for yourself.

So, you may be asking yourself the same question I did, *why is this happening? How could this happen*? In other words, why would medical professionals and drug company advertisers intentionally tell us the wrong thing (at best) or lie to us (at worst)? Two reasons jump out to me. One is the myths I presented above have been established dogma in medical schools and hospital clinics for so many years, it is difficult to fight back against them and be heard with dissenting opinions and research. Unfortunately, this seems to be the wave of the future. In some ways, there's less true, integrity-based scientific debate going on now than ever before. In that same vein, in some circles, it seems it's more difficult than ever before to speak truthfully. Everything that has occurred surrounding COVID-19 proves that.

The other is the potential for profits and commercial gain, plain and simple. $$. There's a lot of money to be made by having lots of people on statin drugs. Some believe this entire cholesterol-heart disease connection is an illogical "red herring" [67] used by the drug industry to divert attention away from the primary issues and to maintain the treatment of the symptom. True or false? Again, you be the judge.

What Have I Decided About My Own Lipid Levels?

Everything I have learned has helped me relax about my own numbers. From my point of view, being as objective as I can be about the facts, I'm at very low risk. My triglycerides are low, HDL is quite high, and everything else looks good. Of course, my doctor doesn't always agree *entirely* with my opinions, but I'm doing my best to educate him. ☺ As always, I'll continue to have regular blood work and watch everything, always seeking to learn more.

As a side note, since doing my own investigation and study, I've learned it's common for people who are following a lower carbohydrate, higher fat diet, to sometimes have elevated cholesterol numbers. Elevated, that is, compared to the accepted standards currently in place. [68] That describes me perfectly at this point in time. Why? Because I am currently eating fewer carbohydrates than I might typically eat due to much lower run-bike "training" volume. This is a smart approach because the amount and types of food we eat (particularly the amount of carbohydrate we eat) should match our activity levels. By the same token, I'll likely increase how much carbohydrate I am eating when I'm training more frequently or for longer duration. Again, this is something I recommend for anyone.

The take home message is *how much carbohydrate you eat should to a large extent, reflect how much you are burning with the activities and exercise you are getting*. Be willing to adjust WHAT you eat and HOW MUCH you eat depending on your activities and lifestyle. For me, right now I'm only doing 45-minutes or so of exercise daily, on average, which isn't a lot compared to the past when I was training for the Ironman triathlon or full marathon distance runs. As such, I've scaled back to a higher fat and protein diet and eat less carbohydrates. Simply put, I don't need nearly as many carbs. To eat more would likely cause some unwanted weight gain and make me feel worse in the process.

What Are the Factors We Should Be More Aware Of?

- **The blood marker most important for you to watch is *triglycerides*.** These are a type of blood fat increasingly correlated with increased risk of heart disease. A high triglyceride level usually means you're eating more calories than you're burning, and those calories are likely coming from high-sugar foods. Too much alcohol can also lead to elevated triglycerides.
- **The most important "ratio" might actually be triglycerides to HDL cholesterol. That is, your triglycerides divided by your HDL.** Make sure you review this ratio with your doctor.
- **Excess sugar intake, in particular fructose, plays an important role in heart disease risk.**[69]
- As you've learned so far in this book, **the presence of insulin resistance and hyperinsulinemia play a central role in not only our risk for heart disease, but every other chronic disease.** It comes back time and again, to these factors as being the most important for our health and risk for disease and too-early death.
- There is some emerging evidence that **thick (viscous) blood and iron overload are commonly overlooked factors for increasing risk of heart disease, stroke, and cognitive decline.** Which, needless to say, is on the rise. Speak with your doctor to learn more.

More On the HDL / Triglycerides Ratio:

I mentioned earlier that perhaps the most important number you should be aware of is the ratio between your HDL and triglycerides. Without getting even more technical than this chapter has already been ☺, let me simply say that triglycerides have taken center stage in the discussion about the MOST important number you need to be aware of. Earlier I told you triglycerides are a type of blood fat increasingly correlated with increased risk of heart disease. I also told you high-sugar foods and alcohol are what raises triglyceride levels.

The bottom line is the ratio of triglycerides to HDL might well be the most important blood fat number to know and perhaps the best predictor of your actual risk for heart disease. Some experts believe that this ratio is five times more predictive of heart attack risk than LDL.[70]

In summary, here's what I recommend to you, the reader:

- **Have regular blood work and discuss everything with your doctor.** If there's a large disagreement between you and that doctor, you may want to find another.

- **Read, research, investigate, and do it all with a healthy dose of skepticism**. That includes what I've presented here. Decide for yourself. I hope what I've presented here inspires you to keep learning!
- **Get serious about cutting back on your sugar intake and in particular, refined processed sugars.**
- **Consider all the information I've shared with you in the context of everything ELSE you're reading in this book**. It is all very much related.
- **To learn more and really get into the nitty gritty if that suits your fancy**, Dr. Peter Attia (who is one expert who I trust and whom I've referenced many times in this book) has done a comprehensive deep dive into the topic with a series of nine articles. You can access those by going here: https://peterattiamd.com/the-straight-dope-on-cholesterol-part-i/

In summary, if you recall, in paragraph three of this chapter, I said what I'll share is a very simplified version of what is actually going on inside your body. That is certainly the truth – what I've shared only scratches the surface. Hopefully you've learned more than you knew before and as a result, have much more to think about and consider. Just remember, there's much more going on than what I've delved into.

I've repeatedly said it is important to be skeptical about everything you read. I've encouraged you to do your own research and even question what I've shared with you. Interestingly, while I highly recommend Dr. Attia's series of podcasts on cholesterol (which I referenced earlier), I have to add that he and I do not agree on the topic of LDL and absolute risk. I've listened to all sides and come to my own conclusions, and even more importantly, am committed to keeping an open mind and continuing to learn moving forward. I hope this chapter and the information I've shared encourages you to do the same.

One last thing: if your doctor wants to prescribe a statin before you've adopted most of the lifestyle changes I'm recommending in this book, run the other way. And then look in the mirror and decide to get to work. You're worth it and your health is worth it!

CHAPTER 14

YOUR GUT MICROBIOME

The immune system cells residing in the gut serve as important sentinels, alerted as soon as a possible invader appears and then coordinating a response from the gut throughout the body to prepare for a widespread scuffle. You can think of the gut microbiota as operating a dial that controls the sensitivity or responsiveness of the entire immune system.

— *Justin Sonnenburg, Ph.D.*

That which is easy to do, is also easy not to do.

— *Jim Rohn*

No self-respecting author writing a book about how to age well and become truly healthy would do so without including a brief section about the microbiome that lives inside us. ☺ So, what is our gut microbiome? And why does it matter? And while I'm asking questions, is it me, or have you noticed over the last several years, there's been a lot of attention paid to our gut and the microbiome that resides inside? I'm speaking specifically about the increased ads and marketing I see for all kinds of special proprietary probiotic "blends," each one claiming to "heal" our gut. At the same time, it seems the number of people who are apparently gluten intolerant or struggling with autoimmune disease is skyrocketing. Have you noticed?

We know if there's a perceived need in the marketplace and the potential for profit, a company somewhere will create products and start selling. The supplement industry is, after all, a multi-billion-dollar industry in the U.S., so there is great potential for huge profits. As an aside, one rule of thumb I've always had is, if someone is giving you advice on how to fix a health problem you have and also has a product for sale with a "guaranteed solution," run away as fast as you can.

That being said, let's move on and make sure we are on the same page with a few definitions, then get straight to the reasons we're seeing this enormous increase in advertising for probiotics.

What Exactly Is Your Gut Microbiome?

Your gut microbiome is the population of microbes such as bacteria, fungi, protozoa, yeast, viruses, and other microorganisms, that live inside your gut. By your gut, I mean your entire digestive tract including your stomach. Your digestive tract is home to roughly 40 trillion of these little bugs that do much more than simply help you digest food. Interestingly, they all have more genes of their own then we do. For example, in Chapter 2 you read about the *epigenome*, which are the multitude of chemical compounds and other processes inside and outside of our bodies that regulate gene expression. Because of the genes that reside inside these microbes, they can have a huge impact on how our own genes act and are ultimately expressed.

As you may be aware, some of these microbes are "good" for our health and some of them are "bad." Nowadays, it's not uncommon for the balance between these two kinds of bugs to become disturbed. When that happens, you have *dysbiosis*, which is routinely "observed in people with a variety of health problems such as Crohn's disease, metabolic syndrome, colon cancer, and even autism."[1] Amazingly, these microbes also impact our emotions, decision making, what foods we crave, the health of our skin, how our immune system functions, and our reaction to certain drugs.[2] These bugs also have a huge impact on our risk for developing some of the other "major human diseases such as obesity, hypertension, cardiovascular disease, diabetes, cancer, inflammatory bowel disease (IBD), gout, depression, and arthritis, as well as infant health and longevity."[3] They're "estimated to account for ~20% of all cancers worldwide."[4] Now, I imagine, if you weren't sure just how important these little bugs are to your health and your ability to become healthier and age well before you got to this chapter, you certainly are aware now. The bottom line is, regardless of which expert you ask, there is universal agreement having a healthy gut microbiome is *critical* for your overall health and ability to age well.

As I've mentioned, several years ago, I operated the Pursuit Athletic Performance gait analysis lab in Connecticut with my partner, Dr. Kurt Strecker. Beyond working with athletes to help them overcome injuries or to help them get faster, one of the additional services we provided was facilitating various types of detailed *metabolic testing* to assist with assorted health problems, most commonly gastrointestinal issues. If you happen to be a runner, cyclist, or triathlete who's ever had to deal with gastrointestinal (GI) problems before, during, or after exercising, you know it can wreak absolute havoc with your ability to perform. Persistent GI issues will also suck the joy out of training and racing, not to mention everyday activities.

So, the big picture questions that come to mind are, why are more of us than ever seeking ways to "heal" our gut microbiome? Why does it seem more people are suffering from food allergies? And what does any of this have to do with our long-term health? Without a doubt, the absolute explosion of probiotic products reflects an increase in the numbers of people having GI problems.

To answer these questions, we need to start by acknowledging there must be many factors at play. Something this broad rarely has only one cause. For starters, I believe many people are being told and sold on taking a *probiotic* to "fix" their issues, when what they actually need is a *prebiotic*. What's the difference? A *probiotic* is living bacteria that is supposed to repopulate your unhappy gut with the good kinds of microbes. On the surface, that sounds like a positive step to take, right? Except there's a problem. If the environment in your gut isn't healthy to begin with, the good bugs won't survive. They'll get overtaken by the bad bugs. When that happens, buying and using a *probiotic* will be a waste of effort and money.

Which Do You Need? A Prebiotic or a Probiotic?

What you actually need is to improve the health of your gut, *first*. How do you do that? You do it with a *prebiotic*. As mentioned earlier, if your gut isn't healthy, a probiotic won't do you any good. The good news is, perhaps the best *prebiotic* you can take is available in any grocery store and it isn't expensive. It's also not a supplement. It's **fiber.** Most experts agree, if you begin to transition to a high-fiber diet, your gut environment will improve, and often very quickly. What is a good source of fiber? As you might imagine by now, fiber comes from *real* food, not processed food.

I haven't talked very much about **fiber** to this point in the book, which is a shame because as you're learning (or being reminded of) right now, having adequate amounts of all types of fiber in your diet is important. It is something I personally focus on, and you should too.

Dr. Justin Sonnenburg, a professor in the department of Microbiology and Immunology at the Stanford School of Medicine, an expert on our microbiota, and author of the book, *The Good Gut: Taking Control of Your Weight, Your Mood, and Your Long-Term Health*, jokes that his family eats what they laughingly "refer to as a Big Mac diet."[5] No, not THAT kind of Big Mac! We know those fast foods aren't the best for us. ☺ The MAC acronym stands for "microbiota accessible carbohydrates." According to Sonnenburg, "MACs are the components within dietary fiber that gut microbes feed on. Eating more MACs can provide nourishment to the microbiota, help gut microbes thrive, and improve the diversity of this community."[6] So, where do you find these MACs in your diet? According to Sonnenburg, it's primarily "complex carbohydrates from fruit, vegetables, legumes, and *unrefined* whole grains."[7] Make a mental note of the key word in italics in the previous sentence, which was *unrefined*. It's important to understand what kinds of foods to get more of and what kinds to avoid. Keep reading.

I will refer to Dr. Sonnenburg's MAC acronym a few more times in this chapter, so be on the lookout for it. When you see it, assume we're talking about the kind of *unrefined* carbohydrates that provide a rich assortment of healthy fiber-rich nutrients your body needs to be healthy.

More About Fiber.

Let's take a step back to learn more about this powerful prebiotic, **fiber**. First, there are two types of fiber we need to be aware of. The first is **insoluble fiber**, the type your GI system *doesn't* absorb. Think of the stringy stuff in celery or the skin of many fruits. You'll find *insoluble fiber* in wheat bran, vegetables like celery, turnip, spinach, peas, radishes, and in legumes and berries, as well as in unrefined grains like quinoa and barley. The *insoluble fiber* in these foods adds bulk to your stool and helps speed digestion through your intestine, leading to easier bowel movements. You may have heard of the word *cellulose*, the woody fiber found in plant walls. If you're ever constipated, look at how much, if any, *insoluble fiber* you're getting in your diet. You may need more of it.

The other type of fiber is **soluble fiber**, which is what holds jelly together. It attracts water and turns to gel during digestion. This type of fiber slows down transit time, which can be helpful if you're battling diarrhea. Whenever I think of *soluble fiber*, I think of the fleshy parts of many fruits, such as an apple or pear. The skin is primarily *insoluble*, and the flesh is mostly *soluble*. If you're thinking this is one of many reasons eating moderate amounts of fresh fruit (hopefully organic) on a regular basis is a good idea, you're right! ☺

It's noteworthy that most plants contain a mix of both types of fiber, although some have higher concentrations of one or the other. According to the Canadian Society of GI Research, these are some of the best high-fiber superstars you can add into your diet.[8]

Food Item	Fibre Content	Serving Size
bran (oat or wheat)	10-12 g	30 g
chia seeds	10 g	30 g
flaxseed	8 g	30 g
artichoke	10 g	1 medium (128 g)
beans and lentils	6-9.5 g	½ cup, cooked (85 g)
avocado	7 g	½ average (100 g)
raspberries	8 g	1 cup (120 g)

Aren't Carbohydrates Supposed to Be "Bad" for Me?

Over the last few years, especially with the rising popularity of "keto" and other low-carb diets like Atkins and South Beach, "carbs" have received quite the bad reputation. The question bolded above, *aren't carbohydrates supposed to be bad for me*, is one I'm often asked. More people than ever are convinced carbs are bad for them. It is true that for some, reducing their carb intake can result in weight loss, which is usually a good thing. The problem is when we throw "the baby out with the bathwater," so to speak. What do I mean?

Let's get something straight: **carbohydrates are not "bad" for you**. While there isn't complete agreement as to how essential they are for our survival, there is no debate about the reason why, in some forms, they've become increasingly problematic for many people. The reason shouldn't come as a surprise to you by the time you've reached this chapter: As a society, we're consuming more of the "simple" carbs found in industrialized, processed foods and junk foods. It's the stuff you've already read about. These "simple" carbs are more basic than complex carbs and as a result, get absorbed very quickly into your bloodstream. In terms of dietary sources, think of fruit juices, cane sugar, candy and "sweets" with added sugar, and fructose from fruits, as some examples.

As you've learned, these "processed" simple carbs cause a quick spike in your blood sugar, resulting in the release of insulin so the circulating glucose can be absorbed. Remember, if insulin levels remain elevated, the body becomes increasingly *desensitized* to it, and must secrete more to control the rise in blood sugar. This is what Chapter 9 is all about. So, you see, when it comes to the health of our gut microbiome, it's the processed, refined sugars in the industrialized foods that are the biggest problem. Remember, if you were to remove ALL the carbs from your diet, you'd also be removing the good, low-glycemic, MAC containing carbs, in addition to the less healthy, refined, high-glycemic variety, hence my "baby with the bath water" reference earlier.

Part of the problem is what is done in manufacturing to "process" some foods that at one time, were healthy for us. And could still be. One prime example is wheat, which today has a poor reputation but in truth, has been consumed by humans for thousands of years. So, what happened to change things and turn this ubiquitous food into something that is now vilified? In his book, Dr. Sonnenburg explains modern manufacturing and processing has resulted in a part of the wheat berry being removed. I became very interested in this processing years ago, simply because understanding it better helps me make smarter choices when shopping.

Dr. Sonnenburg explains this rather elaborate manufacturing process this way: "a kernel of wheat, or wheat berry, is made up of the endosperm, the bran, and the germ. The endosperm contains all the food, in the form of simple starches, to feed a newly growing wheat plant. The bran coats the outside of the wheat berry in a hard shell of fiber. The germ, a fat-filled reproductive organ that also contains fiber, germinates to create a new plant. Thousands of years ago, people began using millstones to grind wheat berries into a meal, bringing about the birth of flour. However, this stone-ground wheat would be unrecognizable next to the factory-produced flour available today. The Industrial Revolution brought about steam-powered mills, allowing for the production of flour on a significantly larger scale. But manufacturers struggled to keep flour fresh during the months it took to transport it from the mill to the consumer. To solve this problem, producers realized if they removed the oily germ (the part that goes rancid) from wheat before milling, they could extend its shelf life almost indefinitely. What they didn't know was that by removing the germ, they were also removing a large amount of the dietary fiber, not to mention all the other healthful micronutrients that are found in wheat germ. Millers then realized by removing the bran as well, they could provide consumers with white, fluffy flour – composed entirely of endosperm – that many people considered to be better looking, more palatable, and easier to bake with. Technology has provided us "rich man's flour" inexpensively, but our microbiota's diet has become poorer."[9] There you have it. To improve shelf life, we are left with a product that is half of what it used to be and should still be. And our guts are worse off because of it. So, what to do?

My recommendation to you is to make sure in addition to whatever else may be on your plate, have equal amounts of "MACs" in the form of beans, roasted vegetables, brown rice, all varieties of nuts, and cooked whole barley, to name just a few ideas. Keep a jar of cooked beans such as chickpeas or kidney beans, as well as nuts and seeds on hand to sprinkle on salads. Cook the beans on a stove, simmering for a few hours, then store them in the fridge. If you're going to keep them for longer than a week, store them in the freezer.

Keep in mind a loaf of refined white flour bread contains almost no "MACs." As Dr. Sonnenburg puts it, today's white bread is "more like the cake your great-grandmother would have eaten,"[10] than the more wholesome variety. The answer is to start by ditching the refined white flour and any other refined starches. Eating bread made from whole wheat flour will give you approximately 2 grams of fiber per slice. But as he points out, "if you go even further and eat a cup of cooked unmilled wheat berries, you will get about 9 grams of fiber, a quarter to one third of your total fiber needs for the day."[11]

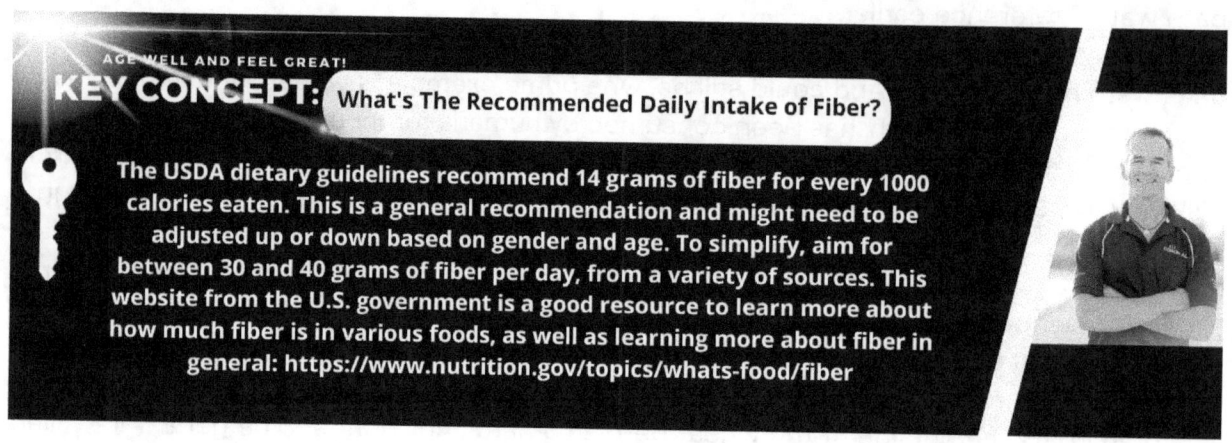

AGE WELL AND FEEL GREAT!

KEY CONCEPT: What's The Recommended Daily Intake of Fiber?

The USDA dietary guidelines recommend 14 grams of fiber for every 1000 calories eaten. This is a general recommendation and might need to be adjusted up or down based on gender and age. To simplify, aim for between 30 and 40 grams of fiber per day, from a variety of sources. This website from the U.S. government is a good resource to learn more about how much fiber is in various foods, as well as learning more about fiber in general: https://www.nutrition.gov/topics/whats-food/fiber

One last thing: some reading this right now are thinking to themselves, as soon as I increase my consumption of fiber, I'm going to have problems with flatulence and a rumbling belly. In my experience, the key is introducing these foods (and MACs) a little bit at a time. Give your GI system time to adapt. It will, but it may take time. If you're not eating many high fiber foods right now and go to 30 grams tomorrow, you may soon regret that decision. If you know what I mean. ☺

What Else Can You Do to Increase Your Fiber Intake?

- Eat the peels on fruits and vegetables.
- Sprinkle some nuts and seeds on a salad. I'm an especially big fan of pistachios, walnuts, and almonds. As far as nuts are concerned, those are the most nutritious nuts and also great sources of fiber. Pumpkin, flax, and chia seeds are also great sources.
- Always eat the whole fruit instead of drinking fruit juice. (As you have already learned, there's little benefit to drinking fruit juice, other than the water they contain. Go with the whole fruit – skip the juice!)

Bottom line, *you need both types of fiber* in your diet as they each perform different functions that help keep your gut and microbiome healthy. In simple terms, they work together to form an impermeable barrier along your intestinal wall that protects it. They also act to slow down or delay absorption, which has the benefit of protecting the liver. One more point worth sharing is a high-fiber diet will also reduce your risk of colon cancer. And I'm sure if you think about it, that makes sense.

At this point you might be asking, besides increasing fiber, what are some more *prebiotic* foods you can add to help improve your gut's health? Here are some ideas: cruciferous vegetables like broccoli and cauliflower, blueberries (certainly pound for pound, these are one of the healthiest fruits you can eat), onions, garlic, different types of seeds, flax, asparagus, and even cocoa, believe it or not.

How Did Our Gut Microbiome Become Unhealthy In the First Place?

The answer to this question should be obvious to you if you're paying attention as you read this book. For the great majority, the answer is *processed foods.* Processed, pre-packaged manufactured foods, starve your gut, they don't feed it. The classic example in my mind is the popularity of canned and packaged juice and energy drinks. These are sometimes all you see when you walk into a convenience store or gas station. Assuming there's actually any "real" fruit juice in any of them, they certainly don't contain any of the healthiest parts of the fruit, starting with the fiber rich peel.

My advice is to skip the juices once and for all and transition to eating REAL food instead. As time goes on and you've hopefully increased the amount of fiber you're getting in your diet, you may find you don't even need a *probiotic* at all. You'll be more regular and you will definitely feel better!

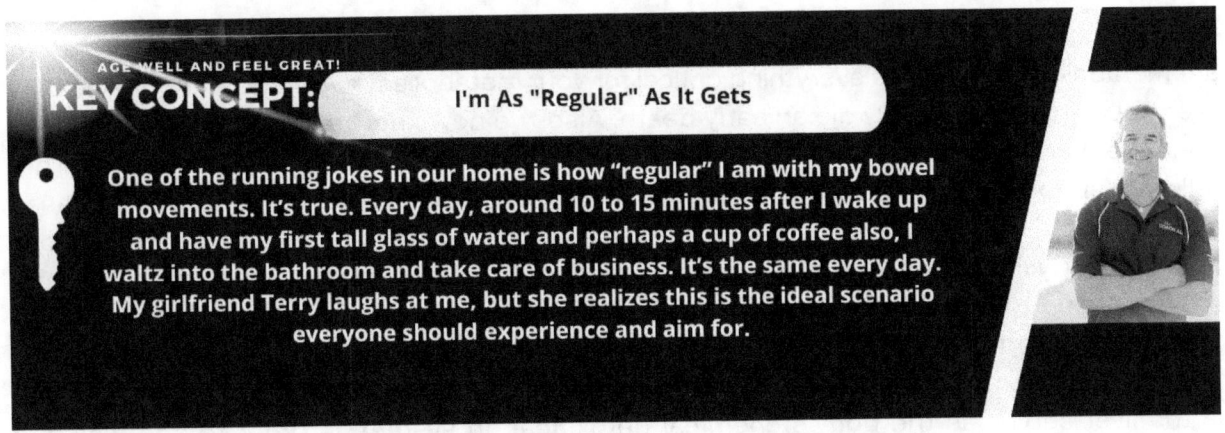

AGE WELL AND FEEL GREAT!

KEY CONCEPT: I'm As "Regular" As It Gets

One of the running jokes in our home is how "regular" I am with my bowel movements. It's true. Every day, around 10 to 15 minutes after I wake up and have my first tall glass of water and perhaps a cup of coffee also, I waltz into the bathroom and take care of business. It's the same every day. My girlfriend Terry laughs at me, but she realizes this is the ideal scenario everyone should experience and aim for.

What are some of the secrets to establishing a regular bathroom routine? The very first thing I do after waking up is throw cold water on my face. Next I drink a tall glass of water. I consider this to be one of the most important things I do and you should too! Always start your day with water! Besides improving hydration status after a night's sleep, drinking some water gets the *gastrocolic reflex* going. Remember, if you're even marginally dehydrated, you'll have more difficulty being regular. Next, I head outdoors for a brief walk to get the blood flowing and expose my eyes to the light, which helps establish my circadian rhythm and again, gets the system churning. I'll sometimes go through a brief, yoga-like movement flow, to loosen up the joints and get the blood moving. This doesn't have to be formal or extensive. Just move! Of course, as you're learning, if the previous day's diet was very low in fiber, you won't be as regular as you should be.

I also believe exercise in any and all forms helps our system keep moving and churning. If you find you're not as regular as you want to be, the answer is to gradually increase the fiber in your diet, and also make sure you are moving, every day. Mix it up with lower and higher intensity exercise. You'll learn more about that in upcoming chapters.

One additional tidbit on the water I splash on my face after waking up. Do you by any chance do this too? Well, there's a good amount of science showing this doesn't just help wake us up, it's also healthy for us. Author James Nestor, in his book, *DEEP: Life, Death & Amphibious Humans at the Last Frontier on Earth,* explores something called the "mammalian dive reflex," the phenomenon by which water triggers an immediate decrease in heart rate as well as a host of other very healthy responses. Numerous studies have been done showing this reflex results in the shunting of blood, called peripheral vasoconstriction, away from the extremities to vital organs. To reap the benefits, you need to get your entire face and nostrils wet with water that is cooler than the air. Nestor believes this phenomenon is among the most extreme transformations ever discovered in the human body and calls it the Master Switch of Life.

What About the Liver?

The liver is the center of the metabolic universe inside our body. It's where glucose and fat are metabolized and where everything critical for your metabolism happens. Without a healthy liver, you will most certainly die an early death. Also, we now know measuring the amount of fat in the liver is the best way to predict whether someone will get diabetes in the future. That tells you all you need to know. It's not a coincidence that one of the most insidious diseases of the modern era, reflecting the increasing amounts of processed foods in our diet, is non-alcoholic fatty liver disease (NAFLD), which can lead to cirrhosis of the liver. And early death.

According to Dr. Sonnenburg, "one of the liver's many functions is to detoxify chemical waste generated by our microbes. If the liver fails, these toxic substances can cause major cognitive problems," wreaking "havoc on normal neurological function."[12] The bottom line is the liver serves as the body's chemical detoxification system. In order to age well and become truly healthy, one of our missions must be to do all we can to make sure we're taking good care of the liver so that it functions optimally.

Age Well and Feel Great!

Key Concept:

What About Your Medications?

According to the latest data from the CDC, nearly ½ of all Americans have taken at least one prescription drug in the previous 30 days.[13] One fact many people aren't aware of is how much our microbiota impacts and is changed by prescription drugs. The microbiota can directly affect the strength of some drugs, which can make these drugs more or less effective in certain people. Dr. Sonnenburg points out, "as we age, we encounter more and more health issues that require the use of medications. This reality makes it important to understand that by taking medication, we are introducing a variable into a highly complex system that consists of numerous still uncharacterized interactions between human cells and microbial cells."[14]

The take home message is, do everything you can to reduce the amount of medications you take. Work with your doctor to get off them whenever possible. As I've already mentioned, and you may be tired of hearing, other than antibiotics after dental work, I've never taken a prescription drug in my life. I'm fortunate to be able to say that, but I will also say it's been a conscious choice. As is always the case, you achieve something like that by looking at your health holistically. There isn't one thing or reason I've been able to achieve it. It comes back to a consistent approach to exercise, eating well (most of the time) and paying attention to the details others might miss.

More on Fiber.

I mentioned earlier one benefit to dietary fiber is it forms a barrier along your intestinal wall that protects it. It's worth remembering that virtually **ALL processed food lacks fiber!** If you're wondering why, the answer is in the processing. The germ of the grain is removed along with the fiber because they can both go rancid.[15]

As you read about in detail in the preceding pages, removing the germ in food processing is a losing proposition for our gut and our health. The rule of thumb for enhancing our microbiome should be to eat low-sugar, high-fiber foods more often. Processed industrialized junk food is just the opposite – high-sugar, low-fiber. **Repeat after me – more LOW-SUGAR, HIGH-FIBER foods!** ☺ **Less HIGH-SUGAR, LOW-FIBER foods!**

What Else Might Be Contributing to Our Sick Gut?

Looking back on the last couple of years where COVID 19 has been front and center, we saw a meteoric rise in the use of hand sanitizers. I believe the kind of thinking that says, "I should be rubbing this stuff on my hands all the time to make sure I don't get germs on my hands," is extreme and misguided. Believing hand sanitizers work to keep us healthy puts way too much emphasis on excessive hygiene to the extent that some of us aren't exposing ourselves to nature, including dirt and plants. Now keep in mind, of course I am not saying you shouldn't wash your hands. What I AM saying is rubbing alcohol sanitizer on your hands at every single opportunity to kill germs, isn't necessary and might not even be very smart.

We all need to spend more time outdoors in nature and maybe even play in the dirt. If you have children this is an absolute must for them. The bacteria kids are exposed to outdoors helps them develop healthy guts and immune systems that will serve them well as they grow and mature. The take home message is get outdoors and play!

Regarding what else might be contributing to our sick gut, there's also the potential **overuse of medications** (as I alluded to earlier) such as antibiotics, nonsteroidal pain relievers like Motrin or ibuprofen, and of course, too much nutrient-poor junk food, which doesn't nurture your gut at all – and often has the reverse effect of causing problems.

Also, have you ever considered the effects of too much **exposure to micro-plastics and pesticides,** and how that might negatively impact our microbiome? What about the increase in autoimmune and allergic diseases, especially in our younger generation? We are playing havoc with our long-term gut health with what we're exposing ourselves to in both our external environment and through many of the poorer quality foods we're eating. And along the way, it's leading to issues like leaky gut, chronic inflammation, and of course, insulin resistance.

What About Our Immune System?

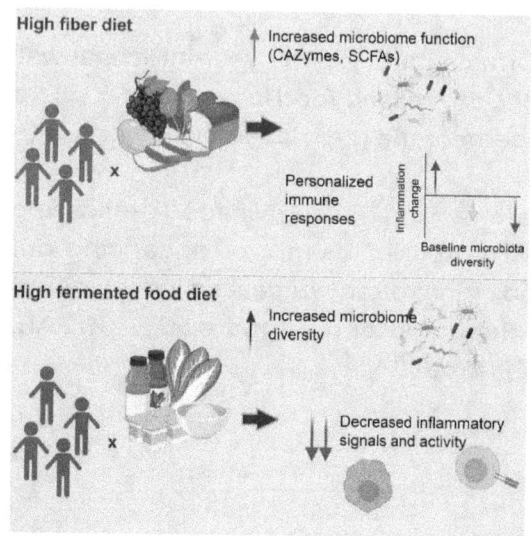

One of the forgotten roles of our gut microbiome is to help fortify our **immune system health and function. In fact, the gut microbiome is our largest immune system organ.** This graphic, taken from a July 2021 study titled *Gut-microbiota-targeted diets modulate human immune status*,[16] illustrates how improving our diet can have a dramatic effect on our gut and thus our immune system.

Believe it or not, about 70% of the immune system is found in the gut. This means if your gut microbiome isn't healthy, by default you don't have a healthy functioning immune system.

Also, your gut wall is the primary barrier between you and the outside world, where certain types of food, bacteria, insects, and toxins can be potential threats. Protecting that barrier is key to keeping out what shouldn't be in.

Have you ever heard of "leaky gut syndrome?" It's described this way: The fragile gut wall loosens up, leaving tiny spaces where bacteria and toxins and even *partially digested food particles* can literally "leak" into your bloodstream. While this condition and the diagnosis for it is still under some debate in medical circles, one thing that isn't debatable is when the symptoms of leaky gut appear, it's an indication your microbiome isn't healthy.

These partially digested food particles can start an inflammatory cascade almost anywhere in your body that can lead to skin rash, depression, brain fog, and joint pain, to name just a few. I believe many of the issues older people struggle with, and typically associate with simply getting older, are really more about unhealthy gut microbiome. Think about it.

Is There a Connection Between Our Microbiome and Cognitive Function?

Have you ever reached the end of the month, looked at the bills you had to pay, and had that sick feeling in your stomach? I know I have. That stressed, sinking feeling is just one example of the brain-gut connection at work. Similarly, the metaphors we often hear and use – that we need to "trust our gut instinct," or we have a "gut feeling," are good examples of the "primal connection" that exists "between our brain and our gut."[17] The association between our brain and our gut is so strong, our gut has often been referred to as our "body's second brain."[18] According to Dr. Kara Fitzgerald, ND, IFMCP, "we've known for a while now about the gut-brain axis and how our GI microbiome affects brain health. After all, our bodies have more microbes than human cells!"[19] In a recent social media post, Dr. Fitzgerald referenced a very recent population study that "found that the diversity of GI microbial community was significantly associated with cognitive function. The study showed that having a robust community of *butyrate producers* is protective against cognitive impairment and decline."[20]

What are butyrate producers and why should we care? Butyrate is a short chain fatty acid produced when dietary fibers are fermented by intestinal bacteria in your gut.[21] A host of scientific studies show butyrate reduces intestinal inflammation, stimulates production and proliferation of healthy intestinal cells, inhibits the proliferation of cancer cells, modulates intestinal motility, and generally restores gut barrier integrity. [22][23] As you can easily see, there's a lot to learn and know about all the various types of bacteria and the kinds of foods that increase good bacteria and serve to maintain a proper balance. It would be easy for me to go deeper into the rabbit hole but I'll stop. If you're experiencing any issues that might be related to this gut-brain superhighway, I encourage you to research and learn more.

What About Adding Fermented Foods to Increase the Health Of Our Gut?

There's no question when you can regularly add real food sources of fermented foods, specifically those that contain live cultures and are refrigerated at the grocery store as a result, you will help your gut stay healthy and happy.

To me, the most obvious sources of fermented foods are sauerkraut, olives, and pickled beets. Since we each have our own unique taste buds, you might not find my list appetizing. I'm personally not a kombucha fan, but if you like it, you can include that on the list, too.

To summarize, I haven't even scratched the surface of all there is to know about this complex topic. What are the biggest take aways to walk away with after reading this chapter? You will notice there are some recurring themes. ☺

- **Rather than try to "fix" GI issues with a probiotic, first try to incorporate more prebiotics like fiber into your diet.** Feed your body prebiotics, such as garlic, onions, asparagus, and even leeks, as well as more fiber rich foods.
- **Start to focus on taking out some of the processed foods that are contributing to an unhappy microbiome.** Anything with added sugars, or made from grains, and sold in a plastic package – you want to eat less of. Included in the list is obviously any kind of fast food.
- **Try to eat organic whenever you can.**
- **Stay clear of any animal meat that has been treated with antibiotics or steroids.** Know where the meat you're eating came from and how it was processed.
- **Of course, only use antibiotics when you absolutely need them.** Discuss your desire to maintain good gut health with your doctor.

As you can see, all the things that are important for good overall health, are also critical for good gut health. Focus on the watch words I shared earlier – make more of what you eat **LOW-SUGAR, HIGH-FIBER**, and you'll be on the right path. That's win/win for your gut! And for your health.

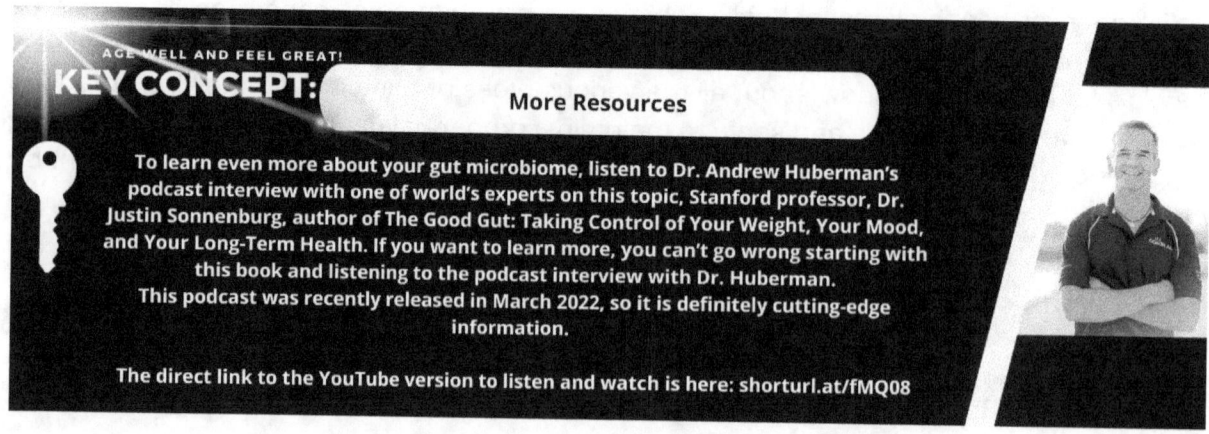

AGE WELL AND FEEL GREAT!

KEY CONCEPT:

More Resources

To learn even more about your gut microbiome, listen to Dr. Andrew Huberman's podcast interview with one of world's experts on this topic, Stanford professor, Dr. Justin Sonnenburg, author of The Good Gut: Taking Control of Your Weight, Your Mood, and Your Long-Term Health. If you want to learn more, you can't go wrong starting with this book and listening to the podcast interview with Dr. Huberman. This podcast was recently released in March 2022, so it is definitely cutting-edge information.

The direct link to the YouTube version to listen and watch is here: shorturl.at/fMQ08

GOOD
FOOD
SOURCES of FIBER

 AVOCADO (raw)
9.2 g per fruit

 **RASPBERRIES (raw)**
8.0 g per Cup

 PRUNES (uncooked)
12.4 g per Cup

 ARTICHOKE (hearts, cooked)
7.2 g per Cup

 **SPINACH (raw)**
6.2 g per 10 oz. bag

 **QUINOA (cooked)**
5.2 g per Cup

 SWEET POTATO (baked, mashed)
6.0 g per Cup

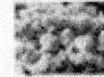 **LENTILS (boiled)**
15.6 g per Cup

 PEAR (with skin)
5.5 per pear (medium-sized)

 BARLEY (cooked)
6.0 g per Cup

 APPLE (raw with skin)
4.4 g per apple (medium)

 KIDNEY BEANS (boiled)
11.3 g per Cup

 BROCCOLI (raw)
2.4 g per Cup

 PEANUT BUTTER (chunky, no salt)
2.6 g per TBSP

 KALE (raw, chopped)
2.4 g per Cup

 COUSCOUS (cooked)
2.2 g per Cup

 BRUSSEL SPROUTS (boiled)
3.3 g per Cup

 GREEN PEAS (boiled)
8.8 g per Cup

CHAPTER 15

MEAT LOVERS VS. VEGETARIANS: *WHO IS RIGHT?*

Four young men sit by the bedside of their dying father. The old man, with his last breath, tells them there is a huge treasure buried in the family fields.

The sons crowd around him crying, "Where, where?" but it is too late.

The day after the funeral and for many days to come, the young men go out with their picks and shovels and turn the soil, digging deeply into the ground from one end of each field to the other.

The find nothing and, bitterly disappointed, abandon the search.

The next season the farm has its best harvest ever.

— **A Parable,** *source unknown*

*Man does not simply exist but always decides what his existence
will be, what he will become the next moment. By the same token,
every human being has the freedom to change at any instant.*

— Victor Frankl

For as long as I can remember, there's been a polarizing difference of opinions between those on one side who follow a strict vegan (or less strict vegetarian) diet, and those on the other side, who believe in the health benefits of eating meat and actually enjoy the taste. This difference in perspective has become even more pronounced with the recent popularity of the keto diet, which as you probably know, is a very low-carbohydrate-based approach to eating.

For as long as I have been training and coaching, I've heard both sides and listened to the arguments. Both sides tend to pick apart the perceived failings of the other side while simultaneously ignoring the weaknesses in their own approach. That's not a big surprise. It's what we human beings like to do – I think of it as cognitive consonance. Basically, confirming in our own minds that what we are doing is the "right" thing because it's what we're already doing. ☺

Many vegan activists believe meat is killing people and cows are killing the planet. Meat lovers and keto devotees believe that carbohydrate is the source of all evil, and eating primarily meat or even only meat, is the healthiest approach. There's always a back/forth debate, it just depends on what you're reading or who you're listening to and whose side you're on.

I've Heard Both Sides.

From my point of view, each side has their own set of problems. You've already heard me say that all things considered, I don't believe it is smart to remove an entire food group, food type, or macronutrient, from our diet. I've seen it from both an individual perspective – how I've experimented over the years trying different approaches, and from a coach or therapist's perspective. I've always tried to be objective and not judge, but that's hard to do when I've naturally formed my own opinions just like everyone else.

When coaching athletes who are either strict vegan or "plant-based" I am concerned they might not be getting all the nutrients they need. The standard vegan diet is often low in iron, omega-3 fats, vitamin B12, and tryptophan, an essential amino acid you must consume because your body cannot make it.

I've also wondered whether they realized that being vegetarian doesn't in and of itself, stop them from indulging in, shall I say, "less-than-healthy" junk foods like chips, soft drinks, and french fries, as these are all "plant-based." My point being, if you're eating industrialized, processed food - but NOT eating "unhealthy" meat, what you're doing doesn't constitute a "healthy" approach.

On the flip side, I've also coached people who proudly proclaimed their love for red meat. And just as with the vegetarians, I wondered about a few things that I knew might impact their health and performance. For example, I wondered if they knew *where* the meat they ate came from. Because where it comes from, how an animal was raised, and how it is processed, matters. Did the meat come from animals raised on grass from birth to slaughter? Or were they raised on corn and other grains and fed nitrates, branch-chain amino acids, and antibiotics?

Similarly, if they don't also eat a wide variety of vegetables and fruits, there is the risk they won't get adequate selenium, magnesium, phosphorus, vitamins B and C, or fiber. (I'm sure after reading Chapter 14 on our gut microbiome, you understand how important both types of fiber are for your health.) These are some of the nutrients that are often lacking in a meat-only or an especially protein-heavy diet. My point is, when it comes to both our individual health and that of the planet, there's a big difference between organic farming on nutrient rich soil, grass fed and finished animals, and industrialized, processed food production.

What's the Advice of Most Medical and Nutrition Professionals?

Most medical and nutrition professionals believe a plant-based diet is *better for us* and might even be better for the planet. Admittedly, I've often said essentially the same thing to others. However, to make sure we're learning all we need to, let's dive in and see if this advice *is* actually the best advice. In other words, is being plant-based or vegetarian truly healthier?

In 2018, a documentary called *The Game Changers* featured a series of interviews with scientists and celebrities around the world and made the case a plant-based diet is much better for both athletic performance and good health. The documentary is now available on Netflix. If you watched and took everything presented at face value, you might come away thinking eating meat is not only bad *for you*, it's even worse *for the planet*. However, I have two issues with this film that make me at least partially question the arguments they present.

The first is the "control group" used for comparison are those eating the typical American diet. In other words, a typically junk-food laden diet loaded with seed oils, cheap grains, dangerous trans-fats, and of course, anything with added sugar. Taking that into account and looking at it honestly, you'd have to admit virtually ANY kind of diet would be an improvement over how most Americans eat. After all, any time someone goes from eating "fast foods to whole foods,"[1] they're going to be healthier and feel better, regardless of whether the switch is primarily to something plant-based or animal based. This poor use of a faulty control group hurts the argument the producers are hoping to make.

The other issue I have is related to something called "the healthy user effect."[2] Think of it as the propensity for people who make one kind of positive lifestyle change, to make additional positive lifestyle changes. In other words, based on my own observations, vegetarians are, as a general rule, more health-conscious people than are non-vegetarians. I'm not saying ALL vegetarians are healthier, just the majority. If you were to take a cross section of all the people in the U.S., and look at those who are *vegetarian*, you'd find they were more health conscious than the non-vegetarians. People who make the decision not to eat meat often adopt other health-oriented changes as well.

On the other hand, in that same cross section of the entire population, when looking at the meat lovers you'd likely find a large percentage eat a lot of *fast food*. It isn't much of a stretch to say they'd be less "health conscious" than vegetarians. I suspect the data would bear this out as true, although I haven't researched it. To me, this healthy user effect means at worst, the producers of the film misused data and based their case of cause and effect on a false premise. At best, they have raised questions about their ability to be objective, assuming that was at least part of their goal in producing the film.

Now, please know that none of what I've said about the film means a vegetarian diet ISN'T also the healthiest. It might be. The thing is, if this *were* true, then India, which has the largest percentage of vegetarians of any country in the world, would be a lot *healthier* than they appear to be. According to data derived from a 2021 study, "estimates in 2019 showed that 77 million individuals in India had diabetes, which is expected to rise to over 134 million by 2045. Approximately 57% of these people remain undiagnosed."[3] If you do the math, it looks like the prevalence of diabetes is about 9% of the population, which makes it very close to our own prevalence here in the U.S., at around 10%.[4]

By comparison, Ireland, which has been referred to as being "Europe's biggest carnivores, consuming the equivalent of more than 70 steaks per person in 2021," is among the two or three countries in the world with the *lowest* prevalence of diabetes, at only 4%.[5] Based on this data alone, one could argue the easiest and most reliable path to good health ISN'T by eating a "plant-based" diet. As I'm sure you're starting to see, you can make a case for either side depending on the criteria you're using and your point of view.

So, who's right? Which approach is "better" than the other and who is it "better" for? For us individually? Or for the planet as a whole? And who decides?

Are These Even the Right Questions to Be Asking?

As we continue our quest for answers, let's take a closer look at the meat we are eating. The word meat means different things to different people and there is a lot of variety in the marketplace. It could be everything from a game meat like venison or grass fed and finished beef (which is considered to be healthier), to the processed variety of ground beef, bacon, sausage, and lunch meats, to name just a few.

When it comes to those processed meats found in the typical grocery store here in the U.S., we have to consider the dangerous long-term health implications of excess branched chain amino acids, nitrates, and choline, to name a few. These additives are part of the diet of corn-fed animals, and drive-up dangerous levels of liver fat and the risk of insulin resistance in humans.[6] With processed meats, there's also evidence of an increased risk of diabetes, cancer, and heart disease.[7] If this data is any indication, it's at least partially the meat processing and what is added or subtracted from the animal's diet that might be the biggest problem. We also cannot ignore the obvious dangers of added preservatives like nitrates in processing, which have been directly implicated in disease and identified as potent carcinogens. The fact is, we don't know what a safe intake is for these, despite what the packaging on these products may say.

There are a lot of other real problems with mass production of meat and meat products. From the use of growth hormone in both the dairy and beef industries, to chicken spiked with estrogen, to preservatives like BHA and BHT, which are used in the meat industry and are known carcinogens. The list goes on and on. When you look at these, it's easy to make the case you're risking your health by eating any kind of *processed* meat.

Then There's the Climate.

Obviously, none of the issues or differences I've alluded to take into consideration the other reasons why people choose a specific approach to eating. Think of religion, animal rights activism, and the global climate crisis as three examples. The first two I won't get into at all. That's a personal choice and goes beyond the scope of what I'd like to discuss. The third - our global climate crisis and the health of our planet - can't be ignored.

If vegan vs. meat lover wasn't controversial enough for you, the debates about the health of our planet are *even more* polarizing. The politics of climate change and global warming have rightly taken center stage. The stakes in the "who's right?" debate are higher than ever! Unless you've been living under a rock, I doubt you'd debate that climate *has to be* the most important issue facing our global community. I've often wondered if it's an overstatement to say in many ways, we're equally effective at killing the *planet* with global greenhouse gas emissions and plastics, as we are at killing *ourselves* through overconsumption of processed, industrialized junk food.

The fact remains the climate crisis is a ginormous topic that goes beyond the scope of this chapter and this book. But I would be remiss if I didn't mention while agriculture and cows are significant producers of methane gas, depending on the data you read and believe, it pales in comparison to the methane production from the gas and oil industry, as well as transportation. There is data that supports livestock only accounts for about 1/7th of global greenhouse gas emissions.[8] [9]

And to drive this point home even further so we don't leave out the plant-lovers among us, ☺ we can't ignore the enormous nitrous oxide (another dangerous greenhouse gas) production from the millions of tons of fertilizer sprayed all over those farmlands producing vegetables for mass sale and consumption. In a recent study from 2020 published in the journal *Nature*, an international team of scientists "discovered that nitrous oxide emissions are increasing at a faster rate than any other type of greenhouse gas emission, due to a rise in nitrogen fertilizer application for food production."[10]

You might respond that the answer is to eat only "organic." And I would agree, in a perfect world that *is* one possible solution. The thing is, organic produce is wildly more expensive and not even available in many areas, especially for those in lower-income brackets. A lot of people are struggling to afford even the cheapest food available to them, let alone organic. Which is one reason processed foods seem more attractive to the majority of consumers.

The unfortunate truth is when it comes to climate change and methane, carbon dioxide, and nitrous oxide gases, as a global community we've got some major challenges ahead of us. And there doesn't appear to be any easy answers.

Although perhaps we ought to start by considering when it comes to the global outcry about the ongoing destruction of the Amazon Rain Forest, we shouldn't lie to ourselves and ignore or forget that the burning of millions of acres in a country like Brazil is at least in part, so that food manufacturers can plant – can you guess? Sugar cane.[11] Pause for a second and think about that. I'll say as someone who lives in Florida, "BIG sugar" has been at the center of a huge controversy surrounding the state's largest lake, Okeechobee, and the run off from thousands of acres of sugar cane fields surrounding the lake. There's real danger the Florida Everglades has been changed forever. And not in a good way. Regardless of your point of view, that has to be a wakeup call to all of us. If it isn't, then I'm not sure what is.

This Is Only the Tip of the Iceberg.

I've only scratched the surface when discussing the major challenges we're facing, both globally and on a local, even internal, level. When it comes to the meat vs. vegan debate, we'd all agree the issues (and questions) go far beyond our own palate – they're among the biggest issues we face as a species moving toward the future. So, where are we at this point in the discussion? Have you made up your mind yet? ☺ Do you have an idea about what is the "best" approach? Is it plant-based or to be a carnivore? Or are you waiting for me to tell you more?

To help answer this question for yourself, which is my ultimate goal of course, I want to go back to an earlier rhetorical question I asked, which was...*are these even the right questions to be asking?* You see, it isn't about where the food comes from or whether it's plant or animal based, *it's about the quality of the food and its preparation*. That's what matters the most.

Perhaps the best first question to ask ourselves is, am I eating *processed*, *industrialized* food, or is it actual, *real* food? Because, my friend, here is the *real* problem: **The ongoing debate and controversy about vegan vs. meat, or plant-based vs. meat lover, *has taken the spotlight OFF where it should actually be*, which is on the food industry. Industrialized, processed food.**

As author, Robert Lustwig M.D., says in his book *Metabolical*, the vegan vs. keto battle is "based on a false premise of metabolic health, and both diets can be abused, as the food industry peddles both processed carbs and processed meats."[12] He goes on to make a valid case that in the end, the food industry is laughing all the way to the bank, as we go about debating the things that *don't matter very much*.

So, here ye hear ye - my message to you is this: Meat lovers and vegans are both right, and they're both wrong. I believe they can and should exist together and both can thrive – in truth they have a lot more in common than many realize. I'd go so far as to say it's really a *fake war*, where the actual enemy they should both be looking to fight *isn't each other*, it's the industrialized food manufacturers. **It's BIG Food (as you've heard me say at least a half-dozen times already) who are producing addictive, sugar and chemical laden foods that are the real culprit in our decaying individual and global health.**

And, I'd add, they're also a major culprit in the climate crisis. If you doubt me, consider the billions of tons of food waste, microplastics, plastic packaging, and greenhouse gases made in the factories operated by the food manufacturing giants, some of which end up in our rivers and oceans and ground water. The cost to our planet is mind-boggling.

No matter what your reasons are for choosing one approach over another, you will *always be able to find* believers and evidence that supports *your choice*. There are a lot of reasons why this is true – too many to cover in this book. But believe it. In the end, you need to do your own thinking and make up your own mind. For me, I'm not vegan or vegetarian and don't believe that being strictly vegan or vegetarian is the smartest approach for good health. It's much more about the quality of the food vs. taking sides on the meat vs. no meat debate.

Finally, remember *cognitive dissonance* is real. Cognitive dissonance is when we hold and believe two *conflicting* ideas or beliefs. It's one of the reasons discussions about diet and our personal choices about food, as well as the climate, are so hard. After all, we're human. It's understandably difficult to cope with the nuances of contradictory ideas - it can be mentally stressful. We all seek consistency in our own attitudes and perceptions - it isn't easy to sit with seemingly opposite ideas or concepts that all seem to be true. Rather than staunchly defend one way or another, I say we should start by accepting our humanity and then seek common ground.

To be clear, I am *both* a meat lover and plant-based. If that sounds like I'm flip-flopping, I don't agree. This balanced approach of eating a primarily plant-based diet that also includes red meat a few times a week reflects my philosophy of eating mostly REAL food, not processed or packaged industrialized food. I believe the greater the variety of quality food I eat from every possible source, the better the chance I'll get what my body needs to thrive. Variety rules when it comes to balanced nutrition and enjoyable eating!

I always consider the quality of the meat first when determining what I eat and when. We buy locally raised, grass-fed and finished ribeye or sirloin almost exclusively. My personal experience and research tells me there are nutrients in meat that are healthful and important for good health, provided the source is as good as it can possibly be.

Do I occasionally eat a hamburger or have a steak when I don't know where the meat came from? Yes, of course. But I don't do it often. And I don't think of it as "cheating" either. As I've said repeatedly, achieving, and sustaining good health is mostly about our daily habits over the long haul, not what we might do very occasionally. It certainly isn't about identifying a certain food as good or bad. Maybe a food or nutrition purist wouldn't agree, but that's what I believe. And I think the occasional indulgence, if you see it that way, makes life more enjoyable.

One thing is certainly true and that is, if you ever want to get into a "spirited" conversation with a group of friends, start talking politics or nutrition. Ha! When it comes to *those two* topics, we all have strong opinions, and those opinions and the choices we make as a result of them, are usually deeply connected to our emotions. For me, when it comes to the foods I eat routinely, I focus on *variety, balance,* and *moderation* and try to keep my emotions in check. Most of the time, I choose foods that will best serve my long-term health. And yes, some of the time it's about what tastes great and will make life a little bit more enjoyable in the moment. ☺

What About Xenohormesis?

I think we'd all agree that exercising is one of the single best things you can do for your health. Have you ever wondered why being active and exercising is so important, beyond the obvious uptick in cardiovascular fitness and strength? The answer is **stress**. Of course, exercise is by definition, the application of various stressors to our bodies, and one type of positive stress we get from exercising is called *hormesis,* or *hormetic stress.* You may recall you learned about *hormesis* in Chapter 2, *Why We Age: Exploring Aging at the Cellular Level.* In Chapter 10 on *Time Restricted Eating,* I also discussed *hormesis* as one of the subtle but important benefits of sometimes being mildly hungry. Discussing *hormesis* brings me back to the topic of diet in general, and *aspirin* in particular. So, what does aspirin have to do with stress and diet and meat eater vs. vegetarian?

An Aspirin a Day?

I recently read an interesting research article from 2019 titled, *Association of Aspirin Use With Mortality Risk Among Older Adult Participants in the Prostate, Lung, Colorectal, and Ovarian Cancer Screening Trial.* The purpose of this research study was to determine whether taking aspirin is associated with a reduced risk of mortality in older people.[13]

The story of the discovery of aspirin stretches back more than 3500 years to when bark from the willow tree was used as a pain reliever and antipyretic, which is a drug used to fight fever. Most pharmacists know aspirin's origins lie with willow bark, but they may be unaware of its role in the development of the pharmaceutical industry. Evolving from salacin (the active ingredient in many plant remedies) to salicylic acid, to the more effective, less toxic acetylsalicylic acid, this pain reliever cornered the nonsteroidal anti-inflammatory market for many years. [14] Aspirin is now not only the most commonly used drug in the world, its role in preventing cardiovascular and cerebrovascular disease has been revolutionary and one of the biggest pharmaceutical success stories of the last century.[15] All that being said, I believe there's even more to learn about aspirin's potential health benefits.

Going back to the research study I referenced earlier, the researchers concluded that in fact, "aspirin use may reduce risk of mortality among older individuals," which is a conclusion that quite honestly, is what I had anticipated before even reading the research article. In *fact, I'll go further and say these findings further strengthen my belief that what the researchers learned could become the single biggest known benefit to eating plants!* To explore just exactly what I mean by that bold statement, let's take a step back to consider not just aspirin and what aspirin is made from (willow bark), but what happens to all plants including the willow tree, as they grow.

Whether you are a meat eater or not, you would have to agree eating some vegetables is good for your health. I don't think that point is debatable. However, it's only recently that science has become more tuned in to the fact some of the most important health-promoting molecules we receive from plants go beyond the more obvious vitamins and minerals, to less obvious compounds that are produced especially *when plants are stressed*. This idea was put forth in Dr. David Sinclair's book, *Lifespan, when he said,* "this, we believe, is evidence of **xenohormesis** - the idea that stressed plants produce chemicals for themselves that tell their cells to hunker down and survive."[16] If you're wondering how a plant might be stressed, consider the "battles" an individual plant has to fight every second of its life that make it hard for it to thrive. Drought, insect invasion, less than ideal soil quality, and environmental factors like high wind, are just a few examples. If you recall, I spoke about one of these factors when discussing the Biosphere 2 experiments in Chapter 2.

It turns out these environmental stressors can jump-start "survival circuits" in plants (just as exercise and hunger can in us) that help them survive. If we eat the plant, we can receive some of the benefits of that *stress*, which is the **xenohormesis** Dr. Sinclair was referring to in his book. These benefits sometimes manifest in the form of compounds in plants such as quercetin (from fruits), allicin (from garlic), resveratrol (from grapes), and of course, aspirin also fits in this category. Why aspirin? As I mentioned, aspirin is made from willow bark, which comes from the bark of several varieties of willow trees. It stands to reason just like any plant or tree, willow trees would experience and have to overcome environmental stress in order to survive, right? As an aside, it is true that organic plants are grown under more stressful environments which is one more reason to eat organic whenever possible!

To circle back to what I said a few paragraphs ago so it's clear why I shared this with you: the findings of this study (as well as the information from Dr. Sinclair and other scientists) suggests to me that perhaps the single biggest benefit of eating plants is the **xenohormetic benefits** passed on from the plants. Which again brings me *back to aspirin*.

If you are thinking this is my way of telling you I take an aspirin daily, you'd be correct. By the way, *xenohormesis* isn't the only reason I take an aspirin every day but it is one of the most important reasons. The other reason is I have Factor-V Leiden, which is a genetic mutation of one of the clotting factors in the blood. This mutation can increase the chance of developing abnormal blood clots, most commonly in the legs or lungs.[17] I've never experienced any evidence of this mutation, but as a precaution, I'm taking the aspirin on the recommendation of my general physician. Which brings me back to two final thoughts on this topic: First, as always, check with your doctor first. Have the conversation. Second, as the great philosopher and thinker, Friedrich Nietzsche, said: "That which does not kill us makes us stronger." ☺

In Summary: I could go on and on. Hopefully, I've given you enough information in this chapter to make you think more broadly about the topic. To summarize, here are some final thoughts:

- **Any approach to eating, whether its vegan or keto or anything else, can be distorted and abused**. Sometimes that's easy to forget. Remember who the "real" enemy is.
- **We all have different basic nutritional needs and unique biochemistry, so what may work well for one person might not work for another**. We can never forget we are all an experiment of one! You'll find that theme throughout this book. Remember, what works for your friend or a celebrity might not work for you, and that's OK! Find what works for you.
- **If you decide to follow one of these stricter approaches, be it vegan or keto, you'll soon find it's increasingly hard to stick with as your motivation to be disciplined begins to wane**. You might also need to monitor blood levels of certain nutrients more closely. You may even find you need to supplement.
- **The real enemy** we all need to be more aware of and who we ought to be fighting against individually and collectively, is processed, industrialized food and the companies that produce it.
- Read the above bullet again. The message? **Eat REAL food**.
- **Rather than try and convince someone else to change what *they* believe by debating them**, be an authentic advocate for what you believe by how you live and act. That will be enough. You are enough. *Be the change you hope to see in the world.*

CHAPTER 16

TAKE HOME NUTRITION TIPS AND COMMON QUESTIONS

The longer your food lasts,
the shorter you will.

— **David Sinclair, Ph.D.,** *author and scientist*

*The indispensable first step to getting what you want
out of this life is this: decide what you want.*
— Ben Stein, *actor and political pundit*

The three word phrase "take home message" appears quite a lot throughout the book. It's my way of letting you know amidst all the knowledge you're taking in, there is something coming up that is specific that you can take immediate action on in your own life. With the goal of becoming truly healthy and aging well, of course.

This chapter follows that theme with a host of different "take home" tips and suggestions. There's also a brief theoretical question and answer segment at the end of the chapter. Enjoy!

Don't Eat After 6 PM Most Days Of the Week.

Going to sleep feeling a little bit hungry is very healthy for you. It's not something you must do every day, but most days it is the ideal. If you avoid late night eating, you go to sleep with less sugar and other nutrients in your blood stream, and that can increase growth hormone release. It will provide you with an automatic near ideal non-eating window, especially when breakfast doesn't come until mid-morning or noontime the next day.

For example, 6 PM until 10 AM the next morning is 16 hours. Waiting until noon to eat will give you 18 hours, which is ideal. Of course, it's not a coincidence one of the most powerful things you can do for your overall health is to not eat when it's often the most socially enjoyable time TO eat, which is obviously later in the evening. This is when the munchies usually hit while hanging out with family or friends or watching TV. Skimping on calories earlier in the day also makes this difficult because you will feel hungrier. As I often say, it won't always be easy but it will be worth it. "Most" days of the week.

Avoid Foods That Contain Processed Seed Oils.

One of the myths the food industry has sold to the general public is that "heart healthy" vegetable oils are, in fact, heart healthy! Nothing could be further from the truth. These oils go rancid quickly and there are a lot of potentially harmful chemicals added when they're manufactured contributing to them being unhealthy for you and me.

The challenge is many of the foods we've become used to eating contain these addictive seed oils. Be aware. My suggestion is to reduce the use of them. If you can cut back to half of what you might have at one time eaten, that will be a positive change. Over time, you may even be able to reduce the use of them to almost zero. These, along with processed sugars and meats are the root cause of so much chronic disease and unwanted weight gain.

Minimize or Eliminate Grazing or Snacking.

On the surface, this sounds like a very unreasonable request for the average person, right? ☺ After all, an occasional snack is enjoyable and always seems to help kill that little pang of hunger that rears its ugly head in between meals, right? And that's part of the problem.

Here's how this works: As you learned in Chapter 9, when you eat, the hormone insulin is secreted to account for the rise in blood sugar. The more frequently you eat, the more insulin stays elevated. Chronically elevated insulin levels damage your health and lead to hyperinsulinemia, insulin resistance, metabolic syndrome and eventually type-2 diabetes.

Chronically elevated insulin levels are the most serious health issue facing people in this country, in part because it's closely associated with every OTHER chronic disease – diabetes, cancer, heart disease, non-alcoholic fatty liver disease, chronic inflammation, and dementias such as Alzheimer's – all of them.

Metabolic illness or metabolic syndrome, as it is sometimes referred to, is the platform upon which every OTHER serious chronic disease develops. **The most recent science and research is showing us that ALL those diseases are, at a basic level, metabolic diseases**. That's what ties them all together. When you snack and eat frequently, cravings increase. A craving isn't hunger, but it feels like it. We are an overfed society, in part because food is available everywhere, as are the constant marketing messages to eat that food.

What to do?

- If you DO need to graze or simply want to snack on something, choose REAL food, not processed food. Blueberries (or some other low-sugar fruits) or raw nuts are great choices in a pinch. Avoid the junk food at all costs.
- Don't focus on calorie restriction or "starving" yourself, focus on when you eat and how often.
- Avoid vending machines and don't buy snack foods of any kind. If it isn't easily available, the odds of you choosing it are lowered.
- **Remember, there's no such thing as a "bad" food. But there are less-than-optimal choices, and "bad" habits that you'd be better off changing.**

There's almost nothing I won't eat – every so often, or on occasion. To put it another way, I haven't cut any specific food entirely from my diet. If I have some ice cream or dessert, I do it without guilt and really enjoy it! But I won't do it every day or even every week, that's the difference.

You see, the path to eating healthier isn't about "this or that" food is "bad." It's about habits. What do you eat routinely and how can you improve upon that? If you want to be healthier and feel better, are there certain kinds of food (such as processed sugar) you'll want to avoid routinely? Yes. The obvious is processed foods, especially cereals, soda, and grains. It's not the added sugar you know, it's the added sugar you don't know, that's the biggest problem. But, focusing on the occasional "bad" choice misses the bigger and more serious problem which is the habits we fall into or form that lead to chronically poor choices.

Humans *are* creatures of habit. And habits are where cravings come from. What matters most are the consistent choices you make over a long period of time, not the occasional less-than-optimal choice. Get out of the "habit" of routinely eating stuff that isn't good for you. Break the habit. Learn to recognize where you can trip on a crack and fall back to bad habits. Occasional "cheat" days are OK – they give you something to look forward to, until you reach a point where that certain food isn't as appealing to you anymore, which you will.

- Focus on what you routinely eat. Your habits.
- Commit to changing habits where you need to. There's no easy way, hack, or quick fix.
- Every day is a new day. Recommit.

There Is No Such Thing As the Perfect Diet For Every Person.

Diets that restrict major food groups bring with them inherent challenges that are often hard to overcome. Vegetarian diets are one example. It's one of the reasons I almost NEVER advocate any kind of approach to eating, or any diet, that excludes a food group or even a type of food. Think about that if you're considering that kind of diet program.

We should all remember we're each an experiment of one. What works for one person might not work as well for another. That's almost assuredly going to be the case a large percentage of the time.

Think about this, too: **Dietary and saturated fat** isn't the enemy. Even though there still remains a lot of misguided messaging surrounding it, it isn't the evil that was once believed.

Meat isn't the enemy. You can have processed chemical-laden, steroid-induced meat, OR you can have grass fed, organic, local farm raised meat. Meat isn't the problem, processed food is.

Salt isn't the enemy. Yes, very often sugar laden food also comes jam-packed with salt. But our kidneys typically do a nice job of excreting extra salt when needed, except when there's insulin resistance. The enemy isn't salt.

If there is an enemy, what is it? Sugar. Processed, especially. The mainstream diet establishment and the government have blamed salt for the problems sugar is responsible for. Processed junk food is high in sugar, and low in nutrients and fiber. "Real" food is the opposite, high in fiber and nutrients and low in sugar. Learn to read food labels. Know what you are buying and eating. Speaking of food labels, keep reading.

Most people seeing CLIF bars on the shelves at the grocery store would think they were a healthy energy bar, right? I used to eat quite a lot of these myself, when I was training more and time was short. There's nothing quite like the ability to grab a quick bar on the go.

Nutrition Facts

6 servings per container
Serving size 1 bar (68g)

Amount per serving
Calories 250

	% Daily Value*
Total Fat 5g	7%
Saturated Fat 1.5g	7%
Trans Fat 0g	
Polyunsaturated Fat 1g	
Monounsaturated Fat 2g	
Cholesterol 0mg	0%
Sodium 140mg	6%
Total Carbohydrate 45g	16%
Dietary Fiber 4g	15%
Insoluble Fiber 3g	
Total Sugars 21g	
Includes 21g Added Sugars	41%
Protein 9g	17%

Vitamin D 2mcg	8%	Calcium 195mg	15%
Iron 2mg	15%	Potas. 207mg	4%
Vitamin A	2%	Vitamin C	6%
Vitamin E	10%	Thiamin (Vit. B₁)	15%
Riboflavin (Vit. B₂)	15%	Niacin	25%
Vitamin B₆	10%	Vitamin B₁₂	25%
Phosphorus	20%	Magnesium	20%

*The % Daily Value (DV) tells you how much a nutrient in a serving of food contributes to a daily diet. 2,000 calories a day is used for general nutrition advice.

INGREDIENTS: ORGANIC BROWN RICE SYRUP, ORGANIC ROLLED OATS, SOY PROTEIN ISOLATE, ORGANIC CANE SYRUP, ORGANIC ROASTED SOYBEANS, RICE FLOUR, CANE SUGAR, UNSWEETENED CHOCOLATE†, ORGANIC SOY FLOUR, ORGANIC OAT FIBER, ORGANIC HIGH OLEIC SUNFLOWER OIL, COCOA BUTTER†, BARLEY MALT EXTRACT, SEA SALT, NATURAL FLAVORS, SOY LECITHIN, ORGANIC CINNAMON. **VITAMINS & MINERALS:** DICALCIUM PHOSPHATE, MAGNESIUM OXIDE, ASCORBIC ACID (VIT. C), DL-ALPHA TOCOPHERYL ACETATE (VIT. E), BETA CAROTENE (VIT. A), NIACINAMIDE (VIT. B3), ERGOCALCIFEROL (VIT. D2), THIAMINE MONONITRATE (VIT. B1), PYRIDOXINE HYDROCHLORIDE (VIT. B6), RIBOFLAVIN (VIT. B2), CYANOCOBALAMIN (VIT. B12).
ALLERGEN STATEMENT: CONTAINS SOY.
MAY CONTAIN PEANUTS, TREE NUTS, MILK, AND WHEAT.

†"Rainforest Alliance Certified"
DISTRIBUTED BY CLIF BAR & COMPANY, EMERYVILLE, CA 94608 U.S.A.
CERTIFIED ORGANIC BY QAI

MEGAN RAPINOE
CLIF® ATHLETE

To stay at the top of my game, I have to keep training all year long. Obviously, that takes dedication, but it also requires a ton of energy. I've tried so many bars, and CLIF BAR® and LUNA® bars are definitely my favorites. They have the protein, fat, and carbs I need to keep my energy levels up, and I love the way they taste! I usually have a CLIF BAR before practice, and I always make sure I have a few bars in my bag when I travel—which is pretty much all the time.

—MEGAN RAPINOE
2-time World Cup champion

1-800-CLIFBAR M–F 8–5 PT
© 2019 CLIF BAR & COMPANY.
TRADEMARKS AND REGISTERED TRADEMARKS ARE OWNED BY CLIF BAR & COMPANY, OR USED WITH PERMISSION.

CLIFBAR.COM

100% Recycled Paperboard

This carton is made from 100% recycled content with a maximum 65% pre-consumer content and a minimum 35% post-consumer fiber content. Please recycle.

RECYCLED Packaging made from recycled material FSC® C106886

66004 014 __R16

7 22252 66004 6

Here's a label from a CLIF bar. At 21g of sugar, I'd say this bar has a lot more in common with a candy bar than anything that's actually healthy. When you add in the organic high oleic sunflower oil, which is an industrialized processed seed oil, you have the makings of a bad food choice. Even with a picture of elite athlete Megan Rapinoe on the package!

Check out the ingredient list for this "therapeutic" nutrition drink called "JEVITY" made by a company called Abbott Nutrition. According to the label, it is advertised as "Complete, Balanced Nutrition with Fiber." It is designed and advertised as a "supplemental or sole source nutrition for tube feeding that is calorically dense and fiber fortified." Apparently, it's supposed to be very good for you! And it's created specifically for a patient population that definitely needs the highest quality nutrition, as it says it should only be used under medical supervision. (Although I don't know how they can say that if you can buy it on Amazon!)

INGREDIENTS: WATER, CORN MALTODEXTRIN, CORN SYRUP SOLIDS, SODIUM AND CALCIUM CASEINATES, CANOLA OIL, CORN OIL, SOY PROTEIN ISOLATE, SHORT-CHAIN FRUCTOOLIGOSACCHARIDES, MEDIUM CHAIN TRIGLYCERIDES, OAT FIBER, SOY FIBER, POTASSIUM CITRATE, CALCIUM PHOSPHATE, GUM ARABIC, SODIUM CITRATE, MAGNESIUM PHOSPHATE, SOY LECITHIN, MAGNESIUM CHLORIDE, CELLULOSE GUM, ASCORBIC ACID, CHOLINE CHLORIDE, POTASSIUM CHLORIDE, TAURINE, L-CARNITINE, ZINC SULFATE, dl-ALPHA-TOCOPHERYL ACETATE, FERROUS SULFATE, NIACINAMIDE, CALCIUM PANTOTHENATE, MANGANESE SULFATE, COPPER SULFATE, THIAMINE HYDROCHLORIDE, PYRIDOXINE HYDROCHLORIDE, RIBOFLAVIN, VITAMIN A PALMITATE, FOLIC ACID, BIOTIN, CHROMIUM CHLORIDE, SODIUM MOLYBDATE, POTASSIUM IODIDE, SODIUM SELENATE, PHYLLOQUINONE, VITAMIN B_{12} AND VITAMIN D_3. **CONTAINS MILK AND SOY INGREDIENTS.**

Abbott Nutrition
Abbott Laboratories
Columbus, Ohio 43219-3034 USA

In other words, it's advertised as a great source of quality nutrients whether you're an adult or a child in need of the best nutrient source you can find. In fact, it's so good, looking on Amazon it appears it's "Amazon's Choice" for this type of product. Well, that's like the gold seal of approval, isn't it? ☺

Look closely at the ingredients list, remembering the items listed first are in higher amounts compared to those things listed later.

Corn maltodextrin.
Corn syrup solids.
Corn Oil.
Soy Protein isolate.
Short-chain Fructooligosaccharides?

Whatever that last ingredient is – I think only a chemist would know – but it looks very close to fructose, which should scare anyone reading this to be very honest. What you have here is a (dirty) laundry list of potentially toxic added sugars of all types, all of them manufactured in a factory, and all of them designed to give this drink a nice, tasty flavor, and most of all, make it very easy and cheap to produce. And the rest of the chemical additives will ensure it'll last on the shelf for a very long time. Another "bonus."

What's the take home lesson here? Thousands of products available in your local supermarket and on Amazon and other retailers are advertised as being "healthy," when the reality is far from it!! To the contrary, you'd be much better off eating a milk chocolate bar than drinking this garbage.

One last thing as it relates to labeling on food. All of the above being said, ironically the most important thing for you to consider as you decide what and how to eat, isn't what is IN the food, it's what HAS BEEN DONE to the food.

When it comes to labeling, the only rules food manufacturers have is for allergies such as peanuts, shellfish, or gluten. Nothing else. My point being the label only tells you what's inside. It doesn't tell you a single thing about how it was produced or what's been done in production. *Food for thought?*

I was inspired one day listening to a podcast with Dr. Peter Attia, M.D., who I've referenced often in this book. Dr. Attia is a trustworthy source of information on all things longevity and aging related – I've learned a lot from him over the years. He shares a ton and has the advantage of working in his own clinic with lots of different kinds of people, so he has firsthand knowledge of so much of what he shares.

In this conversation about eating, he recommended one particular way he advocates for making small positive changes a little at a time. And as you know from having read this far, I highly recommend making changes incrementally – so tiny even, they're almost imperceptible. His advice was simple. I'll paraphrase and share my own spin on it:

Manipulate One of These Three Variables, Every Day.

When it comes to the food you eat and drink, there are three variables you are in control of on a daily basis that you can alter. They are:

1. How much you eat,
2. When you eat, and
3. The quality of the food you eat.

The idea is for you to make a commitment to focus on (at least) one of these variables, every day. In other words, alter them, ideally of course, in a positive way. Always start small.

What are some ways to put this into action? Remember, in the spirit of starting small and making consistent and positive changes that are sustainable, you're only going to try and commit to ONE of these things at a time. Each and every day, of course.

- Eat breakfast later in the day, increasing your "no-eating" window assuming you didn't eat overnight. (That's #2).
- Choose to skip the creamer or even better, the sugar in your coffee or tea. (That's #3). *By the way, black coffee can curb hunger and increase energy. It promotes autophagy by increasing epinephrine and the release of fat from fat cells, it contains healthy polyphenols, and it won't break your "fast." ☺
- Choose to skip dinner. (That's #1 and #2). (Perhaps exercise instead!)

- Choose to leave out a sugar or starch you might normally have at breakfast, lunch, or dinner. An example would be skipping the roasted potatoes or pasta, or breakfast hashbrowns. (That's #1).
- Along the same thinking as the previous bullet, decide to add an in-season vegetable or fruit to your meal you wouldn't ordinarily do. (That's #1 and #3).
- Decide not to buy any food where you buy your gas. (That's #3).
- Decide NOT to eat any foods or food products that contain industrial seed oils like canola, corn, cottonseed, or soy. (That's #3).
- Choose to eat dinner a little earlier in the evening than might be normal for you. (That's #2).

And so on and so forth! The ideas are truly endless. What I like most about this is, in and of themselves, they seem like small changes that won't make a big difference. But nothing could be further from the truth. Small changes add up. Just like compound interest, with a consistent and smart approach, you'll keep these going and little by little, you'll achieve what you are hoping for.

Avoid Exposing Yourself to Toxins in Plastic Packaging.

In Chapter 2, you learned about epigenetics and how behavior and diet are powerful triggers for these epigenetic changes. One example of something which can cause negative changes is the ingestion of certain toxic compounds in some plastics. This process of chemical transfer is known as "migration," and has also been shown to be true for hazardous chemicals and chemicals with unknown toxicity. This makes plastic packaging a relevant source of human exposure to synthetic chemicals. There is some speculation in scientific circles that these chemicals are among a constellation of contributors to the wave of obesity seen in developed countries, and not seen in underdeveloped regions.

The graphic below comes directly from a 2019 study titled *Tackling the Toxics in Plastic Packaging.*[1] This research study focused on the health and environmental impact of microplastics used in packaging, as well as confronting plastic pollution to protect the environment and public health. It's an eye-opening graphic showing how molecules present in the plastic can transfer out of the plastic and into the food.

Clearly, much still needs to be done to weed out the toxic chemicals and reduce the use of these plastics. Your goal should be to reduce consumption of any food contained in plastics and do your best to avoid these containers. That is, bottles, plastic bags, and plastic containers in microwave dinners and other pre-packaged food.

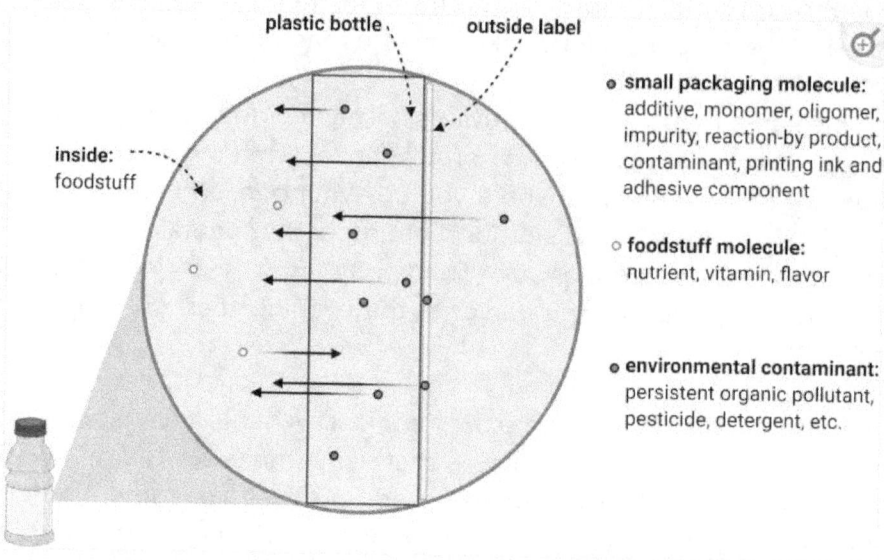

plastic bottle   outside label

inside:
foodstuff

- **small packaging molecule:**
  additive, monomer, oligomer,
  impurity, reaction-by product,
  contaminant, printing ink and
  adhesive component

- **foodstuff molecule:**
  nutrient, vitamin, flavor

- **environmental contaminant:**
  persistent organic pollutant,
  pesticide, detergent, etc.

<u>Fig 1</u>

Schematic illustration of chemical migration from plastic food packaging into food.

Small molecules that are present in the plastic packaging item (red dots) can transfer out of the plastic into the food. The same is true for small molecules present in the food (yellow dot), a process known as flavor scalping. Also, environmental contaminants (blue dots) can be absorbed in the plastic packaging and subsequently be released again, making this an issue for plastics recycling. Chemical migration, flavor scalping, and absorption depend on temperature, time, and the chemical properties of the packaging, the food and the chemicals that are transferring from one medium to another. Created with BioRender.com.

Eat Mostly "Living" Food.

Not sure what I mean? It's about eating foods that will bolster our defenses because their defenses have been bolstered. Think of it this way: many types of food processing and food preservation including cooking can damage and often destroy molecules that would otherwise activate the body's defenses against diseases and aging. These molecules are called "xenohormetic" molecules or "xenohormetins." Most if not all processed foods don't contain any of these molecules. Living or raw, uncooked or only slightly cooked or prepared foods are much better sources. What are some well-known examples of these powerful molecules known as Xenohormetins? For starters there is...

- Resveratrol in red wine,
- Quercetin, a plant flavanol found in many fruits, vegetables, leaves, seeds, and grains; capers, red onions, and kale,

- Fisetin, a plant flavanol found in strawberries, apples, persimmons, onions and cucumbers,
- Oleic acid, a fatty acid found in olive oil,
- Spermidine, a compound found in fresh green pepper, wheat germ, cauliflower, broccoli, mushrooms, and a variety of cheeses, and
- Salicylates, which is in aspirin.
- Foods like red wine, cocoa, nuts, coffee, black tea, regular green tea, and matcha green tea, as well as dark leafy greens, all contain some percentage of these molecules.

Plants make these molecules when they are under stress or experience adversity. These molecules promote survival and improved health. Often, these natural chemicals bind to and modulate just the right enzymes to enhance the plant's defenses and resilience.

When we ingest certain polyphenols, they promote OUR body's defenses by targeting longevity enzymes. Interestingly, scientists now believe this cross-species signaling may exist so animals know when their food supply could run out and allow them to prepare for adversity.

One way to know if plants have an abundance of these molecules is they have a lot of color: red, blue, and dark green. Eating these can offer the benefits of adversity without having to actually experience it.

What Are Some Of the Most Common Questions?

General Nutrition Related:

- "What about salt, I have heard that it's bad and that I should reduce it in my diet."

Salt intake, in my opinion, is one of those things that has been blamed for the problems excess sugar has created. Think about this: Back in the 18th and 19th century, world travelers would often consume as much as 15 grams of salt per day because the fish they caught would have to be cured in salt in order to reduce the risk of contamination. Did they suffer a lot of salt-induced strokes or heart disease? I don't think they did. The reason is simple: the kidneys are very skilled at excreting excess sodium in our diets.

However, maybe this answer should have been posted in the insulin resistance area because there is one thing that WILL inhibit the kidneys from excreting excess sodium effectively, and that's insulin resistance. Also, hyperinsulinemia increases blood pressure, even when salt intake isn't that high. The problem isn't the salt, it's the processed foods and lack of exercise driving insulin resistance. As always, check with your doctor to see how your situation may differ.

- "What the first advice you would give someone who simply wanted to lose bodyfat and also become healthier?"

That's simple! I would tell them to STOP drinking calories. Sugared soda, iced tea, fruit juice, sports drinks, etc., are all sources of calories that contribute to unhealthy weight gain and raise blood sugar levels. This is the first place to begin. If you're drinking calories, stop!

- "I've had difficulty losing weight and getting stronger, and I also still occasionally struggle with cravings. I wonder if my protein intake is part of this. I've read a lot of conflicting advice as to how much protein I should get each day. Can you clear up that confusion?"

Yes! If you're an adult who is eating less than 100 grams of protein per day, it's likely one of the main reasons you keep craving unhealthy foods and are having a difficult time getting stronger or losing unwanted bodyfat. Aim for AT LEAST 1 gram per pound of bodyweight per day, up to even 1.25 grams per pound of bodyweight. In my opinion, the best source is grass fed, grass finished red meat.

On Time Restricted Eating:

- "What If I can't make it the entire 16 or 18 or 24 hours?"

Just do the best you can, that's all that matters. If you truly do your best to make it happen, you will certainly grow and benefit. Even relatively short "breaks" from eating are beneficial for your health!

- "Can I still have my morning coffee or tea?"

In my opinion, the answer is yes, you can. There are some who believe the best answer is not to have anything other than water. I don't think it breaks the "fast" however. Of course, it is better if you don't add milk, cream, and especially sugar. Having it black is ideal. So, if you are accustomed to adding those to your drinks, try to wean yourself off of them. That being said, a small amount of cream shouldn't undo your non-eating window.

- "What If I like to have a snack late at night?"

No can do. Late night eating is not only going to break up and destroy that non-eating window, it'll also mess with your sleep and reduce, among other things, the amount of growth hormone released while you're in REM sleep. The secret to getting past the habit of eating late is to make sure your environment is supporting you! That is, don't have the foods around that you are most subject to cheat with. Keep them out of the house. Access to food is a big part of the problem. Prevent it ahead of time. And remember, sometimes you need to just suck it up and have some self-discipline to get where you want to go. You can do it. And once you put one day on top of another and get into a rhythm with it, it will get easier. You're worth it!

- "What If I exercise in the morning? Should I do this without eating beforehand? "

For exercise sessions up to 90 minutes in length or so, you will be absolutely fine. In fact, you will very likely feel better than ever, for a host of different reasons, not the least of which is your stomach will be clean, and your GI system won't be bogged down trying to digest food while also supplying O2 and nutrients to your working muscles! Remember, as I mentioned earlier in the book, you have stored glycogen and your body likes to use that for energy, especially initially. And then there's the virtually unlimited fat stores. Enjoy exercising in a "fasted" state, it's absolutely the best of both worlds! I'll discuss more in the exercise section of the book.

- "Why do you recommend eating the one meal a day in the evening?"

Eating your main meal at night works best for most people because it likely matches your innate, inner clock, or circadian rhythm. In a nutshell, during the day your sympathetic nervous system (SNS) puts your body in an energy spending active mode, whereas during the night your parasympathetic nervous system (PNS) puts your body in an energy replenishing relaxed and sleepy mode.

Remember your SNS is your "fight or flight" system that often operates on adrenalin, and definitely likes fast-acting sugars as fuel! Your PNS is your recovery, rejuvenation nervous system you want to be in most of the time. Simply put, the SNS is stimulated by fasting and exercise. The PNS is stimulated by night time feeding, which increases sleepiness and relaxation.

- "I'm concerned I may not be getting enough calories, and I am very active. What is the best way to estimate my daily caloric needs?"

That's a great question, because after all, TRE is NOT a caloric restriction approach, exclusively. Yes, it might be a by-product of what you do with this, as I mentioned earlier, but it isn't about generating a caloric deficit. This IS especially important if you are in training of some kind for sports or are extremely active in your job or lifestyle.

Here's the formula I have used most successfully. While it may look complicated, it works, although it will always be only an estimate. Keep that in mind. That being said, it is worth taking the time to get the calculator out and do the math. ☺

Estimating Your Daily Caloric Needs: Your body requires you to take in a certain number of calories every day to supply energy for the work you do and to maintain your present body weight. And while that seems simple enough, it's where some get off track. Eat too little, and the weight you lose can come from your muscle. Eat too much, and you store energy as fat rather than building muscle.

The term used to describe that "daily caloric need" is Basal Metabolic Rate, or BMR, which is defined as "the amount of energy needed while resting in a temperate environment when the digestive system is inactive."

If you'd like to skip doing the math yourself, a fairly accurate calculator for BMR is available online at this website: https://www.calculator.net/bmr-calculator.html

Should you like to dig in and do this yourself, here's the formula:

Women: BMR = 655 + (4.35 x weight in pounds) + (4.7 x height in inches) - (4.7 x age in years)

Men: BMR = 66 + (6.23 x weight in pounds) + (12.7 x height in inches) - (6.8 x age in year)

You'll also want to adjust for your usual activity level during the day. Here are some modifiers to account for that:

If you are sedentary (little or no exercise): Calorie-Calculation = BMR x 1.2.

If you are lightly active (light exercise/sports 1-3 days/week): Calorie-Calculation = BMR x 1.375

If you are moderately active (moderate exercise/sports 3-5 days/week): Calorie-Calculation = BMR x 1.55.

If you are very active (hard exercise/sports 6-7 days a week): Calorie-Calculation = BMR x 1.725.

If you are extra active (very hard exercise/sports & physical job or 2x training): Calorie-Calculation = BMR x 1.9.

What If You Want to Take Your Time Restricted Eating to the Next Level And Maximize Benefits Even More?

If you'd like to get even more out of this lifestyle transformation that might lead to a leaner, healthier you, here is a short **list of foods to eliminate, foods to minimize, and foods to add.**

Two things to keep in mind:

1. Remember carbohydrates, while they've gotten a bad rap in some circles over the past few years, aren't "bad," in and of themselves. The key is to focus on the right kind of carbs – those that come from vegetables and low-sugar fruits are what you

want! And if you are very active and exercising or training for a sport, you may need more "carbs" in your diet in order to perform at your best.

On the other hand, some people are carb intolerant to some degree and will benefit by restricting these. Bottom line, when all else fails or in doubt, remove or at the very least, cut back and minimize the junk and processed sugars. Eat real food instead.

2. Keep in mind this is only a brief list and provides only some suggestions. The list could easily be expanded. Think of it as a simple start.

As much as possible, eliminate these foods:

- Refined sugars: any kind of processed, refined, and pre-packaged, sugar, in all of its forms.
- Artificial sweeteners.
- Candy and baked goods.
- Bread in ALL of its forms.
- Pastas.
- Wheat/grains.
- Any training foods or fuels, such as gels or carb powders.
- Vegetable oils like canola, corn, cottonseed, soybean, rapeseed, rice bran and safflower oils.

Minimize how much you eat these foods:

- Bananas (and other fruits high in sugar).
- Dairy foods such as cheese, milk, yogurt.
- Peanuts and other "junk" nuts.
- Highly processed meats including bacon.
- Condiments.
- Ice cream / frozen yogurt.

Always include these foods – choose organic whenever possible:

- All the veggies, especially leafy greens (organic if possible).
- Lower sugar fruit such as red and blue berries.
- Monounsaturated oils like extra virgin Olive oil, black seed oil, cod liver oil, fish oils.
- Raw nuts and seeds, especially walnuts, pistachios, almonds, and pecans.
- Chicken/turkey from local farms, or organic.
- Eggs.
- Coffee and tea (organic if possible).

What Are Some Additional Common Questions?

1. "Is following a 'keto' diet the answer?"

Keto and ketogenic dieting has been all the rage in fitness and weight loss circles over the last few years. The reasons are obvious to anyone who has followed the hype: people usually DO lose body fat when they go to a keto diet.

So, what is a ketogenic diet? Strictly speaking, it's an extremely LOW carbohydrate diet. What you do is limit your carbohydrate intake to a very low 50 grams per day! This is hardly any at all, which is one of the reasons some folks who think they're fully "keto," are actually only part of the way there, because they're eating more than 50 grams a day of carbohydrate.

Everyone has ketones. If you're not sure what they are, they're a nutrient that can be used for energy that's produced by a process called ketogenesis, which happens when the liver breaks down fat. Ketones are a primary reserve fuel for the brain when glucose is low. Our body makes ketones anytime insulin is low. And as you know by now, when insulin is low, the body wants to naturally shift its energy source to stored body fat instead of glucose. That's a good thing! And of course, this can and usually does happen after a period of time where you haven't eaten, e.g., when you've "fasted."

I could go on and on and this could get even more technical, leaving you blurry eyed and perhaps falling asleep! ☺ So, to keep things simple here, if you'd like to learn more, I recommend you listen to this three-part *The Drive* podcast series on all things Keto, with Dr. Peter Attia, the host, and his guest expert, Dom D'Agostino, Ph.D. There is so much information shared in these episodes, your head will be spinning. Here's the link to episode one of three: https://peterattiamd.com/domdagostinoama01/

2. "What do you think are the things that the mainstream diet experts and our government got WRONG the most during the last 20 years?"

That's a great question. Here's what I believe have been the biggest misinformation and lies that have been told by the government and mainstream diet media. These statements are FALSE.

1. **Too much salt is the problem.**
   a. No, salt isn't the problem for the overwhelming majority of us. The real problem is excess sugar. That's the problem.
2. **Grains are healthy.**
   a. If you followed the advice of the food pyramid, you would think grains should be one of those food types you eat the most! The pyramid is/was lying to you. At best, grains should be limited.
3. **Eggs are bad.**
   a. Boy did they ever get THIS wrong! The egg is a superfood, literally. In my opinion, there isn't anything else you can eat that is more nutritious.

4. **Egg yolks are bad and will raise cholesterol.**
   a. Dietary cholesterol – the cholesterol you eat in animal foods, does NOT raise your blood cholesterol, and even if it did, there's a lot of misinformation about blood cholesterol too.
5. **Low fat food is healthier than food with fat.**
   a. One of the biggest myths and lies that came out of the 90s was this – *the low-fat craze*. To be clear, fat from food is NOT the enemy. Yes, quality matters, of course. You want to stick with higher quality fats from healthy, organic sources when you can.
6. **Polyunsaturated seed oils like canola, soybean, corn, cottonseed, rapeseed, rice bran and safflower oils, are healthy.**
   a. Not ALL polyunsaturated oils are bad for you. For example, flaxseed oil, specifically the oil found in flaxseed, which is alpha-linolenic acid, can be helpful in improving insulin resistance. But you'd be smart to avoid the rest of them. I'd throw margarine in there too, which should be eliminated from your diet in favor of real butter. Keep reading to learn more:

More on the polyunsaturated fats in vegetable oils: Some good research has shown these oils can increase chronic low-grade inflammation and oxidative stress in the body, which is definitely NOT what you want.[2] These oils are also subject to oxidation when they sit on your shelf for too long or are exposed to the air. The oxidation can lead to damaging free radicals and degrade the overall quality of the oil.

Some people might argue the jury is still out and they can be consumed in small amounts without much risk. I agree! I think this is true, the jury IS still out and without question, in small amounts they can be part of a healthy diet. But to be clear, they aren't as good for you as are other "good" fats.

3. "Al, what are the FIVE foods I would always find in your kitchen? Better yet, what about the top 10 or so?"

Here they are and without a doubt, they are my GO-TO because these are literally superfoods for optimal health and satiety.

- Whole eggs.
- Avocado.
- Raw unsalted nuts, especially walnuts, pistachios, and almonds. Raw only.
- Natural peanut or almond butter, or my favorite, macadamia nut butter.
- Organic berries, especially raspberries, blueberries, and blackberries. Organic apples too. I try to select what is in season whenever possible.
- Whole fat yogurt.
- Grass fed and finished red meat, preferably bison.

- Organic leafy greens and other raw veggies of all varieties.
- Olive oil for salads and food preparation.
- Wheat germ (for the fiber).
- Chocolate. ☺ Any and all kinds. I love chocolate! I have it only occasionally, but most of the time I won't deny myself if I am craving it.

4. "I've heard about Omega-3 fats and have been told I should get more of these into my diet. What's the deal?"

Omega-3 fats are a type of essential fatty acid that is typically found in fish oil. And yes, they're important to get into your diet. Omega-3 essential fats play an important role in many processes within the body, so it is assumed a fairly high intake of these is very good for our health. There are three types of Omega 3 essential fats: docosahexaenoic acid (DHA), eicosapentaenoic acid (EPA), and a lesser known but equally valuable form, alpha-linolenic acid (ALA).

The body's capacity to manufacture omega-3 fatty acids is limited and thus we are quite dependent on our food intake to get what we need. Fish oil seems to be the best source of both DHA and EPA – fatty fish like salmon, mackerel, tuna, and trout, and shellfish, such as mussels, oysters and crabs, are good sources. Omega 3-fatty acids are unsaturated fatty acids and the double bonds that make it "unsaturated" can easily react with other molecules. When fatty acids are saturated they are less likely to react with other molecules. One of the molecules the omega-3 fatty acids react with is oxygen. When a fish oil supplement has been exposed to oxygen the fatty acids may be oxidized and this changes the function of the fatty acids.

In addition to DHA and EPA, the alpha-linolenic acid (ALA) from nuts and seeds is important, and while ALA can be turned into DHA and EPA in the body, the conversion isn't easy.

Many people who aren't big fans of fatty fish choose to get their DHA and EPA from fish oil supplements. Generally speaking, supplements have been found to be safe and effective, provided the source is a high quality, reputable brand. Like many things, you get what you pay for. Cheap or inexpensive brands aren't likely to contain as high quality ingredients. Buyer beware.

While there are reputed claims from supplement manufacturers that fish oil supplements can help with a variety of disorders such as macular degeneration or heart disease, the research to date is inconclusive.

Personally, I try to eat as many different kinds of fatty fish as I can but it seems I always come back to solid white tuna. On the other hand, I eat a variety of nuts and seeds every day, something I highly recommend.

Don't Forget! Grab Your FREE Guidebook: Thoughts and Tips for all Chapters!

FREE GIFT

Here are some sample pages from the guide!

THOUGHT:

There is no such thing as a "perfect" way of eating for every person. Some of us would like to believe there is a perfect "diet" plan for everyone that is easy to follow, narrows our choices, and doesn't require much thought. It

CHAPTER 19 - BASICS AND FUNDAMENTALS, WISDOM, AND GOING WITH THE FLOW

THOUGHT:

Only when we open our mind, let go of preconceived ideas and beliefs, and put aside what we thought we knew at one time, can we truly be ready for new and important ideas that will help us grow and improve.

ACTION:

Wherever you are in your own exercise journey, whether novice or experienced, commit today to the *basics and fundamentals*. You won't be sorry.

21

CHAPTER 13 - COLESTEROL: FACTS, MYTHS, AND MISINFORMATION

THOUGHT:

Dietary fat isn't the enemy. It isn't the cause of heart disease, and in fact, there isn't any direct correlation between dietary fat intake, cholesterol, and c of heart disease. food is NOT the e sugar is.

Make sure yo and on your c months. If you disease or are to be, schedule factor to focus

CHAPTER 3 - AGE BELIEFS AND THE AGING PUZZLE: WHAT'S MISSING?

THOUGHT:

Healthy, vibrant aging is not only possible, it is your birthright. However, holding on to *negative* age beliefs and *negative* age stereotypes prevent us from seeing all of the possibilities that are available to us if we act intentionally. And positively.

ACTION:

What is the most important aging "puzzle piece" that is missing? Start today to take one step today toward checking that box. Start small and be consistent.

5

This 32-page guidebook is yours, FREE, by scanning the QR code below.

Scan the QR code or go to this web url:

www.theallyman.com/free-guide

PART 3

MOVEMENT

CHAPTER 17

INTRODUCTION

"Self-awareness is like an onion. There are multiple layers to it, and the more you peel them back, the more likely you're going to start crying at inappropriate times."

— Mark Manson

Movement is life. If you think that is cliché, I agree. But it's cliché for a reason: Everything in life is more meaningful and satisfying when we are fully participating rather than sitting by and watching, especially if we're also in pain. And it doesn't matter whether that pain is psychological, emotional, or physical.

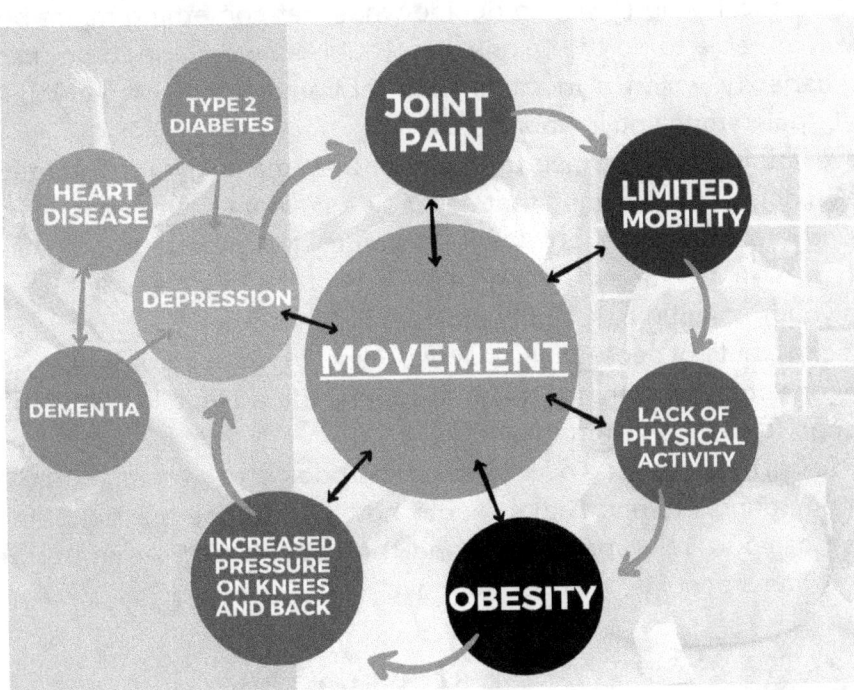

It isn't money, time, or a lack of opportunity that keep us from participating. It's something more subtle and sometimes insidious, especially at first. It might begin with joint pain and stiffness. Or it might begin by feeling lonely, anxious, or lethargic.

When you experience physical pain or struggle emotionally, you often don't even feel like trying. And due to lost desire, you can see your mobility and independence continue to subtly deteriorate as well. It's a vicious cycle that only gets worse unless you do something to turn it around. When we find ourselves in this kind of negative spiral, just getting up and moving – even something as simple as going for a walk can be the linchpin that gets us back on track.

Maybe you know someone caught in this cycle? It's heartbreaking to watch someone's world shrink as they grow weaker, slower, stiffer, month by month and year by year. It seems the less they do, the less they *can* do. The thing is, a small change like starting a morning yoga routine or going for a walk or doing some simple strength exercises, can turn it around.

It's always possible! You just need that little impetus to gain momentum. And then you need to keep it going.

My goal in the upcoming chapters is to expose you to some of what I've learned; why being physical and moving frequently is so important to not only age well, but also to feel more balanced and happy. If I do a good job of sharing what I've learned, you'll begin to think differently about movement. The way we need to consider movement represents a true paradigm shift. If you're wondering what I mean, keep reading. ☺

You'll remember back in the Introduction, I told you the ultimate goal is to be able to die "healthy," someday far off into the future after having done something that is very enjoyable on that day. Of course, it's up to you to decide what that something might be. A happy life is one where you are able to do the things you would like with little to no restrictions. I call this *movement capacity*, which is your tolerance for being active – what you are able to do before fatigue or pain stops you in your tracks.

If you believe you have to exercise for hours or become a "gym rat" to get the benefits, you're wrong. You don't. That's a myth that never dies. It's not about becoming obsessed and turning exercising into a part time job. And it's definitely NOT about that old worn out fitness lie, "no pain, no gain," that's for sure. Don't allow any of the exercise myths to pervade your mind and keep you from acting on what you learn in this book.

Our goal is simple but not necessarily easy: we want to create a few simple daily movement habits and be consistent with them. Never stopping. It's a lifestyle transformation. That's what must happen to reap long-term benefits.

One thing you will hear over and over again in this book is to *start small and be consistent*. Think of it like compound interest. That's exactly how you get the real benefits of movement over the course of your life, especially during the second half. As important, it's about remembering how as a species, we *used to* move.

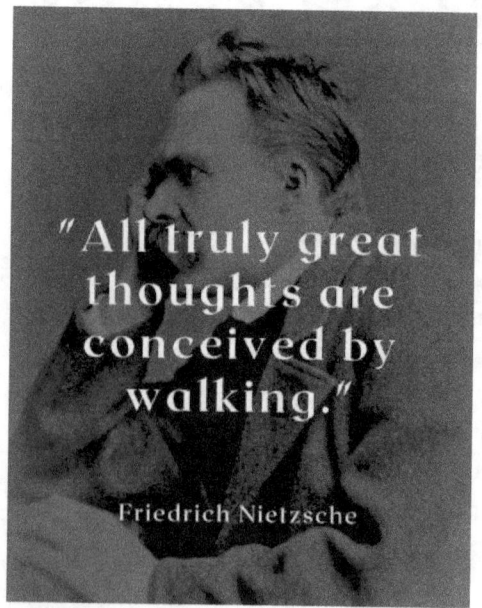

"All truly great thoughts are conceived by walking."

Friedrich Nietzsche

Start Moving – Start Living.

Modern life has unfortunately made *movement* somewhat optional. The conveniences we've all come to cherish and sometimes believe we couldn't live without such as drive thru windows, one stop shopping, remote controls, and the workspaces many of us occupy, where we are chained to a desk in front of a computer screen for hours on end, are all a *double-edged sword.*

Sure, some of us might be setting time aside during our day to squeeze in some "exercise," but as a society, we are *moving less than ever*. There's a difference between these two things and that's the dilemma we're faced with.

As you're reading this you're probably thinking the most practical solution is more exercise, right? That's what you might expect me to say. And some of us are doing just that - trudging off to the gym where we can climb onto a treadmill, run more miles, and yet again, stare into a screen as we countdown the minutes. Or we go into the weight room to grab some dumbbells and start pressing them up and overhead. No, my friend, I don't think the answer is just to get *more* exercise.

Sometimes I hate the word exercise. It's not that being on a treadmill or holding a set of dumbbells is bad. Naturally, I sometimes do these and also recommend it to others. The point I'm hoping to share is that it's moving frequently and consistently, not exercise per se, that is missing. In other words, the **non-exercise movement** – when you aren't at the gym or on your treadmill – *may be a lot more important for your health and wellbeing.* Doing things that require you to exert effort physically. Things like chores around the yard, hiking, climbing stairs - these all replicate the environment your body is adapted for, placing your body in its natural state. It doesn't have to be high intensity, but it should include some movement variety. It can and should include getting to and from places you need to be with your body. It can and should include play and physical work too! Think of it this way: what many of us call "being fit" is what our human ancestors called "being."

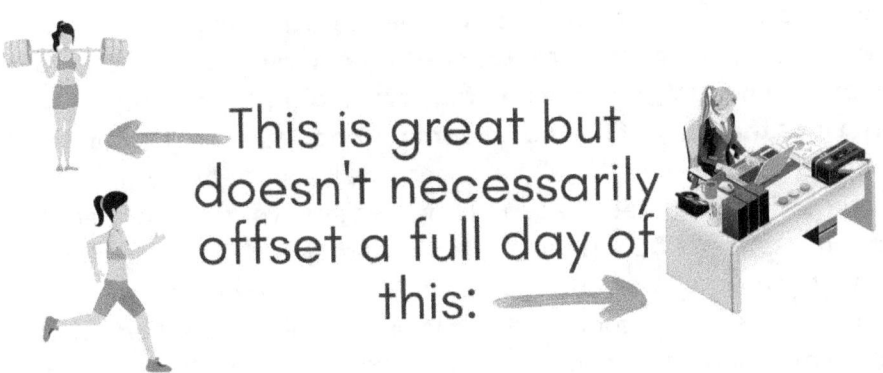

This is great but doesn't necessarily offset a full day of this:

TRY TO ADD MORE OF THIS INTO YOUR LIFE:

My girlfriend Terry, who is the same age as me, is a server at a local breakfast restaurant. She's a retired social worker and now waits tables because she enjoys the opportunity to make new friends and see old friends and customers, doing all she can to make their experience as good as it can be. The tips are usually pretty good too. But there's a side benefit to her work that even she's not aware of, and it often shows up when we're exercising together. In other words, she always surprises me with how well she moves and how strong she is.

One day a few months ago, I asked her to wear my Garmin watch so we could learn how many miles she walks in a typical shift from 7 AM to 2 PM. It turned out it was a busy day for her. At the end of the day, she checked the Garmin: 13.6 miles! I never imagined she was actually walking that much in one day waiting on customers. Keep in mind, this isn't a relaxing jaunt on the beach. She's balancing heavy trays, full glasses, and dishes. Along the way, she'll inevitably have to do a lot of reaching and bending, adding up to all kinds of physically demanding activity. Ironically, none of it is what she or I might categorize as structured "exercise." Also, ironically, while she is hustling and moving around bending, reaching, and carrying things, many of the folks she is waiting on came from work or home where they were doing a lot of, you guessed it, sitting. Up to 12 hours a day or more, in many cases.

There was a time in human history, maybe not that long ago, when the perpetual movement Terry does occurred as part of normal living – and it wasn't that hard and didn't require much thought. Instead, in place of the incidental movement that used to be normal, computers, remotes, and other machines are doing it for us. We don't even have to get out of our cars to eat, we can drive right up or even better, have it delivered right to our door.

We've lost sight of the fact this everyday *movement* and motion is *truly our life force*. I'll even go so far as to say when it comes to our healthspan, it's *as important as any kind of structured exercise.* **Natural, normal, routine 3-dimensional movements are what helps us be human – it simultaneously creates and reinforces our psychological and physiological health in more ways than any of us could ever imagine.** Incidentally, many of Terry's friends her age are "retired" and frequently ask her when she'll also "retire." But why would she stop doing something she enjoys that is also helping her stay younger, longer? Remember this: *We don't wear out our joints from work and activity, they rust out from disuse.*

Thinking about Terry and her work as a server reminds me of a phrase I heard a few years ago when chatting with a college football coach in our Pursuit Athletic Performance gait lab. The coach was telling me about recruiting a local high school player who he described as "farmer strong." So, naturally, I asked what he meant. "The typical high school football player goes to the weight room for an hour or so a day, doing bench pressing and other typical gym exercises, which is fine," he said, except, that kind of training can lead to what he called "isolation strength." In his words, "the gym work helps build stronger muscles, sure, but that strength doesn't always transfer to the football field and can also lead to imbalances that increase injury risk."

Contrast that with this kid he was trying to recruit. He said this boy lived on a farm. His daily chores consisted of lifting and bending and carrying and throwing around hay bales, all a routine part of farming. He said this kid hadn't ever done any "formal" gym training, yet he was stronger than any other kid he'd seen or tested. How's that possible you ask? To do those chores, day after day, the boy's body needed to function holistically – legs, hips, arms, shoulders, all working together – which happens to be the opposite of isolation strength. That's what you call "farmer strong." ☺ I call it a principle that should define all we do in our formal exercise and movement practice: **integrate, don't isolate.**

KEY CONCEPT: Isometric Strength Training IS Integration Training.

In Part 5, I will introduce you to isometric strength training. It is an ideal way to start building strength and can also be a great way to enhance and get more benefit from the strength training you may already be doing.

Our approach to isometric training involves radiating tension from within to integrate every part of the body, which isn't how some approach it. You'll learn more about this powerful and important philosophy when you get to that chapter.

What Is Normal?

Follow along with me so I can paint this mental picture for you, and then let's see if we can learn something along the way, OK? Imagine you're at a gym and you're standing at the back of the room watching a group of weightlifters. These are all muscular guys and gals doing a lot of what weightlifters typically do, squatting with barbells on their back, stepping back and forth with some weight in each hand, and pressing dumbbells overhead. Now the same people are doing the same movements as they were before, but this time *without* any equipment. Can you picture it? There's no equipment, no barbells, squat racks, pull up bars, dumbbells, or anything else.

What you're seeing is people going through *the normal kinds of movements* our body is designed for, movement that can and should be a part of our normal lives *even as we age*. If you're thinking it might also look like watching kids on a playground or on a jungle gym, or perhaps a yoga or tai-chi class, you'd be right. Ironically, they're the kinds of movements our ancestors thought of as *normal*. After all, if you're foraging and digging and climbing to get food, or on the flip side running from a predator, then lunging, squatting, pushing, and pulling are all things you had to do to survive. And just because many of us don't "need" to do these things anymore to survive, the human body is still very good at these "functional" movements and I'd argue, <u>thrives on them.</u>

In a very real way, exercising doesn't make you "fit." What exercising will do is make you "normal." Think about it. Those weightlifters in our imaginary gym without any equipment were simply replicating the environment that our bodies – yours and mine - are naturally selected for. They're simply moving in a totally natural and normal way. As I said earlier, what many of us call "being fit" is what our human ancestors called "being."

Of course, what all that equipment does do is create added resistance which leads to greater strength gains. That's important, but it isn't where we ought to begin. And that's what this chapter is all about. **Too few of us are moving in the ways we are adapted for and that should be our first goal.** We're sitting at desks, behind steering wheels and on couches, all of which are extremely limiting and will ultimately hurt our ability to age well and be able to move well as the years continue to add up.

Where Do Injuries Most Often Happen?

Making the conscious decision to incorporate exercise into your life can be the best feeling in the world. You're taking control of your health. It's great to feel the blood flowing through your veins and your muscles working. Unfortunately, for many people, the feeling is short lived. Why? Because they often end up injured. And that sucks.

In my experience, one place where more people get injured than any other isn't on the playing field or out on the roads – *it's in a gym.* And often they're "working out" with a trainer. The injuries usually happen for three reasons:

1. **Not starting with more general "just move" activity first, heading off to the gym to lift too heavy weights instead**. Start simple and just move. That's where we should all begin. Then if you desire, seek out a trainer or follow the script in this book, which is to learn and groove the basics and fundamentals first. That means basic core stability and joint motion for starters. You'll learn about those in upcoming chapters.
2. **A lack of fundamental movement capacity, that often comes back to core and hip stability or tissue balance**. Always address the basics first before moving on to more complex or advanced movements. If a trainer tells you to do something that makes you nervous or you feel you're not ready for, don't do it!
3. **Trying to lift too much weight too soon.** Very often a heavier weight is the last thing you want to add. Don't become the next person to get injured doing just the thing you thought you should do to avoid injury.

The take home message is this: your body is going to adapt to what you do *most of the time*. You can strength train or stretch for thirty or more minutes a day, every day, but that is a drop in the bucket compared to what you do the other 1410 minutes.

Of course, if you're thinking what you've just read presents a bit of a conundrum about the best way to approach and incorporate exercise into our lives for both overall fitness and healthspan combined, it doesn't have to be that way. Remember these basic tenets which are sure to solve any conundrum:

- **Moderation in all things.** For example, running can be a great activity for improving cardiovascular fitness, but you need to be stable and moving well before embarking on a running program. Running is hard on your body. And running as your only exercise, without other activities to balance it out through the day and even as part of an overall fitness routine, isn't very good for your body or your overall health. The same can be said for cycling, swimming, or any other type of exercise activity that involves repetitive movement patterns that can easily lead to overuse injuries.

- **Variety is the spice of (your movement) life.** For example, to get stronger, you need to engage in a few fundamental movement patterns: hinging, pushing, pulling, and squatting to name the most important, repeating them and progressively loading them. Simple enough. But that repetition isn't enough. In addition to grooving these basic, fundamental patterns, you need variety, too. Think 3-dimensionally. The more varied the movements are and the more they incorporate your entire body, the better. While you certainly don't need to get a job working on a farm, if you can replicate on a much smaller scale, the kind of lifestyle that made that high school football recruit healthier and stronger, you'll be on the right track.

- **It should be your lifestyle.** It shouldn't be something to "fit in" that is drastically different from the way you live. Sure, some of us have jobs that force us into habits that are hard to break or routines that inevitably don't change very much. *It's up to us* to be creative and figure out more ways to get movement variety into our lives without having to think about it much.

If you're even a little bit curious about my emphasis on varied 3-dimensional activity and why it is so important to challenge your body in how you move, there are two main reasons. The first is because of something happening at the cellular level called **mechanotransduction,** defined as "all the various mechanisms by which the cells in our body convert mechanical stimulus into electrochemical activity."[1] I like to think of it a bit simpler by relating it to something I shared with you earlier in the chapter, *Why We Age: Exploring Aging at the Cellular Level.* Remember the word "epigenetics?" If you recall, the word epigenetics comes from "epi" which means above, and "genetics" which is obviously our genes or DNA. Translated, it's simply *above our genes.* To put it succinctly, epigenetics is the study of how our *behaviors and environment* can cause changes that affect the way our genes work and express themselves.

Mechanotransduction is much the same, in that it refers to how **outside forces acting on our body can change how our cells respond.** And that response can make all the difference! For example, cells are sensitive to forces like shear, tension, compression, and rotation to name a few. The key is they will respond to these forces in ways such as multiplying, repairing, migrating, and adapting and ultimately altering metabolism.[2]

The second main reason is because of fascia (pronounced: fashia), the fabric of connective tissues that run through the entire body as a covering and connecting network. It not only gives our body its shape, it also acts like muscle, responds to stress and nerve signals, and

if it becomes stuck and tangled, results in pain and mobility problems. I became so fascinated with what fascia is and how important it is for not only our health and ability to move freely and easily, but also athletic performance, in 2015 I went through a certification program to become a **Fascial Stretch Therapist**.

The Grapefruit Principle: Fascia Keeps Everything In Shape.

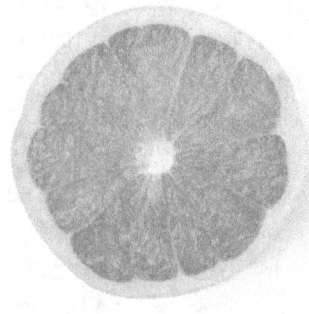

Virtually all organs are surrounded by connective tissue; the whole body is permeated by it, in various surface layers as well as in the deeper layers. To illustrate how fascia keeps the whole body in shape, fascia researcher and author, Robert Schleip, in his book *Fascial Fitness: How to be Resilient, Elegant, and Dynamic in Everyday Life and Sport*, tells how one of his colleagues, author Thomas Myers, uses the vivid picture of a grapefruit to demonstrate fascia in our body. He says "the pulp of a grapefruit is enclosed in small detachments of white skin, and on the outside it is again surrounded by a solid white skin that fits snugly to the peel. If one were to remove all the pulp and leave only the white skin, one could reconstruct the entire fruit and its form, on the basis of this structure alone."[3]

Thomas Myers book, *Anatomy Trains*, has become one of the most important resources for anyone interested in learning more about the body's intricate and totally connected fascial lines and systems. In his book, he reiterates rather than <u>think of your body as being comprised of more than 600 individual muscles, we should think of it as ONE muscle with more than 600 fascial pockets. Our fascial system truly is one large fluid filled membrane that covers us from head to toe.</u> [5]

Because of your fascia, a little bit of tension *anywhere* in your body will create a little tension *everywhere*. Naturally, some of this tension is necessary. In the upcoming chapter on strength and resistance training, I'll discuss this necessary stiffness and tension that helps prevent your body from collapsing against the forces of gravity. You'll learn how to train and improve it. But there's also the tension that isn't necessary and leads to movement problems. To understand what I mean, imagine the restricted motion that happens when someone grabs your shirtsleeve at the top of your shoulder just as you're attempting to move your arm across your body. While they might only be gripping one small area of your shirt, you can quickly feel the rest of the shirt is also restricted and your entire arm and shoulder can't move as easily.

Fascia also has memory. It's similar to somatic recall. This memory is necessary for movement and motion and skill learning, but there's also the memory of trauma and emotion that can get stuck in the fascial sheath by way of interoceptors connected to the insular cortex in the brain. It's referred to in some circles as *somatic recall*. That's right, believe it or not, your past experiences are stored in fascia. In fact, many massage therapists, acupuncturists and other somatic practitioners have frequently reported "uncanny experiences in which vivid images flood into their consciousness as they are working on some part of a client's body. Sometimes there is a transient sensation that "something has happened" within the body they are touching. An avalanche of detailed sensory material may be triggered."[4] These aren't all "bad" memories. Think of the times you smell or feel or taste something that instantly brings back a memory from the past. That's somatic recall in action.

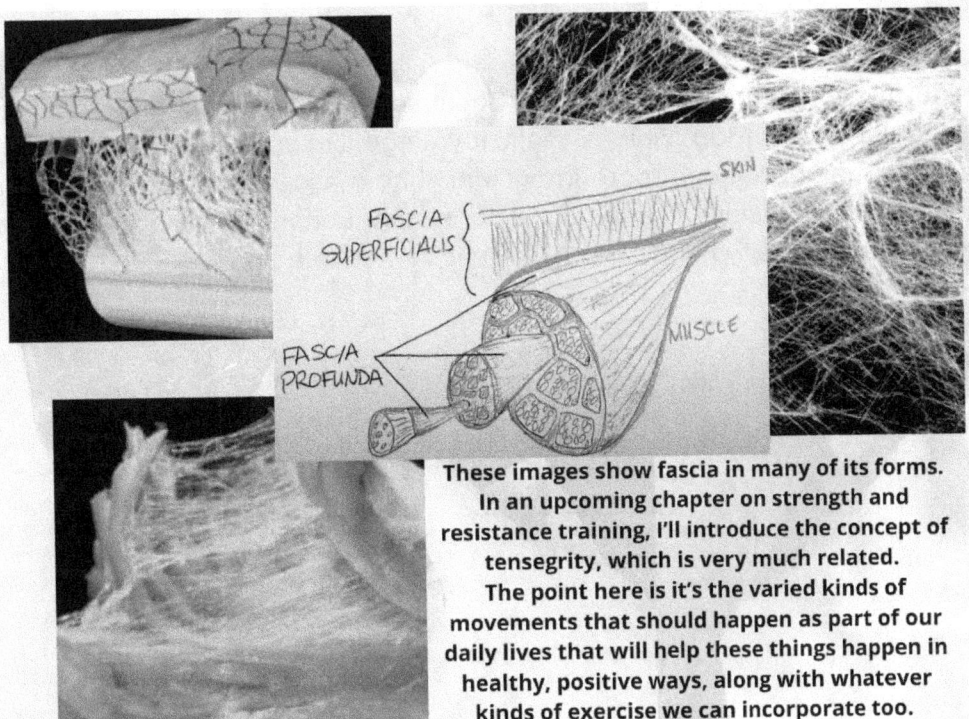

These images show fascia in many of its forms. In an upcoming chapter on strength and resistance training, I'll introduce the concept of tensegrity, which is very much related.

The point here is it's the varied kinds of movements that should happen as part of our daily lives that will help these things happen in healthy, positive ways, along with whatever kinds of exercise we can incorporate too.

Image Source: *Anatomy Trains* by Thomas Myers

(Image: in this photo, the author is taking 5-time Ironman Age Group world champion, Lisbeth Kenyon, through the paces with Fascial Stretch Therapy).

Your Goal is to Start Small and Be Consistent.

Whatever journey you decide to embark on because of this book, whether it is your fitness or exercise habits or your food choices, make it your goal to start small and be as consistent as you can be. That's so much more important than massive change or trying to do too much too soon. Small positive changes and consistent action. Those are your watchwords. Consistency beats intensity hands down when it comes to aging well.

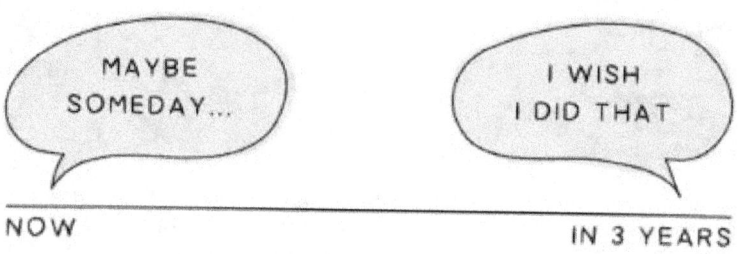

It Doesn't Matter How Old You Are or Where You Begin.

Science as well as my own experience confirms that no matter what age you are when you start, **you CAN improve your energy level, balance, stability, and strength!**

Imagine waking up every morning excited because you'll be able to do almost anything you want with little to no discomfort. Your body will be working with you, not fighting you. You'll feel more confident and comfortable in everything you do, whether it's traveling, hiking a mountain in a faraway land or playing with your grandkids in the backyard.

Being able to do whatever you want is light years better than what I often see when I look around me, which is people who are steadily losing their ability to move without pain and their ability to function. Slow, gradual, physical decline isn't something that *has to happen* as many believe. That's outdated thinking. You have the power to influence it!

Do Your Shoulders and Hips Behave Like Shoulders and Hips Should?

You'd have to have been living under a rock to not see that knee and hip replacement surgeries have skyrocketed over the last several years, nearing almost epidemic levels in the U.S., and they're being performed on younger people. It's not just the fact you literally lose a joint that won't ever come back, it's also the expense associated with the surgery and the pain and hassle of the physical therapy and recovery that follows.

Similarly, low-back pain has become so commonplace in society, if you don't have it you're the weird one. Obviously, it should be the other way around. If you want to age well, go the distance, comfortably doing whatever you want as you get older, you have to prepare the right way. In other words, to get to where you want to be, so you're moving with ease and living life to its fullest right up until the end, you need to go step by step.

Inch by inch, Anything's a Cinch.

For the great majority reading this, you'll need to start at the beginning and approach whatever exercise you try in a smart way. Earlier I mentioned the most common place people get injured is ironically in a gym. That's not a coincidence. Even if you've exercised in the past or are exercising right now and feel like you're fit and ready for something to really challenge you, trust me when I say the smartest thing you could do would be to start where I start here in the book. Don't skip over the basics thinking you already have it nailed. My experience as a trainer, therapist and coach tells me even a professional athlete with lots of athleticism can benefit from a review of some fundamentals.

What Makes This Book Different?

In some ways the fitness industry seems to have gone off the rails a bit. I've seen it over and over again. There's often more attention paid to entertainment than learning and smart progression. There's been too much focus on technology or equipment instead of basic and fundamental skills that create huge opportunities to improve. There also seems to be a collective rush to get to more complex and even unsafe exercises. In the next chapter, you'll hear me say something profound, which is advanced training is nothing more than the basics mastered. More complex is rarely better!

It may not surprise you to hear my approach is different. With this book, you'll be able to proceed at your own pace without feeling rushed or even like you have to move on to something more complex or difficult. You'll get benefit from whatever you decide to do.

You won't need any expensive equipment or a gym for that matter, although there will be times when I may suggest a piece of equipment to perform an exercise. Most importantly, we'll start at the beginning, with the focus on movement first, not just on how to exercise. Years of experience has taught me the smart approach is to learn how to move better, THEN learn how to increase your fitness, not the other way around.

Four Key Areas of The Body to Move Better and Get Stronger.

In upcoming chapters, we'll cover the four most important areas for moving better, feeling better, and getting stronger. We'll start by looking at some basic and fundamental skills, then we'll learn how to create and practice basic core stability, improve how your feet function, and look at some daily movement "snacks" you can and should integrate into your lifestyle that will get you moving 3-dimensionally. Then we'll talk about a 30-day bodyweight squat challenge. In Part 4 of the book, we'll look more closely at how to build strength in a very practical and effective way – by creating tension from within, first.

All these elements represent what is, in my eyes, a beginning. It's where we all need to start regardless of how much experience we have. In fact, very often, I've found that folks who have been going to the gym for a while and think they are beyond the basics, are often the people that are one move away from injury because some element of these basic skills is lacking. Don't be that person.

Think about it: Would you recommend your child begin their math studies by learning Algebra? Of course not. It starts with arithmetic and basic math. You learn that and try to master it before moving on to the next step. Fitness should be the same way, but very few trainers or programs ever start at the beginning anymore.

If you are able, you can progress at breakneck speed and get right into the more advanced exercises. You may even get online at Pursuit Athletic Performance.com, one of my websites with online stability and strength programs where you can find even more advanced programs to follow. But if you'd like to take it slower and simply want to build enough skills to feel great and age well, you can do that too. It's up to you!

Go confidently in the direction of your dreams. Live the life you've imagined.
— Henry David Thoreau

My Promise to You.

If you follow the guidance as I have laid it out, from the beginning, progressing steadily, step by step, I guarantee you will experience dramatic improvements in how easily you're able to stand, move around, and simply enjoy your life. You'll be stronger and more stable and have better balance and more energy. It won't happen overnight, but nothing worth achieving ever happens that way, despite what some false advertising might tell you. And you'll always have the opportunity to take it to the next level once you establish the basics. It's all up to you.

Just M.O.V.E.

I don't think it's an overstatement to say *movement* might be the most powerful medicine available to any of us. Depending on your present health status and how old you are, I don't think I'm overstating it

> The secret of change is to focus all of your energy, not on fighting the old, but building on the new
>
> SOCRATES

when I say <u>what you do with this information and how you act on it may be the most important decision you make in your lifetime.</u> Why?

We're in a bind. As a society, we're in a literal and figurative bind. We are struggling with chronic disease, too much bad stress, and general dissatisfaction within many aspects of life.

We're having trouble getting off our smart phones, out of our desk chairs, and out from behind our steering wheel. We need to just MOVE, and in the process, reconnect with the world around us.

So, if you're just starting out or have had a recent bout of injury or you consider yourself a "couch potato" and have been largely sedentary, your first goal will be to just GET MOVING. I can't emphasize how important it is to start slowly, but you must START. A sedentary lifestyle that has resulted in you being weaker is seriously hazardous to your health. There is definitely truth to the old saying, "use it or lose it." You'll read that repeatedly in Part 3 and 4 of this book. We need to challenge our muscles to maintain our strength and progressively challenge our sensory input and balance. When we do, we're "using" it and will therefore reduce the chance of losing it! That's our goal.

One thing you've already heard me say and I'll repeat again as we go forward: **the best approach is to start small and add just a little bit more than nothing**. In other words, tiny steps forward, done consistently, will lead to much greater long-term improvements. That's not what most people do – they jump in headfirst and try to do too much too soon. Their intention is always positive, but what happens is they can't sustain it. They get frustrated or worse, injure themselves, and then must stop. Don't let that happen. Start slow. Do something today that is just a little bit more than nothing and then repeat it, tomorrow and the next day, gradually adding a little bit more to the mix.

For those who are already active, you'll want to take the next step and improve your stability, mobility, and strength! The same rule applies however – small incremental steps are a lot better than trying to do too much too soon.

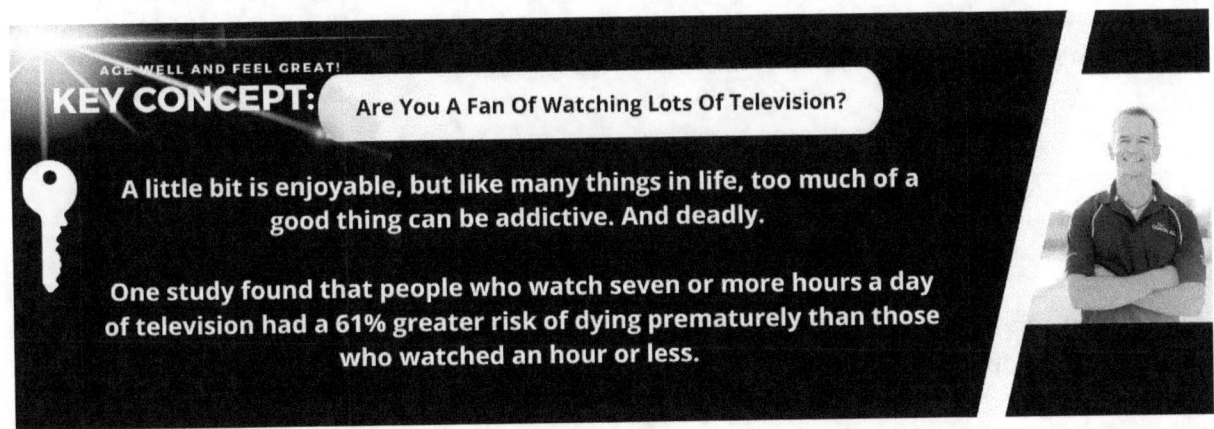

AGE WELL AND FEEL GREAT!

KEY CONCEPT: Are You A Fan Of Watching Lots Of Television?

A little bit is enjoyable, but like many things in life, too much of a good thing can be addictive. And deadly.

One study found that people who watch seven or more hours a day of television had a 61% greater risk of dying prematurely than those who watched an hour or less.

The Fast Track to Frustration.

JUST MOVE. As I said, that's a great place to start. If you've been spending too much time sitting in your comfy chair watching TV, start by making a commitment to get up every ten minutes and walk for one minute. Rinse and repeat. Whatever it takes to get moving. You have to commit to it. There isn't any magic pixie dust I can sprinkle on you, you have to want it and do it. Start small and do it over and over! You can do it.

If you're further down the fitness road though, don't fall victim to the advice you'll often hear from trainers or on TV or read in magazines. Typical advice about starting to lift weights or even worse, a running program can go *drastically wrong*. I want you to have the best chance for success, not just this week or this month or even this year, but for the rest of your life. To achieve that, you have to approach your fitness and exercise the right way. Let me explain.

One Person's Journey: Meet Jane.

I'd like to tell you a story about Jane. She got in touch with me last year to ask about personal training. Jane was in her 50s. When I spoke with her on the phone, I could tell she was particularly excited about strength training – she wanted to be stronger. Which is great! She also said she'd like to start running too. In the course of our conversation, I asked Jane to tell me a little bit about herself - what she did for work, what she did for fun, and if she had exercised at all in the past.

I learned she worked as a paralegal and spent most of her workdays "chained" to a desk. In the past she'd tried some fitness and bootcamp classes at a gym but always got hurt. As could be expected, getting hurt slowed or even halted her progress. Frustrating! I also learned she had tried yoga a few times and always found it very difficult and frustrating to do. Getting into some of the positions was hard, if not impossible.

Hard choices, easy life. Easy choices, hard life.
— Jerzy Gregorek

Can you relate to Jane's situation? Have you ever struggled with some kind of painful setback when you were trying to get in shape or just get moving? When I asked if any of what she had tried was fun for her, she said it absolutely was, until that is, she got hurt and then had to stop. Of course, it makes sense to combine fitness with something fun, but getting hurt is never fun!

Being able to do whatever you want to = fun!

Injury = the opposite of fun = despair, frustration.

As we talked, I asked a few more questions to learn not only about Jane's life history, but more importantly how she was able to *move*. For example...

- I asked if it was easy or hard for her to squat down.
- Could she stand on one leg and balance? And if she could, how about with her eyes closed?
- Did she feel any unusual tightness, soreness or pain anywhere?

It sounds so simple, right? The thing is, most of us don't think about these things until something happens and we can no longer do what we want to. Jane's ability to move freely without pain, to get down on the floor and get back up as one example, had a huge impact on the overall quality of her life. *And the same is true for you, too.*

All along, I knew Jane was motivated to get in shape. I never questioned that. What I didn't know and needed a better sense of, was how physically *ready her body was to do the exercise she was hoping to do.* I call this **movement competency** or *readiness*, and it's something most people never think about, but it is necessary to stay healthy and free from injury.

How to Succeed in Your Fitness Journey.

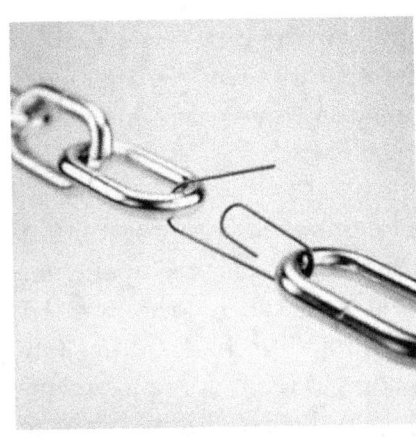

Think about this: You wouldn't give your car keys to someone who didn't have their driver's license and hadn't demonstrated their driving competency, would you?

Jane's *movement competency* – how easily her joints move around or how stable those joints are, as well as things like balance and sensory perception, factor into determining the best way to begin her fitness journey.

When someone decides to start on a path to improve their health and their fitness, the first goal is always simply to get moving. You've heard me say this multiple times. Anything is better than no movement at all. Walking for five minutes straight, if that's something they don't already do. Riding a bike for ten minutes, even if it's the first time since they were a kid. Whatever it is, if it goes beyond what they've done recently, it's a positive step in the right direction. But you can't go from zero to 100 miles per hour without some risk.

Jane thought it was a bit strange that I was asking her about *how she moved*. She wondered if that really mattered in her quest to "get in shape." I explained that all my years of experience had taught me the best path to a successful and sustainable fitness journey begins with moving better *first*, before trying to move *harder or longer*. In other words, *we shouldn't try to put fitness on top of dysfunction.*

Any chain is only as strong as its weakest link.
−unknown

What's Your Movement Story?

Movement is how we experience life and how we learn and develop. It's how we explore, not just the world around us but also *our own body*. From the first day a baby is born their goal is to figure out how to get what they want, and even as much, how to get it more easily.

I think of moving and motion as forms of **self-discovery**. Whatever we decide to do that involves movement, we are in essence, physically demonstrating to the world around us all that has happened to us – it's our movement "story." Not the story about our line of work or even our relationships, but rather, the story of *our body*. The story of lingering effects from an injury like a sprained ankle, from spending lots of time in a certain position, or doing a certain task such as standing for long periods, sitting for long periods at a desk, or performing some kind of manual task over and over, the exact same way. Or the changes to our posture that can happen over the course of many years due to wear and tear. Over time, that all adds up and can change how we move, and not necessarily in a good way. Things that have happened to us in the past dictate where we are today in our movement story, and limit how much we're able to do now and into the future.

If you're like Jane, in your 40s or 50s or even older, at some point in the past you may have vowed to get in shape and then something happened and you fell off the wagon. That's not uncommon. Research shows less than half the people who make a New Year's resolution stick with it beyond a week. And less than a quarter stick with it beyond six months. That's less than one in four, after six months!

When you're 20 or 30 something, it's easy to think you have lots of time to get started. But when you're in your 40s, 50s, or 60s like Jane was, you realize the clock is ticking and you don't have the luxury of time anymore. You know the time to act is now. And Jane knew it too.

So, Jane and I set a date to have her come to my training studio. We had a great first training session together. She was psyched to get at it and anxious to learn some exercises to help her get stronger. She knew she couldn't help getting older but she didn't want to "get old." I like that mindset!

I always start with looking at how someone moves. If you've read this far that probably makes sense to you. I noticed Jane really struggled to stand on a single leg and balance. She also had a very hard time bending at the hips and squatting down to get to the floor. It was no wonder she had been frustrated in yoga class.

I could tell she was frustrated. She had struggled but just assumed it was because she was getting older. Like a lot of people, she had just accepted it as "normal."

KEY CONCEPT: Getting Older Doesn't Have To Mean Pain And Discomfort.

Do you usually attribute any pain or struggle to move easily to simply getting older? Many people do.

I'm here to tell you what I told Jane – don't!

You can get better no matter how old the calendar says you are!

I encouraged and reminded her there was a lot she could still do and told her we would work on the things she struggled with to ensure she improved and felt better. She was curious to learn *why* this happened. She used to be able to squat down pain free or stand on a single leg without almost falling over. She wondered what caused her to lose those abilities? I was happy to hear she had questions, because her inquisitiveness indicated she was on the right track and had the right mindset to improve.

When you focus on learning more and are willing to question and engage in the process rather than just looking for the quick-fix list of exercises to do, you're on the right path! Jane was definitely on the right path. ☺ So, let me ask, when it comes to losing the ability to squat or standing on a single leg, have you also wondered what happened?

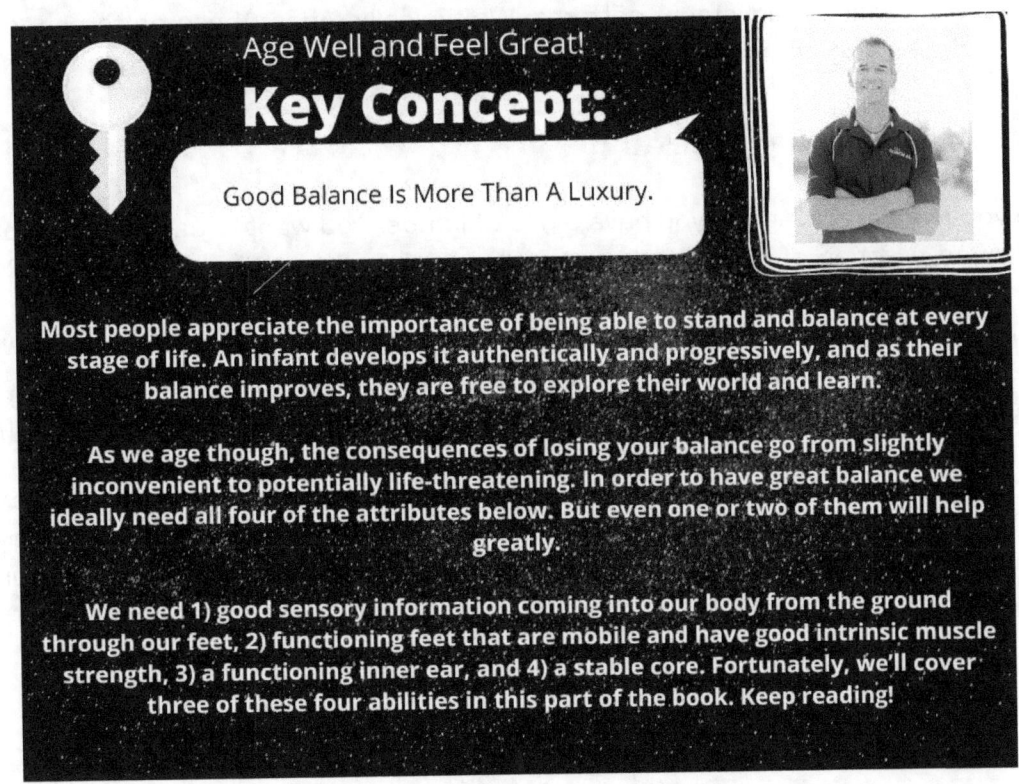

Age Well and Feel Great!

Key Concept:

Good Balance Is More Than A Luxury.

Most people appreciate the importance of being able to stand and balance at every stage of life. An infant develops it authentically and progressively, and as their balance improves, they are free to explore their world and learn.

As we age though, the consequences of losing your balance go from slightly inconvenient to potentially life-threatening. In order to have great balance we ideally need all four of the attributes below. But even one or two of them will help greatly.

We need 1) good sensory information coming into our body from the ground through our feet, 2) functioning feet that are mobile and have good intrinsic muscle strength, 3) a functioning inner ear, and 4) a stable core. Fortunately, we'll cover three of these four abilities in this part of the book. Keep reading!

You Can't Move Where You Can't Move.

Jane possessed good movement skills in quite a few areas. I made sure to include some of the movements and exercises she did well early on so she could feel like she was really working hard.

For those things she struggled with, I explained the best path was to take a step back and see if we could get to the root cause. Squatting down to the floor with relative ease required her hips and ankles and spine to move freely through a wide range of motion – something her joints didn't do. Simply put, *she couldn't move where she couldn't move.*

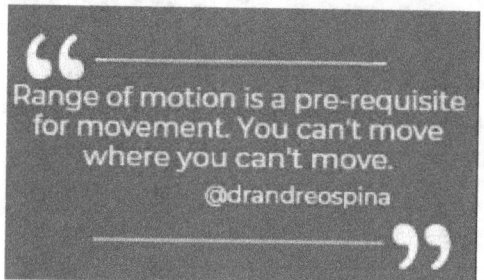

Range of motion is a pre-requisite for movement. You can't move where you can't move.
@drandreospina

Like Jane, you might be asking yourself what that means exactly. I was really glad to see Jane wanted to learn more. I explained it this way: Absolutely any task she asks her body to perform during the course of the day involves a series of **movement patterns**. In many instances, those patterns are habits we've grooved. Think of something very simple like picking up a fork or writing with a pencil – both are tasks that involve a variety of movement patterns involving the hands, arms, fingers, and even our shoulders. We build those habituated patterns through repetition. Tasks such as typing or reaching for something, playing a musical instrument or even something simpler like walking, are all made up of different movement patterns and habits. For most of us, squatting down to the floor also involves a series of movement patterns. We typically repeat these patterns mostly the same way, depending on where we are doing them and how we are feeling in the moment.

Crappy Tools = Crappy Building.

Imagine you're a carpenter and you have a pile of lumber you want to use to build a building. You will need a series of good working **tools** such as a hammer and saw, right? If your hammer or saw doesn't work very well, you won't be able to use that pile of lumber to put together the building you want. The reason is obvious: a carpenter, regardless of how skilled he or she is, *must possess good tools to be able to build a high-quality building. If you want to squat down to the floor easily and not struggle or have to force it, just like a carpenter, you need good* **tools**.

So, what are the tools I'm talking about here? In our analogy, the carpenter's tools are our joints. That's where it all starts - your hips, shoulders, ankles, and knees. And the patterns are the work done by the tools, or the end result of the work. When it comes to our joints, that means the fitness benefits we accrue from exercising or simply moving.

Tools = Joints. Patterns = Fitness.

As human beings who want to be healthy and age well, we need good tools (our joints) to build quality patterns (which build better fitness), that can then be turned into even higher levels of fitness, be it speed, power, or anything else, if that's what we choose.

No matter how much you practice the "pattern" and try to improve your skill, if there is some restriction or limitation in the "joint," there will be a *limitation in the pattern*. To put it another way, if you're attempting to build a great skill or pattern or build "fitness," but have crappy "tools" to do it with, you're going to be bumping up against a limitation that will stop you dead in your tracks and limit how far you can go or how much you can improve.

Let me ask you a question. Have you found that as you get older, your joints get stiffer and don't want to move as easily, so something else has to move instead, to make up for it? I thought so. ☺

That's why our exercise journey won't start with running or lifting weights or any other thing for that matter, it will start with good sound daily movement "snacks" to get you moving in myriad ways and feeling good in the process. You'll read and learn about these daily movement "snacks" in Chapter 23: *Daily Movement "Snacks" and a 30-Day Bodyweight Squat Challenge.*

Our goal should always be to train for the betterment
of the body, not to its detriment.

— Coach Al

Why Do We Lose Joint Motion as We Age?

Use it or lose it. You've already heard me say this once in this chapter, and you've no doubt heard this simple phrase a hundred if not a thousand times in your life. I am sure you know what it means, at least on the surface. There's something going on beneath the skin though, which might bring a new light and enhance your understanding of this often-repeated phrase. Allow me to share it with you. It is something called *tissue turnover.*

Imagine for a moment you are looking at a picture of yourself from three years ago. While you might have shorter hair and perhaps a few other subtle changes, for the most part you look basically the same. Do you realize there's not a single cell in your body today that existed three years ago? Even though you basically look like the same person, underneath the skin every cell is different.

Let's take a step back for a moment and talk about cells, which are the basic building blocks of tissue like muscle, tendon, brain tissue, and of course all our organs. Every single cell in your body has a life cycle, regardless of what tissue it is part of. The whole process of cells being created and cells dying off, which believe it or not happens every second of our lives at the rate of around 3.5 million per day, is known as *tissue turnover*.[6]

The really important question to ask is, when new cells are formed and come together to make muscle or connective tissue or skin or brain tissue, *how do the cells know what to be?* In other words, how do the cells that are being formed every single second know how to lay down and create new tissue? That's a crazy question if you think about it because you obviously don't want there to be miscommunication and poor signaling somewhere and have cells that are supposed to form brain tissue, make bone tissue, right?

If you recall, I briefly introduced the concept of *ex-differentiation* to you in Chapter 2, *Why We Age*. Let's revisit that theory for a moment because it's very closely related to what I hope to share with you here. This theory comes from well-known author and Harvard research professor Dr. David Sinclair, who says that ex-differentiation is akin to "unspooling" or "unpackaging" of the DNA. In the process of that unspooling, cells become more of a generalized cell type vs. a specific cell type, essentially losing their identity and thus beginning to act abnormally. What "abnormally" actually means differs depending upon cell type. He believes this is cell "confusion" – what he refers to as the information theory of aging. Dr. Sinclair believes this *ex-differentiation* or unspooling of the DNA is the root cause, *not just of aging, but of most diseases*. And the key to slowing aging and extending lifespan is to slow down *ex-differentiation*. So, you see, what is happening at the cellular level every single second as cells turnover is incredibly important. Understanding this will help you know why what I tell you to do, matters. Keep reading.

We know there are at least 200 different cell types for different tissues and therefore, each cell type has a different function. For example, there is a type of cell called a "clastic cell," whose job it is to *break down and reabsorb* tissue, such as osteoclast cells that break down bone tissue. There's another type of cell called a "blastic cell," whose job it is to *reform* tissue. In biology and in medicine, the suffix "-blast" refers to immature cells known as precursor cells or stem cells. Blasts give rise to all kinds of different specialized cells. For example, neuroblasts give rise to nerve cells. So, we've got these two different kinds of cells – blastic and clastic - with the exact opposite function or job to do. With me so far?

When the turnover is actively going on, that is to say, while clastic and blastic cells are doing their jobs of breaking down, reabsorbing, and then forming tissue, we also need some kind of signal to the tissues so they know HOW to reform. The signal we're talking about here, is **the demand that was placed on the tissue.** In other words, **when you place a demand on a tissue, whatever the tissue is, be it muscle or ligament or tendon or bone or your skin, the tissue will *adapt* to the *demand* that you recently put on it.** If that isn't enough to consider, then think about this: It's all happening every single second during your entire life.

Recent Demands Determine How the Tissue Reforms.

Remember each one of us is born with almost limitless mobility and range of motion at our joints. If you're wondering what I mean, just think of a newborn baby or an infant and how their hips and arms and legs move so easily. The joints are able to move in extreme ranges of motion. Who hasn't looked at a baby putting their feet in their mouth and thought, *I wish I could do that!*

Somewhere along the way as we get older though, something changes and all of a sudden, we aren't able to put our feet in our mouth any longer. What changed? The answer is, *we stopped doing it.* It's as simple as that. You see, our bodies have evolved to be as efficient as possible with how we move. And that body of ours determines what movements are necessary based on what we've done in the recent past, and essentially eliminates all of the other movements. How? It's not a *conscious* decision, it does it by way of *tissue turnover*, the process I just described. That process reflects the demands that were placed on the tissue earlier.

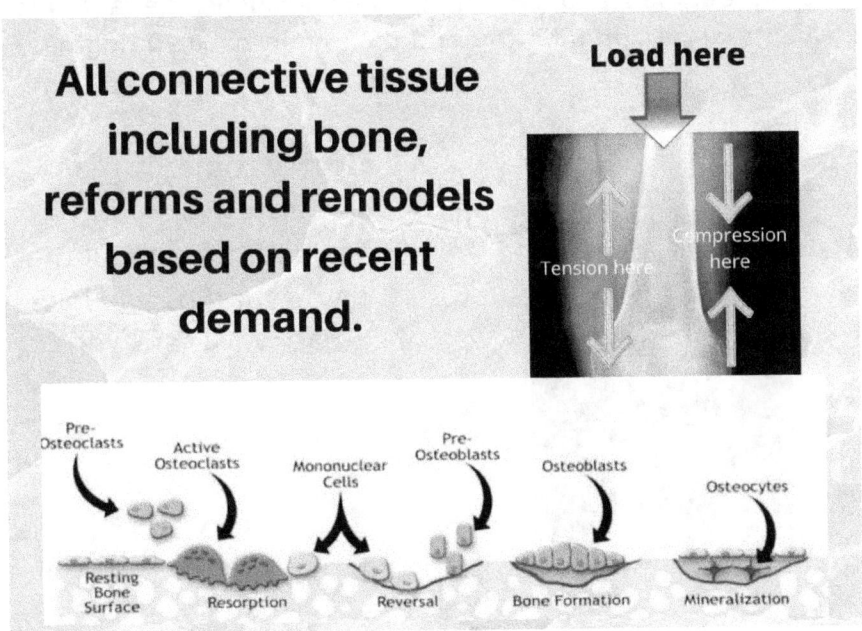

What If You Did a Split Every Day of Your Life?

To help you better understand what this means, I'd like to share a hypothetical situation I heard one of my mentors, Dr. Andreo Spina, say once to a group of students at a lecture. Let's say, hypothetically, that you take a child when they're two or three years old, while they still possess all that mobility they were born with and have them do a split. But not just one split. You're going to have them do it every day for the rest of their life. Can you guess what will happen as they go from child to middle-aged adult to an older person?

Even as they turn 100 years old, they'll still be able to do the split! Those around them will be amazed! Anyone watching them do a split at 100 will assume they possess some kind of freak athletic gift. In reality, all that happened is the child turned adult turned older person has consistently placed that demand on ever changing tissues of the groin, hips, and legs, by doing the split every day. The body responded by maintaining the ability.

What about someone who sits in a chair for most of their life? Let's say they're an office worker sitting in a chair with their knees bent at 90 degrees and their feet flat on the floor and they never actually move into any other range of motion. In other words, they never fully bend their knee or fully extend their knee. You might think this is an extreme example that isn't real, but in truth, it is a microcosm of how many people go through life moving in fewer dynamic ranges. In essence, their 3-dimensional movement world is shrinking.

Not using the range of motion past 90 degrees for a length of time means that when the cells turn over, they will do so in a way that will not allow any more range of motion. In other words, that body never gets any signal or stimulus to the cells that create the tissue length needed to go past 90 degrees, and as such, the new tissue isn't adapted to that demand. And therefore, when that person tries to bend their knee past 90 degrees, they won't be able to do it.

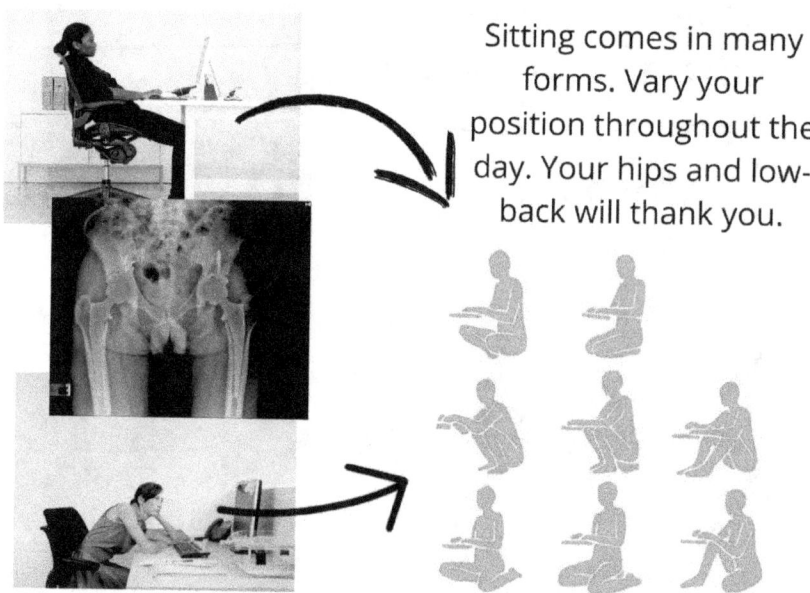

Sitting comes in many forms. Vary your position throughout the day. Your hips and low-back will thank you.

This is why here in the U.S., where many people sit in chairs most of the time with their knees bent at around 90 degrees, those same people can't get down into a full squat. Conversely, if you go to another region of the world where chairs aren't common, such as India or Asia, you will see elderly people who are able to sit into a full squat. They've routinely and consistently placed that demand on their body, and as such, they keep it!

The important take home message here is this: it isn't because of where they live, or their genetics, or the food they eat. It's simply because of the demand they placed on their tissues.

So, as you can see, in order to also maintain or improve how we move, we must *gradually introduce some type of stimulus – some kind of exercise input*, so we can gradually adapt to this stimulus and thus have access to that range of motion. The great news is most of the time, we can restore most of what we've lost. Although, as you can imagine, the longer we wait to turn the ship around, the harder it might be to get back to where we were at one time.

I don't have time is just saying it's not a priority.

— Naval Ravikant

Age Well and Feel Great!

Key Concept:

Is Sitting the New Smoking?

A few years ago, I attended a coaching conference in Orlando. These conferences are typically great events, bringing together a slew of different experts in the industry. It's always a great opportunity to connect (and reconnect) with other coaches and trainers.

Attending this conference reminded me if there's one thing that's a given in the fitness industry, it's the pendulum always swings to the extremes. Whether it's a new research study, book, or article, or even a "cutting-edge" piece of equipment, there is always something new that stirs-the-pot and gets people swaying to the extreme opposite side of things. The classic example right now is how much negative attention sitting gets in both the regular press and in fitness articles. I remember reading a Huffington Post article from 2014, Sitting Is the New Smoking: Ways a Sedentary Lifestyle is Killing You,[7] and thinking to myself, wow, that sounds awfully extreme. And dire!

Is sitting really shortening our lives? You probably know standing work-stations are increasingly popular in offices and schools, and many articles about how sitting "is the new smoking" would sure have you believe it's all bad. Well, let's let that pendulum swing back to the middle a little bit, shall we? ☺

I think our problem as a society isn't necessarily that we sit too much, it's that we don't MOVE enough. *More motion, more movement, is what we really need.* **Motion is the lotion we need.**

This theme has been consistent throughout this entire chapter. Staying static for too long a period of time in any position is the real problem. For example, if you use a standing work-station but keep your feet planted in exactly the same place for thirty minutes straight, you might experience the same stress on your feet, hips and low-back (leaving you sore and stiff) as would sitting in a chair and not moving for the same amount of time. The solution sounds obvious but from a practical point of view, it isn't always easy, right? Sometimes you're working under a deadline or sitting in a meeting and can't just simply get up and move around. If you're smart, you will want to figure out a way.

For me, I like to do a two minute mobility/flexibility "flow" that gets me out of my chair. It's a routine I've developed that gets straight to the heart of the biggest "movement related" challenges I have. While working at my desk, I set the timer and make sure I get up regularly to go through this "flow." That seems to work for me. All or any of the eight movement "snacks" I'll share with you in Chapter 23 are perfect for this kind of short movement burst.

If you've got a long drive planned, build in enough time to allow for stops and get out of the car to move a little bit. Find your own favorite "flow," practice it often and become so familiar with it you could do it in your sleep.

It is true that sitting too much does represent a general trend toward being less active and that can certainly lead to a higher risk of disease. The take home message is **keep moving**. *Motion is lotion.*

OK, we're almost ready to get to the next chapter where you'll read about our universal struggle to exercise and learn more about some basics and fundamentals like stability and how to take care of your feet. Before we wrap this chapter though, let me ask you a simple question: What can you do when your shoulders and hips aren't feeling quite as "new" as they used to, or worse, are causing some chronic or even acute pain? The answer is simple. It comes down to these three things: **Focus, invest, and believe.**

1. Focus On What You Can Control.

That means taking moderate but consistent action every day. I'll give you some specific

things you can do each day in the next few chapters, but remember that it begins by just moving, more. This includes chores, errands, and activities. With everything you might do or have done in the past using some tool to assist and make it easier, try to incorporate more movement into that routine. Walk instead of ride. Use the stairs. Park further from the store entrance. Start small and build from there.

And as you embark on some structured exercise, if this is your first exercise of any kind in a while, **do just a little bit more than nothing at all, but do it consistently.** Focus.

Consistency beats intensity every time, because only when you back off in a smart way but do something consistently can you sustain it over the long haul, and that's our goal.

2. **Invest In Your Future Health By Acting Now to Reverse the Trend.**

Every minute spent moving more and incorporating exercise into your day will pay off down the road by preventing the normal decline in function typical of "old age." You want to stay active and be able to DO the things that will make life more meaningful. Act now to turn the ship around and start moving in the right direction.

3. **Believe In the Process Because It Works.**

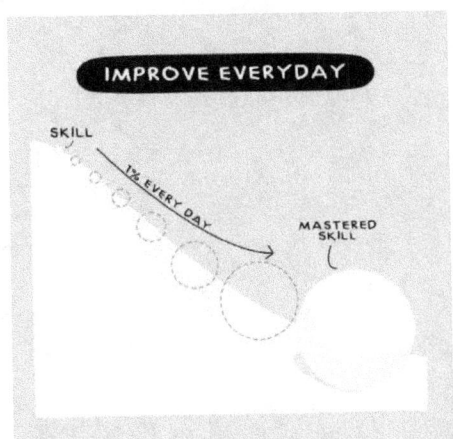

Nothing ever happens without some kind of basic belief that it **can happen**. You must believe, take action, then rinse and repeat. So, what do I mean by the "process?"

I assume you brush your teeth every day, yes? Or do you do it occasionally, whenever you might think about it – maybe once a week or once every couple of weeks?

If you took a "whenever I occasionally think about it" approach to your teeth, you'd soon be discussing dentures with your dentist, or trying to figure out a way to explain to your kids why you have those black holes in your teeth! ☺ We brush daily because it's a habit we've engrained over time, and most importantly because it's the only way to truly care for our teeth and be relatively sure we get to keep them throughout our entire life. This journey is the same thing. Small, consistent action leads to the results you're hoping for. So, again, what are two of your most important keys to success?

1. **Take a deep breath and approach it one step at a time.**
2. **Commit to the process. It won't be easy but it'll be worth it.**

And what are two of our most important goals in this process?

1. **Make sure our joints last a lifetime.** After all, joint replacement surgery is invasive, costly, and no matter how good an artificial joint might be now, compared to the past, it's still never ever going to be as good as your actual joint.
2. **Be able to move pain free, so we can enjoy life more.** Pain robs us of the ability to truly enjoy life to the utmost.

I hope you are as excited and as enthusiastic as I am to get to the next chapter. Let's get to it!

CHAPTER 18

EXERCISE:
THE STRUGGLE IS REAL

Everything that's fun in life is either immoral, illegal, or will make you fat.

— **P.G. Wodehouse,** *author and humorist*

> *Work involves whatever a body is obliged to do. Play involves whatever a body is not obliged to do.*
>
> — Mark Twain, from Tom Sawyer

As you can probably imagine, I've received many strange looks over the years when talking about or describing some of the workouts and hard races I've done in my life: dozens of marathons, Ironman triathlons, and ultra-running races, to name a few. The most frequent question I've gotten is, "why would you do that?" It's been more than 40 years of getting up nearly every single day and thinking about what I was going to do on that day to prepare for the next big challenge.

Most "normal" people, perhaps even you, can't possibly fathom why anyone else would do that. To be honest, I can't *fully* explain it, although there are times when I do have clarity about what has driven me. Certainly, there's a great feeling of accomplishment afterward. But most days, that alone isn't enough to get anyone out the door, including me.

I remember a conversation I had with a former coach. We were sitting together on the shores of Mirror Lake, in Lake Placid, New York, chatting. It was during the week leading up to one of my favorite races, Ironman Lake Placid. We were gazing out toward the water as swimmers went by during their practice swims, each going through their own pre-race swim routine. The crux of the conversation was neither of us could really explain why we, as triathletes, go through the hard and long training days. In the end, we agreed we were being true to ourselves. That's the way I tried to explain it to my kids and friends over the years, that I was just "being myself." I always felt most at peace when I was chasing a goal. We should all try to find that thing that helps us feel more at peace, don't you think?

I also know that some of my childhood experiences have a lot to do with it. In the 5th grade, I was the victim of bullying. As I grew, that experience made me want to prove I was "tough." It's humiliating to think back on it now – the idea that in the 5th and 6th grade, I would find a place to hide when school let out. I would then wait in my secret hiding place for as long as an hour. When I believed most everyone was gone, I'd start my anxious walk home. Invariably, there would be a group of older neighborhood kids waiting for me somewhere along the path. Some days they'd threaten, and other days they'd take it a step or two further and rough me up. When they'd had enough "fun," they'd send me on my way with my tail between my legs. It was awful.

A few years ago, at a funeral for someone in our neighborhood growing up, one of the kids who bullied me (who was now a grown man) sought me out and asked if we could talk. "Sure," I said. Right after the service ended, we found a quiet corner. He looked me straight in the eye and with a trembling voice, said he was very sorry for what he had done. I can only imagine what the people standing right around us must have thought as they listened to him. There we were, two grown men, looking at each other with this very serious, dour look on our faces, and watery eyes - talking about something that had happened 40 years earlier.

To be honest, I'm still stunned he did that. Looking back, I've often believed that maybe I did all those Ironman races simply to prove to myself those bullies were wrong about me.

If you're wondering why I'd share some of these personal experiences, it's simply me recognizing that perhaps there was a deeper reason why I've exercised to such extremes. Obviously, it's not a stretch to say the amount I've done and the dedication I've shown far exceeded what I "needed," to glean the health benefits I desired. To put it another way, I probably "mildly" over did it. ☺

It is important to acknowledge you **DO NOT** need extreme amounts of exercise to reap health benefits. Read that again. Many people believe if they only have the time or desire to do a small amount of exercise – say 1 or 5 or 10 minutes – it's not "worth it" to try. That is NOT true. A little bit is better than nothing at all, 99 percent of time. In fact, I'd add that embarking on extreme endurance exercise, like the marathons and ultra-running and long endurance triathlons I've done over my lifetime will not only not help you age better, it may even be harmful. There continues to be emerging research in an area known as the *Extreme Exercise Hypothesis*, that while largely circumstantial, says "epidemiological studies and observations in cohorts of endurance athletes suggest that potentially adverse cardiovascular manifestations may occur following high-volume and/or high-intensity long-term exercise training, which may attenuate the health benefits of a physically active lifestyle. Accelerated coronary artery calcification, exercise-induced cardiac biomarker release, myocardial fibrosis, atrial fibrillation, and even higher risk of sudden cardiac death have been reported in athletes."[1]

If you're like the great majority of people reading this, chances are you're saying to yourself, *no worries there, Al, I have no intention of embarking on "extreme" endurance exercise*. Which leads me to the title of this chapter and what I hope to share with you: **the struggle is real.**

The struggle I'm referring to is our individual and societal struggle to do even a very modest amount of exercise, far less than what I've done in my life. After all, despite the many different and well-known benefits of exercising, *very few of us are doing it*. Even a very modest amount. According to a 2018 report from the Centers for Disease Control, less than 1/4 of Americans - 23% - met the minimum standard of getting 120 minutes of moderate aerobic and strength training exercise per week. [2] Another article published by the Cleveland Clinic which came from research published in the Journal of the American Medical Association and the Physical Activity Guidelines for Americans, said "about 80% of U.S. adults and children aren't getting enough exercise for optimal health."[3]

So, What Is the Minimum Required to Reap the Health Benefits?

The American College of Sports Medicine recommends adults aged 18-64 get at least **150 minutes a week** of moderate intensity activity such as **brisk walking**, and at least **2 days a week** of activities that **strengthen muscles. This is slightly more than the CDC recommends, which is the 120 minutes I mentioned earlier. Using the ACSM's recommendation:** Since there's 10,080 minutes in a week, that means spending only 2% of the time we have each week doing some kind of exercise. TWO PERCENT.

That isn't much. Yet, the great majority of Americans don't even meet the criteria of this barely perceptible commitment to exercise. For example, despite most of us being very aware that exercise promotes health and agreeing they *should* exercise, a survey done in 2018 reported that 70% of Americans admitted they don't exercise during their leisure time.[4] Additionally, a recent study published on the CDC website showed "only 22% of U.S. adults from 18 to 64 met 2008 guidelines for both aerobic and muscle-strengthening exercise between 2010 and 2015."[5]

And despite these drastically low numbers of people getting even a modest amount of exercise, many experts feel the current guidelines of 150 minutes a week of brisk walking and 2x per week of strengthening, just aren't quite enough.

The chart here, sourced directly from a study titled *The Extreme Exercise Hypothesis: Recent Findings and Cardiovascular Health Implications*, shows what the researchers feel is the optimal amount of exercise.[6]

As you might imagine, their ideal sits at a higher level than current guidelines, but substantially below what is typical for extreme exercisers.

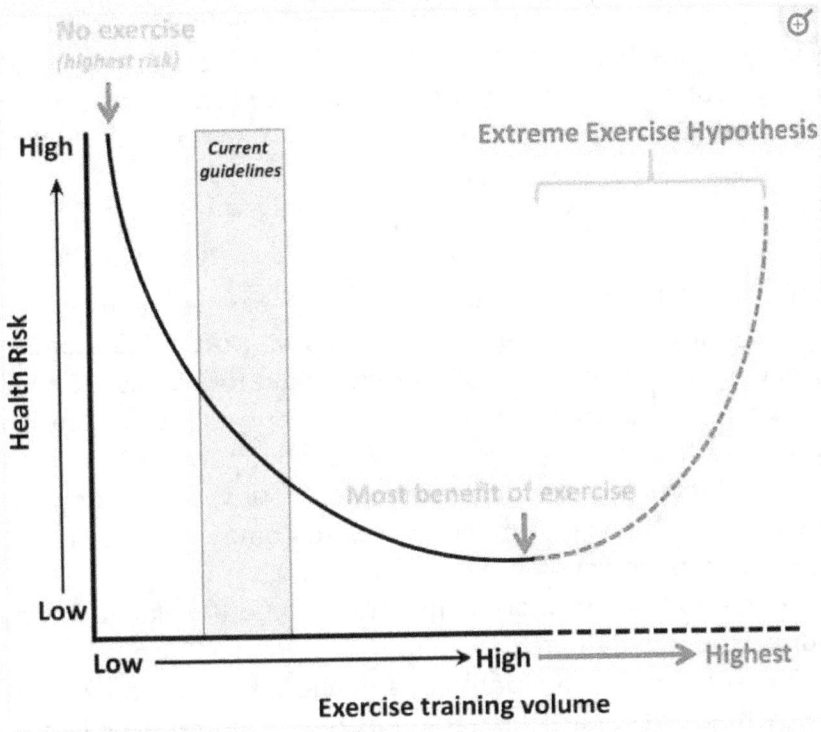

Fig. 1

Conceptual overview of the "Extreme Exercise Hypothesis." Increasing volumes of exercise lead to a curvilinear decrease in health risks, but these health benefits may be partially lost once an individual performs exercise training beyond the optimal exercise dose.

Is Walking the Best Exercise of All? (Hint: It's close. Strength is #1)

For the majority of us, other than resistance exercise to improve strength (along with all the other health benefits of strength training), walking just might be one of, if not the most health and longevity promoting activity of them all. And the bonus is it might be the ultimate human experience blending nature and being more social as well. And there's more, especially as it relates walking to our brain health: a 2018 study of the elderly revealed walking more than 4,000 steps a day makes for a thicker hippocampus, faster information processing, and improved executive function too.[7] Yes, walking is absolutely a brilliant way to keep *movement* in your life. But I'd still argue there are more "pieces to the puzzle" – the strength training box is at least as important to check. In the end, we need both!

There's so much to be gained by a moderate amount of the *right kinds of exercise*, and being extreme is not only *not necessary*, as we're learning, it has the potential to be flat out dangerous to our long-term health.

Which brings us back to our original problem and the *struggle* I alluded to earlier, **most people ARE aware of the benefits of physical activity, yet the overwhelming majority still don't do it with any kind of consistency**. It's ironic because there's nothing else better than physical activity and exercise to maintain a healthy weight, reduce anxiety and stress, increase self-esteem, improve concentration and attention and academic performance, and improve bone and muscle health. So, why aren't more people doing some kind of consistent exercise?

Should and *Need* are Two Different Things.

Nowadays there are a variety of interventions to get non-exercisers moving. Everything from fun technology to play with, to online exercise programs with lots of instruction and motivation, to free gym memberships where people are literally paid to exercise. Some of these work to help people get moving, but the overwhelming majority still don't. Why do you think that is? I've wondered about this for a long time, which is why, many years ago I started digging deeper to learn more. I thought if I could learn more about why so many people have such a distaste for exercise, I could help them find a way to come around to it so that they could reap the benefits, which are indisputable.

My research led me to look back on human history and the Hadza Tribe of Tanzania, to learn more about our hunter-gatherer ancestors. The Hadza Tribe of Tanzania is believed to be one of the last surviving hunter-gatherer societies. It's amazing what we can learn by looking to our ancestors and in particular, the process of natural selection, for some clues.

While opinions vary, most scientists agree when it came to food, our ancestors relied on foraging for wild plants and hunting wild game to survive. The Hadza Tribe spends most of their days foraging for food, climbing trees for a better view of the landscape and picking fruit, digging for root vegetables, hunting with their handmade bows, and building shelter from tree branches and mud.[8] Looking way back to the earliest civilizations, it wasn't uncommon for humans to sometimes go long periods without eating because food was sometimes scarce. Going 12 or 18 or even 24 hours without eating would have been partially dictated by the harsh surroundings, bad weather, or being on the move.

One thing I learned as I researched, was our ancestors were rarely active unless they *needed* to be. Finding food and hunting would have sometimes required moving around tirelessly for hours and scouring the countryside. The exercise they inevitably got was out of necessity to survive.

Yes, they moved a LOT, but only because life dictated it. Because of it, they didn't waste energy. It makes sense if you think about it. There would have been times when they needed to act very quickly to get food, find shelter, or fight off a predator. Common sense tells us they would have been very careful about where they spent extra energy. It wouldn't have made sense to do anything that would use up valuable energy unless it met a very specific need.

We Aren't the Only Ones.

A research study that examined how runners and in fact, all humans, will naturally select the most economical speed when moving and running (unless forced to do otherwise) was published at the time of this writing.[9] One of the lead researchers on the study, Dr. Jessica Selinger, confirmed "from an evolutionary point of view, energy minimization is considered optimal, to the point that it's done across the animal kingdom. Minimizing energy expenditure has evolutionary advantages—it allows us to move farther on fewer calories. We share this trait with other animals, be it flying birds, swimming fish, or galloping horses—there's evidence that we all move in calorie conserving ways out in the wild," said Selinger.[10]

If you've ever seen gorillas in their natural environment or read about their behavior, you know they spend most of their time sitting around doing pretty much nothing at all, except eating. Of course, there's also courtship and finding shelter and families circling around each other where the youngsters are more active, where there's some playtime and fun. All great reasons to exert some energy, especially for the youngsters! The bottom line is, for apes of any age, if the activity and exertion isn't *necessary* to play and have fun or doesn't meet an essential need like getting food or shelter or fighting off a predator, it just doesn't happen. Also, the research study I referenced a few paragraphs earlier confirms while we humans are great "endurance" animals, with the ability to go long distances when needed, we have always done it at the most economical speeds, unless otherwise forced to move faster (and apparently always will.)

If you consider the behavior of both our ancestors and the apes, isn't it logical to believe they would consider the "exercise" we do as somewhat bizarre? Might they see the voluntary things some of us pursue for the sake of health and fitness as a weird creation of modern life? I believe they would.

Combining this with what we have learned before about our collective drive to rest or look for an easier way to do any task, convinces me humans **have evolved to be lazy**, conserving energy whenever possible, unless moving is either necessary to survive, or it's deemed fun.

Doesn't that make you feel better? It's not your fault! ☺ It does me! If nothing else, I believe we should all feel a little less guilty. ☺

Other members of the scientific community also agree. For example, in his book, *Exercised: Why Something We Never Evolved to Do is Healthy and Rewarding*, author and Harvard professor, Daniel Lieberman (who has traveled all over the world studying different hunter-gatherer cultures in the present), says "we evolved to be as *inactive* as possible. Or to be more precise, our bodies were selected to spend *enough but not too much* energy on nonreproductive functions including physical activity."[11]

Could it be our desire to grab a seat whenever we have a chance and just be a "couch potato," doing as little as possible (just like a gorilla), is how *we've evolved* to act? Better yet, is it possible that those of you who have been occasionally labeled as "lazy" because you don't exercise, are actually the normal ones? One thing has occurred to me since learning more about how our modern life compares to our ancestors from millions of years ago: *The day we left the food chain as a species - that's when the sh*t really hit the fan!* In other words, when *some things* about how we live now, such as the amount of exercise we get without trying – have gotten worse to the point where it's leading to early death and increasing dysfunction, we've got a serious problem. ☺

Obviously, I'm not trying to say I'd prefer to be chased by a saber tooth tiger! No! But, when your survival *literally depends* on your ability to run as fast as possible so you can get to a tree and climb it to avoid a predator's jaws, you are going to keep your ability to do that! Or you get eaten. ☺ That's a hell of a motivation to move, wouldn't you say?

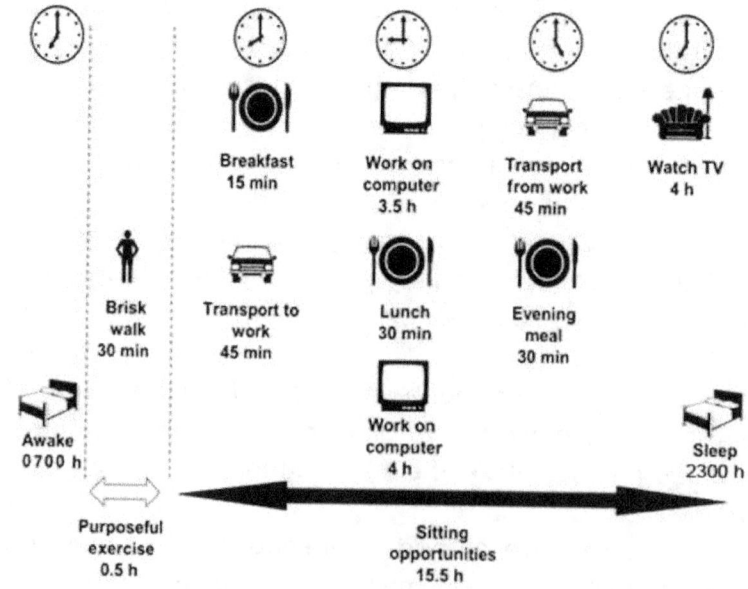

Modern life is predisposed to physical inactivity

Breakfast 15 min
Work on computer 3.5 h
Transport from work 45 min
Watch TV 4 h
Brisk walk 30 min
Transport to work 45 min
Lunch 30 min
Evening meal 30 min
Work on computer 4 h
Awake 0700 h
Sleep 2300 h
Purposeful exercise 0.5 h
Sitting opportunities 15.5 h

Dunstan et al. (2010) *Eur Endocrinol*

Our Collective Obsession with Comfort.

So, we can all let out a big sigh of relief and acknowledge that it's perfectly natural for us to want to only move *as much and as fast* as we have to or that we are intrinsically or extrinsically motivated to. Yay! It is somewhat normal to be lazy! ☺ Yet, here's the problem: acknowledging it doesn't solve the predicament we're in, which is *modern life*. Because we'd all agree that life as we know it, with drive-thru windows, smart phones, remote TVs, and millions of cars, is drastically different than it was thousands of years ago for our hunter-gatherer ancestors. And then there's our modern day "couch potato." ☺

Juxtapose the way our ancestor's lived with what we now have throughout the industrialized world. After all, there's a better than 50/50 chance that if you're reading this right now, you've got a remote control for your TV, a garage door opener, and maybe even a riding lawn mower. And you probably visit a drive-thru window at least once a week if not more.

A potato doesn't have much use for muscles

(Picture source: with permission-20140614 BEgan Muscle matters_ TEDxUCD)

We've become a society built around desks and zoom calls. We have longer commutes and heavier traffic, which causes us to spend more time sitting in our car. And we certainly don't have to hunt for food, as it's always nearby no matter where we are. We've become an overfed, underactive society due to those factors and more.

Have you noticed how coveted those parking spaces close to the stores are? It's crazy watching someone drive around just to park a few feet closer to the entrance. And what about the escalators and stairways that are side by side in airports and shopping malls? Most will not opt to take the stairs instead of the escalator. Only the type-A overachievers, and dogs of course, would be stubborn enough to climb the stairs and exert more energy in the process. Believe it or not there was a study done looking at the numbers of people who took the stairs.[12] What did they find? Only about 5% of the people approaching both the stairs and escalator, took the stairs. 1 out of every 50. I guess that tells you all you need to know. We're going to choose the easy way whenever we can and exert as little energy as possible. Modern life has become so *easy* in many ways. Now, would I trade my way of life for theirs? No, of course not. But the convenience and comfort bring with it a cost. And I'm not talking a financial cost.

So, are we a bunch of lazy bums for taking the escalator and parking close to the door and electing NOT to exercise even when we know we should, or have we simply evolved to avoid exerting energy of any kind unless it's either a real necessity or fun?

By now you're probably wishing I'd get to the point and finally answer this one and remove the mystery. I agree, because it's important and helpful to better understand, at least to some degree, WHY we act the way we do.

It has taken a lifetime of learning for me to accept that natural selection really does matter when it comes to "exercising." We simply aren't wired to run around exerting energy unless it's for fun or out of necessity, that is true. So, I'd like to propose that we finally banish the idea that most humans are lazy, apathetic, indolent bums for choosing inactivity over activity. It's time to stop placing blame and shame on each other and recognize that our innate desire to do less rather than more, is normal, so we can continue to focus on how to actually move forward and find our happy exercise place. That's my goal! Which brings us back to the topic at hand – our struggle with exercise and why we're in the situation we're in at this point – and the ultimate question: what can we do about it?

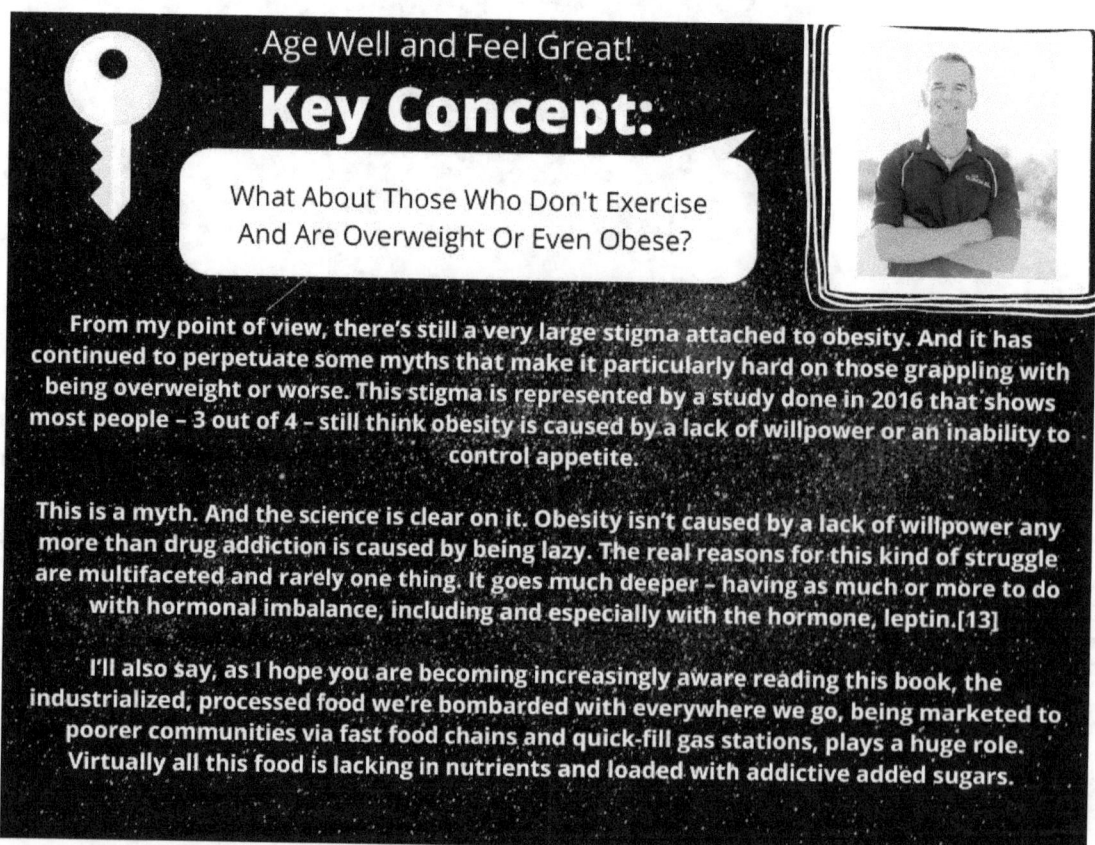

Age Well and Feel Great!

Key Concept:

What About Those Who Don't Exercise And Are Overweight Or Even Obese?

From my point of view, there's still a very large stigma attached to obesity. And it has continued to perpetuate some myths that make it particularly hard on those grappling with being overweight or worse. This stigma is represented by a study done in 2016 that shows most people – 3 out of 4 – still think obesity is caused by a lack of willpower or an inability to control appetite.

This is a myth. And the science is clear on it. Obesity isn't caused by a lack of willpower any more than drug addiction is caused by being lazy. The real reasons for this kind of struggle are multifaceted and rarely one thing. It goes much deeper – having as much or more to do with hormonal imbalance, including and especially with the hormone, leptin.[13]

I'll also say, as I hope you are becoming increasingly aware reading this book, the industrialized, processed food we're bombarded with everywhere we go, being marketed to poorer communities via fast food chains and quick-fill gas stations, plays a huge role. Virtually all this food is lacking in nutrients and loaded with addictive added sugars.

So, we can agree that modern life is vastly different than the life our ancestors lived, especially as it relates to exercise. That still doesn't get to the heart of why you're reading this, so let me get straight to it, because there's one thing we know for sure. **And this really is the TAKE HOME MESSAGE you need to hear right now.**

The Human Body MUST HAVE Regular Physical Stress to Thrive.

To think of it another way, you won't ever die from *overuse*, but you might rust to death from *underuse*.

Earlier in Chapter 2, *Why We Age: Exploring Aging at the Cellular Level*, I discussed the concept of hormesis and how important physical stress is, not only for feeling good and remaining active and fully functioning in the moment, but also as importantly, for slowing down the aging clock. The more you stress your body physically, to a point of course, the more *resilient it becomes*. And one added bonus is that physical stress can and often does alleviate some emotional stress.

When most people hear the word "stress," they immediately think about the negative or bad, emotional kind. The point here is there's another kind of stress that is essential to maintain good health and stay young as you age – to be able to enjoy life – and to be able to have the opportunity to die healthy. **It's physical stress.**

That physical stress can come in many forms. But in my opinion, the best and most important is some form of **strength training**, something I'll discuss and teach you in an upcoming chapter and later here in this chapter.

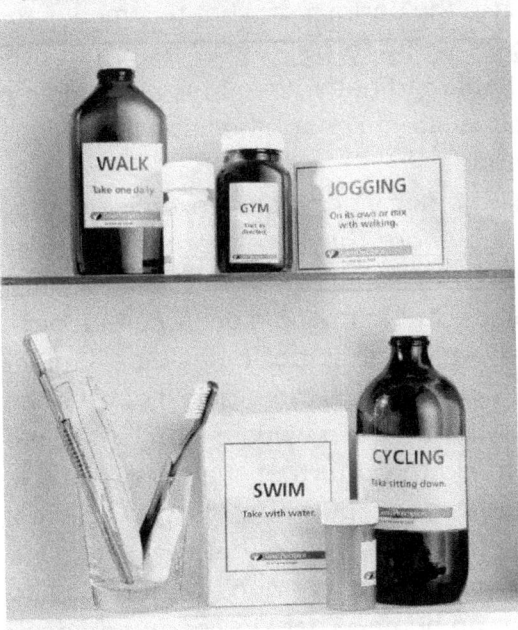

Ask your doctor or nurse about a Green Prescription.
Sometimes the best medicine is a dose of physical activity.

WALK
Take one daily

GYM

JOGGING
On its own or mix with walking.

SWIM
Take with water

CYCLING
Take sitting down

Interestingly, plants that also experience stress are better for us to eat. Some of the molecules that are created because of that stress get passed on to us when we eat the plant.

As I mentioned earlier, all the up-to-date scientific research supports this simple idea that vigorous exercise – that is, physical "stress," of some kind – call it work or exercise or anything else you like - is a powerful activator of "longevity genes" and "survival circuits" which help us age more slowly.

If you don't stress your muscles by forcing them to do work, you will get weaker.

If you don't actively load your bones and skeleton against gravity, they will become brittle.

It's true: *You better use it or you're going to lose it.*

How about what is likely one of the most insidious killers of the elderly in the U.S. right now? Believe it or not, it's falling.

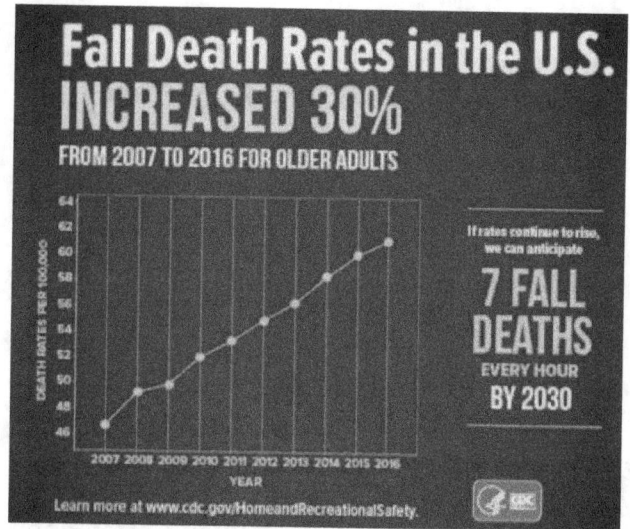

Fall Death Rates in the U.S. INCREASED 30%
FROM 2007 TO 2016 FOR OLDER ADULTS

If rates continue to rise, we can anticipate

7 FALL DEATHS EVERY HOUR BY 2030

Learn more at www.cdc.gov/HomeandRecreationalSafety.

Deaths from falls increased 30% from 2007 to 2016. At this rate, by 2030, there'll be 7 fall deaths every hour! We're simply weaker and frailer than we've ever been.

You've read it here in earlier sections and you've likely read and heard it elsewhere, too. And I'll be talking more about it in upcoming chapters on aerobic exercise and strength training. Use it or lose it. The science couldn't be clearer. And the evidence is all around us. *We don't wear out from overuse; we rust from underuse*. It's that simple.

So, again, I'll go back to the question, what should we do to combat our built-in wiring to not exert ourselves unless our lives literally depend on it? *Because we must each find a way.*

Here are some suggestions to make exercise a little more palatable for anyone and everyone. (Note: if you're training for Ironman or some other long endurance race or are visiting your local CrossFit gym and throwing a massive amount of weight around on a daily basis, you probably don't need these recommendations. My guess is you're an obsessive/compulsive Type-A who does it more for the rush than the health benefits. And that's OK.)

Let's begin with something that in my mind, plays an important role in what I'm about to share. Sir Isaac Newton proposed his First Law of Motion, the law of inertia, in 1687. It says that a *body at rest tends to remain at rest. A body in motion tends to stay in motion*. To put it another way, bodies will continue in their current state whether at rest or in motion, unless acted on by a greater outside force. Let's now put this in the context of what this means for exercise: Until you change your habit of not moving, it's going to be REALLY hard to move. You won't want to. But, when you CAN change that habit and get yourself moving in some way, shape, or form, it gets easier to keep moving. So, how do you adopt the habit of moving? The answer happens to be where most people go wrong.

Here's what I mean: When someone finally makes the decision to start exercising, they will always, and I means **always**, try to do too much too soon. They'll set aggressive goals that, while admirable, almost always set them up to fail.

Why do we tend to do this? There are a few reasons, but in my opinion, it comes back to *ego* and *impatience*. By ego, I mean we remember how it used to be, and what we might have been able to do in the past. And we assume we can get back there quickly, that's the impatience part. For example, I can't tell you how many runners I've worked with who injure themselves over and over because they are always trying to go further than their body is ready for. A mile of running is, after all, the rough equivalent of 1500 one-leg squat jumps! That's a lot of ground touches. But most runners don't think of a mile in that way.

Ego also hurts us because we like doing things we are good at. We don't want to be bad at anything. Many of us live by the mantra of "go big or go home." That kind of an approach is death to a new exercise routine. ☺ Also, we live in a world of instant gratification. We want results yesterday. That impatience means we often start out gangbusters and burn out the motivation before we've had a chance to establish a new habit. So, here's the way I see it. If you want to be successful, you must follow the four rules I'm laying out for you here:

Rule #1: BE WILLING TO BE BAD.

Accept it. Embrace the idea you may not be as good as you hope but that's OK. I love the way Christine Carter, Ph.D., frames this "be willing to be bad" idea in an article she wrote for TED.com, called *Here's How I Finally Got Myself to Start Exercising.*[14] She says, "being good requires that our effort and our motivation need to be equivalent." In other words, the harder a thing is for us to do, the more motivation we need to do that thing. And you might have noticed that motivation isn't something we can always muster on command. Whether we like it or not, motivation comes and goes. When motivation wanes, plenty of research shows that humans tend to follow the law of the least effort and do the easiest thing.

She goes on to say "new behaviors require a lot of effort because change is hard. Change can require a lot of motivation, which we can't count on having. This is why we often don't do the things we really intend to do. To establish an exercise routine, I needed to let myself be bad at it. I needed to stop trying to be an actual athlete."[15] The lesson she's sharing here is this: stop trying to be so good! Abandon your grand plans, at least temporarily.

And that reminds me of something else I must share on the whole idea of motivation, which doesn't work the way most people think it does.

Here's how we think motivation works: We get an **Inspiration** > which then leads to **Motivation** > which then leads to some **Action.**

The problem is, *we're wrong. That isn't how it works.* Inspiration is fleeting. Motivation is fleeting. The constant is and always will be, our ability to act. Here's how it actually works: **Action,** even the tiniest little bit > leads to some **Inspiration** > which then helps increase our **Motivation** to continue.

Action is the linchpin that drives motivation. To think of it another way, action isn't just the effect of motivation, but also the cause of it.

One of my favorite authors, Mark Manson, calls this his "Do Something" Principle. He says he developed it by accident when he was a consultant, helping people who were otherwise immobilized by fears, rationalizations, and apathy to take action. It began out of simple pragmatism: they paid him to be there so they might as well do something. What he found is that often once they did something, even the *smallest of actions*, it would give them the inspiration and motivation to do something *else*. They had sent a signal to themselves, "OK, I did that, I guess I can do more." And slowly they could take it from there.[16]

Which leads me to my second all-important rule if you want to make this exercise thing really work for you long term.

Rule #2: START SMALL.

I mean, really, really small. Reread Newton's First Law one more time. Take note of the words in the second half, "a body in motion tends *to stay in motion*." Consistency means everything when it comes to keeping it going. And keeping it going is *all that matters* at first.

If you can be consistent in whatever change you make, you'll have a much greater chance of turning it into a habit and reaping the benefits. A very small positive change done consistently, is far better than a monumental change that isn't sustainable.

I suggest you think of it this way: *Do something that is only a tiny bit more than nothing at all.* And just in case you're trying to imagine how doing something just a tiny bit more than nothing at all could possibly add up to a dramatic lifestyle change for the better, just remember the power of compound interest. ☺ Baby steps, baby! Tiny, bite-sized, easily sustainable exercise goals allow you to gain a little momentum and use that momentum to power future increases in that activity, but only if you so desire.

In Christine Carter's article, she frames this idea beautifully: "Ask yourself how can you strip down that thing you've been meaning to do into something so easy you could do it every day with barely a thought? So, if your big aim is to eat lots of leafy greens, maybe you could start by adding one lettuce leaf to your sandwich at lunch. Don't worry: You'll get to do more. This *better than nothing* behavior isn't your ultimate goal. But for now, do something ridiculously easy that you can do even when nothing in your life is going as planned. On those days, doing some wildly unambitious act *is* better than doing nothing. A one-minute meditation is relaxing and restful. A single leaf of romaine lettuce has a half-gram of fiber and important nutrients. A one-minute walk gets us outside and moving, which our bodies really need."[17]

She couldn't be more right in my opinion, and that's coming from a guy who's done marathons and ultra-runs and Ironman triathlons during the course of my life. THOSE AREN'T what it's about, at least not in this context. Doing a little something every day IS what it's about.

If you've never exercised before, then one minute a day of walking, done consistently, will lead you down a path that could change your life for the better in unimaginable ways! Sound crazy? I've seen it happen. Even if you've had a high level of fitness in the past but have let some time lapse, you NEED to start small. Be willing to be bad! Just keep at it.

Because you need to do it every day. No excuses. If that seems daunting, then step back your expectations, but commit, nonetheless.

The cool thing is, with your every-day action, you'll be laying down new neural pathways for a new habit. Eventually, you'll be on autopilot and won't even have to think about it. You'll have started what's often called a ritual. Rituals are great because they become a part of how we function and live without us even thinking about it. And they often represent something important to us. Which leads me to rule #3, which is…drum roll please. ☺

Rule #3: DO IT FOR THE RIGHT REASONS.

People start exercising for a whole host of different reasons, but if we were to narrow it down to the most common, it would be these two: 1. To lose weight, and 2. To get in shape to look better.

   If you exercise regularly to lose weight, you're doing it for the wrong reason and focusing on the wrong thing. And here's why: *Excess fat weight is NOT an exercise deficiency problem. It's a hormonal problem driven by your food choices.* Fix the real root cause of the excess weight, which is what you're putting in your mouth. But do continue to exercise to improve your fitness and to look and feel better.

Rule #4: KEEP IT FUN!

One of the places I like to go for a run near my home is an area with a couple of large grassy fields. It's also a favorite place for dogs and their owners. I notice when a car door opens, the dogs typically jump out of the car as fast as possible and sprint off at max speed, sometimes to catch a ball.

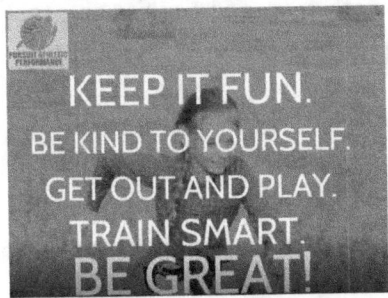

The owners seem to always climb out and walk much more slowly. Every time this happens, I'm reminded people don't have the same urge to bolt off as fast as they can the way dogs do.

   Do the dogs not care about conserving energy? Or do they just need to release some pent-up energy? Maybe it's a bit of both, who knows. One thing I do know is that dogs and cats have lessons to teach us about how to age well. They are both constant reminders of how to live simply and better – stretching when they feel like it and resting when they're tired.

KEY CONCEPT: How To Create An Exercise Habit.

In Chapter 22, Daily Movement Overview: Habits, Rules, Forever Movement Goals, and the Magic Bullet, I'm going to share some additional tips and secrets on how to create a habit that will be so automatic, it will be unconscious.

Keep reading!

I remember reading a triathlon training article years ago titled *How to Train Like a Dog*. I thought it was a great way to look at physical training – to do what a dog would do. I mean, dogs sleep when they want, run around like crazy whenever they can IF they want to, and generally completely and totally act how they feel at any moment. They don't plan activities out in advance, and they certainly aren't shy about stopping the moment they decide they've had enough, right? It's clear we aren't like dogs! ☻ But maybe we should be. Think about it.

Can Something That Is Uncomfortable, Really Be "Fun?"

So, one of the more common things athletes will do before the start of a game, match or if you're a runner or triathlete like me, a race, is to say to another: **"have fun!"** I know I have said it and had it offered to me many times.

Now I imagine you're thinking – what on earth could be *fun* about a long arduous race like an ironman or marathon? I mean, have you ever even seen a runner smile? There's no way they're having fun, right?! Even under the best of circumstances, there's a fair amount of struggle and even some pain and suffering. What could possibly be fun about that?

A few years ago, I spent some time really thinking about that question, because the often repeated "have fun" encouragement from one person to another was virtually universal among everyone who was participating. I thought there had to be more to it than simply encouraging others to succeed.

For most of human history, at least the last few million years, hunter-gatherers rarely ever engaged in hours of exercise solely for the sake of doing it. There was always a greater purpose to their activities. But, when they did go out for whatever reason, they always did it in large groups, rarely ever alone. When the goal was to find food by foraging for berries, digging tubers, etc., the women always traveled in groups of four or more. Men would also typically hunt in pairs and often in much larger groups. After all, for safety reasons, there was always strength in numbers.[18]

Yet, safety doesn't tell the whole story. History as well as our own experiences teach us there was an extra meaning behind why we've always traveled (or done just about anything else of value) in large groups. *We humans are intensely social creatures.*

As I've discussed, for all of human history, we've always done things together. Played together. Hunted together. Supported each other. And research on human behavior points out that we cared what others thought of us while a part of a group. Clearly, gathering in groups is something we are naturally selected to do.

Exercising is certainly no different. When you're exercising in a group, everyone encourages each other. You don't want to miss a class or practice if you think you'll let someone else down. That's a win/win for you and for the others. When you're tired or aren't as skilled, someone is there to lift you up. When you have some success, there's someone to cheer you on and offer some praise. I have always done most of my exercise and training alone, but at the same time, I always really looked forward to races. It's so encouraging to be around others who also enjoy the company of like-minded people. The difficulty and the suffering were always a little bit less because we were all doing it together. And the thought of quitting is so much harder to swallow when you're in a group.

It's simple really: <u>It's just more fun to do almost anything in a group</u>. And there's an evolutionary reason why. We're wired as very social creatures. Plan to exercise with friends, as part of a group, and perhaps even find yourself a trainer for a little bit of accountability too. Being a member of a group or community is often just the kind of "fun" we're looking for to keep us going, but *when it comes to why we do what we do*, there might be more to it.

What is YOUR *Value Hierarchy*?

In his book, *Everything is F*cked - A Book About Hope*, author Mark Manson tells the story of a good friend of his who at one time was one of the hardest *partiers* he'd ever known. She'd "stay out all night and then go straight to work from the party - with zero hours of sleep." In order of importance, awesome Disc Jockeys, drinking, and drugs were tops for her - sleep and work were at the bottom.

Then, as he puts it, "she did one of those volunteer abroad things, where young people spend a couple of months working with orphans in a Third World country." That "changed everything." "Suddenly, as if by magic, the parties stopped being fun. Why? Because they interfered with her top priority: *helping suffering kids*." He went on to describe how she changed careers and was all about her work. "Drinking and doing drugs? A thing of the past." She didn't "lose" the partying. As Manson explained, she didn't *lose* anything by giving up the parties. It's just that they stopped being fun. <u>Her priorities had changed</u>.

"Fun" Is Also a Function of Our Value Hierarchies.

I'll admit I get a little emotional at times when I talk about aging "gracefully," or being able to live a full life and then die healthy. *Passion* is a word that's often used to describe me when I'm speaking about it. It's funny weird, but I often find myself getting so passionate, it can be a little intimidating for the listener. And that can sometimes put people off a little bit. I get it. I ask though, being able to live life on my terms – not suffering from chronic disease or dying a slow death – is there anything more important? Not to me.

I've spent my entire life doing lots of different kinds of exercise day in and day out, all with the goal of keeping me healthy enough to go out and have fun doing the sports I love. I call it the "price I pay to play." Surely a lot of people would look at that exercise and agree it isn't exactly "fun." They might also think to themselves, "that looks boring!" But is it really?

In the Introduction to this book, I said if you don't make time *now* for your wellness, at some point in the future, you'll be *forced* to make time for your illness. I'm not sure I've ever written a truer statement, to be honest.

Sure, we all like to have fun, enjoy the pleasures of life, and sometimes skip the things that are the hardest to do, like exercise. Life is all about balance and doing things in moderation after all, right? Until the suffering from an injury or an illness of some kind, stops us in our tracks. The quality of our health and thus our life is defined most by the values we are willing to struggle for.

Are you willing to commit a few minutes every day to doing something you think of as hard, uncomfortable, or inconvenient, to avoid a much worse "hard" later in life? Because if you aren't, you're going to find getting older is a LOT more difficult. But if you ARE, you'll be amazed at the positives that will be returned to you in every which way, now AND into the future! Trust me on that. In the end, there's just no such thing as a life without some kind of "hard." *It just comes down to YOU choosing which "hard" you want in your life.*

As an aside, have you ever looked back on your years in secondary and high school and considered that the teachers who were hardest on you were the ones who helped you most to grow, and the nicest teachers, much less so? If you're nodding and smiling right now knowing I just hit the nail on the head, you aren't the only one – research shows that experience is universal among most students.[18] Something to remember, I think.

Learn From the Mistakes of Others.

Most of the time it's emotion that drives our actions. It's part of what makes us human. And because of it, our values - somewhat like the hierarchy I'm talking about here - *can't easily be changed* through reasoning alone. If you've been really sick or have struggled with a disease or an injury, you know exactly what I mean. In the end, the only thing that will change what we value - how we live and grow and act, is our experience. Wouldn't we be better off if we could learn more from the mistakes of others, so we don't repeat them ourselves?

I'd like to think that you reading this chapter right now and listening to me go on and on about why you should do "x" or "y" exercise, is going to inspire you to be open to change. I hope it will. Maybe it's just what you needed to hear, I don't know. But I fear it won't do any good until the day arrives when your experience and what you value, ultimately *changes*.

It Comes Back to Me, You, Us. When we value things like aging gracefully and being able to live life on our terms and not on an illness' terms, the daily grind of doing "boring" exercise becomes a lot less boring and a lot more "fun."

It's growth. It's wisdom in action. We're pursuing our hopes and dreams to live life to the bitter end just the way we want to. We're becoming the best version of ourselves. As Manson explains it, in a way, "the ability to sustain boredom constitutes a sort of modern virtue that would enrich your life far more than whatever your phone happened to be showing you that second."

By engaging in the things that help us to grow, like exercise, we're living in a way that represents what is truly most important to us.

So, What's Most Important to You? I guess after thinking about all this, I finally figured it out. Whenever I've shouted out to someone to "have fun," I guess I'm really saying to embrace the opportunity to be doing something that while challenging on the surface, has a much deeper and more profound importance in your life.

Are You Checking All the Boxes?

Where I live in Florida, one of the most popular games played by many retirees is pickleball. It's similar to tennis but played on a much smaller court.

There's also a paved bike trail nearby, one of those converted rails to trails and it's hugely popular for obvious reasons. So many people love to ride their bikes up and down the trail, especially the retired demographic. The path is flat and a safe place to ride. It's a favorite for walkers and runners too.

It's fantastic that these people are enjoying their own favorite brand of exercise. There's absolutely no downside to any of it. Whether it's golf, walking or jogging, pickleball or tennis, or riding a beach cruiser up and down the bike trail, they are all doing something far superior to doing nothing at all. A little bit of something is ALWAYS better than nothing.

But here's the thing. Remember in Chapter 3, I talked about the various pieces to the aging puzzle and taking advantage of our own individual areas of opportunity to improve? I told a little story about one of the scenes from Rocky III, when Apollo Creed, in a desperate and tense moment, corners Rocky and frantically tries to get him to understand that, in his words, "there is NO tomorrow."

The good news is there IS a tomorrow if you decide to act now and start to change. But nailing ONE piece of the "puzzle," while fantastic on so many levels, isn't enough. Not if your goal is to age as well as you can and live on your terms right up until the end. And here's why:

Generally speaking, your body's framework – the "chassis" – is going to fail more quickly than any of the other systems in your body, such as your heart, lungs, or even your mind.

Let's take the pickleball player as an example. It's great cardiovascular exercise. You're forced to move around the court quickly to get to the ball as it comes over the net. You're surely challenging agility, balance, and raising your heart rate. Sounds almost perfect if the goal is to get exercise, doesn't it? It is, almost.

But it lacks one very important component that makes ALL the difference as we age. That component is strength. In other words, if all you're doing to incorporate exercise into your lifestyle as you age is pickleball, whether you realize it or not, you're going to get weaker and become increasingly fragile, despite playing the game with energy and vigor. The same is true for riding a bike on flat roads and trails, and jogging. And just about any other exercise that is similar.

The reason is something called *sarcopenia*, or muscle wasting. In other words, muscle matters, my friend, and in many more ways than most people realize. And it starts to go away – to literally waste away – if we don't challenge ourselves and try to maintain it.

So, yes, *sarcopenia* is inevitable. We are all going to lose some percentage of our muscle as we age. But we can control how fast and to some degree, how much, depending on what we do to slow that process. I'll talk a lot more about HOW in the chapter on strength and resistance training. I'm being intentionally redundant because it is so damn important.

This image from a slide, courtesy of U.K. based scientist, Brendan Egan, Ph.D., a University College Dublin UCD lecturer in sport and exercise science, clearly shows how muscle literally *goes away* via three different cross sections of the leg muscles of three different people.

Age-related muscle wasting is termed "sarcopenia", meaning *poverty of flesh*

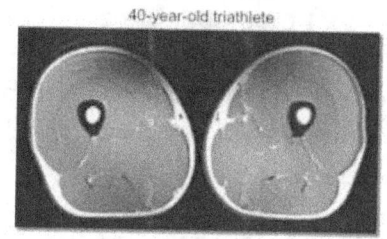

40 y, athlete

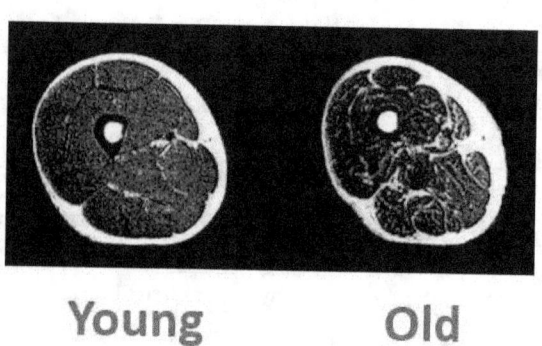

Young   Old

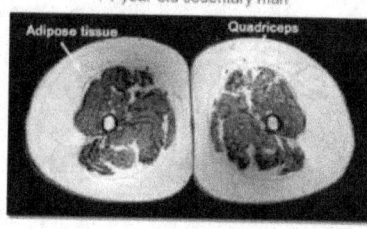

74 y, sedentary

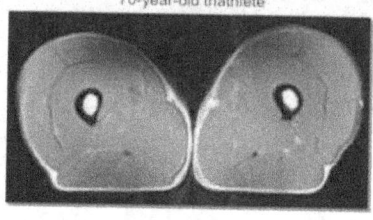

74 y, athlete

Wroblewski et al. (2011) *Phys Sportsmed*

Compare the thickness of the muscle (seen as the darker color) in the 40-year-old athlete, with that of the 74-year-old who is sedentary, and then against the 74-year-old who is an athlete. Wow! It's dramatic, wouldn't you agree? Anyone over the age of 50 has already seen this in themselves. Whether it's baggy skin, or the sensation that the arms and legs are shrinking, it's not a figment of their imagination. It is happening. And the effects can be devastating.

The research tells us starting at age 50, we're going to lose between 1.5 and 2% of our strength every year thereafter. Some studies have shown as much as a 4% loss. Between age 20 and age 80, you can expect to lose at least half your strength, unless you do something to slow the loss.[19] Nursing home residents who spend most of their time sedentary, experience a much greater risk of mortality due to sarcopenia.[20]

Ill and/or hospitalised for a short period?
"Disuse atrophy" is a major threat to ageing well

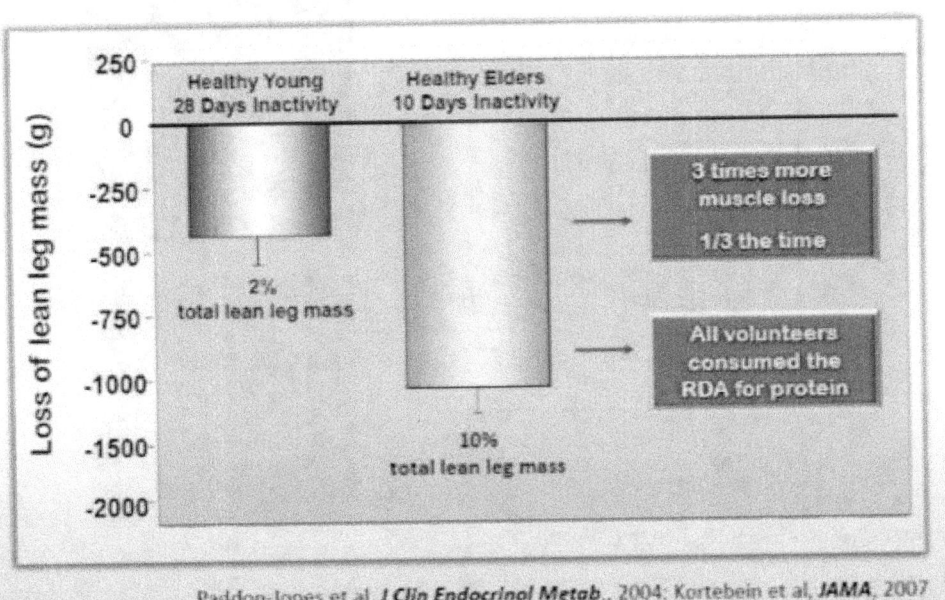

Paddon-Jones et al, *J Clin Endocrinol Metab*., 2004; Kortebein et al, *JAMA*, 2007

There's a dramatic loss of muscle tissue with as little as 10 days of inactivity – three times greater compared to a healthy young person with 28 days inactivity. Three times greater, in one-third the time.

The size of our muscles matters a lot less than our actual strength. When you lose strength, you become frailer, the risk of falling increases dramatically. You eventually lose independence and with it, you'll invariably suffer emotionally. No one wants to be at the mercy of others to move around. Being free to move and take part in life is so important to be happy and content.

It's not a coincidence that *sarcopenia* is also present in most disease states, cancer, kidney disease, HIV-AIDs, heart disease, and osteoarthritis, to name just a few. I could go on and on, and I will in future chapters, but I think you're getting the point. If you want to age well, you can't just choose one type of exercise at the expense of another. And in my experience, the type that rarely gets the attention it so richly deserves, is stability and strength training. Otherwise known as resistance training.

We need cardiorespiratory fitness and strength to age well, there's no two ways around it. We've got to check most if not all the boxes and hit every puzzle piece we can.

Are older adults trainable? Strength training in >85-year-olds increases muscle mass and strength

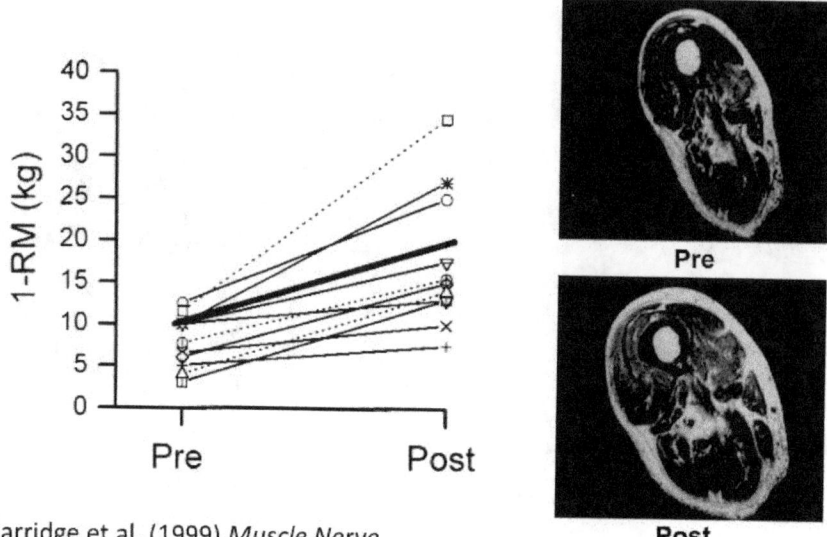

Harridge et al. (1999) *Muscle Nerve*

The great news is no matter how old you are, you can get stronger! There's so much research and my own practical experience that have shown this time and again.[21] One study, as illustrated in the above image again courtesy of Dr. Egan, showed in a group of people OVER the age of 85, after 12 weeks of resistance training there was a 134% increase in their one-rep maximum, and a 44% increase in the density of muscle tissue. That's incredibly exciting in my opinion. You CAN ALWAYS improve strength!

The other bit of great news is I'm going to teach you how you can get stronger and improve your cardiovascular health in a short time and a convenient way in future chapters.

What About Now?

I wouldn't change anything about my life as an endurance athlete, despite the fact, as I mentioned earlier in this chapter, there may be a long-term cost associated with extreme exercise. The marathons, overcoming my PTSD to reach the Ironman, the people I've met, the things I've learned about myself, and the accomplishments themselves – ALL of it - has absolutely been among the most amazing times and experiences of my entire life.

I won't deny the take home from what I've learned over the last decade is that exercising to those extremes carries with it an inherent long-term risk. At the very least, there's certainly been a cost to what I've accomplished for both my cardiorespiratory and musculoskeletal systems. And some days, I can feel that cost in some of the added aches and pains reflecting all the miles I have on my "chassis."

Since we're on the topic, I also want to share with you at this point in my life, my training and exercise goals are focused on shorter races like the 5K where the total "hard" efforts are only 20 to 30 minutes. I'm also focused more than ever on balancing my running and cycling with mobility, flexibility, and strength-based activities, which are a lot of fun. For the most part, excepting the occasional big goal race that I may have always wanted to do, I don't have the desire or the inclination to do the very long, hard racing. The take home message from this information is important:

- **More is definitely NOT better.** In fact, more is often worse. You can get a surprising amount of great health benefits from a small sampling of the right kinds of exercise.
- **Forget forever the stupid phrase: "no pain – no gain."** I know this once popular phrase in training circles has mostly gone by the wayside, but it bears repeating here. Forget this silly and potentially destructive mindset.
- **Steady-state cardio exercise need not, and probably should not be the centerpiece of your fitness program or exercise routine.** *Strength training rules as the MOST important exercise you can do far and away.*

I see all this information as great news for you. After all, I'm quite sure you weren't reading this chapter OR this book so you could improve your marathon Personal Best or to learn how to qualify for the Ironman World Championship. Am I right? ☺

Some TIPS to Make Exercise Work for You.

By this point, it's likely you're saying to yourself, "c'mon!" You've been patiently standing on one foot, waiting for the shortcut, the method, the guarantee. You've heard enough of the preamble and the analysis. You want to know what to do right now. I get it.

I've got a few tips for you to ponder as you move into the next chapters of the book where I'll discuss the HOW for making exercise a part of your life in ways that are both convenient and especially, effective.

Just remember one of the reasons we're collectively struggling in so many ways related to aging and exercise, is we often forget to focus on the questions first – such as WHY - rather than going straight to the answers.

Tip #1: Try Snacking.

"Snacking" on junk food isn't recommended as a general rule, but exercise snacking is one of the best things you could do to incorporate more exercise into your life! The concept is simple. Tiny bites, taken whenever it is convenient, or when the mood strikes you. I'll talk more about this topic in Chapters 22 and 23. In Chapter 23, Your Move-Smart Program: *Daily Movement*

"Snacks" and a 30-Day Bodyweight Squat Challenge, I'll give you specific actionable ways you can begin to include movement snacks in your daily routine.

You don't need to commit an hour or even a half-hour chunk of time in your day, which often isn't practical for the average person. But who doesn't have one minute to do something positive for their health, throughout the course of their day? Here are some of the ways I "snack" during the day, and some things you can do!

- I'll get up from my desk and do one slow push up. That takes about 20 seconds – 10 seconds down, and 10 seconds back up.
- I'll sit into a deep squat. Sometimes it isn't so "deep" depending on how I'm feeling and how I'm dressed. But it always opens up my hips and makes me feel better.
- When I go into our garage from the mudroom, I always pass under my pull up bar. So, I stop and do something virtually every time. Maybe I hang for 20 to 30 seconds, or maybe I do some chin ups or pull ups. Hanging is SO great for grip strength – one of the things that is a great measure of your health and goes quickly as we age.
- If you're at work, move around often and use your break time for a walk up or down the stairs.
- If you have errands to run, do them on foot. Take the hillier route when you can. Park further away from the entrance.

I sometimes refer to exercise "snacking" as "chunking." I've used the term "micro-burst," also. Whatever you want to call it, it's probably the fitness breakthrough of the century and certainly the most practical and reasonable way to get exercise in, no matter how busy you are. And the bonus is if you're learning a new skill, you learn the best when you "chunk" that information, little bits at a time, vs. taking a big bite all at once. It also offers a huge cumulative fitness benefit, and leads to a reduced risk of breakdown, burnout, illness, and injury, compared to full-length workouts and workout protocols.

Tip #2: Weave Exercise into Your Everyday Chores and Activities.

As I said earlier, you don't have to confine your activity to the time you spend in a gym. It's much more important to be moving all day long – to have an active lifestyle. The everyday work of real life provides a great opportunity for you to be physical. It could be moving mulch in the garden, or squatting down to dig up roots and weeds, or helping your neighbor move something.

For me, even though I live in a neighborhood where virtually every single person has someone else come and cut their grass, I always do it myself with a push mower. I not only save the $150-200 a month most people pay for landscape services, I also get the benefits of pushing that mower for 45 minutes.

Obviously, gardening can fit the bill when we're talking truly "functional" exercise. For many, gardening is the ideal way to commune with nature. There's nothing like the feeling of the sun shining down on you with sweat on your brow as you dig into the earth and massage those living, breathing plants. It's like exercise meets microbes in the soil meets sunshine meets fresh air, all rolled into one. Get dirty and enjoy all the benefits. The take home message is, be like me and never outsource your chores! ☺

Tip #3: Be More Childlike.

It seems the older we get, the less childlike we become. And that's especially true when it comes to physical play. I've always believed as soon as we look at any activity or exercise as a "chore," instead of "play," the odds of it continuing into the future are lessened.

Find ways to turn your exercise into play. For me, even a relaxed jog at a slow pace can be made playful by incorporating little sprints from one light post or sign to another, or by some harmless light-hearted competition with a companion. The only limits that exist are those in your imagination.

I'll have a few more tips and suggestions for you in the movement chapters coming up, including how to make that magic bullet, stick!

CHAPTER 19

BASICS AND FUNDAMENTALS, WISDOM, AND GOING WITH THE FLOW

No such thing as spare time.

No such thing as free time.

No such thing as down time.

All you got is life time. Go.

— **Henry Rollins,** *musician, writer, artist, activist*

Only staying active will make you want to live a hundred years.
— Japanese Proverb

I don't know about you, but there was a day a few years ago when I woke up and realized, holy sh*?!, I'm really getting older. Some days it feels like the aging process has accelerated and other days it feels like its slowed. But as the old saying goes, Father Time always wins. The thing is, aging isn't a linear process. Sure, if we look at the calendar and track the weeks, months, and years, and it might appear linear, but it's not. Similarly, we can go along for months and even years feeling like the same person. That is, until one day, something changes. Maybe it's a twinge in your low-back or neck. Or maybe you notice it takes you longer to climb the stairs or get out of bed. Just like that, the little voice inside your head goes, *oh jeez, I guess I'm getting older!*

Chances are, you're not surprised. It's what most expect. Inevitably, you'll also believe it's all downhill from there. Some will outwardly chuckle to themselves, but inwardly, be unnerved, and in our worst moments, depressed. Everyone hitting the half-century mark will at some point experience these feelings. Sooner or later, those jokes we've all heard about "old people" will start to hit a little closer to home. Before you know it, your idea of a "busy" schedule will be the long list of doctors' appointments coming up. It's a fact of life, right?

If accepting what many think of as a "normal" steady decline in health and function doesn't sound appealing, I'm glad! I call it *passive aging*. It's the quintessential example of *negative age beliefs*, something you learned about in Chapter 3. I wrote this book to shake you up and help you realize the worst thing you could do is go along wherever life (and your body) takes you and accept whatever happens, is going to happen and there's not much you can do about it. The irony is, if it's what you believe, it'll soon become a self-fulfilling prophecy. Unless, that is, *you take a more decisive, intentional approach to how you age.* The fact that you're reading this tells me you have what it takes to meet your future head on in the best way possible.

Attitude makes all the difference. Positive age beliefs and the mind-body connection matter. When we believe in the power of our own choices and are willing to act to help steer our course, good things are bound to happen. We'll have a much better chance of making real lifestyle changes as opposed to seeking quick fixes or temporary solutions to those troubling symptoms I described a few paragraphs ago – symptoms that won't lessen or go away completely unless we take action.

Deciding to age *intentionally* should feel really good and be a liberating and empowering force in your daily life. Thinking about this gets me fired up to live every day as though it's my last! At the same time, I want to live every day believing I'll be here past 100, because then I'll be patient enough to learn and do the things I need to do without feeling like I have to rush. I hope you embrace that idea too!

As a distance runner, I've had every injury you can have over the 40 years or so I've been running. Each time I was injured, I was really frustrated and sometimes even a little angry. I am willing to bet you *might* know the feeling; anytime we don't feel our best, it can feel like a setback, sort of like being injured. As I matured, I realized experiencing the injury or setback helped me see there was *something else I needed to learn and discover.* It might have been something about the way I trained or how I was taking care of my body that wasn't being addressed as well as it needed to be. In the end, I always turned those challenging periods into a learning opportunity and a period of intense discovery. I learned how to take a step back and see it from a broader perspective to understand what was happening.

While frustrating at times, as the years went on, these periods of intense discovery and learning also energized me. I became even more passionate about learning more and sharing what I was learning. As time went on, **the more I learned, the more I realized all I didn't know or understand.** The smarter I became, the dumber I realized I was.

The human body is, in so many ways, a mystery. There's far more that scientists don't know than they do know. My goal has always been to approach every day with a beginner's mindset, open to new ideas and concepts that would expand my horizons and improve my understanding, not only of the human body but also of people in general - how they think and the emotions they experience, especially when they were staring an injury in the face, feeling the same frustration I did.

Author, Jason Elias, in his book, *The Seven Graces of Ageless Aging,* says the "Buddhist sages speak of emptiness as openness, which allows us to receive." He goes on to share a teaching story he believes illustrates this beginner's mindset:

> "A university professor approached a master hoping to learn the nature of Zen. 'I know a great deal about the workings of the physical world,' the scholar explained, 'but perhaps you could add to my knowledge by offering some thoughts about the nature of the spiritual world.'
>
> 'Let us have a cup of tea,' said the master, 'and then we shall talk.' The professor held out his cup as the master poured, filling the cup to the brim and then continuing to pour while the tea spilled onto the floor. 'It's overflowing!' protested the professor. 'No more will go in!'
>
> 'Yes, it is so,' said the master. 'Just as this cup is full to overflowing, so is your mind filled with opinions and speculations, leaving no room to receive the teachings. Only when you empty your cup, can we begin.'"[1]

Basics and Fundamentals and Going with the Flow.

Looking back over the last three or four decades of my life as a coach, parent, athlete, and someone simply trying to find my path, there were always concepts I kept coming back to regardless of what role I was in. No matter how many increasingly advanced concepts I would learn and put into practice, it always seemed my ability to master anything new was in large part, <u>dependent on how *deeply* I'd mastered the basic and fundamental concepts I'd learned earlier</u>. What I learned and continue to learn is profound: **Basics and fundamentals are truly what staying healthy and being able to thrive, is all about.** In fact, I'll go further and say "advanced" training is nothing more than the basics and fundamentals, mastered. Sounds simple enough, right? Except this is where many people get off track in their fitness pursuit. What do I mean? It's human nature to want to get to the "fun" stuff, so we sometimes rush the process, without first nailing the basics.

Think of learning to ski or skateboard. Of course, what is fun for one person can be terrifying for another. Our ability to learn more advanced skills, especially as we reach our later years, depends largely on our ability to do more basic skills, such as being able to stand on one leg and balance with our eyes closed. I've learned when I've found I am struggling with something I believe I should be able to do, I just need to scale it back to something more fundamental and look for the weak or missing link. It works every time.

There is something else I've learned – and it took me a long time to learn it. What is it? As you may have already guessed, it's how to *go with the flow*. If that sounds like the opposite of mastering the basics, it shouldn't. They're different ways of looking at the same challenge. They go hand in hand.

Think about this: we've all had those moments when our sense of time seems to disappear. Depending on what we're doing and also how we think about and perceive what we're doing, time can seem to stand still or go by in a flash. When we do something we enjoy that we're also good at, time flies. On the flip side, when it's boring or feels like a chore or is something we aren't good at, time drags. I think it was Albert Einstein who is credited with saying, "put your hand on a hot stove for a minute and it seems like an hour. Sit with a pretty girl for an hour, and it seems like a minute. That is relativity." I would say that about sums it up.

So often I've tried to force things. At one time, I believed the more I dug in and just tried harder, the better my results would be. I was wrong. Some things can't be forced. Anything worth striving for takes time and the process is *never* linear. I've also spent way too much time – wasted time – thinking about the past and being anxious about the future. Both took me away from the present moment. *And being present is really the only way to experience flow.*

My most enjoyable racing and training experiences have always been when I was fully present. The whole experience went by in a flash. That is one thing I love about mountain biking and trail running. You have no other choice than to be "in the moment," or you will surely trip or crash. It's about being completely immersed in what you're doing.

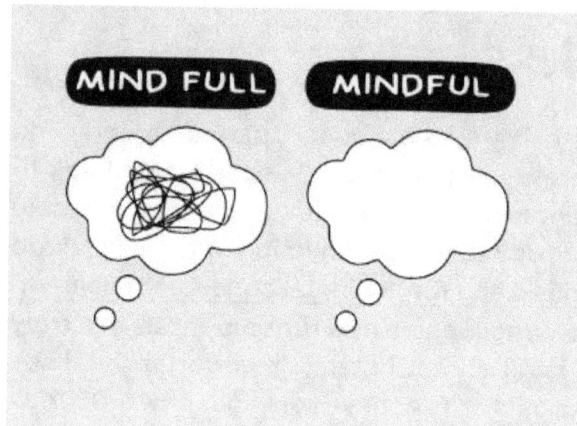

Playing percussion in a symphony orchestra, as one of 75 musicians solely focused on simultaneously following the conductor, reading and interpreting the music, and listening intently to play cohesively with the entire ensemble, brings me squarely back to the present moment. It challenges all the senses!

I'm hardly an expert on Chinese medicine, but one of the elements I've tried to understand better is "Tao," which is at the philosophical heart of traditional Chinese medicine. I interpret Tao as a word to describe a journey or a doctrine. It's sometimes described as the Way. I believe it means to be truly connected and in balance with nature and everything around us and absolutely present and alive in that moment.

Being present and connected and in balance with everything around us is essential to achieve a state of *flow*. Whether you think of it as yin/yang or chi energy or whatever you want to call it, I believe it is essential to be fully present and live mindfully in order to live a long, healthy life. You've no doubt already seen references to this mindfulness in earlier chapters and you'll hear it again. Not coincidentally, as you've already read, these concepts are at the heart of how "Blue Zoners" live.

Kenny Loggins, when asked recently, said he's made a promise to himself about the future...

To be more present so that I can enjoy each moment that I have, because we don't know how many more we've got. So, savor this one.

Speaking of blue zones, in their book, *Ikigai: The Japanese Secret to a Long, Happy Life*, authors Hector Garcia and Francesc Mirallas discuss the *power* of flow: "There is no magic recipe for finding happiness, for living according to your *ikigai*, but one key ingredient is the ability to reach this state of flow and, through this state, to have an optimal experience."[2] The authors say according to the Japanese, *ikigai* is a reason for living, and is key to a happier, healthier life. They add the Japanese, who are among the world's longest living people, describe ikigai as a "place where passion, mission, vocation, and profession intersect – where each day is infused with meaning."[3] That sounds like a state of *flow* to me.

As you go through this book, think about what YOUR *ikigai* might be. Ask yourself this question: what is your reason for getting up in the morning? What is it that when you're doing it, time seems to stand still yet at the same time, hours pass like minutes? That's where you'll find your flow state. Even when this might not happen as "naturally" as we would like, we can help create it with our *attitude* and our *enthusiasm*. Even the most boring tasks can be made fun and more than tolerable with the right attitude and flow.

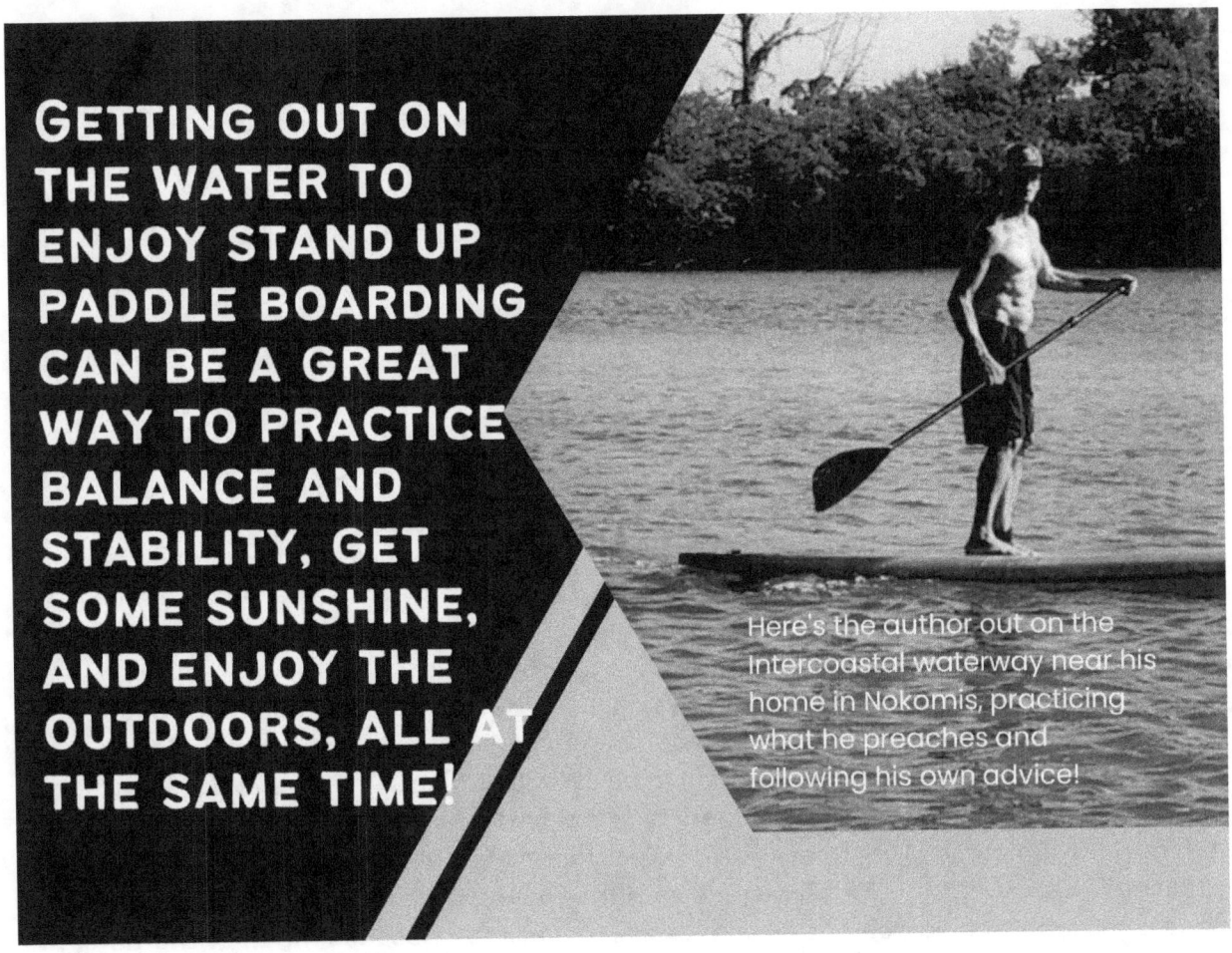

GETTING OUT ON THE WATER TO ENJOY STAND UP PADDLE BOARDING CAN BE A GREAT WAY TO PRACTICE BALANCE AND STABILITY, GET SOME SUNSHINE, AND ENJOY THE OUTDOORS, ALL AT THE SAME TIME!

Here's the author out on the Intercoastal waterway near his home in Nokomis, practicing what he preaches and following his own advice!

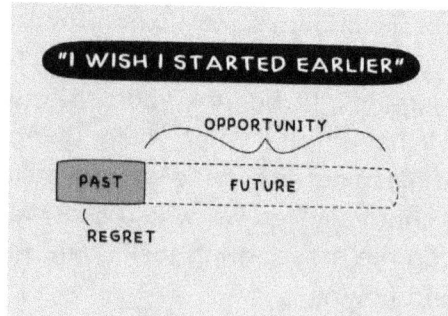

As you embark on the movement practices, hopefully you will embrace the philosophy behind why I've shared them with you. Start by seeking a deeper understanding of the basics and fundamentals. Master them. This is true not just for movement, but also for aging well as a whole. Find your flow. Don't force it. Smile. Enjoy the journey! You won't be disappointed that you did it that way, trust me!

> We often avoid taking action because we think "I need to learn more," but the best way to learn is often by taking action.
>
> — James Clear

Let's Start at the Beginning.

A few years ago, a local musician named Debbie sought me out to ask for help. She had recurring pain in the front of her shoulder and because of it, missed out on some opportunities to play. To say Debbie was frustrated is an understatement. A few months earlier, she went to physical therapy after being diagnosed with tendonitis. This is really just a generic diagnosis that simply means the tendon is inflamed for any number of reasons. We set up a time to go over the exercises she had been doing in therapy and to allow me to do some assessments in order to learn more about her status. So, what did we learn?

One of the major challenges with physical therapy is an all-too-common reductionist approach. What do I mean? For many reasons, therapists often target the *site of the pain* to reduce the symptoms. Of course, it's good to be able to reduce symptoms and help someone feel immediately better, and a side benefit to this approach is targeting a specific area after diagnosis is sometimes the easiest way for the therapist to bill the insurance. So, what's the challenge? Targeting the site of the pain with the focus on treating the symptoms, doesn't necessarily treat the source of the pain. This is a challenge because **much of the time, the site of the pain, where symptoms exist, isn't the *source* of the pain.**

Since Debbie had front shoulder pain, she was given a few exercises using an elastic band to "strengthen" her shoulders, and a few stretching exercises. Of course, the idea of strengthening an area is fine, except in Debbie's case, when she went to set up these exercises and began to move, it was obvious they were too difficult for her to do correctly. She grunted and groaned and contorted her body to compensate for the difficulty. When that happens, the result is an exercise theoretically designed to help, turns into one that makes things worse by aggravating the injured area. Have you ever been treated and had this same kind of experience?

As I watched Debbie attempt this exercise, I could clearly see her excessively arching her back, just one of many ways she was compensating. An intake form allows the clinician to collect the patient's medical history and symptoms. On Debbie's intake form, she reported low-back pain as an issue. I quickly surmised the connection between this exercise and her pain, and determined she needed to establish the important basic and fundamental skills before attempting this advanced exercise.

Debbie's goal was to relieve the pain she was having so she could return to playing. In order for that to happen, she needed to go back to an exercise and progression she could do well, without compensating. This is critical, especially when we start to exercise, whether for rehabilitation or simply to improve fitness. If we must compensate to complete the task, the compensation will likely become exaggerated as the dynamic challenge increases. If you're not sure what I mean, consider this imaginary scenario. You're a third grade teacher meeting with the parents of one of your students, a boy named Johnny. Johnny is struggling to learn addition and subtraction and falling behind his class, and you have an idea that might help. You tell his parents since he's struggling with addition and subtraction, your idea is to start him on multiplication and division, instead. And maybe even algebra or geometry!

Now, I'm sure you're thinking that sounds ridiculous, yes? Anyone knows that learning math, or any other skill for that matter, is about building one set of skills on top of another. There's no way Johnny will be able to learn multiplication and division until he's first learned and then hopefully mastered addition and subtraction. **This obvious and universally understood principle of progressive learning holds true when it comes to fitness and movement skills**. The same is true learning to play a musical instrument, learning how to type, or learning to drive. You always start at the beginning. Think about it.

In assessing Debbie's skill level and ability to move without pain, I determined there were four basic and fundamental skills that stood out as being especially important for her improvement. You'll notice that of these four, only two relate directly to where she felt the pain in her front shoulder.

1. **Head-to-toe whole-body posture**: Posture and good alignment is your starting point. It begins with learning what it is, then getting into a balanced stance and a neutral pelvic position, then working out from the middle to achieve basic whole-body alignment. Debbie's extreme low-back arch showed me she didn't have a solid, foundational movement baseline to then begin to train shoulder function. The idea isn't that she needs to stand as straight as an arrow to reduce her shoulder pain. Rather, it's a simple idea that optimal movement begins in the center of the body and moves outward from there. For this reason, having a good foundation of balanced posture will set up the best opportunity to train her shoulder properly. You'll learn much more about this (including how to do it) in the upcoming chapter on *How to Improve Your Stability*.

What Is Good Posture?

Our body adapts to the positions we spend most of our time in...

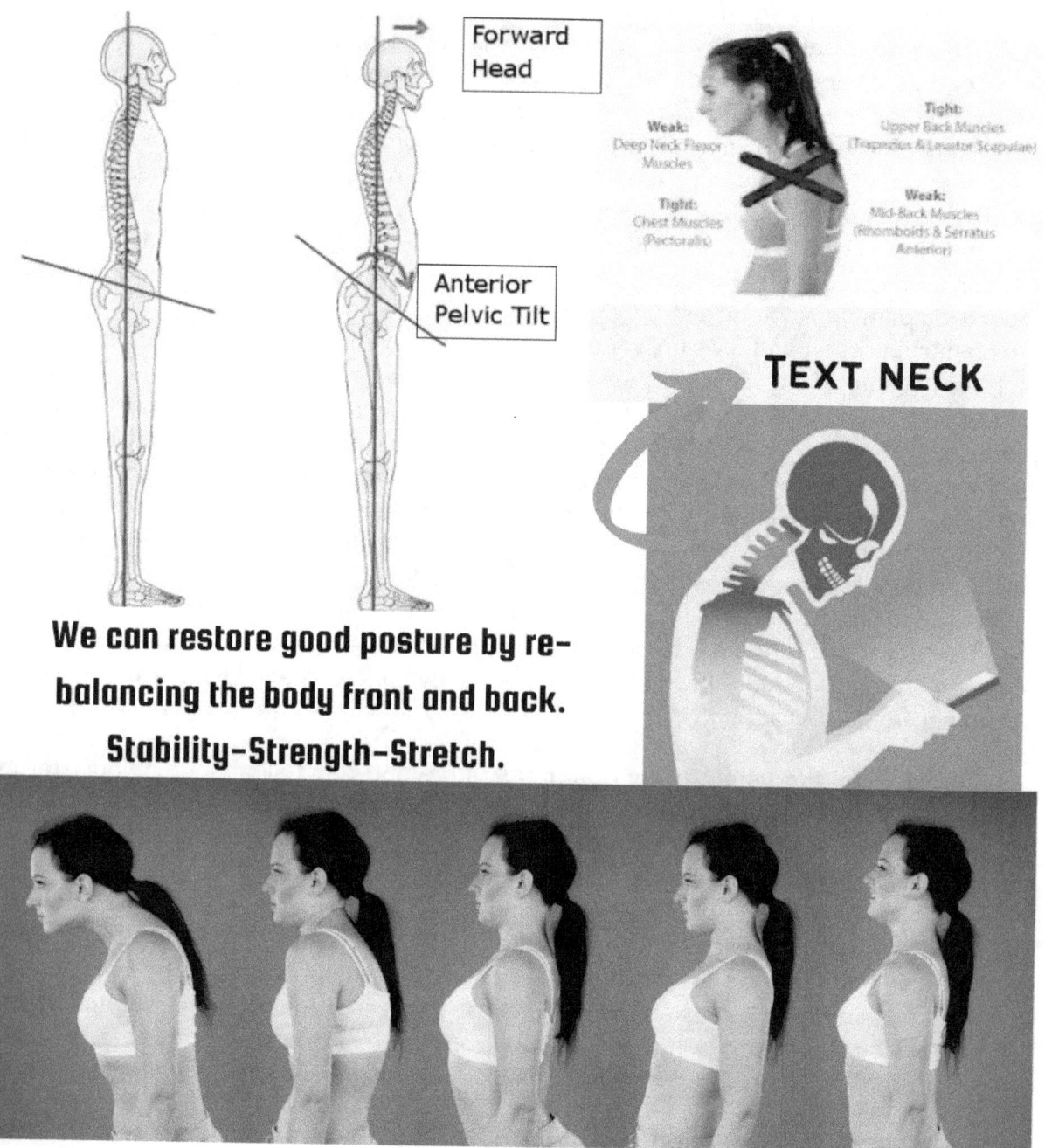

Forward Head

Anterior Pelvic Tilt

Weak:
Deep Neck Flexor Muscles

Tight:
Chest Muscles (Pectoralis)

Tight:
Upper Back Muscles (Trapezius & Levator Scapulae)

Weak:
Mid-Back Muscles (Rhomboids & Serratus Anterior)

TEXT NECK

We can restore good posture by re-balancing the body front and back.
Stability–Strength–Stretch.

2. **Shoulder articulation and shoulder motion**: Ideally, before starting to build strength in the larger muscles that surround the shoulder, the first mission is to assess whether the joints themselves move and articulate normally. You'll learn more about this in the next chapter when I present some mobility-oriented movement "snacks" designed to get you moving on a daily basis. A few of these do focus in on shoulder motion.

3. **Basic core engagement**: Debbie's low-back was very tight and sore, in part because it was being asked to do lots of "work" to stabilize her trunk and shoulders. In other words, her low-back was "compensating" for an unstable core and trunk. The front of her body and deep inside her "core" weren't doing their job. Without good core engagement and stability of the trunk, other areas of the body (like the low-back) will be asked to do more than they should do. You'll learn more about this in the upcoming chapter on *How to Improve Your Stability.*

4. **Shoulder joint stability:** Similar to #2, improving the strength of the larger muscles around the shoulder without first establishing and training stability of the joints themselves, is a recipe for more pain. Stability simply means *control*. In the case of the shoulder, it means the smaller muscles surrounding the joint capsules that are attached to the various bones nearby are all doing their job. When they are, the joint can move freely without pain or impingement. One of the keys to training stability is making sure the exercises don't require much strength, because when they do require lots of force, inevitably the larger muscles have to kick in and compensate.

Taken individually, each of these four movement skills might not be a huge deal, but together, they add up and will jeopardize Debbie's long-term improvement. This is a recurring theme throughout this section because it's often something that is skipped over in other fitness programs and in physical therapy. To put it simply, your body is a little bit like a "union work shop." That is, every area has a responsibility to the whole. If one area isn't doing what it is supposed to, something else has to "pick up the slack." My goal with this chapter and the two that follow is to teach you a few basic but critically important skills so you can feel better and improve your health. I won't teach you every single thing you might want to know, but it will be enough to get you started and on the right path.

When you establish a good baseline of fundamental movement skills, you'll improve more quickly and be able to tackle more challenging exercises without recurrent issues or pain. You get better, faster, and stay that way!

You can practice shooting eight hours a day, but if your technique is wrong, then all you become is very good at shooting the wrong way. Get the fundamentals down and the level of everything you do will rise.

– Michael Jordan

Wisdom from the G.O.A.T.

I'm not sure about you, but I've been a basketball fan since I was a kid. For me, the really fun years were the 1980s. Of course, anyone who knows me knows I'm a Celtics fan. Those Lakers and Celtics battles were fun and so intense!

1% DAILY

YOUR SKILL

TODAY

1 YEAR LATER

A few years ago, a miniseries came on Netflix and ESPN called *The Last Dance*. In case you aren't into these kinds of things, *The Last Dance* is a documentary on the 1997-1998 Chicago Bulls and naturally features Michael Jordan.

Even though he's been retired from the game for a while now, I assume you know who Michael Jordan is. ☺ Most experts on the game of basketball believe "MJ" is the greatest player of all time.

So why am I bringing up a basketball player in a chapter about movement? I figured we could begin by taking a lesson (or two) from a guy who's considered to be *the best* ever or greatest of all time. Not only that, we might also learn from his trainer; the person who worked with him on the "movement" side for fifteen years to help him survive and thrive amidst the rigors of NBA basketball. Just so you know, me sharing this isn't meant to convey that any of us should train like an elite athlete does, or to make you believe you'll get the same results. Rather, it's about what we can learn from his approach, especially as it relates to the basics and fundamentals. After all, given MJ's GOAT status and the fact he was able to achieve incredibly acrobatic, mind-blowing skills on a basketball court, we might assume he never thought much about something as trivial and "easy" as the basics and fundamentals, right?

It just so happens, Mike's trainer, Tim Grover, was interviewed in a video magazine called *GQ Sports*. You can check out the entire interview on YouTube if you'd like – it's called *How Michael Jordan's Trainer Helped Him Become the GOAT*.[4] So, what did Tim have to say about working as MJ's trainer for 15 years? Not surprisingly (to me anyway), Tim said, "the basics and fundamentals, first." Tim felt this was the one thing that helped make MJ the very best at his craft. And it also reflected his own approach to fitness. To save time and also help you get the most from what Tim shared, I'm going to highlight the most important parts of the interview. The numbers inside of the parentheses indicate where during the interview the quote is said, in case you want to hear the actual quotes. Keep reading!

(2:45) "I don't care how fast you are, how high you are, I said none of that matters if you're constantly injured, if you're starting to have little nagging injuries. He was very susceptible to groin pulls and ankle injuries, so I said, let's address those things first."

(3:10) "The healthier you are, the better you'll be able to play. Let's worry about being quicker, stronger, faster, later. Most people put the concept of, we need to make you quicker, stronger, faster, first. The quicker, stronger, faster you make an individual, the more susceptible they are to injury." (3:35) "So my big philosophy was, ok let's deal with the injuries you have, let's take care of those things, first. Doing that...the healthier you get, it's automatically going to improve your game."

(4:30) "Everyone knows Michael is a huge foundation and fundamentals guy. All the crazy stuff you see him doing in the air, all the fancy moves, he never practiced those - he practiced the fundamentals, because he knew if he mastered the fundamentals, mastered the foundation, those other moves would automatically come. That was the same philosophy I had. We started out with the basic compound movements..."

And that's only 5 minutes into a 24-minute interview! Definitely listen in. So, can you guess why I shared this somewhat surprising interview with you in Part 3 of this book focusing on movement? I say surprising because when most people think of Michael Jordan, I don't believe they think of him relentlessly practicing *fundamental movement skills* like those I'll teach you in this book. Rather, they imagine he was probably running up and down the court all day shooting and dunking the ball.

The thing is, just like YOU - the basketball GOAT himself, Michael Jordan, *realizes we are only ever going to be as good and as healthy as our foundation is solid, stable, and strong.* **Success in sport, in life, and especially when it comes to aging well and going the distance will always come back to the basics and fundamentals, first, my friend.** MJ knew it. And now you do, too.

Failure is a few errors in judgement repeated every day.
Success is a few simple disciplines practiced every day. Subtle difference!
— *Jim Rohn*

One last thing before moving on to the next chapter. Get absolutely clear about what you want. **Clarity** is not just something to strive for. It's essential for success, regardless of how you define it. **Clarity** creates *simplicity* and *focus*. Simplicity and focus make *daily action* easier.

Action produces *momentum*. Momentum leads to *more action*. And ultimately, to the *results* you desire. Go ahead, say it with me. *Clarity*.

Decide to get clear about what you want. And then go after it relentlessly. If you do, I know you can't be stopped. I truly believe in you!

CHAPTER 20

HOW TO IMPROVE YOUR STABILITY

Take the words **success** and *failure* out
of your vocabulary.

Replace them with **honesty** and **effort**.

The words success and failure share a
common denominator. Both are temporary.

- unknown

> *Don't pour water into a leaky bucket.*
> – unknown

Way back when I first started running in the early 1980s, I knew very little about the human body and while I had heard the word "core," I figured it was an industry buzzword used by the folks who write those work-out magazines featuring six-pack abs.

As the years went on, I learned more about what the "core" actually is and how important it is if we want to stay active and maintain our quality of life as the years add up. Thinking back on the years I worked in our Pursuit Athletic Performance gait analysis lab, helping people get healthier after their injuries, let's just say there was a lot of focus and learning relating to our core.

In this chapter, you will learn:

1. What the "core" is and why it matters.
2. What "stability" is and why it matters.
3. How to find a "neutral" pelvic position so you can practice core stability.
4. How to create a basic abdominal brace.
5. How to do a different (yet similar) exercise where you can practice what you learned and begin to apply it in progressively challenging ways.

The first three concepts will give you a basic understanding of the "why," so you're empowered to move forward and act. Number four will teach you how to create a basic abdominal brace (aka "ab-brace"), the starting point for learning the most basic way to create stability. It provides the platform for more advanced dynamic exercises, so it's the ideal place to begin with our stability practice. We will finish with a more dynamic exercise as a path to practicing and improving stability.

It's not a coincidence that I use the word "practice." In this chapter, you will learn a new set of skills. That means in the beginning, you might struggle to get the hang of it, but with mindful attention to detail, your skills will improve. As with all "skills," the more you practice these movements, the better you'll get at them. As you practice, you'll get more in tune with your body. For some, this may be the first time they're actually experimenting with their body and moving around to find certain positions. It will be fun!

As you read, don't be overwhelmed by the amount of information. You can always come back to this at a later time. Remember, you're in charge. You decide how fast and how far you want to go with this practice. You can take your time and learn it gradually, or if you're more anxious, fast-track learning the basics and then continue your training with one of the programs online at Pursuit Athletic Performance. It's all up to you!

KEY CONCEPT: Know Thyself.

We should all make it our goal to know our body better than we know anything else, as it's the only one we'll ever get.

It's the "vehicle" that will take us everywhere we want to go in life.

You can't shoot a cannon off of a canoe.

—unknown

Before we learn how to establish stability, I'm guessing that some of you are wondering why you need to learn how to improve core stability? How is this directly related to aging well, being able to live your best life and go the distance?

The typical path many people follow as they reach their later years is to gradually (and painfully) lose their ability to move freely. Tiny little irritating "twinges" when you're in your 40s, can turn into chronic debilitating pain in your 50s and 60s. And it often gets worse. Pain and dysfunction rob you of the chance to enjoy life. Even with repeated visits to the chiropractor and your daily dose of ibuprofen, if you can't move around without some kind of pain, life won't be as enjoyable as it could be. It doesn't have to be that way. And that's what THIS chapter is all about.

If you want to be able to move without pain and enjoy life right up until the last day, you need all your body parts to do their job. Your body, in many ways, is just like a "union shop." Each area or part has a specific function that contributes to the success of the whole. And it all begins with how well we function at the center of our body.

You see, when the middle of our body, specifically the area around our pelvis and trunk right up to our neck, stops functioning the way it was designed to (and how it did when we were much younger), *compensation* rears its ugly head. Compensation is simply when one part of your body has to pick up the slack for another that isn't doing its job. For example, when your core isn't stable, the low-back or the thigh muscles, such as the hamstring or quadricep have to "tighten up" to help restore balance and keep you upright. Since those muscles aren't designed to do that job, the result may be pain or injury.

This kind of low-back compensation can happen as a result of the hips and butt muscles not being stable. The low-back is now forced to "pretend" to be your butt! In fact, much of the chronic low-back pain that so many people in the U.S. experience is due to *compensation*. When the hips and core, also referred to as the trunk, aren't doing their jobs, something else has to pick up the slack, and unfortunately it's often the tiny muscles of the low back that aren't designed for it!

Your *Brain* Doesn't Care How Your *Body* Accomplishes a Task.

The definition for compensation that applies in this context is, "to offset an error, defect, or undesired effect." In other words, to have to make up for something that isn't acting as it should. The human body is a very good compensator. Sometimes it's a wonderful thing, as in the case of someone recovering from a traumatic brain injury. With time and persistence, the person can often recover much of what they lost as a result of the injury. That's the positive side of *compensation* in action.

One of your brain's primary "jobs" is to execute whatever it is you want it to. It doesn't necessarily care how you do it. For example, if you sprain your ankle and limp slightly, the other parts of your body may have to function differently so you can walk. If that ankle doesn't heal as well as it should so it's exactly like it was before the sprain, the way you move has now changed. This is how wear and tear and repeat injuries occur.

As we go through the process of learning what stability is and then practice it, we're relearning something which happened authentically when we were infants. We didn't consciously think about it or try to do it then. It happened as a byproduct of normal growth and development. The great news is that our nervous system learns quickly. And with repetition, it remembers. Especially with our newfound awareness of how things actually *should* feel.

The Four Stages of Learning:

The learning process requires patience and persistence. As we go through that process, we're actually moving through the "four stages of learning." Our primary goal with any new skill is to get to the point where the skill happens automatically, with ease. That is, unconsciously, where we can perform the skill without even thinking about it; where our body just "does it" without having to narrow our focus on it. That is the last stage of learning, stage four.

Think of typing or playing a musical instrument or some kind of sports skill. For example, if you have been typing on a keyboard for years, you probably don't have to think about it anymore. Your fingers just go to the right key without any extra focus. Movement skills are no different!

Here is the way I think of these four stages. Remember these and focus on being where you are throughout the learning journey!

Stage 1: *Unconscious* Incompetence: In the beginning, we are neither skilled nor even aware of how our skill is lacking. Naturally, the only way we can move to the next stage is to become more *aware*. This is how the learning process begins. The truth is most people don't even know what they don't know. ☺ This describes stage one. There's always hope though. A desire to learn takes us to stage two.

Stage 2: *Conscious* Incompetence: We enter stage two when we start to *become aware* of what we don't know and can't do very well. *This is where most of the intellectual learning happens.* For example, right now you're reading this book and as you ponder the concepts I'm presenting, you're becoming more aware of things you may not have thought about before. Of course, becoming more enlightened can be a "double edged sword," as sometimes the more we learn and begin to understand, the more we realize we don't know! In that sense, the saying "ignorance is bliss" can feel true. Don't let yourself become frustrated. Enjoy the journey! Embrace the opportunities that lie ahead due to your newfound knowledge and skills! We want to become more aware of the things we need to know and the skills we eventually want to master.

Stage 3: Conscious Competence: When we put into practice and apply what we've learned, we're at stage three! This is where we are "dancing on the edge of our ability," so to speak. We try to improve, but often fail and have to go back and try again. Tiny little victories give us hope. Yet we're also frustrated at times as the skill may require a lot of conscious focus. It's normal to feel frustrated as we learn something new. We always want progress to happen more quickly than it does. The key at this stage is practice, practice, practice. Perfect practice at the most basic level is how we develop good habits to build on. The better and more frequently we practice, the sooner we reach that final stage where those skills happen unconsciously.

Stage 4: Unconscious Competence: This is our target. We know we've reached stage four when our practice isn't nearly as difficult and doesn't require as much focus. We experience more tiny victories and should feel very good about ourselves. Provided we are grooving those skills in the right way with mindful repetition, we've now set the stage to learn even more dynamic and challenging skills. This is fun! Keep at it!

So, What Is Our "Core" Anyway?

If you ever wanted to experience a heated "discussion" where there might never be complete agreement or one single "right" answer, get a bunch of fitness experts (coaches, trainers, physical therapists, you name it) around a table and ask them each to describe exactly what the "core" is. Holy smokes, talk about fireworks! ☺

They will all have their own opinion and passionately swear by it. There might even be those who say the "core" doesn't exist, or that it can't be defined anatomically. So, let's start right now by acknowledging the "core" can (and will probably always) be defined *differently depending upon the point of view of the person defining it.*

The Core is YOUR FOUNDATION.

The simplest way to think of your "core" or trunk is to think of a barrel. This barrel gives your body an "anchor" or platform for your arms and legs, so they can move freely, forward and backward and every which way. Obviously, we move our arms and legs to get from one place to another, to create balance and rhythm and to generate force, speed and power, regardless of the sport or activity. This barrel (your core) also helps absorb and resist the forces acting on it as you run or do any other physical activity.

When functioning well, the *integration* and *support* the core provides allow for the efficient transfer of energy through your body. That one single sentence is worth reading a few times over. In essence, it means your trunk or core is a transfer station for energy from one side of your body to the other. If you understand this and apply it in all your practice, it will make a huge difference in your success.

Some people think of the "core" as isolated abdominal muscles such as "obliques" or the "rectus abs" that make up that infamous "6-pack" many people long for. But your core is far more than some superficial muscles on the front or side of your body. In fact, *at the very least* your core is the ENTIRE trunk from your hips and pelvis to your neck and cervical spine.

Regardless of how it's defined, the point is the core creates *integration* and a *foundation* for everything we do, whether it's gardening, riding a bike, or simply being active.

The function of the core has little to do specifically with sport. It's not about being a runner, it's about being able to do all the things you love to do for the rest of your life.

What Is the True Purpose of Core Training?

The answer to this question is simple and important. It's the KEY to understanding what you MUST KNOW to get the most from the exercises I will teach you. **The primary function of your core is to stop or control motion, NOT to create it.** *It does that by way of stability first, and strength second.*

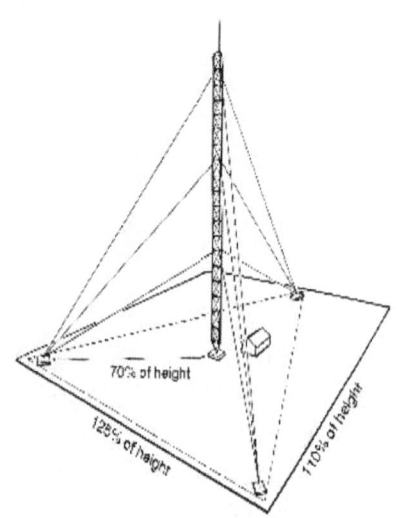

The definition of **stability** in the context of movement is to ***stop or control motion in one area of the body in the presence of motion somewhere else in the body.***

Think of the guy wires attached to a large tower. (See the picture here). You've seen these towers where you live. The base of the tower is attached and solid, but without those guy wires running from the base to help control the position of the tower as the wind is blowing in all directions, it likely wouldn't stay up straight for very long. Our body is somewhat the same way.

For our purposes right now, the pelvic girdle would be the tower – it is the center of our body. It's the base of support for when our arms and legs are swinging around as part of normal, daily life, or when we're running, jumping, or riding a bike. Let me repeat: **The core's primary function is to STOP or control motion, NOT create it.**

THE REAL PURPOSE OF CORE TRAINING?

...TO STOP OR CONTROL MOTION, NOT TO CREATE IT

`01:01`

Your core works *reactively and synergistically*, just like the tower and guy wires, to make sure when you're moving around, the only parts of your body that are moving are the parts that are *supposed* to be moving. For the most part that would be your arms, legs, and hips!

Your Core MUST Be Stable.

I've tossed around the word stability quite a bit in the introduction to this part of the book and in this chapter. I have also repeated your **core's primary function is to STOP or control motion, NOT create it.**

The next and most important concept then, is to understand the **first (and primary) goal of the core training you do is to create STABILITY.**

Creating STABILITY: Why Does This Matter?

Think of it this way: your core is the anchor for how you **transfer power** to your arms and legs, while making sure each body part does only its job, and not the job of any other part. That's a critically important concept, because *compensation* (one body part compensating for another, or trying to do another part's job) is what **frequently leads to injury.**

Stability is about tying everything together in a balanced way, making sure everything is working synergistically and symbiotically. It's very much akin to a large group of rowers all in a boat *pulling as one single unit or person,* to get the boat across the water more quickly and efficiently.

Without *stability* in the trunk and pelvis, your big prime-mover muscles like the glutes, quads, hamstrings, and lats can't function as they should to help you move. The more stable your core is, the better all the smaller AND larger muscles and connective tissue **work together as a synchronous integrated unit. Creating good stability is analogous to a** perfectly functioning sailboat where every rope (and the sails attached to them) have just the right amount of tension and freedom of motion to do their thing as efficiently and effectively as possible.

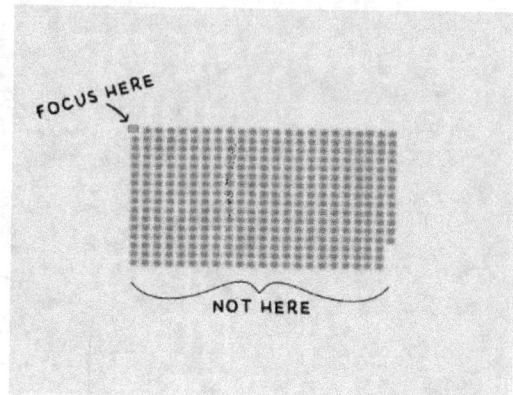

FOCUS HERE

NOT HERE

Working the "Abs"?

Traditional "ab" exercises like sit-ups and crunches are, shall I say, rather DUMB exercises. Why?

Consider again the actual role your core (which is your foundation) plays in how efficiently and effectively you move. When these types of exercises are done in the traditional way, they *initiate motion of the core rather than train it to* **STOP or control motion,** which is its true function. Do you see the difference?

Training abdominal muscles in isolation has no relationship whatsoever to core stability. Exercises like these allow motion to occur through the lumbar spine, negating the functional purpose of that area of the body.

The lumbar spine is not meant to *greatly* twist and flex, and the discs in the back are harmed by those movements. Sit-ups and crunches and the like are completely counterproductive to your goal of becoming a better, healthier human being.

Key Concept:

The Front Plank Exercise Doesn't Improve Core Stability

The Front Plank Is A Dumb Exercise

Here's Why...

As an exercise to improve core stability, the front plank is a terrible choice. Sure, you can create a burn with this exercise and you'll certainly work up a sweat if you do it to extreme. But is that your only goal?

Training the core and your trunk should first be about improving the stability of it. Stability is about timing - it's about all of the muscles around your trunk working together. It's NOT just the strength of the abdomen. And this exercise just doesn't meet the criteria for being able to learn and train that timing and coordination. Why?

You are maintaining four contact points on the ground and as a result, not challenging the core to "stabilize" by keeping only three points of contact with the ground, maintaining stillness, and then moving your arms and legs around that still core.

Is There a Difference Between Core "Stability" and Core "Strength"?

The simple answer is yes, and the difference is critical for you to determine how you're going to approach exercise. It will also determine the benefits you get from that exercise. So, what are the differences?

- **Stability,** sometimes referred to as *motor control*, is *neurological*. **It happens in the brain.** It also happens in your joints and spinal cord. Training stability is essentially "brain training." In other words, it's about neural communication between all the parts of your body starting with your brain and joints.
- **On the other hand, strength** is simply the ability for tissue (or tissues) to *generate force*. It's primarily about **muscle adaptation and growth**. Training strength means forcing recruitment of increasing numbers of motor units within muscle tissue. This forces the body to adapt and get stronger due to increased demands on the tissue.

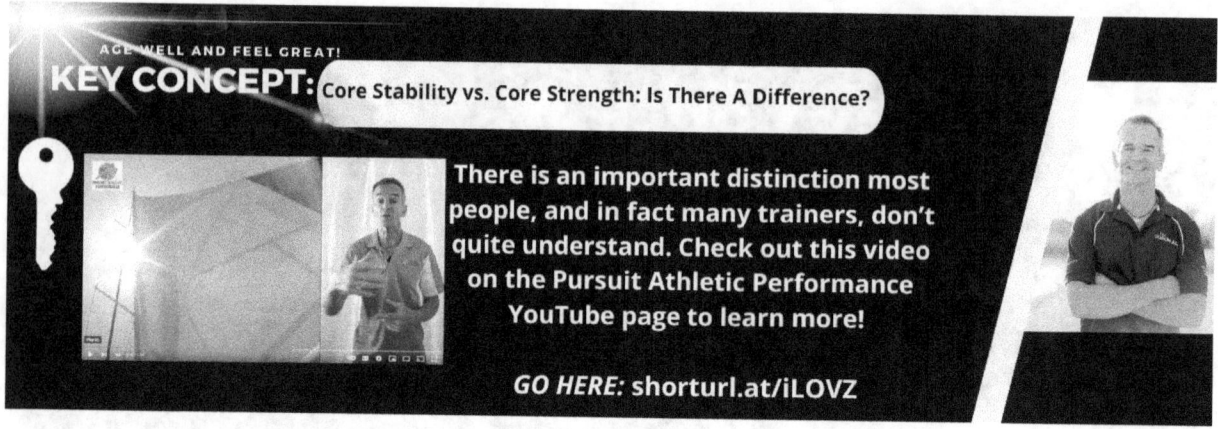

We create stability in our "core" from one shoulder to the opposite hip. The term often used to describe this is the "Serape Effect."[1] It all begins when we are tiny children learning that basic cross-crawl coordination that allows us to first roll, then crawl, and finally walk. The stiffness and integration from your core that develops from appropriate movement practice comes from the diagonal (and spiral) orientation of the tissues from one hip to the opposite shoulder.

To see how this works, check out the image just below, in particular the colored areas of blue and pink forming a corset of sorts around the trunk.

It's the basis for the hip power that helps you do whatever activities you like to do, whether it's running, riding a bike, or playing with your grandkids, safely and efficiently.

Two Things That Make All the Difference.

When you understand stability is neurological - it's in your brain and your joints, and thus core stability training is first and foremost, **brain training and joint training**, you can easily see how important it is to start at the true beginning and build skills the right way from the outset, performing each phase of the movement as well as you can.

Serape Effect

1. **You need to start at the *beginning*.** You should master the first steps, first. Then you're ready to move on and progress to something more challenging.

2. **You should perform each phase of the movement as "perfectly" as you can.** To change behavior (in this case, your stability), you must change the neural engram or existing patterning in the brain. You need a little movement "amnesia" and "re-programming." That can only happen successfully when the new, more desirable pattern, is performed as well as it can be, at a level that is attainable.

What's the Purpose of *All* This Information?

The simple reason I am sharing this information with you is this: Regardless of the skill or practice, I believe it's always more helpful when you truly understand why you're doing what you're doing, you know? When you understand the philosophy and know WHY you're doing any skill, you are guaranteed to bring more energy and enthusiasm to your practice and fully embrace it. Do you need to understand every nuance of the science right now to progress successfully? Absolutely not. You can jump right in and get to work...but...

There's an almost irrefutable truth and training principle that succinctly expresses the WHY behind this type of smart training:

Whether our goal is to simply continue to feel good as we age, or we want to avoid injury and be active right up until the last day - our entire body needs to function as a single integrated unit. Head to toe, top to bottom, inside and out, all working together in synchronous harmony.

With that being said, in this chapter, I will teach you three different skills. They are:

1.   How to establish a neutral pelvic position.
2.   How to create a basic abdominal brace.
3.   How to perform a basic quadraped, or "bird dog."

Each of these skills (when progressed smartly through each phase) will help you create core stability at a basic fundamental level and build a body that functions as a single integrated unit.

In this chapter you will learn:

•   How to set up each movement, then
•   How to create basic stability, and finally
•   How to advance the exercises by adding more dynamic movements.

Age Well and Feel Great!
Key Concept:

Stability: Are You Pulling My Leg?

Stability isn't just about what all the muscles do around the core, it is also very much dependent on having good sensory input.

That simply means having good communication and information entering the body, usually through our feet. That sensory input alerts the central nervous system about interaction between the body and the environment, providing constant feedback and allowing refinement of movement.[2]

We are going to talk a lot more about this sensory input when we get to Chapter 21, How to Improve Your Feet.

STABILITY GOAL #1 Is Learning How to Establish a *Neutral Position.*

In order to get the most from your stability practice, you will need to get into a (relatively) neutral spinal position, specifically around your hips and pelvis. This might sound simple enough, but working with people from all walks of life and all age groups over the past 20 years, I've learned how difficult it is for many people to have good awareness of their body in space. Having a good general sense of the position of your pelvis in particular – as the *center of your body*, is a great place to begin.

At this point, it's important to remember we're all unique and different, especially when looking at our spine and the shape of our body. Yet, at the risk of overstating the obvious, we're all human beings. The point being:

- We are all unique and have unique shapes to our spines. Not every person's "neutral" position will be the same.
- As you read and learn and practice, don't force anything. You're in charge of how fast and how far you go. No one else. Focus on the concept or idea behind what

you're exploring rather than try to get into an exact position. Learning these skills is meant to be a good *starting point*.

- Your goal is to learn how to *dissociate* the upper, middle, and lower portions of your spine, so you can ultimately find "neutral" with your lower (lumbar) spine. This image clipped from one of my instructional videos shows each of these three positions, commonly referred to as your cervical, thoracic, and lumbar spines. You will focus most of your attention on the area in green as you go through this process.

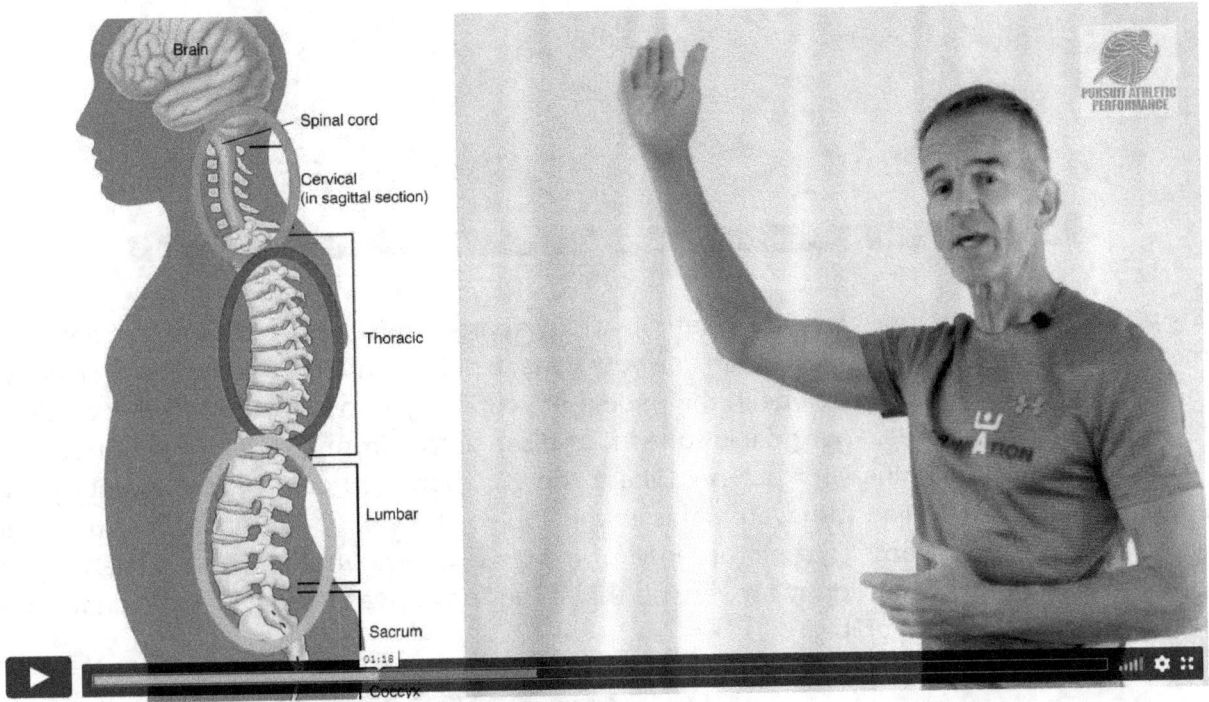

You will have to move around a little bit to find what YOUR neutral pelvic position is.

If you find your hips and back are tight and it's not easy to move around as a result, that's OK! The image below, again clipped from an instructional video, shows from the side how you can tilt your pelvis forward and backward to find "neutral." Explore, have fun with it! Keep reading to learn more.

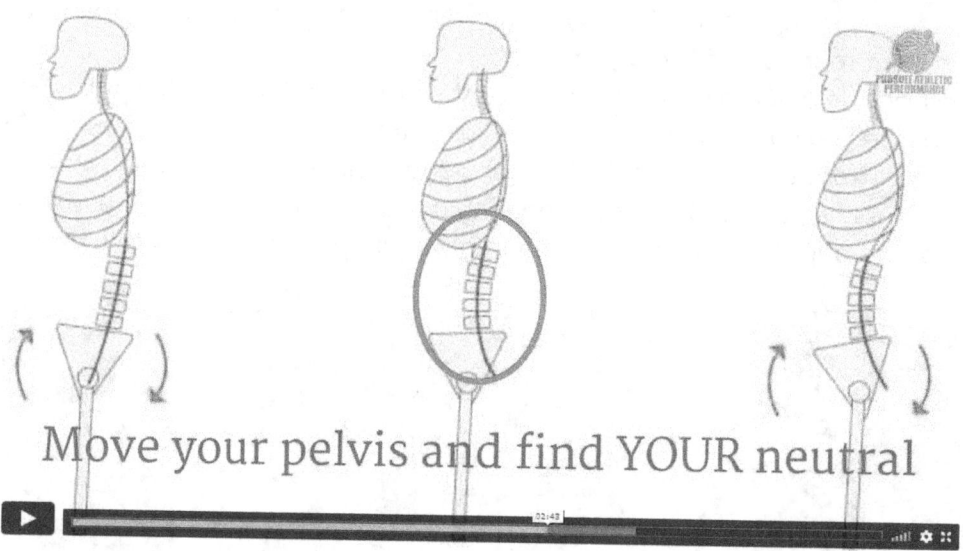

Move your pelvis and find YOUR neutral

Step 1: Stand up straight with your feet hip width apart. It may help to stand in front of a mirror as you are doing this, so you can use your eyes to help "connect" the dots. When ready, locate your pelvis - the large bone in the middle of your body - and start to MOVE it around, forwards and backwards. Your goal is to learn to dissociate it from the rest of your body.

It may help to imagine your pelvis is like a "bowl" where you can "hinge" at your hips. Imagine the "bowl" is filled with water. This image you see here clipped from an instructional video may help you create that picture in your mind's eye. A *neutral position* is likely to be where the "bowl" is tilted slightly forward so that if the "bowl" was filled with water, a tiny bit might leak out the front of it.

Your "pelvic bowl"

Imagine for a second that your PELVIS is like a BOWL, hinging at the hip. Imagine it is filled with water...

This might feel strange because most of us don't spend much time moving around this way. Don't let that stop you from staying with it. The more you move, the easier it will feel, and the more you'll be able to discern the different parts of your spine and see how each part can move independently, yet all together.

Once you've moved around and can find the extremes on each end, you will be ready to move on to Step 2.

Step 2: As you move front and back and your hips start to loosen up, see where the middle is between the two extreme forward and backward positions. Remember as I said earlier, we are focusing primarily on your lower, lumbar spine area. **This is likely where YOUR neutral spine position is.** For most people, this position will result in having a *slight inward curve in the low-back.* Again, remember we're all unique. Some may have a slightly larger curve, and still others might have less. Our spines are unique to each of us.

OK, let's review what we have covered to this point:

Step 1: MOVE! Explore and experiment with moving your pelvis forward and backward. Move the "bowl" so it is tilting in both directions, forward and backward. Learn to dissociate your pelvis from the other parts of your spine and the rest of your body.

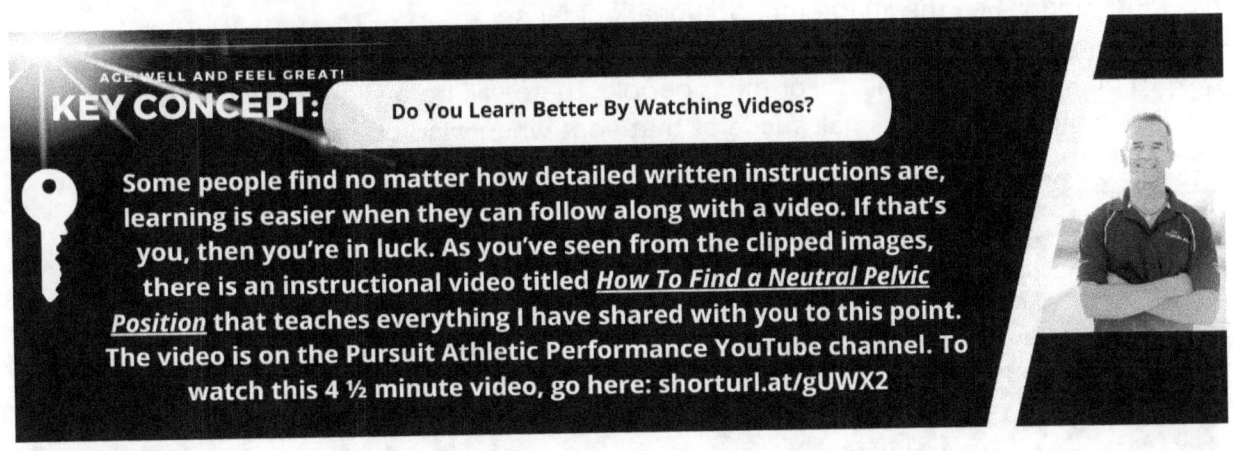

AGE WELL AND FEEL GREAT!

KEY CONCEPT: Do You Learn Better By Watching Videos?

Some people find no matter how detailed written instructions are, learning is easier when they can follow along with a video. If that's you, then you're in luck. As you've seen from the clipped images, there is an instructional video titled *How To Find a Neutral Pelvic Position* that teaches everything I have shared with you to this point. The video is on the Pursuit Athletic Performance YouTube channel. To watch this 4 ½ minute video, go here: shorturl.at/gUWX2

Step 2: Establish YOUR own unique neutral pelvic position. Don't force anything. As you start to loosen up, the middle of the two extreme positions forward and backward is likely a good guesstimate of neutral for you. This position might change depending on how you're feeling, from one day to the next. It's a "moving target," to some degree. The goal is to help you find what **YOUR best starting point is** for learning not only more about your body, but also where to begin when it comes to **stability** of the core and hips.

STABILITY GOAL #2 Is Learning How to Create a Basic Abdominal Brace.

To quickly review, smart core stability training is about *controlling motion*, not creating it. Simply put, **stability starts with *stillness*.** *Especially in your low-back and pelvis.*

The first skill you will now learn after finding your neutral position, is the **Basic Abdominal Brace.** Learning and practicing this skill of creating a slight brace in your lower abdominal area, is the first step to create **stillness** in your core. For our purposes, this **stillness** is measured by the degree of movement (or lack thereof) in your low-back, when performing the exercise.

This is a very simple skill to learn but it isn't always easy, especially at first. It is however, the easiest and best way for your body to learn stability. Why? Because you will be on your back lying on the floor, gravity isn't acting upon your body in the same way as when you're standing or moving in some other way. And because you're only lifting your leg and then extending it, the load placed upon your core (trunk) is small. **Hence, this is the beginning – the easiest and best way to learn how to create a stable core.** Let's get to it and start with Step 1, how to set up the exercise.

Step 1 – Set It Up: Start by lying comfortably on the floor with your feet flat and your knees bent at a comfortable angle. Your arms should be relaxed at your side and your feet about hip width apart. See the image for additional guidance.

Once you get set, go ahead and find that "neutral" low-back pelvic position you just learned how to do. Don't over think it. For most people, there will be a slight curve in the low-back which will mean there's a small space at that spot when lying on the floor.

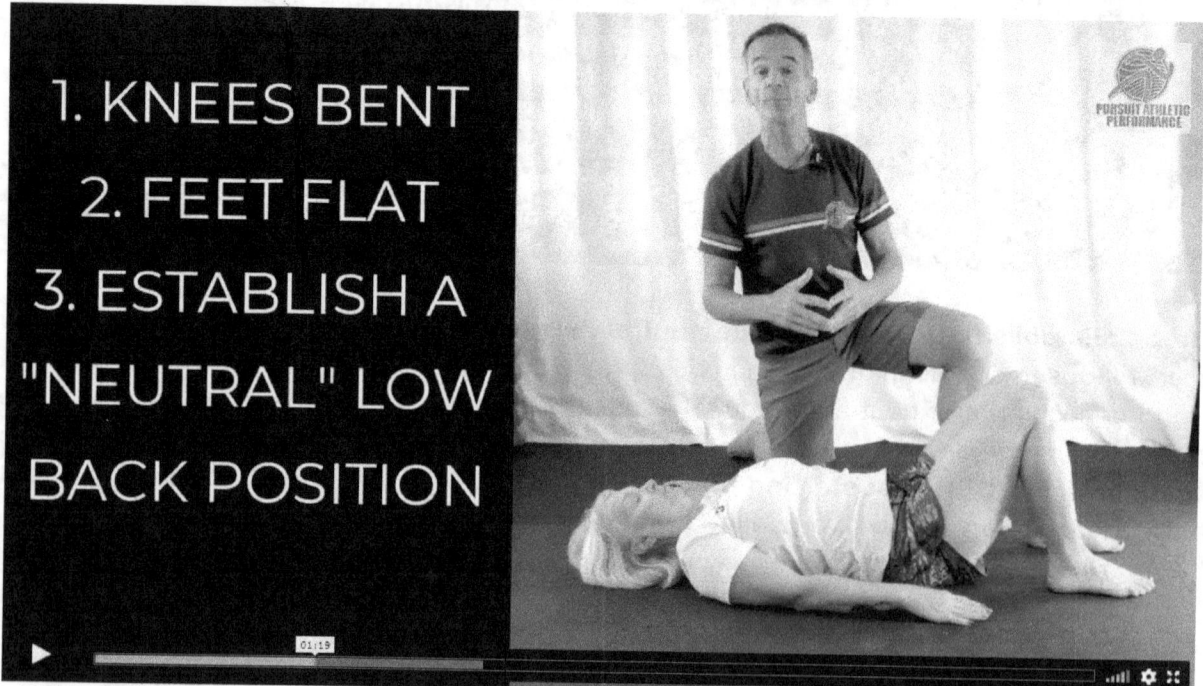

1. KNEES BENT
2. FEET FLAT
3. ESTABLISH A "NEUTRAL" LOW BACK POSITION

Step 2: Practice Creating Your "Ab-Brace:" Create a little bit of stiffness in your lower abdominal area as though you were bracing before being "poked" in the stomach. This isn't a HARD squeeze or "draw-in" at all. It's just a moderate tightening of the lower abdominal area. Simple!

It may feel easier if you hold your breath. And that's OK at first to get the feeling of the brace. Over time and with more practice, see if you can maintain that brace while also breathing normally.

Step 3: Place Your Hands into The Hollow Space You Created When You Found Your Neutral Position. Take note of the amount of pressure on your hands. This will be very important as we get into the exercise.

Now that you've experienced what that "brace" feels like, relax for a moment and place your hands into the hollow space under your low back.

As you move your hands into position, remember your goal is to maintain that same neutral position you found earlier. Your goal is to find neutral, and maintain it throughout the exercise. Good job, you're doing great!

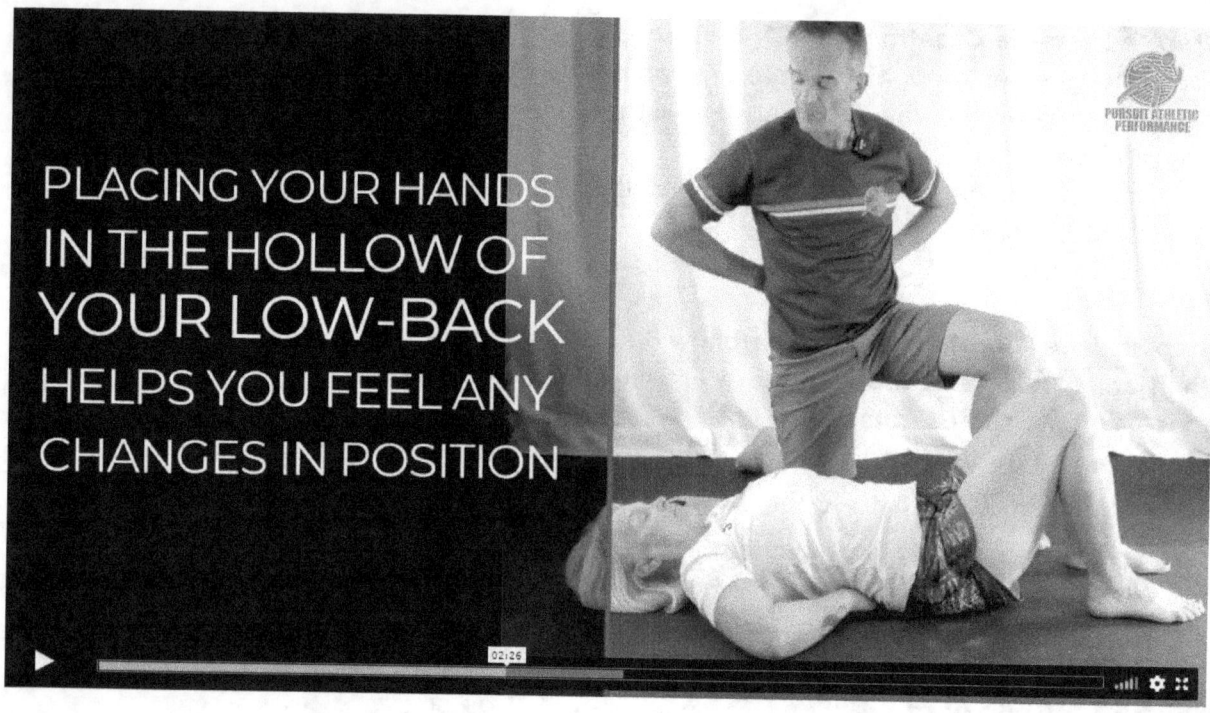

PLACING YOUR HANDS IN THE HOLLOW OF YOUR LOW-BACK HELPS YOU FEEL ANY CHANGES IN POSITION

02:26

Is there a very large space in the hollow of your low back? Or hardly any space at all? Whatever it is you're learning, remember you can always go back to find neutral once again and re-establish it. There's no rush. You're in charge.

You want to be very sensitive to changes in pressure on your hands as you move through the exercise, as this will show you how well you are creating stability!

- *A reduction in pressure* on your hands means you are arching your back and losing your still, stable, low-back position. NOT what you want.
- *An increase in pressure* on your hands means you are flattening your back and again, just like overarching, losing the still and stable position you're looking to maintain.

Take a look at this image. In the skeleton on the right, you can see a large space in the low-back, highlighted by the arrow. This tilts the pelvis forward excessively and isn't what you want.

In the skeleton on the left, you can see there is better vertical orientation and "stacking." Notice the arrows at the front of the abdomen, indicating the moderate brace of the core. This is what you want.

Key Concept:

Finding YOUR Neutral Low-Back Position

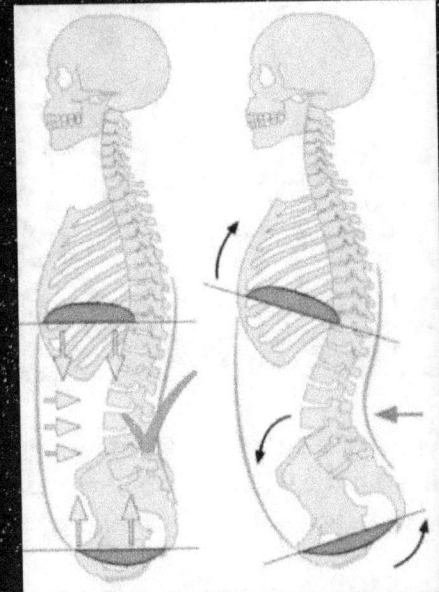

Look at this image to the left of two skeletons.

In the skeleton on the right, you can see a large space in the low-back, highlighted by the arrow. This tilts the pelvis forward excessively and isn't what you want.

In the skeleton on the left, you can see there is better vertical orientation and "stacking." Notice the arrows at the front of the abdomen, indicating the moderate brace of the core. This is what you want.

Step 4: Let's DO the Ab-Brace Exercise and See If We Can Maintain Stillness in Our Low Back!

1. Make sure you are in a neutral position, with your hands under your low-back.

2. Create your "brace," be sure not to change position at all! How will you know? It's simple: **any change in pressure on your hands is a signal your position has changed. If you need to, stop and try again.** Trust me, it's normal to need a few practice reps to get it right. Don't worry, keep it fun. You're learning!

3. When YOU are ready, SLOWLY lift one foot a couple of inches off the floor, pause for a second or two, then return it to the floor. BE VERY sensitive to changes in pressure on your hands. If you sense a change, you need to start over and try again. ☺

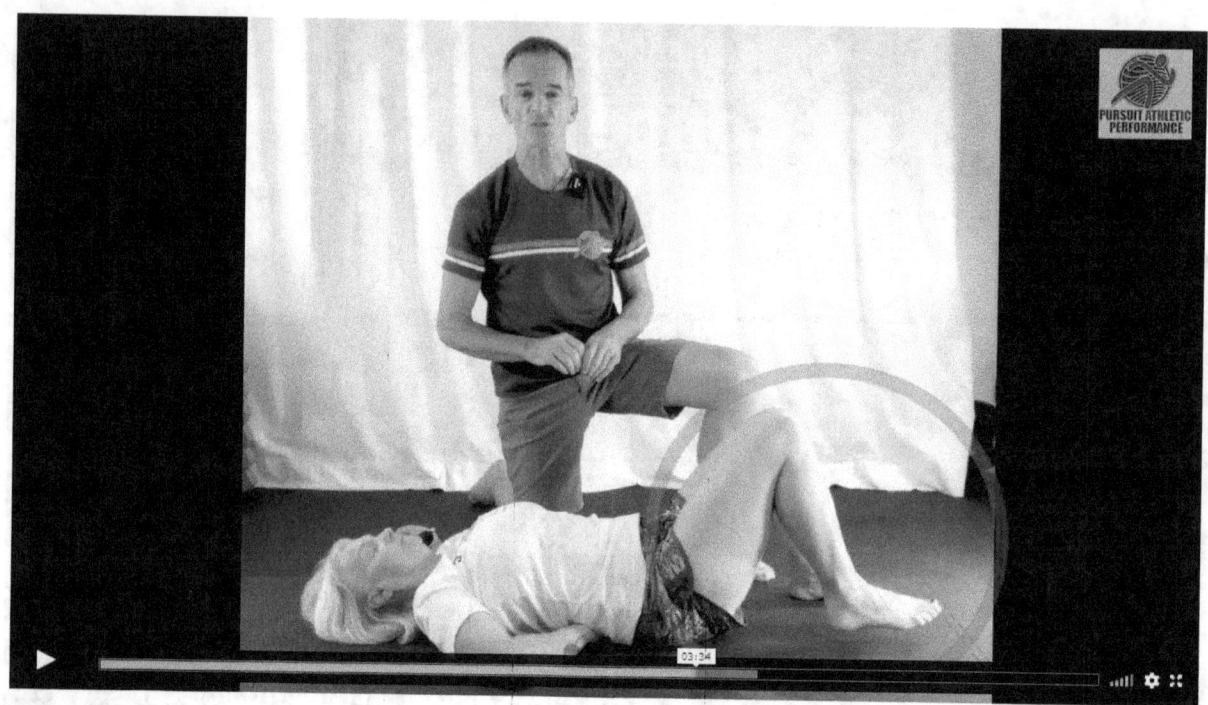

So, what is the most important part of this movement practice? **It's the beginning, right at the moment when you carefully and slowly initiate the lift. That's when the magic happens! Pay attention. Sometimes you will sense a chance when you are just "thinking" about lifting your foot.**

PAY CAREFUL ATTENTION TO THE PRESSURE YOU FEEL WHEN YOU FIRST LIFT YOUR LEG

03:35

This is the moment when you're creating a stable core and learning how to practice and develop it. If in doubt, stop and reset and try again.

Repeat this a few times. Slowly lift your leg and then return it to the floor. Now try the other side. Know right up front it is very common to find that one side is more difficult to maintain stillness, than the other side.

In other words, some differences or an asymmetry is common, although it isn't what you ultimately want. Your goal will be to work on making your "weaker" pattern or side, better! Keep at it!

Be mindful. Your brain, joints, and body are learning! This is truly a whole-body exercise. It isn't about a single body part, it's holistic. Think holistically.

Practice Frequently, and as "Perfectly" as You Can. Since this is the beginning, you want to be sure you get very good at this and make it as good and as natural as you can.

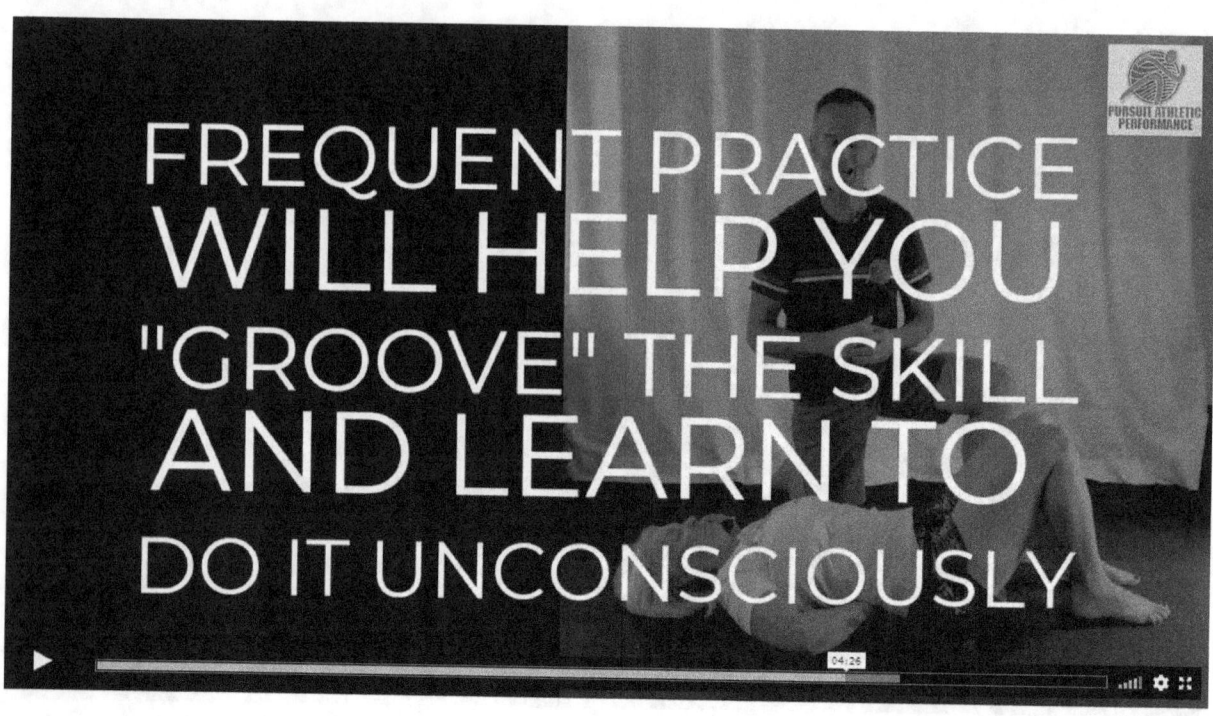

Step 5: Using the Same Approach, Try Extending the Leg. This IS More Challenging to Do Well!

Extending the leg is more challenging because you're moving more of your mass farther from the middle of your body. You're increasing the dynamic load on your core.

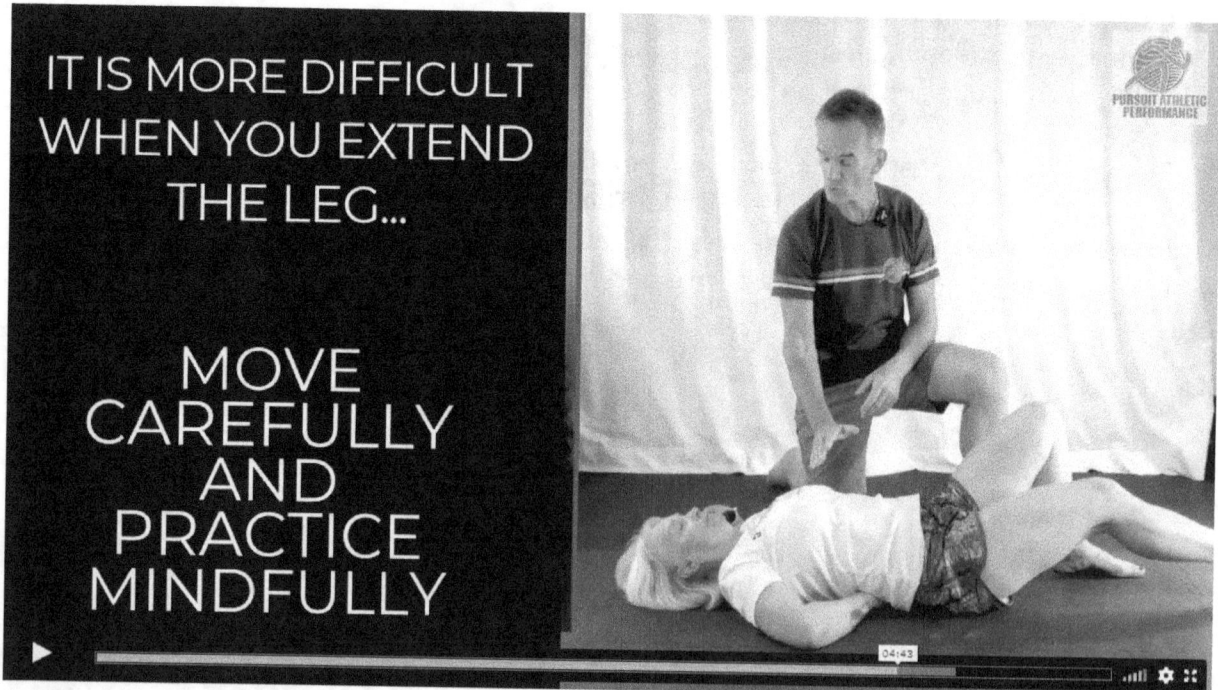

The same goal remains however, which is to make sure there are NO CHANGES IN PRESSURE on your hands.

Maintaining pressure means your low-back is still, which means you are creating good stability throughout your entire core and trunk. ☺

This is the easiest position to learn this important skill. Your goal is to MASTER THIS, then move on to the next exercise. Keep going, you're doing great. Just remember, it is up to you how fast you progress and how far you want to take this. You're in charge!

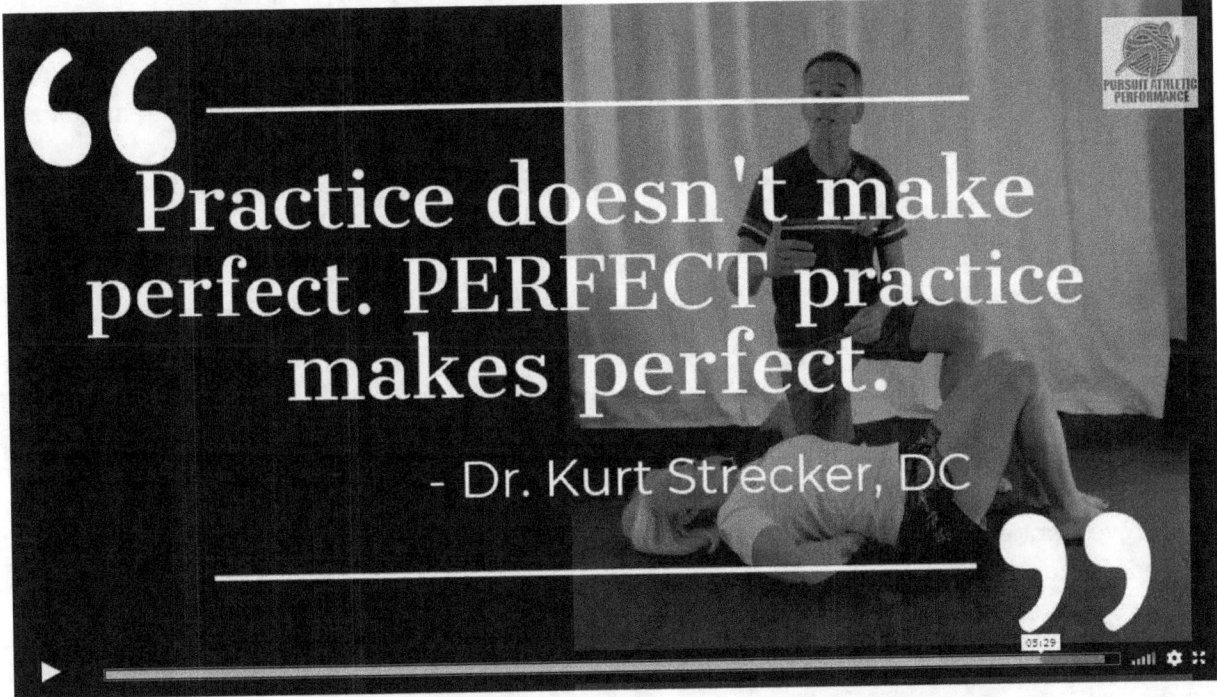

> Practice doesn't make perfect. PERFECT practice makes perfect.
>
> – Dr. Kurt Strecker, DC

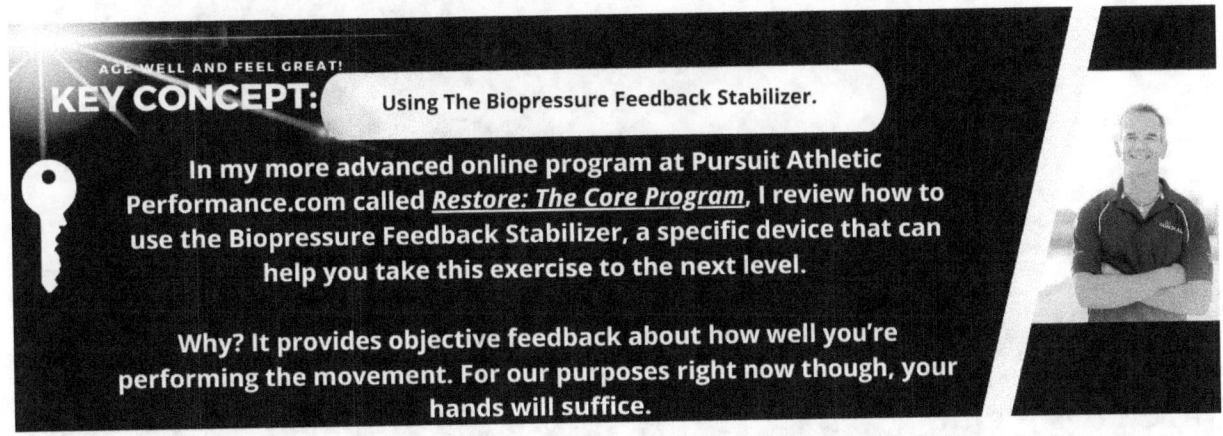

AGE WELL AND FEEL GREAT!

KEY CONCEPT: Using The Biopressure Feedback Stabilizer.

In my more advanced online program at Pursuit Athletic Performance.com called *Restore: The Core Program*, I review how to use the Biopressure Feedback Stabilizer, a specific device that can help you take this exercise to the next level.

Why? It provides objective feedback about how well you're performing the movement. For our purposes right now though, your hands will suffice.

The next step in learning comes when you take what you've learned and practiced and apply it in an exercise. The dynamic challenges are increasing, but I know you're ready for it because you've been reading closely, perhaps even watching the videos online, and you're starting to get the concept of stability – what it means to create STILLNESS instead of motion.

You might even be realizing why a "sit-up," which is one of the old-school ways of training the "core" is actually teaching you to do the OPPOSITE thing you want to do. In a sit-up, you bend at the waist, creating motion through the spine. That's not a stable core! Sure, you might feel a "burn." But is that the goal? No!

You can create a burn doing a lot of different activities and exercises. None will teach you stability at a basic, foundational level. And that matters, a lot. When you learn how to do it the right way from the start, you can progress steadily at your own pace and develop the kind of skill that will truly help you be more durable as you age.

And this IS also the platform we build strength on! You'll learn more about that very important point in the strength portion of the book. Keep going.

So, with that being said, let's move on to the next exercise. If you prefer to watch the video, you can go to the Pursuit Athletic Performance YouTube channel.

Improve Your Stability: The *Basic Prone Quadraped* (also known as a "Bird Dog.")

For our next exercise, you will be down on all fours. If you're thinking this feels like you're going to crawl, you'd be right! And that's not by accident. Crawling is one of the most basic ways we learn stability when we're infants. That "cross-crawl" pattern of hip to opposite shoulder is how we connect and move – right through the middle of our body. It's the *serape effect* you learned about earlier.

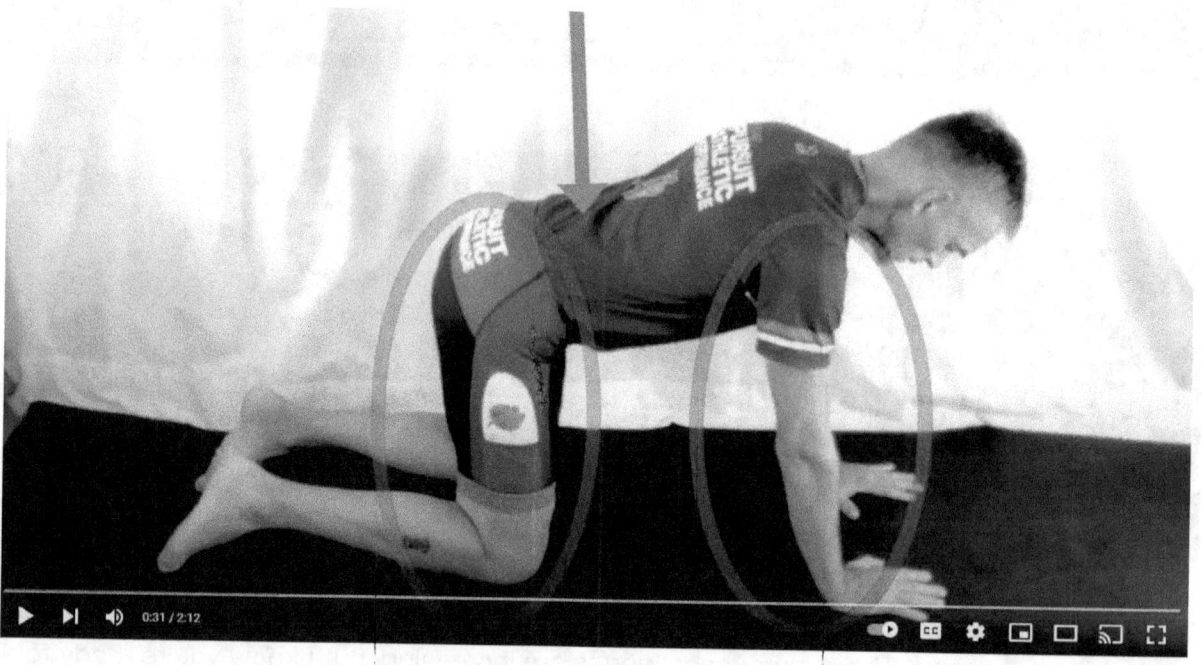

Correct set up is important so you can groove the right groove. As you get into position, make sure to apply the same principles you just learned. **Find that neutral low-back position and create a nice gentle ab-brace. You're going to use all these skills as you create a basic dynamic challenge!**

Stack the shoulders right over your hands and your hips right over your knees. Use extra padding for your knees if you need it. Your knees should be hip width apart. Review the image here and notice the red circles showing the nice vertical alignment of the arms and legs.

So, what is the goal of this exercise? It's simple: **You're moving from a 4-point stance during set up, to a 3-point stance, by moving an arm or a leg.**

This unloading from four points of contact with the ground, to only three points of contact, creates a basic dynamic challenge for your core. Can you remain still around your middle as you move an arm or leg? That's the goal. Nothing else should move except the one part you focus on moving. Here's how:

Step 1: Get yourself set up on all fours. Move your middle around and find that neutral low-back position. Creating a little low abdominal brace (indicated by the red arrow in the picture) will make finding that right position easier. Make sure to keep that brace as you move to step two. Remember it's NOT a large draw-in or a big, forced squeeze. It's a gentle tightening to keep everything still and in place.

Step 2: We'll start with the easiest variation first, which is extending an arm. If it sounds simple, just remember at this most basic level, you're working to move as perfectly as you possibly can. That means absolutely NO MOVEMENT of any kind, other than the reaching arm and shoulder.

- Don't allow your body to twist or rotate.
- Don't move side to side.
- Keep your hands stacked vertically under your shoulders and your knees stacked under your hips.
- Keep your head and neck relaxed and in line with your spine.
- While it isn't easy to see in this photo because of the shirt, I am continuing to maintain a slight curve in my low-back.
- Make sure to practice with both arms. Take note of which side is more difficult. We all have a chocolate and vanilla side! ☺ With every rep, you will learn more about your body and re-develop stability at a truly developmental level.

"Rep" this as often as possible. With every rep you will be building improved core stability

1:04 / 2:12

Step 3: Once you've mastered the arm extensions, move on to extending each leg. This is where it becomes increasingly harder NOT to twist or shift from side to side. It is definitely more challenging.

Don't expect perfection, even though you are trying to do it as perfectly as you can. You're truly "dancing on the edge of your ability," and as that happens, your brain and joints are "learning." You're skill building, at a fundamental level! I don't know about you, but to me this is exciting stuff. We rarely ever go back to the true basics – the nitty gritty – that can often make the biggest difference in how we feel and the results we see over time.

The feeling you want to have as you start to move your leg is one of "sliding it" back. Be mindful and move slowly. You're building fundamental skills that will help your body re-learn how to move authentically.

Also, as you extend the leg, avoid the tendency to OVER ARCH your low-back. Become even more aware of how you're performing this skill by setting yourself up in front of a mirror so you can see yourself as you're practicing. Shoot video of yourself so you can watch and see what you are actually doing. You CAN'T rely solely on feel.

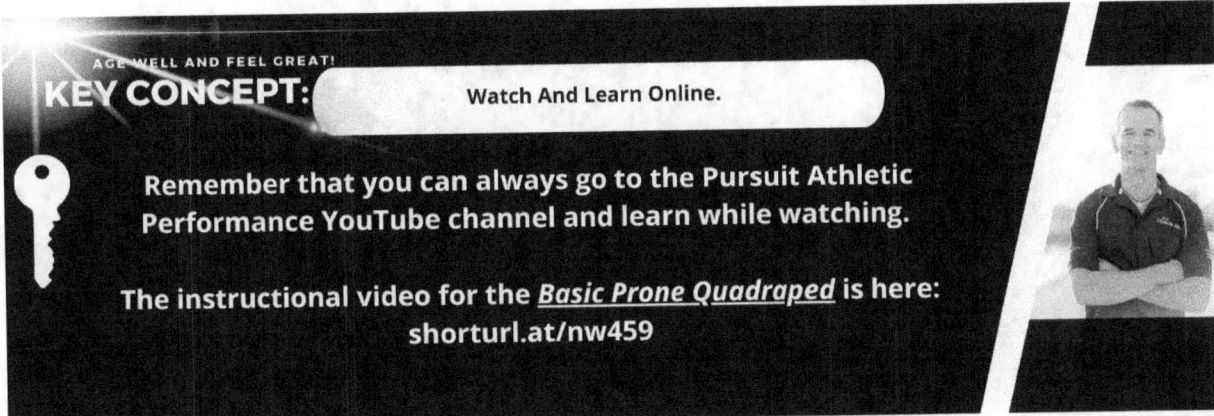

AGE WELL AND FEEL GREAT!

KEY CONCEPT: Watch And Learn Online.

Remember that you can always go to the Pursuit Athletic Performance YouTube channel and learn while watching.

The instructional video for the *Basic Prone Quadraped* is here:
shorturl.at/nw459

Age Well and Feel Great!

Key Concept:

Seek Mastery

People who are successful with any type of skill building seek mastery. Rather than going on to the next best thing, they have a different "relationship" with practice.

Rather than hurrying to a more advanced level of a particular exercise, they look for weak links or mistakes in their current execution. I call it "targeted, mistake-focused practice." So, what do the masters do differently than most of the rank and file? The masters slow it down.

- They stop, correct, and "groove the groove." Then they repeat with attentive repetition.
- They are willing to take baby steps.
- They are engaged in the PROCESS vs. being focused on a potential outcome.
- They push themselves deeply to the sweet spot at the edge of their capabilities.
- They create vivid mental images in their minds of what they want to achieve.

So, what's the last and most advanced progression of the "Bird Dog?"

Step 4: Move your arms and legs at the same time. You are now moving the opposite side arms and legs together without movement anywhere else. For example, reach with your right arm as you slide the left leg back, and vice versa. The reason we do it this way is to practice the "cross-crawl" pattern you learned about earlier, connecting one shoulder to the opposite hip.

You have the same goals as you did earlier. Practice mindfully and move slowly. Take note of asymmetry from one side to the other and practice the "weaker" more difficult pattern or side, more frequently. Focus on the details and the initiation of the movements, that's where the "magic" happens.

Remember at this most basic level, your goal is perfect practice. As you gain mastery, you can continue to increase the challenges by going to more dynamic exercises. Always carry the principles and concepts you are learning to the next phase of your practice, just as you did when you were learning math. **Stability is dynamic. And it should ideally be practiced and grooved progressively.**

Age Well and Feel Great!

Key Concept:

It Isn't About the Exercise, It's About HOW the Exercise Is Done.

When you understand a technique, you know a technique.

When you understand a CONCEPT, you know a thousand techniques.

Another way to think of it is this: Once you learn a concept or principle, you can apply it in a host of different ways. That's the true power behind what you are learning right now!

I've come to realize more as time goes on when it comes to the parts of us we can see and can't see under the skin, the life-long aging process is akin to slowly but steadily changing from filet mignon to beef jerky.

— Coach Al

Thoughts on Stability and Compensation, from My Years Working in our Pursuit Athletic Performance Gait Lab.

When you think about the alignment of body parts, whether it's the hip girdle, the SI joint(s), or the shoulder girdle...ALL of it and ANY of it...is nothing but a bunch of bones and loose body parts...*without* the action of the connective/soft tissue tying it all together and ensuring its integrity. *The soft tissue IS what HOLDS everything together.*

I learned this in a very profound way early on when working alongside my former partner, Dr. Kurt Strecker. Among many tidbits of wisdom Kurt would share with folks he saw in clinic was something he would gently describe to a patient or athlete to help them understand the importance of **stability.**

He'd say, "if you were to remove the very tiny muscles and connective tissue, some barely as thick as a human hair, that run vertically and attach the vertebrae in the neck portion of your spine, as little as **10 pounds would crush the spine** with the vertebrae collapsing upon one another. The average head weighs 15-20 pounds. Think about that!"

The take home message is this: we need each of those muscles and connective tissue to do its job of holding everything together and assuring everything functions at the right time and in unity/synchrony, as we move. I've often said every "movement issue" or injury I've ever seen in an athlete is a **stability problem, first and foremost.** Some people think they have a "unique" issue or set of challenges. I rarely see that, however. What I see, are people who are, at some level of dynamic load, not as stable as they *need* to be. The question comes back to "need" I guess. What do you want to do with your life? How active do you want to be?

For anyone with a history of injury, mastering these challenges (stability) becomes even more important. Your margin of error is smaller. You need to be even more stable than do most other people without an injury history. If you think you're different or unique, you're wrong. If you think you can trust how a stability-oriented movement "feels" when you're training it, you're wrong. You need to use a mirror or video yourself to be sure you're doing it correctly.

Your body is a master at compensation. That's how you got this far in the first place. The right response and what anyone and everyone needs, is to retrain the basics and fundamentals of core and hip stability, relentlessly. Watch yourself performing the most basic stability-oriented movements. Practice perfectly, at the most basic level. If you don't do the most BASIC things perfectly, what do you think will happen when dynamic loads rise? You guessed it. It just gets worse.

Learn from the mistakes of others. You can't live
long enough to make them all yourself.
— Eleanor Roosevelt

What is *Compensation* in the Human Body? Why Does it Matter?

Imagine you go out for a walk one day and you get a pebble in your shoe. That can occasionally happen, right? So, you stop and take the shoe off and turn it upside down and shake it until the pebble drops out. No harm, no foul. You keep walking and all's good.

But what if you ignore the pebble and keep walking, perhaps because you're in a rush and don't want to take the time to stop. A few minutes later the pain is worse and you're really feeling it, now, so you finally stop and shake it out. Now that foot of yours is a little more sore. You've got a little limp in your walk as you continue. Over time though, you walk it off and everything's fine as far as you can tell.

Now, hypothetically, imagine you leave the pebble in there for a full week. By the time you finally take it out, you've got a really nice bruise – it might even be a bit bloody. You remove it, but when you start walking again, you've got a noticeable limp in your walk even without the pebble. And that means your body is a little out of whack and that other leg is taking the biggest brunt of all your activity. In essence, that tiny little innocuous rock that would have been forgotten had you taken it out right away, has manifested into a full-blown injury, that's impacting how everything else in your body is functioning.

Now…stay with me here for one more imaginary scenario. *Imagine leaving it in for a year.* Just think of the impact and damage that would be done to the REST of your body. Even though you eventually take the pebble out, the way your body is now moving has changed. Permanently. Yes, the pebble is gone, but your body is moving as though it is still there in your shoe.

Think about that.

By this point it's likely some of the other parts of your body are now really feeling the effects of that harmless little rock. Maybe your low-back is often "tweaked," or maybe you now have knee pain. And why? Because those other areas are now getting beat up because they had to compensate and take up the slack after your movement fundamentally changed. And not for the better.

That's compensation in your body. Think about old injuries – maybe a sprained ankle when you were a kid. Or a "minor" fall down some steps a while back, or anything else like that. All seemingly innocuous occurrences in the moment. But how did those things change the way you move? What else have you noticed since then, that you didn't realize might be related?

I've always thought of these kinds of compensations as similar to Velcro that gets "stuck" to our body. The purpose of the exercises I've shared with you in this chapter is to tear the Velcro off. If our goal is to move well and remain mostly pain-free throughout our lifetime, then we naturally want to resolve any movement issues before they become permanently ingrained into how we move.

If you'd like more examples of what I mean, just watch any older person move or walk. You're seeing the results of all those "compensations" over the years. Just imagine how much better they might look and feel if they had addressed them earlier. Something to think about…

Is *Compensation* the Reason for Most Running Injuries?

To answer this hypothetical question, no, I don't believe it's fair to say that every single running injury is caused by compensation, in and of itself. There are frequently myriad factors that can lead to an increased risk of injury and ultimately the onset of an injury. Training "errors," such as a too-aggressive volume build is one of many.

That being said, in my more than 40 years of experience as runner/coach/therapist and owner of a gait analysis lab, despite the many factors that are often discovered when an injury actually manifests into symptoms that alter the person's ability to run, **I've ALWAYS found some level of compensation present in an injured runner.** The degree of compensation varies depending upon how long the person has been dealing with the injury, as well as the type of injury. The level of compensation often determines an individual's *margin of error* when it comes to things like volume build and race-specific training. As training becomes more challenging from a speed/volume perspective, the margin of error can decrease and manifest in an injury that might not have otherwise presented with less challenging training.

Similarly, with the athletes I've worked 1 on 1 with, I've found when we can focus training on reducing compensation and making sure all parts of the body are working as they should be, there is a very large margin of error. Their ability to absorb training workload and recover quickly, as well as race hard and bounce back quickly - increases, often dramatically, compared to their past experience. This means they enjoy their training much more and usually go much faster over the short- AND long-term. In very simple terms, it's about large muscles doing their "job" and small muscles doing their job, and not asking either to do the OTHER's job, if you know what I mean.

The fact of the matter is, running as an activity is much harder on the body than most runners realize, at least during the moments when they aren't injured and things are progressing well. There is significant repetitive load - chronic load - 3 to 4x bodyweight with every footstrike from gravity and ground reaction forces. The degree or severity of the effect of these "loads" is unique to each of us, body shape, size, foot mechanics, joint mobility, etc., all have an impact on that risk. I've seen as miles add up, injury often becomes inevitable, UNLESS we do something proactively in training to identify and address these compensations before they turn into an injury.

Lastly, I'll simply say that interestingly, compensation could be considered somewhat "normal" in the human body. It's just not ideal or optimal if your goal is to run injury-free. ☺ What do I mean?

We all marvel at the way someone who has suffered from a traumatic brain injury and loses function of one portion of the brain or spinal cord, is almost miraculously able to adapt (with therapy) over time. As another part of the brain "compensates" in some way – it allows for some part of a movement or skill to be restored. This is the amazing ability of the brain and soft connective tissue to adapt and, thus, "compensate." *If there's one thing I've learned over and over again, our brain doesn't care which tissues are doing which job - just that the job is accomplished!*

But think about it: **what is in one instance miraculous, can, on the other hand, be devastating for a runner** who is challenging themselves to run farther or faster. A low-back "compensating" for weak or unstable glutes/hips or core, as one example. Or a calf muscle "compensating" for a foot or ankle that doesn't move as it should; either too little or more than it should - both can be potentially problematic as miles add up.

In summary, we're all unique and an experiment of one. It's up to each of us (IF our goal is to remain healthy and free of injury and get faster if you're a runner) to learn more about what we can do proactively to reduce our own individual risk of injury, and then DO those things. There are never any guarantees - but for me and the athletes I work with - reducing the risk and increasing the margin of error is incredibly empowering. And exciting. Especially for a runner who has long suffered from one injury after another. And the cool thing is, the same things that reduce compensation also increase speed!

CHAPTER 21

HOW TO IMPROVE YOUR FEET

Our feet tell our stories. They carry us through this life, moving us from one sorrow and season to the next. Our gait can reveal us to be buoyant or bullish, dispirited, or steadfast.

— **Cicely Tyson, from** *Just As I Am*

Growing up, I was always aware of my parent's feet. They were a mess. My mom's feet were very distorted and as a result, didn't work very well. She had a congenital hip issue as a child that resulted in a leg-length difference of 6 inches. That leg-length discrepancy naturally affected her walking gait and contributed to some serious foot abnormality (and pain) as she aged. My dad's feet weren't much better. I still remember his large hammer toes that must have been painful. Hammer toes are so named because the toes can resemble a hammer when stuck in an upright position.

As I type this, my own feet aren't a whole lot better than my dads were when he was my age. In fact, I'll say it up front: my feet don't look or function nearly as well as I would like. I've got some stubborn bunions, especially on the left, and toes that don't function or move independently as well as I would like. There are reasons I'm in this situation that I'll discuss in this chapter.

It all began when I joined the U.S. Coast Guard Band as a percussionist in 1979. Like every other member, part of my dress uniform was a pair of shiny black, plastic chloroform shoes. Little did I know at the time how harmful these unnatural shoes would be. They're narrow at the toes and stiff with a slightly elevated heel. And they don't breathe, resulting in a buildup of excess heat and moisture, making the inside of the shoe the perfect breeding ground for fungus and athlete's foot. Natural footwear should be shaped wider in the front to allow the toes to splay, be more flexible, and lay flat. I didn't recognize back then wearing those shoes would lead to unnatural foot function and the foot challenges I'm dealing with today.

Everything Begins from the Ground Up.

When it comes to moving, our feet truly are our **foundation.** When they're painful or don't work well, it affects every part of our life. So, naturally, any book about how to age well and feel great must include information about our feet. After all, we will have a very difficult time remaining active and enjoying a vibrant life if our feet won't cooperate and function well, right?

In this chapter, I'm going to give you some ideas about how you can care for your feet so they serve you well throughout your life. These ideas will include exercises to strengthen the intrinsic muscles in your feet and improve your proprioception and balance, and to mobilize your feet and toes. I'm also going to tell you more than once to go barefooted as often as possible. You will hear "be barefoot" a lot, for a very good reason: the human foot is perfectly designed for its assigned tasks of walking, standing, and just about anything else you'd do in shoes. The more you wear shoes, especially ill-fitting shoes including high heels, the more foot problems you're likely to have.

In fact, wearing shoes daily is the primary reason most people in the U.S. have **chronic foot problems**. The types of shoes I've worn throughout my life, such as the plastic chloroform shoes I mentioned earlier (and running and cycling shoes too), have definitely been the biggest reason for why my own feet don't function as well as they should. A quick review of some statistics shows Americans are making tens of millions of visits to podiatrists each year to address foot issues. And for whatever reason, Americans in particular have a love affair with shoes! The average person has more than a half dozen pair.

Research from 1905: Comparison of Barefooted and Shod People.

In October 1905, a research paper was published in the American Journal of Orthopedic Medicine titled *Conclusions Drawn from a Comparative Study of the Feet of Barefooted and Shoe Wearing Peoples*.[1] This collection of images below is borrowed from that research article. I don't know about you, but when I discovered this research article and realized it was written early in the 20th century, I was shocked. That's proof positive that even back then, foot deformities related to shoe wear took center stage in the eyes of many experts.

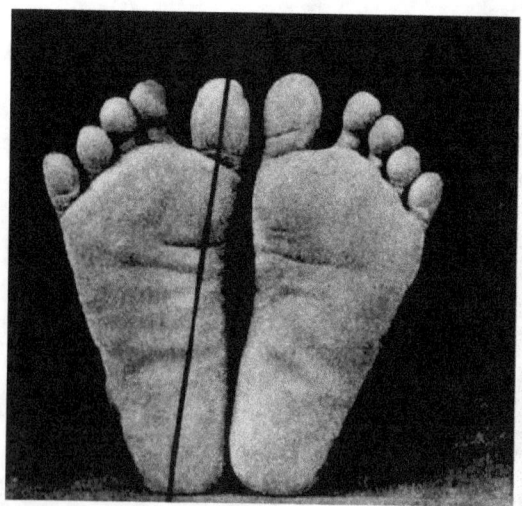 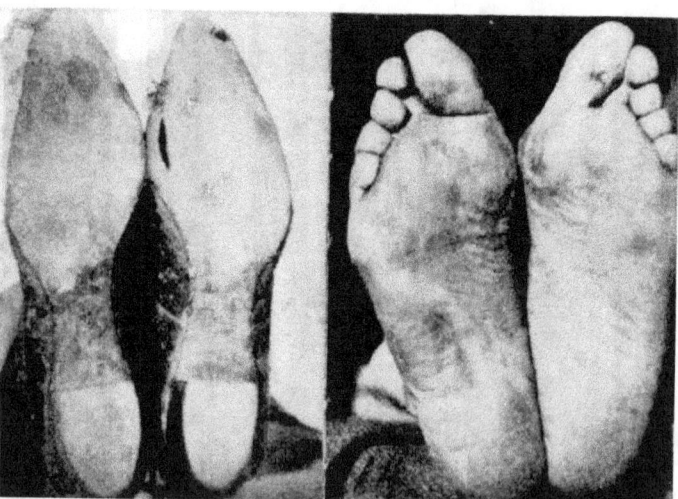

As I'm sure you guessed, the picture on the left is from a person who never wore shoes. Notice how the toes fan out and each toe is in line with its respective metatarsal bone. On the right is someone who wears shoes daily. Particularly obvious are the scrunched-up toes and the beginning of bunion formation, and the hallux valgus, which is the inward turning of the big toe. More often than not, modern people's feet look like the picture on the right, not the left. Only in comparison can you see how different our feet look from the way they are supposed to look, and how much our feet take on the appearance of the shoes we wear. Think about it: If we are to going to wear shoes, shouldn't they look more like our feet?

Think about the millions of visits to the podiatrist, as well as the increase in low-back pain, ingrown toenails, knee issues, and arch and heel pain including plantar fasciitis. You rarely find these problems in societies where people seldom wear shoes. Most of these issues can be traced back to our love affair with shoes! And what's more, not only are our modern feet more dysfunctional, most people can no longer walk barefoot without pain, or balance on one leg without shoes. Whenever I walk around my home (always barefoot, of course!), be it in the yard, or along the sidewalk or even in the road, my neighbors remark how they couldn't possibly walk without shoes. When they say it's just too painful, I usually tell them if they did it more often, their feet would toughen up a bit and they'd find it much easier.

Bacteria and Fungus.

One of the most frustrating issues I've been dealing with for ages is chronic and lingering toenail fungus. It sounds awful, I know! Ugh. Interestingly, a quick check of the statistics will tell you that nearly seven out of ten people in the U.S. experience this problem at some point in their lives. I attribute the beginning of this fungal issue to the 28 years of wearing the previously mentioned plastic shoes, along with running and cycling shoes. Shoes, especially like these, are an incubator for bacterial and fungal infection. The warm, moist environment of a closed shoe provides the ideal home for these organisms. It's ironic that most doctors warn their patients about the dangers of bacteria growing inside their shoes, yet their advice is to wear "breathable" shoes or moisture wicking socks more often. It would be helpful if they also suggested to their patients they go without socks or shoes more often to begin with. In other words, be barefooted.

Age Well and Feel Great!
Key Concept:

Aren't Barefeet At Risk Of Bacterial Invasion?

Most people worry about what their feet are exposed to when they're walking barefooted, without realizing that generally speaking, it's their hands that possess the majority of bacteria, much more than their bare feet.

In his book, *The Barefoot Book: 50 Great Reasons to Kick Off Your Shoes*, author and professor Daniel Howell, Ph.D., says "our hands probably harbor as many microbes as our feet, yet "athlete's hand" and "fingernail fungus" are exceedingly rare.

This is because our hands aren't locked away in gloves all day, every day. Although our hands touch public doorknobs, handrails, money, and a host of other microbe-laden objects throughout the day, microorganisms grow poorly on exposed hands. They also grow poorly on exposed feet."[2]

Of the different types of shoes we wear, those with elevated heels are among the worst, at least when it comes to the long-term health of our feet. I'll admit I like the look of high heeled stiletto shoes on women. My guess is most women who wear them believe the change in body posture gives them a heightened sense of sexuality and empowerment. Part of the reason for this is when the heel is lifted, both the calf and thigh muscles are more engaged, giving the legs a stronger appearance. Also, the pelvis is tilted forward as much as 10 to 15 degrees, leading to an exaggerated curve in the spine that will make the butt stick out. If that's not enough, it will also simultaneously lift the breasts.[3] So, it seems feeling more attractive when wearing these shoes isn't a figment of the imagination! ☺

Unfortunately, despite the enhanced style, high-heeled shoes are disastrous for the health of the feet. Among other things, the body's center of gravity is shifted forward placing a lot more load on the front of the foot, unlike flat shoes that distribute the load evenly between the front and back of the foot. The toes are flexed and strained and the arch is also strained. The knees take a beating too. A study done at Harvard University found high heels put more stress on the knee joint.[4] The constant ankle flexion weakens the arch and the shortened position of the calf and Achilles tendon lead to chronic calf muscle shortening that makes walking in flat shoes or barefooted more difficult. If you're not sure just how much these shoes dramatically alter gait, try it for yourself without the shoes. Try to imitate it. Remember though, you can't let your ankles or toes move. Keep the ankles in full extension. It's not easy to walk and it's obviously not natural.

On the flip side, wearing high-heeled shoes seem to be expected in many business or corporate environments, as well as in certain fashion circles. As a result, there are times when women have less of a choice. The take home message is, there are times when you'll want to and may even feel you must wear them, and that's OK. The point is to limit how much you wear them, and most importantly, follow the advice I provide in this chapter to take care of your feet with regular mobility and strengthening exercises. Doing so will help you undo some of the negative effects so you can keep your feet healthy into your later years and go the distance!

Toe Splay.

The other major issue with most of the shoes worn in this day and age is the size of the toe box. Fortunately, new shoe manufacturers are on the scene with much roomier shoes, but the overwhelming majority of people still wear shoes that are the opposite of what they should be wearing. To see what I mean, check out this graphic comparing one type of shoe that allows the toes to splay and spread out, vs. a typical men's dress shoe, that squishes the toes together.

Toe Freedom

Squished Toes

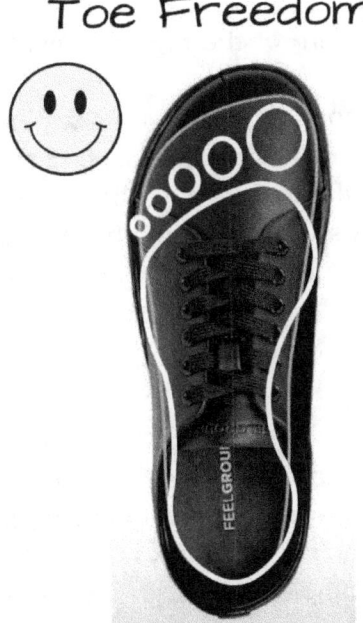

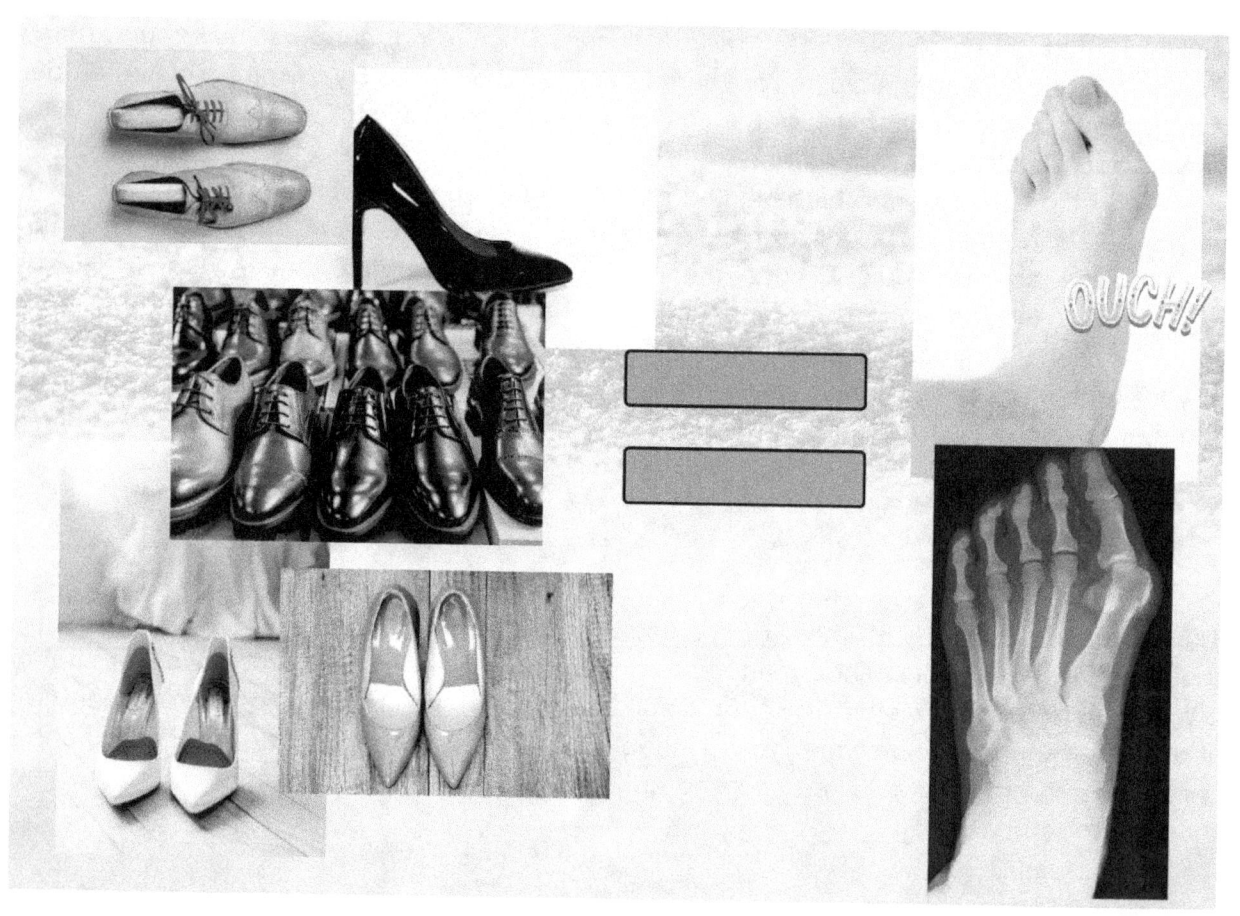

This image shoes the extreme hallux valgus (inward turn of the big toe) resulting from the typical narrow-toed shoes.

If you have the freedom to choose what you wear, choose a shoe with a wider toe box! In my case, during those years as a member of the U.S. Coast Guard Band, I had to conform and wear a certain style. This is also true for some first responders such as policemen and firemen, as well as certain other lines of work requiring a special type of shoe. If this is you, advocate for your foot health. All of your colleagues are in the same position. Perhaps you can band together and seek better alternatives.

I Learned, But Not Before Some Damage Was Done.

In 2010, I opened the Pursuit Athletic Performance gait analysis lab with Dr. Kurt Strecker, and began working with athletes from every sport and background. It was three years after my 28-year career and my feet had seen thousands of running miles. It was then that I really began to understand how important our amazing and complex feet are - all 26 bones, 33 joints, 19 muscles and 107 ligaments! Everyone knows when your feet hurt, it makes doing everything else much harder. I knew my feet were the only contact point between the ground and my body and they played an important role in how I was running and functioning. Yet it wasn't until I started doing this work that I realized just how important our feet actually are.

Kurt was an expert in foot mechanics. He taught me a great deal about foot function and foot health. I learned something every single day from "Doc." Every person who walked through the door was either injured or wanted to avoid injury and was unique in their foot mechanics, health, and athletic history. Have you ever stopped to consider among the 7.9 billion inhabitants of our planet, no two pairs of feet are the same? We are each an experiment of one with a unique bone and soft tissue structure.

Looking back, I wish I had learned more and had done more in those early years to take care of my feet. They would be in better shape now if I had. Unfortunately, I'm now paying the price for my late arrival to the foot-care game. If you're younger than me, or have good functioning feet right now, you get to learn from the error of my ways.

Wear Does Our Ability To Balance Come From?

One of the more fascinating and hidden aspects of the bottoms of our feet, is the outer layers are loaded with what are known as **plantar receptors**. These receptors are sensitive to vibration, which (according to at least one theory) is how your body perceives ground impact, as well as texture, skin stretch, pressure, and touch, making our feet incredibly proprioceptive-rich structures. In case you don't know, proprioception is defined as perception or awareness of position and movement of the body.

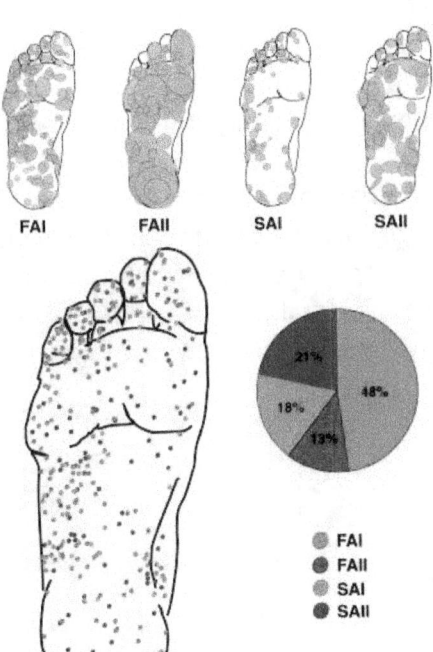

Check out this chart borrowed from a research article titled *Cutaneous Afferent Innervation of the Human Foot Sole: What Can We Learn From Single Unit Recordings?*, that shows how receptors are distributed throughout the fascial layers just below the skin.[5]

As mentioned, all of these receptors are sensitive to different stimuli, such as vibration, texture, stretch, pressure, and touch.

As you can imagine, shoes disturb and block input from the ground. The more time spent in shoes, the *worse* this communication becomes. The more time spent barefooted, the *better* the communication becomes.

It's akin to wearing thick gloves on your hands but expecting to still feel with the same sensitivity as if you didn't have gloves on.

KEY CONCEPT:

Small Nerve Proprioceptors.

Small Nerve Proprioceptors are located in the superficial and deep fascia under the skin. We've got multiple layers of tissue there. This is where the magic happens. What are some of the names of these small nerve proprioceptors and what are they sensitive too?

One receptor, *Ruffini's Corpuscles*, are sensitive to skin stretch. *Merkel's Disks* are sensitive to texture perception. *Pacinian Corpuscles* are sensitive to deep pressure and vibration. And lastly there are *Meissner's Corpuscles*, which are sensitive to light touch.

If you're wondering why these plantar receptors are important, remember without sensory information coming IN, your body won't know where it is in space or be able function. Imagine walking into a very dark room you aren't familiar with. Without the sensory information you are accustomed to from your eyes, you're instantly afraid to move for fear you'll bump into something or worse, fall. The bottoms of your feet are the exact same kind of "window" from the outside world – the ground in particular – to the inside of your body.

When our feet don't function well and our window to the outside world and our environment - otherwise known as **sensory input into our body** isn't as it should be, the result can be:

- Poor joint position sense, leading to...
- Slow joint stability, leading to...
- Poor core stability, leading to...
- Poor reduction of forces acting on our body, leading to...
- An Increased risk of injury, more aches and pains, and more fatigue and tiredness.

Simply put, our feet need to be able to function well in order for our core and trunk to "know" how to act. Think about it: **a joint, be it your ankle or any other joint, will only be as stable as the rate at which it can perceive itself.** ☺ It's easy to see if your perception of the environment isn't very good, your risk of falling rises dramatically. Falls are the #1 fear of many during the late stages of life. Fear of falling may trap you in your home, which you never want to happen.

Key Concept:

Have You Ever Sprained Your Ankle Or Lost Your Balance?

One reason sprained ankles happen, beyond our own clumsiness or lack of awareness, is due to the difference between small nerve and large nerve proprioceptors in our legs and feet.

Large nerve proprioceptors are called Golgi-Tendon Organs and Muscle Spindles and reside in our ankles and legs. It takes roughly 120 milliseconds for these to respond. The small nerve variety layered within the fascia in the bottoms of our feet (that I just told you about) are much quicker.

Consider this: it takes about 80 milliseconds to lose your balance. The difference between the response time of the large nerve proprioceptors (120 milliseconds) and the amount of time it takes to sprain your ankle (80 milliseconds) is the difference between you regaining your balance OR falling down, resulting in a painful sprain.

Balance is much the same thing. As we age our balance becomes progressively worse, due in part to an overreliance on the large nerve proprioceptors in our legs and ankles.
The best path forward is to improve the sensitivity of the small nerve variety, spend more time barefooted and do the exercises as I describe them here in this chapter.

A Lifetime of Wearing Shoes.

Things like **small nerve proprioception** and **foot function** tend to get worse as we age, but we can improve both with specific exercises and by going barefooted more often. Of course, if you're accustomed to wearing shoes most of the time, be patient and wean yourself off them gradually. Going from zero time spent barefooted to multiple hours, quickly, is likely to irritate your feet and legs. Be patient and persistent.

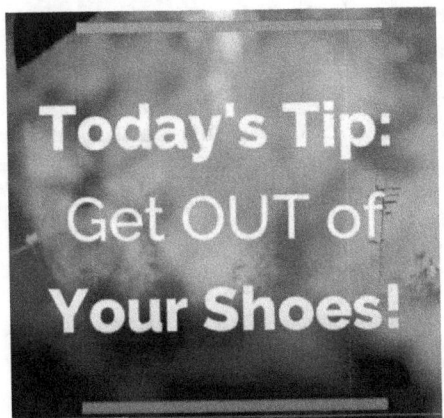

Another reason for that less-than-perfect balance is as time goes on, we naturally tend to rely too much on our other **senses,** especially eyesight. Most people are overly dependent on eyesight and use their other senses less than they should. Consider this classic example to really bring this fact home.

The example involves **single-leg balance**. It seems so simple, doesn't it? Just stand on a single leg and balance. Well, if it's so simple, why is it so challenging for so many people?

Single-Leg Balance.

Give it a try, barefooted of course. Why? Being barefooted forces your foot to adapt to the ground. You'll also have better sensory input from the ground into your foot and above your foot. It's simple, just match the picture here by bringing one thigh up to parallel with the floor and balance there.

If you are able to do that successfully for 30 seconds, <u>try it with your eyes closed</u>. Make sure you have something to hold onto because it's likely you will struggle at first. Why? As I just mentioned, we typically rely more on our eyesight than the sensory input we receive through our feet.

Over the many years I've done gait analysis and worked with injured runners, one thing that always struck me as significant was *every one of them had difficulty standing and balancing on a single leg.* Virtually EVERY one of them.

Understanding *Impact* Forces.

One of the most important jobs of those small nerve proprioceptors is to perceive vibration, and you don't have to be a runner or a field sport athlete to appreciate how important that vibration is. Why? There's one theory that says vibration is how your body perceives and then handles impact forces. Even for someone who walks or spends lots of time on their feet, impact forces matter.

Most people, if asked, would say impact forces are received as **pressure**. And that makes sense, right? Thinking of it logically, there's our old friend gravity pushing down on our body, increasing the pressure as our foot makes contact with the ground. And there is some truth to that. But it isn't the whole truth, and it doesn't tell the whole (or most important part of the) story. So, what is the whole story? How **does** our body *perceive impact forces*? The answer is **vibration**. About 80% of all the **small nerve proprioceptors** in our feet are **sensitive to vibration**, making it the *most important stimulus* for how we perceive impact.

The person who's done the most amount of research and study on impact forces and how our body handles them is biomechanist and longtime shoe researcher, Dr. Benno Nigg.[6] Dr. Nigg's research on **Muscle Tuning Theory** challenged how the science community used to view impact forces and the role our feet play in handling those forces.[7] This theory says <u>our body is able to *anticipate* the impact force we will experience prior to our foot touching the ground through the sensory input from small nerve proprioceptors.</u> The important take home message is those forces are perceived very quickly – less than 50 milliseconds! So, the faster your feet are at anticipating the forces, the better your balance will be and the less likely you'll fall or sprain your ankle.[8] In other words, doing barefoot training exercises and improving at things like single leg balance create anticipatory muscle contractions leading to faster loading responses![9]

What's more, all of the muscles in our body are surrounded by *compartments*, which are *surrounded* by connective tissue known as fascia! ☺ As the vibrations mentioned earlier enter the compartments surrounding the muscles, the **muscles respond by contracting isometrically.** If you're wondering what isometric muscle contractions are, they are those where there isn't any joint movement. In other words, the muscle is firing and contracting but nothing is moving. We'll be talking much more about these contractions in the chapter on strength. Keep reading.

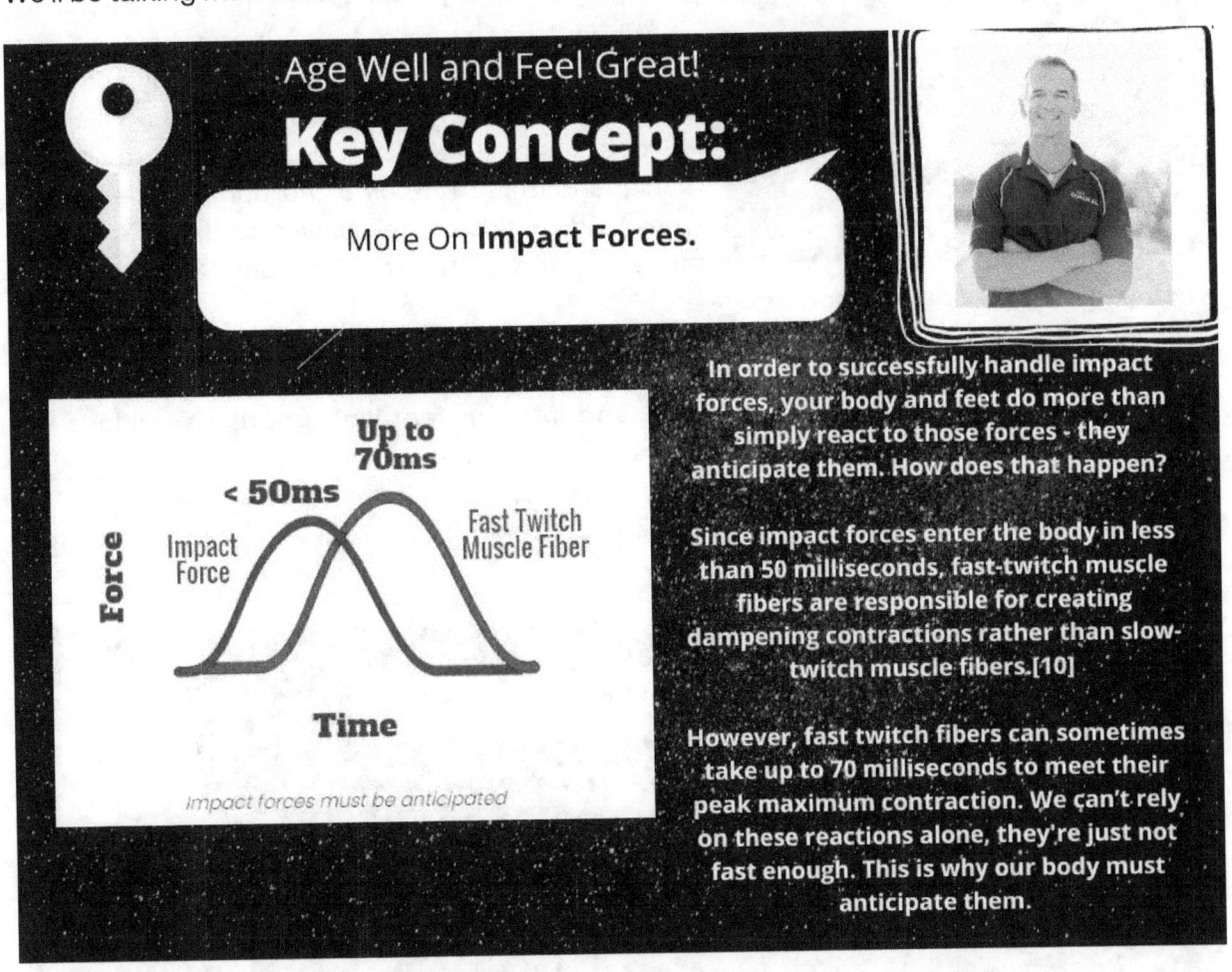

Age Well and Feel Great!
Key Concept:

More On **Impact Forces.**

In order to successfully handle impact forces, your body and feet do more than simply react to those forces - they anticipate them. How does that happen?

Since impact forces enter the body in less than 50 milliseconds, fast-twitch muscle fibers are responsible for creating dampening contractions rather than slow-twitch muscle fibers.[10]

However, fast twitch fibers can sometimes take up to 70 milliseconds to meet their peak maximum contraction. We can't rely on these reactions alone, they're just not fast enough. This is why our body must anticipate them.

(graph labels: Force, Up to 70ms, < 50ms, Impact Force, Fast Twitch Muscle Fiber, Time, impact forces must be anticipated)

If you're having a little trouble grasping this concept of isometric contractions happening in response to vibrations entering muscle compartments, think about a vibrating tuning fork. What happens when you grab it? It instantly stops vibrating of course. Additionally, and importantly, those isometric contractions in the leg muscles ALSO provide a **splinting**

effect that prevents the bones from vibrating OR bending. As you can probably imagine, when I'm working with a runner who has been struggling with a **stress fracture**, it's easy to come to the conclusion that at the very least, <u>their foot and leg muscles</u> **weren't reacting and contracting fast enough to protect (and splint) the bone.** The bone takes a constant beating due to excessive vibration, and the end result is often a "stress" fracture.

It's All About the Fascia!

Remember in Chapter 17, which was the Introduction to Part 3 of this book, I discussed fascia, the grapefruit principle, and how it keeps everything in "shape."

When it comes to proprioception, balance, and handling impact forces, it's our fascial system that really plays arguably the biggest role, and here's how: As those muscles are contracting isometrically, *the fascial sheath surrounding the compartments and within and outside of the muscles,* **is able to slide** and move with the joints, stretching and loading just like when you draw back a rubber band.

The bottom line is:

- If our **proprioception from the ground into our feet isn't good**, we will lose our balance much more easily and have a higher risk of injury.
- If our **fascial system is bound up, dried up, or lacking optimal elasticity**, we'll move like a stiff, non-compliant dried out rubber band, instead of a like-new, super stretchy, very pliable band.

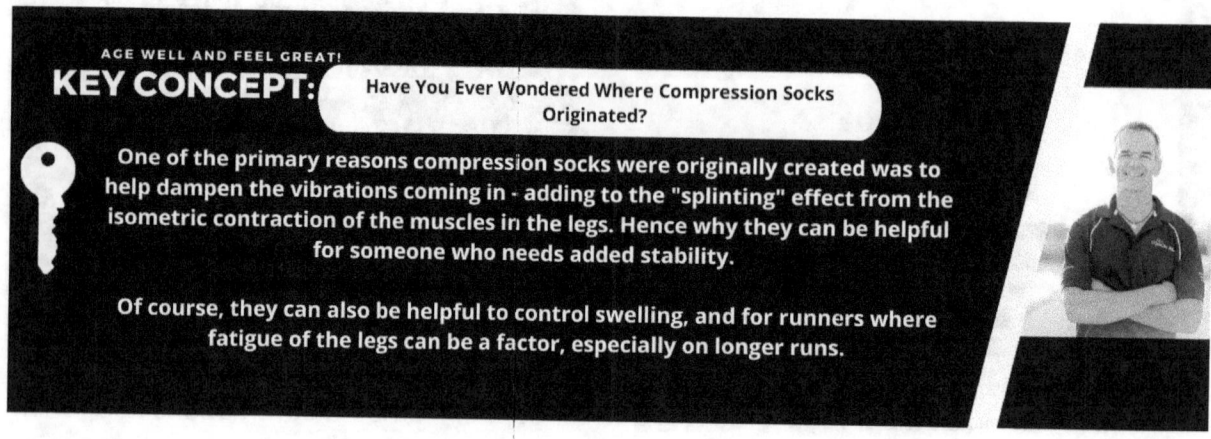

AGE WELL AND FEEL GREAT!

KEY CONCEPT: Have You Ever Wondered Where Compression Socks Originated?

One of the primary reasons compression socks were originally created was to help dampen the vibrations coming in - adding to the "splinting" effect from the isometric contraction of the muscles in the legs. Hence why they can be helpful for someone who needs added stability.

Of course, they can also be helpful to control swelling, and for runners where fatigue of the legs can be a factor, especially on longer runs.

It Gets Even Harder as We Age.

As we age, the fascia throughout our body loses elasticity, and it can also start to get adhesions. (I'll talk more about adhesions soon in the section on diet). This along with worsened sensory input due to a lifetime in shoes, means we can easily lose our ability to "perceive" the ground and "react" to contact with it. The best way to avoid this decline is to focus on training and using those *mechanoreceptors in and on the bottoms of our feet. We want them to be able to react more quickly and effectively!* Naturally, **we do this through effective barefoot training and spending more time barefooted in our daily lives.**

If we're going to age well and keep our ability to function well, we have to place priority on:

1. foot function,
2. intrinsic foot muscle strength, and
3. barefoot exercising.

Without optimal small nerve proprioception and good foot and toe function, we have very little chance for healthier feet as the years pile up. Keep reading for more specific guidance on some exercises to improve foot function!

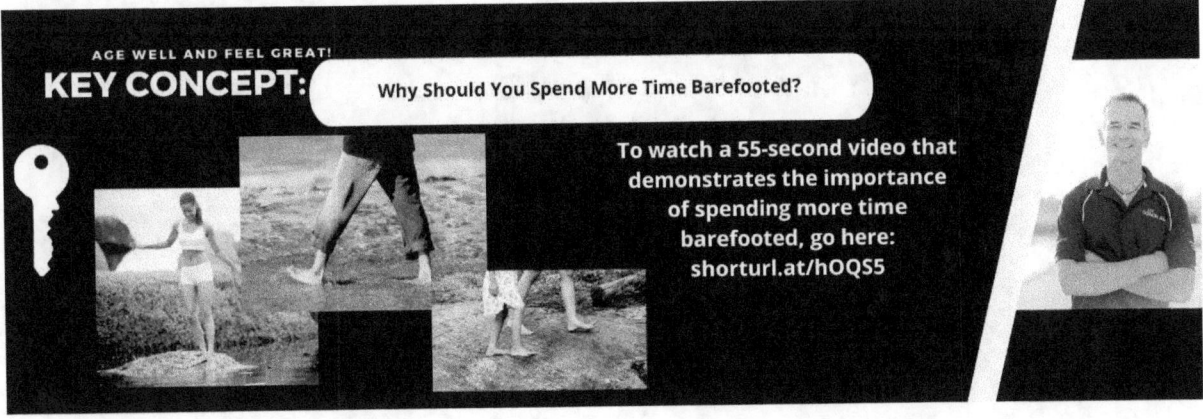

AGE WELL AND FEEL GREAT!

KEY CONCEPT: Why Should You Spend More Time Barefooted?

To watch a 55-second video that demonstrates the importance of spending more time barefooted, go here: shorturl.at/hOQS5

Have You Wondered About Your Calluses?

Anyone over the age of 40 probably has some callus built up on the bottoms and sides of the feet and toes. What are these small, concentrated areas of hardened skin?

Calluses are both a history of "load" and also, on the side of the feet and toes, a result of pressure and friction from wearing too-tight shoes.

Another word for "load" would simply be pressure, or to put it another way, where the majority of your weight is felt during your walking or running gait cycle. Very often, people are surprised to see where they have callus build up. It sometimes appears where you wouldn't necessarily expect it. Remember, loading can occur at various phases of your walk or run gait. After thousands of steps over many years, it's easy to see why you might have a buildup of callus in response to that chronic loading. It's similar to why a bone spur can develop on certain parts of bone tissue. It's important we don't confuse healthy, leather-like skin on the soles of our feet with calluses. Healthy feet have a leather-like feel to the soles that comes from being barefooted more often and walking on a wide variety of surfaces.

One more thing worth mentioning for those north of 60. As we age, we also experience the breakdown of our natural fat pads in the bottoms of our feet. These thinning built-in parts of our feet that help "cushion" impact can cause increasing pain and will often dictate the use of gel pads or extra cushion in shoes to offset this loss. What to do? The recommendations I have for you to strengthen the intrinsic muscles and care for calluses, along with manual massage and strengthening your legs and hips will all help. Of course, avoid restrictive footwear and go barefooted as much as you can!'

Do You Have An Arch? Or Are Your Feet Flat? Does It Matter?

"LOW" ARCH

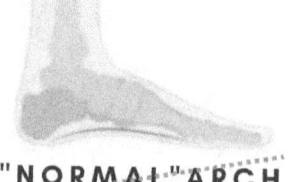

"NORMAL" ARCH

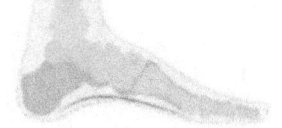

"HIGH" ARCH

These feet have *different* arches, BUT they are all *still* <u>good feet!</u>

With proper *intrinsic muscle strengthening, toe mobilization,* time spent *barefooted,* and *avoiding the use of ill-fitting shoes,* any of these foot types can serve you well.

As you've already learned, no two pairs of feet on the planet are the same. It's also true that we are each an experiment of one when it comes to our foot arch. Remember, it's common to apply labels to certain parts of our body, and the arch is no exception. For example, we might say we have "flat feet" or a "high arch." We like to label one or the other as "good" or "bad." The truth is one isn't really any more "normal" than the other, although the type of feet you have certainly WILL impact your risk of injury, especially if you play sports.

As you look down at your feet and examine them or think back to the past when you were told something about your feet, remember the position your foot is in when you aren't walking or running is a static position that doesn't tell you how it functions when you're moving. This is why I always review video of walking or running when doing a gait analysis. Static positions don't tell the whole story.

Also remember what is happening at your knees and hips will influence what happens with your feet. We're a holistic organism with lots of parts, not only a foot, right? When we walk or run, we do need our feet to flatten (pronate) and unflatten (supinate) in order to perform the natural normal function of absorbing load and providing a rigid lever for us to push off and move forward. Both are vital for natural foot function. One thing is for sure, regardless of what kind of arch you may have, you still need strong intrinsic foot muscles, mobile ankles, and good functioning toes. <u>My best advice is to focus more on those aspects and less on how high your arch may be.</u>

Does Diet Matter?

Were you to walk into any health food or natural food store today, the supplement powder you might see front and center more than any other, is collagen. In case you don't know, collagen is the main structural protein found in the extracellular matrix of connective tissue in the body, including bones, muscles, tendons, ligaments, and skin. Collagen is the main component of connective tissue, making it the most abundant protein in the body. It makes up a whopping 25% to 35% of all of the protein in the human body.[11]

Since it is so important, it's no wonder it's one of the hottest supplements in the diet and fitness industry today. Based on the research I've read to this point, collagen supplementation isn't as helpful in restoring collagen health as we might hope. But collagen supplementation and whether you should or shouldn't, isn't why I'm mentioning collagen here. The real reason is very much diet related.

In an earlier chapter I introduced the concept of *glycation*, which as you may remember, contributes to the aging of our skin. The reason *glycation* is important for our skin is the same reason it's important for our other connective tissue, including our feet and fascia. I believe I've also mentioned in a previous chapter the aging process is akin to going from filet mignon to beef jerky. ☺ That process of slowly turning to beef jerky is why I am sharing this. And *glycation* is that process.

Without getting too technical, collagen hardens and stiffens because the stability of the hydrogen bridges and covalent bonds referred to as *crosslinks* begin to degrade. Normally the crosslinks in collagen provide strength and stability, but according to Dr. Emily Splichal, DPM, who is an expert in the foot and its role in movement longevity, "excessive or what are called non-specific crosslinks create stiffness and a lack of elastic recoil in the connective tissue. It is these non-specific crosslinks that are often called fascial adhesions."[12] What is important to know is these excessive non-specific crosslinks are formed through the glycation process.

Going back to the diet connection, know this: Glycation happens because excess sugar in the bloodstream reacts with protein to form a free radical known as *advanced glycation end products*, or AGEs. These AGEs form crosslinks which create stiffness and make micro-tears much more likely. Think of those "twinges" otherwise known as minor aches and pains we often feel when we're being active or perhaps step the wrong way. These happen in part because our fascia isn't as healthy as it should be. So how do we minimize these *advanced glycation end products*?

You've probably read it at least a hundred times so far so consider this one-hundred-and-one: **CUT BACK ON SUGAR in your diet!** When you reduce the amount of glucose floating through your bloodstream, there's less there to react with protein. It's no wonder people who have eaten lots of sugar throughout their lives look older, and age more quickly, than those who haven't. It comes back to AGEs and glycation.

There's one other diet related tip I want to share with you beyond reducing sugar, that may help with reducing AGEs. If you recall, in Chapter 15, *Meat Lovers vs. Vegetarians: Who Is Right?*, I told you about *xenohormesis*, which is the beneficial stress that plants experience that can be transferred to anyone who eats the plant. I mentioned using aspirin as one way to glean these benefits, since aspirin is made from willow bark. Scientific studies have shown daily aspirin can also offset the formation of collagen crosslinks and AGEs.[13][14] So there you have it! One more potential benefit to a daily aspirin. Please, as always, do not start taking daily aspirin before speaking with your doctor or other healthcare provider, first.

TAKE ACTION: How to Create Bulletproof Feet.

Now that I've shared some of the science behind how our feet function and what can happen as we get older, in this next section, I will give you some specific ways to improve your feet. Some of what I'll share with you is what I've learned as a certified Barefoot Training Specialist. Naturally, because my own feet are compromised, I've learned everything I possibly could do to improve them.

Earlier in the chapter we briefly discussed single-leg balance. Hopefully you tried it and now have a sense of how good your own sensory input is. I highly recommend you continue to practice this every day until you can balance on a single leg for at least 30 seconds with your eyes closed. Expect to find a difference from one side to the other. We all have a chocolate and vanilla side when it comes to skills like this. In other words, we aren't as symmetrical as we

might like to think, especially with something like this. The more you pay attention to these differences, the more you will learn about your body and what it needs most.

We will also review a number of other exercises and skills you can do right now to make your feet more resilient. Say goodbye to plantar fasciitis, heel pain, and the rest of those increasingly debilitating chronic issues!

Step 1: Keep Your Feet Flexible.

Daily massage and mobility work will help make sure all of the bones and soft tissue of the feet move easily and are able to perform their roles. The older you are, the more challenging this may be. Immobility in the foot leads to foot pain, plantar fasciitis, and other foot problems. If you're a lifelong runner like me, it will be even more important.

The link at the end of this sentence will take you to a great video done by my former partner, Dr. Kurt Strecker, sharing his simple approach to keep the feet moving easily: shorturl.at/bdruv

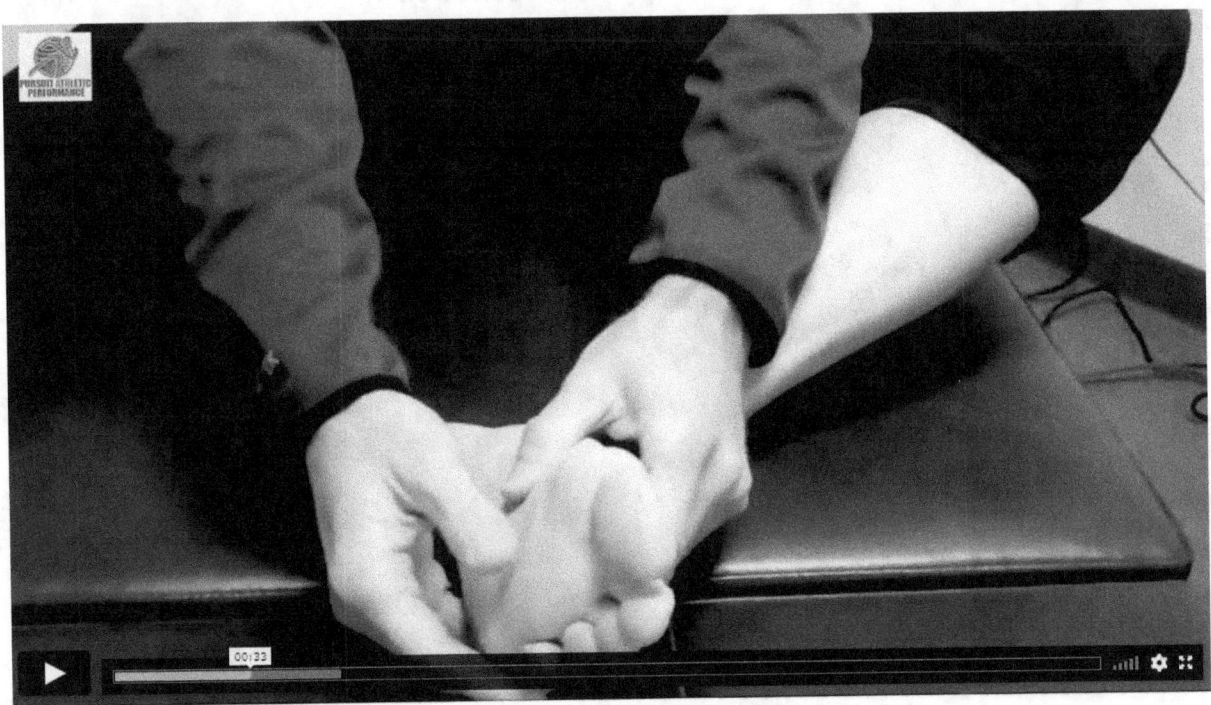

What are some of the other ways you can care for your feet?

- Using a small ball, like a golf ball or slightly larger lacrosse ball, roll your foot around on it, using pain as your guide. The smaller size balls allow for deeper penetration, which can hurt more but in a good way. Don't overdo it. You'll learn more about this on the next page. Check out the graphic images for tips.

- Work your toes with "toe spread" and toe independence exercises. You'll learn more about this in a graphic coming up soon. Keep reading.
- Keep your BIG TOE mobile and healthy. This is often a place where arthritis creeps in and localized inflammation rears its ugly head. Even if you're like me and have lost some mobility, don't let that deter you from working to keep what you still have!

These movements are super helpful for mobilizing your feet and increasing blood flow and overall tissue health.

When you roll with a ball, you will definitely find some tender spots. Pause and let the ball gently sink deeper.

Adjust pressure depending on your pain tolerance.

Massage all of the areas, working lengthwise to gently open up tight areas. Manually separate your toes periodically.

This will feel good!

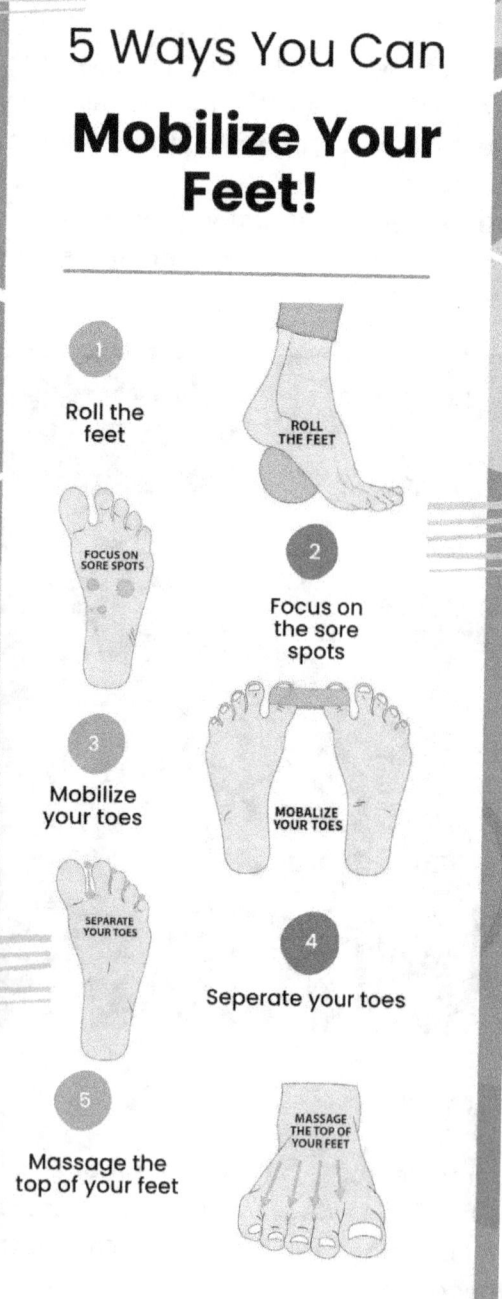

5 Ways You Can
Mobilize Your Feet!

1. Roll the feet
   ROLL THE FEET
2. Focus on the sore spots
   FOCUS ON SORE SPOTS
3. Mobilize your toes
   MOBILIZE YOUR TOES
4. Seperate your toes
   SEPARATE YOUR TOES
5. Massage the top of your feet
   MASSAGE THE TOP OF YOUR FEET

Pull, press, twist, bend, and generally massage your feet!

AGE WELL AND FEEL GREAT!

KEY CONCEPT: Here Are Two Quick and Fun Toe And Ankle Mobility Drills!

Here is a video with two fun and quick mobility drills that are full-body exercises that can be done at any time.

Use this link: shorturl.at/aTY45

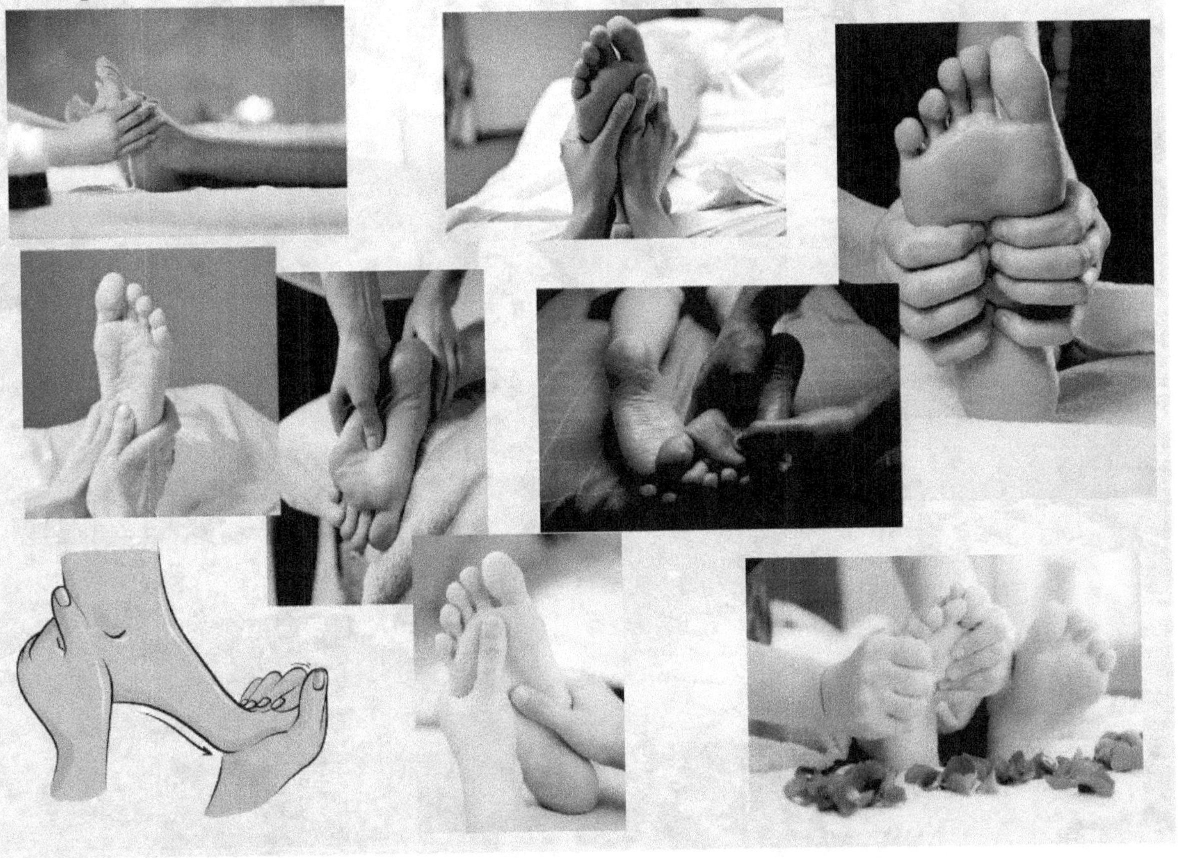

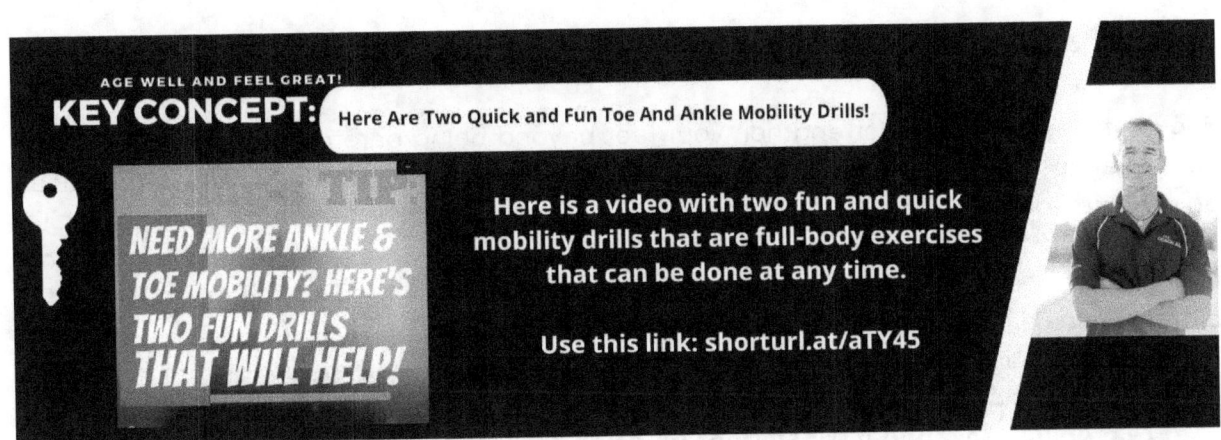

Key Concept:

What Are Intrinsic Foot Muscles?

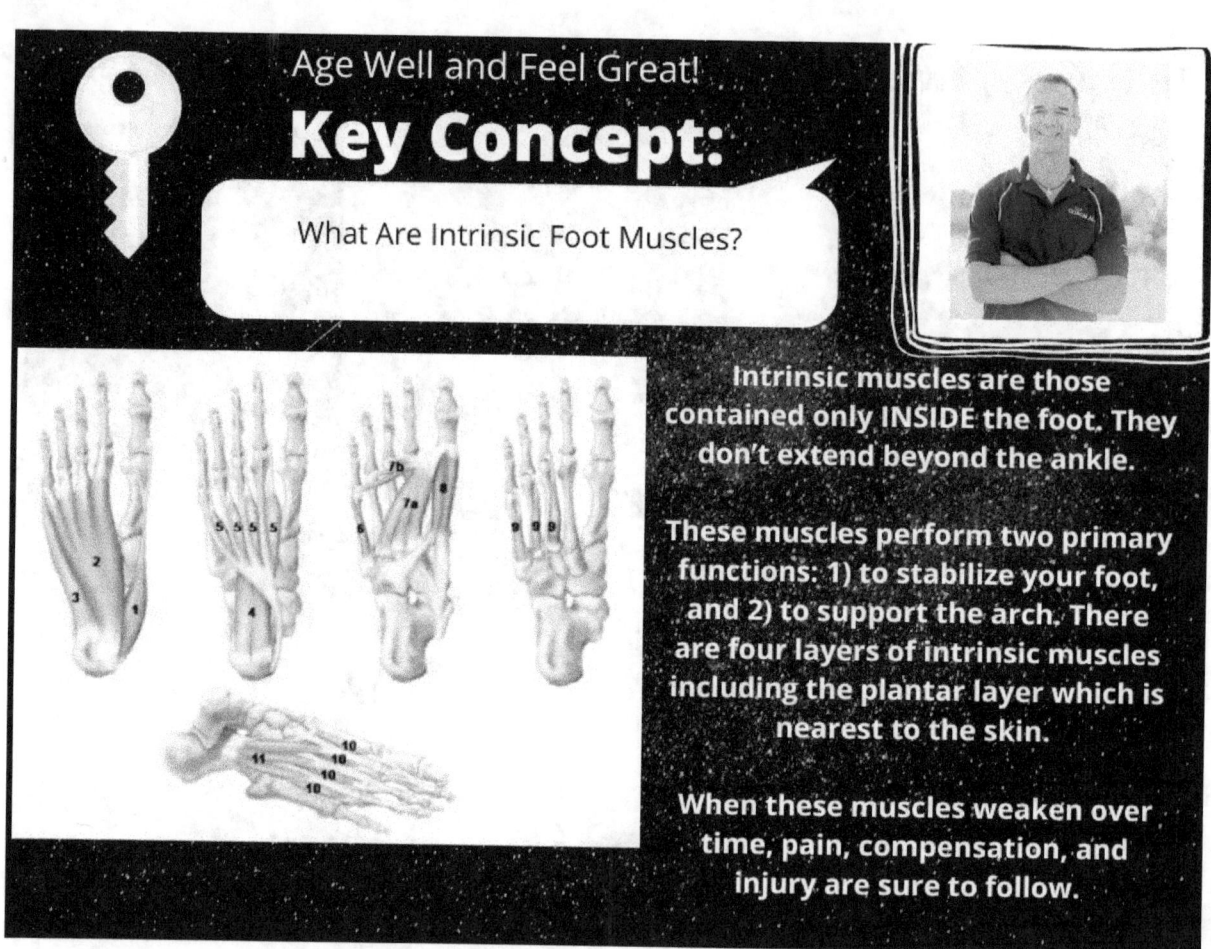

Intrinsic muscles are those contained only INSIDE the foot. They don't extend beyond the ankle.

These muscles perform two primary functions: 1) to stabilize your foot, and 2) to support the arch. There are four layers of intrinsic muscles including the plantar layer which is nearest to the skin.

When these muscles weaken over time, pain, compensation, and injury are sure to follow.

Step 2: Keep Your Feet Strong.

The best way to begin to strengthen your feet beyond being barefooted? Enter the **Short-Foot** exercise, also sometimes referred to as "Small-Foot." When the muscles contained only inside your feet (known as intrinsic muscles) weaken over time and lose their ability to function as they're designed to, the stress and strain take a toll on not only our feet, but all the other connective tissue, joints, and bones, that are nearby. *The calf muscles and the plantar fascia are two examples.*

Want one quick and easy answer as to why so many people suffer with plantar fasciitis, or why runners get calf injuries, stress fractures in the foot, or also suffer from plantar fasciitis? **That reason is weakened intrinsic foot muscles.**

It comes back to the simple idea that compensation, where one part of the body has to take over for the job of another part because that other part isn't doing its job, overstresses a nearby area of the body, be it a joint, bones, or muscle. Injury usually happens when load is added to that pattern of **compensation.**

In order to feel good, function well and perform, every body part must handle its responsibility and not be asked to do some other task it wasn't designed for. This concept is the central focus of so much of this training. It's simple! But oh, so profound.

How To Perform Short Foot Exercise

To strengthen the muscles contained INSIDE the foot.

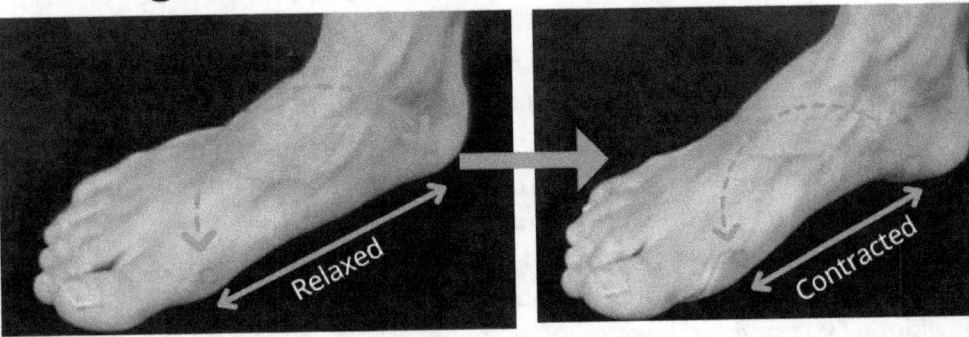

- Begin relaxing your foot and spreading the toes. Keep your entire foot flat on the ground.

- Imagine you're standing on a sandy beach and you are trying to pick up sand with your foot. You do this by contracting the muscles of your arch to "shorten" your foot.

- This may be difficult or even impossible at first. Keep at it. The more you practice, the easier it will become.

- Your toes may want to curl. Try to limit this. Eventually, you will be able to create the arch and also keep your toes relaxed.

- Keep your weight on the outside part of your foot, while keeping your entire foot in contact with the ground.

- **WATCH the full instructional video for SHORT FOOT on YouTube HERE:** shorturl.at/dEFNY

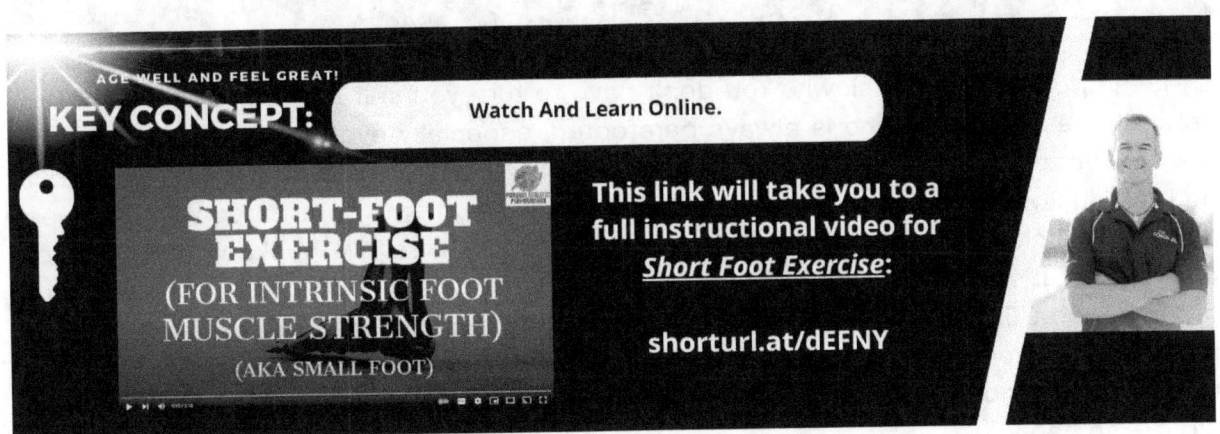

AGE WELL AND FEEL GREAT!

KEY CONCEPT:

Watch And Learn Online.

SHORT-FOOT EXERCISE (FOR INTRINSIC FOOT MUSCLE STRENGTH) (AKA SMALL FOOT)

This link will take you to a full instructional video for *Short Foot Exercise:*

shorturl.at/dEFNY

Putting Your Barefoot Forward.

For most of my life, I didn't understand the importance of spending time barefooted and didn't fully grasp the dangers of being in shoes, especially ill-fitting shoes. I'm paying the price for my ignorance now. My eyes were opened when I started to work with athletes in our gait lab around 2010. Since then, I've made a conscious effort to learn as much as I can about the human foot and spend as much time as possible barefooted. I hope you're inspired to do the same after reading.

One of the most common questions I get is "can I restore my toes and feet to what they were when they were younger?" The answer to that is, it depends. The primary challenge is the degree or severity of the changes in the bony structure. For example, if you have severe bunions and hallux valgus of the big toe (as I do), there isn't anything other than surgery that will restore it to how it was when you were a toddler.

Hope isn't lost however. Improving intrinsic muscle strength with Short-Foot exercise, going barefoot more often, doing frequent mobilization of the toes and feet (following the guidance of the videos I've provided links to in this chapter) and once and for all, ditching the toe-cramping shoes will definitely get you moving in the right direction. I certainly am able to do all of the sports I like to do with minimal limitation. There's always hope if you work at it.

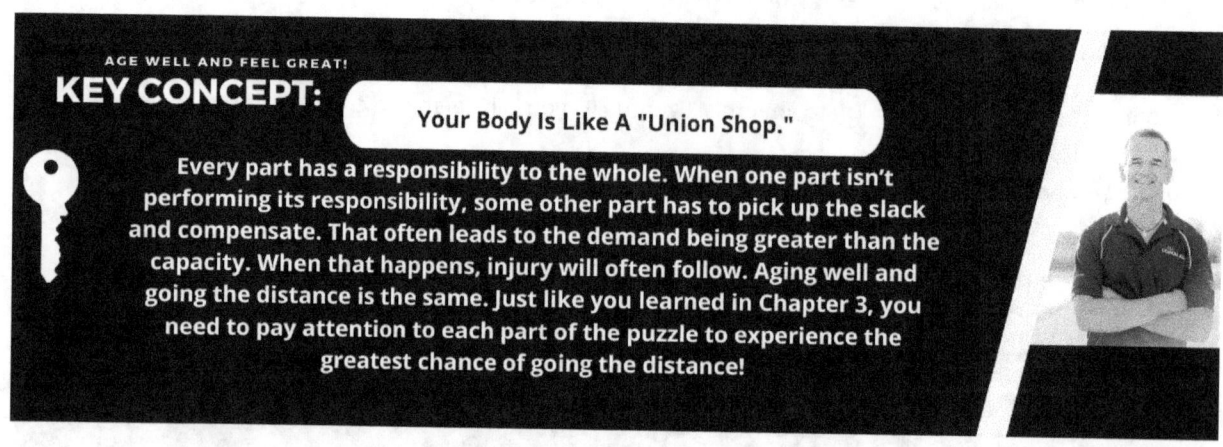

AGE WELL AND FEEL GREAT!

KEY CONCEPT:

Your Body Is Like A "Union Shop."

Every part has a responsibility to the whole. When one part isn't performing its responsibility, some other part has to pick up the slack and compensate. That often leads to the demand being greater than the capacity. When that happens, injury will often follow. Aging well and going the distance is the same. Just like you learned in Chapter 3, you need to pay attention to each part of the puzzle to experience the greatest chance of going the distance!

It's important to start slowly. You don't have to turn yourself into a barefoot expert or be known as someone who is always barefooted, especially overnight. Just like anything else you've exposed your body to for most of your life, when you take it away, you should do it gradually. Remember, anyone who hasn't spent much time barefooted will have weak intrinsic muscles, soft skin, and be injured easily, so the first few weeks will be the most challenging. It's very common to feel every single tiny rock or stick or uneven part of the ground at first. Try kicking your shoes off and heading out into your yard to play around. As time goes on, your feet will toughen up. Think of all of the societies around the world who traditionally do not wear shoes, or our human ancestors from thousands of years ago. They did it – so can you.

In case you're wondering, you don't have to go "cold turkey" and give up shoes entirely. I typically am barefooted around the house, when I go for walks, and often when I'm driving. I always exercise in our home gym barefooted. But I always wear shoes when going out into restaurants, shopping, and of course also for work. Half the time when I'm wearing shoes, it is flip-flops. Other times it's a different soft shoe to provide some covering. And yes, I always wear running shoes for running.

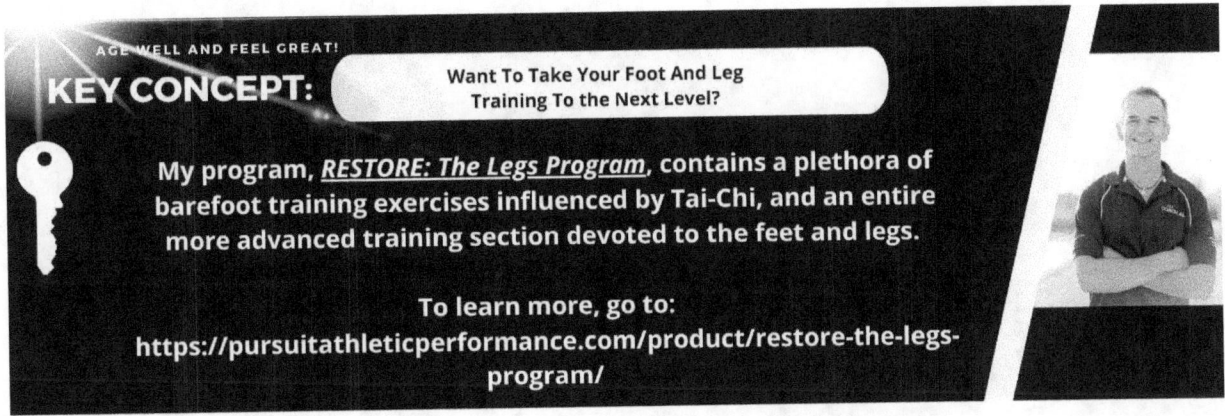

AGE WELL AND FEEL GREAT!

KEY CONCEPT: Want To Take Your Foot And Leg Training To the Next Level?

My program, _RESTORE: The Legs Program_, contains a plethora of barefoot training exercises influenced by Tai-Chi, and an entire more advanced training section devoted to the feet and legs.

To learn more, go to:
https://pursuitathleticperformance.com/product/restore-the-legs-program/

Some reading this will have more challenges when going barefooted. For example, anyone who has had a foot injury in the past or has foot mechanics that result in more stress on the bones, will need to approach it more conservatively. Remember we're all an experiment of one in terms of foot shape, bony structure, and soft tissue. Don't force it by being more aggressive than is smart, for you. If you can very gradually increase your barefoot exposure over a long period of time, and combine that with the mobility, proprioceptive, and strengthening exercises in this chapter, you'll eventually build more resilient feet that will be ready to support you for the rest of your life.

What Else Do You Need To Know About Shoes?

The most important choice you can make to care for your feet is to wear shoes that allow your feet and toes to splay freely. Avoid shoes that cramp your toes at all cost. There are increasing numbers of brands that offer shoes with a wide toe box. Similarly, avoid an elevated heel if you can. Just remember, if you've spent most of your life in shoes with an elevated heel, and then decide to go without that elevation, you will be forcing your calf and Achilles tendon to stretch. So as before, the key is to transition _gradually_. Over time, the muscles will lengthen naturally and become increasingly resilient with the other supplementary work you are doing.

Walking and exercising barefooted are crucial for the health of your feet, despite the myths about being barefooted that prevent people from doing it more often. Are there some risks? Like anything, the answer depends on the environment you're in and whether you've given your body time to adapt. Be smart and take it one step at a time, and your feet will thank you a thousand times over by taking you wherever you may want to go!

CHAPTER 22

DAILY MOVEMENT OVERVIEW:
HABITS, RULES, FOREVER MOVEMENT GOALS, AND THE MAGIC BULLET

Even as our bones and teeth soften, the rest of our body hardens. Blood vessels, joints, the muscles and valves of the heart, and even the lungs, pick up substantial deposits of calcium and turn stiff. Under a microscope, the vessels and soft tissues display the same form of calcium that you find in bone.

When you reach inside an elderly patient during surgery, the aorta and other major blood vessels can feel crunchy under your fingers. As we age, it's as if the calcium seeps out of our skeletons and into our tissues.

— Atul Gawande, M.D.

Forget past failures, forget mistakes, forget everything
except what you're going to do now, and do it.
— Will Durant, *historian*

The most effective way to do it, is to do it.
— Amelia Earhart, *aviator*

For many years I co-owned a gait analysis lab working with injured athletes of all ages, abilities, and from different sport backgrounds. If you're wondering what the term "gait analysis" means, it's an often misunderstood term that describes assessing a person's walking or running gait as well as other movement skills, all with the goal of looking for areas of opportunity for the person to improve their stamina and speed or get out of an injury cycle. Done correctly, it should be an in-depth process looking at every aspect of movement from head to toe.

At the outset of working with someone to help them overcome any fragility in order for them to regain their ability to move freely without pain, I'd tell them that we were going to start by going through what I referred to as "authentic, developmental" movement practice. As we got down on the floor, I'd say, "we're exploring natural reflexes and movement patterns that were at one time, etched deeply into our nervous system. The learning process began for each of us when we were infants." Naturally, at first some would look at me with a puzzled look, but as we got into it, it all made intuitive sense to them. Think about it: How do children learn? How do they develop both their brains and their bodies? The answer is, they explore. They play. They move. If we're going to start somewhere to really change and improve, then we need to be like children.

If it helps, think of it in computer terms. Have you ever noticed if you let your computer run day and night and open lots of programs, it will bog down and not work as well? We used to have to "defragment" the hard drive when this happened. At a minimum, one thing that always works is to shut it down and restart it. What we're essentially doing is "rebooting" that computer, giving it a chance to reset itself. Our body is much the same. It needs that occasional and even frequent "reboot."

It begins with the breath. Always go back to that first and foremost. Take a minute or two each day to revisit 3-D breathing and learn to use it as a basis for changing how you feel and how you move. From there we should move all our joints, especially our hips, neck and ankles, so we retain that ability to move freely.

Our body was designed through evolution to be resilient. We ought to be able to run and jump and crawl and play without sustaining injuries and nagging pain. When we hit our 70s and 80s, we should still be able to have a healthy body that allows us to enjoy life free from pain and restrictions and limitations. The truth is, our body is meant to age, but NOT in the way we are allowing ourselves to do it. We "age" and feel worse due to lack of use. Aging happens when we remain static and don't move in the ways we were designed to. **We don't wear out from overuse, we rust out from non-use!**

In the introduction to this chapter, I shared Jane's story. I also told you how tissue changes and either adapts or not, to what we do on a routine basis. We either use it or we lose it, it's that simple. It's not complicated and it certainly doesn't have to be very structured. The ideas I will share with you in this chapter are just that, ideas. Think about it: do you have to tell a child how to go out and play? Normally, the answer to that question would be an emphatic no. We should look at our own exploration the same way. There isn't any right or wrong way to explore how we move. There are only safe progressions which minimize our risk of injury and maximize time efficiency. I'll share those ideas and suggestions with you.

As you move and explore, start to play around with some of the movement "snacks" I'll suggest. Over time those may turn into "daily habits." That would be great! The truth is you might not get to them every day, but experience has taught me if I plan on doing something every day, I'll probably do it more often than I would if I didn't have a plan. That might sound weird, but I bet it makes sense to you. ☺

Age Well and Feel Great!

Key Concept:

My "Virtual" Gait Analysis process: it is available to you!

This image is taken from video at the start of the analysis. This runner was injured and had many areas of opportunity to improve.

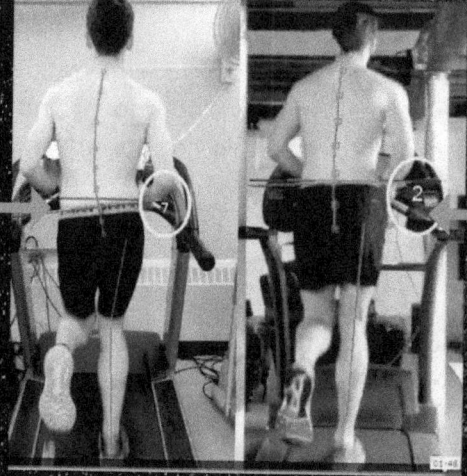

This image is taken from video after some consistent weeks of smart training to specifically address his movement issues.

To learn more about the in-depth virtual gait analysis service I offer, go to this page on my Pursuit Athletic Performance website:
https://pursuitathleticperformance.com/product/virtual-gait-analysis/

> *Don't give up. There are too many naysayers out there*
> *who will try to discourage you. Don't listen to them.*
> *The only one who can make you give up is you.*
> — Sidney Sheldon, *writer*

Is There A Magic Bullet to Moving Better? The Answer is YES!

You might be surprised to read this, but yes, there IS a magic bullet to moving better and unlocking the body of your dreams, where you can watch the years pile on and yet still retain the body of a youngster – the body you were meant to have. That magic bullet is this: **consistency.**

Throughout this book, I know I've said it more than a few times but it's worth repeating. *Consistency.* Think about it. What's the best way to make sure you keep all of your teeth? You brush and floss and care for them, *every day*. The same argument could be made for nearly anything of value. Want to keep your good health? Do the things you need to do, every day. You can have all of the knowledge and information in the world at your disposal but unless you take action almost every day, you simply won't get to where you want to go.

Author, James Clear, whose book *Atomic Habits* is an international best seller, said in an email to his list that "most people need consistency more than they need intensity. Intensity would be running a marathon, writing a book in 30 days, or a silent meditation retreat. Consistency is not missing a workout for two years, writing every week, and a little daily silence. Intensity makes a good story. Consistency makes progress." I agree wholeheartedly!

Of course, the challenge every person has is this: what is the secret to being consistent and not stopping at some point in the future, especially when it comes to exercise? Because odds are, most of the people reading this right now are going to be fired up to get started, but much like with those New Year's resolutions, they will lose steam as time marches on and stop. Isn't there some kind of trick or secret that can help YOU not be one of those statistics? As it turns out, this topic has been studied by scientists, who came up with an interesting answer that may help you solve this potential problem.

The answer comes back to habit formation, something James Clear wrote about eloquently in his book. Habits, regardless of whether they are good or bad, form because of cues. Cues are signals that tell us to do something. In one study, the researchers referred to two types of habits, an "instigation habit" and an "execution habit."[1]

An *execution habit* is when you're following a very specific routine laid out for you. Think of a set of instructions for a complex task you perform over and over. Or relating it to exercise, it's having a specific list of exercises you follow at the gym. It's also referred to as "automated movement through the behavioral sequence."[2] An *instigation habit* is different. This has to do with the cues that prompt you to automatically do something, such as when you awake to an alarm clock or the specific time of day when you know you have to leave for work. In other words, the habit process initiates the behavioral sequence.

In the study referenced earlier, researchers tracked the exercise habits of 118 healthy adults. What they found was *instigation habit*, which is the signal or cue to do something, was the only unique predictor of exercise frequency. When the researchers dug a little deeper, the primary *instigator* for the participants came down to one factor - the time of day.

What this tells me is that it's not how you move that matters when it comes to consistency, it's WHEN you do it. It's about the schedule. In other words, the people who are able to make movement and fitness part of their lifestyle are having success because they do it at a certain time almost every day.

For many people, the instigator is the alarm clock. They get up and go into their exercise or movement routine first thing in the morning. They don't even have to think about it, it's almost unconscious. Of course, that's the very nature of what a habit is, right? For those people, waking up and working out is as routine as flossing and brushing before bed. Preparing for bed is the cue that signals them to brush their teeth. Similarly, waking up is their cue to get moving.

For many years when I was a member of the U.S. Coast Guard Band, during a typical day we'd have a lunch hour between 11:30 AM and 1 PM. That time period was always my cue to run or train. Others are cued by getting off work or getting out of class. As an aside, this explains why it's sometimes hard to keep your exercise routine when your schedule changes or when you're traveling. Similarly, if you sleep in on the weekends it can be harder to get out of bed and do what you need to, because your "wake up, move, go to work" sequence was altered. If you're thinking that one answer is to get up at the same time on weekends to do your thing, that would also be my advice.

So, the next question you might have is, how long does it take to make it a habit? My experience tells me it takes at least four to six weeks. Some researchers have said it takes a month. Others have said as little as three weeks might do it. It's likely going to be different for each of us depending on our experience and schedule. The bottom line is, make sure you stick with it until the habit solidifies. To do that takes discipline and willpower, but only for a little while. Then it becomes habit, which doesn't require the willpower.

If you recall, in Chapter 18, *Exercise: The Struggle is Real*, I gave you four rules to follow to be successful establishing a new exercise habit. Do you remember? Rule #2 is what I want to focus on because it's where many people go wrong. Let's assume the researchers are correct that it takes at least a month to establish an activity as a habit. Does it matter what the activity is and how much you do it? You bet it does! What the researchers neglected to mention was something just as important as the time of day, and that is *starting small* - rule #2 from Chapter 18. I'll repeat what I said in that chapter: *You're going to do something that is only a tiny bit more than nothing at all.* And in case you're trying to imagine how doing something just a tiny bit more than nothing at all could possibly add up to a dramatic lifestyle change for the better, remember the power of compound interest. Tiny, bite-sized, easily sustainable exercise goals, allow you to gain a little momentum and use that momentum to power future increases in that activity, but only if you so desire. Consistency is your magic bullet to keep it going, and as I said earlier, at that early stage especially, keeping it going is *all that matters* at first.

Age Well and Feel Great!

Key Concept:

A Penny For Your Persistence.

Compound interest really is a great metaphor for how each of us can improve our lives every day. If you haven't recently considered how powerful compound interest is, let me tell you a story that will help.

One day there was a young man who was a contestant on a game show, who by the end of the game, was declared the winner! The host told him he had a choice of two prizes. He could choose to received $2.5 million in cash that day, OR he could choose to receive a penny that day, but the game show would double that penny every day for a month. The man paused for a moment and thought to himself, there's no way a penny will ever turn into more than 2.5 million in only 31 days. He told the host he'd take the 2.5 million that day, believing he was way ahead of the game. Would you have made the same choice? If you did, you'd be out a boat load of cash. You see, starting with a penny and doubling it every day for 31 days would total $10,737,418.24! Almost 11 million dollars!

By now you've realized that if the show happened in February, the take home would have been much less. The last few days made all the difference. Never forget the value of tiny improvements over the long haul. It adds up!

Five Rules for Success.

Since we're on the topic of rules to follow, for the upcoming suggested movement "snacks" I'm going to share with you, you will need some general guidelines for how to approach them. In fact, these guidelines can and should be used when engaging in any kind of exercise program. I call them "rules," but they really are just guidelines. Chances are, in my more than 40 years of exercise and coaching experience, I've broken these rules and made just about every mistake too, often more than once. You get to learn from my errors and benefit from my mistakes. Lucky you!

Rule #1.

None of the movements or exercises I share with you, or you read about in this book are ever meant to cause pain, or to be done with pain. If you ever feel pain, STOP immediately. **Do not move through pain or force anything.** That's rule #1.

Pain is your brain telling you something is wrong. If you're ever in doubt, always start with an appointment to see your healthcare provider and find out what may be causing the pain. Get a diagnosis. That's rule #1. No pain!

Rule #2.

The key with any of the movements I may discuss or introduce you to is to **start conservatively, especially if you haven't exercised recently**. That's rule #2.

In fact, my advice is to begin *so conservatively* that it almost feels like you aren't doing much of anything at all. The difference is you will be consistent in how you approach it. Remember, consistency is the magic bullet that will give you results. You have to stay with it! Which means nearly every day or every other day to start.

I love the way author, James Clear, uses this thinking to motivate himself to get moving. It's his, "so easy, I can't say no" approach, a concept he once shared in an email.

For example, let's say you want to get started on an exercise routine but you're finding it hard to get going and take that first step. You could start with only filling up your water bottle. That way, when you don't feel like doing it, you can simply tell yourself, *just fill up the water bottle.* Start there and then see what happens. The next step might be a little easier. Continue from there.

Whatever approach works best for you is what you want to go with, provided you remember that small consistent actions are MUCH more effective than trying to do too much, too soon. Please remember this. That's rule #2. Start conservatively but commit to being consistent.

GO THE DISTANCE RULES FOR MOVEMENT SUCCESS

5

1. Do not move through pain. Do not force anything.
2. Start conservatively.
3. Keep it simple.
4. Take it one step at a time.
5. Bring LOTS of enthusiasm.

Rule #3.

When it comes to beginning something that is brand new to you, it can easily seem overwhelming. That's normal. Therefore, our focus is going to be on **keeping things simple**. That's rule #3. Keep it simple.

Don't allow the knowledge and information and guidance I share with you in this or any chapter complicate what this is really all about, which is simply this: start to incorporate some daily movement habits into your routine so you'll keep what capacity you have or even improve on it as you age. That's it. **It's that simple.**

What IS one way to ensure you keep it simple? *Take it one step at a time, of course! Which is the next rule - rule #4.*

Rule #4.

Take it one step at a time. Why? Well, it doesn't matter what our long-term goal is nor does it matter what the endeavor or activity is. If we bite off too much at any one time, it is easy to become overwhelmed and lose our motivation to continue.

It's natural that motivation wanes a little bit over time, so it's a cup we need to keep refilling, and the way to do that is, you guessed it, **take it one step at a time.** That's rule #4.

You determine how quickly you'll progress through any of these exercises or daily habits. You are in charge! My advice is to *focus on the process, not on the results or on a timetable.* Make progress every day, and you'll get to where you want to go!

Nothing great ever happens in this life without enthusiasm. I think that's a quote from Benjamin Franklin if I remember right. ☺ So, yes, you need to **bring lots of enthusiasm to everything you learn** in this book. That's rule #5.

I love this article, *To Harness Neuroplasticity, Start with Enthusiasm* by Dr. Helen Popovic. In it, she shares that our brain isn't subject exclusively to the commands of our DNA, but rather, is an ever-evolving organ that is "continually altering its structure, cell number, circuitry, and chemistry as a direct result of everything we do, experience, think and believe."[3]

To some degree, the exact same thing could be said for our joints. And maybe, just maybe, even the rest of the muscles and tendons and ligaments in our body. It is possible, you know? It's truly remarkable to consider all the things we **don't yet know** about our bodies – and what amazing discoveries might be made far into the future.

I especially appreciate this, from the article: *"When we practice a skill in our imaginations, the same neurons are firing as if we were performing the skill in real life! If we see ourselves executing a task perfectly in the mind's eye, we become better at it in the real world because mental rehearsal increases the efficiency of electrical transmissions between the involved nerve cells. Mental practice turbocharges our progress!"*[4]

In a book by Dr. Joe Dispenza, called *Breaking the Habit of Being Yourself – How to Lose Your Mind and Create a New One*, several of the concepts he presents align with what Dr. Popovic discusses in her article. He talks about these ideas, not specifically from the skill-building perspective, but from the point of view **if we start with the right thoughts, we can set in motion the rewiring of our neurons, which in turn can change our feelings.** Those thoughts and feelings ultimately lead to actions aligned with, and move us toward our goals, intentions, expectations – those things that we initially thought. Or not.

I've learned this firsthand - the power of our thinking goes so far as to set off the chemical stimulus in the brain and body such that the body is feeling and doing things *as if the "event"/ thought has already happened,* and therefore can make us an agent in influencing the actual situation, all according to our thoughts. This creates a new habit, one that organizes both captain and the crew (to use Dr. Popovic's analogy) more consistently toward the outcomes we want. This is a powerful tool we carry around all day! It is cool to think about how to maximize its potential!

So, what's the point in sharing these concepts and ideas? It's this: **our mental mindset, enthusiasm, thought process, and approach all greatly impact our potential for success.**

The take home is, be enthusiastic and imaginative. Practice in your mind's eye and visualize where you want to be as you learn these movement "snacks" and habits and along the way, keep your practice fun! Make it as playful as possible, in every way you can.

Age Well and Feel Great!

Key Concept:

Is Using A Foam Roller A Waste Of Time?

If you've ever visited a physical therapist or been to your doctor with a soft tissue injury, you've no doubt been exposed to a foam roller or some other similar tool designed for "self-myofascial release."

Without a doubt, these are popular and for good reason. Sometimes it just feels good to use these. Some people really seem to love the feeling (of pain!) as they hammer on their quads, IT band, and hips! The more it hurts, the better we think it is for us...and the more we think we need to do it, right? What are we missing? When it comes to that statement I just made, I believe the truth is, we don't exactly know whether the pain is "good," or whether it's beneficial to do more of it when it hurts. Certainly, among the experts, the jury is out on what's actually happening to our body when we foam roll or use a similar tool, AND whether or not there's real change in the tissue that helps us long-term. In fact, according to quite a few experts, we aren't really doing Self Myofascial Release at all, at least in the way many of us have believed. I happen to agree.

I'm not about to say here that foam rolling is a waste of time or that it's bad for you. It actually feels good, and that may well be enough reason to do it! Many believe the time they spend rolling and doing other soft tissue manipulation IS valuable and feels good, and isn't that what matters? All I am saying is, we've got lots more to learn about the topic.

Your "Forever" Movement Goals.

Can you put on your slacks, socks, and shoes while standing? Whenever I dress, I stand and see how well I can put everything on without leaning on anything else or sitting down. Is it always easy or even doable? The answer is no. Some days, especially the morning after not sleeping well or the day after some hard training, it is challenging. But I never stop trying. The days when I can nail it feels really good.

How about this: Can you get up off the floor and stand without using your hands? For some, it's relatively easy to do. Those who find it easy usually have good hip flexibility and very likely are able to move well. For others with much less flexibility or who might have a specific physical limitation, it can feel almost impossible.

These skills are what I think of as "forever movement goals." I include some variation of these every day as part of my own routine of daily movements. There are certain kinds of movements that represent good overall movement competency. These two skills fall into that category. As such, wherever you fall on the continuum of these skills, I recommend you include some practice in your daily routine. When it comes to putting your clothes on while standing, begin by relearning how to balance on a single leg, something I discussed in the previous chapter on *How to Improve Your Feet*. As your balance improves, and with the aid of a wall to lean on, you'll develop the confidence to give it a try.

As for getting up off the floor, start first by getting comfortable in the 90/90 position. You'll be introduced to that in the next chapter. Adjust yourself on the floor to find the easiest position to elevate to half kneeling. Keep practicing! Get started now and no matter what, never ever give up trying!

What About Flexibility?

If you're bothered by aches and pains or feel stiff and cranky some of the time, it is possible you're losing some flexibility and that might be the culprit for why you feel the way you do. Flexibility is simply the ability of muscles to stretch to their full length or range of motion. We know that as we age, our soft tissue like muscles, ligaments, and tendons, get stiffer and less elastic. Think of an elastic band that's been in the drawer for years and has dried out. It won't stretch as easily and will break if you force it to stretch out too aggressively.

Now, think about a cut or scrape you may get on some part of your body. Notice how as it heals, it tends to leave a little bit of a scar. That scar doesn't stretch quite as easily as the skin around it. That same kind of healing process is happening inside your body every day through the great majority of your life, even though you can't see it. So, what's the answer? As you've already heard more than once, it's to *use it or lose it*.

In Chapter 17, which is the introduction to the movement portion of the book, you learned how tissue turns over based on the latest demands that are placed upon it. It is literally a *use it or lose it* scenario. And the same thing that is true for joint range of motion is also true for muscle flexibility. That being said, in my many years working as a therapist and coach, I've found flexibility is dependent on three major characteristics. What are those?

1. **The first is joint articulation or range of motion**. You learned about this in Chapter 17, the introduction to this part of the book. If your joints can't move through a full range of motion, you won't be able to extend or flex your muscles, increasing the likelihood they become shorter over time.

2. **Joint stability or instability is also related**. If the stability of those joints, which relies on both function and strength of the muscles and connective tissue around the joint worsens, you won't be able to extend or flex your muscles, which also increases the likelihood of them becoming shorter over time. You'll learn more in the chapter on stability.

3. **The other characteristic is muscle strength**. If the muscles become weaker, you will lose the ability to control and use your full joint range of motion. Again, over time, that range of motion will shrink and muscles will shorten, reducing your flexibility.

In summary, when you move frequently through a nice large range of motion and take care of your joints by improving stability and strength, there's much less need for static (non-moving) stretching. Although sometimes that kind of stretching can feel very good!

Still, if you sit too much, your hamstrings on the back of your thighs will get tighter and make it harder for you to bend over. If you spend too much time looking at your smartphone or computer, the front of your chest and shoulders will become tighter and increase the chance of shoulder pain. Muscle imbalances can lead to pain in many areas, so be sure to pay close attention and be aware of where the imbalances exist. Seek help to determine how to rectify the imbalance. The movements I've presented here are a great start.

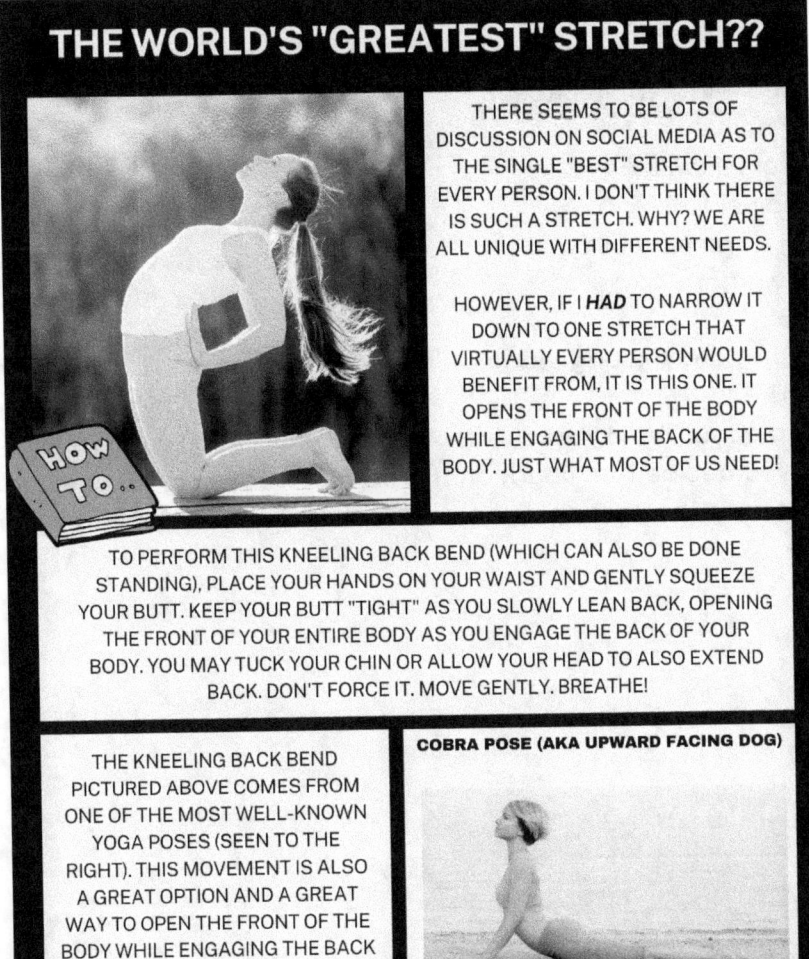

THE WORLD'S "GREATEST" STRETCH??

THERE SEEMS TO BE LOTS OF DISCUSSION ON SOCIAL MEDIA AS TO THE SINGLE "BEST" STRETCH FOR EVERY PERSON. I DON'T THINK THERE IS SUCH A STRETCH. WHY? WE ARE ALL UNIQUE WITH DIFFERENT NEEDS.

HOWEVER, IF I *HAD* TO NARROW IT DOWN TO ONE STRETCH THAT VIRTUALLY EVERY PERSON WOULD BENEFIT FROM, IT IS THIS ONE. IT OPENS THE FRONT OF THE BODY WHILE ENGAGING THE BACK OF THE BODY. JUST WHAT MOST OF US NEED!

HOW TO...

TO PERFORM THIS KNEELING BACK BEND (WHICH CAN ALSO BE DONE STANDING), PLACE YOUR HANDS ON YOUR WAIST AND GENTLY SQUEEZE YOUR BUTT. KEEP YOUR BUTT "TIGHT" AS YOU SLOWLY LEAN BACK, OPENING THE FRONT OF YOUR ENTIRE BODY AS YOU ENGAGE THE BACK OF YOUR BODY. YOU MAY TUCK YOUR CHIN OR ALLOW YOUR HEAD TO ALSO EXTEND BACK. DON'T FORCE IT. MOVE GENTLY. BREATHE!

THE KNEELING BACK BEND PICTURED ABOVE COMES FROM ONE OF THE MOST WELL-KNOWN YOGA POSES (SEEN TO THE RIGHT). THIS MOVEMENT IS ALSO A GREAT OPTION AND A GREAT WAY TO OPEN THE FRONT OF THE BODY WHILE ENGAGING THE BACK OF THE BODY.

COBRA POSE (AKA UPWARD FACING DOG)

One of the ways I like to keep some relaxed stretching and recovery oriented movement in my routine is with this Dynamic Movement Flow. I shot a follow-along video for you, so you too can enjoy this routine. It's 7 ½ minutes long focusing on the spine and hips!

While I refer to this "flow" as being "running-specific," it is wonderful for any person! Don't shy away because of what I call it. In truth, running makes us tighter so any series of stretching that's good for a runner is bound to be great for others, too.

The movements I go through in this follow-along video are:

- Camel stretch
- Quadraped with T-Spine Reach
- Kneeling spinal twist
- Seated spinal twist
- Supine spinal twist
- Standing t-spine mobility
- Twisted warrior

You can find the follow along video on my website and YouTube channel here: shorturl.at/mpq67

In the next chapter, you'll find your daily movement "snacks" guidance and all the information you need should you decide to embark on the 30-day bodyweight squat challenge.

Keep going – this is the best decision you've ever made. Let's keep it fun!

CHAPTER 23

YOUR MOVE-SMART PROGRAM:
DAILY MOVEMENT "SNACKS" AND A 30-DAY BODYWEIGHT SQUAT CHALLENGE

What is action? Action is commonplace, right action is not. As a discipline, it's not any kind of action that will do, but directed action. Everything must be done in service of the whole. Step by step, action by action, we'll dismantle the obstacles in front of us. With persistence and flexibility, we'll act in the best interest of our goals.

Action requires courage, not brashness — creative application and not brute force. Our movements and decisions define us: We must be sure to act with deliberation, boldness, and persistence. Those are the attributes of right and effective action. Nothing else — not thinking or evasion or aid from others. Action is the solution and the cure to our predicaments.

— Ryan Holiday, from his book,
The Obstacle is the Way: The Timeless Art of Turning Trials Into Triumph

> *We must all either wear out or rust out, every*
> *one of us. My choice is to wear out.*
> — Theodore Roosevelt

The key to feeling good and staying healthy for a lifetime is to keep moving and to keep moving *forward*. Over and over again throughout this book, you're hearing how important it is make movement an integral part of your daily life. It doesn't have to be structured movement, although some people can really benefit from a structured approach or they just won't get it done. So, which kind of person are you? It's important to know yourself and then act accordingly. Something as simple as getting out on a Saturday night to dance or jumping into your local Zumba class, or if you like, a Tai-chi or yoga class, all of these options can be great pieces to the aging puzzle. It all depends on what your starting point is. They all get you moving and can be lots of fun, too!

There's another possible solution to where we find ourselves in this modern world of conveniences and for many of us, too much time spent not just sitting in a chair but not moving much at all, and that is to insert some movement "snacks" into our daily routine. That's partly what this chapter is all about.

Over time, the idea is these movement "snacks" become habits that you just do without thinking about it too much. I think of these movement "snacks" as little micro-bursts of activity – as child-like play – that can range all the way from simply shifting positions and getting up out of the chair more often, to going to a stairway nearby and going up and down a flight of stairs, to hitting the deck for a set of pushups, or sitting in a sustained deep squat. Or going through the eight different movements I will share with you shortly.

The goal is to MOVE around and get every part of your body involved. We'll do that by changing positions, getting up and down, and in the process, perhaps even jumpstart our heart rate a little bit while building strength, too. If you remember, in the chapter titled *Exercise: The Struggle is Real*, one of the tips I shared was to start to include some of these movement "snacks." Whatever you want to call it, in this day and age this might end up being the best possible way for busy professionals or anyone else for that matter, to get some healthy movements and exercise into their day. It is certainly among the most practical.

It's no secret there are cultures around the world where people have no back pain, unlike here in the U.S. where back pain is epidemic. There's a few reasons why this is now the norm, but the most obvious and important is in those other cultures, people get up and down off of the ground often, they're able to squat down without pain, and they rarely spend much time sitting.

The way we'll introduce these daily movement "snacks" is with my **Move-Smart Program**. This program consists of two important elements:

1. **Mobility-oriented daily movement "snacks" designed to give you some ideas to get you moving on a daily basis.** They're all quick and snack-like! They can be

done at any time, day or night, in any location – at home, at the gym, at the park or beach – anywhere! They don't require any special equipment and are guaranteed to leave you feeling better than when you started. They don't all need to be done at once or in succession. They don't even need to be done daily, although you'll feel better if you do. They are here for you, to choose from and integrate as you like. It's up to you!

2. **A 30-day Basic Bodyweight Squat challenge**. The goal? To help you relearn the most primal and fundamental movement pattern for a human being, and then by practicing it, build better mobility and strength of the hips, ankles, and legs. The real power in this basic movement is how primal and functional it is!

None of these movements should ever feel intense, at least not at the start. <u>The best approach is to think of this daily movement practice as that space between very relaxed non-moving stretching, and more intense strength training</u>. So, what are the primary goals and intention with this frequent movement practice?

- You are learning about your body and moving in ways that aren't necessarily typical for you in your normal daily routine. As such, you can easily add these to what you might already be doing, be it walking, gardening, riding a bike, or running. If you've been inactive and need something to get you going, these are perfect for that purpose.
- You are pumping blood throughout your body and lubricating your joints to keep them moving freely and easily.
- You are exploring many different joint positions and ranges of motion, all at a low intensity. It should be just enough to drive blood flow but not so much that you get fatigued and feel like you have to recover.

With all of these moves, there's a series of consistent themes. What are they?

- **We're prioritizing our hips and shoulders**. When your hips are moving freely, you'll instantly reduce low-back pain and stiffness. When your shoulders are moving freely, you'll reduce neck stiffness.
- **We're prioritizing movement variety**, by exploring patterns that aren't typical for most of us in our daily lives. The goal is to get out of our movement "comfort zone" (but do so in a comfortable, smart manner that is not intense) and explore some of the other patterns that our body is designed to be able to do.

In order to accomplish these goals, you want to make sure you:

- Stay within your comfort zone in terms of sensations of pain or discomfort, NOT outside of it.

- Always do these in a way that feels "safe" for you. Always work with your body, don't fight it.
- Stay mindful and completely connected to your breath. If you get out of breath, you're working too hard. Don't think of any of these movements as "working out." Rather, think of it as *exploring your body* and *nourishing your body*.
- Anticipate that they should feel a little bit different each time you go through them.
- Remember this isn't and shouldn't ever be "intense."
- Do these barefooted whenever you can!

SUNRISE SALUTES

BEGIN IN A PRAYER POSITION. REACH UP AND OUT SLOWLY AND THEN HIGH UP TOWARD THE SKY. THEN FAN OUT WIDE, KEEPING YOUR ELBOWS BACK. KEEP YOUR SPINE STRAIGHT AND AVOID OVERARCHING YOUR BACK. BREATHE NORMALLY.

GO THE DISTANCE - DAILY MOVEMENT "SNACKS"

TOE TOUCHES

BEGIN STANDING STRAIGHT AND RELAXED. INHALE AND THEN GENTLY HINGE AT THE HIPS AND LET YOUR TRUNK FALL FORWARD, RELAXING YOUR ARMS TO THE GROUND AS YOU RELEASE A SLOW EXHALE. DON'T FORCE IT. LET GRAVITY ASSIST. REPEAT.

GO THE DISTANCE - DAILY MOVEMENT "SNACKS"

CAT - COW: ON ALL FOURS

BEGIN WITH YOUR HANDS AND KNEES ON THE FLOOR IN A NEUTRAL SPINE POSITION - KNEES UNDER YOUR HIPS AND YOUR WRISTS UNDER YOUR SHOULDERS. TAKE A DEEP INHALE THROUGH YOUR NOSE, THEN SLOWLY EXHALE AS YOU ROUND YOUR SPINE UP TOWARD THE CEILING. IMAGINE YOU'RE PULLING YOUR BELLY BUTTON UP TOWARD YOUR SPINE. TUCK YOUR CHIN TOWARD YOUR CHEST, AND LET YOUR NECK RELEASE. THIS IS YOUR CAT-LIKE SHAPE. ON YOUR NEXT INHALE ARCH YOUR BACK, LET YOUR BELLY RELAX, AND GO LOOSE. LIFT YOUR HEAD AND TAILBONE UP TOWARD THE SKY — WITHOUT PUTTING ANY UNNECESSARY PRESSURE ON YOUR NECK OR BACK. THIS IS THE COW PORTION OF THE POSE.

GO THE DISTANCE - DAILY MOVEMENT "SNACKS"

CAT - COW: SEATED

BEGIN SITTING WITH GOOD POSTURE, IN A NEUTRAL SPINE POSITION. JUST AS WHEN PRONE, TAKE A DEEP INHALE THROUGH YOUR NOSE, THEN ON THE EXHALE, ROUND YOUR SPINE UP TOWARD THE BACK OF THE CHAIR. IMAGINE YOU'RE PULLING YOUR BELLY BUTTON TOWARD YOUR SPINE. TUCK YOUR CHIN TOWARD YOUR CHEST, AND LET YOUR NECK RELEASE. THIS IS YOUR CAT-LIKE SHAPE. ON YOUR NEXT INHALE, ARCH YOUR BACK, LET YOUR BELLY RELAX, AND GO LOOSE. LIFT YOUR HEAD AND TAILBONE UP TOWARD THE SKY — WITHOUT PUTTING ANY UNNECESSARY PRESSURE ON YOUR NECK OR BACK. THIS IS THE COW PORTION OF THE POSE.

GO THE DISTANCE - DAILY MOVEMENT "SNACKS"

TOE WALKING - HEEL WALKING

JUST AS IT SOUNDS, THE GOAL IS TO RISE UP ONTO YOUR TOES AND WALK. AND THEN DO THE SAME BY RISING UP ONTO YOUR HEELS. TRY TO GET AS "HIGH" AS YOU CAN IN EACH POSITION, WHICH CAN BE A NICE WAY TO STRENGTHEN THE LOWER LEGS AND FEET. USE A SUPPORT IF NECESSARY.

GO THE DISTANCE - DAILY MOVEMENT "SNACKS"

SHOULDER ROTATIONS: PAGE 1

Explore your shoulder range of motion without forcing it!

BEGIN STANDING. RAISE YOUR ARMS UP STRAIGHT TOWARD THE SKY. LENGTHEN YOUR SPINE BUT DON'T OVERARCH YOUR BACK. FEET ARE HIP-WIDTH. FOCUS ON MOVING YOUR SHOULDERS *ONLY* - NOTHING ELSE. WHEN READY, SLOWLY ROTATE YOUR PALMS OUT (#2) AND BEGIN MOVING SLOWLY AROUND TO THE BACK. KEEP PALMS DOWN.

GO THE DISTANCE - DAILY MOVEMENT "SNACKS"

SHOULDER ROTATIONS: PAGE 2

CONTINUE BY PRESSING YOUR ARMS AS FAR BACK AS YOU CAN. DON'T FORCE IT BUT DO SEEK THE OUTER-MOST RANGE YOU CAN ACHIEVE. THEN ROTATE PALMS UP (#6) AND REVERSE DIRECTION BACK TO THE START POSITION. STAY TALL AND FOCUS ON MOVING ONLY THROUGH YOUR SHOULDERS. REPEAT AS MANY TIMES AS YOU LIKE.

GO THE DISTANCE - DAILY MOVEMENT "SNACKS"

SEATED 90/90 ROTATIONS: NO HANDS

Explore your hip range of motion without forcing it!

BEGIN SEATED AND SEPARATE YOUR LEGS, TURNING ONE KNEE IN AND ONE KNEE OUT. SIT AS "TALL" AS YOU CAN, PLACING YOUR HANDS WHERE YOU LIKE, BUT NOT ON THE GROUND. SLOWLY ROTATE YOUR HIPS FROM ONE SIDE TO THE OTHER, STAYING "TALL" WHILE YOU ROTATE THROUGH YOUR HIPS. MOVE BACK AND FORTH REPEATEDLY.

GO THE DISTANCE - DAILY MOVEMENT "SNACKS"

SEATED 90/90 ROTATIONS: HAND SUPPORT

BEGIN SEATED, THIS TIME LEANING BACK ON YOUR HANDS. SET UP WITH ONE KNEE IN AND ONE KNEE OUT. SIT AS "TALL" AS YOU CAN. SLOWLY ROTATE YOUR HIPS FROM ONE SIDE TO THE OTHER, STAYING "TALL" WHILE YOU ROTATE THROUGH YOUR HIPS. MOVE BACK AND FORTH AS MUCH AS YOU LIKE. KEEP YOUR SPINE "LONG."

GO THE DISTANCE - DAILY MOVEMENT "SNACKS"

LYING 90/90 ROTATIONS

BEGIN LYING ON YOUR BACK, KNEES BENT, FEET FLAT, AND HIPS UP. SEPARATE YOUR FEET WIDER THAN HIP-WIDTH. RISE UP ONTO YOUR HEELS AND ROTATE YOUR HIPS, ONE KNEE IN AND ONE KNEE OUT. TRY TO KEEP YOUR HIPS UP TOWARD THE SKY. MOVE SLOWLY AND ONLY GO AS FAR AS YOU CAN, SEEKING TO EXTEND TO THE GROUND (#5) AS YOU PRACTICE. MAKE SURE TO DO BOTH DIRECTIONS.

GO THE DISTANCE - DAILY MOVEMENT "SNACKS"

KNEE QUARTER BENDING:FEET TOGETHER

BEGIN STANDING WITH YOUR FEET TOGETHER. GENTLY BEND STRAIGHT DOWN AT THE HIPS, KNEES, AND ANKLES. PLACE YOUR HANDS WHERE THEY ARE MOST COMFORTABLE. GO AS LOW AS YOU ARE ABLE TO, SEEKING TO GO EVEN DEEPER WITH PRACTICE. BREATHE NORMALLY.

GO THE DISTANCE - DAILY MOVEMENT "SNACKS"

KNEE QUARTER BENDING: FEET APART

BEGIN STANDING WITH YOUR FEET FAR APART. GENTLY BEND AT THE HIPS, KNEES, AND ANKLES. PLACE YOUR HANDS WHERE THEY ARE MOST COMFORTABLE. GO AS LOW AS YOU ARE ABLE TO SAFELY, SEEKING TO EXPAND THE DEPTH WITH PRACTICE.

GO THE DISTANCE - DAILY MOVEMENT "SNACKS"

KNEE QUARTER BENDING: FRONT - BACK

BEGIN STANDING WITH ONE FOOT IN FRONT OF THE OTHER. KEEP YOUR FEET HIP-WIDTH APART. BEND BOTH KNEES ABOUT QUARTER DEPTH, GOING DEEPER AS YOU GAIN PRACTICE. PLACE YOUR HANDS WHERE THEY ARE COMFORTABLE.

GO THE DISTANCE - DAILY MOVEMENT "SNACKS"

KNEE QUARTER BENDING: KNEE CIRCLES

BEGIN STANDING WITH YOUR FEET TOGETHER. GENTLY BEND AT THE HIPS, KNEES, AND ANKLES AND THEN MOVE YOUR KNEES IN A CIRCULAR MOTION. START WITH SMALL CIRCLES AND EXPAND THE RANGE OF MOTION AS YOU LIKE. GO IN BOTH DIRECTIONS.

GO THE DISTANCE - DAILY MOVEMENT "SNACKS"

KNEE QUARTER BENDING: SIDE WAYS

BEGIN STANDING WITH YOUR FEET APART. KEEP ONE LEG STRAIGHT AND BEND THE OPPOSITE KNEE, HIP AND ANKLE. BEND ABOUT QUARTER DEPTH, GOING DEEPER AS YOU GAIN PRACTICE. PLACE YOUR HANDS WHERE THEY ARE COMFORTABLE.

GO THE DISTANCE - DAILY MOVEMENT "SNACKS"

RISE UP FROM THE FLOOR WITHOUT USING YOUR HANDS: OPTION 1 (EASIER)

BEGIN IN A 90/90 POSITION. KEEP YOUR HANDS WHEREVER YOU LIKE AS LONG AS YOU DON'T TOUCH THE GROUND. RISE UP BY PRESSING YOUR LEG INTO THE GROUND. ONCE YOU ARE ON YOUR KNEES, YOU CAN MOVE INTO HALF KNEELING AND STAND!

GO THE DISTANCE - "LIFETIME" MOVEMENT GOALS

RISE UP FROM THE FLOOR WITHOUT USING YOUR HANDS: OPTION 2 (HARDER)

GO THE DISTANCE - "LIFETIME" MOVEMENT GOALS

PUSH UP:

A STRENGTH EXERCISE CAN ALSO BE A GREAT DAILY MOVEMENT "SNACK"

TO LEARN HOW TO DO A BASIC PUSH-UP. <u>WATCH A 1.5 MINUTE INSTRUCTIONAL VIDEO</u> ON THE PURSUIT YOUTUBE PAGE.
Go Here:
shorturl.at/qrswy

If you're just starting o[ ]
with this, keep the range of
motion small to start.
That's quite OK!

*2 or 3 REPS

*5 seconds down

*2 second pause at the

easier range of motion

*5 seconds back up

GO THE DISTANCE - DAILY MOVEMENT "SNACKS"

THREE DAILY HABITS

FOR FOOT, ANKLE, KNEE, AND HIP HEALTH

1
Sitting on your legs (full knee flexion) with feet plantar flexed.

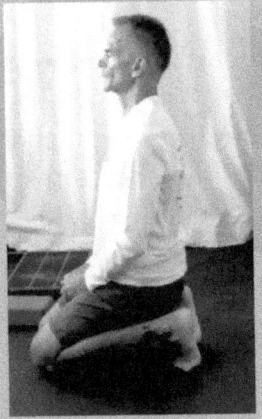

2
Sitting on your legs with ankles dorsiflexed, toes curled under.

3
Deep squat with elevated heel/slant board.

What Is One Other Thing You Can Do To Enhance the Health Of Your Feet, Ankles, and Knees?

The answer is....

Backwards Walking!

Backwards Walking?

You've read how important it is to including plenty of walking in your routine. What you might not have thought of is how valuable it can be to do some backward walking also.

It's a totally different way to move than "normal." You're pressing off your toes and extending the knee in a unique way vastly different than forward walking. Just be sure you are on safe ground and you know what is behind you! 😊

How Much Should You Do? The Answer Is:

Do Only What You *Can Do* Safely.

Find out where you are right now. Be mindful and know that to rush the *process* might end up stalling your *progress* long term. One step at a time! When you're ready, then move on to the more advanced skills, but only when you're ready.

Within each practice, remember that one or two minutes of relaxed mindful movement is much better than 20-minutes of forced frustration. How you feel and move from one day to the next will always be a "moving target," especially as you age. For example, you won't always come back to an exercise or movement the next day and feel like you've improved. Some days you'll feel as though you took a step back, and other days you'll feel like you have made a quantum leap forward. It's all OK. Life, and our bodies, have a habit of reminding us it moves at its own pace. We need to respect that and honor our body along the way.

All of these movement variations are different and represent some ideas about how we can incorporate moving more dynamically into our daily routine. They are by no means all you can or should do. If you aren't familiar with any of these, you need to take it slow and easy and do only what you can. There's nothing remotely competitive about any of this, and you definitely do NOT need to do them all, every day. Select a few to play around with. It's about exploration and play. You are always welcome to add more to your routine once you are ready and able. It's up to you.

Don't force any of it, and don't get frustrated if you find something is beyond your capacity right now. Scale it to make it easier. The future is limitless, if you look at it as one step, one skill, one day, one habit, at a time. You simply need a smart approach that has you very carefully and gradually moving forward. If you end up sore or feel like you did too much at one time, then you absolutely did too much. Always remember that in one individual practice or session, less is more. Focus on being consistent day in and day out. Consistency is your watch word. Consistency is the key. Consistency is the magic bullet you seek. Progress at your own pace. Enjoy the journey!

LET'S HANG OUT!
Improve Grip Strength AND Healthspan.

PERHAPS THE SINGLE BEST THING YOU COULD DO FOR IMPROVING SHOULDER AND BACK STABILITY AND STRENGTH...

...AND IMPROVE GRIP STRENGTH, WHICH IS HIGHLY CORRELATED WITH LONGEVITY AND HEALTHSPAN, IS TO....

Just Hang!

AS ALWAYS, KEEP IT SIMPLE AND BE SAFE, WHICH MEANS BEING SURE THAT WHATEVER YOU ARE HANGING ON IS SECURE.

YOU DON'T NEED ANY SPECIAL EQUIPMENT, JUST A COMMITMENT TO DO IT AS OFTEN AS POSSIBLE. SET YOUR TIMER AND MAKE IT YOUR GOAL TO BE ABLE TO HANG FREELY FOR AT LEAST ONE MINUTE!

THERE'S NOTHING MORE PRIMAL OR FUNDAMENTAL TO GOOD TOTAL BODY HEALTH THAN A BASIC BODYWEIGHT SQUAT.

THIS COMPOUND MOVEMENT IS ABOUT AS GOOD AS IT GETS FOR TARGETING THE ENTIRE BODY, ESPECIALLY THE HIPS, LEGS, AND CORE.

The Basic Bodyweight Squat (and 30-Day Challenge).

Before we discuss the Bodyweight Squat "30-day challenge," let's talk about how to execute the basic bodyweight squat in a smart way so you get all the benefits of doing them.

Remember, the goal with this practice is simply to help you relearn the most primal and fundamental movement pattern for a human being, and then by practicing it, build better mobility and strength of the hips, ankles, and legs. You will feel amazing if you do these consistently, trust me!

One NOTE: Unless you have lots of ankle mobility, you will very likely need to elevate your heels. How will you know?

Here's how: try the squat first. <u>If you can go all of the way down such that your thighs touch your calves while keeping your feet flat on the floor and toes pointed straight ahead, you're good to go.</u>

IF YOU ARE FINDING IT DIFFICULT BECAUSE OF IMMOBILE ANKLES, YOU SHOULD ELEVATE YOUR HEELS USING BOOKS OR WHATEVER ELSE YOU HAVE AVAILABLE. START WITH ONLY 1 TO 2 INCHES. REMEMBER TO KEEP YOUR FEET POINTED STRAIGHT AHEAD AND ONLY GO AS DEEPLY AS YOU CAN. AS YOU PRACTICE, YOU SHOULD IMPROVE!

GO THE DISTANCE - DAILY MOVEMENT "SNACKS"

If you can go only half that far down, then you will find it much easier to elevate your heels. It's easy to do. Use two books (or something similar that is firm) of equal thickness, perhaps 2 to 3 inches thick to start. Less is more. Experiment until you find just the right height (not too high, but high enough) that allows you to sink deeply without any pain. I've provided you with the image to the left so you can see how to set this up. Make it your goal to eventually do these without the books. To do that, reduce the thickness of the lift as time goes on.

What other technique pointers should you remember as you learn the bodyweight squat?

- Set up with your toes pointed straight ahead. If this is difficult, you may turn your feet out *slightly*. Straight ahead is preferred, however.
- As you lower, keep your knees tracking over your toes so that your knees don't move toward each other. You may want to use a mini-elastic exercise band around your knees to keep your hips fully engaged.
- Once you're ready to move, take a moderately deep breath through your nose and then exhale slowly through your nose and mouth as you create the moderate brace of your low-abs to "stabilize." If you're unsure what this means, go back to the chapter on stability and review how to create that slight abdominal brace. You'll be bringing your arms up to parallel at the same time as your exhale.
- As you lower down as far as you can without pain, seek to maintain the normal curvature (that neutral position) of your low back. Keeping the moderate ab-brace throughout will help.
- Lower down as far as you can without pain. The eventual goal is to get your thighs to your calves. Do the best you can, working on increasing the depth over time. Depending on the health of your knee joints, you may not end up getting that low. That's OK! Just do the best you can.

You'll read more specific guidance on the pictures which follow. That being said, here's HOW:

Set Up - Starting Position: You'll begin standing up straight with your feet hip-width apart and toes pointed straight ahead or very slightly turned out. Take a nice deep breath in through your nose, then exhale slowly through your nose and mouth to a count of three or four as you brace your low-ab to stabilize. At the same time, extend your arms straight ahead. This is your start position.

Execution: Lower slowly, think "back pockets to heels." Your hips and knees should crease at the same time. Think "slow and controlled." Pause for a brief moment at your bottom position. Avoid bouncing off the bottom position to come back up. Go only as low as you can go without any pain. If you have a history of knee pain or experience any knee pain, slow down even more and do not go as deep - reduce the range of motion. You can also lessen knee pain by focusing on creating more full-body tension throughout your entire body, or by widening your stance. If in doubt, do less. Continue to brace your low-ab to maintain a neutral spine and good posture.

How to Decrease the Challenge: To lessen the challenge, don't go as deep. Yes, your goal is to continue to develop the ability to go more deeply over time. For some people, depending on age, knee health, and injury history, this may take weeks or months or never happen at all. That is OK. Your only goal is to be consistent (that is your magic bullet!) and to try to improve as time goes on.

THE BASIC BODYWEIGHT SQUAT: PAGE 1

SET UP WITH YOUR TOES POINTED STRAIGHT AHEAD OR TURNED OUT SLIGHTLY. KEEP YOUR KNEES TRACKING OVER YOUR TOES – DON'T ALLOW THEM TO MOVE TOWARD EACH OTHER. ONCE YOU'RE READY, TAKE A DEEP INHALE, BRACE, AND THEN BRING ARMS UP TO PARALLEL AS YOU BEGIN TO SQUAT DOWN. THINK "POCKETS TO HEELS." ALSO SLOWLY EXHALE. LOWER DOWN AS FAR AS YOU CAN WITHOUT PAIN. SEEK TO MAINTAIN THE NORMAL CURVATURE (NEUTRAL) OF YOUR LOW BACK. THE GOAL IS TO GET YOUR THIGHS TO YOUR CALVES. DO THE BEST YOU CAN, WORKING ON INCREASING THE DEPTH OVER TIME.

GO THE DISTANCE - DAILY MOVEMENT "SNACKS"

THE BASIC BODYWEIGHT SQUAT: PAGE 2

IF YOU ARE FINDING IT DIFFICULT BECAUSE OF IMMOBILE ANKLES, YOU SHOULD ELEVATE YOUR HEELS USING BOOKS OR WHATEVER ELSE YOU HAVE AVAILABLE. START WITH ONLY 1 TO 2 INCHES. REMEMBER TO KEEP YOUR FEET POINTED STRAIGHT AHEAD AND ONLY GO AS DEEPLY AS YOU CAN. AS YOU PRACTICE, YOU SHOULD IMPROVE!

GO THE DISTANCE - DAILY MOVEMENT "SNACKS"

What Are Some Of the More Common Mistakes When Performing the Basic Bodyweight Squat?

- **Moving too quickly without good control, such as bouncing off the bottom**. To prevent this from happening, move slowly and with control.
- **Leaning too far forward**. To prevent this, think "tall, long spine."
- **Losing your ab-brace and rounding or flattening your low-back**. To prevent this, keep that core engaged!
- **Letting the feet float off of the ground or the heels to rise**. To prevent this from happening, keep your feet flat.
- **Letting the knees move toward the middle**. To prevent this, keep your knees tracking over your toes. Use a mirror to see how you are doing.
- **Turning the feet out during lowering**. To prevent this, be aware and focus on keeping them straight.

Start where you are. Do only what you can do. Don't try to be "perfect" but do seek to improve each time you come back to it.

The Basic Bodyweight Squat 30-Day Challenge.

Virtually everyone likes a challenge! Many also like having a plan to follow that will guide them from the start to a more advanced level, right? Those reasons are why I included this simple, easy-to-follow 30-Day Challenge.

On the next page, you'll find your plan. Please read all of the notes and "top priorities" carefully. Most importantly, make sure to focus first on form.

In the beginning it isn't important to go "deeply." However, over time make it your goal to go deeper into the squat. The ultimate goal is to get your thighs to your calves, however that may not be possible for those who have wonky knees or limited hip mobility. If you do this the right way, you will not only do more reps as time goes on but also be going slightly deeper as well. The bottom line is this: Just try to do your best and try to get better each day! If you do that, you win!

Always remember if you're just starting out, adjust the volume down by at least 20%. You can always come back to the challenge in the future and hit the numbers as they are. If you're more experienced, you can do this with a weight! The bottom line, train smart and keep it fun!

MON	TUE	WED	THU	FRI	SAT	SUN	WEEK TOTAL
2 sets of 5	Rest	3 sets of 5	Rest	1 set of 8 / 1 set of 5	Rest	1 set of 10 / 3 sets of 5	63!
Rest	Rest	2 sets of 8 / 2 sets of 5	Rest	3 sets of 8 / 2 sets of 5	Rest	2 sets of 10 / 4 sets of 5	105!
Rest	3 sets of 10	3 sets of 5	3 sets of 10	Rest	4 sets of 10	2 sets of 10 / 5 sets of 5	135!
Rest	3 sets of 12	Rest	3 sets of 15 / 1 set of 5	Rest	2 sets of 20 / 4 sets of 5	4 sets of 10	176!
Rest	2 sets of 25						

TOP PRIORITIES

1. Go only as deeply as you can go safely.
2. Focus on form and your breath, first.
3. Elevate your heels if you need to.
4. Rest as much as needed between sets.
5. Move slowly, with control. Breathe.
6. If in doubt, do less. Train smart!

NOTES

This plan gives any person a starting point. Depending on your experience and health, you may want to adjust the volume down or up. If this is your first time doing anything like this, subtract 20% from each days' total.

It's a good idea to shoot video of yourself or watch yourself in a mirror so you can check your form. Two things to look for are 1. Don't allow your knees to move inward as you descend. 2. Maintain a nice "braced" low-ab and keep that neutral position as you move up and down.

If in doubt, do less! Always respect your health and allow time for your body to adapt! Keep it fun!

PART 4

STRENGTH

CHAPTER 24

INTRODUCTION:
RESPONSIBILITY, REGRET, AND RESISTANCE EXERCISE

For the greatest enemy of truth is very often not the lie - deliberate, contrived, and dishonest - but the myth - persistent, persuasive, and unrealistic.

Too often we hold fast to the clichés of our forebears. We subject all facts to a prefabricated set of interpretations. We enjoy the comfort of opinion without the discomfort of thought.

— **John F. Kennedy,**
Yale University commencement address
(June 11, 1962)

I have this neighbor, his name is Don. He's a tad angry with me right now. Won't talk to me. And honestly, it makes me a little sad. We've had a really cordial relationship since we met about 5 years ago. I consider him and his wife good friends. The thing is, since I've lived next door to him, *every time* I see him, he'll always stop me, and tell me how much *getting older,* stinks.

"Man, it really stinks to get old," he'll say. "You wait until you get to be my age, you'll see - you'll see!" Up until a couple of weeks ago, I always nodded and smiled back at him, chuckling and agreeing with him to make him feel better. "I hear you, Don!" "Sure does, yup."

He's in his late-70s. Older, yes, but not *that much* older than I am. He's had one health issue after another over the last couple of years – gastrointestinal and heart issues, foot and ankle problems, you name it. He spent some time in the hospital a couple of months ago for what he said was "some minor" colon surgery." (Is there such a thing actually, as "minor" colon surgery? Hmm...)

Everything changed a couple of weeks ago. I was just finishing up a run and walking past his house, soaking wet with sweat and feeling that kind of "beat" that is typical after a run in the Florida heat and humidity. Don had just come out of his house, hobbling as he walked to his car. As sure as the sun rises in the morning, he yells out to me just as he's done dozens of times: "you wait until you get to be my age – you won't be running like that anymore!"

I just looked at him and sighed. It was a typical summer morning run in Florida with weather not exactly tailor made for running. But make no mistake, I love being here. So, I tolerate these few months of blistering heat and humidity while looking toward the fall. I just didn't want to play the game at that moment. And that's really all our banter back and forth had been – a game. He continued on.

"So ...listen to this...I tried to make another appointment with my doctor about this stupid ankle... his receptionist says they can't see me for another three weeks because their schedule is booked up...can you believe that? What a crock."

Whose Responsibility Is It?

Now, I have to be honest and tell it like I see it. Don eats some version of processed junk food every day and does nothing to help himself feel better or age more gracefully. He sits in front of the TV, leaving the house only when he wants to drive to the store to bargain shop. Like many others his age, most of his trips away from home are going to the doctor's office. **He blames how he feels solely on getting older. He doesn't believe he has any control over *how* he ages.**

Of course, Don has every right to live his life the way he wants. We all have that fundamental right as long as we're not hurting anyone else. There's no rule that says he should do anything any differently than he does. And if I am being completely honest with myself, I have to accept that I've only known him for a few years and don't know *his complete "story."* And we ALL have a story.

This is the challenge *we all face at some point in our lives*—reaching out to others and trying to help them in any way we can, while also accepting there are things we don't know about them and may never know. I'll admit I've spent years as a coach and mentor and parent and partner, trying to better understand the vagaries, as well as uniformities, of life - the vast spectrum of realities going on in the interconnected lives of those around me. But that doesn't mean I can easily understand what *his unique challenges are* or the path he's followed to reach this point in his life. And that's important for me to remember.

You can lead a horse to water but you can't make it drink.

– a proverb

Firing Back.

I listened as he went on and on, and finally in an irrational moment of sweat-induced fatigue, I thought, *man, that's it, I've had enough.* It had been a few years and more encounters at the end of the driveway than I could count. And in that moment, it seemed like I'd heard enough complaining and blaming to last two lifetimes. I looked at him and said something like this:

"Listen my friend...your health is your responsibility, no one else's. It isn't easy, but you've got to work at it. Don't wait for the doctor to give you the answers! You think he really cares about your health? I hate to break it to you...the only one that has the power to do anything about how you feel, is you. I get it! It's not easy. It sucks. But only you can do it!"

He laughed sarcastically, as though I'd just made a bad joke, about him no less! Looking at me with a teeny bit of anger in his eyes, he said, "Wow...looks like we're getting a little pep talk here! Alright!"

It was sarcastic and obviously reflected the idea he never expected to hear THAT from me, especially at that moment. I'd put him on the spot and turned it back around to him, putting the mirror right in his face, and he didn't want any part of it.

I continued, trying to ease the shock of the moment and not sound like a jerk. "I'm sorry man. I've seen it more times than I can count. Sure, there's no guarantees, no matter what you do, but damn man...this is just the way it is - we've got to own responsibility for our health and take care of it. If we don't, no one else will." He turned away and walked back toward his car...mumbling. Clearly irritated. I'd given him a piece of the truth, my truth – and he didn't appreciate it one bit. Maybe I was out of line. After all, what he does is his choice. It's none of my business, right?

I walked toward my home thinking of the question I've asked myself a million times: why do so many people not care for the most important thing in their life – **their health** – in the same way they do their material possessions? It's difficult for me to understand why it's so hard for Don to accept that his health is HIS responsibility and no one else's.

The Pain of Regret.

Some might say that I have no right to judge his reaction to what I said. That might be true, but the question still remains: if the primary responsibility for his own health isn't HIS, then *whose is it?* And since I'm asking rhetorical questions, is it worth asking whether his choices and behavior impact others? I can assure you his wife isn't happy with how he chooses to live, nor does she enjoy listening to him complain. And I know his kids feel the same way.

Don is bitter, frustrated, and even resentful. He believes both his body and the healthcare system have let him down and that is the reason he is struggling. The problem is, the system is complex and can be difficult to navigate. In truth, while it is good at trauma when we need immediate medical care, it doesn't do a very good job at helping us *prevent* disease.

If Don wants to live, not just longer, but *better - healthier*, he needs to avoid chronic disease. Prevention must be the priority for him, and for ALL of us! Unfortunately, our current healthcare system is structured and primarily geared toward helping us live longer *once we develop* chronic disease.

Not a single one of us can ignore this undeniable truth which admittedly is sometimes hard to hear: **our health is our own responsibility, and no one else's.** Sure, sometimes we get tough breaks in life. But most of the time, we simply haven't done what we needed to and suffer because of it. We can blame it on genetics or bad luck but pointing fingers won't change our circumstances. No one wants to feel the pain of regret as they age. It's no fun when the quality of life is poor, because of pain and health issues.

How Old Would You Be If You Didn't Know How Old You Was?

I really love that Satchel Paige quote at the beginning of this chapter: *How old WOULD you be if you didn't know how old you was?* Satchel Paige, in case you don't know, was a baseball pitcher who started his career in the Negro league and later, played in the major leagues with the Cleveland Indians. A truly gifted athlete, his career spanned five decades – he played professionally well into his 50s and always amazed the fans with his youthful performances even as he aged. Many teammates and adversaries said he was the greatest they ever saw.

I'm not one of those people who says off handedly that "age is only a number." I think there's more to it than that, including the fact we really do have to respect how old we actually are chronologically. But the thing is, how old we "feel" is important in assessing the quality of our life to some degree, you know?

For me, I feel pretty darn good all things considered – not a lot different than I did 20 or 30 years ago. In some ways, I feel better than I did when I was in my 20s. I'm fortunate to be in this position. Of course, when I look in the mirror and see the receding hairline and graying temples, I'm reminded I'm definitely not 20 or 30 anymore, that's for sure. ☺ I'm also reminded of the years having passed when I go out and try to run fast. But that's not the point I hope to share with you. What is the point? It's this:

What is Normal ...Is Not Common.

Here's a picture of me taken on the 62nd anniversary of my birth. ☺

You probably think I'm an outlier- that I'm not "normal." I mean, looking at this picture quickly, I would admit I don't look like the "typical" 62-year-old, that's for sure.

But am I really an outlier? Am I not "normal?" **Well, I believe, with all of my heart, that I AM normal.** I believe there's a very good chance if we could see pictures of our male hunter-gatherer ancestors at my age right now, many, if not most of them would look similar.

Think about it: They didn't eat processed foods or refined sugars because those foods just didn't exist. They certainly got a good amount of different kinds of exercise foraging, hunting, and escaping predators, because they had no choice if they wanted to survive. They didn't have a convenience store or drive-thru window only a minute's drive away, like we do.

What you see, my friend, IS normal. And it's available to anyone willing to do some work and be disciplined and accountable to themselves. You CAN thrive and feel good as you go into your 50s and 60s. And beyond. Now, repeat after me: This is normal. This is NORMAL. Of course, the problem is, **what is normal, isn't common.**

You're probably thinking it's not common because it is a nearly impossible achievement for the average person. You probably think I'm not average. You probably think I...

1. Exercise relentlessly, for hours and hours each week.
2. Am incredibly "strict" with my diet.
3. Am not much fun to be around because I'm so "disciplined."

Well, nope, I don't exercise for hours and hours each week. I average only around 30-45 minutes of exercise most days, built primarily around strength training, with some running and cycling thrown in. I don't think that's extreme at all. The great thing is, YOU could do as little as 10 minutes a day and get nearly the same results as I do <u>if you do it consistently</u>. I'll show you how.

And while I do eat very well most days of the week, I don't have to think about it very much. It isn't forced. Because I don't eat very much processed food, I don't have cravings that drive me to the cupboards often looking for something to "munch on." And as you know, I practice Time Restricted Eating most of the time, but that isn't at all forced either. On the contrary, it feels very natural and normal for me to approach eating that way. It'd feel normal for you, too, if you allowed

yourself some time to practice it so that it became a habit. And combined it with eating REAL food and not processed junk most of the time.

As for the third thing, I'm probably not much fun to be around but it isn't because of my health or training habits! ☺ And in case you're wondering, I am quite average. Perhaps the way I think isn't average, but I am very average, especially athletically.

How I might look and the fact that at 62, I'm able to do just about anything I want to physically – that is *every single person's birthright*. It's YOUR birthright. *It should be common.* And as I've said, you *don't need to become an exercise junkie* or the least fun person to be around. What you do need is to <u>commit to getting the processed food out of your diet and start eating REAL food. Also incorporate a little bit of smart strength training into your daily routine and stress the body physically</u>, so it can remain resilient and relatively youthful. The amount you need to do to get great results is less than you think!

So, *what is* common? For one, how about the fact that in 2022, more than 75% of those 50 and older in the U.S. take at least one prescription drug every day. The average is four prescription drugs for every American. More than 90% of those 80 and older are taking prescription drugs. According to a study done by the Mayo Clinic back in 2013, more than 70% of Americans are on at least one prescription drug and more than half take two. One study found that antibiotics, antidepressants and painkilling opioids are the most commonly prescribed.[1] The number is surely even higher today. And we haven't even talked about the side effects and expense.

Other than some occasional antibiotics after dental work, I've never taken a prescription drug. You probably think that isn't normal. **I'm here to tell you it IS normal. It's just not common**. But it should be.

I'm also here to tell you that many, if not virtually all the chronic diseases of our modern age, including our pathologic addiction to prescription drug use to cure our various ills, comes back primarily to one single thing: **the loss of muscle mass.**

Muscle Matters.

Muscle is what gives you the ability to move freely, and it's what will prevent you from falling as you get older. Muscle is what allows you to perform in whatever ways you want to. It's what will keep you from becoming tired, weak, and frail. It is what will afford you independence and the ability to live your life. If you want to be leaner, you need muscle. Muscle is active tissue. It burns calories. Fat does not, it just sits there.

Do you want to be able to keep playing and enjoying the activities which bring you joy? Do you want to avoid joint replacements? Muscle strength will give you that opportunity.

And herein lies the problem: ***Muscle goes away if we don't use it or stress it.***

If you don't actively work to keep your muscles, they'll start to shrink up and gravity will keep trying to crush you down. Your joints will take the beating and you'll be in more and more pain. You may even eventually need a replacement. In clinical circles, it's called **sarcopenia**, which is simply *age-related muscle wasting*.

After the age of 30, we lose up to 8% per decade. That's the equivalent of up to 10 pounds. And if you spend most of a 24-hour day sitting or lying down, you may lose it much faster. As you get older, if you spend any time in bed inactive, due to an illness, the loss increases exponentially, compared to when you were younger. You could lose as much as a year's worth in a single day. That sounds crazy, I know, but it's true.

Nothing has as direct an effect on the quality of your years as does **muscle strength.** The very latest research has shown conclusively **there is a direct relationship between strength and all-cause mortality.** There is also a direct relationship between strength and your ability to enjoy life.

Yes, if you're eating processed foods, that needs to change. And no matter what, you can't ever exercise a bad diet away. But beyond the quality of the food you eat, **maintaining muscle mass is the absolute single most important thing you can do to extend your healthspan and improve the chances of you dying healthy.**

Key Concept:

"I Exercise So I Can Eat Whatever I Want To."

This quote is something I've heard a lot over the years. I have occasionally been guilty of uttering it myself, although not in a very long time. The truth is, as I stated earlier, you CAN'T exercise away a poor diet.

For one thing, exercise burns relatively few calories compared to the amount in processed foods. For example, a 3 mile run which might take 30 minutes, burns only about 300 calories. That's about a medium sized bagel with nothing on it.

As you're reading this book, you're learning it's about processed seed oils and sugary snacks, how they've been manufactured and what they contain, and the impact on our body and health. No amount of exercise can UNDO the negative impact to your health AND your waistline, that comes from eating a poor diet on a regular basis.

Strength Training ISN'T Just About Getting Stronger.

When you're stronger, you obviously can do anything and everything more easily. You're able to play with your kids, climb a set of stairs more easily, do your chores, or enjoy traveling, all with less pain and a lot more enjoyment. But the benefits that come from strength and resistance training AREN'T limited to looking and functioning better.

Many of the benefits from doing strength training are because of chemicals called myokines. These are released by muscle cells during muscle contractions and then sent cascading throughout the entire body.[2]

This graphic from Dr. Doug McGuff, a well-known lecturer and author of the book Body by Science, shows how myokines from muscle cells travel to many different locations throughout the body and can positively and dramatically impact the health of our bones, internal organs, and brain. Importantly, they also help the body use up sugar in the bloodstream and give up fat from fat cells. You'll recall from the chapter on Insulin Resistance and Hyperinsulinemia, how important it is to maximize the uptake of sugar and tap into fat depots in the body for both health and body composition.

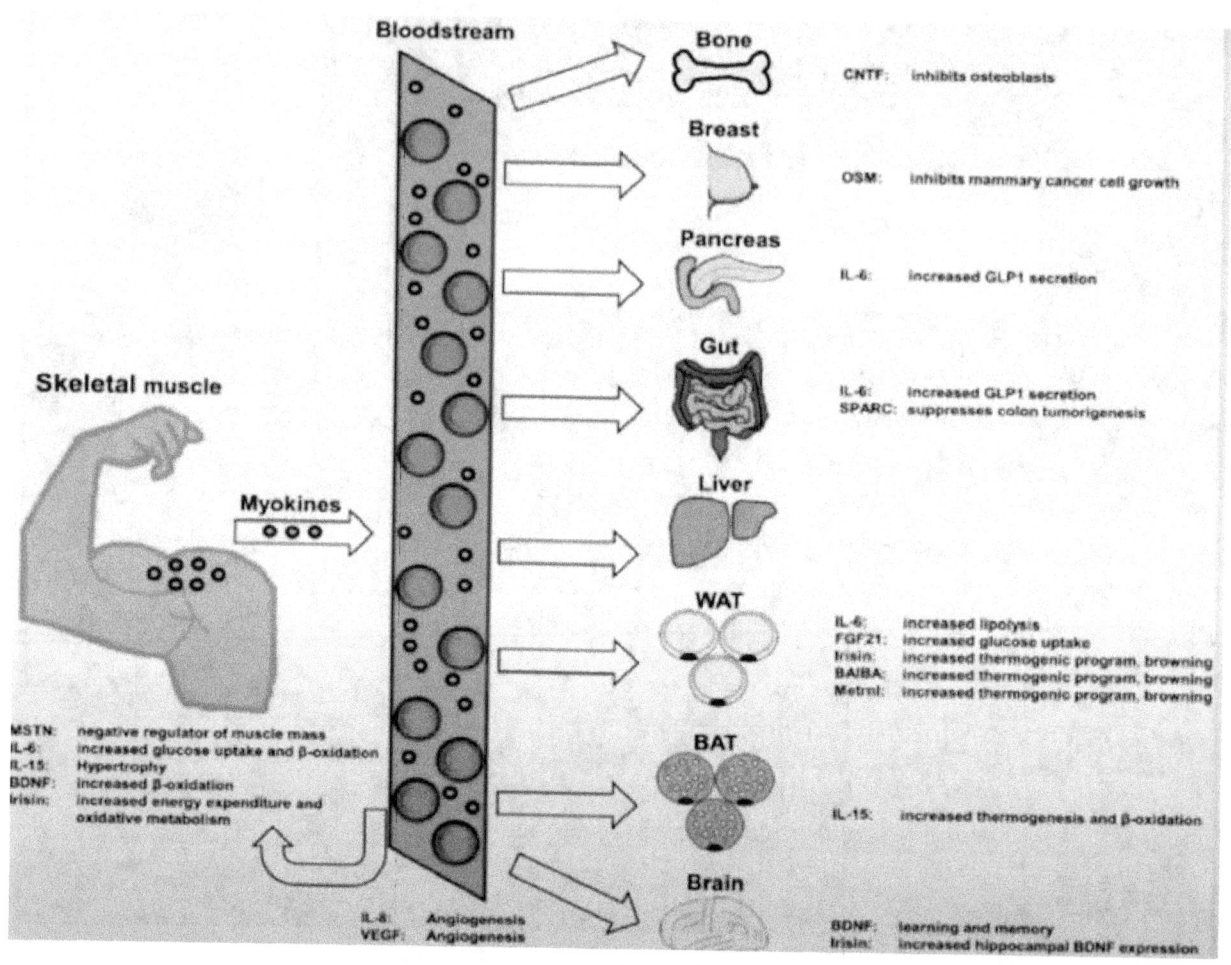

Think of it this way: **skeletal muscle is the largest portion of the body that also has the potential to have the greatest positive impact on the health and function of the other parts of your body!** That's the truth. So, we'd better do all we can to help it do its job, by incorporating strength and resistance training into our lifestyle.

What About Bone Density, Osteoporosis, and Resistance Exercise?

Increasingly brittle bones can lead to dramatic increases in the risk of falling, and other serious traumatic injuries. Osteoporosis, which is a loss of bone density, becomes increasingly common as we get older, and it seems to be more prevalent in women. We start to lose the ability to improve bone density at about age 30. From that point on, everything we're doing as far as exercise and diet is essentially helping to maintain what we have.

A gradual loss of strength and muscle wasting always precedes a loss of bone density. One leads to the other. Among other things, resistance or strength training creates bone stress as contracting muscles tug and pull on the attachment to the bone. This kind of stress makes the bone stronger.

Weight bearing activities like walking and running are critically important to maintain bone density too. One exercise that isn't nearly as helpful for maintaining bone, is riding a bike. You're not able to load your skeleton against gravity when sitting on a bike saddle. I'll talk more about this in Chapter 26, when I discuss cycling as a great option for low impact cardio exercise. The bottom line, still, is the best possible way to maintain bone density is weight bearing movement and resistance training.

What About Arthritis and Resistance Exercise?

There are few things more debilitating for the average person entering their 50s and beyond than increasing chronic pain in the joints due to arthritis. If you're in your 6th decade and beyond, I'm sure you know what I mean.

Arthritis happens due to changes to the cartilage inside our joints. Wear and tear beat down the cartilage, leading to bone-on-bone contact, more inflammation, and more pain, as it progresses. It seems everyone will eventually see some kind of reduction in cartilage, so it might seem hopeless. But fortunately, there are a lot of things we CAN do to stave off loss of cartilage, reduce chronic pain, and reduce the likelihood of joint replacement surgery.

Resistance exercise, as you might imagine, is the most effective thing we CAN do to reduce the loading on our joints and thus the wear and tear. If you're wondering why, consider this: your skeleton is essentially nothing more than a collection of bones held together and supported nearly entirely by the muscles and connective tissue, wrapped in a fascial envelope. Your head alone weighs about 10 to 12 pounds. Were it not for all of the muscles and fascia around your neck, shoulders, and trunk, the weight of that head of yours would eventually crush your skeleton. Literally!

To understand even more how important the strength of our muscles is and the connection between soft tissue and bone, consider this: in essence, our body, specifically our muscular-skeletal system, is a tensegrity structure. It's the muscles and fascia both inside and around our entire body that manages the balance between tension and compression in the body.

From Thomas Myer's book, *Anatomy Trains*: "There are two ways to support something in this physical universe – via tension or compression; brace it up or hang it up. No structure is utterly based on one or the other; all structures mix and match these two forces in varying ways at different times."[3]

In the case of the human body, the forces work simultaneously as "our myofascial system provides a continuous network of restricting but adjustable tension around the individual bones and cartilage as well as the incompressible fluid balloons of organs and muscles, which push out against this restricting tensile membrane."[4]

Bio-Tensegrity:
What it is...
and why it matters...

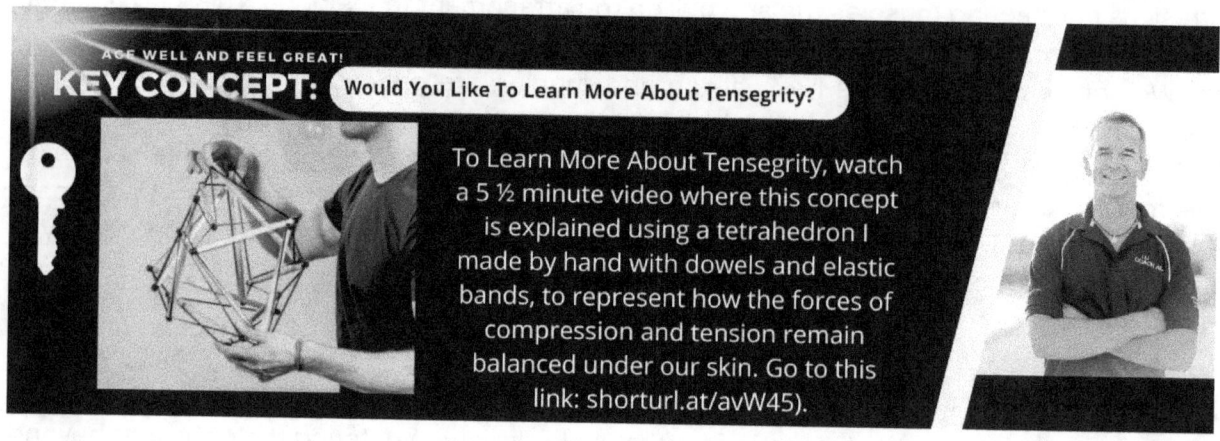

KEY CONCEPT: Would You Like To Learn More About Tensegrity?

To Learn More About Tensegrity, watch a 5 ½ minute video where this concept is explained using a tetrahedron I made by hand with dowels and elastic bands, to represent how the forces of compression and tension remain balanced under our skin. Go to this link: shorturl.at/avW45).

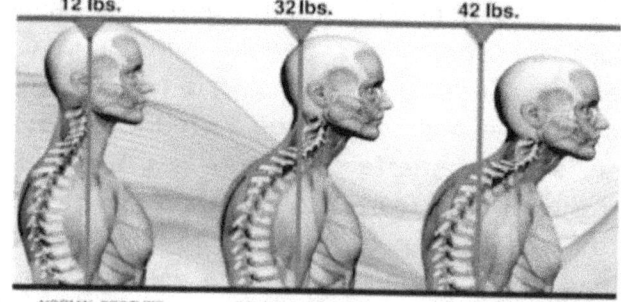

How Heavy is Your Head?

12 lbs.   32 lbs.   42 lbs.

NORMAL POSTURE   2 INCHES FORWARD   3 INCHES FORWARD

As we get weaker and start to show the effects of gravity pushing down on us, we will typically experience changes in posture where our body is much less aligned, top to bottom, than it should be. Check out this picture that shows how the net effect of a change in posture to a more forward head position, essentially increases the weight of our head. These changes put more stress on joints and contribute to more wear and tear.

So, what is the take home?

- **You need to do some resistance exercise**. The thing is, one of the biggest mistakes many people make is trying to do too much too soon, which can lead to injury. Read the next chapter carefully to learn how little is actually required to keep what you have and reduce the loading on joints.

- **Make sure you have some good basic movement skills first**. Read Chapter 20 titled How to Improve Your Stability. In that chapter, I discuss why stability is important. The best approach to building a resilient body that can go the distance is to focus on becoming more stable first, before focusing on strength.

- **Make sure to focus on form.** There's no question that repetitive exercises done with poor form reduce the benefits you get and can dramatically increase your risk of injury. My former partner in our Pursuit gait analysis lab often said it "isn't about the exercise, it's about how the exercise is done." You'd be very smart to remember those wise words. Pay close attention to form. Go to my YouTube page for additional instructional videos, and always remember you can get a more in-depth set of instructions and guidance with one of the many programs that are available on my website at http://PursuitAthleticPerformance.com

- **Do regular weight bearing exercise as often as you can, starting with walking.** When you load your body against gravity, the bone gets the message to continue to remodel and will remain dense and strong. And of course, whenever you can, do that walking barefooted. Keep reading.

What Other Benefits Are There to Getting Stronger?

- **When you contract muscle by creating internal tension and integration and using isometric contraction, you will experience an increase in your heart rate**. In other words, resistance training CAN BE great cardiovascular exercise too, when done the right way! Talk about a double bonus! ☺ I'll teach you how to do this in the next chapter.
- **When you contract muscle, you will experience improved blood flow through all the arteries and veins, improved left ventricle pumping power and improved venous return**. Resistance training is a very powerful mechanism for protecting against vascular diseases. You'll learn one reason why this is important in the last chapter, Final Thoughts, when I discuss sex, among other topics. ☺
- **When you contract muscle, you improve blood glucose uptake and control**. Why? Well, skeletal muscle is the single largest reservoir in your body of stored sugar, known as glycogen. You'll remember that in Chapter 9 on **Insulin Resistance and Hyperinsulinemia**, I discussed glycogen "depletion" and its importance in improving insulin sensitivity.
- **Don't forget eating a diet of processed foods increases inflammation in the body**. Go back and read the chapter on Chronic Inflammation to learn more.

The Fountain of Youth?

Remember epigenetics and DNA methylation from the chapter Why We Age: *Exploring Aging at the Cellular Level*? In one of the most fascinating studies ever done on the benefits of resistance exercise, in the mid-2000s, researchers at the Buck Institute for Aging at the University of California at San Diego used statistical analysis to look at gene expression at younger and older ages. They then put elderly patients on a resistance training program for around six months. After the training period, they again measured the gene expression and found DNA expression had returned to more youthful levels![5] That's incredible.

Other studies have shown the same effect. For example, in another beautiful scientific study showing how gene expression seems to revert back to a more youthful expression by way of DNA methylation, [6] there was another very interesting finding. The researchers trained the participants for seven weeks, and then let them detrain for the next seven weeks. When they returned to training again, they were able to pick up and return to their previous level much more quickly. Apparently, this happens because the methylation sites are marked from memory. How cool is that? ☺

The fountain of youth is right here in front of us, despite many of us refusing to see it. **It's strength training!** Not surprisingly, that same group of researchers has also shown how resistance exercise can literally reverse aging in skeletal muscle.[7]

Do Running and Biking Make You Stronger?

One question I am frequently asked is, "do running and cycling make me stronger?" I think many people assume that it DOES strengthen our body, but they are not aware of just how much. In fact, I've heard more than a few runners and cyclists who believe the strength benefits are so good, they don't need to engage in any other type of strength work. Well, I hate to burst their bubble, but cycling and running won't improve your strength. This is one of the biggest myths in all of endurance sports.

It's a Fact: We Lose Muscle Tissue as We Age. And Cycling and Running Won't Help Reverse the Trend.

If you're older than 40, that gradual "weakening" and loss of muscle tissue is happening at a faster and faster rate. It's scary how fast muscle goes away once you hit your 50s and beyond. Unless you do something about it, that is. Here are a few more truths for you. Chew on these:

- **If you include lots of high-intensity hill work in your training,** that will help you build more "*sport-specific*" strength. The keywords here are "sport-specific." Your calves will become stronger from uphill running, and certainly your quads - from cycling and the downhill running. You'll need lots of volume in order to push beyond a threshold - and you will STILL be lacking the kind of balanced strength essential for injury resistance and good health. Think about it.
- **What about how strong professional grand tour riders are?** Whatever strength they have in their legs (which I'll certainly admit is significant) comes from a massive amount of volume (600-700 miles a week!), combined with gym work for most of them.
- **When you're on a bike, your butt is planted on the saddle** and your trunk is basically going along, for the ride. The only muscles really working (assuming you are riding "hard") are your leg muscles, specifically the quads. That's it. Cycling sucks as a way to build "total body" strength and fitness. What's worse, you're not loading against gravity AT ALL so your bones also weaken.
- **What about your "muscular" friend who has never strength trained?** It's possible that friend might simply be naturally muscular. There are those kinds of folks. If

you've seen my girlfriend Terry's legs, you'll know what I mean. Her quads have always looked strong - even at a young age. It's just how she is, naturally.

- **What really happens when you run?** *Your body is progressively and gradually breaking down.* And while your body is resisting the forces acting against it (gravity and ground reaction) and breaking down in the process, it happens at a threshold that is WAY below your peak level of strength. The end result is this: In one respect your body adapts to the specific demands placed upon it - BUT it is also simultaneously weakening AND becoming more imbalanced.

- **Are you one of those folks who head to the gym to strength train?** If your go to is those expensive-looking machines, you may want to rethink your strategy. While you can "build" beach-body muscle using them, your body won't learn how to better control that strength and use it to perform more athletically and holistically in an integrated way. To get that important benefit, you need some bodyweight strength work.

And here's a secret: If you believe you are "tight" and inflexible, the type of exercise you NEED to improve once and for all, MUST include a strength training component. It isn't just about stretching more, that's for sure. Why? One simple reason: **Force input is the language of the cell.** If there's no force input, no engagement of muscle, no specific challenge to the muscle, then there will be minimal or zero adaptation or change. Which is another way of saying, stretching might feel good at the moment and there might be a temporary improvement, but it isn't likely to last.

There is one last thing I'd like to share with you on how important and beneficial strength training can be when it comes to gene expression, our immune system health, and reducing chronic inflammation, which are all linked. To do this, I'd like to again refer back to Chapter 9 on glycogen storage and energy utilization. As well as Chapter 2 where I discussed the relationship between AMPK and mTOR.

When you perform consistent resistance and strength exercise, you're creating an energy deficit by using up blood glucose and stored muscle and liver glycogen. Along the way, you're also restoring hormonal balance because of the low-energy state you created by doing the exercise. Remember the term? It's hormetic stress, the kind of stress that is SO GOOD for your health. Not coincidently, the same thing happens when you are hungry, or fasting, or when you expose yourself to extremes in temperature – both hot and cold. Also, senescent cells, otherwise simply known as dead cells, are more efficiently removed from the body before they can cause other damage, such as mistakenly turning on a cancer oncogene. Senescent cells that aren't appropriately discarded in the body drive chronic inflammation and can often start a disease cascade due to a variety of factors, such as incorrect signaling.

Think about it: Strength training, through mechanisms like using up stored energy, cell turnover, and DNA methylation, has been shown scientifically to actually reverse the age of muscle tissue and change DNA and gene expression to a more youthful level. As I said earlier, strength and resistance training is your true fountain of youth!

To summarize, the precipitous decline we see happening in aging folks around us, not only in terms of functional capacity but also the onset of disease, does not have to happen the way it does for most people. As you've read before in this book, and yes I'm being redundant because sometimes we need to hear the message more than once for it to really sink in: **You have a choice.** You have some control over how your life plays out over the second half.

Resistance training must be near the top of the list of choices you make in order to take control of your health and your life. Yes, it requires hard work and some discipline. And that's probably the reason it hasn't "taken off" and gotten the press that so many expensive supplements have.

You have to do the work and put in some effort. In truth, the tools don't matter nearly as much as the effort does. And you know what? It doesn't take much time or skill. It's convenient and can be done pretty much anywhere. I'll show you how in the next chapter. Let's keep going!

CHAPTER 25

HOW TO – RESISTANCE TRAINING FOR EVERYONE:
ISOMETRIC STRENGTH TRAINING

The best way to accomplish goals is not through sheer willpower or grit, but through creating small habits and circumstances that make the goals inevitable.

— **Mark Manson,** *author*

Over the course of my life as a coach and therapist, I've studied, experimented with, practiced, and employed just about every type of strength training method there is. Traditional barbell and dumbbell strengthening and Olympic lifting, kettlebell training, bodyweight training and calisthenics, resistance band training, mobility training, and let's not forget the rehabilitative "functional" exercises that were part of the system of exercises we used in our Pursuit Athletic Performance gait analysis lab. If it exists as a way to build strength, I've studied it and used it.

However, there exists one method I've used more successfully as a coach and athlete than any other. I'll even go so far as to say it is a cornerstone of virtually all the strength training I do myself and with those I coach and train. And there are great reasons why. Which is exciting. ☺ After all, in my opinion, this type of strength training is:

- The easiest to learn, especially if this is your first time doing any strength training,
- The safest for anyone to do, reducing the risk of joint pain or injury to near zero,
- The easiest to scale to make harder or easier, regardless of your experience,
- The most practical, because it can literally be done anywhere at any time,
- The best mode of strength training because it teaches and reinforces important principles that apply to any other form of training,
- The most time-efficient. You won't waste a single minute.

If you happen to be one of those folks between the ages of 30 and 80, that's been dragged down by joint pain, niggling injuries, and other ailments commonly accepted as "part of getting older," you'll be thrilled with this type of training. What is this almost magically effective form of strength training? It's called **isometrics**.

If there's one thing I've learned over the course of my lifetime, it's that *knowledge is power*. You can rest assured everything I will share with you in this chapter is backed by science and represents the most practical, efficient, and effective way for you to improve your strength.

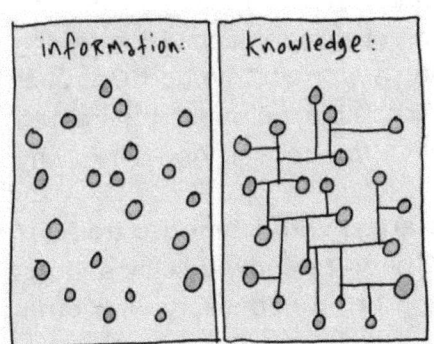

So, what is *isometric training?* It is simply **creating muscle tension *without* joint movement**. That's it. The word isometric comes from two Greek words "isos" meaning equal and "metria" meaning measuring - equal measuring if you will.

Some athletes and coaches hear the word *isometrics* and think it's a new type of training, but this isn't true. Isometric training has been around for as long as we have as a species. Cave paintings, carvings and statues dating as far back as 3000 BC depict ancient martial artists and yogis performing isometric poses and routines. It is said that Buddhist monks brought different forms of static training and exercises to China in the 1100's.

Moving forward, strongmen and body builders of the late 1800's, early 1900's explored isometrics to gain a competitive advantage. During the 1920s, the famous American body builder, Charles Atlas, marketed his Dynamic Tension Training Method, which was certainly influenced and somewhat based on isometric tensioning using your own body for resistance.

Even the legendary kung fu expert and actor, Bruce Lee, used isometrics extensively. The martial arts and gymnastics communities have probably used isometrics more than any other, although its popularity in all facets of strength and conditioning is rising steadily. Over the last decade, more isometrics textbooks have appeared and more scientific research completed to learn about and confirm the true effectiveness of isometrics. While isometrics have been around forever, in some ways this approach DOES represent a true *paradigm shift* - a "new" way of thinking about building strength effectively and efficiently.

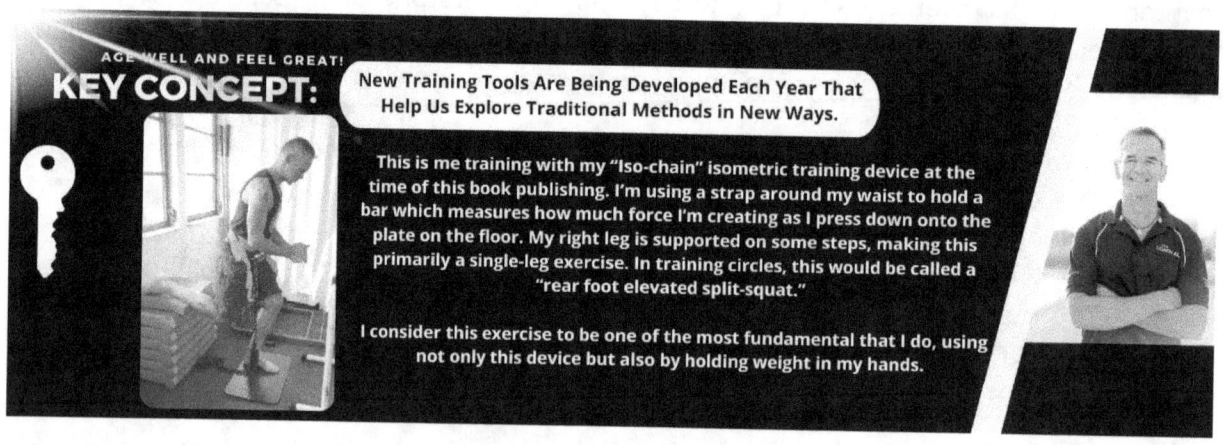

AGE WELL AND FEEL GREAT!

KEY CONCEPT: New Training Tools Are Being Developed Each Year That Help Us Explore Traditional Methods in New Ways.

This is me training with my "Iso-chain" isometric training device at the time of this book publishing. I'm using a strap around my waist to hold a bar which measures how much force I'm creating as I press down onto the plate on the floor. My right leg is supported on some steps, making this primarily a single-leg exercise. In training circles, this would be called a "rear foot elevated split-squat."

I consider this exercise to be one of the most fundamental that I do, using not only this device but also by holding weight in my hands.

So, what has the scientific community learned in the research that's been done? The research supports the concepts I and other coaches and athletes who have experimented with this method have learned. And we're learning more every day. As I said earlier in the book, my motus operandi has typically been to experiment and test things on my own and then wait patiently for the research to appear that validates what my own experience taught me. New tools that make isometric training even more practical and easy to do are appearing. I own one such tool and train with it right now – the "Iso-Chain."

Isometrics aren't "perfect." If we use the simplest and most practical approach to the training, which we will, there are a couple of things that keep it from being a "perfect" method. One such thing is not having an easy way to measure load or progress. That's big, no doubt, but in truth, no method is perfect. That being said, it IS the best method for OUR purposes. And here's why:

- **You won't need to learn many new skills to get started with isometric training.** Because of that, you'll be able to pick up what you need to know quickly and get started right away without the learning curve that's often necessary with other types of training.

Of course, there's nothing inherently wrong with having to learn new skills, right? The thing is, having a high skill demand at the outset of starting a new program often creates frustration, when the goal from the outset is just to get moving and start exercising. I learned this a long time ago when training other athletes. When someone is starting out, I'll always give them the lowest skill-requirement exercises so they can build some momentum and achieve a feeling of accomplishment and satisfaction right from the start. Of course, should you choose to progress beyond what I'll share with you in this book, the skill demands will likely increase as you go.

- **Isometric training takes less time than more traditional strength training, yet is as effective.**

There are many reasons why isometrics strength training is more efficient and takes less time to perform. First, as you will read soon, I'll recommend you do contractions lasting only 6 seconds. These short contractions are ideal because you can achieve maximum effort very quickly. Even with multiple sets and including a variety of exercises, the bulk of any "workout" can be done in 10 to 15 minutes or sometimes less, compared to 45 minutes (more or less) for traditional dynamic training. Also, because you can do isometrics virtually anywhere - you don't need a gym or special equipment for most exercises, you will save the time normally spent driving to and from a gym.

- **Isometric training is just as effective at improving strength as any other kind of strength training.** To understand one reason why, we need to consider what constitutes "effective" training.

In my mind, when it comes to strength training, effective means maximal *fiber recruitment*, and maximum recruitment of *motor units*. In other words, when your goal is to increase strength, you want to recruit as many fibers as possible during your training. The only way to recruit more fibers is through higher intensity contractions.

Isometric training allows you to recruit the most fibers and generate the highest overall intensity in the shortest amount of time more easily and efficiently.

To understand why this is, let's use an example of a simple, traditional dynamic biceps curl exercise that most people are familiar with.

Imagine you are doing slow repetitions, curling the weight up and then lowering it down.

The picture here shows this exercise at the start position (on the left) and the finish position (on the right).

Now let's look at the image of a *sine wave* to understand how the intensity of the curl fluctuates as you move it up and down during these traditional repetitions.

Notice the high points of the sine wave and also the low points.

The low points of the wave represent the lowest point when the weight is at your side, AND the highest point when you complete a repetition, before beginning to lower the weight. The horizontal line represents the midpoint of the movement when intensity is at its highest.

In other words, **there is an intensity fluctuation with a traditional dynamic exercise like this**. It goes from easy where there is very little force involved at the start, to harder at the midpoint when your forearms are parallel to the floor. Then as you pass that point, the force required to keep moving decreases to the top, just like the sine wave graphic you see here. And when you reverse and lower down, there's less force required at every moment because gravity is assisting.

With isometric training, you won't see this fluctuation in intensity because, when performed correctly, you'll hold a single static position that allows you to maintain a maximum muscular contraction. This allows you to create fatigue much more quickly, due to no fluctuation in intensity, which is the goal.

In addition to increasing the total time at maximal contraction, you'll also be *generating tension from within* and *radiating the tension*, NOT JUST in your biceps (or any other targeted muscle) but throughout your whole body. This is one of the most important training principles of this approach and also applies to bodyweight training. All of this results in increased intensity in a shorter amount of training time and better integration, which means better carryover to sport performance and everyday life.

- **Isometric training *is safer* than traditional dynamic strength training, and suitable for ANY person, regardless of age.**

For years, in our Pursuit Athletic Performance gait analysis lab, we used isometric training because it allowed people who were unable to move their joints without pain, the opportunity to still do some exercises to get stronger. This is why it's been popular in physical therapy circles as well.

There is less risk of acute injury with this type of training because you are either moving very slowly or not at all. There's nothing ballistic about this training. Not that ballistic training is "bad," but there's no question that bounding and jumping with high force increases the risk of injury, especially for someone who has dealt with injury in the past and is at higher risk for a repeat injury. Because you're not moving a joint while contracting the muscles, you reduce the risk of acute injuries to ligaments or tendons.

There are also cutting edge studies showing not only does isometrics not lead to increased joint pain like some other traditional methods can, isometrics can actually REDUCE joint pain. I've seen this happen over and over working one on one with others as a trainer. It can also improve injury resistance by improving tendon stiffness and total-body integration.

And as mentioned, when you generate muscular tension from within, you do create better integration of all parts of the body, which is a strong protective mechanism to ensure exercise safety.

- **Isometric training is better for compromised or painful joints, as it creates less joint abrasion**. Anyone who has reached their 50s or later and has a "bad" knee or hip, knows what joint pain feels like. Very often the idea of even attempting strength training when a joint or joints are compromised, is difficult.

And even if you don't have painful, arthritic joints, nearly anyone who has ever done any kind of traditional strength exercise or even just hard physical work, knows what it's like to have niggling aches and pains like sore elbows or shoulders. These types of temporary injuries usually clear up with rest and ibuprofen, but over time, the micro-trauma from the abrasion can lead to more chronic issues.

The joint pain I'm talking about is most often caused by that cumulative wear and tear – mechanical abrasion - which can eventually lead to the breakdown of cartilage inside the joint leading to inflammation and eventually, chronic arthritis. Joints are, after all, designed to give us greater range of motion and thus freedom, but the downside is they typically suffer greater friction, especially as cartilage wears down.

With isometrics, you can reduce and even eliminate pain by slowing down and experimenting to find just the right joint angle that feels the best. You then train at that angle statically. The result? No more joint abrasion.

GO THE DISTANCE!

HERE'S THE AUTHOR FINISHING A SET OF TRAP-BAR DEADLIFTS IN HIS GARAGE!

ONCE YOU MASTER THE BASICS, IF YOU CHOOSE TO, YOU CAN MOVE ON TO TRAINING WITH KETTLEBELLS, BARBELLS, AND ASSORTED OTHER TRAINING "TOYS."

BUT ONLY WHEN THE FUNDAMENTALS ARE IN PLACE, FIRST!

None of this is to say that you don't want to MOVE joints. You do! In fact, movement is what stimulates healthy cartilage and synovial fluid circulation. Unfortunately, with repeated abrasion, the synovial fluid can become weakened or damaged. How? With compromised exercise form, you can have impingements in the joint (think of your painful shoulder!), and ultimately the friction increases, sometimes leading to less lubrication. I can tell you I know this first hand because I am dealing with it in a few joints in my body – after all, I've got a lot of running miles on my "chassis." When lubrication is compromised, friction increases and gliding surfaces roughen up, damaging the cartilage and creating adhesions in soft tissue like tendons and ligaments, which in turn increases surface area, leading to more friction. It's a vicious cycle.

There's a great analogy of how isometric training can reduce this friction in author Paul Wade's book, *The Ultimate Isometrics Manual*. He's discussing a physics principle that says, "the coefficient of friction decreases as force is added, but as mass is added, frictional force increases proportionately."[1] If your head is spinning after reading those words, Coach Wade's analogy will make it much easier to understand. He says it this way: "Imagine pressing a piece of sandpaper onto a wall. No matter how hard you press on the sandpaper, it's very hard to do damage to the wall if *it remains still*. Now begin to move the sandpaper up and down, still in contact with the wall. What happens? The sandpaper begins to noticeably damage the wall, even if you don't apply much pressure. If you do begin to push hard, the damage becomes worse, much quicker."[2] Think about that in the context of your joints. I'd say that describes it quite clearly and makes me cringe a little bit thinking about it. ☺

- **Isometric training, done correctly, can provide great heart health benefits and an effective cardiovascular training effect.** I often read and hear from others they need to do both strength AND cardio. And obviously, to a large degree this is true and something I do discuss in this book. The thing is, when it comes to isometrics, you can effectively achieve both strength and cardiovascular benefits with one type of exercise.

This might seem counterintuitive to someone who runs or rides a bike for their "cardio." But it is true and has been well studied and proven scientifically. One such study says "both systolic and diastolic pressure markedly rise with isometric exercise to maintain blood flow to actively contracting skeletal muscles, thus producing a marked increase in both heart rate and mean arterial pressure."[3]

To think of it from a practical point of view, you're generating tension from within, squeezing your muscles and holding position. As you do, blood vessels become mechanically constricted by the increasingly tight muscles, forcing your entire cardiovascular system to work harder to pump blood all around your body. Your heart and blood vessels get a great workout.

As you can imagine, while this is happening, your blood pressure will also rise. During rest periods, it will return to normal levels. This temporary rise in pressure, which happens to some degree regardless of the type of exercise, is safe for any healthy person. In fact, studies have shown that with consistency, this effect results in lowering blood pressure, which could be life-saving for some people. As always, if you have questions or concerns, please consult with your doctor or healthcare provider to assess your risk and decide what is best for you.

As you'll read soon, one important element that is also related to heart health, blood pressure, and safe execution of isometrics, is **to breathe continually throughout each repetition.** You'll take a short inhale of 2-3 seconds, and then slowly release air through pursed lips and your nose for about 6 seconds. Ideally, you should never hold your breath during isometrics.

The zero (or near zero) equipment type of isometric training I will teach you in this chapter is arguably the most natural way to train to improve strength. In fact, it's been said this type of "training" is already wired into our "mammalian neurological software: when we yawn and stretch, we are actually contracting our muscles hard, to refresh them."[4]

- **Isometrics is the ideal way to improve strength for older populations,** for many of the reasons already mentioned, including and especially because it is kinder to joints and there's a lower overall risk of injury. Add in convenience and the fact you don't need much special equipment or a high level of skill, and there's clearly no better way for someone who is older and feels vulnerable or at risk of injury, to get stronger!

Interestingly, there is some research that demonstrates isometrics may be helpful in protecting older populations from Alzheimer's Disease,[5] and that being older might even be an advantage because older people seem to have a greater tolerance for discomfort.[6]

- **You recover faster and thus are able to do isometrics more frequently than traditional dynamic strength training.** There are many reasons this is the case, beginning with the fact that more traditional methods take longer to recover from. Why? In a nutshell, it's because muscle soreness occurs due to damage at the cellular level, and that happens to a larger extent with traditional training. Again, why? Microtrauma at the cellular level ISN'T caused by tension or contraction of the muscles – *it is caused primarily by movement while contracting or under tension.* Especially if that movement involves lowering a load, or for runners, going downhill. Those involve something called *eccentric* contractions. The simple and important take home message is this: you can do isometric training of some kind every single day with low risk of muscle soreness. Just remember, don't equate how sore you get to how much progress you will make! It's not the same thing and isn't necessarily correlated.

One extra tidbit? About one hundred years ago, a biologist named Wallace Fenn discovered muscle actions that involve movement – think of it as some kind of mechanical work – seem to need more energy and thus produce more internal heat than comparable isometric contractions, which would theoretically increase the recovery time necessary following the exercise.[7] Admittedly, there isn't complete agreement in the science community about whether there truly is a "Fenn Effect," but in my mind, it makes intuitive sense. Movement generates heat.

- **You are able to generate more force with Isometrics compared to traditional dynamic strength training.** My primary goal with the strength training I do is to simply get stronger, without losing flexibility along the way and without getting much bigger muscles, and I hope that is the same for you. I also want to be able to do it in the shortest time possible and make the greatest gains in strength. I want to feel good, function better, and maintain my quality of life and ability to play and enjoy life as I age.

Scientific studies have repeatedly shown one critical key to improving strength is to *exert as much force as possible during an exercise*, to create as much localized fatigue as possible. It's the muscular fatigue that is central for increases in strength.

Assuming this is true, and it is, you might be asking the question: Can you generate as much fatigue with isometric training as you can with traditional dynamic training? The answer is a definitive YES. And here's why: **How tired you get and how much fatigue you create from an exercise, is directly proportional to the force you generate times how long you take to generate that force.**[8]

With isometric training, as you will learn, the key variable we're focusing on is *TIME*. Specifically, **TIME UNDER TENSION**. This goes back to the earlier point using the sine wave to illustrate how changes in tension (up and down) with traditional dynamic training result in lower time under tension. Simply put, with isometrics, you maintain more tension and increasing TIME under tension compared to traditional training. Many research studies confirm greater time under tension leads to greater muscle fiber recruitment and muscle growth.[9]

So, force + time under tension = increased fatigue which leads to greater gains in strength.

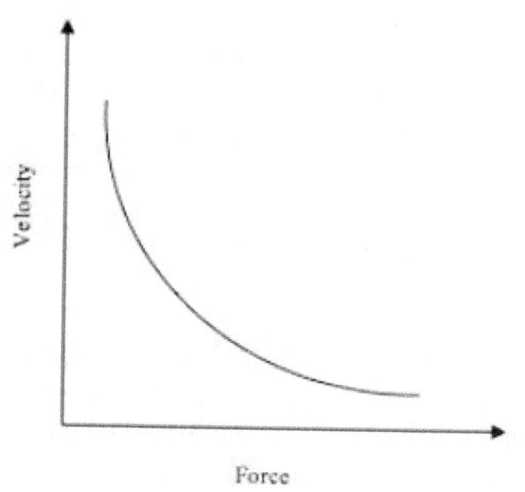

If you're following along, you might then be asking why isometrics allows for greater force development to begin with? The answer is, because of something called the *force-velocity relationship*.[10] It's also known as "Hill's Law," which simply states that **when muscle force is high, contraction speed must be low.**[11]

If you think about it, it makes sense. You can't move a heavy load where you have to generate a LOT of force very fast. If you're still not sure what this means though, maybe this will help: Think about when you grab an object, whatever it might be, and try and move it. The lighter it is, the easier it is to move and the faster you can move it. But, if it's heavier, you will have to generate more force to move it and you won't be able to move it as fast. And as it gets heavier still, your speed will get slower and slower, until it reaches a point where the object is SO heavy, you can't move it at all. This relationship between force (or load) and the speed at which you can move that load (or how much force you create) is Hill's Law.

So, how does this directly relate to isometric training? It's simple: with isometrics, you aren't moving at all. Thus, because of this *force-velocity relationship*, you are able to generate much higher forces than if you were moving.

None of the above means traditional dynamic strength training isn't valuable or important to do, it is! And this isn't meant to say isometric training is "perfect," because it isn't. In fact, there are two major drawbacks to isometrics, and one of them relates to the force production idea I just told you about. That is, with isometrics, one thing which is absent is something called *the loading reflex*.

So, what is *the loading reflex* and why does it matter? Perhaps this example paraphrased from Coach Paul Wade, will help to understand the *loading reflex* better. Imagine you are pushing against an object as hard as you can that won't move, no matter how hard you push. Think of a tree or a wall. Even though you are pushing as hard as you can, you won't be able to generate as much strength as you could if the wall or tree could be moved, or in other words, if the load was "live." This is because our nervous system does a good job of protecting our muscles from damage by putting "blocks" in place to prevent us from creating too much tension, which might effectively tear and thus damage the muscles. Now imagine the supports which were holding the wall or tree in place suddenly break and it's now falling on top of you. You have to lock your arms and use all your strength to keep it from crushing you.[12]

Because the load from the tree or wall is falling on you and is therefore "live," your brain will release the block, allowing you to generate more of your ultimate strength potential. This is related to something called *cortical inhibition*, and Hooke's law.[13] It's also what is known as the stretch reflex. Thankfully, it is one reason isometrics are safer, but it does limit how much force we can generate compared to pressing or pushing against a "live" load.

The other drawback to isometrics is the lack of an easy way to measure how much force or work we are actually doing. In truth, this lack of measurability is probably the main reason isometrics fell out of favor with many athletes over the years. Without a way to measure how much force you're creating, it becomes much harder to quantify improvements. With weights, it's easy. You just go to a heavier weight.

Do either of these drawbacks make isometrics a less than optimal choice for you? In my opinion, absolutely not, and here's why: <u>The advantages for the majority of people who will read this book far outweigh any negatives or drawbacks</u>.

And we know the advantages are...

- you can do isometrics anywhere,
- it doesn't require a high level of skill at first,
- it's extremely safe regardless of your age or experience level,
- no expensive or special equipment is necessary to get started,

- and you CAN still generate lots of force and improve your strength as a result.

In this chapter, what I'm hoping to provide for you is a **starting point with isometric training**. The great majority of people who will read this book haven't been doing strength training at all and need a way to begin. This is it. It isn't meant as a be all-end all, nor is it intended for someone who desires a more complex way to improve strength. It surely is a great starting point though – and that IS the point. And even if you have experience in the gym and are performing more complex exercises, you can absolutely use the principles I'm providing to enhance the quality of that training.

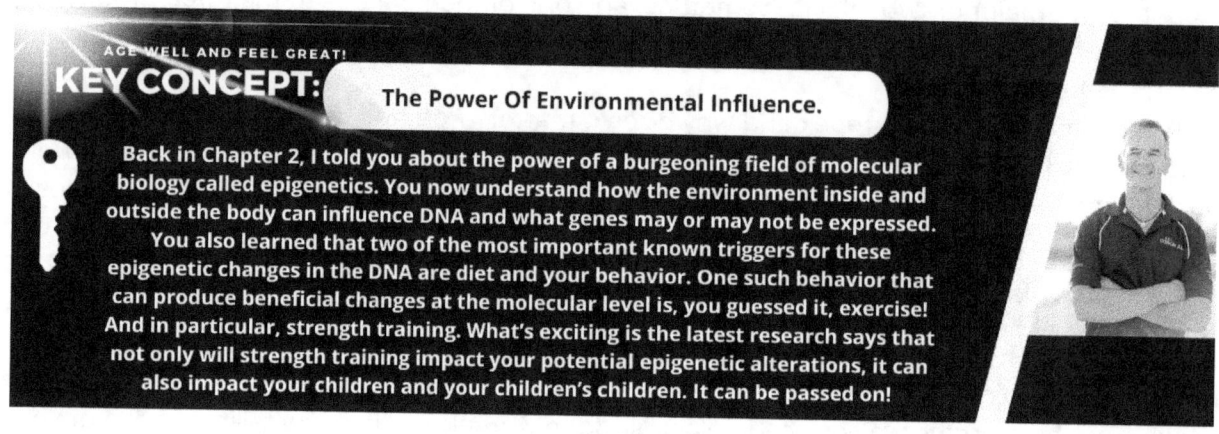

AGE WELL AND FEEL GREAT!

KEY CONCEPT: The Power Of Environmental Influence.

Back in Chapter 2, I told you about the power of a burgeoning field of molecular biology called epigenetics. You now understand how the environment inside and outside the body can influence DNA and what genes may or may not be expressed. You also learned that two of the most important known triggers for these epigenetic changes in the DNA are diet and your behavior. One such behavior that can produce beneficial changes at the molecular level is, you guessed it, exercise! And in particular, strength training. What's exciting is the latest research says that not only will strength training impact your potential epigenetic alterations, it can also impact your children and your children's children. It can be passed on!

If it doesn't suck, don't do it.
-Coach Al

Important Principles.

Before I get to the actual exercises and offer some specific guidelines for how to do them, I want to share just a little bit more about some important principles that will help you get the most from your effort. These are *radiating tension from within*, training at *different joint angles*, your *maximum contraction (MC)*, and a bit more about *time under tension (TUT)*.

Let's Start With Radiating Tension From Within.

Our ability to improve **how we move** and **get stronger** comes back in part to *better integration and connection among all the parts of our body:* the trunk, legs, hips, shoulders, arms, and feet! How can we best accomplish better integration and connection? One answer is to literally

create tension from within, radiating that tension with total muscular contraction. This has so many benefits, it's impossible to overstate it. Don't worry if at first glance it sounds complicated or intimidating, it's not. It's very simple actually. Not "easy" mind you, but simple.

Here's the deal:

- As you get into position, before beginning, think of "ramping up" the tension by squeezing and forcefully contracting every muscle in your body, especially those involved in the exercise you're doing. Remember, nothing you do with isometrics is passive other than the rest intervals between reps and sets.
- The "ramp up" period of up to 2 seconds is important. The goal is to progressively engage muscles and connective tissue such that there's moderate total radiation of tension. It's sort of like turning up the dimmer switch on a light – don't push it to the top right at first so it's full-on, but perhaps three-quarters of the way, then keep pushing it up slowly. Think about it. Then, practice it! As time goes on and you do this more, your skill will improve and along with it, you'll be smoother and more integrated. Yes, these are skills! The more you do it, the better you get at it.
- Anytime your feet are in contact with the ground when doing these movements, think **STATIC STOMP** into the ground: the idea is to engage and press your feet into the ground actively. Stomp the ground statically without lifting your feet! If it sounds strange, trust me, and just try it! You'll instantly feel more connected and integrated. Your overall body position awareness will improve. Everything will feel stronger and more stable. Try it!
- If you're wondering how breathing plays into all of this, I suggest you inhale for 2 seconds as you ramp up. Once you hit maximum tension, hold the tension and exhale throughout a full 6 second contraction. Resist the temptation to hold your breath for extended periods or hyperventilate at any time. You will find sometimes it feels natural to hold your breath for very short periods of time - that's fine and can sometimes help you increase your effort and intensity. By and large though, don't overthink it, just keep breathing in and out!
- Remember, to get the most from this program takes focus and conscious effort. *Nothing is passive.* The more you bring to it, the more you'll get from it. And the bonus? You'll be rewarded with a buzz throughout the muscles and your body telling you that you worked hard and didn't let momentum, gravity, or elasticity create a false sense of work or fatigue.

Now let's discuss the next concept, time under tension.

Time Under Tension: This is sometimes also referred to as time under load, and simply means that we'll count the amount of time we are under tension versus completing a set or pre-planned number of repetitions ("reps"). This might be very different than what you're accustomed to. Most programs and gyms typically tell you to do "x" number of reps and "x" number of sets. Sure, when you're performing these movements, you'll still accomplish a certain number of "reps," but the critical difference is the number of reps isn't your focus as much as is the length of each rep, or in other words, the amount of time under tension. Intensity is also a focus – the more intensely you work, all things being equal, the better the results!

To better understand WHY the concept of Time Under Tension is so important, let's back up and talk about <u>basic muscle physiology</u>. Trust me, while this might seem complicated when you first read it, it will become simpler the more you think about it. And understanding this is powerful because you'll then understand WHY this training is so effective. OK?

So, let's start with this: **The smallest unit of a muscle is a *motor unit*.** Motor units work much like a regular light switch – they are either on or off. There's no in-between. There are very *small* motor units, *medium-sized* motor units, and very *large* motor units. Your body will only use as many (and as large) a unit as it needs to do work – to perform a certain task. That's it, and it's important. Remember, it's an all or none principle, they're either on or off.

For example, say you reach down to pick up a pencil. Because the pencil is very light, only the smallest motor units will kick on, and not very many of them. If you squeezed that pencil very hard and tried to break it in half, some of the larger motor units would have to kick in and turn on in order for you to be able to generate more force to be able to break the pencil. And if you continued to squeeze hard for more than a few seconds, eventually those smaller motor units that first turned on would become fatigued. They'd tire out. So eventually more motor units would have to turn on in order for you to be able to continue to squeeze and generate the force required to break the pencil.

If you squeezed hard and long enough, you would get really tired and your hands and fingers would start to hurt like hell! Even though you would feel like the smaller muscles in your hands and fingers were exploding, the reality is they'd be generating less and less force as time went on, due to fatigue. As you are get increasingly tired and feel quite a bit of significant discomfort, the actual amount of force you generate is getting lower and lower. It doesn't feel that way, I know!

Now imagine, instead of a pencil, you bent over to pick up a much heavier steel rod. You would need more motor units (and larger ones) to kick in and turn on. Are you following me here?

What's the take-home message? It is this: *exercising doesn't make us stronger,* STRESS to our body followed by recovery, leads to an adaptive response, and that is what makes us stronger. You get positive stress that forces adaptation to a higher level of strength more efficiently – more quickly, with time under load. It's that simple.

The Difference Between "Reps" and "Time": If you keep the "pressure" on the muscle, more motor units will need to kick in. And perhaps even larger ones, too. But conversely, if you rest or pause, the units can regenerate or recharge, and as a result, not as many will need to be involved.

Think about doing a regular push up. You get into position, lower quickly and then rebound back up to the starting position. At this point you'd rest momentarily, and then drop back down again. Short bouts of work with rest in between. Momentum and rebound all contributing. With a big dose of passive lowering because of gravity! Think about it: at no point are the larger motor units really ever asked to contribute. For the most part, the work is accomplished with a minimum number of smaller motor units. Yes, you'll get tired eventually. But it may take a dozen or more reps and a few sets.

However, think about this: if you KEEP THE TENSION ON and focus on **time under tension instead of reps**, moving slowly and actively or not at all as we'll do with our isometric training, more and more motor units MUST kick on to help do the work and keep the tension up! If you are squeezing hard from within and really generating a lot of tension yourself, EVEN MORE motor units and larger ones will have to kick on to contribute! This is the true secret to training via time under load, vs training the more traditional way where you are just counting reps! It works like magic to help you get stronger.

Age Well and Feel Great!
Key Concept:
Time Under Tension

Watch a 5-minute video where I discuss Time Under Tension in the context of my RESTORE: The Bodyweight Strength Program, by going to the Pursuit Athletic Performance YouTube channel here: shorturl.at/knPQ8

In case you're curious, my *RESTORE: The Bodyweight Strength Program* is a powerful and effective training course available online.

You'll get all of the instructional videos, a plan to follow and lots of additional bonus content. And it's all available whenever it is convenient for you because it'll be in your own online account.

To learn more, go to this link:
https://pursuitathleticperformance.com/get-strong-move-right/

Now that we've discussed time under tension and radiating tension, let's talk about maximum contraction.

- **Your *Maximum* Contraction:** This is very simply the greatest amount of tension you can achieve after ramping up gradually. The focus of this tension is the primary muscles involved in the specific exercise, but don't forget this is also much more effective when you create whole-body tension from within. Don't forget to "static stomp" into the ground with your feet.

The amount of tension you're able to generate will vary depending on the position of your body including your arms, legs, and hips. For example, it is more difficult to generate high tension with your arms and hands overhead or behind you, than it is with your arms and hands right in front of you.

Age Well and Feel Great!

Key Concept:

What Happens To Your Strength As You Perform A Set?

When you do these exercises as I describe, you will make steady improvements in your strength. Ironically, as you fatigue, you may feel as though you are producing more force but in actuality, force is going down. Here's what I mean: At the beginning of a set, you are fresh so you're ready to put maximum effort into the rep. However, once you have built up to maximum effort, with each passing second your strength level diminishes.

At the same time, your breathing rate goes up and you will begin to feel the burning sensation indicating you are working hard. As time goes on, you're losing strength but the discomfort increases. Your goal at the end of each rep is to reach temporary muscular failure. Keep in mind that this is only temporary. After a short pause, you'll be ready to get back after it. The key take home message is; even though it may be very uncomfortable, due to increasing fatigue, you're actually producing less force, hence the risk of injury is nil. It may hurt, but in a good way. And it's safe.

Three GROUPS of Isometric Exercises:
1. No Equipment 2. Doorway 3. Strap, Rope, or Towel

The three groups of exercises in this chapter represent an ideal starting point, as well as the perfect foundation for more complex and advanced exercises. I've chosen a sampling of exercises that work all of the muscle groups in the body. You could easily use these principles and come up with your own positions. Again, these are a starting point to help you get going. Each group of exercises uses the same principles. The difference between the groups is in the equipment (or lack thereof) needed. I wanted to be sure to give you different options so that you could literally strength train anywhere, anytime.

- **Group 1 exercises don't require any equipment at all**. All you need is a few minutes of time, and the focus and desire to do some work.
- **Group 2 exercises use a doorway**. Any doorway, whether it's in your home, at work, in a hotel, or even in a gym.
- **Group 3 exercises use a towel, rope, or nylon strap**. These provide an additional challenge because you're required to hold onto the towel or strap, thereby providing a stimulus to improve grip strength!

Numerous scientific studies have demonstrated that grip strength is an important biomarker for aging.[14] Biomarkers are medical signs at the level of pathology, body function or structure, or activity/participation that provide an objective indication of medical status. In other words, these studies all show that grip strength is largely "consistent as an explanator of concurrent overall strength, upper limb function, bone mineral density, fractures, falls, malnutrition, cognitive impairment, depression, sleep problems, diabetes, multimorbidity, and quality of life."[15] There is also lots of evidence showing a predictive link between grip strength and all-cause and disease-specific mortality, future function, bone mineral density, fractures, cognition and depression, and problems associated with hospitalization.[16]

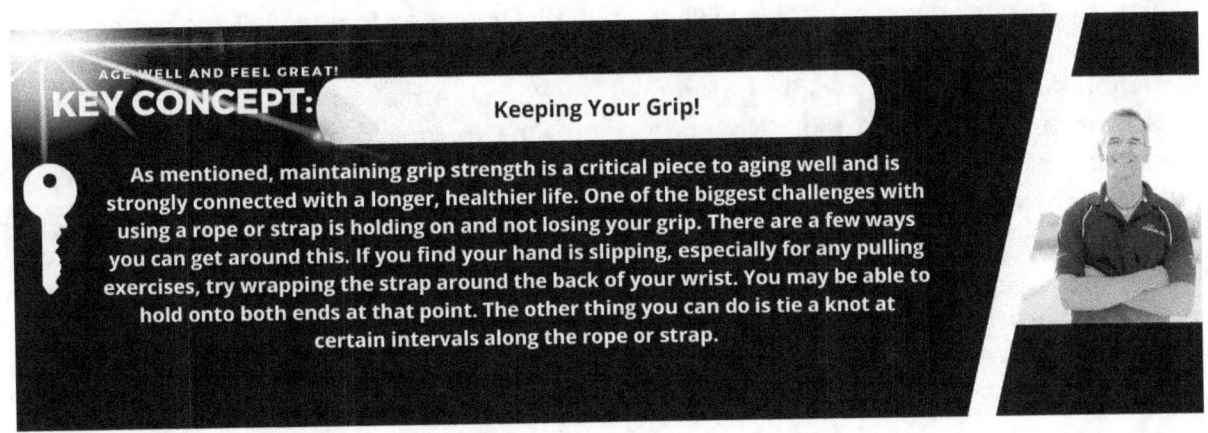

AGE WELL AND FEEL GREAT!

KEY CONCEPT: **Keeping Your Grip!**

As mentioned, maintaining grip strength is a critical piece to aging well and is strongly connected with a longer, healthier life. One of the biggest challenges with using a rope or strap is holding on and not losing your grip. There are a few ways you can get around this. If you find your hand is slipping, especially for any pulling exercises, try wrapping the strap around the back of your wrist. You may be able to hold onto both ends at that point. The other thing you can do is tie a knot at certain intervals along the rope or strap.

Which group of exercises you choose will depend on where you are, whether you have a rope, strap or towel on hand, and what your inclination might be at that moment. I encourage you to vary your approach and use them interchangeably. You might find one particular approach is more convenient for you. You might also find one or another approach feels more beneficial for you. It's up to you!

Always remember exercise set up will make a huge difference in the amount of benefit you receive from the exercises. That means breathing, radiating tension from within, building into each rep, static stomping, and of course, finishing each rep as intensely as possible.

What Are Some Other Tips?

- While you will radiate tension from within, contracting all of the muscles in your body and making the most of the mind/body connection, keep your head and neck still and don't allow tension to radiate up into this part of your body. In other words, relax your head and neck. You don't need tension from the neck up. With practice, you'll be able to better differentiate different areas of your body.
- Follow my guidance for breathing during the exercises, but remember, if in doubt, breathe normally.
- Move quickly between each exercise. This will help you achieve a better cardiovascular response.
- At the start of each exercise, create the lower-abdominal brace you learned in Chapter 20. Don't overdo this by squeezing very hard. You simply want to create a mild brace as though you were guarding against someone poking you. This will help you establish a neutral low-back and pelvic position and help protect your low-back.

Should you choose to advance your training, my **Restore: The Bodyweight Strength Program** would be an ideal choice. All of the principles you will learn with this isometric training are important in calisthenics and bodyweight training, as well as more traditional strength training. Keep in mind you can achieve all the benefits you need to age well and remain active with this program. The key to getting the most from this is consistency and effort. You can learn more about this Bodyweight Program at my Pursuit Athletic Performance website.

Strength Training Is A Skill: Now is a good time for me to remind you that strength training is a skill. Like any skill, the more you practice it, the better you get at it. For example, radiating tension from within often feels strange the first few times you try it. It's common to not feel like you're getting enough of the requisite tension to make a difference. Don't worry though, because the more you do it, the better you become. Practice it often, even when you're not actually performing the exercises. It literally is as simple as focusing your mind and your attention on a certain muscle group and squeezing hard!

How Will You Perform These Exercises?

Follow these guidelines for each exercise. The same protocol is used for each group of exercises.

- Take a moderately deep inhale through your nose for 1 to 2 seconds. Pause momentarily while you "ramp up" the tension for about 2 seconds to what feels like your maximum contraction. This is where you radiate tension fully throughout your entire body. The more tension you create from within, the greater the benefit!
- Hold and squeeze hard for 6 seconds, while also slowly exhaling at the same time, releasing air through your nose and pursed lips. The exhale should be a "pssssssssttt" sound like air leaking from a tire.
- Rest for around 10 seconds.
- Repeat the 2 second ramp, 6 second hold, 10 second rest cycle for up to 6 total sets, totaling around 1.5 to 2 minutes for each exercise.
- Finish with some kind of relaxing activity, such as a few dynamic yoga poses or other preferred relaxed stretching to release the tension.

This assortment of exercises is only a start. There are limitless variations you can employ once you have a good understanding of the principles of training strength isometrically. Experiment on your own and find different positions that work best for you. You can grab the rope or strap and hold it in a variety of positions. Just remember to create a good solid low-ab brace and build tension from within. Have fun with it!

Smart Considerations For Maximum Safety.

Properly approached and performed, isometric strength training done in the way I am teaching you is among the safest possible ways to get stronger. The key is the words "properly approached and performed," because any kind of exertion that isn't approached smartly and progressively can cause injury. To reduce your risk of injury from this training, there are some basic safety guidelines that you should follow. I've listed each of these safety "tips" and guidelines below. Please make sure you understand them all and follow all precautions to ensure you don't injure yourself or prevent yourself from making the progress you desire.

1. Build tension from within and increase force gradually.

Always begin from within by radiating tension inside your body BEFORE you put any pressure on any other surface or training tool. When you create your OWN tension, you create integration. This integration is a safety net that produces stability around joints and protects them. Similarly, build and increase force gradually, a little at a time. Yes, you are prescribed

2 seconds to ramp and 6 seconds to hold and increase force, but you can always take more time if you need it. There are no hard and fast "rules" other than proper form. Connect every part of your body and build into the tension. Then finish strong!

2. Don't let yourself get overheated.

When you are contracting muscles hard and repeatedly, heat will build up inside your muscles and you'll begin to perspire to offset that increase in temperature. Make sure you have plenty of water handy to stay well-hydrated and use a fan to avoid overheating. A small fan placed close to where you are performing the exercises might become your best friend. When you have a light breeze, you can work harder without overheating and you'll improve faster as a result.

3. Breathe!

At first, it may seem natural to hold your breath when doing these kinds of exercises. Avoid that by focusing on continuing to breathe even when it may seem normal to hold your breath. Taken to extreme, holding your breath while you exercise can lead to increased blood pressure, dizziness, and in certain case cause exertion-induced headache. Breathe continuously throughout the exercises! ☺ If you find yourself holding your breath, stop immediately and breathe. Reset, then try again.

4. Know the difference between normal training "discomfort" and pain from or leading to injury.

When you are creating tension and squeezing muscles hard and trying to produce as much force as you can, you will feel a burning sensation in your muscles and notice your heart rate is increasing. Your breathing will become increasingly labored and you will also notice fatigue is mounting. These are all normal signs of you working hard to get stronger. You might also notice you are feeling some lightheadedness or dizziness in the late stages of pushing hard to improve. These are also normal, although if they continue or become chronic, are indications you should stop and pause before continuing. Of note, one great benefit of this kind of strength training IS that you can stop immediately if you need to, without having to put a weight down. If you feel any unusual sensations that your intuition is telling you isn't normal, stop immediately and consult with your doctor or healthcare provider. Do NOT PUSH through pain that may end up causing even more injury or illness down the road. Be smart and honor your health first!

What Will You Find In The Upcoming Pages?

I'm providing you with specific guidance for three different groups of isometric strength exercises, each using different equipment and set up.

In Group 1, which requires zero equipment and can be done anywhere, you will find these six exercises:

- Low Abdominal Press
- Chest Press: Low-Medium-High
- Monkey Pull: Low-Medium-High
- Arm Curl: Low-Medium
- Seated Thigh Hold: Inside-Outside
- Wall Sit

In Group 2, which requires only a doorway to perform the exercises, you will find these seven exercises:

- Doorway Overhead Press
- Doorway Side Press
- Doorway Horizontal Press
- Doorway Lateral Leg Raise
- Doorway Leg Press
- Doorway Leg Curl
- Doorway Calf Raise

In Group 3, which requires a strap, rope, or towel to perform the exercises, you will find these eight exercises:

- Deadlift
- Pull: Low-Medium-High
- Leg Extension
- Press: Standing-Lying
- Lateral Raise
- Chest/Shoulder Press
- Triceps Press
- Seated Row

Final Questions.

- You may be asking, is this the only "best" way to approach isometric strength training? The answer is, there is no "best" for every single person, but I do believe this IS the best approach for the majority of people. It's time-efficient and effective, you have different options in terms of equipment and won't need anything expensive or fancy, and it is very safe. No excuses!

That being said, there are other approaches that are also effective, such as using LONGER continuous holds of 30 seconds up to 90 seconds. Those longer holds are also effective but because there is a slower buildup of tension, the exercises will take more total time.

- If you're curious about the strap I use in some of these photos, it is a polyester car towing strap purchased at an auto parts store that I cut to about 15 feet in length. I've also tied a series of knots in the strap to make it easier to grip. You can do the same thing with a soft cotton rope. This is a great plus to using a strap or rope. Give it a try!

Begin by creating that abdominal brace you learned in Chapter 20. That brace will be where you will put your primary focus in this exercise. Then hinge at the hips and place your hands on your thighs. Keep your head in line with your spine and focus on the lower abdominal area.

Once you're ready to go, squeeze your abdominals hard and press down on your thighs hard. Imagine your arms are helping transmit force to your lower body. Radiate tension throughout!

LOW ABDOMINAL PRESS

GROUP 1 EXERCISES

NO EQUIPMENT REQUIRED

GO THE DISTANCE - ISOMETRIC STRENGTH TRAINING

For the chest press, you may interlink your hands any way that is most comfortable for you. Start with the low-ab "brace." For each position, lower, middle, and high, find the most comfortable position, grip tightly and always make sure to drop your shoulders so you aren't hunched. When you're ready to go, begin to press your hands together, radiating tension not just through your arms and shoulders, but your entire body.

CHEST PRESS: LOW-MEDIUM-HIGH

GROUP 1 EXERCISES

NO EQUIPMENT REQUIRED

GO THE DISTANCE - ISOMETRIC STRENGTH TRAINING

Interlock your fingers in a "monkey grip." As before, set up with a solid low-ab brace, a static stomp, and make sure to radiate tension after your short inhale. Then pull apart with maximum force! This is great for your back, shoulders, hands, and fingers! Grip strength matters.

MONKEY PULL: LOW-MEDIUM-HIGH

GROUP 1 EXERCISES

NO EQUIPMENT REQUIRED

GO THE DISTANCE - ISOMETRIC STRENGTH TRAINING

With your hands in front of your body, put your hands together with the top facing down and the lower facing up. When you're ready, brace and radiate tension and try to "curl up" the lower arm while pressing down hard with the upper arm.

ARM CURL: LOW-MEDIUM

GROUP 1 EXERCISES

NO EQUIPMENT REQUIRED

GO THE DISTANCE · ISOMETRIC STRENGTH TRAINING

You should be seated for this exercise. Knees should be bent, hip-width, feet flat on the floor. INSIDE: Place your palms on the inside of your knees and brace. When you're ready, push out hard against your knees while simultaneously trying to close your legs together. OUTSIDE: place your hands on the outside of your thighs. When you're ready, brace yourself and push in hard against your knees, while simultaneously trying to open your legs.

▼

SEATED THIGH HOLD: INSIDE-OUTSIDE

GROUP 1 EXERCISES

NO EQUIPMENT REQUIRED

GO THE DISTANCE · ISOMETRIC STRENGTH TRAINING

You will need a blank wall for the "wall sit." Make sure the floor or ground isn't slippery - wear sticky shoes if needed. To perform this, lean up against the wall and assume a "seated" position (as though you were actually sitting). Knees and hips should be at 90 degree right-angles. Place your hands and arms where they are most comfortable. Extend forward as in the photos is the most challenging.

WALL "SIT"

GROUP 1 EXERCISES

NO EQUIPMENT REQUIRED

GO THE DISTANCE · ISOMETRIC STRENGTH TRAINING

Standing in the middle of a doorway, place your hands on the upper frame. Set up as before with good posture and your head in line with your spine.

Place your feet about hip width so you have a solid base of support. If the doorway is too high, stand on a box or on your toes.

When ready, press up hard.

DOORWAY OVERHEAD PRESS

GROUP 2 DOORWAY EXERCISES

NO GYM REQUIRED

GO THE DISTANCE - ISOMETRIC STRENGTH TRAINING

Stand in the center inside a doorway and place your hands on the inner frames. Choose a height around shoulder height that is most comfortable.

Stand tall and make sure to brace, keeping your head in line with your spine and your chin tucked.

When ready, press hard sideways into the door inner frames.

DOORWAY SIDE PRESS

GROUP 2 DOORWAY EXERCISES

NO GYM REQUIRED

GO THE DISTANCE · ISOMETRIC STRENGTH TRAINING

Position yourself sideways in the door frame so that you are looking at the frame.

Make sure to place your foot and low back tight against the frame and then reach out to the opposite side frame. Place your hands where you're most comfortable to be able to generate maximum force into the frame.

When you're ready, push hard against the frame, using the opposite side as support.

DOORWAY HORIZONTAL PRESS

GROUP 2 DOORWAY EXERCISES

NO GYM REQUIRED

GO THE DISTANCE - ISOMETRIC STRENGTH TRAINING

Standing in the middle of the doorway so that you can position one leg against the door frame. You have the option of positioning your hands as I do in the photo, or keeping them both down. Whatever is most comfortable and allows you to generate maximum force.

Balance on one leg and place the other foot sideways against the door frame, pressing hard into the frame. Do both sides.

DOORWAY LATERAL LEG RAISE

GROUP 2 DOORWAY EXERCISES

NO GYM REQUIRED

GO THE DISTANCE · ISOMETRIC STRENGTH TRAINING

You will sit down onto the floor sideways in a doorway, positioning your body so that your back is up tight and supported by the doorway. It may help to cushion your back by using a pillow.

Place one foot against the other side of the doorway and when ready, press hard against the doorway. Make sure to do both sides.

DOORWAY LEG PRESS

GROUP 2 DOORWAY EXERCISES

NO GYM REQUIRED

GO THE DISTANCE · ISOMETRIC STRENGTH TRAINING

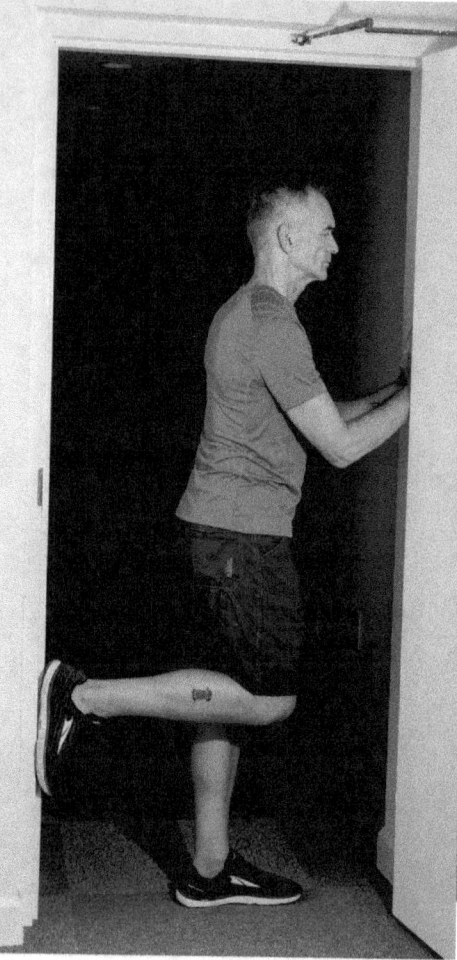

Stand sideways in the doorway. Your goal is to grip one side of the door frame tightly while you place the sole of one foot against the opposite door frame.

Make sure to create the ab brace and then radiate tension throughout your body, from your fingertips to the soles of your feet. Once you're ready, press back with your foot while gripping the frame tightly with your hands. Do both sides!

DOORWAY LEG CURL

GROUP 2 DOORWAY EXERCISES

NO GYM REQUIRED

GO THE DISTANCE - ISOMETRIC STRENGTH TRAINING

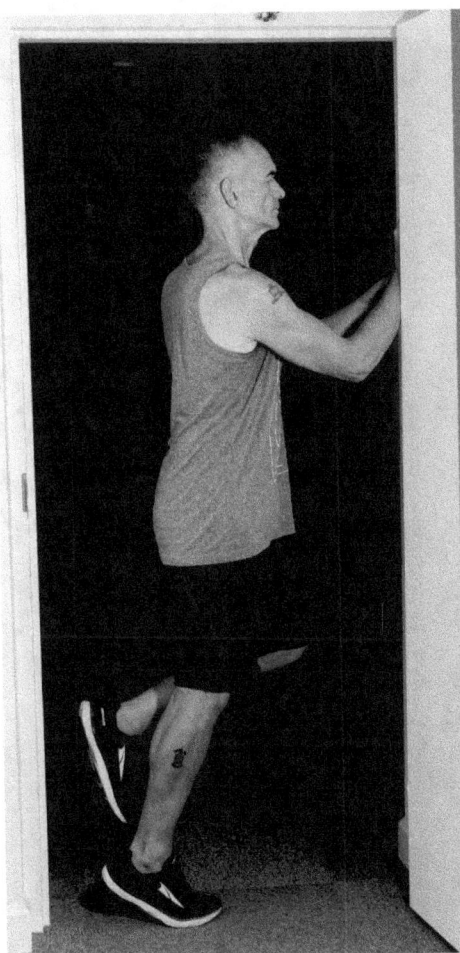

Standing sideways in the doorway, focus on one leg and foot at a time as you grip the doorframe with your hands.

On one leg, raise the heel and press up on the ball of your foot, pushing up as high as you can. Get right up on the ball of your foot and toes! Make sure to do both sides and radiate tension throughout! Do both sides.

DOORWAY CALF RAISE

GROUP 2 DOORWAY EXERCISES

NO GYM REQUIRED

GO THE DISTANCE · ISOMETRIC STRENGTH TRAINING

Place the towel, rope, or strap beneath your feet, gripping the ends of whatever you're using, keeping your arms straight. Feet should be hip width apart.

Create that solid ab-brace and make sure to keep the low-back neutral. Keep your head in line with your spine.

When ready, grip tightly and pull up hard.

ROPE DEADLIFT

GROUP 3 EXERCISES

TOWEL - STRAP - ROPE REQUIRED

GO THE DISTANCE - ISOMETRIC STRENGTH TRAINING

Grip a rope, towel, or strap in front of you. Create that solid low-ab brace. Once you are set, grip tightly and pull your hands apart. Make sure to keep your shoulders down and back throughout! Radiate tension from within to create maximum integration and total body strength.

▼

ROPE PULL: LOW-MEDIUM-HIGH

GROUP 3 EXERCISES

TOWEL - STRAP - ROPE REQUIRED

GO THE DISTANCE - ISOMETRIC STRENGTH TRAINING

Using a towel, strap, or rope, lie on your back with one foot flat on the floor, knee bent. Place the strap underneath the foot of the other leg and bring your thigh to your chest while holding tightly onto the strap. Maintain a slightly bent knee. Grab tightly and push your leg to the sky.

▼

STRAP LEG EXTENSION

GROUP 3 EXERCISES

TOWEL · STRAP · ROPE REQUIRED

GO THE DISTANCE · ISOMETRIC STRENGTH TRAINING

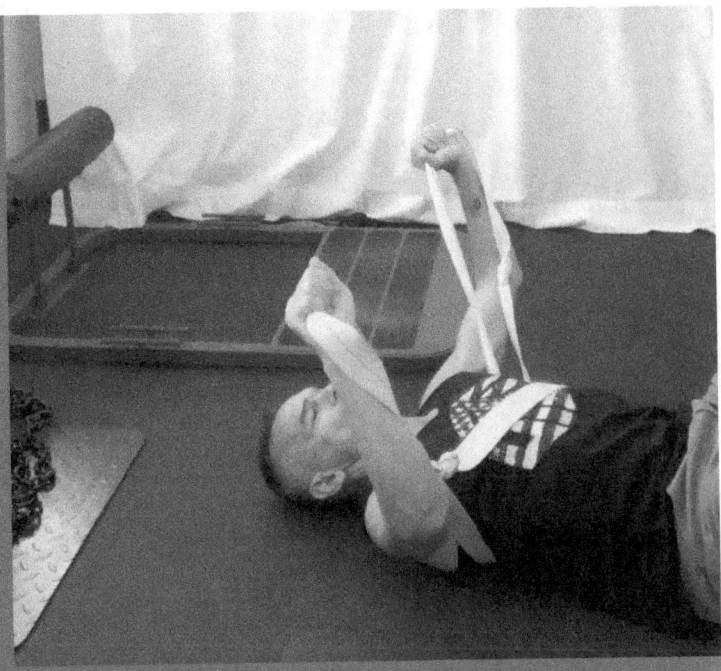

You have two different options here with a rope, towel, or as the picture shows, a strap. For either variation, wrap the strap under your arms and grab it tightly. Adjust the length so that you are positioned to be able to press overhead or directly in front of your chest.

▼

STRAP PRESS: STANDING/LYING

- -

GROUP 3 EXERCISES

TOWEL · STRAP · ROPE REQUIRED

◄ GO THE DISTANCE · ISOMETRIC STRENGTH TRAINING

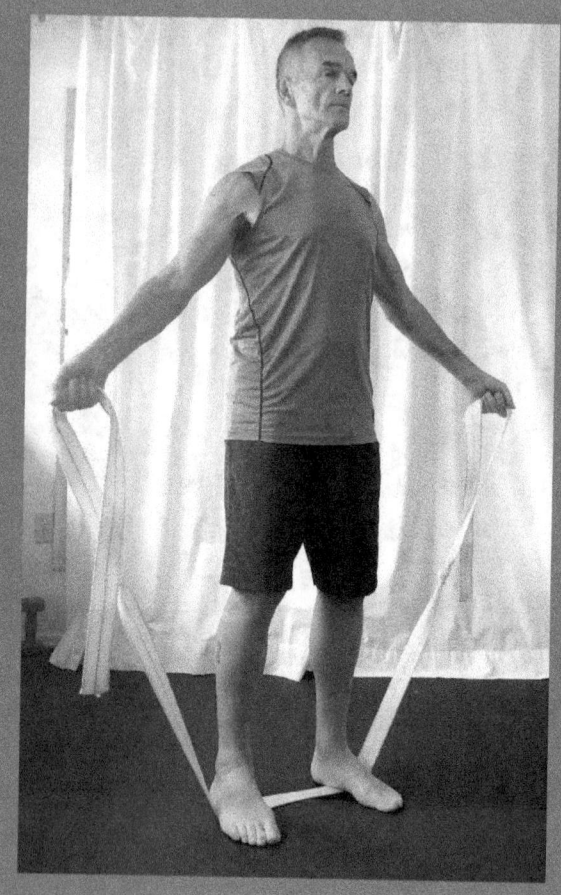

Place a towel, strap, or rope on the ground and place your feet inside so you are standing on it.

Grab the ends such that you can extend your arms straight out to your side.

Keep the elbows straight and palms facing out and up. Wrap your wrist or tie a knot to increase your grip.

When ready, radiate tension throughout your body and try to raise your arms toward the sky.

LATERAL RAISE

GROUP 3 EXERCISES

TOWEL · STRAP · ROPE REQUIRED

GO THE DISTANCE · ISOMETRIC STRENGTH TRAINING

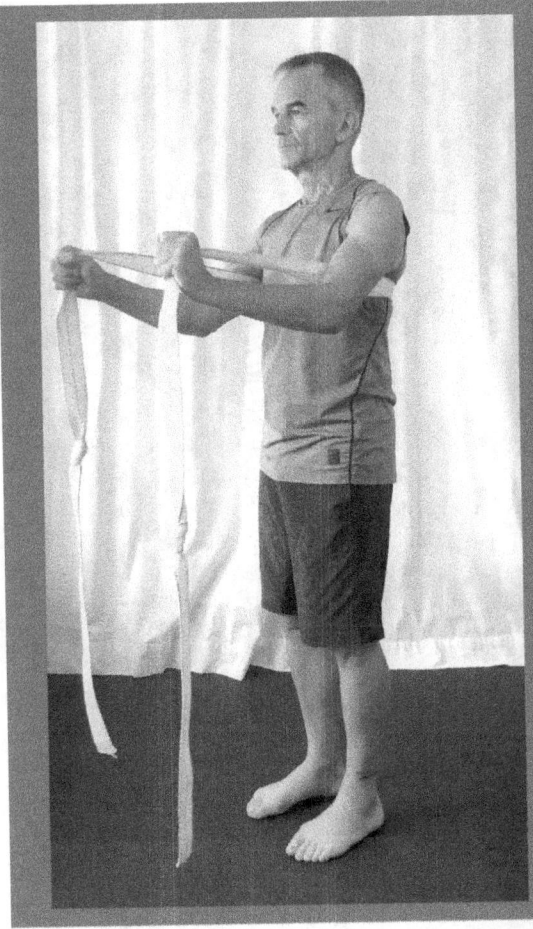

Wrap a towel, strap, or rope around the back of your trunk about chest high.

Grab the ends such that you can place your hands straight ahead for a chest or shoulder press. If necessary, wrap your wrists or tie a knot to hold onto.

When ready, brace and radiate tension throughout your body and try to press the strap away from your body.

CHEST/SHOULDER PRESS

GROUP 3 EXERCISES

TOWEL · STRAP · ROPE REQUIRED

GO THE DISTANCE · ISOMETRIC STRENGTH TRAINING

You will need a long rope or strap for this exercise.

You should stand on the rope or strap with your feet together, grabbing the ends.

Move your arms overhead and raise your elbows toward the ceiling, allowing your hands to lower behind your head. Be careful not to overarch your back.

When ready, brace and radiate tension throughout your body and try to press your hands toward the sky.

TRICEP PRESS

GROUP 3 EXERCISES

TOWEL - STRAP - ROPE REQUIRED

GO THE DISTANCE - ISOMETRIC STRENGTH TRAINING

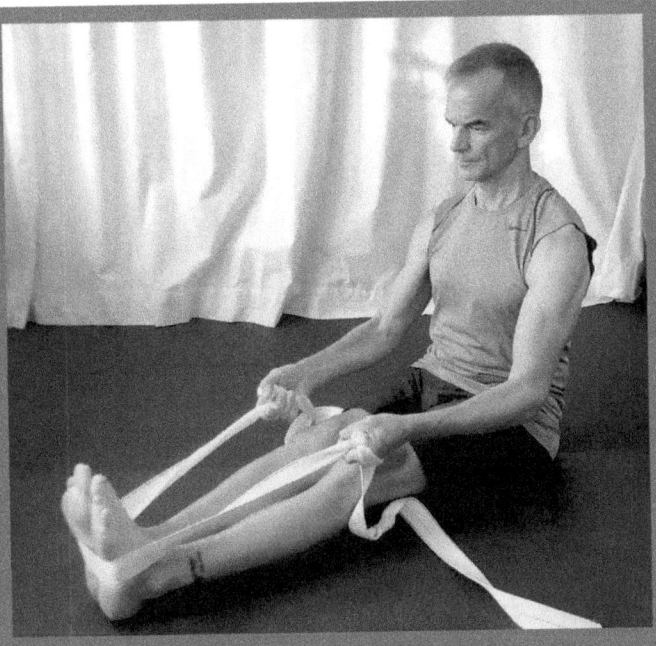

Get into a seated position with your feet together and legs straight out in front of you. Place a towel, strap, or rope, under your feet and grab the middle of the strap with bent arms. Grip tightly, brace and attempt to pull the strap back in a rowing motion.

▼

SEATED ROW

- -

GROUP 3 EXERCISES

TOWEL · STRAP · ROPE REQUIRED

GO THE DISTANCE · ISOMETRIC STRENGTH TRAINING

PART 5

CARDIO

CHAPTER 26

CARDIOVASCULAR FITNESS:
THE OPTIMAL APPROACH FOR LONG TERM HEALTH AND FITNESS - TYPE 1 AND TYPE 2.

Your entire life happens inside your body. It's the one home you'll always occupy and can never sell. But you can renovate it. If you can only pick one habit to build, exercise is probably the one. Everything is downstream from how your body is functioning.

— **James Clear,** *author of Atomic Habits*

In this chapter, I'm going to share lots of important information about cardiovascular exercise and make some specific recommendations for how you can start to incorporate it into your life, even if you've never done any "cardio" exercise before. Just in case you're concerned, I'm not going to recommend you embark on a running program, although if you ARE a runner, I will share some specific recommendations for you in the upcoming pages.

Unless you've been living under a rock, you're well aware of the health benefits of doing some kind of cardiovascular exercise. It's been studied scientifically more than any other form of exercise and the research results have been consistent. Even as little as 15 minutes a day, 3 to 4 days a week, has been shown to improve heart health and blood flow, lower your risk of cancer and diabetes and other serious diseases, lower blood pressure, boost immune function, burn calories, and improve your mood, too. But believe me when I say, the benefits from committing to consistently doing cardiovascular exercise don't stop there. There's something else as important. To show you what I mean, I'd like to share a story.

In my early running days, the singular goal that pushed me more than any other was to get better at the marathon so I could eventually qualify for "Boston." And then, once I did qualify, to get even faster – to see what my true potential was. In the mid-1980s, the qualifying standard for Men's Open was 2 hours, 50 minutes, which is an average of around 6 minutes, 30 seconds per mile. Needless to say, becoming an "official" qualified runner wasn't easy in those days!

Training to run a "fast" marathon can be tricky. You need a balance of speed and endurance to hit your goal pace and hold it to all the way to the finish line. Early on I learned the marathon distance, like a lot of other long endurance events, is sort of an "eating and drinking contest." In other words, beyond run fitness to resist inevitable muscular fatigue, your body needs an almost limitless supply of nutritional energy to finish strong. And, that energy – as I learned – needs to come in part, from *stored fat*. Why? For one, relying on sugar, regardless of where it might come from, doesn't work for a run of that distance. There's simply not enough of it available in storage and you can't take it in, absorb and digest it quickly enough to get you to the finish line. The point being, to do your very best at the marathon, you have to be really good at accessing body fat and using it as a fuel source. In other words, a good "fat burner." If you recall, I discussed all of these elements including storing sugar and also "fat burning" back in Chapter 9 on *insulin resistance* and *hyperinsulinemia*. As you'll soon see, there's a strong health connection between these elements that goes well beyond running a marathon, or running at all, for that matter. To reiterate, this ISN'T about running per se, it's about the long term health benefits of burning body fat as a fuel source for whatever activity we might embark on. Keep reading.

Even if you've never run a marathon, it might be easy to imagine during 26+ miles of running at your fastest possible speed, there's going to be lots of ups and downs. A marathon rarely ever evolves in linear fashion, there's always ebb and flow. To be successful, you have to be present in the moment, be a good problem solver, and just keep moving forward and doing your best. You sort of take your punches and keep working at it in a smart way, never allowing yourself to get too far ahead nor to look back. If you think about it, that sounds an awful lot like *life*, doesn't it? Which is another thing I learned early on - running a marathon well and finishing strong is in many ways, a *lot like life*.

The idea of a marathon being a microcosm of life is certainly one I pondered early on in my running journey, and in many ways it has become cliché. Lots of runners and runner/writers have written about it. But there's something important about how a marathon run exists as a microcosm of life that isn't often discussed. And in my opinion, it's more important than the inevitable ebb and flow and need to be present that I just mentioned. The "it" I'm talking about is being a *good fat burner*. That's the health connection I alluded to earlier. And it's one of the most important connections between cardiovascular exercise and the kind of good health that will help us go the distance!

Simply put, you won't be good at the marathon without being a good fat burner, and you certainly WON'T be healthy and live a long time free of disease, without also being a good fat burner. Both of these things – running a marathon and living healthfully for a long time - require us to get most of the energy we need from stored fat, NOT from sugar.

Does Intensity Matter?

If you're thinking how "hard" something is determines where the fuel for it comes from, you are absolutely right. And this matters, as you will read and learn soon.

Simply put, your body "chooses" where to get energy, whether it's sugar floating in your bloodstream or stored in muscles and liver, or fat stored in fat cells, **based on the intensity of whatever it is you're doing**. Harder/faster = more from sugar. Slower/easier = more from fat. We'll get into some details about this shortly. I will tell you how to get the greatest benefit of fat burning from your aerobic exercise, yet still retain your youthful vigor. Both are important.

Aerobic Exercise Isn't Just About Improving "Cardio" Fitness.

Before we talk about the specifics of what kind of exercise and how hard, I'd like to delve a bit deeper into this exercise/health/stored fat connection I alluded to when I told you how life and a marathon run are much the same. It's important to understand; it will empower you to dial in the right effort if your goal is to age well.

Remember from Chapter 9 on *insulin resistance* and *hyperinsulinemia*, I shared how important it is to tap into stored sugar in our muscles and liver for optimal metabolic health and body composition. When we use up the stored sugar in muscles and the liver, we create that "storage depot" for the food we're eating, so *less is stored as bodyfat* in fat cells. If we don't tap into stored sugar (and bodyfat), it means we're relying more on the glucose floating around in our bloodstream, which will mean insulin will be chronically elevated and we will become increasingly *insensitive* to it. As you now know, that's a recipe for disaster for your health. And, <u>if you're not sure why this is the case, please go back and read that chapter again.</u> I fully admit that it can be a complex topic to delve into, but it IS arguably **the most important thing you can learn from this book that will dramatically impact your health, which is why I'm being redundant.**

As well, in Chapter 10 on **Time Restricted Eating**, I wrote about how having an eating window and all that goes with it, is largely about "teaching your body to become more fat adapted – a fat burning machine." While there isn't complete agreement in the scientific community as to what is actually happening and whether or not we're "teaching" our body anything, I will tell you from first-hand experience over many years, that there is something very important going on that your body can learn.

In this chapter, we're going to tie all of these elements together and talk about how cardiorespiratory exercise or whatever you may want to call it – aerobic fitness, cardio, or endurance training – plays an important role not just in improving heart health and blood flow and all the other things I mentioned, but also, as importantly, *in your metabolic health.*

If what I've shared so far comes as a bit of a surprise to you, I get it. You're probably thinking since I've spent my life as an endurance athlete and coach, it would make sense that I might harp primarily on the pure "fitness" benefits of this type of exercise. Nope! When it comes to aging better, feeling younger, functioning better as we age, and creating our best chance to die healthy, **it's the metabolic health benefits that matter the most.**

How Do You Teach Your Body To Become a Fat-Burning Machine?

Get leaner, improve insulin sensitivity, have more energy, and age well!

 1 TAP INTO STORED SUGAR IN MUSCLES AND LIVER, CREATING A STORAGE DEPOT FOR THE FOOD YOU EAT.

HOW?

 2 TAP INTO STORED BODY-FAT AS A PRIMARY FUEL SOURCE FOR MORE OF YOUR DAILY ACTIVITY, INSTEAD OF RELYING ON SUGAR FLOATING IN YOUR BLOOD STREAM!

HOW?

- STRENGTH TRAINING
- MOVE AND STAY ACTIVE - SPRINT!
- DON'T EAT 2 TO 3 HOURS PRIOR TO EXERCISING
- TYPE 2 CARDIO
- YARD WORK AND CHORES

- EAT LESS OFTEN
- MOVE AND STAY ACTIVE
- DON'T EAT 2 TO 3 HOURS PRIOR TO EXERCISING
- TYPE 1 CARDIO
- REDUCE THE SUGAR IN YOUR DIET - EAT MORE FAT

It's the activity you get combined with what and when you eat and the hormonal response to it that matters the most.

To learn even more, let's continue to explore this topic of the health benefits of cardio exercise and fat burning a bit more before I discuss some of the changes that can happen to our cardiovascular fitness as we age. I'll also give you my recommendations for how to best incorporate this kind of aerobic exercise into your routine.

Know this: If you've never exercised before, now is YOUR time to get started. There's no time like the present. While there is no magic "hack," there is a smart approach. Which is:

1. Commit to doing it long enough so there's enough time to establish a new lifestyle habit, and
2. Make sure to start small enough so that it's easy to do and so that you can be consistent, no matter what might happen.

There are no mistakes, only learning and opportunities.

— Tina Fey

The Relationship Between Cardio Exercise and Metabolic Diseases.

First, let's review a few terms and keep it simple. Remember the word *metabolism* simply means all the chemical processes that go on in our body that turn food energy into energy we can use. *Metabolic syndrome* is the term used to describe a plethora of conditions, such as insulin resistance, that are linked to a dysfunctional *metabolism*. At the center of these processes, inside every cell, we have *mitochondria* that are the main powerhouse of the cell in which *metabolism* occurs. An example of metabolism would be the conversion of glucose and fat into energy through a series of enzymatic reactions. Other organs also play a vital role, such as the liver.

The role of "cardio" exercise and *metabolic syndrome* has been extensively studied. One such study led by well-known researcher and physiologist, Inigo San Milan, Ph.D., looked at how athletes with good cardiovascular fitness and healthy mitochondria (remember these are the energy producers within the cell) are able to clear sugar and lactic acid more efficiently from the bloodstream, [1] and access fat better as a source of energy. By now you know, this means they are more *metabolically healthy*. We also now know that cardio exercise directly mobilizes special transporters inside the cell which remove glucose. You also now know that this is a good thing and why.

In a podcast interview Dr. Milan stated, "a typical characteristic that we know of people with pre-type 2, or type 2 diabetes, is that they have a poor metabolic flexibility that is also a poor capacity to oxidize fuels. One of them is fat. We know that fat can only be oxidized in the mitochondria. Thus, by measuring the fat oxidation of these patients, we can indirectly see the mitochondrial function, especially when we put them in context or in comparison with those ones who are healthy individuals."[2]

What is he saying in simpler terms? And what does this really mean for you? He simply means <u>people who are pre-diabetic or who have already been diagnosed with type 2 diabetes</u> – <u>who are essentially in poorer metabolic health</u> – **have less of an ability to use fat as a fuel**. Their blood sugar levels are higher and are much more dependent on blood glucose for energy. Obviously, this is not good.

Remember in Chapter 9 on insulin, I shared how improving our insulin sensitivity and thus our ability to burn fat as a primary source of energy would lead to a healthier *metabolism*. That's exactly what he is saying is compromised in folks who are pre-diabetic.

And what is really scary is, according to a 2018 report from the Centers for Disease Control (who in my opinion typically *under* reports these findings), "approximately 100 million American adults—almost 2 out of 3 —have prediabetes. Of those, more than 80% don't know they have it."[3] At the time of this writing, the number is likely higher.

It is important to understand the relationship between the health of our metabolism, the mitochondria, and our risk for chronic disease. We know to some extent, mitochondrial function does deteriorate as we age, but *we can* impact and slow the rate of deterioration through our exercise habits.

Simply put, the more we improve our cardiovascular fitness and health through appropriate cardio exercise:

- The healthier our metabolism will be,
- The better we'll be at tapping into fat stores for energy,
- The less sugar we'll have floating around in our bloodstream,
- The more sensitive (and less resistant) we will be to insulin,
- The more storage space or depots we will have for glucose to enter as it is metabolized from the food we eat,
- The less risk we will have for mitochondrial related chronic diseases such as heart disease, diabetes, cancer, and Alzheimers and other dementias, among others.

And...drum roll, please! We will absolutely feel better mentally, emotionally, and physically, and have more energy for all the activities we want to do right up until the end. If all that doesn't convince you of how important a little cardio exercise is in your life, then I guess nothing will.

What Happens to Our Cardiovascular Fitness as We Age?

The improvements in cardio function we might expect to see when embarking on an exercise program depend largely on our background and experience with it. All things being equal, the less aerobic exercise we've done in our lives, the greater likelihood we'll see big improvements moving forward. This can be fairly exciting for a 40 or 50 year old who has never done any cardio exercise to speak of, and then embarks on a cycling or running or swimming routine. These folks have the potential to see some encouraging results with consistent effort, largely because they're starting from ground zero. For those who have more experience, the improvement potential isn't quite as high, depending of course on many factors.

As we age, generally speaking, we lose cardiac capacity along with some inevitable other physiological changes. These are all well documented.[4] Among these less-than-desirable changes are:

- Decreased maximal aerobic capacity (max VO2) and maximum oxygen consumption, perhaps as much as a 30-40% reduction in the 65-year old compared to the 25-year old,[5]
- A reduction in maximum heart rate during maximal exertion,
- Reduced capacity of the left ventricle of the heart to propel a large volume of blood with each beat,[6]
- An increase in the left ventricle's wall and total ventricular mass, reducing its potential to contract completely,[7]
- A decrease in the amount of oxygen received by the muscles, known as temporary ischemia,[8]

- Arterial walls become more rigid with age and are less able to dilate to accommodate increases in blood flow,[9]
- And because there is generally less muscle mass in older people, there's also a lowered demand for oxygen by those tissues, thus less oxygen is extracted by the muscles.[10]

While that list might look daunting, don't let the inevitable changes deter you from making a conscious choice to start if you haven't already. We know these changes are potentially worse in those who are sedentary and don't get any exercise, which is reason enough to start right now.

We ALSO know we can improve our cardiac capacity at any age, especially if we're coming from a background where we haven't done much to begin with. Very often the goal is to slow the loss or simply to maintain what we have for a longer period of time.

In his interview on *The Drive* podcast with Dr. Peter Attia, M.D., Dr. San Milan noted that he has personally "seen people in their 60s and 70s make unbelievable improvements in their metabolic health, often achieving the metabolic parameters of active 30-year olds."[11] He says "we should think of this level of training the same way as accumulating wealth. It's day in and day out, small, compounded gains over years and years. This is why a 40-year-old overweight smoker can become a world champion cyclist at 80 because he probably never once again got out of shape in that 40 years."[12]

While I think it's questionable as to the likelihood that a 40-year-old overweight smoker can become a cycling world champion, I do absolutely believe the news is positive IF we are consistent and make sure to look at every piece to the aging puzzle, starting with exercise and how, what, and when we eat. Certainly, this encouraging information confirms we can positively impact our quality of life and increase our odds of dying healthy with a smart, consistent, aerobic exercise program. Never forget there is always hope, no matter how old you are!

The Ideal Approach for Optimal Cardiovascular Fitness:

Type 1 and *Type 2*

Now that we've looked at the powerful benefits of 1) being a better fat burner, 2) discussed how cardiovascular fitness declines as we age, and 3) reviewed all the amazing benefits of beginning and then maintaining a cardio fitness program to improve your cardiorespiratory fitness, I'm now going to teach you how I recommend you approach it, regardless of your experience level. If the goal is to age well, minimize risk of injury, and get the most benefits in the least amount of time, you have some objectives to consider.

First is that you'll need to balance this along with some of the other elements that are needed for a holistic approach to fitness and health, such as **strength training** and **moving better**. With that in mind, the ideal cardio program for novices beginning for the first time is

4 to 5 times per week of an activity of your choice for a total of 30 minutes. For more experienced exercisers, the goal is up to 1 hour.

More experienced exercisers have the opportunity to include **TWO different types of sessions, which I'll call Type 1 and Type 2. Anyone just beginning or coming back to this kind of activity after a long layoff should focus only on Type 1.**

Even for more experienced exercisers, **Type 2** sessions should be done sparingly and balanced with other types of movement like strength training, to ensure you remain durable and injury-free. _Focus first on improving stability and strength_, then use that as a foundation for incorporating more cardio type training into your routine.

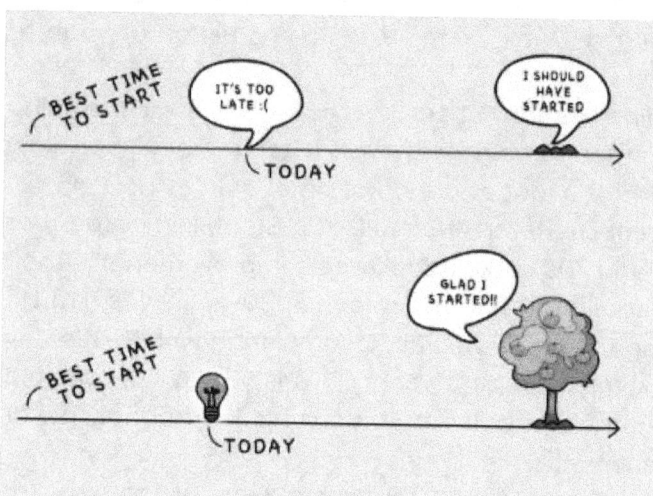

Variety Keeps You Healthy:

Remember mixing it up and maintaining some variety is the best approach. The more varied your routine, the better. Variety keeps your body nimble and helps with motivation. You could ride a bike one day and go dancing on another. Your goal is to move at the right effort level and not get hurt doing it. ☺

What Are the Different Types of Cardio Exercise?

Type 1 cardio is where you keep a "steady state" moderately comfortable effort that is optimal for fat burning and building cardio fitness. The most important thing to remember is you should be able to breathe entirely through your nose without gasping for air and even carry on a short conversation. Again, this intensity level is ideal if you're just beginning after a layoff or if regular exercise is new to you. You want to challenge yourself to maintain a consistent effort, but the effort should be comfortable.

You are squarely in your "fat burning zone" and optimizing metabolic health when you can maintain nose breathing but have to focus to keep your effort up and consistent.

Refer to the Rating of Perceived Exertion chart coming up shortly for some specific guidance. Rather than making it complex or relying on gadgets to determine how "hard" you are working, pay attention to how it feels to you and how you are breathing. Focus in on the 4 to 5 scale (Moderate Activity), which is appropriate for this type of cardiovascular exercise (see the blue shaded area inside the pink box).

You may even begin at 2 to 3 (Light Activity) and raise effort until you reach 4 to 5. Always listen to your body and connect to your breath. Why? Your breathing is a window into your body telling you how it is responding to the exertion. This is important and one way to become more in tune with your body.

Some ideas for this type of cardiovascular exercise are brisk walking, hiking, moderately vigorous dancing such as with Zumba or belly dancing, biking or elliptical at a moderate effort, easy to steady running or jogging, swimming, and rowing.

RPE SCALE RATING OF PERCEIVED EXERTION

10	**Max Effort Activity** Feels almost impossible to keep going. Completely out of breath. Unable to talk. Can only maintain for a short period of time.
8 - 9	**Very Hard Activity** Difficult to maintain intensity. Heavy breathing through nose and mouth. Can speak only a few words.
6 - 7	**Vigorous Activity** Borderline uncomfortable. Some gasping. Can speak only in very short sentences.
4 - 5	**Moderate Activity** *(This is Type 1 Cardio)* Still able to breathe through the nose. Can hold short conversation. Comfortable but becoming challenging.
2 - 3	**Light Activity** Easy to breathe and carry on a conversation. Could go for many hours. Relaxed strolled, easy cycling.
1	**Very Light Activity** Hardly any exertion, but more than sleeping or watching TV.

For **Type 1**, the ideal rise in heart rate should be moderate in order for it to be true "aerobic" exercise. This type of exercise isn't meant to be "hard." If you're gasping for air or out of breath, you're doing it too hard. Most of the activities that are ideal for this should all be done at a relatively easy to moderate effort level.

Reminder, if you're new to exercise or coming back after a long layoff, focus on **Type 1** only until you're able to build some consistency, making sure you don't get injured along the way.

First-time exercisers and "weekend warriors": Don't be that person who blasts out of the gate, going too hard too soon, and getting out of breath quickly and having to stop, or worse, get injured. Regardless of your experience level, your primary mission is to stay healthy so you can continue and be consistent.

You still want to be able to breathe entirely through your nose and not feel like you have to gasp for air. Similarly, you should be able to talk in short sentences during this exercise. Also, as you now know from a previous chapter, strength training can also elevate your heart rate and give you cardiovascular benefits depending upon how you approach it.

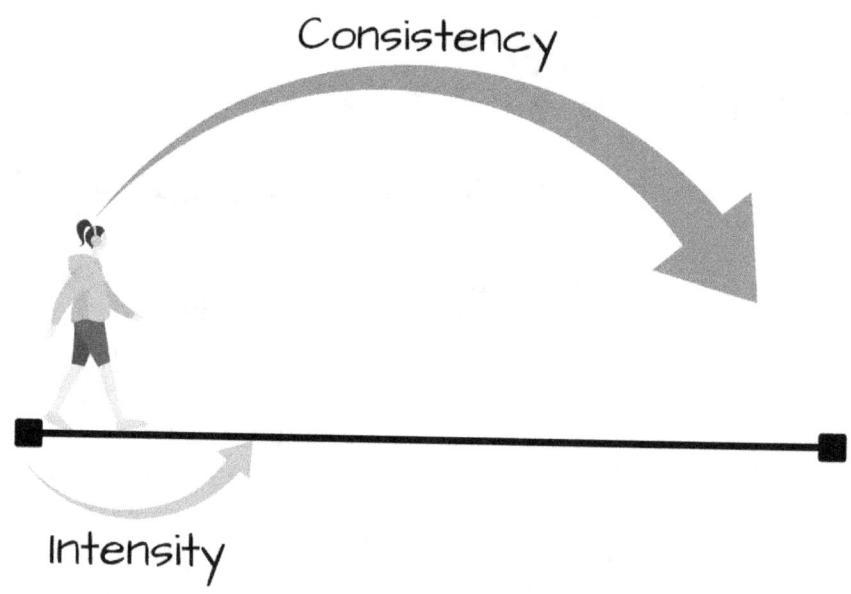

Type 2 cardio is where you will vary the effort much more than for **Type 1**, allowing yourself to get "out of breath" for short periods. For those new to this type of exercise, keep the duration to around 10 to 30 seconds at a time, as you raise the effort. More experienced exercisers including cyclists and runners might extend the duration of these "accelerations" or "surges" up to 1 to 3 minutes. Always use caution as stress rises quickly.

What are some examples of **Type 2** cardio? Playing sports such as soccer, tennis, or basketball, short sprinting (interspersed into Type 1 steady state efforts), riding your bike or hiking on hilly terrain or including some out-of-the-saddle "jumps," calisthenics, short "strides" during a steady state run or jog, using a stair master or other stair climbing machine, and of course, strength training.

For Type 2 cardio, refer to the Rating of Perceived Exertion chart for some specific guidance. The 8 to 9 scale is appropriate for this type of cardiovascular exercise (see Very Hard Activity). You may even begin at 6 to 7 (Vigorous Activity) and raise effort until you are 8 to 9.

You do want to continue to connect to your breath, while remembering that for very short exertions, your breathing will LAG BEHIND your efforts. Keep this in mind. For **Type 2** cardio, it may be helpful to focus more on RPE than your breath.

RPE SCALE — RATING OF PERCEIVED EXERTION

10	**Max Effort Activity** Feels almost impossible to keep going. Completely out of breath. Unable to talk. Can only maintain for a short period of time.
8 - 9	**Very Hard Activity** *(This is Type 2 Cardio)* Difficult to maintain intensity. Heavy breathing through nose and mouth. Can speak only a few words.
6 - 7	**Vigorous Activity** Borderline uncomfortable. Some gasping. Can speak only in very short sentences.
4 - 5	**Moderate Activity** Still able to breathe through the nose. Can hold short conversation. Comfortable but becoming challenging.
2 - 3	**Light Activity** Easy to breathe and carry on a conversation. Could go for many hours. Relaxed strolled, easy cycling.
1	**Very Light Activity** Hardly any exertion, but more than sleeping or watching TV.

AGE WELL AND FEEL GREAT!

KEY CONCEPT: Maximal Aerobic Capacity (Max VO2)

Dr. Peter Attia, M.D., a well-known longevity expert who I've referenced frequently throughout the book, states that "VO2max[13] is one of the strongest predictors of longevity. The hazard ratio for all-cause mortality when you compare the top 2.5% to the bottom 25% is just over 5x. That's more significant than comparing smokers to non-smokers (1.41), comparing people with diabetes to those without (1.4) and even those with end-stage renal disease to those without (2.78).[14]

Do you remember reading in Chapter 18, *Exercise: The Struggle is Real*, how our collective and individual strain to exercise consistently is actually normal? In that chapter, I also discussed the *Extreme Exercise Hypothesis*. One of the take home messages I shared with you was that *steady-state cardio* may not be the ideal choice for those of us who want to age well. I want to clarify that statement now by saying:

- **Your recent history and experience with exercise matters**. **Type 1** is ideal for someone who hasn't been very active or is just starting out. If that's you, **Type 1** is just what you need to create a consistent cardio exercise routine where your risk of injury is low. Keep in mind that you can also glean **Type 1** benefits from strength training! How? If you move quickly between strength exercises, you will get an aerobic "boost" and raise heart rate, achieving both a **strength session** and a **Type 1** cardio session simultaneously. Win!
- **Our first and most important goal is to move frequently and consistently**. Once we establish this habit, the next goal is to mix things up and keep things playful and varied.

The best path to being able to create a consistent routine of cardiovascular exercise is to start by building good movement skills and strength, first. Then add some cardio exercise focusing on **Type 1**, and then eventually adding short bits of intensity with **Type 2**.

Of course, you can always walk or spin easily on your bike. That's a given. This advice is more focused on the higher intensity efforts, where injury often occurs. Be smart. You're in this game for the long haul.

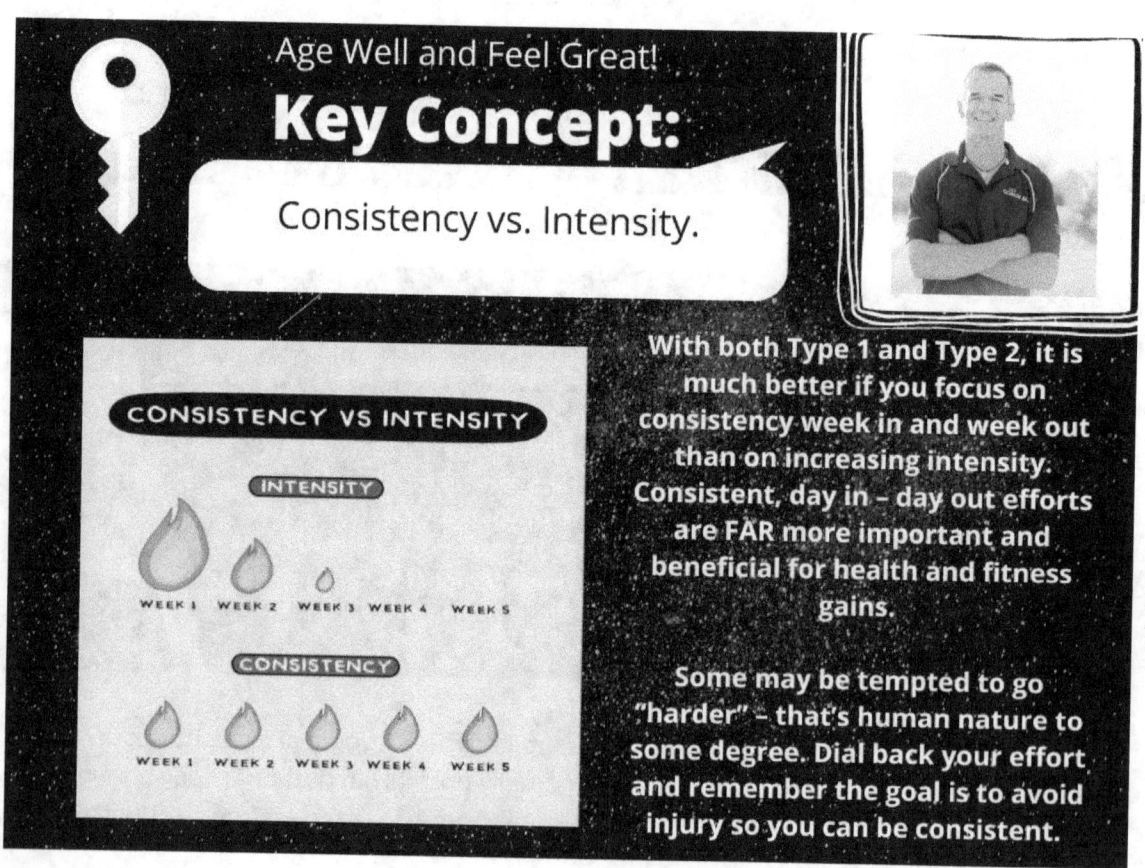

Age Well and Feel Great!

Key Concept:

Consistency vs. Intensity.

CONSISTENCY VS INTENSITY

INTENSITY

WEEK 1   WEEK 2   WEEK 3   WEEK 4   WEEK 5

CONSISTENCY

WEEK 1   WEEK 2   WEEK 3   WEEK 4   WEEK 5

With both Type 1 and Type 2, it is much better if you focus on consistency week in and week out than on increasing intensity. Consistent, day in – day out efforts are FAR more important and beneficial for health and fitness gains.

Some may be tempted to go "harder" – that's human nature to some degree. Dial back your effort and remember the goal is to avoid injury so you can be consistent.

Are You a Runner or Would You Like to Try Running?

If you're already running for cardio or hope to start a running program, when it comes to aging well and staying youthful, the better choice is to do less "distance" running and more playful kinds of running, including sprinting. That may not be what you wanted to read, but trust me, distance running carries with it an orthopedic cost that will always come back to bite you if you don't prepare for it. And steady-state distance running without mixing it up maximizes the potential negatives without tapping into the positives available to you. Sprint and play more!

If you're not sure what I mean by "orthopedic cost," think about this: Statistics have consistently shown more than 7 of 10 recreational runners get injured in a calendar year. More than 70%. That tells you all you need to know. And I speak from experience here. As you probably know, I've spent my life studying running injuries. I operated a gait analysis lab with a sports physician. I've coached runners and triathletes for more than 20 years AND...I've had every running injury you can think of myself. I speak from experience. ☺

The fact is, **distance running is really hard on your body.** One mile is essentially the approximate equivalent of ~1500 *one-leg squat jumps.* Every mile. I'm willing to bet you've never thought about it that way...but any way you slice it, that's a LOT OF chronic, repetitive load, which adds up and builds up with every step you take. Mile after mile.

For the most part when we distance run, the pattern rarely changes much. This repetitive stress is one primary reason most runners get injured. The chronic loads from all those foot strikes are much greater and have a more profound impact than most runners realize. The other primary reason? Most runners progress their mileage too quickly before their body and musculoskeletal system has had time to adapt.

This is one reason I am a big-time stickler for details when it comes to building a more stable, mobile, and strong chassis**. When it comes to how I expect the folks I work with to practice and progress the basic and fundamental exercises that I give them to help them, I can sometimes be the proverbial pain-in-the-ass. But the goal is to make them more durable.

Whatever your goals are, whether it's to simply run a few miles to get your heart rate up, or run your first 5k, or even a marathon...you won't get very far without injury unless you first build a body that can handle the repetitive, chronic loads.

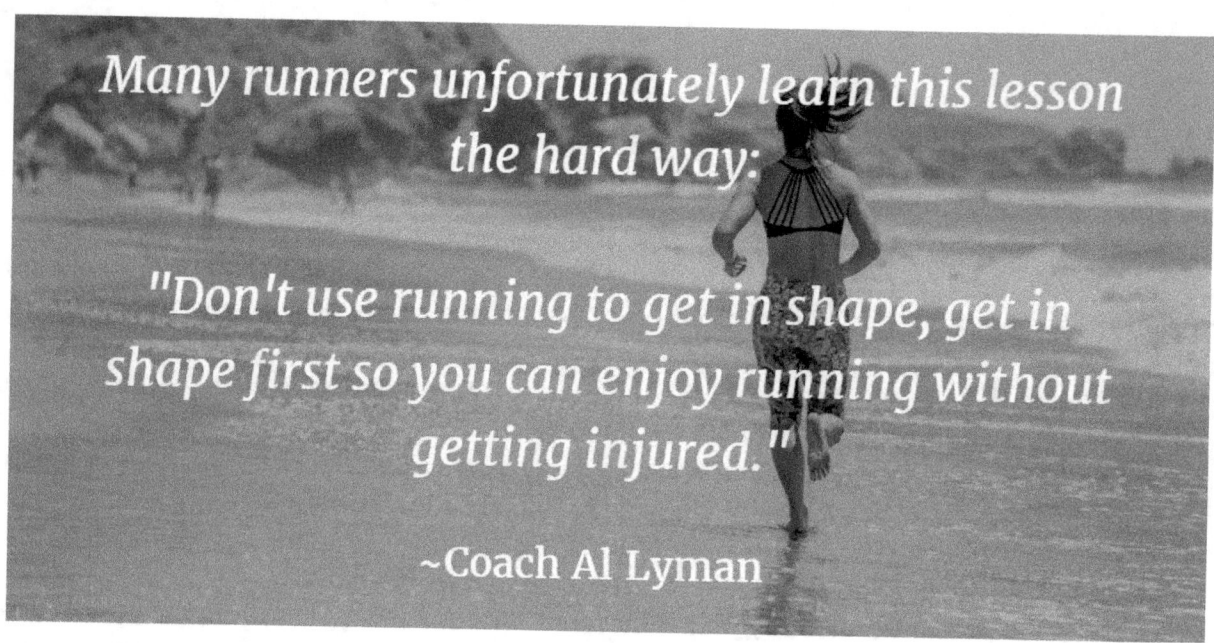

Many runners unfortunately learn this lesson the hard way:

"Don't use running to get in shape, get in shape first so you can enjoy running without getting injured."

~Coach Al Lyman

Type-2 Training for the Experienced Runner.

This morning, I ran a one-mile effort *as hard as I could*. It hurt in a good way. I always say, it never gets easier, you just get older. ☺ There are a number of things about training that aging runners don't like very much. In other words, there's stuff we are less inclined to do as we get older. It's human nature. Some examples? I bet not too many older runners reading this are routinely jumping, sprinting, bounding, or including regular changes in speed and variation in training. There are some things that come *so naturally to us when we're young* but we avoid like the plague as we get older. But...there's one thing many aging runners dislike more than all of these, and it might be the best anti-aging thing you can possibly do. Of course, it hurts a little bit, in a good way. What is it? It's **metabolic acidosis,**[15] which is a complex sounding term that for our purposes, simply means the increase of hydrogen ions in the blood resulting from very intense exertion. The increase in acidity means the effort is going to feel very uncomfortable.

Embrace the Suck: Running as hard as you can for 1-mile (or about 6 to 10 minutes) brings you up close with "your friend," the suck. So, why am I referring to it as "your friend?" If you want to stay and feel younger and get maximum bang-for-your-buck from run training, there's *nothing you could do* that would be as valuable as engaging in some of these short, but very intense efforts.

It doesn't have to be a 1-mile all-out effort, although that is among the best kinds of efforts you could do. Mixing it up by going harder for 30 seconds, then easing off for 30 seconds, and repeating that strategy for up to 10 or 15 minutes is also great. It doesn't need to be structured. You can go "harder" for a bit and then ease off. The point is to mix it up by varying speeds and intensity. You can also mix it up by varying terrain. For example, when it comes to variable stress and intensity, nothing works better than going up and down hills!

One additional way you can get the benefits of varying intensity and also enjoy mother nature more is to get out into the woods and on trails. Trail running and hiking provides multiple benefits that are magnificent for both aging well and building total body fitness and strength. As always, the key is making sure to choose a trail that matches your skill level or provides a slight challenge above your present skill level. That way you minimize the risks and maximize the benefits! Make sure you take whatever you bring with you and don't leave any trace behind. Let's care for mother earth.

The take home message is this: for any person regardless of their age, the bulk of any cardio exercise program should be steady-state, **Type 1.** Perhaps as much as 80 to 90% of all of the cardio you might do. **Type 1** gets you moving and provides a nice boost to your heart and lungs and vessels. This is where you should be most of the time. **Type 1 is certainly THE most beneficial cardio you can do.** It will keep you moving forward and feeling good.

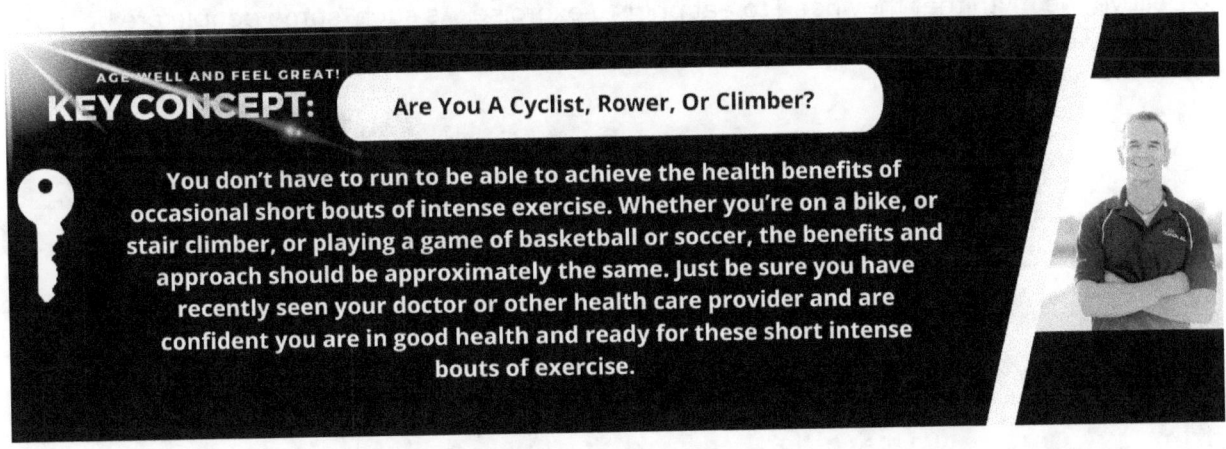

AGE WELL AND FEEL GREAT!

KEY CONCEPT: Are You A Cyclist, Rower, Or Climber?

You don't have to run to be able to achieve the health benefits of occasional short bouts of intense exercise. Whether you're on a bike, or stair climber, or playing a game of basketball or soccer, the benefits and approach should be approximately the same. Just be sure you have recently seen your doctor or other health care provider and are confident you are in good health and ready for these short intense bouts of exercise.

If you are experienced or as you gain experience, the other 10 to 20% of your cardio exercise should be comprised of more intense exertions that get your heart and breathing rate up! Just remember, as we age, there's a tendency to skip out on those short, intense efforts. Be willing to sometimes challenge yourself and show a little grit. **Do the hard things**. The benefits will be worth it. *The truth is, we have to work hard to retain the skills and abilities that don't come easiest for us and resist the natural tendency to go slower and longer as we get older.*

Eating Before and After/Around Your Exercise Sessions: Here's What You Need To Know.

When it comes to HOW you should approach eating around exercise, your goal is three-fold, starting with 1) maintaining an optimal hydration level. Always have a tall glass of water prior to any exercise session. You should pay close attention to your thirst and drink regularly throughout the session. You won't need anything other than plain water unless you are exercising in the heat. In extreme cases you may want to also consume a drink containing salt.

That being said...your other primary objectives beyond hydration are 2) to have normal insulin levels and 3) maintain a clean stomach. By "clean" stomach, I mean a relatively empty one that isn't upset, bloated, or otherwise unhappy.

To achieve these objectives, avoid eating 2 to 3 hours prior to the start of any exercise session. This will keep your stomach mostly empty and happy and also establish a normal insulin level at the start of the exercise. A "clean" or relatively empty stomach ensures your body won't have to send blood to your gut to facilitate digestion, when that blood and nutrients should be going to your working muscles.

If this sounds extreme or you're accustomed to eating before exercising, refer back to the chapter on insulin resistance and also **Time Restricted Eating**, where you learned that you have an ample supply of glycogen (stored sugar) in your muscles and liver, as well as nearly unlimited stores of fat in fat cells. Truth be told, many people have been foolishly told to believe the myth that they need to eat prior to exercise. As such, some people are hesitant to try. However, when they do, they always feel better and gain confidence as a result.

A common path to failure is ignoring the fundamentals while searching for a better way to do things. A common path to success is ignoring things while searching for a better way to do the fundamentals.

— James Clear

It Isn't About THE Exercise, It's About HOW the Exercise Is Done.

When it comes to exercising and practicing the skills you've learned in Part 3 and Part 4 of this book, especially in the Part 3 movement chapters where I discuss and show you how to become more stable, one of the things you've read once or twice is it *isn't about the exercise itself, it's how the exercise is done.*

What that simply means is form matters. Details matter. Doing it correctly at the most fundamental level, matters. Anyone who's ever learned new skills and wants to learn them the right way so they can progress as quickly as possible, understands why. Here's how I think of it...

The POWER of Exponentially Increasing Dynamic Load.

So, what does this really mean and *why should it matter to you?* Do you remember the story of Milo of Criton, who carried a calf each day as it grew, which allowed him to also grow in strength?[16] That is an example of exponentially increasing dynamic load.

Then there's the example of throwing a baseball...which reminds me of an imaginary story I'd like to share. Let's see if this helps explain what I am hoping to convey to help you get what you want from whatever exercise you decide to embark on.

Close your eyes and imagine you're standing in someone's driveway in any town in California. You've got a baseball in your hand, and you're going to attempt to throw it across the street with the goal of hitting the neighbor's driveway. To actually be able to do that successfully, you'd have to calculate the angle at which you'd cock your arm back and the angle at which you'd throw the ball into the air, right? (Your brain will probably do this all on its own - you wouldn't have to think much about it). If you did a good job of calculating that angle, you'd probably have a VERY good chance of hitting the neighbor's driveway without too much trouble, yes? Most kids do this all of the time when playing ball!

Ok, good. Let's keep going. Now, what if you were to attempt to throw that baseball, *not just* across the street, but to a different driveway that is two blocks away. All of a sudden, the exact angle you'd use as you attempted to throw the ball into the air becomes a *LOT more critical.* Because for every foot or yard that the baseball travels in the air, *the initial angle you throw it, will inevitably become more important.*

In fact, if you were only throwing the ball across the street, a slight miscalculation of the angle of only 1 or 2 degrees might not be that big a deal. But if you were attempting to have it land in a driveway two blocks away, a 1 or 2 degree error at your release point, might result in the ball landing 100 feet or more from where you wanted it to land, potentially hitting another unsuspecting neighbor in the head! Ouch!!!

A tiny infinitesimal error of a micromillimeter or so at the release point, would become *exponentially greater* as the distance of your throw increased. What seemed like such an inconsequential thing, turned into something which might totally change the landing point, and thus, have dramatic effects on the result.

What if you attempted to throw the baseball from that driveway in California, **not** to a neighbor's driveway or to a driveway two blocks away, *but* ...to a driveway of someone who lived in, say...the city of Chicago, which is more than 1000 miles away? I get that sounds far-fetched, but can you tell where I'm going here? Every single tiny little error in the trajectory of the ball becomes exponentially more important as the distance of the throw increases.

If you apply this analogy to movement practice, distance running, strength training or any other kind of exercise program, it's easy to see every single tiny little error in a basic fundamental movement (at the lowest dynamic loads), becomes exponentially more important and potentially harmful, at the highest dynamic loads.

- The difference between practicing and developing the *optimal neural pathways* to establish a stable trunk and core and hips on the floor at the most basic level, while you're well rested and consciously focusing on the task at hand, is the dynamic equivalent of *throwing that baseball across the street*.
- Running two or three miles is the equivalent of you attempting to hit Chicago with the baseball.
- Running a half marathon or more, is likely the equivalent of you attempting to hit a driveway in New York City with that baseball, all the way from that driveway in California!

If I could help more people see and understand this simple yet profound concept about how important our training is at the most basic level, it could change the world. *I swear it's that important.*

And in case you haven't already thought about this analogy and figured it out (I bet you have), this is also true at NASA, where scientists use calculations to determine where a spaceship will land in the ocean from space. And if you're a golfer, do you get frustrated when the tiniest error in club angle sends your ball into the pond or worse? ☺

There's no other way I know of to build the skills and strength that could ultimately lead to the sustainable performance potential you'd love to have! Or, perhaps it's not so much about racing results. Maybe it's simply aging gracefully without the need for a hip replacement at too young an age, or maintaining the ability to "play" until the day you go to sleep and don't wake up. Just pick the "goal" you want to achieve, and then...

- *Master the basics and fundamentals.*

- *Build quality skills with focus on form first, then fitness, not the other way around.*
- *Be accountable to them.*
- *Get faster and stronger and have more fun along the way!*
- *Then go out and enjoy playing!*

---

*...what differentiates those who are gritty vs. those who aren't is not just the hours of work they're putting in. They are putting the **hardest kinds of work in.** They're not working on things they already know, they isolate what they DON'T know, isolate their own weaknesses, and then they work just on that. And that seems to be characteristic of high achievement and what grit enables you to do. Basically, being in a very uncomfortable place for some part of your day, working extremely hard, and then to get up and do it all over again.....and again and again.*

-Angela Lee Duckworth, Ph.D., from her TedXBlue on grit

Common Questions and Answers:

Q: Should I focus on a certain heart rate or heart rate range for my cardio exercise?

A: The simplest and easiest tool for determining "how hard" you are working is your breathing. My advice is to focus on that, and not heart rate. The heart rate charts that are typically used to recommend a certain range based upon age aren't accurate for everyone. Why? Because your true "maximum" heart rate is genetic and unique to you. As an aside, some guidelines recommend you learn your maximum heart rate through some kind of field test. I don't recommend this as it is difficult and for some, risky, to raise effort high enough to get a true estimate of what your "max" is. It is much better to simply focus on your breathing. Keep it simple! For Type 1, focus on breathing through your nose and notice when you start to gasp for air. Back off a little bit. If you're running or cycling and come upon a hill that causes an increase in your breathing, that's OK. Listen to your body, keep working at it until you're over the hill, and then recover down the other side. We're focused more on the average breathing rate and intensity, rather than short increases because of terrain. Note that you'll need to adjust effort down when it is hot and humid.

Q: How should I warm up for my exercise sessions?

A: For both of these types of cardio sessions, you have a variety of options, depending on how you are feeling. Using some of the movement "snacks" you learned in the Part 3 Movement portion of the book, such as the 90-90 hip rotations or standing shoulder rotations or doing some single-leg balance and barefoot proprioception exercises, are ideal for any person. You might also do some simple light active warm up movements like hinging, squatting, toe and heel walking, or lunging. In either case, it is always a good idea when you start out at a very easy effort level and build gradually from there to the appropriate effort level. Always trust your intuition and vary your warm up depending on how you feel. For example, if you feel stiff or sore, starting out at a very easy effort level to loosen up and warm up your body is probably better than immediately bending and lunging.

Q: Earlier in the book, you mentioned exercising is a good form of hormetic stress. Which is better for this, Type 1 or Type 2?

A: Virtually any type of exercise or activity you would consider self-induced "stress," that raises your heart rate and forces you to work a bit harder than if you were at rest, is beneficial for fitness and health and can be thought of as hormetic stress. Naturally, the higher the effort, the more stressful the activity is, and in theory, the better for inducing hormesis. However, remember you can easily over extend yourself especially if you're a novice, and create more stress than is ideal for health purposes. By definition, hormetic stress is moderate, not extreme, and should be introduced consistently, day in and day out, in order to realize the benefits that are most associated with optimal health and healthy aging. [17]

Q: I've done some running in the past and would like to do so again. My problem is I've been injured a few times, which stopped my progress and was super frustrating. How can I avoid it happening again?

A: Speaking from experience personally and as a coach and therapist, I'll say running is a very hard activity for your body and carries with it an orthopedic risk. Most runners don't think of the fact that a single mile of running is the equivalent of approximately 1500 one-leg squat jumps! Think about that. Do the math – it can be an eye opener. What this means is there is a lot of repetitive stress on your body when you consider you're landing with 3 to 4 times your bodyweight with each footstrike due to gravity and ground reaction forces. Based on this, my advice is simple:

- **Make sure you focus on moving well, first.** That means being stable, having good overall flexibility, and of course, the stronger you are, the better, all things being equal. Good movement competency is important. If you aren't sure the best approach, get in touch with me via my Pursuit Athletic Performance website and I'll be happy to offer some additional suggestions. Consider a Virtual Gait Analysis to be sure all of the "boxes" are checked and you are moving well.
- **Start VERY conservatively and build running volume even more conservatively**. Most runners are excited at the start of their program and aren't injured, so they mistakenly believe they can increase their miles substantially as the weeks go on.

The problem with this is, your musculoskeletal system adapts to the loads your body has to deal with, much more slowly than does your cardiovascular system or breathing. If you keep pressing and increasing mileage, you will inevitably do more than your body is ready for. At that point, you "tweak" something and boom – your progress stops and frustration begins. Aim for no more than a 10% increase from one week to the next, and every three to four weeks, step BACK by 10% to allow extra time for your body to catch up and recover. If in doubt, do less, not more. Rest is when you actually are improving!

Q: I'm an older, "masters" age runner. Do you have any tips or advice to help me and other masters age runners to stay healthy and feel good as I age?

A: Here are THREE of the most important tips I can share with you as a masters runner. I hope it helps.

1. **Be flexible with the structure and your plan:** Masters runners, more than their younger counterparts, need to take each day as it comes and not force the issue if "it" isn't there. In other words, it takes longer to recover from longer or harder training. This means don't be a slave to the plan, whether you wrote it or a coach wrote it. Because sometimes the plan says to do "x" but your body just isn't ready for "x". Rather than force the issue, keep things easy that day and perhaps try again tomorrow. At our age, recovery just takes longer. Respect it. Don't force it. In the end, being able to actually DO the quality training in the way it was intended, even if it took a day or two more to get it in, is what matters.

2. **Running makes you stiff.** One thing that many older runners refuse to accept is that running is the activity that, while it keeps you younger in many respects, also makes you stiffer. Stiffer in every way. (and longer, slower running makes you even more stiff!) **To counteract that, commit more time and energy to flexibility and mobility.** Whether it's getting out of bed in the morning, or the lingering stiffness in the evening after you sit in a chair for a few minutes, running unfortunately contributes to that stiffness. So, what to do? The more you run and the higher quality your running is, the more time you'll need to spend counteracting that stiffness with some stretching, and also addressing mobility deficits. Even if you never stretched when you were younger, you'll need to as you get older.

3. **Quality vs. quantity (less is more):** To state it simply, as we age, it seems as though every force in nature is working against us and trying to break us down and forcing us to slow down, or even stop. Think of it as entropy, or the natural order of things. Look all around you. People age, and they slow down. You need to FIGHT these negative forces with every ounce of your energy, every day. The key is to focus

more time and energy on stability and strength training and keeping some element of quality running in your plan. It doesn't have to be a lot. And in fact, focusing on volume or quantity can end up being very counterproductive and putting you at a higher risk of injury.

Here's a few examples of what I mean....

- Instead of running every day, alternate run days with flexibility and strength days. Mixing things up keeps you younger. And healthier.
- Even as few as 6 or 8 "strides" in a run can get you out of a rut of chronically slower running.
- Hamstrings, calves, and quads can get and feel tight from faster paced running, OR too much sitting. Spend a little extra time on these areas.
- If you have a choice between going LONG and slower, or going SHORTER and faster, choose SHORTER and faster! Every time. You don't lose endurance as you age nearly as fast as you lose speed.

CHAPTER 27

CARDIOVASCULAR FITNESS:

CYCLING: THE LOWER IMPACT CARDIO CHOICE.

> The bicycle has done more for the emancipation of women than anything else in the world.
>
> — **Susan B. Anthony,** *women's rights activist*

> *The phrase "functional movement" is time and again misused and misunderstood - a single isolated exercise is not functional movement training. To know if your movement is "functional," you simply must put it to the test with its true purpose:* **overcoming obstacles and navigating terrain.**
>
> – Dan Edwardes, Creator of Parkour Generations

I remember as a kid I looked forward to weekends, when I could ride my bike over to my friend's house. We spent hours playing, working on our take-offs with our "home-made" ramps (made out of whatever scrap wood we could find) and chasing each other around the driveway, creating our own little backyard trails and laughing our butts off the entire time! Thinking back, I never got into BMX riding but I sure wish I had. Do you have any memories like that? Take a minute and think back. *Riding bikes was so much FUN when we were kids!*

Riding a bike might be the only activity that can boost your heart rate and give you that little adrenaline rush from speeding along and is accessible to virtually every person regardless of their fitness level. At a basic level it doesn't take a lot of skill, and you certainly don't need an expensive bike to go out and enjoy pedaling. It's also a great platform if you want to push the effort up and lift your fitness to a higher level. And as I said earlier, it's a helluva lot of fun! Think about it: spinning your legs and getting your heart rate up while having some fun sure beats sitting in a chair watching the world go by, you know? In this day and age, don't we ALL need more pure, unadulterated (and legal!) fun in our lives, as well as some childlike joy in our exercise routine? Of course, the answer is YES!

One thing I've learned since living here in Florida is a lot of people who reach retirement age start riding bikes again. The reasons are obvious: a bike is a great choice for low impact exercise, the terrain is generally flat, and there are lots of paved bike trails. It's easy to get out and start moving. For someone who hasn't exercised much before, riding a bike is a great choice to get exercise into your routine.

Still though, as I watch people in their 50s and 60s and beyond on a bike, I believe something could be missing if that is their only form of exercise. What is it? As great as riding is for low-impact cardio, on a bike you aren't loading your body against gravity and thus not challenging bone density. The reason? When you're on a bike, your bodyweight is supported entirely by the bike. It's somewhat akin to being an astronaut in space and not having gravity's effect of pressuring your skeleton. You may recall in Chapter 23, I discussed bone density, osteoporosis, and resistance exercise. Age-related bone loss has received lots of attention in the media. Everyone knows about the progressive decline associated with osteoporosis, the degenerative disease that makes bone fracture and breaks more likely, especially with an increasing risk of falls. Studies have demonstrated there are many factors, such as vitamin D and calcium intake, as well as hormonal changes related to bone loss.[1]

At the top of the list of how to combat contributing factors leading to osteoporosis and other similar maladies, is making sure we stay active and get some kind of weight bearing exercise to load our entire body against gravity. We also need to maintain strength and muscle mass to slow down the effects of sarcopenia.[2] When you walk, run, dance, or hike, with each step you're loading your entire body against both the forces of gravity as well as ground reaction forces. That's hormetic stress for your bones, which will help keep them strong.

The bottom line is, if we simply plant our butts on that saddle and spin our legs, it is possible that while we can get our heart rate up, we might also be fast-tracking our own deterioration and accelerating aging. Literally fast-tracking old-age.

If that sounds too strong, I hope you will consider some other ways riding a bike, as your only form of exercise, can come up short:

- **When you're sitting relatively still on your bike, you're not challenging your hips or trunk** very much at all. Your legs are doing virtually all the work.
- **There's no other activity as repetitive as cycling,** especially when you're clipped into your pedals. Every single pedal stroke is virtually the same, up to 200 times in a minute. Some muscle groups get worked, but most others get left behind. As a prime example, look at the professional riders in races like the Tour De France. They might be the single most imbalanced athletes you could find. Huge legs, huge lungs - everything else? Well, not so much.
- **On that bike, you're never loading your bones or joints against gravity**. As I said earlier, much like an astronaut living in the Space Station, without that gravitational load, you lose bone density. The more you ride, the older your bones become, figuratively speaking.
- **All the muscles you're not using are atrophying**. Especially if you're over the age of 40.

What I hope for those older folks I see out on their bike is they're combining riding with strength training, walking, and doing physical chores around the home. This combination is the ideal mix of low-impact cardio from cycling, and the other activities like strength training to help maintain muscle mass.

All that being said, if your only goal is to get a good cardio workout, provided you put in the effort - you can get one on a bike. And certainly, compared to doing nothing, riding a

bike is a HUGE win. But the truth is, it provides a very one-sided benefit. You'll be left with stronger legs and more cardio fitness, only IF you ride quite hard some percentage of the time.

If you're one of those folks who rides a lot and really enjoys cycling, right about now you might be feeling left out. I'll admit I haven't exactly painted the brightest picture when it comes to the general health benefits of cycling. Well, what if I told you there was something you could do that would offset the decline, help you slow the aging clock, and be lots of fun too? Would you be interested?

The answer is (drum roll please....) getting off road and on the trails on a **mountain bike**. Now if you already ride off road, there's no reason to read on. You're a *believer*. *You get it.* You've smiled, sweated, laughed, gasped for breath, been humbled, scared, euphoric, and even bloodied and bruised. And....you've never been happier while riding a bike.

But if you haven't ventured off road and are curious, read on! Because exploring forests and trails on a mountain bike is the *most challenging fun you will ever have on two wheels*.

There's nothing that makes you feel more like a kid than a flowy, wooded single-track, dotted with rocks, roots, and berms twisting and turning down a slope. And...conversely, there's nothing that will challenge your *strength, focus, balance, power production, movement quality, and mental toughness,* than will pushing those pedals across an ever changing landscape to get back up the trail.

Simply put, off road riding is a much better full-body workout. If you can improve your skills so you can ride increasingly technical trails, *your balance, hand-eye coordination, and full-body stability and strength* will instantly be challenged!

Every moment, you're adapting to changing terrain, weight shifting forward and backward, and you're likely UP and out of the saddle which engages and trains the hips and trunk much more effectively. In between and under trees, handling roots and rocks and off-camber terrain - it changes in the blink of an eye. There's zero chance of zoning out. I LOVE IT!

Off Road Riding Is Ideal If You Want to Slow the Aging Clock.

In the previous introductory chapter on cardio exercise, I referenced Chapter 18, *Exercise: The Struggle is Real*, reminding you of how our collective and individual strain to exercise consistently is actually normal. I also referenced how in Chapter 18, I discussed the *Extreme Exercise Hypothesis*. As you remember I'm sure, one of the take home messages I shared with you was that *steady-state cardio* probably *isn't the ideal choice* for those of us who want to age well. Well, guess what? Off road riding ISN'T steady state! That aspect can make it more challenging, but it is definitely one reason why it's a great option for those who want to benefit more from riding.

Getting OFF ROAD on your bike is absolutely the most challenging fun you will ever have on two wheels!

Here's a picture from one of my local trail systems!

Going off road forces you to react quickly, because the terrain and the obstacles in front of you are always changing. It challenges your eyesight and your reflexes. Of course, the faster you ride, the faster you must react. So, you always have the option to slow down and give yourself more time to react. It's all about pacing yourself so you keep it both fun AND challenging.

Off road riding also challenges your balance. You will find yourself moving more on the bike and getting up out of the saddle more often, which improves mobility, stability, and strength. It's nearly the perfect blend of movement training, strength training, and cardio, all in one. Of all the many things I do now, riding my mountain bike is without a doubt, the most rewarding, challenging, butt-kicking fun I have as an athlete!

Regardless of what kind of bike you are riding, consider this mini chapter as simply me *encouraging you to consider getting started if you haven't already.*

Just in case you're hoping for some *basic tips* to get you started on the right path, here are a few that will help keep you focused on staying healthy and increase the fun factor.

- **Get all the right equipment.** You don't need a lot of high-tech equipment to enjoy off road riding, but you do need high quality gear. That includes the bike, a good helmet, glasses, gloves and appropriate shorts, for starters. Remember the old saying you get what you pay for because it's usually true.
- **Don't let yourself be intimidated.** The secret is starting out on easy, non-technical terrain and progressing at your own pace. Seek out like-minded riders in a local bike club and ride with folks who are at your skill level or slightly better. Enjoy the learning.
- **Riding a mountain bike safely and enjoyably on more technical terrain requires good skills.** (Doesn't anything worth doing well?) Learning those skills gradually and building upon them will help you have more fun. Why not consider attending a camp/workshop or find a friend or fellow rider who can help you learn what you need to know.
- **Take the time to find the right group of fellow riders to learn with who are at, or perhaps slightly above, your skill and experience level.** Ride behind someone you trust who is more skilled than you are and learn by watching how they ride.
- **Find trail systems that are appropriate for your skill level.** Don't get caught on highly technical or hilly terrain if you're not quite ready for it. Nothing sucks the fun out of riding more than crashing a lot.
- **Be patient and persistent.** Don't take yourself or the riding too seriously and *keep smiling*. You'll improve consistently and have a ton of fun learning along the way!
- **Regardless of what kind of riding you do, make sure to get properly fit to your bike.** A good bike fit is probably more important for road riding. But regardless of which bike you end up with, make sure to get the sizing and adjustments right on the bike. If you'd like to learn more, the best bike fit expert in the world also happens to be a good friend of mine. And he can help you remotely, which is a huge bonus. To get in touch, on the internet go to: https://ttbikefit.com and speak with Todd. You won't be disapointed you did.

Now let's go out and play! Happy Trails!

PART 6

FINAL THOUGHTS AND RECOMMENDATIONS

CHAPTER 28

DENTAL HEALTH, ANTI-AGING SUPPLEMENTS: WORTH THE RISK OR THE COST?

THE DANGERS OF MODERN LIFE, THE FUTURE IN LONGEVITY SCIENCE: WHAT'S TO COME? AND MORE.

The fact is that almost all of us can live to be at least one hundred, regardless of our current age or health status.

But you must decide your fate now— while you are still relatively young!

—**Sergey Young,** founder of the $100M Longevity Vision Fund—one of the few funds specializing exclusively in longevity and helping to accelerate longevity breakthroughs

I was thinking about how people seem to read the bible a lot more as they get older, and then it dawned on me—they're cramming for their final exam.
- George Carlin

No one's life ever goes as they planned. That truth alone should bring a sense of relief to everyone.
- Andrena Sawyer

The older I get, the more I realize aging is a rite of passage. It's also a blessing. Everyone knows of someone who they wished could experience the indignities of getting older but didn't make it that far. Which reminds me, we've all heard the phrase, "you're only as old as you feel." Well, some days I feel I must be an exhumed mummy or something! That's right, some days are definitely harder than others, even for me. Trust me. I often think to myself, *it never gets easier, we just get older*. The goal is to keep on keeping on!

Earlier today I was trying to remember when I'd first heard "Anthem," the signature song from deceased singer, poet, and novelist, Leonard Cohen. If you haven't ever listened to it, you should.

"Ring the bells that still can ring, Forget your perfect offering, There is a crack a crack in everything, That's how the light gets in."[1]

We're all broken – *cracked* – in some way. Each of us needs all the help we can get to navigate this life journey successfully. And after all, no one gets out alive, right? ☺ As author Jason Elias says about aging, "it takes courage, compassion, and community to live it well."[2]

I'm sure it won't come as a surprise to you, writing this book over these past few months has been cathartic. And none of the more than 215,000 words I've shared in this book have lessened my own challenges to grab hold of those things I CAN control...and *let the rest go*. And man, oh man, is it ever hard sometimes to just *let it go*. We must though, because there IS so much we can do to make sure our story ends as well as it possibly can.

If we are going to be successful, we will have to fight the one thing I've seen derail the best laid plans, which is <u>complacency</u>. It's a well-known and accepted aspect of our humanity that we begin to become somewhat *numb* to the inputs or energy we're exposed to on a routine basis. It's even true with sunshine. I mean, does the sun shine every single day where you live? If so, a sunny day is *routine - no big deal*. Easy to take for granted.

What about our experiences? How about this - think of your favorite performer or singer. I'll wait. ☺ Ok, got it? Now, am I correct in assuming you'd be really excited if you had tickets to hear or see that person in concert? But... what if you got to hear that person every single week for a year straight. After those 52 performances, you would become somewhat numb to their performance. It'd be, dare I say it, routine. Nothing special.

You've gotten through most of this book – certainly the meat of it. You've been exposed to all manner of information, tips, suggestions, knowledge, and principles gleaned from thousands of hours of study and many years of experience. After a while, reading the same words, over and over, you become numb to it. **Complacent.**

As soon as any complacency sets in, you start to live on your past accomplishments or assume because you read something yesterday or last week, that it's now yours. You start to take for granted what you have in front of you, and what your responsibility is when it comes to taking action. Learning and understanding are one thing. <u>Doing is another.</u>

If you're interested, you'll do what's easy and come up with excuses if things don't work out. When you're committed, you'll do whatever it takes. You'll accept the discomfort of changing your beliefs and habits. So, are you just interested or are you committed?

— Coach Al

Over my more than 20 years of coaching, I've seen complacency set in with a few of the folks I've worked with. They were psyched to get started, they tasted a little success, and then started to take it for granted. As they took their eyes off the prize, struggles often reappeared. One thing I'm sorry to say, it doesn't get easier as you get older. *But that's what makes the finish line so special.*

So, the question you'll be facing as you peer straight into your mirror and stare yourself down: Are you willing to do what it takes to **fight complacency** with all your might? Are you willing to wake every day ready to take action and renew your commitment to yourself? Trust me, your health and your future success will depend on it.

"Anti-Aging" Supplements: Worth the Risk or the Cost?

Anyone remotely interested in increasing their lifespan or healthspan has no doubt wondered if there was a supplement they could take that would improve their odds. I'll be the first to admit that I certainly have. Over the years, when I'd hear about an "aging" supplement or see something referenced in a book or article, I couldn't wait to learn more. I never doubted there would be many companies working on developing a "wonder drug" that would give humans the youthfulness they crave. Our collective anxiety about growing old means there will be no shortage of snake oil salesmen ready to capitalize. If any of these companies were successful, it might change the aging game forever and earn them a fortune in profits. That being said, as I peer out onto the landscape of what's available to us now, I'll start with some books and of course, what we can learn with a few clicks of the keyboard.

Dr. David Sinclair's book, *Lifespan*, along with many similar books, initiated the discussion about new advances in supplementation, or so-called "anti-aging" drugs. The discussion is primarily about this group: NAD+ precursors, Resveratrol (the compound that comes from red wine), and two molecules, Rapamycin and Metformin. Those seem to be the big four. If you're not at all familiar with these, no worries. A little research online will certainly expose you to a plethora of marketing and even a little science if you dig really deep. ☺ Additionally, any of the books and podcasts I've referenced in THIS book will have some information about supplementation.

It isn't just the "anti-aging" supplements keeping these manufacturers busy. Think about this: According to the website Fortune Business Insights, in an update published in May 2021, "The global vitamins and supplements market in the U.S. is anticipated to grow from $129.60 billion in 2021 to $196.56 billion in 2028!"[3] One Hundred and Twenty Nine Billion! Another website projected the global market would top $307 billion by 2026.[4] All I can say is...wow. The obvious take home message here is, whenever the public is anxious to spend their hard earned dollars for a pill that will possibly give them the edge or the quick fix they're looking for, there will always be profit hungry entrepreneurs and businesses lining up to provide those products. It's that simple. Welcome to capitalism.

If you're wondering what I think about what's available to us at the time of this writing, I wouldn't recommend you start taking any of it. Perhaps this comes as a surprise, but to put it bluntly, I say "no thanks" to any supplements at this moment. Maybe two or three or five years from now, research and the resultant science will show there is something worth taking. This is only my opinion, of course. And I will say, this is the view I've pretty much always taken on most supplements. And here's why:

There are four primary reasons I say "no." Note I am not naming any of the companies making these supplements. If you have any interest in them, please take the time to do a deep dive on your own.

1. **Long term risks aren't well-known or established:** Most, if not all these supplements have NOT been studied in humans' long term. Meaning, you and I have no idea what the long-term effects are. Some have been studied in mice and other animals, but a mouse is not a human. Of course, there is something to learn from animal studies, and short-term human studies might show promise. But what we do not know, for example, is the effect of taking something like a NAD+ precursor such as NMN or NA, for three or five or more years. Does it affect the body's ability to produce this on its own? Are there potential changes to the body's chemistry that could cause a different set of problems? Simply put, are there risks that haven't yet been determined? Are you willing to roll the dice and just hope the effect will be positive?

2. **You can't know for sure that any perceived positive effect is *from* the supplement:** Let's say you take a supplement, and after a few days or weeks or months, you "think" it helps in some way, such as you are sleeping better or have more energy. Is that the placebo effect? After all, if you believe it WILL help you feel better, odds

are increased it will. Is it because of the supplement or is it something else? My point is <u>you can't know for sure.</u>

Assuming you're making positive changes in any number of areas including diet, exercise, or stress management, maybe the positive results are because of those? And if you become attached to those short-term results and suspect it's because of the supplement, have you locked yourself into taking it for an indefinite period of time? So, you're now caught between a rock and a hard place. Do you keep taking it, hoping it is the reason, or do you stop taking it because you're not sure if it's the reason? Do you simply believe the advertising from companies whose primary goal is to increase their profits? <u>There's no right answer.</u>

3. **You have no way of knowing which one is "best" or worth the expense:** How do you decide which one to take, the more expensive NAD+ precursor, NMN, or the less expensive NR? Or the B vitamin, niacin, which is even less expensive. They vary in cost as of this writing, but none are inexpensive if taken indefinitely. Before long, you could be spending hundreds per month for a minimum daily supply.

4. **Supplementing might draw your attention away from easily accessible behavior changes that cost less and actually work:** Putting energy and money into supplementation increases the risk you'll focus less on making positive changes in your lifestyle and habits. Simply put, it's easier to let yourself off the hook on something like daily exercise, if you know you're taking a pill that might give you similar benefits without having to do the work. Think about it.

<u>My advice is to stop looking for the quick fix</u>. Put the effort into deciding what's most important to you and then commit to doing the little things, even if you don't get the immediate results you want. There's no secret hack. No magic pixie dust. In the end, how fast you age and how healthy you are from now until the end will reflect the sum total of all your habits, lifestyle, and genetics. Supplements, regardless of what they are, won't have nearly the impact. Embrace the idea that what matters the most is what you do (or don't do) day in and day out.

Along the same line, as I briefly alluded to in the Introduction to this book, be skeptical and avoid taking advice from books or so-called "experts" whose advice is attached to something they are selling.

Longevity expert, Dr. Peter Attia, MD., who I've referenced a great deal in this book has often said (I'm paraphrasing) the best "supplement" for aging is available to anyone and it doesn't cost a thing. What is it? **Exercise**. ☺

It's really hard to know, in my view, how important sirtuins are as longevity factors...If we accept that, then it's difficult to know [the importance of] activation of sirtuins by NAD as a longevity mechanism.

—**Matt Kaeberlein, PhD.**, is a biogerontologist best known for his research on evolutionarily conserved mechanisms of aging.

Should You Avoid the Sun and Use Sunblock? What About Vitamin D?

I'll admit I was a little shocked when I learned from a blood test that I was low in vitamin D. After all, living in Florida where the sun shines so often, you'd think I'd have plenty. And that is the first tip you ought to take from this: even when you do get quite a bit of sun exposure, it's not a guarantee your vitamin D level is where it should be.

Before going any further, let's discuss a few basics. Your body, specifically your skin, produces vitamin D, but it needs the sun's UV rays to do so. The sun produces two types of UV rays – UVA and UVB. UVA rays penetrate deeply into your skin. These are the rays that are generally responsible for skin cancer. UVB rays don't penetrate nearly as far into your skin. Your body uses UVB rays to produce vitamins. You can also get vitamin D from the food you eat. Sources include eggs, cheese, beef liver, fatty fish and fish oil, and mushrooms, which are perhaps the best vegetable source of vitamin D.

If you took a moment to do some research online, you would quickly find lots of information on what vitamin D does for your body, and the various ways you can get it. Rather than repeat all that here, my goal is to make sure you're aware it's important for your bone health, immune system health, and overall well-being. So, what's my advice on the topic of the sun, sunblock, and vitamin D? Here are my thoughts:

- There is a lot of focus in the media on possible vitamin D deficiency, with some "experts" even pointing out more people might be deficient than was previously believed. Some of the heightened awareness came from COVID-19 research. So, is this true? Well, it might be. That's one of the reasons I'm including it. The only way to know for sure is to be tested. Find out for yourself, then have the conversation with your healthcare provider. Staying on top of regular blood work and other important diagnostic testing is essential for everyone's health.
- There has understandably been lots of emphasis on the dangers of excess sun exposure. Many of these concerns are real. And of course, "excess" means different things for different people. For example, having a darker complexion compared to a lighter complexion makes a difference. Many are spending more time indoors than ever before and as a result, might be missing out on adequate sun exposure, along with the other benefits of being active and outdoors.

After all, the sun's rays not only provide vitamin D, there is good research that points to sun exposure also helping with the intake and absorption of many important molecules, including dopamine, serotonin, melatonin, sirtuins, nitric oxide, and perhaps even more. It can also help with hormesis, mood and your overall outlook on life. <u>My advice is to get outside!</u> More to the point, **the sun *isn't evil nor the sole reason for skin cancer* as many think.** We need to respect the sun but not fear it! The smart approach is to use caution, especially if you have a lighter complexion and are susceptible to burning, which is absolutely something <u>you want to avoid.</u> That's not debatable: <u>sunburns are bad news</u>. Regardless of your skin type or recent exposure, if you're expecting to be outdoors for a long period of time, you should use a good quality sunscreen, applied liberally and often.

- Speaking of sunscreen, my recommendation if you do plan to use it, is to use something mineral based, not chemical based. One mistake people often make is putting on lots of sunscreen with all kinds of potentially harmful chemicals in it, when moderate sun exposure would have been much healthier. Chemical sunscreens were introduced in the 1970s, yet the incidence of melanoma has been rising. If these sunscreens worked, the incidence of melanoma should be decreasing. Remember, you need a little sun exposure to be healthy. The sun is a source of life and seeing it more often will surely make you smile more. ☺

- In a recent post on Instagram, Dr. Kara Fitzgerald, ND IFMCP, shared some fascinating new research posted on the website of the American Journal of Clinical Nutrition, titled *Vitamin D and Brain Health: an Observational and Mendelian Randomization Study*.[5] What was the result of the study? According to Dr. Fitzgerald, it's that "17% of dementia could be prevented by simply correcting vitamin D deficiency." That's quite a profound statement. About the study and research article, she went on to say, "Participants with a vitamin D status <25 nmol/L had a 54% higher risk of dementia compared to those within the range of 50-75.9 nmol/L. Limited benefits were found at levels beyond 50 nmol/L. The researchers also noted a threshold effect for vitamin D, where both lower and HIGHER concentrations were associated with lower total brain, white and gray matter volumes. We also know correcting vitamin D deficiency decreases bio age. So, we can conclude from these two studies, vitamin D alone increases both healthspan and lifespan!"[6]

- While I typically don't advocate taking many supplements, as you may have gathered, vitamin D is one supplement I do take daily. The National Institute of Health recommends a daily intake of 400-800 IUs. I take substantially more than this daily. Check with your healthcare provider to find out what is your best approach. Another supplement I take is *astaxanthin* (10-12mg daily), which is a little known carotenoid found in certain algae. Astaxanthin has been extensively studied in recent years, particularly its role in protecting against cancer and damage from UV rays.[7]

Carotenoids are naturally occurring pigment colors which promote health; you have probably heard of beta carotene which has an orange color. Astaxanthin is red and it lends its color to many marine creatures like lobsters, crab, shrimp and ocean salmon as well as secondarily, giving flamingos their trademark pink hue. Interestingly, I've heard through secondhand sources that some native Hawaiians have added microalgae into their diet to protect their eyes and skin from the UV rays that cause sunburn. At least one study does support that substances derived from marine algae can be protective.[8] If you're interested in learning more about the potential health benefits of *astaxanthin*, I recommend you research it on your own and then speak with your doctor or other healthcare provider if you have additional questions.

> *The story of aging is the story of our parts. Experts say they can gauge a person's age to within five years from the examination of a single tooth.*
> —Atul Gawande, M.D.

Dental Health.

It may seem a little strange to read about oral health in a book about aging well, especially from someone who hasn't traditionally enjoyed going to the dentist. (I mean, does anyone, really?) But it really shouldn't, as you'll soon learn. ☺ Let's just say, I've had my fair share of challenges when it comes to my teeth. I didn't get great dental care as a kid (am I the only one that remembers getting a lollipop after a visit to the dentist?), didn't learn very good flossing or brushing habits early on, and all that carried over into young adulthood. My dad had dentures very early in life too – I think he had all his teeth pulled before his 50th birthday. It happened so early, I can't really remember him ever having had teeth. I think he'd have looked very strange with teeth. Now that IS strange.

Dental visits have always been stressful for me, although they're less so now than they used to be. Truth be told, I've always been embarrassed about my teeth. The "bad" news? Receding gums and some borderline periodontal disease has been something I've had to deal with for as long as I can remember. The "good" news? I still have all my teeth! Which ironically isn't very common for someone my age.

In his book, *Being Mortal: Medicine and What Matters in the End,* author, doctor, and professor, Atul Gawande writes "by the age of sixty, people in an industrialized country like the United States have lost, on average, a third of their teeth. After eighty-five, almost 40% have no teeth at all."[9] If you're still wondering WHY this chapter is in the book, hear this: **The truth is there's a strong correlation between our oral or dental health and our risk for whole-body, systemic chronic diseases**. I wasn't always aware of this to the degree I am now. I wish I had been.

Have you ever stopped to think that cavities are a relatively modern phenomenon? According to most fossil records, our ancestors didn't have as many cavities as we do, although it is clear as soon as humans started eating more of certain types of refined carbohydrates like fructose and glucose (sugar), the incidence of cavities increased. A study done on the frequency of cavities in four different historical periods indicates "the direct, continuous impact of starch and sugar consumption on caries incidence is visible from the Chalcolithic Age to the present time, around the world and across civilizations."[10] And that's really the point. *Soda and other sugary, acidic drinks, along with all the processed foods containing refined sugars, are destroying lots of teeth and leading to a host of other related health issues.*

So let me ask, have you ever heard of "mountain dew mouth?" An article on NPR.org from 2013 titled *Mountain Dew Mouth Is Destroying Appalachia's Teeth,* highlights how this highly sugary and caffeinated drink has become ingrained in the culture of the region and "dentists have also found that the effects of soda on teeth are strikingly like the effects of methamphetamine or crack on teeth."[11]

In another article, Mohamed Bassiouny, a researcher and professor of dentistry at Temple University, says "even people who wouldn't consider themselves soda addicts are at risk of dental erosion if they exceed the recommended intake limit." And Bassiouny says that it's also the cumulative impact of the chemicals in certain beverages that matters. "Citric acid, a preservative that enhances flavor and shelf life in soda, is the main culprit. It erodes the enamel and eventually the dentin — the core of the tooth. Energy drinks and citrus juices also have a lot of citric acid. It all contributes to the damaging effect on dentition," says Bassiouny. And it means that even if you limit your soda intake to one can a day, you should "avoid other beverages that could contain citric acid."[12]

Simply put, everything I've learned from both personal experience and the latest science about dental/oral health, diet and nutrition, and healthy aging, clearly demonstrates how these are all closely linked. In the words of Dr. Patricia Corby, DDS, "It's all based on the insult of the bacteria, causing inflammation and systemic health problems."[13] In other words, **there IS a strong mouth – body (oral/systemic) health connection!**

It won't come as a huge shock to you to learn that prevention is the key. No matter your history, commit to taking steps now, especially if you haven't paid close attention to this. Rectify it. And yes, I know how expensive dental visits are. I'm living it, trust me. But every dollar spent on improving our oral health and reducing systemic inflammation is money well spent!

Poor oral health leads to poor or substandard amounts of inflammatory environment, and that's the driver of (these) diseases.

– Dr. Peter Attia, M.D.

Should We Be Concerned About Fluoride Safety?

If there's one dental-related thing you could ask about that is guaranteed to elicit different opinions based on who you ask, it's fluoride. Virtually any dentist will tell you fluoride is essential for hardening the enamel and fighting cavities, especially for children. It has certainly been the gold standard for that purpose for as long as I can remember. In recent years, questions have been raised about possible safety concerns, especially for folks my age who have been exposed to fluoride in many forms, for most of our lives.

According to Dr. Mark Burhenne, DDS, who hosts a popular podcast on functional dentistry, "fluoride gained support due to an observation one man made many years ago, which has progressed into many cities fluoridating their water and most dentists singing its praises. But over the years the research on fluoride has greatly evolved, to the point that we can now see large differences in how it works topically versus internally and identify risks that come with consumption."[14]

He goes on to point out there is "emerging research that supports connections between fluoride and IQ changes, neurotoxicity, arthritis, osteosarcomas, and changes in metabolism, how fluoride works in the body, and why using it topically is very different than consuming it, and why the root cause of cavities is not a deficiency in fluoride, but the sugary and starchy foods making up the Standard American Diet, an altered oral microbiome, and mouth breathing."[15] The take home for you is simply to consider all your options, have that honest talk with your dentist, and make the best choice for you. As always, make sure you know all the facts, first.

Some Suggestions and Tips:

These come from my experience and the expertise of other professionals in this field that I've done my best to learn from.

- See your dentist *at least* twice a year. More often if you have a history of issues.
- Get your teeth cleaned at least twice a year, and again, more often if you need it. I go every three months, or four times a year. It makes the cleaning itself relatively effortless and ensures I stay on top of any issues that might be lurking.
- Brush and floss every day. Honestly, I haven't missed a day of flossing in at least 30 years. I am crazy about doing it! Brush your tongue too.
- Avoid using a mouthwash, despite what the marketing tells you. The mouth isn't meant to be disinfected. The microbiome there contributes to good health!
- Almost every person over the age of 60 has some amount of periodontal disease. The key to treatment is frequent dentist visits and appropriate hygiene to monitor it. Don't wait, it won't get easier or less expensive.
- Those who are prediabetic or have type-2 diabetes definitely have a higher incidence of periodontal disease. Those folks need more frequent cleanings and would be smart to follow my lead by going every three to four months.
- Always brush lightly with a very soft bristle brush! It seems counterintuitive, but hard brushing can lead to gum damage. Don't make the mistake I did. ☺

What's My Regimen?

- I typically rinse and brush at least once, and sometimes twice a day with my Oral-B electric toothbrush. In the morning after coffee or around noontime after my first meal, and always in the evening before bedtime.
- I floss in the evening. I do this first, rinse with a water pik, and then brush. I will almost always floss at least one other time during the day, usually after a meal.

- Right now, I'm using a non-fluoride toothpaste whose primary ingredient is nano-hydroxyapatite, which comprises 97% of your tooth enamel. In case you're wondering, at least one well-done study from 2019 shows this type of toothpaste is equally effective at preventing cavities as a fluoride toothpaste and is completely non-toxic. [16] If you'd like to try it, choose a brand that has at least a 15% nano-hydroxyapatite concentration.

- I don't use a mouthwash like Listerine. Why? Any antibacterial mouthwash made to kill "bad" bacteria also kills the good kind, which isn't what you want. If bad breath is a problem, look to your gut microbiome or your diet as the potential cause. Be sure to floss well. Pay attention to any problem foods that might be disturbing sleep or increasing your stress. You can also try an "elimination" diet to find the culprit.

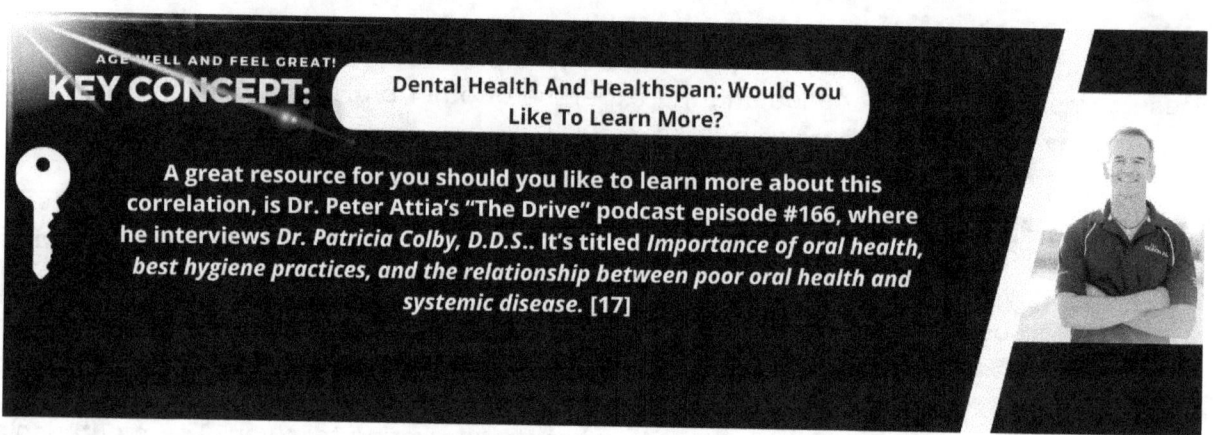

AGE WELL AND FEEL GREAT!
KEY CONCEPT: Dental Health And Healthspan: Would You Like To Learn More?

A great resource for you should you like to learn more about this correlation, is Dr. Peter Attia's "The Drive" podcast episode #166, where he interviews *Dr. Patricia Colby, D.D.S.*. It's titled *Importance of oral health, best hygiene practices, and the relationship between poor oral health and systemic disease.* [17]

We've been wrong about what our job is in medicine. We think our job is to ensure health and survival. But really it is larger than that. It is to enable well-being. And well-being is about the reasons one wishes to be alive. Those reasons matter not just at the end of life, or when debility comes, but all along the way.

Whenever serious sickness or injury strikes and your body or mind breaks down, the vital questions are the same: What is your understanding of the situation and its potential outcomes? What are your fears and what are your hopes? What are the trade-offs you are willing to make and not willing to make? And what is the best course of action that best serves this understanding?
— Atul Gawande, M.D.
...from his book, *Being Mortal: Medicine and What Matters in the End*

The Future in Longevity Science: What's to Come?

"Age reversal is real and it is here...at least, if you are a mouse."[18] Those are the words of author, founder of the Longevity Fund, and visionary, Sergey Young. Are you a believer? Because whether or not you're ready for it, seemingly outrageous developments in the longevity field are happening right now. They're not hyperbole or purely science fiction. In many ways, the future is now. So, what are the longevity-related innovations that are coming down the road? To answer this question, I once again turn to a group of researchers and visionaries who are in the trenches doing the work. They're all people I've referenced many times in this book.

In his book, *Lifespan*, author and researcher, David Sinclair says that right now, today, he "can read an entire human genome of 25,000 genes in a few days for less than a hundred dollars on a candy-bar sized DNA sequencer called a MiniION that I plug into (his) laptop. And that's for a fairly complete readout of a human genome, plus the DNA methyl marks that tell you your biological age."[19] In Sinclair's view, as he looks through the lens of his own research and that of his colleagues in the field, he sees the development of a vast array of drugs that could completely change the aging landscape. He discusses many of these in his book – I've made mention of a few in earlier chapters. He clearly views technology as also playing a large role in "reducing the noise in our epigenomes and keeping watch over the biochemical systems that keep us alive and healthy."[20] He says, while some technological breakthroughs might let us down, there's no way they all will. "Taken separately, any of these innovations in pharmaceuticals, precision medicine, emergency care, and public health would save lives, providing extra years that would otherwise have been lost. When we take them together, though, we are staring up the road at decades of longer, healthier life."[21]

Author and researcher, Nir Barzilai, MD., who is probably most well-known for his research on the drug, Metformin,[22] is the founding director of the Institute for Aging Research, the Nathan Shock Center of Excellence in the Basic Biology of Aging, and the Paul F. Glenn Center for the Biology of Human Aging Research at Albert Einstein College of Medicine. He also directs the Longevity Genes Project, a genetics study of over 600 families of centenarians and their children. Metformin, as you might know, is a medication widely used to treat type 2 diabetes. There is lots of excitement about its prospects as an aging drug. Along with his ongoing research on Metformin, one of Dr. Barzilai's beliefs is that new advances in *artificial intelligence* will allow for a huge amount of data to be processed. He refers to this data as *omics and* says "it's transforming our ability to solve aging riddles that would otherwise take years if not decades to figure out."[23] Just like Sinclair, Barzilai sees *personalized medicine*, which Sinclair referred to as *precision medicine*, to be at the forefront of new advances that will save lives. It makes sense the closer you can target a treatment, the greater the chance it will be effective.

In 2006, researcher Shinya Yamanaka[24] won the Nobel Prize for discovering that a particular set of four genes could reprogram adult cells into immature cells that could in turn develop into any type of cell. Barzilai says, Yamanaka "laid the groundwork for scientists to grow new blood cells, tissues, and organs that are already being transplanted into people."[25]

This kind of discovery is certain to expand and become a linchpin for more exciting discoveries that will surely impact aging and disease.

Aging visionary and entrepreneur, Sergey Young, sees a future where we might live to be 200, and more than that, he's working in the trenches toward that end. His book, *The Science and Technology of Growing Young*, is loaded with a huge variety of concepts and ideas about how the future of aging research and discovery might unfold. There's artificial intelligence, which I've already mentioned and which he feels will radically change every aspect of healthcare from drug development to diagnosis to disease management.

Then there's genetic engineering, which he feels may eventually end "all hereditary diseases and most forms of cancer within (your) lifetime,"[26] the most important of which may be CAR T-cell therapy, which he describes as a "cancer treatment method by which scientists change a patient's own immune-system T cells to fight the specific type of cancer they have."[27] And then there is "organ and tissue regeneration and replacement, so that getting a new heart, lung, kidney, or liver may someday soon be as easy as having eye surgery or getting a tooth replaced."[28] And we can't forget the pharmaceuticals that Young feels might "soon make living to 150 years old possible and practical."[29]

Despite all the money he's personally invested in his Longevity Vision Fund, and all the outrageous technologies he sees coming down the road soon, he doesn't appear to believe these new advances will change the idea that in the end, aging well is still primarily up to us. I happen to agree. ☺ He says, "diet, exercise, and lifestyle habits are probably more important than you ever understood or imagined." Likewise, "mind-set, sleeping habits, and social connections are all also remarkably important to living a long healthy life."[30]

In summary, there's consensus among all these experts that any kind of possible intervention in the near or distant future, be it a drug or some form of technology, **will very likely work best when the individual is also doing all they can to maximize their own health and well-being**. In other words, how we live each day – our lifestyle habits!

All truth passes through three stages. First, it is ridiculed. Second, it is violently opposed. Third, it is accepted as being self-evident.

— Arthur Schopenhauer

The Dangers of Modern Life.

Modern life has certainly brought its own set of perils. Among those are the constant sea of chemicals we're all exposed to on a daily basis. Certainly, our ability to live a long, healthy life free of disease will depend to some degree on how we navigate these often hidden dangers of modern life all around us. I'm talking about all manner of chemicals found in personal care products and household and consumer products, heavy metals, electro-magnetic fields (EMF) from smart phones and other electronic devices, and indoor air pollution such as mold and other contaminants that might be in the air around us. And this is just for starters.

I'm not an expert on this topic. There is much more I don't know than I do, that's for sure. The primary reason I'm including this in this chapter is simply to make sure you're aware. Like you perhaps, on a daily basis I'm attempting to strike the sometimes delicate balance between fear of the unknown, and learning more every day, so I can improve the health implications of the environment I spend most of my time in.

Perhaps you saw the 2019 film *Dark Waters*, starring actor Mark Ruffalo playing the role of attorney Robert Bilott. The movie dramatized the case Bilott brought against Dupont, the chemical manufacturing giant, after they contaminated a town with chemicals. The story was first told in the 2007 book *Stain-Resistant, Nonstick, Waterproof and Lethal: The Hidden Dangers of C8,* written by Callie Lyons, a Mid-Ohio Valley journalist who covered the controversy as it was unfolding. Seeing the Hollywood-made movie made me realize once again there are potential dangers lurking in the air, water, and soil around us, and in the products many of us use on a daily basis.

What to do? One reliable source of information is the **Environmental Working Group (EWG)**. You can learn more about this organization by going to **http://ewg.org**. On their website, they state their mission is "to empower you with breakthrough research to make informed choices and live a healthy life in a healthy environment." Among other things, they make in-depth consumer guides, work to create change on Capitol Hill, and help to lead and fund breakthrough research that hopefully creates the opportunity for better health. Who is EWG? According to their website, they are a "team of scientists, policy experts, lawyers, and communications and data experts that work tirelessly to reform our nation's broken chemical safety and agricultural laws. We push industries to adopt our standards and stand against chemicals of concern. We educate consumers with actionable information and inspire demand for safer products."[31]

The EWG has identified the following chemicals as the **"Dirty Dozen Endocrine Disrupters."** Endocrine disruptors are harmful substances sometimes found in our food, water, and many common products. These chemicals can disrupt our hormones, creating potentially significant health risks. Avoiding endocrine disruptors is possible by shopping smarter for products WITHOUT these chemicals.

1. BPA (found in some canned foods and plastics).
2. Dioxin (found in some processed foods, especially commercial animal products).
3. Atrazine (an herbicide sometimes found in tap water).
4. Phthalates (found in plastics, PVC, fragrances, personal care products).
5. Perchlorate (found in rocket fuel, also sometimes in tap water).
6. Fire retardants (found in clothing, carpet, upholstery, bedding).
7. Lead.
8. Arsenic.
9. Mercury.

10. Per-fluorinated chemicals (PFCs) (found in nonstick cookware, stain- and water-resistant coatings on clothing, furniture, and carpets). *PFCs were the subject of the movie *Dark Waters*.
11. Organophosphate pesticides (found in some non-organic foods).
12. Glycol ethers (found in some cleaning products).[32]

As I mentioned earlier, I'm not an expert by any means, but it does make sense to me that it's smart to do everything we can to rid our lives of these substances. The less we expose ourselves to them, the better our health will be.

Check EWG's website for more information on cosmetics, healthy cleaning products, and different foods along with a shopper's guide to pesticides in produce.

What else can we do?

- Avoid foods and products that contain high levels of mercury and other heavy metals like aluminum, nickel, and cadmium. That means avoiding cheaply made jewelry, cheap cookware, tobacco and e-cigarettes, and car exhaust!
- If you do eat shellfish and seafood, be aware of how they are raised and harvested.
- Reduce your exposure to your cell phone. Keep it away from your head when talking, using speakerphone whenever possible. You may want to consider carrying it in an EMF-blocking bag or case.
- Make it a habit to limit or even turn off electricity in your bedroom at night.
- Consider trading in your microwave oven for a steam convection oven instead.
- Decorate your home with more plants to help eliminate and absorb EMF radiation.
- Make sure you get outdoors and exercise. Work up a good sweat on a regular basis.
- If you have in-house air conditioning and heating with ducts in your attic, to reduce any exposure to poisonous mold, hire a professional to come in and clean and disinfect these ducts on an annual basis. I hired a company and had this done last year. It was a day-long process and fairly expensive, but in my mind, well worth it.
- Get rid of carpets where you can and opt for bare floors instead.
- Be aware of any symptoms you experience that can't easily be diagnosed just in case any are caused or increased by environmental pollution. Have the discussion with your doctor or other healthcare provider.

If you sign up for EWG's newsletter, you will be able to download their guide to avoiding PFAS chemicals. These chemicals are Per- and Polyfluoroalkyl substances. According to EWG, they can be found in "coatings on carpets and clothing, in microwave popcorn bags and on fast-food wrappers. Most waterproof or stain-repellent clothing is coated with them, and while many responsible clothing companies are seeking safer alternatives, PFC coatings remain common in the marketplace. The fabric may be labeled with brands such as TEFLON, SCOTCHGARD, STAINMASTER, POLARTEC OR GORE-TEX, but these are only a handful of the brands that still contain these chemicals."[33]

Odds and Ends - *What Have I Missed?*

I couldn't write a book like this without touching on some of the topics nearest and dearest to my heart, not only because of their impact on health but also because they're some of the things that add to life's richness and enjoyment. So where to begin? Java, of course! ☺

Coffee: I'd like to think of myself as a coffee connoisseur, but the truth is, I'm not. A true connoisseur could probably sip a few varieties and tell the difference between Columbian, Kona, or French Roast. I doubt I ever could. A true connoisseur also wouldn't be caught drinking anything but the finest roast. Me? I'm not that picky. But I *do love the taste* of the stuff. Always have. As long as it is black and as strong as an ox!

I love seeking out the "cool" coffee shops wherever I travel. There's almost always a relaxed vibe that creates a great atmosphere for reading or meeting old and new friends. I like some of our local places just because of the décor and how they make me feel, which is, well, "cool." ☺ I remember once traveling through California and visiting San Luis Obispo. If you've never been there, it's a cool little town on the coast with a variety of awesome coffee shops and coffee bars. I found one that was both a bike shop and a coffee bar combined! I thought that combo was the greatest thing and vowed someday, I'd own a bike shop and coffee bar together in one location, too. Maybe someday. Goals!

So, for years, I've combed all the literature I could find and read every scientific study I could get my hands on looking for some inkling – anything - that perhaps I should ease off my two to four cups a day habit. For as long as I can remember, I've always thought of coffee as my one true vice. In the 80s and 90s, coffee and caffeine were both thought by some to be unhealthy. It's a debate that's been ongoing for a long time. Thankfully, the scientific community has finally come to their senses and confirmed that not only is coffee not harmful to our health, it might even be beneficial. Which is music to my ears.

According to Dr. Kara Fitzgerald, ND, IFMCP, who I have referenced numerous times in this book, one of the reasons for the health benefits is "coffee is a methylation adaptogen thanks to two amazing polyphenols it contains: caffeic acid and chlorogenic acid." But that isn't the half of it. For example, one study published in 2012 in the *New England journal of Medicine* found, within a population of more than 400,000 men and women, regular coffee drinkers were 10% less likely to die during a thirteen year period.[33] A much more recent study published only last month (May 2022) in the *Annals of Internal Medicine*, showed moderate consumption (defined as 1.5 to 3.5 cups per day) of unsweetened or sugar-sweetened coffee is associated with a lower mortality risk.[34] The study involved following 171,616 participants (with a mean age of 55.6 years) for a period of 7 years. None of the participants had cardiovascular disease or cancer at baseline. They were asked several dietary and health behavior questions to determine their coffee drinking habits. The researchers found during the 7-year follow up period, participants who drank any amount of unsweetened coffee were 16-21% *less likely to die* than participants who did not drink coffee. They also found that participants who drank 1.5 to 3.5 daily cups of coffee sweetened with sugar were 29-31% *less likely to die* than participants who did not drink coffee. An article published in the magazine, *Sci-News*, shared the good news.[34] So, when it comes to coffee, the news does seem to be good news! Of course, like anything else, moderation is smart. And as I said earlier in the book, for me, anything after noon or so is decaf only. Sleep is just too important to risk drinking the real stuff any later.

Chocolate: My girlfriend Terry and I have a running joke that we often laugh about: As long as no one touches MY chocolate, no one will get hurt. ☺ She knows we can run out of any assortment of things in the pantry and it probably won't be a big deal, but she doesn't dare run out of chocolate. So, if you're starting to get the picture that I like chocolate, you'd be right. And I mean, after all, is there any person on the planet who doesn't???

Chocolate drinks were the first kind of chocolate to come into the world in the 16th century when Central Americans learned how to brew an apparently somewhat bitter drink from cacao beans. The original drinkers of this concoction were immediately hooked on the taste and the caffeine buzz, I'm sure, and from what I've been able to learn, used it especially in religious ceremonies. Later, in 1866, Henri Nestle made the first solid milk chocolate bar and soon after, John Cadbury introduced chocolate candies to the market. For as long as any of us has been eating it, chocolate has been thought of as a delicious treat that was notoriously bad for both our teeth and our waistlines, primarily due to its high sugar and fat content. Similarly, dark chocolate was always believed to be the much healthier alternative with less added sugar and fat, and higher cocoa content compared to milk chocolate.

While consuming it only occasionally seems like a smart idea – moderation after all – the health benefits of the cocoa, which is the prime ingredient, seem to be piling up. Many of the benefits come back to the high content of polyphenols, a class of antioxidant contained in cacao. One study showed very positive benefits for cardiovascular health markers from moderate consumption, with the authors saying, "regular consumption of chocolate bars containing plant sterols and cocoa flavanols may support cardiovascular health by lowering cholesterol and improving blood pressure."[35]

Regarding cognitive function, one study done by scientists at Harvard Medical School, "suggested that drinking two cups of hot chocolate a day could help keep the brain healthy and reduce memory decline in older people."[36] Another study showed consuming chocolate moderately could reduce heart disease risk by one-third.[37] There was even one study in 2012 showing that men and women who ate a small amount of chocolate regularly weighed five to seven pounds less than those who didn't eat any![38]

There's surely someone reading this right now thinking I'm cherry picking these studies. But regardless, no one can discount the amazing taste and how, even a small bite can boost your mood and bring a smile to your face like few other things. The only problem? The taste and the mood enhancing effects are short lived. ☺

The other potential problem? Quality matters. For example, the earlier study I referenced on the possible benefits of hot chocolate didn't consider the brand or the quality. There are some brands with lots of added sugar and other added chemicals – you should avoid those most of the time. Similarly, there are brands where ingredients and manufacturing practices make them better choices. How do you know the difference? Read the labels and do some research. Again, it's not about being "perfect." It's about habits. <u>What you eat or drink most of the time</u>.

Age Well and Feel Great!
Key Concept:
What About Caffeine?

As I'm sure you know, both coffee and chocolate, as well as some other foods, contain caffeine. If you elect to drink coffee or tea or consume any other food containing caffeine, you certainly know it can be addictive. So, be aware. Proceed with caution.

In the chapter on sleep, I fully intended to discuss a naturally occurring chemical in our body largely responsible for the sleepiness we feel as the day goes on. Alas, I never did. Now's my chance. That chemical? It's called adenosine. Your desire and "drive" for sleep as the day goes into night, comes primarily because this neurotransmitter, adenosine, is building up in your bloodstream. Then, while you sleep, your body gradually breaks down the adenosine, which is one reason why you (in theory) wake up in the morning feeling much more rested. Well, as fate would have it, caffeine is directly connected to adenosine. How?

Caffeine and adenosine have very similar chemical structures. When you consume caffeine or a food containing it, the caffeine molecules attach themselves to adenosine receptors in the brain and block them, making you feel less tired, more alert, and if you're lucky, even euphoric. Blocking adenosine receptors with caffeine can do more than reduce tiredness. It also dilates and constricts blood vessels. Different people have different reactions to this impact on the cardiovascular system. On the flip side, caffeine will usually increase blood pressure in people who do not ingest it regularly. In case you're wondering, caffeine can also increase breathing rate, the need to urinate, and the need to defecate.[39]

Alcohol: It's difficult if not impossible to put all alcoholic drinks into one category. That is, on the surface, most people would assume that drinking wine in moderation is healthier than beer or liquor. It is true that red wine certainly shines as being healthier overall, than either of the other two. The question becomes, to what degree? And does it really matter?

Entire books, articles, and scientific studies have been done on drinking alcohol. I'm not going to try and recapture it all here, that would be impossible. What I would like to start with though, is a drink late in the day or the evening can ruin a good night's sleep like few other things. Yes, alcohol is a depressant, but it's a myth that it helps you sleep better. While we are all an experiment of one, meaning it impacts certain people differently, these quotes from sleep expert, Dr. Matthew Walker, taken directly from his podcast interview with Dr. Peter Attia, shed some light on this important topic:

- "Alcohol is a sedative—you actually 'lose consciousness' faster when you put yourself in bed, but you're not going into naturalistic sleep."
- "Your sleep becomes more fragmented because the alcohol will actually stimulate the fight or flight branch of the nervous system which are wake promoting chemicals making you wake up more frequently throughout the night."
- "Alcohol will decrease the amount of REM sleep that you get." In Dr. Attia's opinion, having a drink to help relax after a stressful day, can become a "self-fulfilling prophecy." He says, "if you're downscaling the amount of REM sleep that you get at night with alcohol, you may not be getting the necessary emotional benefit that you need to de-risk the emotional experiences and the anxiety that's building up. Then the next night you find yourself reaching for another glass of wine because of the increased stress from not enough REM sleep which then takes away the REM sleep once again."[40] Clearly that's a no win situation for anyone.

So, how is alcohol made and what is its primary ingredient? Ethanol is used in the drinks most people enjoy. To make alcohol, you need to put grains, fruits or vegetables through a process called fermentation, which is when yeast or bacteria react with the sugars in food. The by-products are ethanol and carbon dioxide.[41]

The important thing to remember is ethanol is a toxin. The amount we consume can turn it from a toxin into something much worse, a poison. The exact same thing can be said of sugar. Also, the calories in alcoholic drinks are largely "empty" calories. They don't contain any of the nutrients that would enhance our health, with the exception of a small amount of polyphenols in red wine and beer.

You're probably thinking something like, *yeah, I know all that. Who cares? Having a drink is something I enjoy, especially when I'm hanging out with friends.* Which leads to perhaps the most important question to ask ourselves: why are we drinking it? Are we using it moderately in a way that enhances our enjoyment of life? Or is it something else? For many people, a drink can lessen their inhibitions and that can feel good. Certainly, having a drink in a social setting is something many people enjoy. Like many other things, using alcohol responsibly can and should enhance our physical and emotional health, when used responsibly and in moderation.

The bottom line from my perspective is overindulging, whether it's chocolate, coffee, or alcohol, isn't healthy and won't help you **go the distance**. But enjoyed in moderation, to compliment a balanced, healthy lifestyle, seems like a good strategy to me. This again reinforces the prevailing theme throughout this book. It's not about "perfect," it's about the overriding habits, day in and day out. It's about being *mostly* healthy, *most* of the time. And enjoying life too!

The best activities for your health are pumping and humping.
— Arnold Schwarzenegger

Sex: Speaking of enjoying life. ☺ So, a few weeks ago I was having breakfast with a good friend named Joan at one of my favorite local restaurants, The "Original Word of Mouth." WOM is a great breakfast/lunch restaurant in Venice, Florida, if you're ever in the area, you won't be disappointed. After ordering, Joan asked me how the book was coming along, so I proceeded to give her a detailed update, letting her know that for all intents and purposes, the rough draft was done. Out of the blue, she asks me, "so what about sex?" I was like, "huh?" To say I was a little taken aback by her question is an understatement. It just wasn't what I expected her to ask about.

My immediate response? "Well, to this point I haven't written anything about it. I thought about it, but just haven't, yet."

She pipes right up with, "what do you mean? You have to, Al. I mean, how on earth can you write a book about aging well and not write about sex?" Since Joan is an older lady who I think of as more like a mom, I was trying to carefully script a respectful response. I have to admit though, inside I was hooting and hollering like a nudist in a cactus patch at midnight. That is, I was actually very excited she brought it up. (no, not excited in THAT way!) ☺ Immediately I realized this book wouldn't be complete without me sharing my take on remaining sexually active into our later years!

Dr. Ruth Westheimer is perhaps the most well-known sex therapist who, besides being a holocaust survivor and college professor, has written more than 40 books on sex and sexuality. [42] As of this writing, she's still kicking at age 94, maintaining an active Twitter account and YouTube channel, all of it promoting the physical and emotional health benefits of an active sex life. Certainly, the research agrees with Dr. Ruth. There are enough research studies showing that sex can and should remain a driving force in the lives of those of us who are north of 60 years old. Simply put, you are NEVER too old to enjoy a healthy, happy sex life!

To dig in a little deeper and find out what's really happening, let's skip over the stigma of sex and aging and get right to the facts, discussing briefly, some of the known health benefits of sex in all its various forms, OK? So, what are the overall health benefits?

- It's not only an act of intimacy, it's also a form of exercise and stress reducer! ☺ Which means you get the cardio and strength training benefits.[43]

In actuality, sex and strenuous exercise (such as strength training and type 2 cardio exercise) have lots in common, which is one of the reasons it's just plain good for you. The stress response involves a reduction in T cell count and beta endorphin levels. T cells are white blood cells, or lymphocytes, that fight off invading germs and pathogens. Endorphins are brain chemicals that help us tune out pain and tune in a feeling of euphoria. Both are produced during sex (and strenuous exercise).

- It improves your sleep quality.
- It improves the body's defenses, strengthening the immune system.

- It increases the secretion of hormones that can aid in improving your health, such as testosterone and oxytocin. In case you don't know what oxytocin is, is defined as a peptide hormone and neuropeptide normally produced in the hypothalamus and released by the posterior pituitary. It plays a pivotal role in social bonding, reproduction, and childbirth. It's released into the bloodstream in response to sexual activity.[44][45]

What are some emotional health benefits?

- It improves your mood.
- It improves self-confidence.
- It improves intimacy and trust between couples and results in greater satisfaction from the relationship.

What are some genital system benefits?

- It reduces the risk of prostate cancer and improves recovery from prostate-oriented diseases.[46]
- It strengthens the pelvic floor and along with that, reduces the risk of incontinence, improving bladder control and enhancing vaginal function.
- It promotes blood flow, oxygenation, and function of the penis and vagina.

What are some cardiovascular health benefits?

- It reduces blood pressure.
- As mentioned, it relieves stress.
- As mentioned, it's a good (albeit brief) form of cardiovascular exercise.

If frequent sex is so good for us and also enjoyable, why don't more of those over 60 enjoy it more often? While there aren't a lot of studies that point this out, there is one research article saying only 3 out of 10 of the "happiest" couples have sex at least once per week. [47] That's not a lot when you consider it's a reflection of those who are "happiest" in their relationships. What about those who aren't so happy? ☹

Equally as interesting (and unnerving) is the research that says 6% of those 3 out of 10 mentioned earlier make love more than once per week, and half of those people in relationships for 21 years or more feel that their partner has sex with them out of a sense of obligation. [48] Doesn't sound very encouraging, does it? So, what gives?

Perhaps it's overstating the obvious to mention when it comes to impotence or erectile dysfunction (ED), the statistics are staggering. For example, as of 2022, erectile dysfunction will happen to 33% of men by age 50, to 42% of men by age 60. Eighteen million American males suffer from ED and 44% of all men suffering from ED experience this problem due to a chronic health issue. And finally, worldwide incidence of ED is predicted to increase from 152 million men in 1995 to 322 million men by the year 2025.[49]

These statistics are, as I said, staggering. Of note is the 44% suffering from ED due to some other health issue, which points to the fact it's much harder to be fully present and engaged in the bedroom when you aren't healthy or feeling very good.

What are a few of the other factors for why many of us aren't enjoying sex as much as we should be?

- A high-sugar diet of processed foods is inflammatory and may restrict blood flow throughout the body, including sex organs.
- Hormone disruptors in our environment, including some known as *xenoestrogens*, can throw our entire body out of whack and destroy our libido in the process. Xenoestrogens are chemical imposters that mimic estrogen in the body. They can come in the form of plastics, pesticides, solvents, car exhaust, industrial chemicals and food additives.
- Arthritic changes and other age-related changes to our hands, blood vessels, and nerves may play a role in arousal and sensitivity to touch.
- The impact of prescription medications that can destroy libido, increase vaginal dryness, and reduce vaginal elasticity.

Age Well and Feel Great!

Key Concept:

The Pelvic Floor

PELVIC FLOOR TRAINING

The pelvic floor muscles play a key role in ejaculation. The bulbocavernosus muscle (BC) is the motor of ejaculation. It supplies the "horsepower."

The BC surrounds the inner, deepest portion of the urinary channel. It's a compressor muscle that during sex engorges the spongy erection chamber that surrounds the urethra and engorges the head of penis. At the time of climax, this BC muscle expels semen by virtue of its strong rhythmic contractions, allowing ejaculation to occur and contributing to orgasm. (Note ejaculation happens in the penis but an orgasm happens in the brain).

A weakened BC muscle may result in semen dribbling with diminished force or trajectory, whereas a strong BC can generate powerful contractions that can forcibly ejaculate semen at the time of climax.[50]

Fortunately for you, I created a 5 ½ minute instructional video to teach you how to strengthen your pelvic floor. It's available to view on the Pursuit Athletic Performance YouTube page here: https://youtu.be/IyUTt0b7DQQ

How to Stay Sexy at Any Age.

To enjoy love making and **going the distance** in the bedroom or whatever location you find yourself in depends on a wide variety of physical and emotional factors, just like virtually every other topic I've discussed. It rarely comes down to a single element. Ironically, much of the time the most important element isn't physical, it's what happens between the ears and what is said between two people. I often say we make love with our voices and our words!

I can't imagine a relationship can thrive in or out of bed without a strong mutual sense of trust and open communication. Trust takes time to nurture, and it can quickly be torn down when there's a violation of that trust or a loss of transparency. Trust creates an opportunity to show one's vulnerability and still feel safe. The feeling of safety is important for a long lasting loving relationship. Trust takes effort to build and it usually remains fragile.

Regularly expressing affection and devotion are vital, not just on a birthday or special occasion but more often. You might think you have your own special and unique way of saying or showing another person, "I love you," but are you absolutely sure your way aligns with your partners?

Great communication starts with meeting people where they are, not where we want them to be, and that includes expressing feelings in a way that makes the other person feel safe and valued and appreciated for who they are. I'm proud of the fact I'm known among Terry's friends as the guy who brings flowers often, and that I always try to be there to provide support and show affection, not only for her, but also for anyone in her life that she cares about.

The little things are what is most important when it comes to fostering a strong bond that creates the opportunity for a long-term love affair. What do I mean by "little things?" Do the laundry every so often. Run the vacuum cleaner! Always be there for support. For example, when Terry is performing in the local community theater, I not only attend a performance, I go to many performances. I bring flowers more than once. I make an effort to meet and support the other cast members, too.

At the same time, when I'm performing with the local symphony orchestra or have a gig, she comes to be a part of the experience in every way she can. My colleagues know her and appreciate how she is there, not just for me but also to support them. To foster a thriving relationship requires striking a balance between allowing the other person to express themselves individually, yet also feel like they're an integral part of a loving pair. It's sometimes a delicate balance, but very much worth finding and keeping. Also, I'll admit I'm a cornball. I often sit with her and watch the Hallmark channel and even sometimes cry at the end. There are some movies I've seen repeatedly and I always cry. I'm just corny like that. Yeah, I admit it. It's OK gentlemen. A little corniness can go a long way! ☺

At the same time, regardless of your age, it's hard to feel very attractive and sexy if you don't feel good about yourself or feel anxious or depressed. Feelings of boredom, fear, fatigue, and grief also add to the list of items that will destroy any interest in sex. Those kinds of feelings often arise during the middle and later years, *especially* if there are health issues to deal with.

I know that being physically fit contributes mightily to feeling desirable and attractive. And it doesn't hurt when it comes to achieving a quick erection. Why? Consider that the active ingredient in Viagra is nitric oxide, which besides being a colorless gas and a free radical, is a vasodilator. A vasodilator helps expand and widen blood vessels. Circulatory insufficiency is the most common cause of impotence in men. Studies have shown that one of the best natural vasodilators is, you guessed it, exercise![51] Clearly, keeping artery walls free of plaque is not only good for your heart, it's good for the bedroom. If there's one big reason to keep exercise as part of your daily routine that goes beyond the obvious benefits, the fact that it helps maintain healthy blood vessels is at the top of my list.

Speaking of erections, does diet play a role? In 2016, researchers from Harvard published results of a large, population-based study in which they monitored over 50,000 men over the course of 30 years. The men were periodically asked about their ability to achieve and maintain an erection, tracking back to 1986. The study found those who regularly ate foods rich in certain polyphenols (e.g., anthocyanins, flavanones, and flavones) had improved sexual function and were far less likely to suffer from any kind of erectile dysfunction. Foods that contain these particular polyphenols and were prevalent in the diets of strong-erection men include blueberries, cherries, blackberries, and radishes. Encouragingly, according to lead researcher Aedin Cassidy, you can achieve positive benefits with "just a few portions a week."[52]

There are as many ways to make love and express your love for someone else as there are stars in the sky. Or close to it. But when considering the more well-known ways, we should acknowledge that any of those are difficult if not impossible if you have severe back pain or can't otherwise move around very much. Having a physical limitation or dysfunction doesn't mean making love is impossible, but it could certainly be a lot more difficult. Why? It's obvious: depending on the severity of course, being in pain robs us of our ability to be fully present with love making and expressing ourselves in many of the ways we would like to.

Hormones such as estrogen, testosterone, progesterone, and human growth hormone, also play a critical role in our health and sexual performance. There's much more to know. If in doubt or you want to learn more, speak with your doctor or healthcare provider and do some research.

In summary, when we're healthy and feeling good, the sky's the limit for our sex life up until our very last day. While there are certainly more hurdles to overcome that are a natural byproduct of getting older, there's not really a single significant reason in the world that it shouldn't be enjoyable and fulfilling right up until the end. In the end, it comes down to the words of George Bernard Shaw, who said "*we don't stop playing because we get old, we get old because we stop playing.*" Cheers to that!

Our Immune System:

Over the last few years during the height of the COVID-19 pandemic, our immune system took center stage due to a lot of confusion about immunity. There was a great deal of fear of older people becoming infected and dying. The truth is, anyone with compromised immune system vitality or who was fighting a chronic disease, <u>regardless of their age</u>, were at higher risk of infection and tended to suffer more from infection.

Our immune system is what protects us from the onslaught of fungus, viruses, bacteria, mold, parasites, heavy metals, and chemicals. **If you are metabolically unhealthy, you will have a compromised immune system.** All the advice and recommendations in this book, from the quality of your sleep and diet, to the amount of exercise and hormetic stress you expose yourself to, is designed to <u>build immune system resilience</u>. I could go on and on, but the bottom line is, how well your immune system functions is a direct result of how you take care of yourself.

Every day, each one of us is exposed to millions of pathogens. Scientists say trillions of viruses live inside of each of us and we're exposed to almost as many every moment, something you learned about in the chapter on the gut microbiome. Down the road, there will be more viruses that come along and threaten the health of the most vulnerable.

A healthy immune system is one that is balanced and doesn't overreact or underreact to pathogens. What we saw with COVID-19 was the occurrence of something called a cytokine storm – which is an overreaction of the immune response and an uncontrolled release of inflammatory particles.[53] This overreaction can result in severe damage to the lungs. So, why would this overreaction occur? In my estimation, it's because the immune system wasn't functioning well, perhaps not being well-calibrated. How does that happen? As I said earlier, it's all of the aspects that have been discussed in this book: high quality sleep, "bad" stress reduction, Time Restricted Eating resulting in positive hormetic stress, unhealthy gut microbiome from too-high sugar and processed food intake, and too little exercise. In a nutshell, when the body is exposed to the right kinds of stressors repeatedly and isn't exposed to a poor diet devoid of nutrients like vitamin D, it becomes more resilient in every way, and that includes the immune system.

Proactively doing all you can to support your immune system by making positive lifestyle changes including eating healthfully most of the time, clears a path for your body to be able to stay resilient so you can age well and die healthy. **There's no secret hack, no quick fix, no prescription drug, that can take the place of consistent, high quality self-care**! Believe it!

EPILOGUE

Start before you're ready.
Don't prepare. Begin.

Remember our enemy is not the lack of
preparation; it's not the difficulty of the
project or the state of the marketplace
or the emptiness of our bank account.

The enemy is resistance.

The enemy is our chattering brain, which,
if we give it so much as a nanosecond,
will start producing excuses, alibis,
transparent self-justifications, and a
million reasons why we can't/shouldn't/
won't do what we know we need to do.

Start before you're ready.

•

— Steven Pressfield, from his book, Do The Work.

Reflect on your present blessings on which every man has many,
but not on your past misfortunes, on which all men have some.
— Charles Dickens

There comes a time when each of us realizes we're not going to live forever - that life truly is short. Some of us come to this realization because of an event - perhaps losing someone close. Or watching someone we care about fight a serious, devastating disease like cancer. And much like the inevitable process of getting older, the dying part that always happens at the end of it isn't something we like to talk about. But it's always there, invisible, ever present.

Some people will take the realization that life is short and use it to fire things up. They'll recommit to a goal they had set for themselves at one time and let slip away. For others, it'll be about recommitting to their most important relationships, or rekindling one that had slipped away through time, as so often happens. Others won't be nearly as proactive. Time will just go by. They'll let whatever happens, just happen, moving forward aimlessly thinking it'll be what it'll be.

In his book, *Being Mortal*, author Atul Gawande, tells the story of the *Laches*, a dialogue written by Plato detailing a conversation between Socrates and two Athenian generals, where they collectively seek to answer the question, *what is courage?*

As Gawande tells it, the three of them go back and forth with different ideas to answer this quintessential question but can't seem to find the perfect definition. Finally, Gawande surmises that perhaps the reader might have come to one possible definition. He says, "courage is strength in the face of knowledge of what is to be feared or hoped."[1]

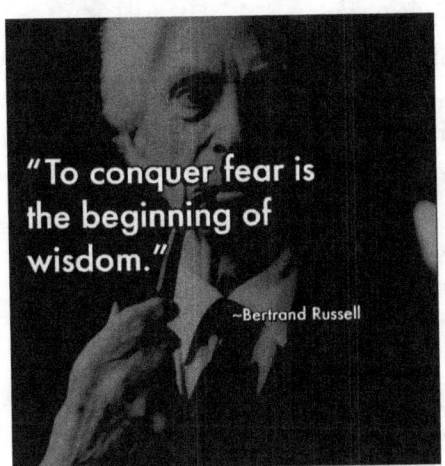

"To conquer fear is the beginning of wisdom."

~Bertrand Russell

There are many negative age beliefs and myths that seem to pervade the news cycle and continue to live inside people's minds about aging, which is one reason so many still don't believe they can exert influence over how their health and life might play out. Science is moving at breakneck speed and helping us realize how powerful the mind-body connection is - that things like memory loss, hearing loss, cancer, and cardiovascular events, are often influenced by existing negative age beliefs. And these things can potentially be turned around and improved by changing our outlook, and our belief system. But still, many of us resist. And turn away.

In what's a profound observation, Gawande follows with this: "At least two kinds of courage are required in aging and sickness. The first is the courage to confront the reality of mortality – the courage to seek out the truth of what is to be feared and what is to be hoped. Such courage is difficult enough. We have many reasons to shrink from it. But even more daunting is the second kind of courage – *the courage to act on the truth we find*. The problem is that the wise course is so frequently unclear. For a long while, I thought that this was simply because of uncertainty. *When it is hard to know what will happen, it is hard to know what to do*. But the challenge, I've come to see, is more fundamental than that. *One has to decide whether one's fears or one's hopes are what should matter the most*."[2]

So, I ask you: *What matters most to you? Is it your fears or your hopes?* The answer to that question will reflect your own age belief and determine in large part what you do with the information you've found here in this book. And what you do with the remaining years you have on this planet.

My hope is what you've learned will change your perception of what's *possible*. If there's one thing I know, it's when you start to act intentionally on your own behalf, and never give up or give in, you can change your life in powerfully positive ways. You have more influence over how you feel and how healthy you can become then you could possibly imagine. *But you have to believe*.

Perhaps it comes back to the word from the Okinawans, *ikigai*, that you learned about in Chapter 6, *The Mainstays of a Long, Healthy Life*. The French have "raison d'etre," which means reason for existence. In Costa Rica, it's "plan de vida," which translates as bread of life. In other words, *your why*. WHY are you reading this book right now? WHY does any of what I've shared with you matter to you? Even more fundamentally, WHY do you get up in the morning?

What is YOUR WHY – your purpose?

I'd like to tell you the story of a German TV commercial released at Christmastime in 2020,

that poignantly conveys the true meaning of *purpose* – of having a *why*. There's only one word that's spoken in the entire commercial – it's "Papa" – a word any person would know the meaning of regardless of their own language.

The opening setting is an old man's bedroom. It's early in the morning before dawn, and the old man hears his alarm as he's lying in bed. He glumly turns it off and forces himself to sit up, staring at the floor pondering his next move. The music is quiet, restless, anticipatory. As he forces himself up, a troubled look on his face gives the viewer the sense that he's got something important on his mind.

He glances toward a wall with some pictures, and grabs another from his dresser and looks, then shifts his glance to some people he notices passing by his window carrying a Christmas tree. This is the first time you know it's Christmastime. Inspired and with a tiny more spunk in

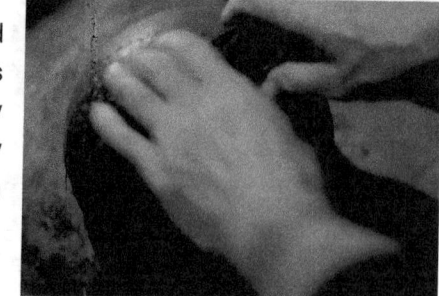

his step, he walks outside and into the garage. Still in his bathrobe, he flicks on the dim light. The music seems a little more spirited, hopeful.

The garage is typical of most garages – disheveled, filled with all kinds of stuff. He grabs and lifts a blanket, putting it aside. Underneath is a kettlebell. It looks heavy, maybe 40 to 50 pounds. Reluctantly, he bends down and grabs the kettlebell by the handle and drags it slowly across the floor and then outdoors. It's too heavy for him to lift, but he won't be deterred.

Just as soon as he gets it outside, he spots a nosy neighbor curiously gazing over the fence at him. She's clearly intrigued - wondering what on earth he's doing. Feeling a bit self-conscious and embarrassed, he sheepishly turns around and pulls the bell back inside the garage. Finally, he sets himself, gets a firm grip on the handle and slowly lifts it as high as he can in front of him. Struggling mightily and gritting his teeth, he barely manages to get it chest high.

Soon the alarm is again going off. It's the next morning. Once again he sits up, grabs the picture on his dresser and gazes. There's a sense of urgency now – he seems more committed.

Soon he's back in his garage. This time he's brought the picture with him and stares intently at it as he lifts, again. And again. And again.

The nosey neighbor from the day before is now outside his window, peering in. She shakes her head, wondering what this old man is doing. Why is he lifting this kettlebell, struggling, grunting - over and over again?

A family of three nearby hears his groaning and stops to see what is going on inside the garage. There's also a young woman nearby looking curiously at the old man. You get the sense she might be his daughter.

The next day, he rises and goes into his bathroom, and looks at himself intently in the mirror, shaking his head. He's doubting himself as we all sometimes do. He seems to be thinking to himself: *can he actually do what it is he's set out to do?*

Before you know it, it's the next day and the alarm is going off again. We're learning this is his new routine, his challenge, his struggle - *his purpose*.

But this time, there's a different aura – a newfound confidence to his walk. And he's dressed in workout clothes now – not a bathrobe. He gladfully strides out through his garage to his deck and again, picks up the kettlebell.

His nosy neighbor watches, but he won't lose his focus or be dismayed. Astonished, she watches as he repeatedly lifts the kettlebell, clearly stronger than before. Finally, the neighbor grabs her cellphone and makes a call.

Soon the young woman seen earlier, who the nosy neighbor called, is slowly walking toward the old man.

The neighbor sees her and points to the old man, as if to say, *look at him. Look at your father. What on earth is he doing?*

Concerned, the woman appraises the old man, and then says pensively, "Papa?"

He looks back - but doesn't stop moving, lifting. Over and over and over. He won't be dissuaded. He's clearly on a mission.

Soon a couple of children walking nearby see him lifting and squatting. Up and down. Standing just outside his garage window, the children begin mirroring his every move. He smiles, but only for a moment. Then it's back to work.

The days change and soon you see the old man getting dressed up in a tie and jacket. He's got a package that's beautifully wrapped - a Christmas gift.

He straightens his tie one last time then heads out the door to his car. Soon he arrives to someone else's home and is greeted by the woman we saw earlier and her husband. It's now clear this woman is his daughter. They walk toward each other and hug.

The old man then looks around the living

area as though he's searching for something or someone.

Sure enough, a lovely little girl appears on the stairway. It's his granddaughter. They smile at each other, with the kind of heart-felt loving smiles that can't be described with only words.

You quickly realize the picture he was looking at during all those days in the garage, was of her.

He gives her the boxed gift. She's surprised and so excited. She begins to open it as her parents look on, wondering what might be in the box and what this has all been about. She sees the gift is a star, the kind that goes on top of a Christmas tree.

She's holds the star tightly in her hand as the old man, her grandfather, grabs her by the waist and effortlessly lifts her high up so she can place the star on the tree. She's so happy. *And he makes it look so easy.*

As he puts her back down carefully, she joyfully runs straight to her mom and gives her a gigantic hug.

The old man and the little girl's mom – who you now know is his daughter - look at each other with tears in their eyes. The emotion is palpable.

She now realizes what her father was doing all of those days with the kettlebell.

He wanted more than anything to be able to gift his granddaughter the star, and then be able to lift her up with ease, and in the process, create a lasting memory that will endure for a lifetime, for all of them.

The commercial finishes with some words that come across the screen (in German).

Roughly translated, they say...

...*so that you can take care of what really matters most in life.*

So, again, I'll ask, *what matters most to you? Is it your fear or your hopes?* What really matters most in your life?

Getting older isn't something to be "cured," in the same way that youth shouldn't be glorified. The problem isn't that we're all getting older. The problem is as a society and culture, we're not doing a very good job of it.

As I said in the Introduction, when you don't have good health, nothing else matters nearly as much. You want to feel good and healthy to be able to take care of the things that matter the most.

I also said and acknowledged that *life is hard*.

Being intentional and doing the things we each need to do *is also hard*. In the end, we must *choose our hard* - something the old man was willing to do. In the process, he showed us all what truly *mattered most to him*.

We don't beat the reaper by living longer. We beat the reaper by living well and living fully. For the reaper is always going to come for all of us.

The question is: What do we do between the time we are born and the time he shows up? Because when he shows up, it's too late to do all the things that you're always gonna, kinda get around to.

– Randy Pausch, from his *Last Lecture*

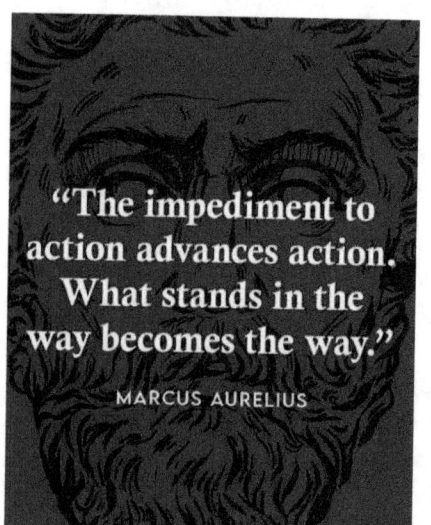

"The impediment to action advances action. What stands in the way becomes the way."

MARCUS AURELIUS

As author Kindra Hall teaches in her book, *Choose Your Story – Choose Your Life*, we're not the people we are because of our DNA, our jobs, our looks, or anything else.

We are who we are because of the stories we tell ourselves – the endless conversations that go on inside our minds about not only what we do with the limited time we have, but also our own worthiness, pain, or the hopes and dreams we have, for our future and the future of those we cherish.

Again, I'll ask, *what matters most to you? Is it your fear or your hopes? What stories are you telling yourself that are holding you back from taking action?*

I had a heartfelt conversation with my now 91 year-old mom a few years ago. Here's a picture of us that is now about 10 years old. Our talk

came about, in part, because of my own frustration stemming from my inability to *help* her. If you're wondering what I mean by "help," keep reading. And yes, as you might imagine, the conversation wasn't easy or comfortable - but I felt I needed to be honest with her.

It hurts to say it but the truth is, for most of the last 30 years or so, she's been reluctant to take my suggestions or advice on how to improve her health so she could feel better as she grew older.

Now you might be thinking to yourself, *Al, if she's 91, it seems like she's doing pretty well.* If that's what you're thinking, you'd be only partially correct. Yes, in some ways, she's aged very well. Many never make it to 91. But in other ways, it's been a major struggle. And this is one of the reasons I wrote this book. After all, it isn't the length of our life that matters as much as the quality of it. You see, she's spent a significant amount of time hospitalized with a whole variety of ailments, many of which nearly ended her life. Over her lifetime, she's had more than 40 surgeries, including both shoulders, both hips, and both knees replaced. She's in near constant pain and just not happy or enjoying life very much. She and everyone close to her has made significant practical adjustments so she can deal successfully with the constraints she has. Avoiding stairs, managing transport of her walker or wheelchair, rearranging furniture, handling and acquiring medications, adjusting bath and bedroom facilities, are just a few. If you're now thinking she's tough as nails, you'd be 100% correct. Also, despite it all, she's a great mom and "nana" to her many grandchildren and great grandchildren.

The bottom line is, *change is hard*. Especially for someone who has been stuck in their ways. Changing our habits, changing how we think, losing ourselves in the doing of what needs doing, that is all *really hard*. She hasn't changed how she eats, nor has she acted on the advice I've given her to improve her strength and hopefully, her independence and her ability to live out life on her own terms. With less pain and more freedom.

No one including me can force her or anyone else to act on advice or recommendations. We can help show the way, be there to extend a helping hand on occasion, and offer encouragement. In the end, the desire to do something to change our situation has to come from within. We have to want it. And then do something about it.

Have you ever had one of those "difficult" talks with someone you love? Some days the people you care about just need you to listen and show them you care. Other days, they need you to give them a little kick-in-the-pants, urging them to fight hard and never give up or give in. When it comes to my Mom's health, you could say she's a little bit of a paradox. On the negative side, she's aging quickly and getting progressively weaker; she's had some serious falls and at this point, is at risk of one that will end her independence, forever. She relies entirely on her walker to go anywhere in her house or out of it. Every step appears to be agonizing. Despite this, the truth is, whether she realizes it or not, she *could continue to live for many more years*.

Her toughness and love for others belies the emotional pain she also endures. She spends most of her days sitting, watching TV and thinking about the past, the "good old days" when she was happier and life seemed simpler. She loves to be active and involved in various activities, yet her ability to do that lessens with each passing day. Some days she'll burst into tears for no apparent reason or talk about someday soon having to go to a convalescent home. Or about dying, as though it's something she wishes would just happen. Naturally, she misses my Dad, who's been gone for more than twenty years now, and so many of her closest friends who have also passed. None of what she has faced has been easy.

In that conversation, I started with a simple question. "Mom, what would you do differently today, if you *knew* you were *guaranteed* to live to 100?" I told her the caveat was she wouldn't be guaranteed good health or vitality for those years, only that she would live to that age.

She immediately brushed me off. The look on her face implied she thought that was a stupid thing to talk about. I knew she didn't want to talk about it. In what is a strange yet common dichotomy, the thought of living that much longer is too frightening for her to even consider, yet the fear of dying or losing her independence is even more frightening. If those years included losing her independence, it would mean being bedridden or entirely reliant upon others for *everything*. She'd hate that. In a way, it would be a form of torture.

So, let me ask YOU the same question I asked her.

What would you do differently today, if you knew you were guaranteed to live to be 100 years old?

Most of the people I know either live with a sense of urgency or simply let the time pass by. Some rush around, afraid they'll miss out on something - proud members of the "rat race." Others seem to be waiting for the end to come. After all, if you believe it's too late, you won't take the time to learn a new set of skills or start a new career or take up a new hobby. OR... take control of your health. Or even finally learn how to swim.

But what if you knew you were going to live to be 100 years old? Would that change your perspective?

One of the reasons I wrote this book is my belief that *the same habits – the same mindset that can add life to our years, can also add years to our life.* Like the old man in the commercial - I challenge you to look at yourself in the mirror and think about where you might be a little short-sighted, selling yourself short. Selling your loved ones short. *Selling life short.*

You know, I've heard and read so many times that age is "just a number." I believe for some, it can be. In her research, author and professor, Dr. Becca Levy, a leading expert on the psychology of aging, has demonstrated that "people's memory performance, gait, balance, speed, and even will to live," can be improved dramatically by "activating positive age stereotypes for just ten minutes or so."[3] Clearly, her work has shown that "people with positive perceptions of aging" and who think of age as just a number, "performed better physically and cognitively than those with negative perceptions; they were more likely to recover from severe disability, they remembered better, they walked faster, and they even lived longer."[4] The thing is, <u>only if we believe</u>. And then I'd add, <u>take action</u>.

So, let me ask you for a fourth time: *what matters most to you? Is it your fears or your hopes?* What stories are you telling yourself that are holding you back from taking action?

I'm not suggesting you while away time because you know you've got lots more of it. *Every single day is precious and none are ever guaranteed.* What I am suggesting is there may be a better way to approach every day so you can become healthier and thus spend more of the time you have, doing the things that matter most to you, with the people who matter most to you.

> *Trust that still, small voice that says, this might work and I'll try it.*
> — Diane Mariechild

As you learned in the Preface, when I was 10 years old I nearly drowned. That experience left me scared to death of the water. 26 years later, inspired by watching the Ironman on TV with my daughter Erin, and caught up in the excitement of the Mark Allen and Thomas Hellriegel late-race "duel" on the Queen Kaahumanu highway, I shouted out to Erin that I was *going to DO the Ironman!*

Now let me ask you - who in their right mind would ever even think about trying to overcome a deathly fear of water and learn how to swim - at the age of 36?? No one in their *right* mind would do that, would they? A lot of things in life are hard, but few are as challenging as learning how to swim as an adult, and that's not even taking into consideration being afraid of the water. A fear I might add, that is hard to explain or rationalize. Looking back, it was clearly a form of PTSD.

It's now more than *21 years later....who would have imagined* I would compete and finish nine ironman races including the Hawaii Ironman three times. Or that I would be the fortunate coach to so many awesome people and athletes. Or that I would write a book about how to become truly healthy and feel good for the rest of your life! Not me, that's for damn sure.

The choice is yours.

I'm no different than you are. I'm a regular guy who, for some reason, believed I needed to follow my heart. I didn't know the future, but I believed if I committed to learning *everything* I could about swimming, worked relentlessly, and didn't give up, perhaps, just maybe, I might be able to swim well enough to someday get through a triathlon. I guess I was right!

My hope is this book has given you a starting point for how to become truly healthy, age well, and feel great, so that you can live your life believing you WILL live to be 100, or even more. At the same time, I implore you to live each day with passion, determination, and purpose. If you're not sure what your purpose is right now, keep looking. You'll find it if you listen and trust your heart and take action. I promise you won't regret it. Amazing things await you.

Thank you for reading. All my best to you!

Al Lyman

AUTHOR OF
AGE WELL AND
FEEL GREAT!

TOP 10 WORDS OF WISDOM BY GANDHI

1. BE THE CHANGE

2. WHAT YOU THINK YOU BECOME

3. WHERE THERE IS LOVE THERE IS LIFE

4. LEARN AS IF YOU'LL LIVE FOREVER

5. YOUR HEALTH IS YOUR REAL WEALTH

6. HAVE A SENSE OF HUMOR

7. YOUR LIFE IS YOUR MESSAGE

8. ACTION EXPRESSES PRIORITIES

9. OUR GREATNESS IS BEING ABLE TO REMAKE OURSELVES

10. FIND YOURSELF IN THE SERVICE OF OTHERS

Find Your Purpose. The wonderful commercial I told you about (did I just say a commercial was wonderful?) ☺ is on YouTube. Please take a few minutes and go watch this. You won't be disappointed – my written description doesn't do it justice. Go HERE: shorturl.at/cptv2

ACKNOWLEDGEMENTS

There are so many people I need to convey my thanks and gratitude to. Each played a role in helping me turn this dream of being an author and sharing what I've learned, into a reality.

- I've often said we all get here on the backs of those that come before us, and that is certainly true for me. As such, I'd like to thank all of the scientists, teachers, coaches, mentors, and authors, who through their various books, articles, lectures, and teachings, have helped us all learn and grow. The world is a better place because of your efforts and desire to share.

- Thank you to the hundreds of athletes I've worked with over many years, especially those I've worked with 1 on 1. During the times when I was struggling the most and doubting whether I was on the right path, your desire to learn and commitment to training for the betterment of your body, not to its detriment, not only helped ME learn and grow, it gave me a reason and the courage to continue to forge ahead and keep fighting for what I believed was right. And speaking of coached athletes...

- Thank you, Lisbeth. You, more than any other person I've ever worked with or known, through your grace, humility, talent, and hard work, helped me to believe in myself. You stayed with me when almost no one else would and have always remained a close friend to support me in whatever way you could. You are special - simply one of a kind. As a coach, having the opportunity to coach YOU will always be the greatest gift I've ever received. 5-TIME IRONMAN World Champion sounds amazing. You earned each one!

- Thank you to everyone who contributed to this manuscript in some way, especially Beth, for your inspiration and willingness to help with editing. And to my models for the movement and strength chapters, Terry, Alison, and Zack.

And finally...

- To Erin and A.J., who ironically aren't "kids" anymore. I know your mom would agree, you both are the best things we've ever done. Nothing is more important to me than your health and happiness. To say I love you more than words can say doesn't seem adequate enough. Know that every day since you were born, you've been my greatest inspiration to love more, learn more, do more, share more. You've made me so incredibly proud to be your dad.

- To Mom and Pops. You taught me more than you'll ever know. Your love for each other was always inspiring and life-affirming. Your work ethic and character set a high bar that I've always tried to live up to, not always successfully. ☺ For as long as I can remember, I just wanted you to be proud of me. #makehimproud

- Lastly, to Ter. Thank you sweetie. Simply put, this book wouldn't have been possible without your support, amazing editing and proofreading, modeling, constant encouragement and affirmation, smiles, and endless love. Even more, given how difficult the last few years have been, I simply wouldn't be here without you.

REFERENCES

Preface.

[1] https://www.cancer.gov/about-cancer/understanding/statistics
[2] https://www.who.int/news-room/fact-sheets/detail/cancer
[3] https://www.statista.com/topics/6701/
health-expenditures-in-the-us/#dossierKeyfigures
[4] https://www.cdc.gov/childrensmentalhealth/data.html
[5] https://www.beckershospitalreview.com/hospital-management-administration/pediatric-suicide-attempts-mental-health-cases-rose-53-percent-in-2021-stanford-children-s-ceo-says.html
[6] https://www.cnbc.com/2019/02/11/this-is-the-real-reason-most-americans-file-for-bankruptcy.html

Introduction.

[1] Population Division of the Department of Economic and Social Affairs of the United Nations Secretariat, World Population Prospects: The 2006 Revision and World Urbanization Prospects: The 2005 http://wisdom.unu.edu/en/ageing-societies/; Image source: Brenden Egan from his Ted Talk, "Muscle Matters."

Chapter 1 - What Does it Mean to *Die Healthy?*

[1] https://www.mayoclinic.org/diseases-conditions/glioblastoma/cdc-20350148
[2] https://www.cdc.gov/cancer/dcpc/research/update-on-cancer-deaths/index.htm
[3] David A Sinclair, Ph.D., *Lifespan: Why We Age and Why We Don't Have To.* Simon and Schuster, 2019, p.72
[4] Ibid., p79
[5] Atul Gawande, M.D., *Being Mortal: Medicine and What Matters in the End,* Metropolitan Books, 2014, p 26.
[6] Ibid.
[7] Ibid, p 27.
[8] https://www.nytimes.com/2021/12/24/health/james-f-fries-dead.html

[9]   https://www.researchgate.net/
      publication/15816171_Aging_Natural_Death_and_the_Compression_of_Morbidity
[10] https://www.nytimes.com/2021/12/24/health/james-f-fries-dead.html
[11] James A. Swartz, *James Fries: healthy aging pioneer. Am J Public
      Health.* 2008;98(7):1163-1166. doi:10.2105/AJPH.2008.135731
[12] Ibid.
[13] https://www.lifespanpodcast.com/the-science-behind-why-we-age/
[14] https://markmanson.net/delayed-gratification
[15] https://markmanson.net/how-to-stop-procrastinating

Chapter 2 - Why We Age: *Exploring Aging at the Cellular Level.*

[1]   https://en.Wikipedia.org/wiki/Cellular_senescence
[2]   Jiang H, Ju Z, Rudolph KL. Telomere shortening and ageing. Z Gerontol Geriatr.
      2007 Oct;40(5):314-24. doi: 10.1007/s00391-007-0480-0. PMID: 17943234.
[3]   https://en.Wikipedia.org/wiki/Oxidative_stress
[4]   Hayflick L. *Entropy explains aging, genetic determinism explains
      longevity, and undefined terminology explains misunderstanding both.
      PLoS Genet.* 2007;3(12):e220. doi:10.1371/journal.pgen.0030220
[5]   Harman D. *The aging process. Proc Natl Acad Sci U S A.*
      1981;78(11):7124-7128. doi:10.1073/pnas.78.11.7124
[6]   https://www.nutraceuticalsworld.com/contents/view_breaking-news/2017-01-26/
      global-antioxidants-market-expected-to-reach-45-billion-by-2022/
[7]   https://www.genome.gov/genetics-glossary/Deoxyribonucleic-Acid
[8]   https://www.lifespanpodcast.com/the-science-behind-why-we-age/
[9]   Ibid.
[10] Ibid.
[11] Dr. Kara Fitzgerald, ND, IFMCP, *Younger You*, Hatchett Book Group, 2022, p. xiii
[12] https://en.wikipedia.org/wiki/Epigenetics
[13] Moore, L., Le, T. & Fan, G. *DNA Methylation and Its Basic Function.*
      Neuropsychopharmacol 38, 23–38 (2013). https://doi.org/10.1038/npp.2012.112
[14] Dr. Kara Fitzgerald, ND, IFMCP, *Younger You*, Hatchett Book Group, 2022, p. 4.
[15] Ibid.
[16] https://en.Wikipedia.org/wiki/Adaptogen
[17] https://www.lifespanpodcast.com/the-science-behind-why-we-age/
[18] Elizabeth Blackburn, PhD., Elissa Epel, PhD., *The Telomere Effect: A Revolutionary
      Approach to Living Younger, Healthier, Longer,* Orion Books, 2017, p. 16
[19] Brydon L, Lin J, Butcher L, Hamer M, Erusalimsky JD, Blackburn EH, Steptoe
      A. Hostility and cellular aging in men from the Whitehall II cohort. Biol
      Psychiatry. 2012 May 1;71(9):767-73. doi: 10.1016/j.biopsych.2011.08.020.
      Epub 2011 Oct 5. PMID: 21974787; PMCID: PMC3657139.

[20] O'Donovan A, Lin J, Tillie J, Dhabhar FS, Wolkowitz OM, Blackburn EH, Epel ES. Pessimism correlates with leukocyte telomere shortness and elevated interleukin-6 in post-menopausal women. Brain Behav Immun. 2009 May;23(4):446-9. doi: 10.1016/j.bbi.2008.11.006. Epub 2008 Dec 11. Erratum in: Brain Behav Immun. 2012 Aug;26(6):1017. Tillie, J M [corrected to Tillie, J]; Wolkowitz, O [corrected to Wolkowitz, O M]; Blackburn, E [corrected to Blackburn, E H]; Epel, E [corrected to Epel, E S]. PMID: 19111922; PMCID: PMC2719778.

[21] Ikeda A, Schwartz J, Peters JL, Baccarelli AA, Hoxha M, Dioni L, Spiro A, Sparrow D, Vokonas P, Kubzansky LD. Pessimistic orientation in relation to telomere length in older men: the VA normative aging study. Psychoneuroendocrinology. 2014 Apr;42:68-76. doi: 10.1016/j.psyneuen.2014.01.001. Epub 2014 Jan 9. PMID: 24636503; PMCID: PMC4070424.

[22] Elizabeth Blackburn, PhD., Elissa Epel, PhD., *The Telomere Effect: A Revolutionary Approach to Living Younger, Healthier, Longer*, Orion Books, p. 107.

[22] Ibid.

[23] David Sinclair, PhD., *Lifespan: Why We Age and Why We Don't Have To*, Simon and Schuster, 2019, p. 149.

[24] *Wandering Minds and Aging Cells* - https://journals.sagepub.com/doi/full/10.1177/2167702612460234

[25] https://www.ted.com/talks/matt_killingsworth_want_to_be_happier_stay_in_the_moment

[26] https://markmanson.net/your-two-minds

[27] https://markmanson.net/diversify-your-identity

[28] https://en.wikipedia.org/wiki/Biosphere_2

[29] https://bluemala.com/articles/learning-about-anxiety-from-biosphere-2

[30] Ibid.

Chapter 3 - Age Beliefs and the Aging Puzzle: *What's Missing?*

[1] Becca Levy, Ph D., *Breaking the Age Code: How Your Beliefs About Aging Determine How Well and Long You Live*, Harper Collins Pub, 2022, p. 15.

[2] Sheree T. Kwong See, Carmen Rasmussen & S. Quinn Pertman (2012) Measuring Children's Age Stereotyping Using a Modified Piagetian Conservation Task, Educational Gerontology, 38:3, 149-165, DOI: 10.1080/03601277.2010.515891

[3] Becca Levy, Ph D., *Breaking the Age Code: How Your Beliefs About Aging Determine How Well and Long You Live*, Harper Collins Pub, 2022, p. 11.

[4] Ibid.

[5] https://www.ageism.org/what-is-ageism/

[6] Officer A, de la Fuente-Núñez V. A global campaign to combat ageism. Bull World Health Organ. 2018 Apr 1;96(4):295-296. doi: 10.2471/BLT.17.202424. Epub 2018 Mar 9. PMID: 29695887; PMCID: PMC5872010.

[7] Ibid.

[8] Becca Levy, Ph D., *Breaking the Age Code: How Your Beliefs About Aging Determine How Well and Long You Live*, Harper Collins Pub, 2022, p.21.

[9] https://en.wikipedia.org/wiki/Norman_Lear

[10] https://www.washingtonpost.com/national/john-williams-90-steps-away-from-film-but-not-music/2022/06/23/26b97ac2-f2f2-11ec-ac16-8fbf7194cd78_story.html

[11] Ibid.

[12] Ibid.

[13] Ibid.

[14] Ibid.

[15] Becca Levy, Ph D., *Breaking the Age Code: How Your Beliefs About Aging Determine How Well and Long You Live*, Harper Collins Pub, 2022, p.95.

[16] Levy BR, Slade MD, Pietrzak RH, Ferrucci L. When Culture Influences Genes: Positive Age Beliefs Amplify the Cognitive-Aging Benefit of APOE ε2. J Gerontol B Psychol Sci Soc Sci. 2020 Sep 14;75(8):e198-e203. doi: 10.1093/geronb/gbaa126. PMID: 32835364; PMCID: PMC7489069.

[17] https://www.cdc.gov/aging/aginginfo/alzheimers.htm

[18] https://www.alzheimersorganization.org/alzheimers-gene-apoe4

[19] Becca Levy, Ph D., *Breaking the Age Code: How Your Beliefs About Aging Determine How Well and Long You Live*, Harper Collins Pub, 2022, p.63.

[20] Ibid.

[21] Ibid.

[22] VanderWeele TJ, Kubzansky LD. Facets of optimism: Comment on Scheier et al. (2021). Am Psychol. 2021 Oct;76(7):1191-1193. doi: 10.1037/amp0000864. PMID: 34990174; PMCID: PMC8939852.

Chapter 4 - Conscious Aging: *How to Rewrite the Narrative.*

[1] https://naomiwoodspring.com/2018/10/age-appearance-and-beauty-the-face-in-the-mirror/

[2] Ibid.

[3] https://www.ted.com/talks/dan_buettner_how_to_live_to_be_100?language=en

[4] https://timesofindia.indiatimes.com/life-style/relationships/love-sex/72-women-find-grey-haired-men-more-attractive-than-others-says-study/photostory/73961818.cms

[5] Part of this book writing process has been also preparing the topic of this book, *Conscious Aging,* onto the speaking circuit. To that end, I've been working with a company called The Speaker Lab, to learn more about how to create a compelling talk and build a speaking business.

[6] https://www.huffpost.com/entry/fear-of-aging_l_627030f5e4b0bc48f57e5293

[7] https://glistencounseling.com/about/

[8] https://www.huffpost.com/entry/fear-of-aging_l_627030f5e4b0bc48f57e5293

[9] Ibid.

[10] Ibid.

[11] Kindra Hall, *Choose Your Story, Change Your Life*, Harper Collins pub., 2022, p.162.

[12] Ibid., inside cover.

[13] Ibid., pp 164-171.

[14] http://drannkearneycooke.com/

[15] https://www.huffpost.com/entry/fear-of-aging_l_627030f5e4b0bc48f57e5293

[16] https://www.deepakchopra.com/articles/the-genius-of-second-maturity/

[17] Jason Elias, *The Seven Graces of Ageless Aging*, Five Element Healing Press, 2021, p. 90.

[18] Deepak Chopra, M.D., *Ageless Body, Timeless Mind: The Quantum Alternative to Growing Old*, Three Rivers Press, p. 157.

[19] Jason Elias, *The Seven Graces of Ageless Aging*, Five Element Healing Press, 2021, p. 94.

[20] https://en.wikipedia.org/wiki/Dunning%E2%80%93Kruger_effect

[21] https://www.goodreads.com/quotes/24141-ignorance-more-frequently-begets-confidence-than-does-knowledge-it-is

[22] https://dailystoic.com/amor-fati-love-of-fate/

[23] Plato is widely considered a pivotal figure in the history of Ancient Greek and Western philosophy, along with his teacher, Socrates, and his most famous student, Aristotle. He has often been cited as one of the founders of Western religion and spirituality. https://en.wikipedia.org/wiki/Plato

[24] https://tim.blog/2022/06/01/primatologist-isabel-behncke/

[25] Ibid

Chapter 5 - The Mainstays of a Long, Healthy Life: *Early Diagnosis, Stress, Sleep, Finding Happiness and a Long, Healthy Life the Blue Zone Way*

[1] Randy Pausch: Last Lecture-Achieving Your Childhood Dreams, https://www.youtube.com/watch?v=ji5_MqicxSo

[2] https://www.cancer.org/cancer/pancreatic-cancer/detection-diagnosis-staging/survival-rates.html

[3] Irving G, Neves AL, Dambha-Miller H, *et al*, International variations in primary care physician consultation time: a systematic review of 67 countries, *BMJ Open* 2017;**7**:e017902. doi: 10.1136/bmjopen-2017-017902

[4] Sergey Young, *The Science and Technology of Growing Young*, Benbella Books Inc, 2021, p 52.

[5] Ibid. p 58.

[6] https://moffitt.org/taking-care-of-your-health/taking-care-of-your-health-story-archive/how-often-should-you-get-a-colonoscopy/

[7] Robert Sapolsky, Ph.D., *Behave: The Biology of Humans at Our Best and Worst*, Penguin Books, Random House, LLC, 2017, p. 127.

[8] Dr. Kara Fitzgerald, ND, IFMCP, *Younger You*, Hatchett Book Group, 2022, p. 4

[9] Ibid, p 70.

[10] Ibid.

[11] Venditti S, Verdone L, Reale A, Vetriani V, Caserta M, Zampieri M. *Molecules of Silence: Effects of Meditation on Gene Expression and Epigenetics. Front Psychol.* 2020;11:1767. Published 2020 Aug 11. doi:10.3389/fpsyg.2020.01767

[12] https://peterattiamd.com/robertsapolsky/

[13] Robert Sapolsky, Ph.D., *Behave: The Biology of Humans at Our Best and Worst*, Penguin Books, Random House, LLC, 2017, p. 136.

[14] Steptoe A, Kivimäki M. Stress and cardiovascular disease. Nat Rev Cardiol. 2012 Apr 3;9(6):360-70. doi: 10.1038/nrcardio.2012.45. PMID: 22473079.

[15] Dr. Kara Fitzgerald, ND, IFMCP, *Younger You*, Hatchett Book Group, 2022, p. 172.

[16] https://peterattiamd.com/robertsapolsky/

[17] https://abcnews.go.com/GMA/OnCall/story?id=5851269&page=1
https://www.nytimes.com/2011/07/15/science/15baboon.html

[18] Nobles J, Weintraub MR, Adler NE. Subjective socioeconomic status and health: relationships reconsidered. *Soc Sci Med.* 2013;82:58-66. doi:10.1016/j.socscimed.2013.01.021

[19] Becca Levy, Ph D., *Breaking the Age Code: How Your Beliefs About Aging Determine How Well and Long You Live*, Harper Collins Pub, 2022, p. 77.

[20] Gretchen van Steenwyk, Martin Roszkowski, Francesca Manuella, Tamara B Franklin, Isabelle M Mansuy, Transgenerational inheritance of behavioral and metabolic effects of paternal exposure to traumatic stress in early postnatal life: evidence in the 4th generation, *Environmental Epigenetics*, Volume 4, Issue 2, April 2018, dvy023, https://doi.org/10.1093/eep/dvy023

[21] https://ideas.ted.com/
emotionally-exhausted-burnout-completing-stress-response-cycle/?

[22] Triage is defined as the assignment of degrees of urgency to wounds or illnesses to decide the order of treatment of a large number of patients or casualties.

[23] Steinberg RJ, Figart DM. Emotional Labor Since: The Managed Heart. The ANNALS of the American Academy of Political and Social Science. 1999;561(1):8-26. doi:10.1177/000271629956100101

[24] https://www.precisionnutrition.com/what-causes-stress

[25] Evy Poumpouras, *Becoming Bulletproof: Protect Yourself, Read People, Influence Situations, Live Fearlessly*, Simon and Schuster, Inc,. 2020, p 49-50.

[26] Don B. Ardell, *High Level Wellness: An Alternative to Doctors, Drugs, and Disease*, Rodale Press, 1977, p. 138.

[27] https://www.brainyquote.com/authors/marcus-aurelius-quotes

[28] Kindra Hall, *Choose Your Story, Change Your Life*, Harper Collins, 2022, p. 25.

[29] Ibid.

[30] Jack Canfield and Mark Victor Hansen, *The Aladdin Factor*, Berkley Publishing Group, 1995.

[31] https://www.mindbodyonline.com/sites/default/files/public/education/learning-assets/2022-MWI-Fitness-Report.pdf

[32] https://www.mindbodyonline.com/sites/default/files/public/education/learning-assets/2019_Fitness_in_America-Report.pdf

[33] https://www.amazon.com/Scott-Allan/e/B00GG165RO/ref=aufs_dp_fta_dsk

[34] https://www.badwater.com/event/badwater-135/

[35] https://pubmed.ncbi.nlm.nih.gov/6857280/

[36] https://www.ted.com/talks/matt_walker_sleep_is_your_superpower?language=en

[37] https://peterattiamd.com/matthewwalker1/

[38] Sergey Young, *The Science and Technology of Growing Young*, Benbella Books, 2021, p 203.

[39] Ibid.

[40] https://peterattiamd.com/matthewwalker2/

[41] Ibid.

[42] https://peterattiamd.com/matthewwalker2/

[43] Fischer D, Lombardi DA, Marucci-Wellman H, Roenneberg T. Chronotypes in the US - Influence of age and sex. PLoS One. 2017 Jun 21;12(6):e0178782. doi: 10.1371/journal.pone.0178782. PMID: 28636610; PMCID: PMC5479630.

[44] Dr. Mark Burhenne, DDS, *The 8-Hour Sleep Paradox*, Sunnyvale, CA., 2015, p. 13-15.

[45] Mark Burhenne, The 8-Hour Sleep Paradox: How We Are Sleeping Our Way to Fatigue, Disease, and Unhappiness, 2015, p 12.

[46] Ibid, p. 13.

[47] Chang AM, Aeschbach D, Duffy JF, Czeisler CA. Evening use of light-emitting eReaders negatively affects sleep, circadian timing, and next-morning alertness. Proc Natl Acad Sci U S A. 2015 Jan 27;112(4):1232-7. doi: 10.1073/pnas.1418490112. Epub 2014 Dec 22. PMID: 25535358; PMCID: PMC4313820.

[48] https://peterattiamd.com/?s=melatonin; https://peterattiamd.com/matthewwalkerama/

[49] Nedeltcheva AV, Kilkus JM, Imperial J, Schoeller DA, Penev PD. Insufficient sleep undermines dietary efforts to reduce adiposity. *Ann Intern Med.* 2010;153(7):435-441. doi:10.7326/0003-4819-153-7-201010050-00006

[50] Dan Buettner, *The Blue Zones: Lessons for Living Longer From the People Who've Lived the Longest*, National Geographic, 2008, p. xiii

[51] Ibid, p. xv.

[52] Ibid, p. xiv.

[53] Hector Morales and Francesc Miralles, *Ikigai: The Japanese Secret to a Long and Happy Life*, Penguin Random House pub, 2017, p. 3.

[54] Nir Barzalai, M.D., *Age Later: Healthspan, Lifespan, and the New Science of Longevity*, St Martins Press, 2020, p. 24.

[55] https://www.ted.com/talks/dan_buettner_how_to_live_to_be_100?language=en

[56] Nir Barzilai, M.D., *Age Later: Healthspan, Lifespan, and the New Science of Longevity*, St Martins Press, 2020, p. 31.

[57] Ibid, p 36.

[58] Ibid.

[59] https://www.ted.com/talks/dan_buettner_how_to_live_to_be_100?language=en

[60] Nir Barzilai, M.D., *Age Later: Healthspan, Lifespan, and the New Science of Longevity*, St Martins Press, 2020, p. 46.

[61] Hector Garcia and Francesc Miralles, Ikigai: The Japanese Secret to a Long and Happy Life, Penguin Random House Pub, 2016, p. 123.

[62] https://www.ted.com/talks/dan_buettner_how_to_live_to_be_100?language=en

[63] Ibid.

[64] Ibid.

[65] https://en.wikipedia.org/wiki/Mens_sana_in_corpore_sano

[66] Hector Morales and Francesc Miralles, *Ikigai: The Japanese Secret to a Long and Happy Life*, Penguin Random House pub, 2017, p inside cover.

[67] Ibid, p. 2.

[68] https://www.ted.com/talks/dan_buettner_how_to_live_to_be_100?language=en

[69] Hector Morales and Francesc Miralles, *Ikigai: The Japanese Secret to a Long and Happy Life*, Penguin Random House pub, 2017, p. 4.

[70] https://einsteinmed.edu/news/releases/798/personality-genes-may-help-account-for-longevity/

[71] Ibid.

[72] Hector Morales and Francesc Miralles, *Ikigai: The Japanese Secret to a Long and Happy Life*, Penguin Random House pub, 2017, p. 172

[73] Ibid.

[74] Ibid. p. 183.

Chapter 6 - Self-Assessment: *What Are Your Risk Factors and Family History?*

[1] https://peterattiamd.com/heart-disease-begin-tell-us-prevention/

[2] https://www.ahajournals.org/doi/pdf/10.1161/01.cir.103.22.2705

[3] https://www.diabetes.org/diabetes/a1c/diagnosis

[4] Ibid

[5] https://www.testing.com/tests/apoe-genotyping-alzheimer-disease/

[6] https://www.nia.nih.gov/news/study-reveals-how-apoe4-gene-may-increase-risk-dementia

[7] Alper JS, Beckwith J. Genetic fatalism and social policy: the implications of behavior genetics research. *Yale J Biol Med*. 1993;66(6):511-524.

Chapter 7 - Introduction: *Confusion and Chaos.*

[1] Nightshades are a botanical family of foods and spices that come from flowering plants, that contain chemical compounds called alkaloids. In addition to tomatoes, common edible nightshades include potatoes, eggplant, bell peppers, and spices

sourced from peppers such as cayenne and paprika. These vegetables (some of which are actually fruits) are highly nutritious diet staples in many cultures. https://health.clevelandclinic.org/whats-the-deal-with-nightshade-vegetables/

[2] Robert Lustwig MD., *Metabolical*, Harper-Collins Pub, 2021, p 69.

[3] Ibid.

Chapter 8 - Myths, Magic Bullets, and the Enemy.

[1] Matt Fitzgerald, *Diet Cults: The Surprising Fallacy at the Core of Nutrition Fads*, Pegasus Books, 2014, p.

[2] https://health.usnews.com/best-diet/search

[3] https://www.npd.com/industry-expertise/books/

[4] https://www.cdc.gov/nchs/products/databriefs/db360.htm

[5] https://www.healthline.com/health/fitness/skinny-fat

[6] Sam Apple, *Ravenous: Otto Warburg, the Nazis, and the Search for the Cancer-Diet Connection*, WW Norton and Co, 2021, p 317.

[7] Robert Lustwig MD., *Fat Chance: The Hidden Truth about Sugar, Obesity, and Chronic Disease*, 2013, Harper-Collins pub, p. 7

[8] Ibid.

[9] Robert Lustwig MD., *Metabolical*, Harper-Collins Pub, 2021, p 167.

[10] https://my.clevelandclinic.org/health/diagnostics/10683-dexa-dxa-scan-bone-density-test

[11] https://www.thelancet.com/journals/landia/article/PIIS2213-8587(18)30288-2/fulltext

[12] The Fat Acceptance movement began in the 1960s and was originally called the "National Association to Aid Fat Americans" when it was founded in 1969, NAAFA was groundbreaking in addressing weight bias and discrimination against fat people as a civil rights issue.

[13] https://drweightcontrol.com/myth-2-weight-and-health-are-mutually-inclusive-or-exclusive/

[14] https://osf.io/preprints/nutrixiv/w3zh2/

[15] Robert Lustwig MD., *Metabolical*, Harper-Collins Pub, 2021, p 66.

[16] Michael Moss, *Hooked: How Processed Food Became Addictive*. (Penguin Books, 2021). Pg 105.

[17] Aldi is a fast-growing German based discount food chain that has more than 1900 stores in the U.S. and a cult-like following that is willing to tolerate any inconvenience in exchange for lower prices.

Chapter 9 - Insulin Resistance and Hyperinsulinemia.

[1] https://www.cdc.gov/nchs/pressroom/nchs_press_releases/2021/202107.htm

[2] Joana Araújo, Jianwen Cai, and June Stevens. *Metabolic Syndrome and Related Disorders*. Feb 2019.46-52. http://doi.org/10.1089/met.2018.0105

[3] Chiarelli, F. and M.L. Marcovecchio, *Insulin resistance and obesity in childhood.* Eur J Endocrinol, 2008. P. 67-74

[4] https://www.theguardian.com/society/2015/sep/16/type-2-diabetes-three-year-old-girl-obesity

[5] https://peterattiamd.com/jasonfung/ This opinion was also expressed by Dr. Fung as a guest on episode #29 of The Drive, Dr. Peter Attia's podcast.

[6] Glucagon is another pancreatic hormone that acts opposite to insulin. It brings glucose levels up when they get too low. Both work together to maintain balance, which is described by the word, homeostasis.

[7] https://www.cdc.gov/diabetes/basics/type1.html

[8] https://www.ncbi.nlm.nih.gov/pmc/articles/PMC4283517/

[9] Jones, D.S., et al., The burden of disease and the changing task of medicine. NEJM, 2012. https://www.nejm.org/doi/full/10.1056/NEJMp1113569

[10] https://peterattiamd.com/geraldshulman/

[11] Bikman, Benjamin, PhD., *Why We Get Sick*, Benbella Books 2020, p. 7

[12] https://peterattiamd.com/jasonfung/

[13] De novo lipogenesis is a complex enzymatic pathway for converting dietary carbohydrate (CHO) into fat in the liver. To learn more, go here: https://www.sciencedirect.com/science/article/abs/pii/S0026049514001115

[14] Metabolism refers to the chemical (metabolic) processes that take place throughout your body as liver and muscle glycogen and fat stores are converted into energy that ultimately fuels body functions.

[15] https://peterattiamd.com/jasonfung - *Fasting as a potent antidote to obesity, insulin resistance, type 2 diabetes, and the many symptoms of metabolic illness, min. 00:39 of the podcast.*

[16] https://www.pnas.org/doi/abs/10.1073/pnas.1110105108

[17] *Enhanced peripheral and splanchnic insulin sensitivity in NIDDM men after a single bout of exercise.* https://pubmed.ncbi.nlm.nih.gov/3102297/

[18] Liu J, Li Y, Zhang D, Yi SS, Liu J. Trends in Prediabetes Among Youths in the US From 1999 Through 2018. *JAMA Pediatr.* Published online March 28, 2022. doi:10.1001/jamapediatrics.2022.0077

[19] https://en.wikipedia.org/wiki/Glycation

[20] Kraft, Joseph R. *Diabetes Epidemic and You.* Trafford Publishing, Bloomington, IN., 2008, pg. viii

[21] https://www.health.harvard.edu/staying-healthy/understanding-acute-and-chronic-inflammation

[22] Ridker PM, Rifai N, Rose L, Buring JE, Cook NR. *Comparison of C-reactive protein and low-density lipoprotein cholesterol levels in the prediction of first cardiovascular events.* N Engl J Med. 2002 Nov 14;347(20):1557-65. doi: 10.1056/NEJMoa021993. PMID: 12432042.

[23] Fishel MA, Watson GS, Montine TJ, Wang Q, Green PS, Kulstad JJ, Cook DG, Peskind ER, Baker LD, Goldgaber D, Nie W, Asthana S, Plymate SR, Schwartz MW, Craft S. Hyperinsulinemia provokes synchronous increases in central inflammation and beta-amyloid in normal adults. Arch Neurol. 2005 Oct;62(10):1539-44. doi: 10.1001/archneur.62.10.noc50112. PMID: 16216936.

[24] Bikman, Benjamin, PhD., *Why We Get Sick*, Benbella Books 2020, p. 22.

[25] https://www.lifespanpodcast.com/the-science-behind-why-we-age/

[26] Ibid.

[27] Ibid.

[28] https://nutritionandmetabolism.biomedcentral.com/articles/10.1186/1743-7075-7-7

[29] Ibid., p. 291

[30] Apple, Sam, *Ravenous: Otto Warburg, the Nazis, and the Search for the Cancer-Diet Connection,* W.W. Norton and Co., New York, NY., 2021, p. 289.

[31] Ibid.

[32] Ibid., p. 294

[33] https://peterattiamd.com/geraldshulman/

[34] Ibid.

[35] Bikman, Benjamin, PhD., *Why We Get Sick*, Benbella Books 2020, p. 61

[36] Ibid.

[37] https://journals.physiology.org/doi/full/10.1152/ajpendo.00586.2013

[38] https://rdcu.be/cJ0ea

[39] Bikman, Benjamin, PhD., *Why We Get Sick*, Benbella Books 2020, p. 63

[40] Ibid.

[41] https://pubmed.ncbi.nlm.nih.gov/19240815/

[42] https://medicine.yale.edu/news-article/small-amounts-of-liver-fat-lead-to-insulin-resistance-and-increased-cardiometabolic-risk-factors-yale-researchers-find/

[43] Ibid.

[44] https://aasldpubs.onlinelibrary.wiley.com/doi/full/10.1002/hep.28431

[45] https://www.ncbi.nlm.nih.gov/pmc/articles/PMC6051295/

[46] https://www.liebertpub.com/doi/abs/10.1089/rej.2011.1289

[47] Bikman, Benjamin, PhD., *Why We Get Sick*, Benbella Books 2020, p. 31

[48] Ibid.

[49] https://academic.oup.com/brain/article/136/2/374/287025

[50] https://peterattiamd.com/amandasmith/

[51] Verma N, Jain V, Birla S, Jain R, Sharma A. *Growth and hormonal profile from birth to adolescence of a girl with aromatase deficiency.* J Pediatr Endocrinol Metab. 2012;25(11-12):1185-90. doi: 10.1515/jpem-2012-0152. PMID: 23329769.

[52] Carr MC. *The emergence of the metabolic syndrome with menopause.* J Clin Endocrinol Metab. 2003 Jun;88(6):2404-11. doi: 10.1210/jc.2003-030242. PMID: 12788835.

[53] Muller M, Grobbee DE, den Tonkelaar I, Lamberts SW, van der Schouw YT. *Endogenous sex hormones and metabolic syndrome in aging men.* J Clin Endocrinol Metab. 2005 May;90(5):2618-23. doi: 10.1210/jc.2004-1158. Epub 2005 Feb 1. PMID: 15687322.

[54] https://kokumura.medium.com/the-order-in-which-to-properly-eat-food-inspired-by-kaiseki-ryori-62a7d52860d9

[55] Shukla AP, Andono J, Touhamy SH, Casper A, Iliescu RG, Mauer E, Shan Zhu Y, Ludwig DS, Aronne LJ. Carbohydrate-last meal pattern lowers postprandial glucose and insulin excursions in type 2 diabetes. BMJ Open Diabetes Res Care. 2017 Sep 14;5(1):e000440. doi: 10.1136/bmjdrc-2017-000440. PMID: 28989726; PMCID: PMC5604719.

[56] According to many experts, polycystic ovarian syndrome (PCOS) is the most common cause of female infertility. It affects as many as 10 million women worldwide. As the name suggests, the ovaries of the affected woman become burdened with cysts. PCOS is a disease of too much insulin.

Chapter 10 - Time Restricted Eating.

[1] Julie Fink, https://www.businessinsider.com/how-breakfast-became-known-as-the-most-important-meal-of-the-day-2016-6

[2] https://www.nytimes.com/2019/03/29/sunday-review/biosphere-2-climate-change.html

[3] Sinclair, David, PhD., *Lifespan-Why We Age and Why We Don't Have To.* Simon and Schuster, 2019, p 26.

[4] Ibid.

[5] Ibid.

[6] Fontana, Luigi, PhD., *Path to Longevity*, Hardy Books, 2020, p 51.

[7] Kozumbo, W.J. & Calebrese, E.J., Two decades (1998-2018) of research progress on Hormesis: advancing biological understanding and enabling novel applications. *Journal of Cell Communication and Signaling*, 13, 273-275 (2019).

[8] https://peterattiamd.com/paulgrewal/

[9] Trans-fat, also called trans-unsaturated fatty acids, or trans fatty acids, is a type of unsaturated fat. It became widely produced as an unintentional byproduct in the industrial processing of vegetable and fish oils in the early 20th century for use in margarine and other processed foods. The World Health Organization in 2018 introduced a 6-step guide to eliminate industrially-produced trans-fatty acids from the global food supply. Artificial trans-fat has been banned in many nations, including the United States, but it is still widely consumed in developing nations, resulting in more than 500,000 excess deaths per year. https://en.wikipedia.org/wiki/Trans_fat

[10] https://pubmed.ncbi.nlm.nih.gov/20678538/

[11] https://journals.sagepub.com/doi/abs/10.1106/1898-plw3-6y6h-8k22

[12] Rong S, Snetselaar LG, Xu G, Sun Y, Liu B, Wallace RB, Bao W. Association of Skipping Breakfast With Cardiovascular and All-Cause Mortality. J Am Coll Cardiol. 2019 Apr 30;73(16):2025-2032. doi: 10.1016/j.jacc.2019.01.065. PMID: 31023424.

[13] https://www.cancer.gov/publications/dictionaries/cancer-terms/def/autophagy

[14] Wegman MP, Guo MH, Bennion DM, et al. Practicality of intermittent fasting in humans and its effect on oxidative stress and genes related to aging and metabolism. *Rejuvenation Res.* 2015;18(2):162-172. doi:10.1089/rej.2014.1624

[15] Benjamin Bikman, PhD., *Why We Get Sick*, Benbella Books 2020, p. 148

[16] Moro T, Tinsley G, Pacelli FQ, Marcolin G, Bianco A, Paoli A. Twelve Months of Time-restricted Eating and Resistance Training Improves Inflammatory Markers and Cardiometabolic Risk Factors. Med Sci Sports Exerc. 2021 Dec 1;53(12):2577-2585. doi: 10.1249/MSS.0000000000002738. PMID: 34649266.

[17] https://peterattiamd.com/are-you-eating-enough-protein/

[18] https://peterattiamd.com/the-impact-of-fasting-on-muscle-mass/

[19] Harari, Yuval Noah, Sapiens – A Brief History of Humankind, 2015,Harper Collins pub, p 77

[20] Ibid. p 78

[21] Ibid. p 81

[22] Ibid. p 79

[23] Ibid. p 81

[24] https://www.nytimes.com/2022/04/20/health/time-restricted-diets.html

[25] https://www.nejm.org/doi/full/10.1056/NEJMoa2114833

[26] https://www.cell.com/cell-metabolism/fulltext/S1550-4131(20)30319-3?dgcid

[27] https://www.cell.com/cell-metabolism/fulltext/S1550-4131(20)30319-3?dgcid

[28] Dr. Jason Fung is a best-selling author of many books including The Obesity Code and The Diabetes Code.

Chapter 11 - Sugar.

[1] https://www.dhhs.nh.gov/dphs/nhp/documents/sugar.pdf

[2] Robert Lustwig, MD., *Fat Chance: The Hidden Truth about Sugar, Obesity, and Disease*, Harper-Collins pub, 2013, p 239.

[3] Ibid, p 50.

[4] Michael Moss, *Hooked: How Processed Food Became Addictive*, Penguin Random House pub, 2021, p. 43.

[5] https://journals.plos.org/plosone/article?id=10.1371/journal.pone.0047948

[6] Brian Johnson, *The Philosopher's Notes*, volume 1, 2010, Entheos Enterprises, p.82.

Chapter 12 - Chronic Inflammation.

[1] https://peterattiamd.com/neddavid/ (How Cellular Senescence Influences Aging and What We Can Do About It)

[2] Daniel J. Levitin, *Successful Aging: A neuroscientist Explores the Power and Potential of Our Lives*, Penguin Random House, 2020, p.331.

[3] Ibid.

[4] David Sinclair, Ph D., *Lifespan: Why We Age and Why We Don't Have To*, Simon and Schuster, 2019, p.150.

[5] Furman, D., Campisi, J., Verdin, E. *et al. Chronic inflammation in the etiology of disease across the life span. Nat Med* **25,** 1822–1832 (2019). https://doi.org/10.1038/s41591-019-0675-0

[6] https://en.wikipedia.org/wiki/C-reactive_protein

[7] Adjibade M, Andreeva VA, Lemogne C, et al. The Inflammatory Potential of the Diet Is Associated with Depressive Symptoms in Different Subgroups of the General Population. *J Nutr.* 2017;147(5):879-887. doi:10.3945/jn.116.245167

[8] Mejías-Peña Y, Estébanez B, Rodriguez-Miguelez P, Fernandez-Gonzalo R, Almar M, de Paz JA, González-Gallego J, Cuevas MJ. *Impact of resistance training on the autophagy-inflammation-apoptosis crosstalk in elderly subjects.* Aging (Albany NY). 2017 Feb 2;9(2):408-418. doi: 10.18632/aging.101167. PMID: 28160545; PMCID: PMC5361672.

Chapter 13 – Cholesterol: *Facts, Myths, and Misinformation.*

[1] https://en.wikipedia.org/wiki/Ancel_Keys

[2] https://www.sevencountriesstudy.com/about-the-study/investigators/ancel-keys/

[3] https://www.heart.org/en/health-topics/cholesterol/hdl-good-ldl-bad-cholesterol-and-triglycerides

[4] Brown MS, Goldstein JL. How LDL receptors influence cholesterol and atherosclerosis. Sci Am. 1984 Nov;251(5):58-66. doi: 10.1038/scientificamerican1184-58. PMID: 6390676.

[5] Boren J, Chapman MJ, Krauss RM et al. Low-density lipoproteins cause atherosclerotic cardiovascular disease: pathophysiological, genetic, and therapeutic insights: a consensus statement from the European Atherosclerosis Society Consensus Panel. Eur Heart J 2020.

[6] David Diamond Ph.D., *Should You Be Concerned about High LDL-cholesterol on a low-carb diet?* https://www.youtube.com/watch?v=VUMUhp1pSyM&t=2223s

[7] https://www.usf.edu/news/2018/bad-cholesterol-may-not-be-so-bad-after-all.aspx

[8] Uffe Ravnskov, Michel de Lorgeril, David M Diamond, Rokuro Hama, Tomohito Hamazaki, Björn Hammarskjöld, Niamh Hynes, Malcolm Kendrick, Peter H Langsjoen, Luca Mascitelli, Kilmer S McCully, Harumi Okuyama, Paul J Rosch, Tore Schersten, Sherif Sultan & Ralf Sundberg (2018) LDL-C does not cause cardiovascular disease: a comprehensive review of the current literature, Expert Review of Clinical Pharmacology, 11:10, 959-970, DOI: 10.1080/17512433.2018.1519391

[9] https://symbiosisonlinepublishing.com/endocrinology-diabetes/

[10] Mundal L, Sarancic M, Ose L et al. Mortality Among Patients With Familial Hypercholesterolemia: A Registry-Based Study in Norway, 1992-2010. Journal of the American Heart Association 2014; 3.

[11] Robinson JG, Williams KJ, Gidding S et al. Eradicating the Burden of Atherosclerotic Cardiovascular Disease by Lowering Apolipoprotein B Lipoproteins Earlier in Life. J Am Heart Assoc 2018; 7:e009778.

[12] Hovland A, Mundal LJ, Igland J et al. Risk of Ischemic Stroke and Total Cerebrovascular Disease in Familial Hypercholesterolemia: A Register Study From Norway. Stroke 2019; 50:172-174.

[13] Harlan WR, Graham JB, Estes EH. Familial Hypercholesterolemia - a Genetic and Metabolic Study. Medicine 1966; 45:77-&.

[14] Williams RR, Hasstedt SJ, Wilson DE et al. Evidence That Men with Familial Hypercholesterolemia Can Avoid Early Coronary Death - an Analysis of 77 Gene Carriers in 4 Utah Pedigrees. Jama-Journal of the American Medical Association 1986; 255:219-224.

[15] Sijbrands EJ, Westendorp RG, Defesche JC et al. Mortality over two centuries in large pedigree with familial hypercholesterolaemia: family tree mortality study. BMJ 2001; 322:1019-1023.

[16] David Diamond on Deception in Cholesterol Research: *Separating Truth from Profitable Fiction*, https://www.youtube.com/watch?v=inwfSkSGvQw

[17] Ravnskov U, Diamond DM, Hama R, *et al Lack of an association or an inverse association between low-density-lipoprotein cholesterol and mortality in the elderly: a systematic review. BMJ Open* 2016;**6:**e010401. doi: 10.1136/bmjopen-2015-010401

[18] https://openheart.bmj.com/content/openhrt/8/2/e001680.full.pdf

[19] Harcombe Z, Baker JS, Cooper SM, Davies B, Sculthorpe N, DiNicolantonio JJ, Grace F. *Evidence from randomised controlled trials did not support the introduction of dietary fat guidelines in 1977 and 1983: a systematic review and meta-analysis.* Open Heart. 2015 Jan 29;2(1):e000196. doi: 10.1136/openhrt-2014-000196. Erratum in: Open Heart. 2015;2(1). pii: openhrt-2014-000196corr1. doi: 10.1136/openhrt-2014-000196corr1. PMID: 25685363; PMCID: PMC4316589.

[20] Menke A, Casagrande S, Cowie CC. Contributions of A1c, fasting plasma glucose, and 2-hour plasma glucose to prediabetes prevalence: NHANES 2011-2014. Ann Epidemiol 2018; 28:681-685 e682.

[21] Gast KB, Tjeerdema N, Stijnen T et al. Insulin Resistance and Risk of Incident Cardiovascular Events in Adults without Diabetes: Meta-Analysis. Plos One 2012; 7.

[22] Bhat SL, Abbasi FA, Blasey C et al. Beyond fasting plasma glucose: The association between coronary heart disease risk and postprandial glucose, postprandial insulin and insulin resistance in healthy, nondiabetic adults. Metabolism-Clinical and Experimental 2013; 62:1223-1226.

[23] Garg PK, Biggs ML, Kaplan R et al. Fasting and post-glucose load measures of insulin resistance and risk of incident atrial fibrillation: The Cardiovascular Health Study. Nutrition Metabolism and Cardiovascular Diseases 2018; 28:716-721.

[24] Zhang XH, Li J, Zheng SP et al. Fasting insulin, insulin resistance, and risk of cardiovascular or all-cause mortality in non-diabetic adults: a meta-analysis. Bioscience Reports 2017; 37.

[25] Diabetes Prevention Program Research G, Knowler WC, Fowler SE et al. 10-year follow-up of diabetes incidence and weight loss in the Diabetes Prevention Program Outcomes Study. Lancet 2009; 374:1677-1686.

[26] Volek JS, Feinman RD. Carbohydrate restriction improves the features of Metabolic Syndrome. Metabolic Syndrome may be defined by the response to carbohydrate restriction. Nutr Metab (Lond) 2005; 2:31. 23

[27] Volek JS, Fernandez ML, Feinman RD, Phinney SD. Dietary carbohydrate restriction induces a unique metabolic state positively affecting atherogenic dyslipidemia, fatty acid partitioning, and metabolic syndrome. Prog Lipid Res 2008; 47:307-318.

[28] Dashti HM, Mathew TC, Khadada M et al. Beneficial effects of ketogenic diet in obese diabetic subjects. Molecular and Cellular Biochemistry 2007; 302:249-256.

[29] Feinman RD, Pogozelski WK, Astrup A et al. Dietary carbohydrate restriction as the first approach in diabetes management: Critical review and evidence base. Nutrition 2015; 31:1-13.

[30] Karam JG, McFarlane SI, Feinman RD. Carbohydrate Restriction and Cardiovascular Risk. Curr Cardiovasc Risk 2008; 2:88-94.

[31] Kelly T, Unwin D, Finucane F. Low-Carbohydrate Diets in the Management of Obesity and Type 2 Diabetes: A Review from Clinicians Using the Approach in Practice. Int J Environ Res Public Health 2020; 17.

[32] Norwitz NG, Loh V. A Standard Lipid Panel Is Insufficient for the Care of a Patient on a High-Fat, Low-Carbohydrate Ketogenic Diet. Front Med (Lausanne) 2020; 7:97.

[33] Barrea L, Caprio M, Watanabe M et al. Could very low-calorie ketogenic diets turn off low grade inflammation in obesity? Emerging evidence. Crit Rev Food Sci 2022.

[34] Chi JT, Lin PH, Tolstikov V et al. Serum metabolomic analysis of men on a lowcarbohydrate diet for biochemically recurrent prostate cancer reveals the potential role of ketogenesis to slow tumor growth: a secondary analysis of the CAPS2 diet trial. Prostate Cancer P D 2022.

[35] Gram-Kampmann EM, Hansen CD, Hugger MB et al. Effects of a 6-month, lowcarbohydrate diet on glycaemic control, body composition, and cardiovascular risk factors in patients with type 2 diabetes: An open-label randomized controlled trial. Diabetes Obesity & Metabolism 2022; 24:693-703.

[36] Volek JS, Phinney SD, Krauss RM et al. Alternative Dietary Patterns for Americans: Low-Carbohydrate Diets. Nutrients 2021; 13.

[37] Bailey WA, Westman EC, Marquart ML, Guyton JR. Low glycemic diet for weight loss in hypertriglyceridemic patients attending a lipid clinic. Journal of clinical lipidology 2010; 4:508-514.

[38] Foley PJ. Effect of low carbohydrate diets on insulin resistance and the metabolic syndrome. Curr Opin Endocrinol Diabetes Obes 2021; 28:463-468.

[39] Harvey C, Schofield GM, Zinn C et al. Low-carbohydrate diets differing in carbohydrate restriction improve cardiometabolic and anthropometric markers in healthy adults: A randomised clinical trial. Peerj 2019; 7:e6273.

[40] Stoica RA, Diaconu CC, Rizzo M et al. Weight loss programmes using low carbohydrate diets to control the cardiovascular risk in adolescents (Review). Exp Ther Med 2021; 21:90.

[41] Siri-Tarino PW, Krauss RM. Diet, lipids, and cardiovascular disease. Curr Opin Lipidol 2016; 27:323-328.

[42] Wood RJ, Volek JS, Davis SR et al. Effects of a carbohydrate-restricted diet on emerging plasma markers for cardiovascular disease. Nutr Metab (Lond) 2006; 3:19. 24

[43] Faghihnia N, Tsimikas S, Miller ER et al. Changes in lipoprotein(a), oxidized phospholipids, and LDL subclasses with a low-fat high-carbohydrate diet. Journal of Lipid Research 2010; 51:3324-3330.

[44] Westman EC, Yancy WS, Jr., Olsen MK et al. Effect of a low-carbohydrate, ketogenic diet program compared to a low-fat diet on fasting lipoprotein subclasses. Int J Cardiol 2006; 110:212-216.

[45] Volek JS, Phinney SD, Forsythe CE et al. Carbohydrate restriction has a more favorable impact on the metabolic syndrome than a low fat diet. Lipids 2009; 44:297- 309.

[46] Norwitz NG, Loh V. A Standard Lipid Panel Is Insufficient for the Care of a Patient on a High-Fat, Low-Carbohydrate Ketogenic Diet. Front Med-Lausanne 2020; 7.

[47] Pinto A, Bonucci A, Maggi E et al. Anti-Oxidant and Anti-Inflammatory Activity of Ketogenic Diet: New Perspectives for Neuroprotection in Alzheimer's Disease. Antioxidants-Basel 2018; 7.

[48] Dupuis N, Curatolo N, Benoist JF, Auvin S. Ketogenic diet exhibits antiinflammatory properties. Epilepsia 2015; 56:e95-e98.

[49] O'Neill BJ. Effect of low-carbohydrate diets on cardiometabolic risk, insulin resistance, and metabolic syndrome. Curr Opin Endocrinol Diabetes Obes 2020; 27:301-307.

[50] Krebs JD, Bell D, Hall R et al. Improvements in Glucose Metabolism and Insulin Sensitivity with a Low-Carbohydrate Diet in Obese Patients with Type 2 Diabetes. Journal of the American College of Nutrition 2013; 32:11-17.

[51] Boden G, Sargrad K, Homko C et al. Effect of a low-carbohydrate diet on appetite, blood glucose levels, and insulin resistance in obese patients with type 2 diabetes. Annals of Internal Medicine 2005; 142:403-411.

[52] Westman EC, Tondt J, Maguire E, Yancy WS. Implementing a low-carbohydrate, ketogenic diet to manage type 2 diabetes mellitus. Expert Rev Endocrino 2018; 13:263- 272.

[53] Ahmed SR, Bellamkonda S, Zilbermint M et al. Effects of the low carbohydrate, high fat diet on glycemic control and body weight in patients with type 2 diabetes: experience from a community-based cohort. Bmj Open Diab Res Ca 2020; 8.

[54] Kelly T, Unwin D, Finucane F. Low-Carbohydrate Diets in the Management of Obesity and Type 2 Diabetes: A Review from Clinicians Using the Approach in Practice. International Journal of Environmental Research and Public Health 2020; 17.

[55] Westman EC, Tondt J, Maguire E, Yancy WS, Jr. Implementing a lowcarbohydrate, ketogenic diet to manage type 2 diabetes mellitus. Expert Rev Endocrinol Metab 2018; 13:263-272.

[56] Westman EC, Yancy WS, Jr. Using a low-carbohydrate diet to treat obesity and type 2 diabetes mellitus. Curr Opin Endocrinol Diabetes Obes 2020; 27:255-260.

[57] Yancy WS, Jr., Mitchell NS, Westman EC. Ketogenic Diet for Obesity and Diabetes. JAMA Intern Med 2019; 179:1734-1735.

[58] Athinarayanan SJ, Hallberg SJ, McKenzie AL et al. Impact of a 2-year trial of nutritional ketosis on indices of cardiovascular disease risk in patients with type 2 diabetes. Cardiovasc Diabetol 2020; 19:208. 25

[59] Sharman MJ, Kraemer WJ, Love DM et al. A ketogenic diet favorably affects serum biomarkers for cardiovascular disease in normal-weight men. J Nutr 2002; 132:1879-1885.

[60] Bazzano LA, Hu T, Reynolds K et al. Effects of low-carbohydrate and low-fat diets: a randomized trial. Ann Intern Med 2014; 161:309-318.

[61] Sackner-Bernstein J, Kanter D, Kaul S. Dietary Intervention for Overweight and Obese Adults: Comparison of Low-Carbohydrate and Low-Fat Diets. A Meta-Analysis. PLoS One 2015; 10:e0139817.

[62] Volek JS, Sharman MJ, Forsythe CE. Modification of lipoproteins by very lowcarbohydrate diets. The Journal of nutrition 2005; 135:1339-1342.

[63] Tzenios N, Lewis ED, Crowley DC et al. Examining the Efficacy of a Very-LowCarbohydrate Ketogenic Diet on Cardiovascular Health in Adults with Mildly Elevated Low-Density Lipoprotein Cholesterol in an Open-Label Pilot Study. Metab Syndr Relat Disord 2022; 20:94-103.

[64] Wakabayashi I, Daimon T. Comparison of discrimination for cardio-metabolic risk by different cut-off values of the ratio of triglycerides to HDL cholesterol. Lipids in health and disease 2019; 18:156.

[65] https://health.gov/our-work/nutrition-physical-activity/dietary-guidelines/previous-dietary-guidelines/2015

[66] https://jcp.bmj.com/content/jclinpath/s1-5/1/1.full.pdf

[67] https://en.wikipedia.org/wiki/Red_herring

[68] Nicholas G Norwitz, David Feldman, Adrian Soto-Mota, Tro Kalayjian, David S Ludwig, Elevated LDL Cholesterol with a Carbohydrate-Restricted Diet: Evidence for a "Lean Mass Hyper-Responder" Phenotype, *Current Developments in Nutrition*, Volume 6, Issue 1, January 2022, nzab144, https://doi.org/10.1093/cdn/nzab144

[69] Stanhope KL, Bremer AA, Medici V, Nakajima K, Ito Y, Nakano T, Chen G, Fong TH, Lee V, Menorca RI, Keim NL, Havel PJ. *Consumption of fructose and high fructose corn syrup increase postprandial triglycerides, LDL-cholesterol, and apolipoprotein-B*

in young men and women. J Clin Endocrinol Metab. 2011 Oct;96(10):E1596-605. doi: 10.1210/jc.2011-1251. Epub 2011 Aug 17. PMID: 21849529; PMCID: PMC3200248.

[70] https://prevmedhealth.com/more-important-than-ldl-the-triglyceride-hdl-ratio/

Chapter 14 - Your Gut Microbiome.

[1] Justin Sonnenburg, PhD, *The Good Gut: Taking Control of Your Weight, Your Mood, and Your Long-Term Health*, Penguin Books, 2015, p. 32.

[2] https://www.nationalgeographic.com/magazine/article/how-trillions-of-microbes-affect-every-stage-of-our-life-from-birth-to-old-age-feature

[3] Ding RX, Goh WR, Wu RN, Yue XQ, Luo X, Khine WWT, Wu JR, Lee YK. Revisit gut microbiota and its impact on human health and disease. J Food Drug Anal. 2019 Jul;27(3):623-631. doi: 10.1016/j.jfda.2018.12.012. Epub 2019 Feb 1. PMID: 31324279.

[4] Wong SH, Kwong TNY, Wu CY, Yu J. Clinical applications of gut microbiota in cancer biology. Semin Cancer Biol. 2019 Apr;55:28-36. doi: 10.1016/j. semcancer.2018.05.003. Epub 2018 May 18. PMID: 29782923.

[5] Justin Sonnenburg, PhD, *The Good Gut: Taking Control of Your Weight, Your Mood, and Your Long-Term Health*, Penguin Books, 2015, p. 112.

[6] Ibid.

[7] Ibid.

[8] https://badgut.org/information-centre/health-nutrition/dietary-fibre/

[9] Justin Sonnenburg, PhD, *The Good Gut: Taking Control of Your Weight, Your Mood, and Your Long-Term Health*, Penguin Books, 2015, p. 131

[10] Ibid, p 132.

[11] Ibid.

[12] Ibis, p. 146.

[13] https://www.cdc.gov/nchs/fastats/drug-use-therapeutic.htm

[14] Justin Sonnenburg, PhD, *The Good Gut: Taking Control of Your Weight, Your Mood, and Your Long-Term Health*, Penguin Books, 2015, p. 200.

[15] https://www.hsph.harvard.edu/nutritionsource/processed-foods/

[16] https://www.cell.com/cell/pdf/S0092-8674(21)00754-6.pdf

[17] Justin Sonnenburg, PhD, *The Good Gut: Taking Control of Your Weight, Your Mood, and Your Long-Term Health*, Penguin Books, 2015, p. 137

[18] Ibid, p. 138.

[19] https://www.instagram.com/p/Cc-7saBvJ1K/ Gut diversity associated with better cognitive function – Dr. Kara Fitzgerald, ND, IFMCP

[20] Meyer K, Lulla A, Debroy K, Shikany JM, Yaffe K, Meirelles O, Launer LJ. Association of the Gut Microbiota With Cognitive Function in Midlife. JAMA Netw Open. 2022 Feb 1;5(2):e2143941. doi: 10.1001/jamanetworkopen.2021.43941. PMID: 35133436; PMCID: PMC8826173.

[21] https://www.sciencedirect.com/topics/pharmacology-toxicology-and-pharmaceutical-science/butyrate

[22] Boesmans L, Valles-Colomer M, Wang J, Eeckhaut V, Falony G, Ducatelle R, Van Immerseel F, Raes J, Verbeke K. Butyrate Producers as Potential Next-Generation Probiotics: Safety Assessment of the Administration of *Butyricicoccus pullicaecorum* to Healthy Volunteers. mSystems. 2018 Nov 6;3(6):e00094-18. doi: 10.1128/mSystems.00094-18. PMID: 30417112; PMCID: PMC6222043.

[23] Potential beneficial effects of butyrate in intestinal and extraintestinal diseases; https://www.ncbi.nlm.nih.gov/pmc/articles/PMC3070119/

Chapter 15 - Meat Lovers vs. Vegetarians: *Who is Right?*

[1] https://peterattiamd.com/191027/ (Is Ditching Meat a Game Changer for Your Health?)

[2] Shrank WH, Patrick AR, Brookhart MA. Healthy user and related biases in observational studies of preventive interventions: a primer for physicians. *J Gen Intern Med.* 2011;26(5):546-550. doi:10.1007/s11606-010-1609-1

[3] https://journals.lww.com/ijo/Fulltext/2021/11000/Epidemiology_of_type_2_diabetes_in_India.6.aspx

[4] https://www.cdc.gov/diabetes/pdfs/data/statistics/national-diabetes-statistics-report.pdf

[5] https://endocrinenews.endocrine.org/u-s-leads-developed-nations-in-diabetes-prevalence/

[6] https://www.nature.com/articles/nrendo.2014.171

[7] https://link.springer.com/article/10.1007/s11883-012-0282-8

[8] Food and Agriculture Organization of the United Nations. 2006. *Livestock's long shadow: Environmental issues and options.* http://www.fao.org/docrep/010/a0701e/a0701e00.HTM

[9] https://www.fao.org/3/i3437e/i3437e.pdf

[10] https://e360.yale.edu/digest/fertilizer-use-driving-rapid-rise-in-potent-nitrous-oxide-emissions

[11] https://news.mongabay.com/2019/11/in-a-surprise-move-even-to-the-sugarcane-industry-president-bolsonaro-has-removed-restrictions-on-sugarcane-production-in-the-brazilian-amazon-experts-expect-land-speculators-to-benefit/

[12] Robert Lustwig, MD., *Metabolical*, Harper-Collins Pub., 2021, p. 9.

[13] *Association of Aspirin Use With Mortality Risk Among Older Adult Participants in the Prostate, Lung, Colorectal, and Ovarian Cancer Screening Trial.* https://jamanetwork.com/journals/jamanetworkopen/fullarticle/2756258

[14] Wick JY. Aspirin: a history, a love story. Consult Pharm. 2012 May;27(5):322-9. doi: 10.4140/TCP.n.2012.322. PMID: 22591976.

[15] Desborough MJR, Keeling DM. The aspirin story - from willow to wonder drug. Br J Haematol. 2017 Jun;177(5):674-683. doi: 10.1111/bjh.14520. Epub 2017 Jan 20. PMID: 28106908.

[16] David Sinclair, PhD., *Lifespan-Why We Age and Why We Don't Have To*. Simon and Schuster, 2019, p 131.

[17] https://www.mayoclinic.org/diseases-conditions/
      factor-v-leiden/symptoms-causes/syc-20372423

Chapter 16 - Take-Home Nutrition Tips and Common Questions.

[1]   Muncke J. Tackling the toxics in plastics packaging. PLoS
      Biol. 2021 Mar 30;19(3):e3000961. doi: 10.1371/journal.
      pbio.3000961. PMID: 33784315; PMCID: PMC8009362.
[2]   https://www.jandonline.org/article/S2212-2672(12)00464-9/fulltext

Chapter 17 - Introduction.

[1]   https://en.wikipedia.org/wiki/Mechanotransduction
[2]   Sharon L. Dunn, Margaret L. Olmedo, Mechanotransduction: Relevance to
      Physical Therapist Practice—Understanding Our Ability to Affect Genetic
      Expression Through Mechanical Forces, *Physical Therapy*, Volume 96, Issue
      5, 1 May 2016, Pages 712–721, https://doi.org/10.2522/ptj.20150073
[3]   Robert Schleip, *Fascial Fitness: How to be Resilient, Elegant, and
      Dynamic in Everyday Life and Sport,* Lotus Publishing, 2014, p. 23.
[4]   Somatic Recall Part 1 – Soft Tissue Memory: @
      inproceedings{Oschman2012SomaticRP,title={Somatic Recall Part 1 — Soft
      Tissue Memory},author={James L. Oschman and Nora H. Oschman},year={201}
[5]   *The Distribution of Cellular Turnover in the Body* - https://
      www.nature.com/articles/s41591-020-01182-9
[6]   https://www.huffpost.com/entry/sitting-is-the-new-smokin_b_5890006

Chapter 18 - Exercise: *The Struggle is Real.*

[1]   Eijsvogels TMH, Thompson PD, Franklin BA. The "Extreme Exercise
      Hypothesis": Recent Findings and Cardiovascular Health Implications.
      Curr Treat Options Cardiovasc Med. 2018 Aug 28;20(10):84. doi: 10.1007/
      s11936-018-0674-3. PMID: 30155804; PMCID: PMC6132728.
[2]   https://www.cdc.gov/nchs/fastats/exercise.htm
[3]   https://health.clevelandclinic.org/80-of-americans-dont-get-
      enough-exercise-and-heres-how-much-you-actually-need/
[4]   Physical Activity Guidelines Advisory Committee (2018), Scientific Report,
      (Washington, DC, U.S. Department of Health and Human Services). https://
      health.gov/sites/default/files/2019-09/PAG_Advisory_Committee_Report.pdf
[5]   https://www.cdc.gov/nchs/data/nhsr/nhsr112.pdf
[6]   Eijsvogels TMH, Thompson PD, Franklin BA. The "Extreme Exercise Hypothesis":
      Recent Findings and Cardiovascular Health Implications. *Curr Treat Options
      Cardiovasc Med.* 2018;20(10):84. Published 2018 Aug 28. doi:10.1007/s11936-018-0674-3

[7]   Siddarth P, Rahi B, Emerson ND, et al. Physical Activity and Hippocampal Sub-Region Structure in Older Adults with Memory Complaints. *J Alzheimers Dis.* 2018;61(3):1089-1096. doi:10.3233/JAD-170586

[8]   https://www.nationalgeographic.org/encyclopedia/hadza/

[9]   Running in the wild: Energetics explain ecological running speeds, https://www.cell.com/current-biology/pdfExtended/S0960-9822(22)00563-2

[10] https://phys.org/news/2022-04-runners-pace-distance.html

[11] Daniel Lieberman, *Exercised*. Pantheon Books- Penguin Random House LLC, 2020, p 52.

[12] Webb, O.J. et al. (2011), A statistical summary of mall-based stair-climbing intervention, *Journal of Physical Activity and Health* 8:5 56-65. https://journals.humankinetics.com/view/journals/jpah/8/4/article-p558.xml

[13] https://en.Wikipedia.org/wiki/Leptin - Leptin is a hormone predominantly made by adipose cells and enterocytes in the small intestine that helps to regulate energy balance by inhibiting hunger, which in turn diminishes fat storage in adipocytes. Leptin acts on cell receptors in the arcuate and ventromedial nuclei, as well as other parts of the hypothalamus and dopaminergic neurons of the ventral tegmental area, consequently mediating feeding.

[14] https://ideas.ted.com/heres-how-i-finally-got-myself-to-start-exercising/

[15] Ibid.

[16] https://markmanson.net/how-to-get-motivated

[17] https://ideas.ted.com/heres-how-i-finally-got-myself-to-start-exercising/

[18] Marlowe, F.W.. (2010). The Hadza: Hunter–Gatherers of Tanzania.

[19] https://papers.ssrn.com/sol3/papers.cfm?abstract_id=3767273

[20] Keller K, Engelhardt M. Strength and muscle mass loss with aging process. Age and strength loss. *Muscles Ligaments Tendons J.* 2014;3(4):346-350. Published 2014 Feb 24.

[21] Zhang X, Wang C, Dou Q, *et al,* Sarcopenia as a predictor of all-cause mortality among older nursing home residents: a systematic review and meta-analysis, *BMJ Open* 2018;**8**:e021252. doi: 10.1136/bmjopen-2017-021252

[22] Puthucheary, Zudin MRCP; Harridge, Stephen PhD; Hart, Nicholas PhD Skeletal muscle dysfunction in critical care: Wasting, weakness, and rehabilitation strategies, Critical Care Medicine: October 2010 - Volume 38 - Issue 10 - p S676-S682, doi: 10.1097/CCM.0b013e3181f2458d

Chapter 19 - Basics and Fundamentals, Wisdom, and Going with the Flow.

[1]   Jason Elias, *The Seven Graces of Ageless Aging*, Five Element Healing Press, 2021, p. 166

[2]   Hector Garcia and Francesc Miralles, Ikigai: The Japanese Secret to a Long, Happy Life, Penguin Random House, 2016, p 56.

[3]   Ibid, inside cover.

[4]   How Michael Jordan's Trainer Helped Him Become the GOAT: https://www.youtube.com/watch?v=iTFtY6KgS58

Chapter 20 - How to Improve Your Stability.

[1]   https://en.wikipedia.org/wiki/Serape_effect
[2]   Hodges PW. Core stability exercise in chronic low back pain. Orthop Clin North Am. 2003 Apr;34(2):245-54. doi: 10.1016/s0030-5898(03)00003-8. PMID: 12914264.

Chapter 21 - How to Improve Your Feet.

[1]   http://www.bsmpg.com/hs-fs/hub/52884/file-5411032-pdf/docs/1905hoffman.pdf
[2]   Daniel Howell, Ph.D., *The Barefoot Book: 50 Great Reasons to Kick Off Your Shoes,* Hunter House Publishers, 2010, p. 15.
[3]   Why Shoes Make Normal Gait Impossible - https://www.barefooters.org/wp-content/uploads/2018/10/Rossi-WhyShoesMake.pdf
[4]   Kerrigan DC, Todd MK, Riley PO. Knee osteoarthritis and high-heeled shoes. Lancet. 1998 May 9;351(9113):1399-401. doi: 10.1016/S0140-6736(97)11281-8. PMID: 9593411.
[5]   Strzalkowski, Nicholas & Peters, Ryan & Inglis, John & Bent, Leah. (2018). Cutaneous afferent innervation of the human foot sole: What can we learn from single unit recordings?. Journal of Neurophysiology. 120. 10.1152/jn.00848.2017.
[6]   Benno M Nigg, Wen Liu, The effect of muscle stiffness and damping on simulated impact force peaks during running, Journal of Biomechanics,Volume 32, Issue 8, 1999, Pages 849-856, ISSN 0021-9290, https://doi.org/10.1016/S0021-9290(99)00048-2. (https://www.sciencedirect.com/science/article/pii/S0021929099000482)
[7]   Ibid.
[8]   Dr. Emily Splichal, DPM *Barefoot Strong*, 2015, p. 37.
[9]   Ibid.
[10] Ibid.
[11] https://en.wikipedia.org/wiki/Collagen
[12] Dr. Emily Splichal, DPM, *Barefoot Strong*, 2015, p. 67.
[13] https://www.researchgate.net/publication/6423306_Aspirin_inhibits_the_formation_of_pentosidine_a_cross-linking_advanced_glycation_end_product_in_collagen
[14] Collagen as a model system to investigate the use of aspirin as an inhibitor of protein glycation and crosslinking; https://www.sciencedirect.com/science/article/abs/pii/S0968432800000

Chapter 22 - Daily Movement Overview: *Habits, Rules, Forever Movement Goals, and the Magic Bullet.*

[1]   Phillips LA, Gardner B. Habitual exercise instigation (vs. execution) predicts healthy adults' exercise frequency. Health Psychol. 2016 Jan;35(1):69-77. doi: 10.1037/hea0000249. Epub 2015 Jul 6. PMID: 26148187.

[2] Rhodes BJ, Bullock D, Verwey WB, Averbeck BB, Page MP. Learning and production of movement sequences: behavioral, neurophysiological, and modeling perspectives. Hum Mov Sci. 2004 Nov;23(5):699-746. doi: 10.1016/j.humov.2004.10.008. PMID: 15589629.

[3] https://sharpbrains.com/blog/2012/01/31/to-harness-neuroplasticity-start-with-enthusiasm/

[4] Ibid.

Chapter 23 - Your Move-Smart Program: *Daily Movement "Snacks" and a 30-Day Bodyweight Squat Challenge.*

Chapter 24 - Introduction: *Responsibility, Regret, and Resistance Exercise.*

[1] https://newsnetwork.mayoclinic.org/discussion/nearly-7-in-10-americans-take-prescription-drugs-mayo-clinic-olmsted-medical-center-find/

[2] Gomarasca M, Banfi G, Lombardi G. Myokines: The endocrine coupling of skeletal muscle and bone. Adv Clin Chem. 2020;94:155-218. doi: 10.1016/bs.acc.2019.07.010. Epub 2019 Aug 8. PMID: 31952571.

[3] Thomas Myers, *Anatomy Trains*, Elsevier Limited pub., 2009, 2nd edition, p 45.

[4] Ibid.

[5] Golden TR, Hubbard A, Dando C, Herren MA, Melov S. Age-related behaviors have distinct transcriptional profiles in Caenorhabditis elegans. *Aging Cell.* 2008;7(6):850-865. doi:10.1111/j.1474-9726.2008.00433.x

[6] Seaborne, R., Strauss, J., Cocks, M. *et al. Methylome of human skeletal muscle after acute & chronic resistance exercise training, detraining & retraining. Sci Data* **5,** 180213 (2018). https://doi.org/10.1038/sdata.2018.213

[7] Melov S, Tarnopolsky MA, Beckman K, Felkey K, Hubbard A. *Resistance exercise reverses aging in human skeletal muscle. PLoS One.* 2007;2(5):e465. Published 2007 May 23. doi:10.1371/journal.pone.0000465

Chapter 25 - How To: Resistance Training for Everyone - *Isometric Strength Training.*

[1] https://www.sciencedirect.com/topics/engineering/friction-law

[2] Paul Wade, *The Ultimate Isometrics Manual*, Dragon Door Publications, 2020, p. 50.

[3] Carl J Lavie, Richard V. Milani, Patrick Marks, Helen de Gruiter, *Exercise and the Heart: Risks, Benefits, and Recommendations for Providing Exercise Prescriptions.* Ochsner Journal, Oct 2001, 3 (4) 207-213.

[4] Paul Wade, *The Ultimate Isometrics Manual*, Dragon Door Publications, 2020, p. 217

[5] Isometric Exercise Training for Managing Vascular Risk Factors in Mild Cognitive Impairment and Alzheimer's Disease, https://www.frontiersin.org/articles/10.3389/fnagi.2017.00048/full

[6] Bäckman E, Johansson V, Häger B, Sjöblom P, Henriksson KG. Isometric muscle strength and muscular endurance in normal persons aged between 17 and 70 years. Scand J Rehabil Med. 1995 Jun;27(2):109-17. PMID: 7569820.

[7] https://journals.biologists.com/jeb/article/218/13/2075/13779/ Muscle-force-work-and-cost-a-novel-technique-to

[8] Ibid. p. 32.

[9] https://physoc.onlinelibrary.wiley.com/doi/full/10.1113/jphysiol.2011.221200

[10] Sugi H, Ohno T. Physiological Significance of the Force-Velocity Relation in Skeletal Muscle and Muscle Fibers. *Int J Mol Sci.* 2019;20(12):3075. Published 2019 Jun 24. doi:10.3390/ijms20123075

[11] https://en.wikipedia.org/wiki/Hill%27s_muscle_model

[12] Paul Wade, *The Ultimate Isometrics Manual*, Dragon Door Publications, 2020, p. 81-82

[13] https://www.britannica.com/science/Hookes-law

[14] Bohannon RW. Grip Strength: An Indispensable Biomarker For Older Adults. Clin Interv Aging. 2019 Oct 1;14:1681-1691. doi: 10.2147/ CIA.S194543. PMID: 31631989; PMCID: PMC6778477.

[15] Ibid.

[16] Zammit AR, Robitaille A, Piccinin AM, Muniz-Terrera G, Hofer SM. Associations Between Aging-Related Changes in Grip Strength and Cognitive Function in Older Adults: A Systematic Review. J Gerontol A Biol Sci Med Sci. 2019 Mar 14;74(4):519-527. doi: 10.1093/gerona/gly046. PMID: 29528368; PMCID: PMC6417444.

Chapter 26 - Cardiovascular Fitness: *The Optimal Approach for Long Term Health and Fitness - Type 1 and Type 2.*

[1] Assessment of Metabolic Flexibility by Means of Measuring Blood Lactate, Fat, and Carbohydrate Oxidation Responses to Exercise in Professional Endurance Athletes and Less-Fit Individuals, https://pubmed.ncbi.nlm.nih.gov/28623613/

[2] https://peterattiamd.com/inigosanmillan/

[3] https://www.cdc.gov/diabetes/data/statistics-report/prevalence-of-prediabetes.html

[4] Adami, A., Sivieri, A., Moia, C. *et al.* Effects of step duration in incremental ramp protocols on peak power and maximal oxygen consumption. *Eur J Appl Physiol* **113,** 2647–2653 (2013). https://doi.org/10.1007/s00421-013-2705-9

[5] Stamford BA. Exercise and the elderly. Exerc Sport Sci Rev. 1988;16:341-79. PMID: 3292262.

[6] S.K.Whitbourne, *The Aging Body*, Springer-Verlag New York, Inc. 1985, p 34-36.

[7] Ibid.

[8] Ibid.

[9] Ibid.

[10] Ibid.

[11] https://peterattiamd.com/inigosanmillan2/

[12] Ibid.

[13] VO2max stands for maximal aerobic capacity, also known as the maximal rate of oxygen consumption during incremental exercise. To put it simply, it's how much O2 your muscles can use as intensity rises. https://en.wikipedia.org/wiki/VO2_max

[14] https://www.instagram.com/p/Cei_qEljXrs/

[15] Robergs RA, Ghiasvand F, Parker D. Biochemistry of exercise-induced metabolic acidosis. Am J Physiol Regul Integr Comp Physiol. 2004 Sep;287(3):R502-16. doi: 10.1152/ajpregu.00114.2004. PMID: 15308499.

[16] http://gavinnoble.com/winter-training-milo-of-croton

[17] Kouda K, Iki M. Beneficial effects of mild stress (hormetic effects): dietary restriction and health. J Physiol Anthropol. 2010;29(4):127-32. doi: 10.2114/jpa2.29.127. PMID: 20686325.

Chapter 27 - Cycling: The Lower Impact Cardio Choice.

[1] Demontiero O, Vidal C, Duque G. *Aging and bone loss: new insights for the clinician.* Ther Adv Musculoskelet Dis. 2012 Apr;4(2):61-76. doi: 10.1177/1759720X11430858. PMID: 22870496; PMCID: PMC3383520.

[2] Mödder U., Achenbach S., Amin S., Riggs B., Melton L., Khosla S. (2010) *Relation of serum serotonin levels to bone density and structural parameters in women. J Bone Miner Res* 25: 415–422

Chapter 28 - Your Dental Health, Anti-Aging Supplements: Worth the Risk or the Cost?, The Future in Longevity Science: What's to Come?, and More.

[1] https://www.azlyrics.com/lyrics/leonardcohen/anthem.html

[2] Jason Elias, *The Seven Graces of Ageless Aging*, Five Element Healing Press, 2021, p. 192

[3] https://www.fortunebusinessinsights.com/vitamins-and-supplements-market-104051

[4] https://www.globenewswire.com/news-release/2021/01/19/2160500/0/en/Industry-Statistics-Global-Dietary-Supplements-Market-Size-Will-Grow-to-USD-306-8-Billion-by-2026-Says-Facts-Factors.html

[5] Shreeya S Navale, Anwar Mulugeta, Ang Zhou, David J Llewellyn, Elina Hyppönen, Vitamin D and brain health: an observational and Mendelian randomization study, *The American Journal of Clinical Nutrition*, 2022;, nqac107, https://doi.org/10.1093/ajcn/nqac107

[6] https://www.instagram.com/p/CgEvRWtKucA/

[7] Tanaka T, Shnimizu M, Moriwaki H. Cancer chemoprevention by carotenoids. Molecules. 2012 Mar 14;17(3):3202-42. doi: 10.3390/molecules17033202. PMID: 22418926; PMCID: PMC6268471.

[8] Pangestuti R, Siahaan EA, Kim SK. Photoprotective Substances Derived from Marine Algae. Mar Drugs. 2018 Oct 23;16(11):399. doi: 10.3390/md16110399. PMID: 30360482; PMCID: PMC6265938.

[9] Atul Gawande, *Being Mortal: Medicine and What Matters in the End*, Metropolitan Books, 2014, p. 29.

[10] Grimoud AM, Lucas S, Sevin A, Georges P, Passarrius O, Duranthon F. *Frequency of dental caries in four historical populations from the chalcolithic to the middle ages. Int J Dent.* 2011;2011:519691. doi:10.1155/2011/519691

[11] https://www.npr.org/sections/thesalt/2013/09/12/221845853/mountain-dew-mouth-is-destroying-appalachias-teeth

[12] https://www.npr.org/sections/thesalt/2013/05/29/187050058/soda-mouth-can-look-a-lot-like-meth-mouth

[13] https://peterattiamd.com/patriciacorby/

[14] https://askthedentist.com/podcast/what-are-the-dangers-of-fluoride-ingestion/

[15] Ibid.

[16] Amaechi, B.T., AbdulAzees, P.A., Alshareif, D.O. *et al.* Comparative efficacy of a hydroxyapatite and a fluoride toothpaste for prevention and remineralization of dental caries in children. *BDJ Open* **5,** 18 (2019). https://doi.org/10.1038/s41405-019-0026-8

[17] https://peterattiamd.com/patriciacorby/

[18] Sergey Young, *The Science and Technology of Growing Young*, Benbella Books pub, 2021, p.16.

[19] David Sinclair, PhD, *Lifespan: What We Age and Why We Don't Have To*, Simon and Schuster, 2019, p. 181.

[20] Ibid, p. 214.

[21] Ibid, p. 209.

[22] https://en.wikipedia.org/wiki/Metformin

[23] Nir Barzilai, MD., *Age Later: Health Span, Life Span, and the New Science of Longevity*, St Martin's Press, 2020, p. 246.

[24] https://www.nobelprize.org/prizes/medicine/2012/yamanaka/facts/

[25] Nir Barzilai, MD., *Age Later: Health Span, Life Span, and the New Science of Longevity*, St Martin's Press, 2020, p. 256.

[26] Sergey Young, *The Science and Technology of Growing Young*, Benbella Books, 2021, p.17.

[27] Ibid, p. 27.

[28] Sergey Young, *The Science and Technology of Growing Young*, Benbella Books, 2021, p.17.

[29] Ibid.

[30] Ibid, p.19.

[31] https://www.ewg.org/

[32] https://www.ewg.org/consumer-guides/dirty-dozen-endocrine-disruptors

[33] https://static.ewg.org/ewg-tip-sheets/EWG-AvoidingPFCs.pdf

[34] https://www.nejm.org/doi/full/10.1056/NEJMoa1112010

[35] https://www.acpjournals.org/doi/10.7326/M21-2977

[36] http://www.sci-news.com/medicine/sugar-sweetened-unsweetened-coffee-consumption-10861.html

[37] Allen RR, Carson L, Kwik-Uribe C, Evans EM, Erdman JW Jr. Daily consumption of a dark chocolate containing flavanols and added sterol esters affects cardiovascular risk factors in a normotensive population with elevated cholesterol. J Nutr. 2008 Apr;138(4):725-31. doi: 10.1093/jn/138.4.725. PMID: 18356327.

[38] *Neurovascular coupling, cerebral white matter integrity, and response to cocoa in older people,* Farzaneh A. Sorond, Shelley Hurwitz, David H. Salat, Douglas N. Greve, Naomi D.L. Fisher, Neurology Sep 2013, 81 (10) 904-909; DOI: 10.1212/WNL.0b013e3182a351aa

[39] https://www.bmj.com/content/343/bmj.d4488

[40] https://health.ucsd.edu/news/releases/Pages/2012-03-26-chocolate-and-weight-loss.aspx

[41] https://www.sleepfoundation.org/how-sleep-works/adenosine-and-sleep

[42] https://peterattiamd.com/alcohol-sleep-and-stress/

[43] https://www.drinkaware.co.uk/facts/alcoholic-drinks-and-units/what-is-alcohol-ingredients-chemicals-and-manufacture

[44] https://twitter.com/askdrruth

[45] Liu H, Waite LJ, Shen S, Wang DH. Is Sex Good for Your Health? A National Study on Partnered Sexuality and Cardiovascular Risk among Older Men and Women. J Health Soc Behav. 2016 Sep;57(3):276-96. doi: 10.1177/0022146516661597. PMID: 27601406; PMCID: PMC5052677.

[46] https://en.wikipedia.org/wiki/Oxytocin

[47] LaFerla, J.J., D.L. Anderson, and D.S. Schalch, *Psychoendocrine response to sexual arousal in human males.* Psychosom Med, 1978. 40(2): p. 166-72.

[48] Jacobsen SJ, Jacobson DJ, Rohe DE, Girman CJ, Roberts RO, Lieber MM. Frequency of sexual activity and prostatic health: fact or fairy tale? Urology. 2003 Feb;61(2):348-53. doi: 10.1016/s0090-4295(02)02265-3. PMID: 12597946.

[49] Press, The Associated. "Happiest Couples in Study Have Sex After 60 ." The New York Times, The New York Times, 4 Oct. 1992, www.nytimes.com/1992/10/04/us/happiest-couples-in-study-have-sex-after-60.html.

[50] Chrisanna Northrup, Dr. Pepper Schwartz. "Sex at 50-Plus: What's Normal? - Older Married Couples, Having Sex, Re..." AARP, www.aarp.org/home-family/sex-intimacy/info-01-2013/seniors-having-sex-older-couples.html.

[51] https://www.trendstatistics.com/health/erectile-dysfunction-statistics/

[52] https://njurology.com/ejaculation-what-to-expect-as-you-age/

[53] Maiorana A, O'Driscoll G, Taylor R, Green D. Exercise and the nitric oxide vasodilator system. Sports Med. 2003;33(14):1013-35. doi: 10.2165/00007256-200333140-00001. PMID: 14599231.

[54] Cassidy A, Franz M, Rimm EB. Dietary flavonoid intake and incidence of erectile dysfunction. Am J Clin Nutr. 2016 Feb;103(2):534-41. doi: 10.3945/ajcn.115.122010. Epub 2016 Jan 13. PMID: 26762373; PMCID: PMC4733263.

[55] Hafezi B, Chan L, Knapp JP, Karimi N, Alizadeh K, Mehrani Y, Bridle BW, Karimi K. Cytokine Storm Syndrome in SARS-CoV-2 Infections: A Functional Role of Mast Cells. Cells. 2021 Jul 12;10(7):1761. doi: 10.3390/cells10071761. PMID: 34359931; PMCID: PMC8308097.

Epilogue. What's Your WHY? What Would You Do Differently If You Knew You Were Going to Live to 100?

[1] Atul Gawande, *Being Mortal: Medicine and What Matters in the End*, Metropolitan Books pub, 2014, p. 232

[2] Ibid.

[3] Becca Levy, Ph D., *Breaking the Age Code: How Your Beliefs About Aging Determine How Well and Long You Live*, Harper Collins Pub, 2022, p. 6.

[4] Ibid, p. 5.

URGENT PLEA!

Thank you for reading my book!

I really appreciate all of your feedback and I love hearing what you have to say.

Please take two minutes now to leave a helpful review on Amazon letting me know what you thought of the book.

Thanks so much!

Al Lyman

AUTHOR OF

A G E   W E L L   A N D
F E E L   G R E A T !

PURSUIT ATHLETIC PERFORMANCE
MOVE BETTER - GET STRONGER - FEEL GREAT

ONLINE COURSES AND PROGRAMS

Are you ready to take your fitness and strength to a NEW level? Would you benefit from having an online course that you could access in the comfort of your own home, that would guide you every step of the way?

- **Circuits that can be done in 10 minutes or less!**

- **Follow-Along Workout Videos**

- **Detailed instructional videos and a plan to follow!**

To learn more, go to:

PursuitAthleticPerformance.com/store

On my Pursuit Athletic Performance **website, I have a full assortment of easy-to-use online programs to improve your mobility, stability, and strength!**

- **RESTORE: The Foundation Program**
- **RESTORE: The Bodyweight Strength Program**
- **RESTORE: The Core Program**
- **RESTORE: The Hips Program-Stability**
- **RESTORE: The Hips Program-Mobility**
- **RESTORE: The Legs Program**

And More!

About The Author

Al attended the Boston Conservatory of Music and completed his undergraduate studies at the University of Connecticut. At 19 years old, he joined the U.S. Coast Guard Band and embarked on a career as a percussionist. Since then, in addition to performing, he's competed at hundreds of different events and continues to amass a wide variety of athletic achievements, most notably a 2:39:37 **Boston Marathon** personal best, and finishing 9 Ironman Triathlons to date, including qualifying three different times for the **Ironman Triathlon World Championship** in Kailua-Kona, Hawaii.

He began coaching runners and triathletes part-time in 1999. In an effort to continue to share what he learned through a lifetime of health and wellness study and endurance sports training, he co-founded **Pursuit Athletic Performance** in 2010, where he provides movement therapy, gait analysis, coaching, and online exercise programs suitable for any person, regardless of age or experience. He has been certified as a Sports Therapist, Fascial Stretch Therapist, Strength and Conditioning Specialist, Functional Range Conditioning Mobility Specialist, USA Triathlon Coach, USA Weightlifting Coach, Barefoot Training Specialist, Functional Movement Screen Provider, and in clinical gait analysis.

From overcoming being bullied and a near-fatal drowning at 10 years old, to overcoming PTSD and learning to swim at 36 years old, to transitioning from a career in music to being a business owner, to becoming an author, Al has learned firsthand the importance of failing forward, being a life-long learner, and never giving up. Above it all, every step of his journey has been focused on becoming **truly healthy** and **aging well,** so he could extend not only his lifespan, but more importantly, his **healthspan.** His ultimate goal is to be able to do what he enjoys with those who matter the most, right up until his last day. As this book attests, Al has always been passionate about sharing all that he's learned with others.